Fodor's New EDITION

Greece

"When it comes to information on regional history, what to see and do, and shopping, these guides are exhaustive."

—*USAir Magazine*

"Valuable because of their comprehensiveness."

—*Minneapolis Star-Tribune*

"Fodor's always delivers high quality...thoughtfully presented...thorough."

—*Houston Post*

"An excellent choice for those who want everything under one cover."

—*Washington Post*

Fodor's Travel Publications, Inc.
New York • Toronto • London • Sydney • Auckland
http://www.fodors.com/

Fodor's Greece

Editor: Caragh Rockwood

Editorial Contributors: Robert Andrews, Toula Bogdanos, Michael Boyd, Stephen Brewer, David Brown, Jeffrey Carson, Audra Epstein, Eva Kanellis, Laura M. Kidder, Lea Lane, Susan Lupack, Terrence Moloney, Heidi Sarna, Helayne Schiff, Mary Ellen Schultz, M. T. Schwartzman (Gold Guide editor), Dinah Spritzer.

Creative Director: Fabrizio La Rocca

Cartographers: David Lindroth, Inc.; Mapping Specialists

Cover Photograph: Jeffrey Aaronson/Network Aspen

Text Design: Between the Covers

Copyright

Third Edition

ISBN 0–679–03227–4

"A Word about Greek Architecture," "A Short Glossary of Technical Terms," and "Greek Mythology" are reprinted from the *Swan Hellenic Cruise Handbook* by generous permission of Swan Hellenic Limited.

Special Sales

Fodor's Travel Publications are available at special discounts for bulk purchases for sales promotions or premiums. Special editions, including personalized covers, excerpts of existing guides, and corporate imprints, can be created in large quantities for special needs. For more information, contact your local bookseller or write to Special Marketing, Fodor's Travel Publications, 201 East 50th Street, New York, NY 10022. Inquiries from Canada should be directed to your local Canadian bookseller or sent to Random House of Canada, Ltd., Marketing Department, 1265 Aerowood Drive, Mississauga, Ontario L4W 1B9. Inquiries from the United Kingdom should be sent to Fodor's Travel Publications, 20 Vauxhall Bridge Road, London, England SW1V 2SA.

PRINTED IN THE UNITED STATES OF AMERICA

10 9 8 7 6 5 4 3 2 1

CONTENTS

Maps

ON THE ROAD WITH FODOR'S

WE'RE ALWAYS THRILLED to get letters from readers, especially one like this:

It took us an hour to decide what book to buy and we now know we picked the best one. Your book was wonderful, easy to follow, very accurate, and good on pointing out eating places, informal as well as formal. When we saw other people using your book, we would look at each other and smile.

Our editors and writers are deeply committed to making every Fodor's guide "the best one"—not only accurate but always charming, brimming with sound recommendations and solid ideas, right on the mark in describing restaurants and hotels, and full of fascinating facts that make you view what you've traveled to see in a rich new light.

About Our Writers

Our success in achieving our goals—and in helping to make your trip the best of all possible vacations—is a credit to the hard work of our extraordinary writers and editors.

Toula Bogdanos is a journalist working in Athens, where she also teaches Media Studies at Coventry University–Mediterranean.

Terrence Moloney has a master's in classics from the University of Toronto. While studying at the American School of Classical Studies in Athens, he did some stellar sleuthing for Fodor's.

Susan Lupack is a doctoral candidate in classics at the University of Texas at Austin and is researching her thesis at the American School of Classical Studies in Athens.

For more than 25 years, native New Yorker **Jeffrey Carson** has lived on Paros, Greece, where he teaches and writes—when not swimming in the dazzling Mediterranean. Most recently, he edited *The Collected Poems of Odysseus Elytis.*

Athens-based archaeologist **Michael Boyd** is researching the mainland Bronze Age and

studied at Glasgow, Liverpoo inburgh universities.

Stephen Brewer is a New York–L writer who spends as much time as p sible on Crete and other Mediterranea shores. He reports on his travels for various national magazines and guidebooks.

Lea Lane, a frequent contributor to guidebooks and a cruise expert, first traveled to the Greek islands 25 years ago and still finds them among her favorite destinations.

A special thanks is due to **Stavros Kavalaris,** from the New York Greek National Tourist Organization, for his generous assistance.

New This Year

This year we've reformatted our guides to make them easier to use. Each chapter of *Fodor's Greece* begins with brand-new recommended itineraries to help you decide what to see in the time you have; a section called When to Tour points out the optimal time of day, day of the week, and season for your journey. You may also notice our fresh graphics, new in 1996. More readable and more helpful than ever? We think so—and we hope you do, too.

New to this edition is coverage of the island Tinos in the Cycladic archipelago. Also, a new chapter on the Southern Peloponnese completes our coverage on the Peloponnese.

On the Web

Also check out Fodor's Web site (http://www.fodors.com/), where you'll find travel information on major destinations around the world and an ever-changing array of travel-savvy interactive features.

How to Use This Book

Organization

Up front is the **Gold Guide.** Its first section, **Important Contacts A to Z,** gives addresses and telephone numbers of organizations and companies that offer destination-related services and detailed information and publications. **Smart Travel Tips A to Z,** the Gold Guide's second sec-

n how to
n Greece
oth sec-
opic.

nged
ith
ded
ction rec-
driving tour and
habetical order. Each re-
pter is divided by geographical
a; within each area, towns are covered
iogical geographical order, and attrac-
ve stretches of road and minor points of
interest between them are indicated by
the designation En Route. Throughout, Off
the Beaten Path sights appear after the places
from which they are most easily accessible. And within town sections, all restaurants and lodgings are grouped together.

To help you decide what to visit in the time
you have, all chapters begin with recommended itineraries; you can mix and match
those from several chapters to create a complete vacation. The A to Z section that ends
all chapters covers getting there, getting
around, and helpful contacts and resources.

At the end of the book you'll find Portraits,
enlightening essays about Greek architecture and mythology, a glossary of technical terms, Greek vocabulary, and
interesting books and videos to give travelers a perspective of Greece.

Icons and Symbols

★ Our special recommendations
✕ Restaurant
🏠 Lodging establishment
✕🏠 Lodging establishment whose restau-
     rant warrants a detour
⚙ Campgrounds
☺ Rubber duckie (good for kids)
☞ Sends you to another section of the
     guide for more info
✉ Address
☎ Telephone number
FAX Fax number
🕐 Opening and closing times
💰 Admission prices (those we give
     apply only to adults; substantially
     reduced fees are almost always
     available for children, students,
     and senior citizens)

Numbers in white and black circles—②
and ❷, for example—that appear on the

maps, in the margins, and within the tours
correspond to one another.

Dining and Lodging

The restaurants and lodgings we list are
the cream of the crop in each price range.
Price charts appear in the Pleasures and
Pastimes section that follows each chapter introduction.

Hotel Facilities

We always list the facilities that are available—but we don't specify whether they
cost extra: When pricing accommodations, always ask what's included.

Assume that hotels operate on the **European Plan** (EP, with no meals) unless we
note that they use the **Full American Plan**
(FAP, with all meals), the **Modified American Plan** (MAP, with breakfast and dinner daily), or the **Continental Plan** (CP, with
a Continental breakfast daily).

Restaurant Reservations and Dress Codes

Reservations are always a good idea; we
note only when they're essential or when
they are not accepted. Book as far ahead
as you can, and reconfirm when you get
to town. Unless otherwise noted, the
restaurants listed are open daily for lunch
and dinner. We mention dress only when
men are required to wear a jacket or a jacket
and tie. Look for an overview of local
habits under Dining in Smart Travel Tips
A to Z and in the Pleasures and Pastimes
section that follows each chapter introduction.

Credit Cards

The following abbreviations are used: **AE**,
American Express; **D**, Discover; **DC**, Diners Club; **MC**, MasterCard; and **V**, Visa.

Please Write to Us

You can use this book in the confidence
that all prices and opening times are based
on information supplied to us at press
time; Fodor's cannot accept responsibility for any errors. Time inevitably brings
changes, so always confirm information
when it matters—especially if you're making a detour to visit a specific place. In addition, when making reservations be sure
to mention if you have a disability or are
traveling with children, if you prefer a
private bath or a certain type of bed, or
if you have specific dietary needs or any
other concerns.

Were the restaurants we recommended as described? Did our hotel picks exceed your expectations? Did you find a museum we recommended a waste of time? If you have complaints, we'll look into them and revise our entries when the facts warrant it. If you've discovered a special place that we haven't included, we'll pass the information along to our correspondents and have them check it out. So send your feedback, positive *and* negative, to the *Greece* Editor at 20 New York, New York . a wonderful trip!

Karen Cure

Karen Cure
Editorial Director

Black Sea

T U R K E Y

Istanbul

Sea of Marmara

Xanthi

THRACE

Makri

Thassos

Samothrace

N

0   50 miles

0   75 km

Limnos

Aegean Sea

Lesbos

T U R K E Y

N O R T H E R N   I S L A N D S

Chios

Izmir (Smyrna)

Andros

A E G E A N

I S L A N D S

Samos

Tinos

Ikaria

Siros   *Mykonos*

Delos

Patmos

Paros

Sifnos

Naxos

Leros

Kalimnos

Bodrum

Kos

C Y C L A D E S

Amorgos

Kos

Ios

Astypalea

Nissyros

Symi

Rhodes

Santorini   *Anafi*

D O D E C A N E S E

Tilos

Chalki

Rhodes

Sea of Crete

Karpathos

C R E T E

Heraklion

Ay. Nikolaos

Kassos

Ierapetra

Mediterranean Sea

Greek Ferries

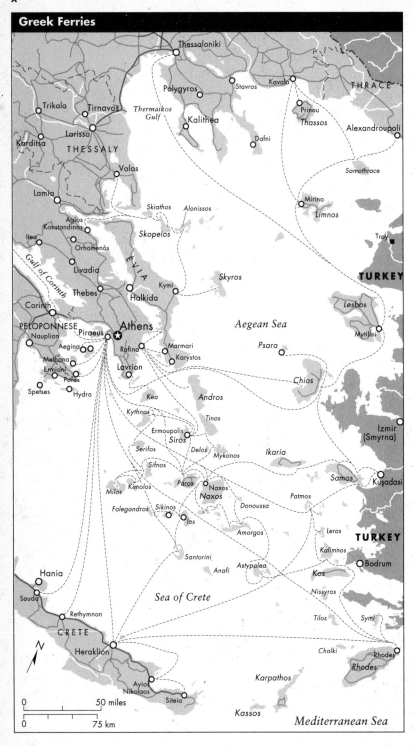

IMPORTANT CONTACTS A TO Z

An Alphabetical Listing of Publications, Organizations, and Companies that Will Help You Before, During, and After Your Trip

A

AIR TRAVEL

Athens's major gateway is **Ellinikon Airport,** which has two terminals. The west terminal (☎ 011–30–01/936–3363 through 3367; dial any four-digit sequence for flight information) serves **Olympic Airways** international and domestic flights only; the east terminal (☎ 011–30–1/969–4466 through 4467) is used by all other international carriers.

CARRIERS

Greece's national airline, **Olympic Airways** (☎ 212/838–3600 or 800/223–1226 outside New York) flies nonstop to Athens from both the U.S. and Canada.

U.S. carriers flying nonstop to Athens include **Delta** (☎ 800/241–4141) and **TWA** (☎ 800/892–4141).

European national airlines that fly to Athens from the United States and Canada via their major cities include **Austrian Airlines** (☎ 800/843–0002), **Sabena Belgian World Airlines** (☎ 800/955–2000), **Air France** (☎ 800/237–2747), **LOT Polish Airlines** (☎ 212/869–1074), **Lufthansa** (☎ 800/645–3880), **British Airways** (☎ 800/247–9297), **Virgin Atlantic** (☎ 800/862–8621), **KLM Royal Dutch**

Airlines (☎ 800/777–5553), **Alitalia** (☎ 800/223–5730), **TAP Air Portugal** (☎ 800/221–7370), **Iberia Airlines** (☎ 800/772–4642), and **Swissair** (☎ 800/221–4750). Remember that these are connecting flights that include at least one stop and may require a change of planes.

FROM THE U.K.➤ Carriers serving Greece from the United Kingdom include **British Airways** (☎ 0181/897–4000 or 0345/222–111 outside London), **Air UK** (☎ 0345/666777 or 01293/535353), and **Olympic Airways** (☎ 0171/409–3400).

COMPLAINTS

To register complaints about charter and scheduled airlines, contact the U.S. Department of Transportation's **Aviation Consumer Protection Division** (✉ C-75, Washington, DC 20590, ☎ 202/366–2220). Complaints about lost baggage or ticketing problems and safety concerns may also be logged with the **Federal Aviation Administration (FAA) Consumer Hotline** (☎ 800/322–7873).

CONSOLIDATORS

For the names of reputable air-ticket consolidators, contact the **United States Air Consolidators Association** (✉ 925 L St., Suite 220, Sacramento, CA

95814, ☎ 916/441–4166, FAX 916/441–3520). For discount air-ticketing agencies, *see* Discounts & Deals, *below.*

FLYING TIME

Flying time to Athens is 8 hours from New York, 10 hours from Chicago, and 14 hours from Los Angeles.

PUBLICATIONS

For general information about charter carriers, ask for the Department of Transportation's free brochure **"Plane Talk: Public Charter Flights"** (✉ Aviation Consumer Protection Division, C-75, Washington, DC 20590, ☎ 202/366–2220). The Department of Transportation also publishes a 58-page booklet, **"Fly Rights,"** available from the Consumer Information Center (✉ Supt. of Documents, Dept. 136C, Pueblo, CO 81009; $1.75).

For other tips and hints, consult the Consumers Union's monthly **"Consumer Reports Travel Letter"** (✉ Box 53629, Boulder, CO 80322, ☎ 800/234–1970; $39 1st year).

WITHIN GREECE

Scheduled (i.e., non-chartered) domestic air travel in Greece is provided only by **Olympic Airways** (☎ 01/966–6666 for reservations; ☎ 01/936–3363 through 3367 for

THE GOLD GUIDE / IMPORTANT CONTACTS

daily arrival and departure information, FAX 01/966–6111), which operates out of Athens's West Terminal. There is service to Alexandroupolis, Astypalaia, Ioannina, Kastoria, Kavala, Kozani, Preveza, and Thessaloniki, all on the mainland; Kalamata in the Peloponnese; the Aegean islands: Karpathos, Kassos, Kythira, Crete (Hania, Heraklion, and Sitia), Chios, Kos, Lesbos, Limnos, Leros, Milos, Mykonos, Naxos, Paros, Rhodes, Samos, Skiathos, Syros, Skyros, Kastellorizo (only via Rhodes), and Santorini; Corfu, Kefalonia, and Zakynthos in the Ionian Sea. All domestic flights are no-smoking.

Charter companies include **Air Greece** (☒ Nikis 20, Athens ☎ 01/325–5011 through 5014), which operates from the East Terminal. In summer there are daily flights from Athens to Thessaloniki, Heraklion, and Rhodes, as well as between all four destinations.

AIRPORT TRANSFERS

In Athens **Yiannis Yiannakopoulos Limousines** (car phone ☎ 094/316798) provides limousine transfers from the airport to city hotels for 12,000 dr. For bus and taxi information, *see* Airport Transfers *in* Smart Travel Tips A to Z, *below.*

B

BETTER BUSINESS BUREAU

For local contacts in the hometown of a tour operator you may be considering, consult the **Council of Better Business Bureaus** (☒ 4200 Wilson Blvd., Suite 800, Arlington, VA 22203, ☎ 703/276–0100, FAX 703/525–8277).

BOAT TRAVEL

For information on boats departing from Piraeus, Greece's main port, contact a travel agency or the **Piraeus port authority** (☎ 01/451–1311 and 01/417–2657). Boats for some of the Cyclades islands closer to Athens (Andros, Tinos, Mykonos) leave from **Rafina** (port authority ☎ 0294/22300). The Greek National Tourist Organization (GNTO or EOT) also distributes weekly lists for boats leaving Athens, or you can call ☎ 143 for a **recording** (in Greek) of the day's departures. At 1 PM, a new recording lists boats leaving the following morning. Outside Athens, contact the port authority nearest you.

BUS TRAVEL

FROM THE U.K.

You can travel to Greece from the United Kingdom via Italy. The route, operated by **Eurolines** (☒ 52 Grosvenor Gardens, London SW1W 0AU, ☎ 0171/730–0202), takes four days of essentially nonstop travel and begins at Victoria Coach Station (☒ 164 Buckingham Palace Rd.); luggage space is severely restricted.

WITHIN GREECE

The price of public transportation in Greece has risen steeply in the last couple of years, but it is still cheaper than in other western European cities. In Athens, the **Organization for Urban Public Transportation** (☒ Metsovou 15, Athens, ☎ 185 or 01/883–6076, ☼ weekdays 8–2:30), one block north of the National Archaeological Museum, answers questions about city routes and distributes maps.

Greece has an extensive, inexpensive, and reliable regional bus system (**KTEL**) made up of local operators. Each city has connections to towns and villages in their vicinity; visit the local KTEL office to check routes. Buses from Athens, however, travel throughout the country. **Terminal A** (☒ Kifissou St. 100, ☎ 01/512–4910) is the arrival and departure point for bus lines that serve parts of northern Greece, including Thessaloniki, Epirus, and Macedonia, and the Peloponnese destinations of Epidauros, Mycenae, and Corinth. Each line has its own Athens phone number; the EOT offices distribute a list. **Terminal B** (☒ behind Liossion 260, ☎ 01/831–7153), serving Evia and eastern and central Greece, including Delphi, is in a remote area northwest of Omonia Square. To get into the city center, take Bus 51 from Terminal A, Bus 24 from Terminal B.

The **Tavlaridou** travel agency (☒ Chalkokondili 31 and Triti Septemvriou, Omonia Sq., Athens, ☎ FAX 01/522–1048) offers luxury coach trips (air-conditioning, bar, toilet, and video) to Thessaloniki daily at 4 PM and midnight (6,000 dr. one-way).

C

CAR INSURANCE

In general, auto insurance is not as expensive as in other countries. You must have third-party car insurance to drive in Greece. If possible, get an insurance "green card" valid for Greece from your insurance company before arriving. You can also buy a policy with local companies; keep the papers in a plastic pocket on the inside right front windshield. For more information, or to locate a local representative for your insurance company, call the **International Insurance Company** (✉ Xenofontos 10, Athens 10557, ☎ 01/323–6733).

Rental agencies offer a full range of insurance: collision damage waiver costs from $8–$14 a day, depending on the deduction, personal insurance $2, theft, $3.

CAR RENTAL

The major car-rental companies represented in Greece are **Avis** (☎ 800/331–1084; in Canada, 800/879–2847), **Budget** (☎ 800/527–0700; in the U.K., 0800/181181), **Hertz** (☎ 800/654–3001; in Canada, 800/263–0600; in the U.K., 0345/555888), and **National InterRent** (sometimes known as Europcar InterRent outside North America; ☎ 800/227–3876; in the U.K., 0345/222–

525). Rates in Greece begin at $33 a day and $163 a week for an economy car with unlimited mileage. This does not include tax on car rentals, which is 18% (13% on some islands).

Other companies operating in Athens include **Thrifty** (✉ Syngrou 24, Athens, ☎ 01/922–1211 through 1213 and 01/921–6000); **Greece Rent-A-Car** (✉ Syngrou 7, ☎ 01/924–9802 through 9804), which has weekly and monthly rates; **Pappas Rent-A-Car** (✉ Amalias 44, ☎ 01/322–0087 and 01/323–4772); and **Swift Car Rental** (✉ Nikis 21, ☎ 01/324–7855 and 324–7875).

RENTAL WHOLESALERS

Contact **Auto Europe** (☎ 207/828–2525 or 800/223–5555), **Europe by Car** (☎ 800/223–1516; in CA, 800/252–9401), or the **Kemwel Group** (☎ 914/835–5555 or 800/678–0678).

CHILDREN & TRAVEL

BABY-SITTING

Contact the **Pan-Athenian Union of Baby-Sitters** (✉ Glafkonos 5, Omonia, ☎ 01/383–5798); be sure to give two to three days' notice. The basic charge is 1,200 dr. per hour.

FLYING

Look into **"Flying with Baby"** (✉ Third Street Press, Box 261250, Littleton, CO 80163, ☎ 303/595–5959; $4.95 includes shipping), cowritten by a flight attendant. **"Kids and Teens in Flight,"**

free from the U.S. Department of Transportation's Aviation Consumer Protection Division (✉ C-75, Washington, DC 20590, ☎ 202/366–2220), offers tips on children flying alone. Every two years the February issue of *Family Travel Times* (☞ Know-How, *below*) details children's services on three dozen airlines. **"Flying Alone, Handy Advice for Kids Traveling Solo"** is available free from the American Automobile Association (AAA) (✉ Send stamped, self-addressed, legal-size envelope: Flying Alone, Mail Stop 800, 1000 AAA Dr., Heathrow, FL 32746).

KNOW-HOW

Family Travel Times, published quarterly by Travel with Your Children (✉ TWYCH, 40 5th Ave., New York, NY 10011, ☎ 212/477–5524; $40 per year), covers destinations, types of vacations, and modes of travel.

LODGING

At the **Best Western** hotels (reservations ☎ 800/528–1234) in Athens, Olympia, Tinos, Ayios Constantinos, Arachova, and Glyfada, one child under 6 may stay free with an adult; there is an extra charge if the child needs his own roll-away bed. The **Hilton** hotels (reservations ☎ 800/445–8667) in Athens and Corfu allow one child under 12 to stay free in his or her parents' room. They also maintain lists of baby-sitters.

THE GOLD GUIDE / IMPORTANT CONTACTS

Grecotel Rhodos Imperial (⊠ Ixia, Rhodes, ☎ 0241/75000) runs recreational "mini clubs" for children (activities include swimming and other water sports, games, and arts and crafts) and offers special children's meals.

TOUR OPERATORS

If you're outdoorsy, look into programs from the **American Museum of Natural History** (⊠ 79th St. and Central Park W., New York, NY 10024, ☎ 212/769–5700 or 800/462–8687).

CRUISING

Cruising is experiencing a resurgence in popularity. It can be a pleasant, leisurely way to travel without the complications of rental cars, trains, reservations, frequent packing and unpacking, and the rest. Cruises on big ships often include stops in countries other than Greece. Among the major lines sailing to the four most popular islands—Mykonos, Rhodes, Crete, and Santorini (April through October)—is **Royal Olympic Cruises**, which was created in January 1996 when Sun Line Cruises and Epirotiki Cruises merged (⊠ One Rockefeller Plaza, New York, NY 10020, ☎ 212/397–6400; ⊠ in Greece: Akti Miaouli 87, 18538 Piraeus, ☎ 01/429–1000 or book at their downtown office, Karitsi Square 11, 10561 Athens, ☎ 01/324–7181). Other Greek cruise agencies are **Chandris** (⊠ Akti Miaouli 95, Piraeus, ☎ 01/429–0300); and **Hydrodynamic Cruises** (⊠ Xenofontos 14, Athens, ☎ 01/323–4292).

Other major cruise lines that call in the Greek Islands include **Club Med, Costa Cruise Lines, Crystal Cruises, Cunard Line, Holland America Line, Orient Lines, Princess Cruises, Radisson Seven Seas Cruises, Renaissance Cruises, Seabourn Cruise Line, Silversea Cruises, Star Clippers, and Windstar Cruises.** These cruises often call at ports outside Greece as well, and may begin or end in Italy or Turkey. For more information and exact itineraries contact a cruise-only travel agency.

For a cruise of the islands aboard a small yacht, contact **Club Voyages** (⊠ 43 Hooper Ave., Atlantic Highlands, NJ 07716, ☎ 908/291–8228), **Valef Yachts** (⊠ Box 391, 7254 Fir Rd., Ambler, PA 19002, ☎ 215/641–1624 or 800/223–3845), or **Zeus Tours and Yacht Cruises** (⊠ 566 7th Ave., New York, NY 10018, ☎ 212/221–0006 or 800/447–5667). The refurbished 1931 **Sea Cloud** sailing yacht cruises the Greek islands and Turkey; contact the **Cruise Company of Greenwich** (⊠ 31 Brookside Dr., Greenwich, CT 06830; ☎ 800/825–0862) for information. The Greek-based **Viking Star Cruises** (⊠ Artemidos 1, 16674 Glyfada, ☎ 01/898–0829 and 01/894–9279) offers a weeklong cruise to Mykonos, Santorini, Delos, Paros, Naxos, Ios, and Tinos on a 14-cabin yacht.

BY HYDROFOIL

Flying Dolphin hydrofoils carry passengers from Zea in Piraeus to the Saronic Gulf Islands and eastern Peloponnesian ports, including Aegina, Hermioni, Hydra, Kyparissi, Kythera, Leonidion, Methana, Monemvassia, Nauplion, Neapolis, Poros, Porto Heli, and Spetses. In summer there is additional service. These boats are somewhat pricey, but fast and fun to ride on. Tickets can be purchased through authorized agents or in downtown Athens at the Spirou Milou Arcade 4 near Syntagma Square. For more information or to reserve seats on the Rafina-Evia-Cyclades-Rhodes-Mytilini routes, call **Ilio Lines** (in Athens: ⊠ Stoa Spirou Milou 4, ☎ 01/322–5139; in Piraeus: ⊠ Gounari 2, ☎ 01/422–4980; and in Rafina harbor: ☎ 0294/23500 and 0294/25100).

CUSTOMS

U.S. CITIZENS

The **U.S. Customs Service** (⊠ Box 7407, Washington, DC 20044, ☎ 202/927–6724) can answer questions on duty-free limits and publishes a helpful brochure, **"Know Before You Go."** For information on registering foreign-made articles, call ☎ 202/927–0540 or write ⊠ U.S. Customs Service, Resource Management, 1301 Constitution Ave. NW, Washington, DC 20229.

COMPLAINTS➢ Note the inspector's badge number and write to the commissioner's office

(✉ 1301 Constitution Ave. NW, Washington, DC 20229).

CANADIANS

Contact **Revenue Canada** (✉ 2265 St. Laurent Blvd. S, Ottawa, Ontario K1G 4K3, ☎ 613/993–0534) for a copy of the free brochure **"I Declare/Je Déclare"** and for details on duty-free limits. For recorded information (within Canada only), call ☎ 800/461–9999.

U.K. CITIZENS

HM Customs and Excise (✉ Dorset House, Stamford St., London SE1 9NG, ☎ 0171/202–4227) can answer questions about U.K. customs regulations and publishes a free pamphlet, **"A Guide for Travellers,"** detailing standard procedures and import rules.

D

DISABILITIES & ACCESSIBILITY

COMPLAINTS

To register complaints under the provisions of the Americans with Disabilities Act, contact the U.S. Department of Justice's **Disability Rights Section** (✉ Box 66738, Washington, DC 20035, ☎ 202/514–0301 or 800/514–0301, FAX 202/307–1198, TTY 202/514–0383 or 800/514–0383). For airline-related problems, contact the U.S. Department of Transportation's **Aviation Consumer Protection Division** (☞ Air Travel, *above*). For complaints about surface transportation, contact the Department of Transportation's **Civil Rights Office** (✉ 400 7th St., SW, Room 10215, Washington, DC 20590, ☎ 202/366–4648).

LODGING

The **Hotel Inter-Continental** (reservations ☎ 800/327–0200) in Athens has seven rooms specifically adapted for travelers with disabilities (wider doors, handrails, storage space for wheelchair) and most public areas are accessible. The **Hilton** hotel (reservations ☎ 800/445–8667) in Athens (one room) and Kanoni on Corfu (two rooms) have accommodations equipped with extra-wide doors and accessible bathrooms, but some public areas, such as the pool, may be difficult to get to by wheelchair.

ORGANIZATIONS

TRAVELERS WITH HEARING IMPAIRMENTS➤ The **American Academy of Otolaryngology** (✉ 1 Prince St., Alexandria, VA 22314, ☎ 703/836–4444, FAX 703/683–5100, TTY 703/519–1585) publishes a brochure, "Travel Tips for Hearing Impaired People."

TRAVELERS WITH MOBILITY PROBLEMS➤ Contact **Mobility International USA** (✉ Box 10767, Eugene, OR 97440, ☎ and TTY 541/343–1284, FAX 541/343–6812), the U.S. branch of a Belgium-based organization (☞ *below*) with affiliates in 30 countries; **MossRehab Hospital Travel Information Service** (☎ 215/456–9600, TTY 215/456–9602), a telephone information resource for travelers with physi-cal disabilities; the **Society for the Advancement of Travel for the Handicapped** (✉ 347 5th Ave., Suite 610, New York, NY 10016, ☎ 212/447–7284, FAX 212/725–8253; membership $45); and **Travelin' Talk** (✉ Box 3534, Clarksville, TN 37043, ☎ 615/552–6670, FAX 615/552–1182), which provides local contacts worldwide for travelers with disabilities.

TRAVELERS WITH VISION IMPAIRMENTS➤ Contact the **American Council of the Blind** (✉ 1155 15th St. NW, Suite 720, Washington, DC 20005, ☎ 202/467–5081, FAX 202/467–5085) for a list of travelers' resources or the **American Foundation for the Blind** (✉ 11 Penn Plaza, Suite 300, New York, NY 10001, ☎ 212/502–7600 or 800/232–5463, TTY 212/502–7662), which provides general advice and publishes "Access to Art" ($19.95), a directory of museums that accommodate travelers with vision impairments.

IN THE U.K.

Contact the **Royal Association for Disability and Rehabilitation** (✉ RADAR, 12 City Forum, 250 City Rd., London EC1V 8AF, ☎ 0171/250–3222) or **Mobility International** (✉ rue de Manchester 25, B-1080 Brussels, Belgium, ☎ 00–322–410–6297, FAX 00–322–410–6874), an international travel-information clearinghouse for people with disabilities.

PUBLICATIONS

Several publications for travelers with disabilities are available from the **Consumer Information Center** (✉ Box 100, Pueblo, CO 81009, ☎ 719/948–3334). Call or write for its free catalog of current titles. The Society for the Advancement of Travel for the Handicapped (☞ Organizations, *above*) publishes the quarterly magazine **Access to Travel** ($13 for 1-year subscription).

The 500-page **Travelin' Talk Directory** (✉ Box 3534, Clarksville, TN 37043, ☎ 615/552–6670, FAX 615/552–1182; $35) lists people and organizations who help travelers with disabilities. For travel agents worldwide, consult the **Directory of Travel Agencies for the Disabled** (✉ Twin Peaks Press, Box 129, Vancouver, WA 98666, ☎ 360/694–2462 or 800/637–2256, FAX 360/696–3210; $19.95 plus $3 shipping).

TRAVEL AGENCIES & TOUR OPERATORS

The Americans with Disabilities Act requires that all travel firms serve the needs of all travelers. That said, you should note that some agencies and operators specialize in making travel arrangements for individuals and groups with disabilities, among them **Access Adventures** (✉ 206 Chestnut Ridge Rd., Rochester, NY 14624, ☎ 716/889–9096), run by a former physical-rehab counselor.

TRAVELERS WITH MOBILITY PROBLEMS➣ Contact **Hinsdale Travel Service** (✉ 201 E. Ogden Ave., Suite 100, Hinsdale, IL 60521, ☎ 630/325–

1335), a travel agency that benefits from the advice of wheelchair traveler Janice Perkins; and **Wheelchair Journeys** (✉ 16979 Redmond Way, Redmond, WA 98052, ☎ 206/885–2210 or 800/313–4751), which can handle arrangements worldwide.

TRAVELERS WITH DEVELOPMENTAL DISABILITIES➣ Contact the nonprofit **New Directions** (✉ 5276 Hollister Ave., Suite 207, Santa Barbara, CA 93111, ☎ 805/967–2841).

TRAVEL GEAR

The **Magellan's** catalog (☎ 800/962–4943, FAX 805/568–5406) includes a section devoted to products designed for travelers with disabilities.

DISCOUNTS & DEALS

AIRFARES

For the lowest airfares to Greece, call 800/FLY–4–LESS.

CLUBS

Contact **Entertainment Travel Editions** (✉ Box 1068, Trumbull, CT 06611, ☎ 800/445–4137; $28–$53, depending on destination), **Great American Traveler** (✉ Box 27965, Salt Lake City, UT 84127, ☎ 800/548–2812; $49.95 per year), **Moment's Notice Discount Travel Club** (✉ 7301 New Utrecht Ave., Brooklyn, NY 11204, ☎ 718/234–6295; $25 per year, single or family), **Privilege Card International** (✉ 3391 Peachtree Rd. NE, Suite 110, Atlanta, GA 30326, ☎ 404/262–

0222 or 800/236–9732; $74.95 per year), **Travelers Advantage** (✉ CUC Travel Service, 49 Music Sq. W, Nashville, TN 37203, ☎ 800/548–1116 or 800/648–4037; $49 per year, single or family), or **Worldwide Discount Travel Club** (✉ 1674 Meridian Ave., Miami Beach, FL 33139, ☎ 305/534–2082; $50 per year for family, $40 single).

HOTEL ROOMS

For hotel room rates guaranteed in U.S. dollars, call **Steigenberger Reservation Service** (☎ 800/223–5652).

PASSES

☞ Train Travel, *below*.

STUDENTS

Members of Hostelling International–American Youth Hostels (☞ Students, *below*) are eligible for discounts on car rentals, admissions to attractions, and other selected travel expenses.

PUBLICATIONS

Consult **The Frugal Globetrotter,** by Bruce Northam (✉ Fulcrum Publishing, 350 Indiana St., Suite 350, Golden, CO 80401, ☎ 800/992–2908; $16.95 plus $4 shipping). For publications that tell how to find the lowest prices on plane tickets, *see* Air Travel, *above*.

Also see Fodor's **Affordable Europe** (available in bookstores, or ☎ 800/533–6478; $18.50 plus $4 shipping).

DRIVING

AUTO CLUBS

The **Automobile Touring Club of Greece** or ELPA (✉ Athens Tower, 2–4

Messogion St., Athens, ☎ 01/748–8800) has a special telephone line (☎ 174) for tourist information that works throughout the country; staff is extremely helpful. Other branches include **Patras** (✉ Patroon-Athinon 18, ☎ 061/425411 or 061/426416), **Heraklion** (✉ Knossou Ave and G. Papandreou 16, ☎ 0181/289440), **Thessaloniki** (✉ Vas. Olgas 230, ☎ 031/426319 and 031/426386), and **Volos** (✉ Iolkou 89, ☎ 0421/47404).

BREAKDOWNS

You must put out a triangular danger sign if you have a breakdown. Roving repair trucks, manned by skilled ELPA mechanics, patrol the major highways (☎ 104 in all of Greece). They assist tourists with breakdowns for free if they belong to AAA or to ELPA; otherwise, there is a charge.

FERRIES

Superfast Ferries (✉ Amalias 30, Athens, ☎ 01/331–2252 and reservations ☎ 01/969–1111) sails from Patras to Ancona. The **Orient Express** (✉ 20 Upper Ground, London SE1 9PD, ☎ 0171/928–6000) sails from Venice to Simplon. Details about the **Adriatica Lines** services from Brindisi to Igoumenitsa and Patras and from Venice to Piraeus can be obtained from the Stena–Sealink Travel Centre (✉ Charter House, Park St., Ashford, Kent TN24 8EX, ☎ 01233/647047) opposite

Platform 2 in Victoria Station. For information on the **Minoan Lines** car ferries between Ancona and Igoumenitsa and Patras contact P&O European Ferries (✉ Channel House, Channel View Rd., Dover CT17 9TJ, ☎ 01304/203388; ☞ Driving *in* Smart Travel Tips A to Z, *below*).

IMPORTING YOUR CAR

Contact the **Greek Consulate** for a six-month duty-free license to import your car. To receive an additional six-month extension, contact the **Directorate for the Supervision and Control of Cars** or DIPEA (✉ Amvrosiou Frantzi 14, 11473 Athens, ☎ 01/922–7315; ☞ Driving *in* Smart Travel Tips A to Z, *below*).

MAPS

The EOT distributes regional and city maps, but the most detailed is published by S. Kapranidis and N. Fotis in cooperation with ELPA. It is simply called **Ellas** and is available at all major bookstores, ELPA offices, and even some kiosks. The same company puts out an easy-to-understand street guide to the capital, **Athens-Piraeus-Suburbs,** essential if you're going to remain more than a few days.

E
EMERGENCIES

Police, ☎ 100, **National Ambulance Service (EKAV),** ☎ 166 (a taxi is faster), **Fire,** ☎ 199, **Poison center,** ☎ 01/779–3777). The **Tourist**

Police (☎ 171 in Athens, call the local police in other regions or see specific chapters for phone number) can provide general information, help in emergencies, and can mediate in disputes.

G
GAY & LESBIAN TRAVEL

LOCAL INFO

To Kraximo and *Greek Gay Guide* (available from kiosks in Omonia Square in Athens and near the Thessaloniki train station) are both published by Kraximo publications (✉ Box 4228, 10210 Athens).

ORGANIZATIONS

The **International Gay Travel Association** (✉ Box 4974, Key West, FL 33041, ☎ 800/448–8550, ℻ 305/296–6633), a consortium of more than 1,000 travel companies, can supply names of gay-friendly travel agents, tour operators, and accommodations.

PUBLICATIONS

The 16-page monthly newsletter **"Out & About"** (✉ 8 W. 19th St., Suite 401, New York, NY 10011, ☎ 212/645–6922 or 800/929–2268, ℻ 800/929–2215; $49 for 10 issues and quarterly calendar) covers gay-friendly resorts, hotels, cruise lines, and airlines.

TOUR OPERATORS

Cruises and resort vacations for gays are handled by **R.S.V.P. Travel Productions** (✉ 2800 University Ave.

SE, Minneapolis, MN 55414, ☎ 612/379–4697 or 800/328–7787). **Olivia** (✉ 4400 Market St., Oakland, CA 94608, ☎ 510/655–0364 or 800/631–6277) specializes in such bookings for lesbians. For mixed gay and lesbian travel, **Atlantis Events** (✉ 9060 Santa Monica Blvd., Suite 310, West Hollywood, CA 90069, ☎ 310/281–5450 or 800/628–5268) and **Toto Tours** (✉ 1326 W. Albion Ave., Suite 3W, Chicago, IL 60626, ☎ 773/274–8686 or 800/565–1241, FAX 773/274–8695) offer group tours to worldwide destinations.

TRAVEL AGENCIES

The largest agencies serving gay travelers are **Advance Damron Travel** (✉ 1 Greenway Plaza, Suite 890, Houston, TX 77046, ☎ 713/682–2002 or 800/292–0500), **Club Travel** (✉ 8739 Santa Monica Blvd., W. Hollywood, CA 90069, ☎ 310/358–2200 or 800/429–8747), **Islanders/ Kennedy Travel** (✉ 183 W. 10th St., New York, NY 10014, ☎ 212/242–3222 or 800/988–1181), **Now Voyager** (✉ 4406 18th St., San Francisco, CA 94114, ☎ 415/626–1169 or 800/255–6951), and **Yellowbrick Road** (✉ 1500 W. Balmoral Ave., Chicago, IL 60640, ☎ 773/561–1800 or 800/642–2488). **Skylink Women's Travel** (✉ 2460 W. 3rd St., Suite 215, Santa Rosa, CA 95401, ☎ 707/570–0105 or 800/225–5759) serves lesbian travelers.

H
HEALTH

FINDING A DOCTOR

For its members, the **International Association for Medical Assistance to Travellers** (IAMAT, membership free; ✉ 417 Center St., Lewiston, NY 14092, ☎ 716/754–4883; ✉ 40 Regal Rd., Guelph, Ontario N1K 1B5, ☎ 519/836–0102; ✉ 1287 St. Clair Ave. W., Toronto, Ontario M6E 1B8, ☎ 416/652–0137; ✉ 57 Voirets, 1212 Grand-Lancy, Geneva, Switzerland) publishes a worldwide directory of English-speaking physicians meeting IAMAT standards.

MEDICAL ASSISTANCE COMPANIES

The following companies are concerned primarily with emergency medical assistance, although they may provide some insurance as part of their coverage. For a list of full-service travel insurance companies, *see* Insurance, *below.*

Contact **International SOS Assistance** (✉ Box 11568, Philadelphia, PA 19116, ☎ 215/244–1500 or 800/523–8930; ✉ Box 466, Pl. Bonaventure, Montréal, Québec H5A 1C1, ☎ 514/874–7674 or 800/363–0263; ✉ 7 Old Lodge Pl., St. Margarets, Twickenham TW1 1RQ, England, ☎ 0181/744–0033), **Medex Assistance Corporation** (✉ Box 5375, Timonium, MD 21094, ☎ 410/453–6300 or 800/537–

2029), **Near Travel Services** (✉ Box 1339, Calumet City, IL 60409, ☎ 708/868–6700 or 800/654–6700), **Traveler's Emergency Network** (✉ 1133 15th St. NW, Suite 400, Washington, DC 20005, ☎ 202/828–5894 or 800/275–4836, FAX 202/828–5896), **TravMed** (✉ Box 5375, Timonium, MD 21094, ☎ 410/453–6380 or 800/732–5309), or **Worldwide Assistance Services** (✉ 1133 15th St. NW, Suite 400, Washington, DC 20005, ☎ 202/331–1609 or 800/821–2828, FAX 202/828–5896).

I
INSURANCE

IN THE U.S.

Travel insurance covering baggage, health, and trip cancellation or interruptions is available from **Access America** (✉ 6600 W. Broad St., Richmond, VA 23230, ☎ 804/285–3300 or 800/334–7525), **Carefree Travel Insurance** (✉ Box 9366, 100 Garden City Plaza, Garden City, NY 11530, ☎ 516/294–0220 or 800/323–3149), **Tele-Trip** (✉ Mutual of Omaha Plaza, Box 31716, Omaha, NE 68131, ☎ 800/228–9792), **Travel Guard International** (✉ 1145 Clark St., Stevens Point, WI 54481, ☎ 715/345–0505 or 800/826–1300), **Travel Insured International** (✉ Box 280568, East Hartford, CT 06128, ☎ 203/528–7663 or 800/243–3174), and **Wallach & Company** (✉ 107 W. Federal St., Box 480,

Middleburg, VA 22117, ☎ 540/687–3166 or 800/237–6615).

IN CANADA

Contact **Mutual of Omaha** (✉ Travel Division, 500 University Ave., Toronto, Ontario M5G 1V8, ☎ 800/465–0267 in Canada or 416/598–4083).

IN THE U.K.

The **Association of British Insurers** (✉ 51 Gresham St., London EC2V 7HQ, ☎ 0171/600–3333) gives advice by phone and publishes the free pamphlet **"Holiday Insurance and Motoring Abroad,"** which sets out typical policy provisions and costs.

L
LODGING

APARTMENT & VILLA RENTAL

Among the companies to contact are **At Home Abroad** (✉ 405 E. 56th St., Suite 6H, New York, NY 10022, ☎ 212/421–9165, FAX 212/752–1591), **Europa-Let/Tropical Inn-Let, Inc.** (✉ 92 N. Main St., Ashland, OR 97520, ☎ 541/482–5806 or 800/462–4486, FAX 541/482–0660), **Property Rentals International** (✉ 1008 Mansfield Crossing Rd., Richmond, VA 23236, ☎ 804/378–6054 or 800/220–3332, FAX 804/379–2073), **Rent-a-Home International** (✉ 7200 34th Ave. NW, Seattle, WA 98117, ☎ 206/789–9377 or 800/488–7368, FAX 206/789–9379), and **Villas International** (✉ 605 Market St., Suite 510, San Francisco, CA 94105, ☎ 415/281–

0910 or 800/221–2260, FAX 415/281–0919). Members of the travel club **Hideaways International** (✉ 767 Islington St., Portsmouth, NH 03801, ☎ 603/430–4433 or 800/843–4433, FAX 603/430–4444; $99 per year) receive two annual guides plus quarterly newsletters and arrange rentals among themselves.

CAMPING

There are numerous campgrounds, most privately owned, throughout Greece. One or more can usually be found in close proximity to popular archaeological sites and beach resorts—they aren't intended for those who want to explore the wilds of Greece. Their amenities range from basic to elaborate and those operated by the tourist organization are cushier than most. Contact the **Greek Camping Union** (✉ 76 Solonos St., 10680 Athens, ☎ 01/362–1560, FAX 01/346–5262) for more information. The EOT distributes a free brochure called **"Camping in Greece"** with site listings. Keep in mind that what the Greeks call "freelance" camping is also available, (though technically illegal). These informal sites spring up annually, often around an island's nudist beaches. Usually there is some form of running water and a nearby taverna—ask around.

HOME EXCHANGE

Some of the principal clearinghouses are **HomeLink International/ Vacation Exchange Club**

(✉ Box 650, Key West, FL 33041, ☎ 305/294–1448 or 800/638–3841, FAX 305/294–1148; $78 per year), which sends members five annual directories, with a listing in one, plus updates; and **Loan-a-Home** (✉ 2 Park La., Apt. 6E, Mount Vernon, NY 10552, ☎ 914/664–7640; $40–$50 per year), which specializes in long-term exchanges.

HOTELS

Greek hotels are classified as luxury (L) and A–E, though don't expect hotels in each government-set category to have the same amenities as their American and Northern European counterparts. Within each category, quality varies greatly but prices don't. Still, you may come across an A-class hotel that charges less than a B-class, depending on facilities. The EOT distributes lists of hotels for each region, although it will not make recommendations. Annual hotel directories are available at most English-language bookstores in Athens and Thessaloniki and at city kiosks in late spring. One of the most complete guides is **Hellenic Traveling Pages** (✉ Info Publications, Pironos 51, 16341 Athens, ☎ 01/994–0109, FAX 01/99–6564), a monthly publication available at most Greek bookstores; it also lists travel agencies, bus, boat, and airplane routes, and museum hours.

RENTAL ROOMS

Although you will be approached by owners of rental rooms upon your arrival at most islands in summer, you may want to check a new annual publication in English that details prices and facilities of rental rooms, with photos of accommodations to help you decide. *Holiday Rentals in Greece: Rooms, Apartments and Studios,* is published by Touristiki Ekdotiki (⊠ P. Tsaldari 48, 16232 Vironas, ☎ 01/765–1065) and is available at Athens kiosks.

TRADITIONAL SETTLEMENTS

In an effort to provide tourist accommodations in traditional settings, the EOT has begun a restoration program, converting older buildings into guest houses. Some of the villages developed so far include Oia on Santorini; Makrinitsa on Mt. Pelion; Mesta on Chios; Papingo in Epirus; Vathia in the Mani with its curious tower homes; and Monemvassia in the southern Peloponnese. For reservations call the **Greek Hotel and Cruise Reservation Center** (☎ 714/641–3502 or 800/736–5717, or FAX 714/641–0303). Many of these settlements are detailed and photographed in an EOT handout, **"Traditional Settlements,"** as well as in a new guide called **Traditional Inns in Greece: Alternative Forms of Tourism,** in English, published by Vertical Advertising (⊠ 61A Katehaki St., 11525 Athens, ☎ 01/691–2219, FAX 01/649–6782) and sold in Athens foreign-language bookstores.

M
MAIL

RECEIVING MAIL

You can have your mail sent to the **American Express** office in Athens (⊠ Ermou 2, 10225 Athens). The service is free for cardholders or those with AmEx traveler's checks; otherwise, there is a 400 dr. charge for each pickup. Any Greek post office will hold your mail, if the address includes the words **"poste restante,"** though you need your passport to collect the letters. The main Athens post office (⊠ Aeolou 100, 10200 Athens) is open weekdays 7:30 AM–8 PM, Sat. 7:30–2, Sun. 9–1:30.

MONEY

ATMS

For specific foreign **Cirrus** locations, call ☎ 800/424–7787; for foreign **Plus** locations, consult the Plus directory at your local bank.

CURRENCY EXCHANGE

If your bank doesn't exchange currency, contact **Thomas Cook Currency Services** (☎ 800/287–7362 for locations). **Ruesch International** (☎ 800/424–2923 for locations) can also provide you with foreign banknotes before you leave home and publishes a number of useful brochures, including a "Foreign Currency Guide" and "Foreign Exchange Tips."

WIRING FUNDS

Funds can be wired via **MoneyGram℠** (for locations and information in the U.S. and Canada, ☎ 800/926–9400) or **Western Union** (for agent locations or to send money using MasterCard or Visa, ☎ 800/325–6000); in Canada, ☎ 800/321–2923; in the U.K., ☎ 0800/833833; or visit the Western Union office at the nearest major post office).

P
PACKING

For strategies on packing light, get a copy of **The Packing Book,** by Judith Gilford (⊠ Ten Speed Press, Box 7123, Berkeley, CA 94707, ☎ 510/559–1600 or 800/841–2665, FAX 510/524–4588; $7.95 plus $3.50 shipping).

PASSPORTS & VISAS

U.S. CITIZENS

For fees, documentation requirements, and other information, call the State Department's **Office of Passport Services** information line (☎ 202/647–0518).

CANADIANS

For fees, documentation requirements, and other information, call the Ministry of Foreign Affairs and International Trade's **Passport Office** (☎ 819/994–3500 or 800/567–6868).

U.K. CITIZENS

For fees, documentation requirements, and to request an emergency passport, call the London **Passport Office** (☎ 0990/210410).

PHOTO HELP

The **Kodak Information Center** (☎ 800/242–2424) answers consumer questions about film and photography. The **Kodak Guide to Shooting Great Travel Pictures** (available in bookstores; or contact Fodor's Travel Publications, ☎ 800/533–6478; $16.50 plus $4 shipping) explains how to take expert travel photographs.

S
SAFETY

"Trouble-Free Travel," from the AAA, is a booklet of tips for protecting yourself and your belongings when away from home. Send a stamped, self-addressed, legal-size envelope to Trouble-Free Travel (✉ Mail Stop 75, 1000 AAA Dr., Heathrow, FL 32746).

SENIOR CITIZENS

CLUBS

Sears's **Mature Outlook** (✉ Box 10448, Des Moines, IA 50306, ☎ 800/336–6330; annual membership $14.95) includes a lifestyle/travel magazine and membership in ITC-50 travel club, which offers discounts of up to 50% at participating hotels and restaurants. (☞ Discounts & Deals *in* Smart Travel Tips A to Z, *below*).

EDUCATIONAL TRAVEL

The nonprofit **Elderhostel** (✉ 75 Federal St., 3rd Floor, Boston, MA 02110, ☎ 617/426–7788), for people 55 and older, has offered inexpensive study programs since 1975. Courses cover everything from marine science to Greek mythology and cowboy poetry. Costs for two- to three-week interna-

tional trips—including room, board, and transportation from the U.S.—range from $1,800 to $4,500.

Interhostel (✉ University of New Hampshire, 6 Garrison Ave., Durham, NH 03824, ☎ 603/862–1147 or 800/733–9753), for travelers 50 and older, has mostly two-week trips that cost $2,000–$3,500, including airfare.

ORGANIZATIONS

Contact the **American Association of Retired Persons** (✉ AARP, 601 E St. NW, Washington, DC 20049, ☎ 202/434–2277; annual dues $8 per person or couple). Its Purchase Privilege Program secures discounts for members on lodging, car rentals, and sightseeing.

SPORTS

BICYCLING

Bicycling is impossible on the crowded city streets, although some use bikes to go to and from work in smaller towns. For recreational biking programs contact the **Greek Cycling Federation** (✉ Bouboulinas 28 St., 10682 Athens, ☎ 01/883–1414).

GOLFING

Golfing in Greece is possible, but there aren't many 18-hole courses. Those with complete facilities include the **Glyfada Golf Course and Club** (☎ 01/894–6820) near Athens, the **Afandou Golf** (☎ 0241/51451 or 0241/51256) on Rhodes, the **Porto Carras Golf Club** in Chalkidiki (☎ 0375/71221), and the **Corfu Golf Club** (☎ 0661/94220).

HIKING & MOUNTAIN BIKING

The country offers plenty of rugged terrain for serious hiking and mountaineering. The **Greek Skiing and Alpine Federation** (✉ 7 Karageorgi Servias St., 10563 Athens, ☎ 01/323–4555) operates more than 40 mountain refuge huts that are available to the public by prior arrangement. The **Greek Federation of Mountaineering Associations** (✉ Milioni 5, 10673 Kolonaki, ☎ 01/364–5904) can also supply details on refuges, mountain paths, and contact numbers for local hiking clubs. The **Greek Touring Club** (✉ Politechniou 12, 10433 Athens, ☎ 01/524–0854, October through May only) arranges hiking trips throughout Greece, and the **Federation of Excursion Clubs of Greece** (✉ Dragatsaniou 4, 10559 Athens, ☎ 01/323–4107) provides information on mountain paths, as well as guides.

Treks throughout Greece are organized by adventure travel agencies, which also offer kayaking, rafting, mountain biking and camping trips; try **Trekking Hellas** (✉ Fillelinon 7, Syntagma, 10557 Athens, ☎ 01/325–0317 or 01/325–0853); and **Ev Zin** (✉ Syngrou 132, 11745 Athens, ☎ 01/923–0263 and 01/921–6285).

HORSEBACK RIDING

The helpful **Greek Equestrian Federation** (✉ Messinias 55, 15341 Ayia Paraskevi, ☎ 01/652–8139) provides a list of riding clubs throughout the country.

RAFTING & KAYAKING

Alpine Club (⌧ Michalakopoulou 39, Ilisia, 11528 Athens, ☎ 01/721–2773) organizes trips, including transportation, guides, and equipment, to rivers throughout Greece.

SAILING & WINDSURFING

The **Greek Sailing Federation** (⌧ Leoforos Poseidonios 51, Moschato, 18344 Athens, ☎ 01/930–4826) can recommend clubs with equipment and lessons available for both sailing and windsurfing. The International Aegean Sailing Rally, held for 10 days in July, is the most important regatta in Greece—information and entry applications can be obtained from the **Hellenic Offshore Racing Club** (⌧ Akti Dilaveri 3, 18533 Mikrolimano, ☎ 01/412–3357).

SKIING

Ski Centre Parnassos (☎ 0234/22689 and 0234/22693) is one of the country's best resorts, about three hours north of Athens. The **Greek Skiing and Alpine Federation** (⌧ Karageorgi Servias 7, 8th floor, Syntagma, 10563 Athens, ☎ 01/323–0182) can give you a bilingual brochure with addresses for other ski centers as well as mountain refuges.

SPELUNKING

Tourists with troglodyte tendencies are welcome to subterranean Greece. Twelve of the caves

have some facilities for tourists, and three more are being developed. Spelunkers in search of wild caves should contact the **Hellenic Speleological Society** (⌧ Mantzarou 8 St., 10672 Athens, ☎ 01/361–7824).

SWIMMING & DIVING

In Athens **EOT** outlets (main info office ⌧ Karageorgi Servias 2, Athens, ☎ 01/322–2545) can give you a list of their local beaches, which have snack bars and beach umbrellas, chairs, dressing rooms, and sports equipment for rent, and occasionally windsurfing and waterskiing lessons.

Scuba diving is heavily restricted to protect underwater artifacts. Areas where limited diving is permitted include Corfu, Chalkidiki, Mykonos, and Rhodes. A travel agent can steer you to a supervised dive trip, or you can call the **Greek Diving Center** (⌧ Vas. Pavlou 26, Kastella, 18533 Piraeus, ☎ 01/412–1708), which offers lessons up to the instructor's level, rents equipment, and organizes one- to two-day diving excursions on weekends. For those who want an introduction to the sport, **Scuba Diving Club of Vouliagmeni** (⌧ Leoforos Poseidonos behind Albatross candy shop, 16671 Ormos Vouliagmeni, near Athens, ☎ 01/696–4609) runs a one-day orientation called Discover Scuba, where you learn basic theory and then dive with an instructor. The center also offers regu-

lar diving courses, equipment, boat rentals with accompaniment for expeditions, and water sports. Call a few days ahead to arrange matters.

TENNIS

There are tennis clubs in most large cities and island resorts. Call the **Hellenic Tennis Federation** (⌧ Olympic Stadium offices, Kalogreza, ☎ 01/685–2511/2) for information on tennis clubs, from which you can rent courts by the hour, or check with your hotel concierge to help you find one that admits nonmembers.

STUDENTS

HOSTELING

In the U.S., contact **Hostelling International–American Youth Hostels** (⌧ 733 15th St. NW, Suite 840, Washington, DC 20005, ☎ 202/783–6161, ℻ 202/783–6171); in Canada, **Hostelling International–Canada** (⌧ 205 Catherine St., Suite 400, Ottawa, Ontario K2P 1C3, ☎ 613/237–7884); and in the United Kingdom, the **Youth Hostel Association of England and Wales** (⌧ Trevelyan House, 8 St. Stephen's Hill, St. Albans, Hertfordshire AL1 2DY, ☎ 01727/855215 or 01727/845047). Membership (in the U.S., $25; in Canada, C$26.75; in the U.K., £9.30) gives you access to 5,000 hostels in 77 countries that charge $5–$40 per person per night.

You can also contact the **Greek Association of Youth Hostels** (⌧ 4, Dragatsaniou St., Athens, ☎ 01/323–

4107), but because of some bureaucracy with the EOT, not all hostels fall under their jurisdiction. For the moment, hostels (whether called that or not) are operating in Athens and Delphi on the mainland; Nauplion and Olympia in the Peloponnese; Corfu; Santorini; and Ayios Nikolaos, Hania, Heraklion, Mallia, Rethymnon, and Sitia on Crete. The **YWCA** in Athens (⊠ Amerikis 11, ☎ 01/362–4291) also takes overnight guests, women only.

ORGANIZATIONS

A major contact is the **Council on International Educational Exchange** (mail orders only ⊠ CIEE, 205 E. 42nd St., 16th Floor, New York, NY 10017, ☎ 212/822–2600, FAX 212/822–2699). The **Educational Travel Centre** (⊠ 438 N. Frances St., Madison, WI 53703, ☎ 608/256–5551 or 800/747–5551, FAX 608/256–2042) offers rail passes and low-cost airline tickets, mostly for flights that depart from Chicago.

In Canada, also contact **Travel Cuts** (⊠ 187 College St., Toronto, Ontario M5T 1P7, ☎ 416/979–2406 or 800/667–2887).

PUBLICATIONS

Check out the *Berkeley Guide to Europe* (available in bookstores; or contact Fodor's Travel Publications, ☎ 800/533–6478; $18.95 plus $4 shipping).

T

The country code for Greece is 30. For local access numbers abroad, contact **AT&T** USADirect (☎ 800/874–4000), **MCI** Call USA (☎ 800/444–4444), or **Sprint** Express (☎ 800/793–1153).

TOUR OPERATORS

Among the companies that sell tours and packages to Greece, the following are nationally known, have a proven reputation, and offer plenty of options.

GROUP TOURS

SUPER-DELUXE➤ **Abercrombie & Kent** (⊠ 1520 Kensington Rd., Oak Brook, IL 60521-2141, ☎ 708/954–2944 or 800/323–7308, FAX 708/954–3324) and **Travcoa** (⊠ Box 2630, 2350 S.E. Bristol St., Newport Beach, CA 92660, ☎ 714/476–2800 or 800/992–2003, FAX 714/476–2538).

DELUXE➤ **Globus** (⊠ 5301 S. Federal Circle, Littleton, CO 80123, ☎ 303/797–2800 or 800/221–0090, FAX 303/795–0962) and **Maupintour** (⊠ Box 807, 1515 St. Andrews Dr., Lawrence, KS 66047, ☎ 913/843–1211 or 800/255–4266, FAX 913/843–8351).

FIRST-CLASS➤ **Brendan Tours** (⊠ 15137 Califa St., Van Nuys, CA 91411, ☎ 818/785–9696 or 800/421–8446, FAX 818/902–9876), **Central Holidays** (⊠ 206 Central Ave., Jersey City, NJ 07307, ☎ 201/798–5777 or 800/935–5000), **Collette Tours** (⊠ 162 Middle St., Pawtucket, RI 02860, ☎ 401/728–3805 or 800/832–4656, FAX 401/728–1380), **DER Tours** (⊠ 11933 Wilshire

Blvd., Los Angeles, CA 90025, ☎ 310/479–4140 or 800/937–1235), **General Tours** (⊠ 53 Summer St., Keene, NH 03431, ☎ 603/357–5033 or 800/221–2216, FAX 603/357–4548), **Insight International Tours** (⊠ 745 Atlantic Ave., #720, Boston, MA 02111, ☎ 617/482–2000 or 800/582–8380, FAX 617/482–2884 or 800/622–5015), and **Trafalgar Tours** (⊠ 11 E. 26th St., New York, NY 10010, ☎ 212/689–8977 or 800/854–0103, FAX 800/457–6644).

BUDGET➤ **Cosmos** (☞ Globus, *above*) and **Trafalgar** (☞ *above*).

PACKAGES

Independent vacation packages that include round-trip airfare and hotel accommodations are available from major airlines and tour operators. Among U.S. carriers, contact **Delta Dream Vacations** (☎ 800/872–7786). Leading tour operators include **Central Holidays** (☞ Group Tours, *above*), **DER Tours** (☞ Group Tours, *above*) and **General Tours** (☞ Group Tours, *above*).

FROM THE U.K.

For holiday packages to Greece, contact **First Choice** (⊠ First Choice House, Peel Cross House, Peel Cross Rd., Salford, Manchester M5 2AN, ☎ 0161/745–7000), **Inspirations** (⊠ Victoria House, Victoria Rd., Horley, Surrey RH6 7AD, ☎ 01293/822–244), and **Unijet** (⊠ Sandrocks, Rocky Lane, Haywards Heath, West Sussex RH16 4RH, ☎ 01444/451–515).

THE GOLD GUIDE / IMPORTANT CONTACTS

ORGANIZATIONS

The **National Tour Association** (✉ NTA, 546 E. Main St., Lexington, KY 40508, ☎ 606/226-4444 or 800/755-8687) and the **United States Tour Operators Association** (✉ USTOA, 211 E. 51st St., Suite 12B, New York, NY 10022, ☎ 212/750-7371) can provide lists of members and information on booking tours.

PUBLICATIONS

Contact the USTOA (☞ Organizations, *above*) for its **"Smart Traveler's Planning Kit."** Pamphlets in the kit include the "Worldwide Tour and Vacation Package Finder," "How to Select a Tour or Vacation Package," and information on the organization's consumer protection plan. Also write for a copy of the Better Business Bureau's **"Tips on Travel Packages"** (✉ Publication 24-195, 4200 Wilson Blvd., Arlington, VA 22203; $2).

THEME TRIPS

Travel Contacts (✉ Box 173, Camberley, GU15 1YE, England, ☎ 01/27667-7217, FAX 01/2766-3477), which represents over 160 tour operators, can satisfy just about any special interest in Greece.

ADVENTURE➤ Action-packed tours of Greece are also sold by **Adventure Center** (✉ 1311 63rd St., #200, Emeryville, CA 94608, ☎ 510/654-1879 or 800/227-8747, FAX 510/654-4200).

ARCHAEOLOGY➤ **Archeological Tours** (✉ 271

Madison Ave., New York, NY 10016, ☎ 212/986-3054, FAX 212/370-1561) explores the rich history of Greece.

BICYCLING➤ A bike tour through Greece and Turkey is available from **Backroads** (✉ 1516 5th St., Berkeley, CA 94710-1740, ☎ 510/577-1555 or 800/462-2848, FAX 510/527-1444).

HISTORY➤ History buffs should contact **Herodot Travel** (✉ 775 E. Blithedale, Box 234, Mill Valley, CA 94941, ☎ FAX 415/381-4031).

JUDAISM➤ Jewish life in Greece is the subject of a tour from the **American Jewish Congress** (✉ 15 E. 84th St., New York, NY 10028, ☎ 212/879-4588 or 800/221-4694).

LEARNING VACATIONS➤ For educational programs contact **Earthwatch** (✉ Box 403, 680 Mt. Auburn St., Watertown, MA 02272, ☎ 617/926-8200 or 800/776-0188, FAX 617/926-8532), which recruits volunteers to serve in its EarthCorps as short-term assistants to scientists on research expeditions, and **Smithsonian Study Tours and Seminars** (✉ 1100 Jefferson Dr. SW, Room 3045, MRC 702, Washington, DC 20560, ☎ 202/357-4700, FAX 202/633-9250).

SINGLES AND YOUNG ADULTS➤ Travelers 18-35 looking to join a group should try **Contiki Holidays** (✉ 300 Plaza Alicante, #900, Garden Grove, CA 92640, ☎ 714/740-0808 or 800/266-8454, FAX 714/740-0818).

VILLAS➤ Contact **Villas International** (✉ 605 Market St., San Francisco, CA 94105, ☎ 415/281-0910 or 800/221-2260, FAX 415/281-0919).

YACHT CHARTERS➤ Try **Alden Yacht Charters** (✉ 1909 Alden Landing, Portsmouth, RI 02871, ☎ 401/683-1782 or 800/662-2628, FAX 401/683-3668), **Huntley Yacht Vacations** (✉ 210 Preston Rd., Wernersville, PA 19565, ☎ 610/678-2628 or 800/322-9224, FAX 610/670-1767), **Lynn Jachney Charters** (✉ Box 302, Marblehead, MA 01945, ☎ 617/639-0787 or 800/223-2050, FAX 617/639-0216), **The Moorings** (✉ 19345 U.S. Hwy. 19 N, 4th floor, Clearwater, FL 34624-3193, ☎ 813/530-5424 or 800/535-7289, FAX 813/530-9474), **Ocean Voyages** (✉ 1709 Bridgeway, Sausalito, CA 94965, ☎ 415/332-4681, FAX 415/332-7460), **Russell Yacht Charters** (✉ 404 Hulls Hwy., Southport, CT 06490, ☎ 203/255-2783 or 800/635-8895), and **Sail Away** (✉ 15605 S.W. 92nd Ave., Miami, FL 33157-1972, ☎ 305/253-7245 or 800/724-5292, FAX 305/251-4408).

TRAIN TRAVEL

For information on trains, contact the Greek Railway Organization **(OSE)** at your local station, or at their main offices in Athens (✉ Karolou St. 1 near Omonia Sq., ☎ 01/524-0646 through 0648; ✉ Sina St. 6, ☎ 01/362-4402 through 4406; and ✉

Filellinon St. 17 near Syntagma Square, ☎ 01/323-6747 and 01/323-6273). You may also call ☎ 145 for a recorded departure timetable, in Greek, of trains within Greece; call ☎ 147 for information on trains to Europe and Russia. In Athens, OSE has two stations: trains from northern Greece and abroad use **Stathmos Larissis** (☎ 01/823-7741), and from the Peloponnese **Stathmos Peloponnisou** (☎ 01/513-1601), next door. **OSE buses** for Albania, Bulgaria, and Turkey also leave from this station (☎ 01/513-5768 or 01/513-5769).

DISCOUNT PASSES

EurailPasses are available through travel agents and **Rail Europe** (✉ 226-230 Westchester Ave., White Plains, NY 10604, ☎ 914/682-5172 or 800/438-7245; ✉ 2087 Dundas E., Suite 105, Mississauga, Ontario L4X 1M2, ☎ 416/602-4195), **DER Tours** (✉ Box 1606, Des Plaines, IL 60017, ☎ 800/782-2424, FAX 800/282-7474), or **CIT Tours Corp.** (✉ 342 Madison Ave., Suite 207, New York, NY 10173, ☎ 212/697-2100 or 800/248-8687 or 800/248-7245 in western U.S.).

TRAVEL AGENCIES

For names of reputable agencies in your area, contact the **American Society of Travel Agents** (✉ ASTA, 1101 King St., Suite 200, Alexandria, VA 22314, ☎ 703/739-2782), the **Association of Canadian Travel Agents** (✉ Suite 201, 1729 Bank St.,

Ottawa, Ontario K1V 7Z5, ☎ 613/521-0474, FAX 613/521-0805), or the **Association of British Travel Agents** (✉ 55-57 Newman St., London W1P 4AH, ☎ 0171/637-2444, FAX 0171/637-0713).

TRAVEL GEAR

For travel apparel, appliances, personal-care items, and other travel necessities, get a free catalog from **Magellan's** (☎ 800/962-4943, FAX 805/568-5406), **Orvis Travel** (☎ 800/541-3541, FAX 540/343-7053), or **TravelSmith** (☎ 800/950-1600, FAX 415/455-0554).

ELECTRICAL CONVERTERS

Send a self-addressed, stamped envelope to the **Franzus Company** (✉ Customer Service, Dept. B50, Murtha Industrial Park, Box 142, Beacon Falls, CT 06403, ☎ 203/723-6664) for a copy of the free brochure "Foreign Electricity Is No Deep, Dark Secret."

U

U.S.
GOVERNMENT
TRAVEL BRIEFINGS

The U.S. Department of State's American Citizens Services office (✉ Room 4811, Washington, DC 20520; enclose SASE) issues **Consular Information Sheets** on all foreign countries. These cover issues such as crime, security, political climate, and health risks as well as listing embassy locations, entry requirements, currency regulations, and providing other useful infor-

mation. For the latest information, stop in at any U.S. passport office, consulate, or embassy; call the interactive hot line (☎ 202/647-5225, FAX 202/647-3000); or, with your PC's modem, tap into the department's computer bulletin board (☎ 202/647-9225).

V

VISITOR
INFORMATION

Contact the **EOT.**

IN THE U.S.

✉ 645 5th Ave., New York, NY 10022, ☎ 212/421-5777, FAX 212/826-6940; ✉ 611 W. 6th St., Suite 2198, Los Angeles, CA 90017, ☎ 213/626-6696, FAX 213/489-9744; ✉ 168 N. Michigan Ave., Suite 600, Chicago, IL 60601, ☎ 312/782-1084, FAX 312/782-1091.

IN CANADA

✉ 1233 Rue de la Montagne, Suite 101, Montréal, Québec H3G 1Z2, ☎ 514/871-1535, FAX 514/871-1498; ✉ 1300 Bay St., Toronto, Ontario M5R 3K8, ☎ 416/968-2220, FAX 416/968-6533.

IN THE U.K.

✉ 4 Conduit St., London W1R 0DJ, ☎ 0171/734-5997.

W

WEATHER

For current conditions and forecasts, plus the local time and helpful travel tips, call the **Weather Channel Connection** (☎ 900/932-8437; 95p per minute) from a Touch-Tone phone.

THE GOLD GUIDE / IMPORTANT CONTACTS

The *International Traveler's Weather Guide* (✉ Weather Press, Box 660606, Sacramento, CA 95866, ☎ 916/ 974–0201 or 800/972– 0201; $10.95 includes shipping), written by two meteorologists, provides month-by- month information on temperature, humidity, and precipitation in more than 175 cities worldwide.

SMART TRAVEL TIPS A TO Z

Basic Information on Traveling in Greece and Savvy Tips to Make Your Trip a Breeze

A

ADDRESSES

To make finding your way around as easy as possible, it's wise to learn to recognize letters in the Greek alphabet. Most areas, even Athens, have few signs in English. Sometimes there are several spelling variations in English for the same place: Agios or Ayios, Georgios or Yiorgos. Also, the English version may be quite different from the Greek, or even what locals use informally: Corfu is known as Kerkyra, island capitals are often just called Chora (town) no matter what their formal title, Vassilis Sofias (Queen Sofia), a main Athens boulevard now reads Venizelou on maps since royalty was banned, but if you ask for that name, no one will know what you're talking about. A street may change names several times, and a city may have more than one street by the same name, so it's best to know the district you're headed for, or a major landmark nearby, especially if you're taking a taxi.

AIR TRAVEL

If time is an issue, **always look for nonstop flights,** which require no change of plane. If possible, **avoid connecting flights,** which stop at least once and can involve a change of plane, even though the flight number remains the same; if the first leg is late, the second waits.

For better service, **fly smaller or regional carriers,** which often have higher passenger satisfaction ratings. Sometimes they have such in-flight amenities as leather seats or greater legroom and they often have better food.

CUTTING COSTS

The Sunday travel section of most newspapers is a good place to look for deals.

MAJOR AIRLINES➤ The least-expensive airfares from the major airlines are priced for round-trip travel and are subject to restrictions. Usually, you must **book in advance and buy the ticket within 24 hours** to get cheaper fares, and you may have to **stay over a Saturday night.** The lowest fare is subject to availability, and only a small percentage of the plane's total seats is sold at that price. It's smart to **call a number of airlines, and when you are quoted a good price, book it on the spot**—the same fare may not be available on the same flight the next day. Airlines generally allow you to change your return date for a $25 to $50 fee. If you don't use your ticket, you can apply the cost toward the purchase of a new ticket, again for a small charge. However, most low-fare tickets are nonrefundable. To get the lowest airfare, **check different routings.** If your destination has more than one gateway, **compare prices to different airports.**

FROM THE U.K.➤ To save money on flights, **look into an APEX or Super-PEX ticket.** APEX tickets must be booked in advance and have certain restrictions. Super-PEX tickets can be purchased right at the airport.

CONSOLIDATORS➤ Consolidators buy tickets for scheduled flights at reduced rates from the airlines, then sell them at prices below the lowest available from the airlines directly—usually without advance restrictions. Sometimes you can even get your money back if you need to return the ticket. Carefully read the fine print detailing penalties for changes and cancellations. If you doubt the reliability of a consolidator, **confirm your reservation with the airline.**

ALOFT

AIRLINE FOOD➤ If you hate airline food, **ask for special meals when booking.** These can be vegetarian, low-cholesterol, or kosher, for example; commonly prepared to order in smaller quantities than standard fare, they can be tastier.

JET LAG➤ To avoid this syndrome, which occurs when travel disrupts your body's natural cycles, try to maintain a normal routine. At night, **get some sleep.** By day, move about the cabin to **stretch your legs, eat light meals, and drink water—not alcohol.**

SMOKING➤ Smoking is not allowed on flights of six hours or less within the continental U.S. Smoking is also prohibited on flights within Canada. For U.S. flights longer than six hours or international flights, **contact your carrier in regard to their smoking policy.** Some carriers have prohibited smoking throughout their system; others allow smoking only on certain routes or even certain departures of that route.

WITHIN GREECE

The frequency of flights varies according to the time of year, and it is essential to book well in advance for summer or for festivals and holidays. Domestic flights are a good deal for many destinations. In summer 1996 the one-way Athens–Rhodes fare was 23,100 dr.; to Corfu, 19,200 dr.; to Santorini, 20,200 dr.; and to Heraklion, 20,500 dr. Unless the flight is part of an international journey, the baggage allowance is only 15 kilos (33 lbs.) per passenger.

AIRPORT
TRANSFERS

In Athens yellow-and-blue double-decker express **buses** connect the two terminals, Syntagma Square, and Omonia Square (Bus 91), running every half hour. To Piraeus Bus 19 runs hourly until 11 PM; night service on both is less frequent. The fare is 160 dr., 200 dr. after 11:30 PM. It's much easier and faster just to queue at the **taxi** stands in front of each terminal: 1,000 dr. between terminals, 1,700 dr. to the city center, 1,800 dr. to Piraeus; the price goes up by about two-thirds between midnight and 5 AM. In Thessaloniki, a municipal shuttle picks up travelers every half hour for the 30-minute bus ride into town. At other airports throughout Greece, especially on the islands, public transportation from the airport is either infrequent or nonexistent; ask your hotel to make arrangements or take a taxi, keeping in mind that rates are usually set to fixed destinations, and there is a 300-dr. pick-up charge from the airport.

B
BOAT TRAVEL

Cruise ships and ferries to and from the Aegean islands leave from **Piraeus,** 10 km (6 mi) southwest of Athens, although some northern islands, like Thassos and Limnos, are more easily reached from Thessaloniki. The metro (100 dr.) is the fastest way to get from the Athens city center to the port. Ships for the Ionian islands and Italy sail from ports on the west coast, such as Patras and Igoumenitsa. Timetables change frequently, and boats may be delayed by weather conditions, especially when the northwestern winds called *meltemi* hit in August, so your plans should be flexible. Travel agents in the cities can call the port to check for you; on the islands, each shipping agency posts a board with departure times, or you can call the port authority (limenarchio), where some English is usually spoken. Buy your tickets several days in advance if you are traveling between July 15 and August 30, when most Greeks vacation, or if you're taking a car. Reserve your return journey soon after you arrive.

The other main port in Attica is **Rafina,** on the eastern coast, where boats to and from Evia and nearby Cyclades (Kea, Andros, Tinos, Mykonos) dock. To get there, take a KTEL bus (☎ 01/821–0872, fare: 400 dr.), which leaves every half hour from Aigyptou Square near Pedion Areos park in Athens.

If the journey will be more than a few hours, take supplies, as food and refreshments on board are quite expensive, and the washrooms always seem to run out of toilet paper. Most of the shops aboard ferries sell Dramamine, as do the kiosks on the harbors.

BUS TRAVEL

Organized bus tours can be booked together with hotel reservations by your travel agent. Many tour operators have offices in and around Syntagma or Omonia squares in Athens. Bus tours often depart from Syntagma or adjacent streets.

The EOT distributes KTEL regional bus schedules, including prices for each destination and phone numbers for the ticket desk (☞ Bus Travel *in* Important Contacts A to Z, *above*). Make reservations at least one day before your planned trip, earlier for holiday weekends. Board early, because Greeks have a very loose attitude about assigned seating, and ownership is nine-tenths possession. Although smoking is forbidden on the bus, and the bus takes a break every two hours or so, drivers are exempt from the rule; don't sit near the front seat if smoking bothers you.

In Athens and Thessaloniki avoid riding buses during rush hours. Upon boarding, validate your ticket in the canceling machines, at the front and back of buses (this goes for the yellow trolleys, too). Keep your tickets until you reach your destination, as inspectors who occasionally board are strict about fining offenders. On intra-city buses, an inspector boards to check your ticket, so keep it handy. On islands and in smaller towns, you buy tickets from the driver's assistant once seated; try not to pay with anything more than a 1,000-dr. bill to avoid commotion.

BUSINESS HOURS

BANKS

Banks are normally open Monday–Thursday 8–2, Friday 8–

1:30. In Athens, the Ionian Bank of Greece (✉ In the Athens Hilton, Vasilissis Sofias 46, Hilton, 11528, ☎ 01/722–1182) stays open weekdays 8–2 and 3–9, and the National Bank of Greece (✉ Syntagma Sq., ☎ 01/323–6481) has weekend hours for foreign exchange only (Sat. 9–3, Sun. 9–1). Hotels and tourist shops also will cash traveler's checks on weekends.

CHURCHES & MONASTERIES

There is absolutely no rhyme or reason as to when churches and monasteries are open to the public; in numerous cases monasteries are merely ruins, no longer functioning or looked after. The best time to find churches unlocked is during mass, especially on Sunday; otherwise try from about 8 AM to noon and 5:30 to 7:30 on any day, unless where noted. The hours for monasteries are dependent upon their keepers, but they are generally more likely to be open in the morning to early afternoon; specific hours are noted.

MUSEUMS & SITES

The days and hours for museums and sites vary; they are usually open daily 8–3 except one weekday (usually, Monday), although in summer, depending on personnel available that year, the hours are extended to as late as 7 PM. The Acropolis is open summer evenings when there is a full moon. On major holidays, most sites and museums are closed; on

minor holidays they may have Sunday hours or close at 12:30. In Athens, for instance, the Byzantine Museum, Kerameikos cemetery, and Agora Museum are closed Monday; the Goulandris Museum of Cycladic Art is closed Tuesday and Sunday. Admission to most museums and archaeological sites is free on Sunday November through mid-March.

SHOPS

Nominally shops are open Monday, Wednesday, and Saturday 9–3 (8:30–3 in summer); Tuesday, Thursday, and Friday 9–3 (8:30–3 in summer) and 5:30–8:30 (5:30–9 in summer). Supermarkets are open Monday through Saturday 8–8. Be warned that shop hours are liable to change at any moment. In tourist areas, shops are allowed to extend their hours; those in Plaka, Athens's popular tourist bazaar, stay open until late into the night.

C

CAMERAS, CAMCORDERS, & COMPUTERS

IN TRANSIT

Always **keep your film, tape, or disks out of the sun;** never put these on the dashboard of a car. Carry an extra supply of batteries, and **be prepared to turn on your camera, camcorder, or laptop computer for security personnel** to prove that it's real.

X-RAYS

Always **ask for hand inspection at security.**

Such requests are virtually always honored at U.S. airports, and are usually accommodated abroad. Photographic film becomes clouded after successive exposure to airport X-ray machines. Videotape and computer disks are not harmed by X-rays, but **keep your tapes and disks away from metal detectors.**

CUSTOMS

Before departing, **register your foreign-made camera or laptop with U.S. Customs.** If your equipment is U.S.-made, call the consulate of the country you'll be visiting to find out whether it should be registered with local customs upon arrival.

Upon arrival, show your equipment to Greek Customs, who will register the model in your passport. Technically, you then must check in again at Customs upon departure from Greece (the desk is located after the security check), to show you haven't sold it in Greece; your passport will be stamped again. You may never be stopped coming or going and even if you are, Customs is unlikely to do anything if you have a foreign passport, but to avoid unforeseen hassles, it's best to follow the legal procedure. It's a good idea, also, to locate **the Greek representative at your destination** before you leave the U.S., in case you should need repairs.

CAR RENTAL

Because driving in Greece can be harrow-

ing, car rental prices are higher than in the U.S., and transporting a car by ferry hikes up the fare substantially, think twice before deciding on car travel. It's much easier to take public transportation or taxis, which are among the cheapest in Europe. The exception is large islands where the distance between towns is greater—and taxi fares higher—then, you may want to rent a car or a moped for the day for concentrated bouts of sightseeing.

CUTTING COSTS

It will be considerably cheaper if you **book through a travel agent who is willing to shop around.** Ask your agent to **look for fly-drive packages,** which also save you money, and **ask if local taxes are included** in the rental or fly-drive price. These can be as high as 20% in some destinations. Don't forget to find out about required deposits, cancellation penalties, drop-off charges, and the cost of any required insurance coverage.

Always **find out what equipment is standard** at your destination before specifying what you want; automatic transmission and air-conditioning are usually optional—and very expensive.

Be sure to **look into wholesalers**—companies that do not own their own fleets but rent in bulk from those that do and often offer better rates than traditional car-rental operations. Prices are best during off-peak periods; rentals booked through

wholesalers must be paid for before you leave the U.S.

FINDING QUALITY

Also **ask your travel agent about a company's customer-service record.** How has it responded to late plane arrivals and vehicle mishaps? Are there often lines at the rental counter, and—if you're traveling during a holiday period—does a confirmed reservation guarantee you a car?

INSURANCE

When driving a rented car, you are generally responsible for any damage to or loss of the rental vehicle. Before you rent, **see what coverage you already have** under the terms of your personal auto insurance policy and credit cards.

If you do not have auto insurance or an umbrella insurance policy that covers damage to third parties, purchasing CDW or LDW is highly recommended.

Collision policies that car-rental companies sell for European rentals typically do not cover stolen vehicles. Before you buy additional coverage for theft, find out if your credit card or personal auto insurance will cover the loss.

LICENSE REQUIREMENTS

In Greece your own driver's license is not acceptable unless you are an EU citizen. An International Driver's Permit is necessary; it's available from the American or Canadian automobile associations, or, in the United Kingdom, from the AA or RAC.

SURCHARGES

Before you pick up a car in one city and leave it in another, **ask about drop-off charges or one-way service fees,** which can be substantial. Note, too, that some rental agencies charge extra if you return the car before the time specified on your contract. To avoid a hefty refueling fee, **fill the tank just before you turn in the car**—but be aware that gas stations near the rental outlet may overcharge.

CHILDREN & TRAVEL

Greek parents, who dote on their children to the point of spoiling them, believe this is the natural order of things: You marry, have children, then shower them with attention. They will dote on your children, too, if you take them along. Couples traveling without children, on the other hand, are likely to be interrogated: How many do you have at home? When do you expect your first child? Despite this fondness for children, organized child-care services are scarce. You'll have to make arrangements for special activities and baby-sitting on an ad hoc basis.

When traveling with children, **plan ahead** and **involve your youngsters** as you outline your trip. When packing, **include a supply of things to keep them busy** en route (☞ Children & Travel *in*

Important Contacts A to Z, *above*). On sight-seeing days, try to **schedule activities of special interest to your children,** like a trip to a zoo or a playground. If you **plan your itinerary around seasonal festivals,** you'll never lack for things to do. In addition, **check local newspapers for special events** mounted by public libraries, museums, and parks.

BABY-SITTING

For recommended local sitters, **check with your hotel desk.**

DRIVING

If you are renting a car, don't forget to **arrange for a car seat when you reserve.** Sometimes they're free.

FLYING

As a general rule, infants under two not occupying a seat fly at greatly reduced fares and occasionally for free. If your children are two or older **ask about special children's fares.** Age limits for these fares vary among carriers. Rules also vary regarding unaccompanied minors, so again, check with your airline.

BAGGAGE➤ In general, the adult baggage allowance applies to children paying half or more of the adult fare. If you are traveling with an infant, **ask about carry-on allowances** before departure. In general, for infants charged 10% of the adult fare you are allowed one carry-on bag and a collapsible stroller, which may have to be checked; you may be limited to less if the flight is full.

FACILITIES➤ When making your reservation, **request children's meals or freestanding bassinets** if you need them; the latter are available only to those seated at the bulkhead, where there's enough legroom. If you don't need a bassinet, **think twice before requesting bulkhead seats**—the only storage space for in-flight necessities is in inconveniently distant overhead bins.

SAFETY SEATS➤ According to the FAA, it's a good idea to **use safety seats aloft** for children weighing less than 40 pounds. Airline policies vary. U.S. carriers allow FAA-approved models but usually require that you buy a ticket, even if your child would otherwise ride free, since the seats must be strapped into regular seats. However, some U.S. and foreign-flag airlines may require you to hold your baby during takeoff and landing—defeating the seat's purpose. Other foreign carriers may not allow infant seats at all, or may charge a child rather than an infant fare for their use.

GAMES

Milton Bradley and Parker Brothers have travel versions of some of their most popular games, including Yahtzee, Trouble, Sorry, and Monopoly. Prices run $5–$8. Look for them in the travel section of your local toy store.

LODGING

Most hotels allow children under a certain age to stay in their parents' room at no extra charge; others charge them as extra adults. Be sure to **ask about the cutoff age.**

CRUISES

To get the best deal on a cruise, **consult a cruise-only travel agency.**

Many travelers with limited time find traveling by boat an ideal way to see Greece's mainland ports and islands. It spares you the planning headaches of solitary island-hopping, when you can be stranded en route, waiting several days for the next ferry. The disadvantage: though cruise ships cover great distances at night, leaving days free for exploring, the usual stop in a port of call is often only a few hours, allowing for only a superficial visit. Often, an island's harbor is some distance from the main town, the more attractive, traditional villages, and the better beaches. Cruises are best for an overview that's useful for planning a return trip to the more appealing stops. Three-day cruises of the Greek islands, for instance, can be combined with a longer land tour. For information on specific lines and ships that offer these sails, consult a travel agent.

CUSTOMS & DUTIES

To speed your clearance through customs, **keep receipts for all your purchases abroad** and **be ready to show the inspector what you've bought.** If you feel that you've been incorrectly or unfairly charged a duty, you can **appeal assessments in dispute.** First ask to see a supervisor. If you are still unsatisfied, **write to the port director** at your point of entry, sending your customs receipt and any other appropriate documentation. The address will be listed on your receipt. If you still don't get satisfaction, you can take your case to customs headquarters in Washington.

IN GREECE

You may bring into Greece duty-free: food and beverages up to 22 pounds (10 kilos); 200 cigarettes, 100 cigarillos, or 50 cigars; one liter of alcoholic spirits or two liters of wine; and gift articles up to a total of 51,000 dr. Foreign bank notes amounting to more than $2,500 must be declared for reexport, but there are no restrictions on traveler's checks. Foreign visitors may take in 100,000 dr. in Greek currency and export up to 40,000 dr.

Only one per person of such expensive portable items as cameras, camcorders, tape recorders and the like is permitted into Greece. Sports equipment, such as bicycles and skis, is also limited to one (pair) per person.

To bring in a dog or a cat, you need a health certificate issued by a veterinary authority and validated by the Greek consulate and the appropriate medical authority (in the U.S., the Department of Agriculture). It must state that your pet doesn't carry any infectious diseases and that it received a rabies inoculation not more than 12 months (for cats, six months) and not fewer than six days before arrival. Dogs must also have a veterinary certificate that indicates they have been wormed against echinococcus.

The export of antiquities from Greece is forbidden. If any such articles are found in a traveler's luggage, they will be confiscated and the individual will be liable for prosecution. Reproductions of ancient works of art, some of very high quality, can be purchased throughout Greece, and may be exported freely.

IN THE U.S.

You may bring home $400 worth of foreign goods duty-free if you've been out of the country for at least 48 hours and haven't already used the $400 allowance, or any part of it, in the past 30 days.

Travelers 21 or older may bring back 1 liter of alcohol duty-free, provided the beverage laws of the state through which they reenter the U.S. allow it. In addition, regardless of their age, they are allowed 100 non-Cuban cigars and 200 cigarettes. Antiques, which the U.S. Customs Service defines as objects more than 100 years old, are duty-free. Original works of art done entirely by hand are also duty-free. These include, but are not limited to, paintings, drawings, and sculptures.

Duty-free, travelers may mail packages valued at up to $200 to themselves and up to $100 to others, with a limit of one parcel per addressee per day (and no alcohol or tobacco products or perfume valued at more than $5); on the outside, the package must be labeled as being either for personal use or an unsolicited gift, and a list of its contents and their retail value must be attached. Mailed items do not affect your duty-free allowance on your return.

IN CANADA

If you've been out of Canada for at least seven days, you may bring in C$500 worth of goods duty-free. If you've been away for fewer than seven days but for more than 48 hours, the duty-free allowance drops to C$200; if your trip lasts between 24 and 48 hours, the allowance is C$50. You cannot pool allowances with family members. Goods claimed under the C$500 exemption may follow you by mail; those claimed under the lesser exemptions must accompany you.

Alcohol and tobacco products may be included in the seven-day and 48-hour exemptions but not in the 24-hour exemption. If you meet the age requirements of the province or territory through which you reenter Canada, you may bring in, duty-free, 1.14 liters (40 imperial ounces) of wine or liquor *or* 24 12-ounce cans or bottles of beer or ale. If

you are 16 or older, you may bring in, duty-free, 200 cigarettes, 50 cigars or cigarillos, and 400 tobacco sticks or 400 grams of manufactured tobacco. Alcohol and tobacco must accompany you on your return.

An unlimited number of gifts with a value of up to C$60 each may be mailed to Canada duty-free. These do not affect your duty-free allowance on your return. Label the package "Unsolicited Gift— Value Under $60." Alcohol and tobacco are excluded.

IN THE U.K.

If your journey was wholly within European Union (EU) countries, you no longer need to pass through customs when you return to the United Kingdom. If you plan to bring back large quantities of alcohol or tobacco, check in advance on EU limits.

D

DINING

One of the pleasures of traveling in Greece is lingering over regional specialties and barrel wine in a taverna or ordering an ouzo by the sea with a plate of *meze* (appetizers). Unless you are in the middle of nowhere, try to avoid eating all your meals in the hotel dining room. Be bold; don't just go to establishments that have menus posted in three languages. Let your senses guide you—visit the kitchen and point to what looks appetizing. You can create a great meal by ordering several appetizers, often the

most interesting dishes on the menu. If you're in a fish taverna, ask to see the daily catch to check for freshness, choose your fish, and have it weighed before it's cooked; prices are by the kilo. Keep in mind that Greeks usually eat lunch around 2 PM, although restaurants may open earlier in tourist areas. Rarely will an establishment open for dinner before 8:30 PM, since Greeks eat around 10 or 11. Meals, except in foreign restaurants, tend to be reasonably priced.

DISABILITIES & ACCESSIBILITY

Visitors will probably find it easier to manage in the modern resorts and hotels than in rented rooms. Many cruise ships are equipped to accommodate people with disabilities, but access to archaeological sites can present some difficulty, and most two-story museums do not have elevators. Call ahead to find out exactly what obstacles you might face and to enlist extra help from staff. Public transportation is generally crowded, and few special provisions are available. The easiest solution is to use taxis to get between different points, or hire a taxi for the day (about 10,000 dr. for five hours in Athens); most hotels can arrange this. You may encounter stares— until recently Greeks with disabilities were encouraged to stay at home—but people will usually lend a helping hand, since this is a country where hospitality is a time-honored virtue. Athens has some parking spaces to accommodate people with disabilities, but these are often illegally occupied by other drivers. Traveling with a companion or a group is advisable.

When discussing accessibility with an operator or reservationist, **ask hard questions.** Are there any stairs, inside *or* out? Are there grab bars next to the toilet *and* in the shower/tub? How wide is the doorway to the room? To the bathroom? For the most extensive facilities, meeting the latest legal specifications, **opt for newer accommodations,** which more often have been designed with access in mind. Older properties or ships usually must be retrofitted and may offer more limited facilities as a result. Be sure to **discuss your needs before booking.**

DISCOUNTS & DEALS

You shouldn't have to pay for a discount. In fact, you may already be eligible for all kinds of savings. Here are some time-honored strategies for getting the best deal.

LOOK IN YOUR WALLET

When you **use your credit card to make travel purchases,** you may get free travel-accident insurance, collision damage insurance, medical or legal assistance, depending on the card and bank that issued it. American Express, Visa, and MasterCard provide one

or more of these services, so **get a copy of your card's travel benefits.** If you are a member of the AAA or an oil-company-sponsored road-assistance plan, always **ask hotel or car-rental reservation agents for auto-club discounts.** Some clubs offer additional discounts on tours, cruises, or admission to attractions. And don't forget that auto-club membership entitles you to free maps and trip-planning services.

DIAL FOR DOLLARS

To save money, **look into "1-800" discount reservations services,** which often have lower rates. These services use their buying power to get a better price on hotels, airline tickets, and sometimes even car rentals. When booking a room, always **call the hotel's local toll-free number** (if one is available) rather than the central reservations number—you'll often get a better price. Ask the reservationist about special packages or corporate rates, which are usually available even if you're not traveling on business.

JOIN A CLUB?

Discount clubs can be a legitimate source of savings, but you must use the participating hotels and visit the participating attractions in order to realize any benefits. Remember, too, that you have to pay a fee to join, so **determine if you'll save enough to warrant your membership fee.** Before booking with a club, **make sure the hotel or other supplier isn't offering a better deal.**

GET A GUARANTEE

When shopping for the best deal on hotels and car rentals, **look for guaranteed exchange rates,** which protect you against a falling dollar. With your rate locked in, you won't pay more even if the price goes up in the local currency.

SENIOR CITIZENS & STUDENTS

As a senior-citizen traveler, you may be eligible for special rates, but you should mention your senior-citizen status up front. If you're a student or under 26 you can also get discounts, especially if you have an official ID card (☞ Senior Citizens *and* Students on the Road, *below*).

DRIVING

Regular registration papers and an international third-party insurance certificate (green card) are required, in addition to a driver's license (EU or international). If you insist on bringing in your own car, contact your local Greek consulate to pick up necessary forms and the latest information. You may import your vehicle duty-free for six months, if you have the car's registration and proof of ownership. You may then receive a six-month extension by applying to the DIPEA (✉ Driving *in* Important Contacts A to Z, *above*). After providing proof (foreign currency transactions called pink slips) that you are not working in Greece, you will be issued a free usage certificate, which exempts you from import duty and the circulation tax. Cars with foreign plates and rental cars are exempt from the alternate-day ban in Athens on driving in the center according to whether the license plate is odd or even. Full insurance, including coverage against collision with an uninsured motorist, is recommended. Accidents must be reported (something Greek motorists often fail to do) before the insurance companies consider claims.

The two main highways, both called Ethniki Odos (National Road), leave Athens going north and south. At the city limits, signs in English clearly mark the way to Syntagma and Omonia squares in the center. When you exit Athens, signs are well marked for the highway, usually naming Lamia for the north and Corinth or Patras for the southwest. Gas pumps and service stations are everywhere, and lead-free gas is widely available. Be aware that many stations in cities close after 8 PM.

FERRIES

On the west coast the local ferry between the island of Corfu and Igoumenitsa runs many times daily in each direction. The coastal highway leads directly to Preveza and the ferry across the strait to Action. You then go via Messolonghi to the Rion–Antirion ferry, which crosses to the Peloponnese and the National Road that leads to Athens. Ferries leave frequently from Piraeus (the port of Athens) to the Saronic Gulf islands, the Cyclades, Dodecanese, and Hania and Heraklion on Crete. Shorter crossings to the Cyclades can be made from the other side of Attica, from Rafina to Andros, Tinos, and Mykonos, and from Lavrio to Kea and Kythnos. You can cross to Turkey from the northeastern Aegean islands, from Lesbos to Dikeli, from Chios to Cesme, and from Samos to Kusadasi. Note that British passport holders must have 10 pounds sterling with them to purchase a visa on landing in Turkey and U.S. citizens need $20.

FROM THE U.K.

Driving to Greece from Britain is now possible, though keep in mind that gas may be difficult to find in the former Yugoslavia, especially unleaded. Though it is expensive, you can take a car to Greece (and at the same time greatly reduce your driving and save gasoline and hotel costs) by using the Paris–Milan and Milan–Brindisi car sleeper and then a car ferry to Corfu, Igoumenitsa, or Patras.

There are frequent sails between Italy and Greece—at least seven a day in summer from Brindisi, two each from Bari and Ancona, one from Otranto, and two–three a week from Trieste; all go to Corfu and/or Igoumenitsa and Patras (three a week call at Kefalonia). There is also one sailing (sometimes more) a week from Venice to Piraeus.

Some of the shipping lines are Adriatic Ferries, Adriatica, Anek, European Seaways, Hellenic Mediterranean, Karageorgis, Marlines, Minoan, Strintzis, and Ventouris. A few years ago Superfast Ferries were introduced; although about one-third more expensive, they make the trip from Patras to Ancona in 20 hours, about 16 hours faster than conventional ferries.

British Ferries operates a weekly service from Venice to Athens on their luxury car ferry *Orient Express* from May to October. For info contact the Venice–Simplon Orient Express (☞ Driving *in* Important Contacts A to Z, *above*). Adriatica Lines services routes from Brindisi to Igoumenitsa and Patras and from Venice to Piraeus; contact the Stena–Sealink Travel Centre (☞ Driving *in* Important Contacts A to Z, *above*). The Minoan Lines car ferries sail from Ancona and Igoumenitsa and Patras; contact P&O European Ferries (☞ Driving *in* Important Contacts A to Z, *above*). Bookings for summer should be made well in advance and reconfirmed shortly before sailing.

ROAD CONDITIONS & TRAFFIC

Driving defensively is the key to safety in Greece. In the city and on the highways, the streets are riddled with potholes, motorcyclists seem to come out of nowhere, often passing on the right, and cars may even go the wrong way down a one-way street. In the countryside, you must watch for herds of goats and sheep crossing the road, as well as tourists shakily learning the motorbikes they've recently rented.

The many motorcycles and scooters weaving through traffic and the aggressive attitude of fellow motorists can make driving in Greece's large cities less than enjoyable—and the life of a pedestrian actively dangerous; Greeks often run red lights on side streets or round corners without stopping. In the countryside, off the toll roads (tolls range from 200 dr. to 800 dr.), traffic is light, and driving is more pleasant, but highway route numbers are largely nonexistent. The National Road is very slick when wet—avoid driving in rain and on the days preceding or following major holidays, when traffic is at its worst as urban dwellers leave for their villages. If air pollution has reached dangerous levels in Athens, all cars are banned from the center.

RULES OF THE ROAD

International road signs are in use throughout Greece. You drive on the right, pass on the left, and yield right-of-way to all vehicles approaching from the right (except on posted main highways). The speed limits are 120 kph (74 mph) on the National Road, 90 kph (54 mph) outside built-up areas, and 50 kph (31 mph) in cities, unless lower limits are posted. Often, no speed limits are posted, and even when they are, many Greeks don't obey them. In many streets, alternate-side-of-the-street parking rules are in effect. Although it's illegal, sidewalk parking is common. The police have become far more strict, regularly inspecting cars (which must have a fire extinguisher, emergency triangle, and first-aid kit) and introducing alcohol tests. You must always carry a valid driver's license (EU or international), car registration, and insurance contract or green card. The use of seat belts and helmets is compulsory, though Greeks tend to ignore these rules. Police are empowered to impose on-the-spot fines.

G
GAY & LESBIAN TRAVEL

In Greece, homosexuality has been very much a part of life from antiquity to today. Indeed, many prominent figures of the country's cultural life (both past and present) are openly gay. Others, such as the late Minister of Culture, Melina Mercouri, have strongly supported gays. One should be aware, however, of the special mentality of the Greek male vis-à-vis homosexuality. Many Greeks—both men and women—are bisexual, though this does not indicate a conscious recognition of being gay. Greek society remains conservative regarding open declarations of homosexuality by either sex, although homosexual relations for men over 17 have been legal for many decades in Greece. The nearest thing to a gay scene in the Western sense of the word exists in Athens, Thessaloniki, Mykonos, Rhodes, and Ios for men; for women, at Eressos on Lesbos.

H
HEALTH

Greece's strong summer sun and low humidity can lead to sunburn or sunstroke if you're not careful. A hat, long-sleeve shirt, and long pants or a sarong are essential for a day at the beach or visiting archaeological sites. Sunglasses, a hat, and sunblock are necessities, and insect repellent may keep the occasional horsefly and mosquito at bay. Drink plenty of water. Most beaches present few dangers, but keep a lookout for the occasional jellyfish, and in some areas, sea urchins. Should you step on one, don't break off the embedded spines, which may lead to infection, but remove them with heated olive oil and a needle.

Food is seldom a problem, but the liberal amounts of olive oil used in Greek cooking may be indigestible for some. Tap water in Greece is fine, and bottled spring water is readily available.

For minor ailments, go to the local pharmacy first, where the licensed staff can make recommendations for over-the-counter drugs. Most pharmacies are closed in the evenings and on weekends, but each posts the name of the nearest pharmacy open off-hours. Newspapers also carry a listing of pharmacies open late or, in large cities, all night. In an emergency you can call an ambulance at ☎ 166, but waving down a taxi is faster, since cars in big cities give way reluctantly to ambulances. Most hotels will call a doctor for you. In Athens, you can locate a doctor on call 2 PM–7 AM on Sunday and on holidays by dialing ☎ 105, but the message is in Greek. For a dentist, check with your hotel, embassy, or the tourist police.

SHOTS & MEDICATIONS

No special shots are required before visiting Greece. If you take any medication regularly, have your doctor write a prescription using the drug's generic name, as brand names vary from country to country. Birth control pills are available from pharmacies without a prescription.

You can get vaccinations or immunizations free at the National Public Health Center (✉ Leoforos Alexandras 196, Ambelokipi, Athens), from 8:30–12:30 PM.

I

INSURANCE

Travel insurance can protect your monetary investment, replace your luggage and its contents, or provide for medical coverage should you fall ill during your trip. Most tour operators, travel

agents, and insurance agents sell specialized health-and-accident, flight, trip-cancellation, and luggage insurance as well as comprehensive policies with some or all of these coverages. Comprehensive policies may also reimburse you for delays due to weather—an important consideration if you're traveling during the winter months. Some health-insurance policies do not cover preexisting conditions, but waivers may be available in specific cases. Coverage is sold by the companies listed in Important Contacts A to Z; these companies act as the policy's administrators. The actual insurance is usually underwritten by a well-known name, such as The Travelers or Continental Insurance.

Before you make any purchase, **review your existing health and homeowner's policies** to find out whether they cover expenses incurred while traveling.

BAGGAGE

Airline liability for baggage is limited to $1,250 per person on domestic flights. On international flights, it amounts to $9.07 per pound or $20 per kilogram for checked baggage (roughly $640 per 70-pound bag) and $400 per passenger for unchecked baggage. Insurance for losses exceeding the terms of your airline ticket can be bought directly from the airline at check-in for about $10 per $1,000 of coverage; note that it excludes a rather extensive list of

items, shown on your airline ticket.

COMPREHENSIVE

Comprehensive insurance policies include all the coverages described above plus some that may not be available in more specific policies. If you have purchased an expensive vacation, especially one that involves travel abroad, comprehensive insurance is a must; **look for policies that include trip delay insurance,** which will protect you in the event that weather problems cause you to miss your flight, tour, or cruise. A few insurers will also sell you a waiver for preexisting medical conditions. Some of the companies that offer both these features are Access America, Carefree Travel, Travel Insured International, and Travel Guard (☞ Insurance *in* Important Contacts A to Z, *above*).

FLIGHT

You should **think twice before buying flight insurance.** Often purchased as a last-minute impulse at the airport, it pays a lump sum when a plane crashes, either to a beneficiary if the insured dies or sometimes to a surviving passenger who loses his or her eyesight or a limb. Supplementing the airlines' coverage described in the limits-of-liability paragraphs on your ticket, it's expensive and basically unnecessary. Charging an airline ticket to a major credit card often automatically provides you with coverage that may also extend to travel by bus, train, and ship.

HEALTH

Medicare generally does not cover health care costs outside the U.S.; nor do many privately issued policies. If your own health insurance policy does not cover you outside the U.S., **consider buying supplemental medical coverage.** It can reimburse you for $1,000–$150,000 worth of medical and/or dental expenses incurred as a result of an accident or illness during a trip. These policies also may include a personal-accident, or death-and-dismemberment, provision, which pays a lump sum ranging from $15,000 to $500,000 to your beneficiaries if you die or to you if you lose one or more limbs or your eyesight, and a medical-assistance provision, which may either reimburse you for the cost of referrals, evacuation, or repatriation and other services, or automatically enroll you as a member of a particular medical-assistance company. (☞ Health *in* Important Contacts A to Z, *above*.)

TRIP

Without insurance, you will lose all or most of your money if you cancel your trip regardless of the reason. Especially if your airline ticket, cruise, or package tour is nonrefundable and cannot be changed, it's essential that you **buy trip-cancellation-and-interruption insurance.** When considering how much coverage you need, look for a policy that will cover the cost of your trip plus the nondiscounted price of a one-way airline ticket should you need to return home early. Read the fine print carefully, especially sections that define "family member" and "preexisting medical conditions." Also **consider default or bankruptcy insurance,** which protects you against a supplier's failure to deliver. Be aware, however, that if you buy such a policy from a travel agency, tour operator, airline, or cruise line, it may not cover default by the firm in question.

U.K. TRAVELERS

You can buy an annual travel insurance policy valid for most vacations during the year in which it's purchased. If you are pregnant or have a preexisting medical condition make sure you're covered before buying such a policy.

L

LANGUAGE

Greek is the native language not only of Greece but also of Cyprus, parts of Chicago, and Astoria, New York. Though it's a byword for incomprehensible ("it was all Greek to me," says Casca in Shakespeare's *Julius Caesar*), much of the difficulty lies in its different alphabet. Not all the 24 Greek letters have precise English equivalents, and there is usually more than one way to spell a Greek word in English. For instance, the letter *delta* sounds like the English letters "dh," and the sound of the letter *gamma* may be transliterated as a "g," "gh," or "y." Because of this the Greek for Holy Trinity might appear in English as *Agia Triada, Aghia Triada, Ayia Triada,* or even (if the initial aspiration and the dh are used) *Hagia Triadha.* It seems complicated, but don't let it throw you. With a little time spent learning the alphabet and some basic phrases, you can acquire enough Greek to navigate—i.e., exchange greetings, find a hotel room, and get from one town to another. Many Greeks know some English, but will appreciate a two-way effort.

If you only have 15 minutes to learn Greek, memorize the following: *miláte angliká*? (do you speak English?); *den katalavéno* (I don't understand); *parakaló* (please/you're welcome); *signómi* (excuse me), *efharistó* (thank you); *pósso*? (how much?); *pou eéne ee trápeza*? (where is the bank?), *...ee toiléta*? (...the toilet?); *...to tahidromío*? (...the post office?); *kaliméra* (good morning), *kalispéra* (good evening), *kaliníhta* (good night). Also *see* Greek Vocabulary at the back of this guide.

LODGING

The array of accommodations ranges from luxury island resorts to traditional settlements that incorporate local architecture to inexpensive rented rooms peddled at the harbor. Family-run pensions and guest houses outside Athens and Thessaloniki are usually clean, bright, and recently built; they also let you get better acquainted with the locals. Self-catering apartments are available as well in most resort areas.

Although lodging is less expensive in Greece than in most of the EU and the U.S., the quality tends to be a little lower. Sometimes you can reduce the price by eliminating breakfast, by bargaining when it's off-season, or by going through a travel agency for the larger hotels on major islands and in Athens and Thessaloniki. Many Greeks rent rooms in their houses, which can be less expensive and more homey than a hotel, but you might have to scout around a bit to find them, and it's a good idea to see them first, for quality and location. Owners wait for tourists at the harbor, and signs in English throughout villages indicate rooms available. Accommodations may be hard to find in smaller resort towns during the winter and beginning of spring. Remember that the plumbing in most low-end hotels (and restaurants, shops, and other public places) is delicate enough to require that toilet paper and other detritus be put in the wastebasket and not flushed.

APARTMENT & VILLA RENTAL

If you want a home base that's roomy enough for a family and comes with cooking facilities, **consider taking a furnished rental.** This can also save you money, but not always—some rentals are luxury properties (economical only when your party is large). Home-exchange directories list rentals—often second homes owned by prospective house swappers—and some services search for a house or apartment for you (even a castle if that's your fancy) and handle the paperwork. Some send an illustrated catalog; others send photographs only of specific properties, sometimes at a charge; up-front registration fees may apply.

HOME EXCHANGE

If you would like to find a house, an apartment, or some other type of vacation property to exchange for your own while on holiday, **become a member of a home-exchange organization,** which will send you its updated listings of available exchanges for a year, and will include your own listing in at least one of them. Arrangements for the actual exchange are made by the two parties involved, not by the organization.

HOTELS

The government classifies hotels into six categories: L (luxury), and A–E, which govern the rates that can be charged. Ratings are based on room size, size of the lobby and other public areas, bathroom facilities, and other amenities. There is a great deal of variation from one town to the next, and the classifications can be misleading—a hotel rated C in one town might qualify as a B in another. For the categories L, A, and B, you can expect something along the lines of a chain motel in the U.S., although the room will probably be somewhat smaller. A room in a C hotel can be perfectly acceptable; with a D the bathroom may or may not be shared. Ask to see the room before signing. You can sometimes find a bargain if a hotel has just renovated but has not yet been reclassified.

Prices are posted in each room, usually on the back of the door or inside the wardrobe. The room charge varies over the course of the year, peaking in the high season when breakfast or half board (at hotel complexes) may also be obligatory.

M

MAIL

Post offices are open weekdays 8–2, although in city centers they may stay open in the evenings and on weekends. The main post offices in Athens (✉ Aeolou 100 and Syntagma Sq.) are open weekdays 7:30 AM–8 PM, Saturday 7:30–2, and Sunday 9–1:30. At press time (October, 1996), airmail letters and postcards to North America weighing up to 20 grams cost 150 dr., and 240 dr. for 50 grams (120 and 200 dr. to the United Kingdom and Europe). If you are mailing a package, you must bring it open with

THE GOLD GUIDE / SMART TRAVEL TIPS

your wrapping materials to the post office so it can be inspected.

RECEIVING MAIL

Mail service in Greece is not the fastest, but it is generally reliable. If you're expecting something important, have the sender register it, since mail does get lost and Greek postal agents will not make the most strenuous effort to relocate it. Mail marked "poste restante" sent to post offices in Greece will be held until picked up by the addressee, who must show identification, usually your passport. You can have mail (not registered or certified mail or parcels) sent to you c/o American Express offices; there is no pick-up charge for clients of American Express (i.e. cardholders and those with Amex travel vouchers, tickets, or traveler's checks); others pay 400 dr. It can be collected in person with identification and will be returned after 30 days. A forwarding address can be left for a nominal charge. Amex offices in Greece providing this service are in Athens, Corfu, Heraklion, Mykonos, Patras, Rhodes, Santorini, Skiathos, and Thessaloniki.

MEDICAL ASSISTANCE

No one plans to get sick while traveling, but it happens, so **consider signing up with a medical assistance company.** These outfits provide referrals, emergency evacuation or repatriation, 24-hour telephone hot lines for medical consultation, cash for

emergencies, and other personal and legal assistance. They also dispatch medical personnel and arrange for the relay of medical records. Coverage varies by plan, so **read the fine print carefully.**

MONEY

The drachma (dr.) is the Greek unit of currency. Bills are in denominations of 10,000, 5,000, 1,000, and 500 drachmas (100- and 50-drachma bills are going to be taken out of circulation). Coins are 100, 50, 20, 10, 5. At press time (October, 1996) the average exchange rate was 240 drachmas to the U.S. dollar, 176 drachmas to the Canadian dollar, and 373 drachmas to the pound sterling.

ATMS

CASH ADVANCES➤ Before leaving home, **make sure that your credit cards have been programmed for ATM use in Greece.** Note that Discover is accepted mostly in the U.S. Local bank cards often do not work overseas either; **ask your bank about a Visa debit card,** which works like a bank card but can be used at any ATM displaying a Visa logo.

TRANSACTION FEES➤ Although fees charged for ATM transactions may be higher abroad than at home, Cirrus and Plus exchange rates are excellent, because they are based on wholesale rates offered only by major banks.

COSTS

Although prices have risen since Greece joined the EU, the

country will seem inexpensive to travelers from the U.S. and Great Britain. Popular tourist resorts (including some of the islands) and the larger cities are markedly more expensive than the countryside. Though the price of eating in a restaurant has increased over the past several years, it remains a bargain. Hotels are generally reasonably priced, and the extra cost of accommodations in a luxury hotel, compared to an average hotel, often seems unwarranted.

Transportation is a good deal in Greece. Bus and train tickets are inexpensive, though renting a car is costly; there are relatively cheap—and slow—ferries to the islands, and express boats and hydrofoils that cost more. If your time is limited, domestic flights are a fair trade-off in cost and time saved, compared with sea and land travel.

Some sample prices: Admission to archaeological sites: 500 dr.–2,000 dr.; authentic Greek sponge: 2,000 dr.; coffee: 400 dr.–700 dr.; beer (500 ml): 500 dr.–800 dr.; Coca-Cola: 300 dr.; spinach pie: 250 dr.; taxi ride: about 1,700 dr. from the airport to downtown Athens; local bus: 75 dr. in one zone; foreign newspaper: 400 dr.–700 dr.

EXCHANGING CURRENCY

For the most favorable rates, **change money at banks.** You won't do as well at exchange booths in airports or rail and bus stations, in hotels, in restaurants, or in stores, although you may find their hours more convenient. Exchange rates don't vary much from bank to bank, but what can vary significantly are the commission fees charged. Usually, there is no fee for cashing traveler's checks. To avoid lines at airport exchange booths, **get a small amount of the local currency before you leave home.**

TAXES

Taxes are always included in the stated price, unless otherwise noted.

HOTEL➤ An 8% government tax, 4.5% local tax, and 1.2% stamp tax (total 13.7%) is added to the bill, though usually the rate quoted to you will include the taxes. Ask.

VAT➤ Value-added tax, ranging from 8% to 36% is included in the cost of hotels, restaurant meals, car rentals, and most consumer products. As an individual, you may get a VAT refund on products worth 40,000 dr. or more bought in Greece from stores that have a tax-free sticker in their window. The shop will give you an application, which you must fill out and show at Greek Customs, along with the item to prove you are taking it out of the country. Customs—at the airport or port— will stamp the paper, which you then must send back to the shop. Within a month or so, they will refund your

money through the Greek post office.

TRAVELER'S CHECKS

Whether or not to buy traveler's checks depends on where you are headed; **take cash to rural areas and small towns, traveler's checks to cities.** The most widely recognized checks are issued by American Express, Citicorp, Thomas Cook, and Visa. These are sold by major commercial banks for 1%–3% of the checks' face value—it pays to **shop around.** Both American Express and Thomas Cook issue checks that can be countersigned and used by either you or your traveling companion. So you won't be left with excess foreign currency, **buy a few checks in small denominations** to cash toward the end of your trip. Before leaving home, **contact your issuer for information on where to cash your checks** without incurring a transaction fee. Record the numbers of all your checks, and keep this listing in a separate place, crossing off the numbers of checks you have cashed.

WIRING MONEY

For a fee of 3%–10%, depending on the amount of the transaction, you can have money sent to you from home through Money-Gram^{SM} or Western Union (☞ Money *in* Important Contacts A to Z, *above*). The transferred funds and the service fee can be charged to a Master-Card or Visa account.

Take what you *will* need, not what you *might* need. You can rent a cart at the airport (300 dr.), but from then on you'll have to carry your own luggage. Getting on and off the train, buses, and boats can be easy or difficult, depending on how much you're hauling around. Also, remember that you'll be carrying souvenirs on your way out. It's a good idea to itemize the contents of each bag and keep the list, in case you need to file an insurance claim. Be certain to put your home or business address on each piece of luggage, including carry-on bags.

Outside Athens, Greek dress tends to be middle of the road—you won't see patched jeans *or* expensive suits, though locals tend to dress up for nightclubs and bouzoukia. In the summer bring lightweight, casual clothing and good walking shoes. A light sweater or jacket is a must for cool evenings, especially in the mountains. There's no need for rain gear in high summer, but don't forget sunglasses and a sun hat. Be prepared for cooler weather and some rain in spring and fall, and in winter, add a warm coat.

Casual attire is acceptable everywhere except in the most expensive restaurants in large cities, but you should dress conservatively

THE GOLD GUIDE / SMART TRAVEL TIPS

when visiting churches or monasteries. It's not appropriate to show a lot of bare arm and leg; men wearing shorts must cover up as well, as must women in pants, in some stricter monasteries. Monasteries (e.g., in Meteora) and churches will not admit improperly dressed men or women, though they often provide long skirts or some sort of draping at the entrance. In cities, and everywhere in winter, revealing too much skin may lead to unwelcome harassment. Swimsuits are technically required, but most beaches are topless, except those near the harbor or town center. The number of beaches where nude bathing is acceptable is slowly growing. Watch to see what others do, and err on the conservative side.

For dimly lit icons in churches and moonless island walks, a small flashlight comes in handy, as does a jack-knife with a corkscrew and screwdriver, though they may show up on the airport security scanner and cause you to open your bag. It's a good idea to bring zip-closing plastic bags, mosquito repellent for more verdant areas, moist towelettes, a roll of transparent tape, and a pocket calculator, all indispensable. A pair of opera glasses can greatly enhance the appreciation of an archaeological site or give the tourist a better view of wall paintings in a church, for example.

Bring an extra pair of eyeglasses or contact lenses in your carry-on luggage, and if you have a health problem, **pack enough medication** to last the trip or have your doctor write you a prescription using the drug's generic name, because brand names vary from country to country (you'll then need a duplicate prescription from a local doctor). It's important that you **don't put prescription drugs or valuables in luggage to be checked,** for it could go astray. To avoid problems with customs officials, carry medications in the original packaging. Also, don't forget the addresses of offices that handle refunds of lost traveler's checks.

ELECTRICITY

To use your U.S.-purchased electric-powered equipment, **bring a converter and an adapter.** The electrical current in Greece is 220 volts, 50 cycles alternating current (AC); wall outlets take Continental-type plugs, with two round prongs.

If your appliances are dual-voltage, you'll need only an adapter. Hotels sometimes have 110-volt outlets for low-wattage appliances near the sink, marked FOR SHAVERS ONLY; don't use them for high-wattage appliances like blow-dryers. If your laptop computer is older, carry a converter; new laptops operate equally well on 110 and 220 volts, so you need only an adapter.

LUGGAGE

Airline baggage allowances depend on the airline, the route, and the class of your ticket; ask in advance. In general, on domestic flights and on international flights between the U.S. and foreign destinations, you are entitled to check two bags. A third piece may be brought on board, but it must fit easily under the seat in front of you or in the overhead compartment. In the U.S., the FAA gives airlines broad latitude regarding carry-on allowances, and they tend to tailor them to different aircraft and operational conditions. Charges for excess, oversize, or overweight pieces vary.

If you are flying between two foreign destinations, note that baggage allowances may be determined not by piece but by weight—generally 88 pounds (40 kilograms) in first class, 66 pounds (30 kilograms) in business class, and 44 pounds (20 kilograms) in economy. If your flight between two cities abroad *connects* with your transatlantic or transpacific flight, the piece method still applies.

SAFEGUARDING YOUR LUGGAGE➤ Before leaving home, **itemize your bags' contents** and their worth, and label them with your name, address, and phone number. (If you use your home address, cover it so that potential thieves can't see it readily.) Inside each bag, **pack a copy of your itinerary.** At check-in, **make sure that each bag is correctly tagged** with the destination airport's three-letter code. If your bags arrive damaged—or fail to arrive at all—file a written report with the airline before leaving the airport.

PASSPORTS & VISAS

If you don't already have one, **get a passport.** It is advisable that you **leave one photocopy of your passport's data page** with someone at home and keep another with you, separated from your passport, while traveling. If you lose your passport, promptly call the nearest embassy or consulate and the local police; having the data page information can speed replacement.

U.S. CITIZENS

All U.S. citizens, even infants, need only a valid passport to enter Greece for stays of up to 90 days. Application forms for both first-time and renewal passports are available at any of the 13 U.S. Passport Agency offices and at some post offices and courthouses. Passports are usually mailed within four weeks; allow five weeks or more in spring and summer.

CANADIANS

You need only a valid passport to enter Greece for stays of up to 90 days. Passport application forms are available at 28 regional passport offices, as well as post offices and travel agencies. Whether for a first or a renewal passport, you must apply in person. Children under 16 may be included on a parent's passport but must have their own to travel alone. Passports are valid for five years and are usually mailed within two to three weeks of application.

U.K. CITIZENS

Citizens of the United Kingdom need only a valid passport to enter Greece for stays of up to 90 days. Applications for new and renewal passports are available from main post offices and at the passport offices in Belfast, Glasgow, Liverpool, London, Newport, and Peterborough. You may apply in person at all passport offices, or by mail to all except the London office. Children under 16 may travel on an accompanying parent's passport. All passports are valid for 10 years. Allow a month for processing.

S

SAFETY

Greece is still one of the safest countries in Europe; even Athens has a low crime rate, with serious crimes rare, although the number of bank robberies has gone up in the last five years. You will often see people sitting at cafés with their handbag carelessly dangling over chairs, or women and elderly people walking home late at night. If you take the normal precautions of carrying your money in a security pouch, and if you avoid isolated places at night, you should have little problem. If you feel unsure about the safety of an area, ask your hotel before setting out. For example, in the last few years, crime has gone up around Omonia Square in Athens, because of the large transient population that congregates there.

In general, women traveling alone are safe in Greece, though Greek men will try to talk to them, especially if they look foreign. It's best to do as the Greek women do, and ignore the amorous overtures; responding will only be interpreted as a sign that you're interested. If you feel threatened, don't hesitate to shout; this will be enough to scare off most offenders. Greeks, especially in Athens, where people are out until all hours, will usually come to your aid. One way to avoid unwanted advances is to try to blend in with the Greeks: dress as they do, walk like you know where you're going, and don't openly carry a map or a foreign newspaper. If you are taking a taxi at night, the driver won't usually pick up a male passenger; if he does, he is obligated to ask your permission.

SENIOR CITIZENS

Despite the dearth of facilities at hotels, museums, and archaeological sites for those with impaired movement, traveling in Greece can be quite pleasurable. Elders are treated with respect: most Greeks still take care of their parents at home, and crimes against the elderly are rare. Most people—even taxi drivers—will go out of their way to make sure senior citizens receive good treatment.

DISCOUNTS

Always ask about senior citizen discounts, although these tend to be limited in Greece to about one-third off at museums and archaeological sites, Olympic Airways fares (about 13% less), and public transportation (again, about a third less). Identification to prove you are over 60 is required. To qualify for age-related discounts, **mention your senior-citizen status up front** when booking hotel reservations, not when checking out, and before you're seated in restaurants, not when paying the bill. Note that discounts may be limited to certain menus, days, or hours. When renting a car, **ask about promotional car-rental discounts**—they can net even lower costs than your senior-citizen discount.

SHOPPING

Because of hefty taxes, most items in Greece, especially electric appliances and clothing, cost more than in the U.S. and Canada, though Greece does have inexpensive shoes, furs, and leather goods. Good gift ideas are the natural Kalymnos sponges, flokati rugs made from longhaired goat wool, handicrafts such as embroidery, ceramics, and kilims, fisherman's caps and hand-knit sweaters, *koboloi* (worry beads) in plastic, wood, and onyx, and blue and white amulets that protect against *mati* (the evil eye). What is cheaper in Greece is silver and gold jewelry, often original and unusual pieces. In some stores, chains are sold by the gram. Always bargain in tourist shops and with street vendors (except for sponges—prices are set by the government), and always get a receipt from shops. In an attempt to diminish tax fraud, the government heavily fines buyers who walk out of a store without proof of purchase. Most stores will not give you a cash refund, but they may give you a credit slip.

A delightful institution in Greece is the *laiki* (open-air market), which offers fresh produce at prices lower than in produce stores, as well as items sold by political and economic refugees, such as linen tablecloths (sold by the meter), caviar, and Russian lacquered dolls. Every town has a laiki, and big cities like Athens have several a day in different neighborhoods.

STUDENTS ON THE ROAD

For students, Greece is an inexpensive destination. Not only are museums and archaeological sites cheaper (you must have an ISIC card), but student and youth rates are offered on public transportation as well as domestic and EU flights. Many travel agencies catering to students are on Fillelinon and Nikis Streets in Athens, off Syntagma Square. Rented rooms and camping are the most inexpensive lodging—in summer, you can rent roof space if you've brought a sleeping bag. Take advantage of souvlaki stands (the filling fast food of Greece), local tavernas, and the open-air market; convenience stores in tourist areas are wildly overpriced. Finally, watch expenditures in bars—in most, an alcoholic drink, even a beer, costs at least 1,500 dr.

To save money, **look into deals available through student-oriented travel agencies.** To qualify, you'll need to have a bona fide student ID card. Members of international student groups are also eligible (☞ Students *in* Important Contacts A to Z, *above*).

T

TAXIS

"On our three-week vacation, we were faced with some form of overcharging *every other day*. Taxi drivers were the worst—about half tried or succeeded to charge more. We found that being firm with the price we thought appropriate, combined with a demand for them to call the police, usually worked." So wrote a Fodor's reader. In Greece, as everywhere, unscrupulous taxi drivers will try to take advantage of out-of-towners or foreigners. Rather than memorize all the allowable surcharges, you might ask your hotel concierge or owner before engaging a taxi what the fare to your destination ought to be. You are more likely to be overcharged in Athens and vicinity than elsewhere, especially when traveling to and from airport terminals. It should cost no more than 1,700 dr. from the airport to city center. Make sure that the driver turns on the meter to Tarifa 1, unless it's between midnight and 5 AM when the price goes up. Remember that an extra 300 dr. is expected when taking a taxi from the airport and 160 dr. from ports and bus and train stations. Each item of baggage is likewise charged (55 dr.). If you suspect a driver is overcharging, demand to be taken to the police station; this usually brings them around. As a last resort contact the tourist police (☎ 171 in Athens).

When you're taking an early morning flight, it's a good idea to reserve a radio taxi the night before (400 dr. surcharge, 300 dr. for immediate response). They are usually quite reliable and punctual; if you're not staying in a hotel, the local tourist police can give you some phone numbers for companies.

TELEPHONES

The Greek telephone company, the OTE (pronounced "oh-tay"), has card phones virtually everywhere, though some may not be in working order. Phone cards (up to 10,000 dr.) used for intercity and overseas calls can be purchased at kiosks or the local OTE office. You can also make calls from OTE offices, which tend to have limited hours, and from kiosks (a local call is about 20 dr.). Avoid making calls from your hotel, where the surcharge can be quite hefty.

Doing business over the phone in Greece can be extremely frustrating—the lines always seem to be busy, and English-speaking operators and clerks are few. You may also find people too busy to address your problem—the independent-minded Greeks are not very service-conscious. It is far better to develop a relationship with someone, for example a travel agent, to get information about train schedules and the like, or to go in person and ask for information face-to-face. Though OTE is updating its archaic phone system, it may take you several attempts to get through. Try dialing slowly, and if you get a wrong number, don't assume it's your mistake—the lines frequently get crossed. Don't discuss highly sensitive matters on the phone; party lines are still a social hazard in Greece. Local and international calls are cheaper in the evenings (after 10 or 11 PM, depending on where you're calling, and on the weekends after 3 PM on Saturday).

FAXING

If you need to send a fax and can't find a hotel or travel agency to let you use theirs, you may send one from most post offices.

LONG-DISTANCE

The long-distance services of AT&T, MCI, and Sprint make calling home relatively convenient, but in many hotels you may find it impossible to dial the access number. The hotel operator may also refuse to make the connection. Instead, the hotel will charge you a premium rate—as much as 400% more than a calling card—for calls placed from your hotel room. To avoid such price gouging, travel with more than one company's long-distance calling card—a hotel may block Sprint but not MCI. If the hotel operator claims that you cannot use any phone card, ask to be connected to an international operator, who will help you to access your phone card. You can also dial the international operator yourself. If none of this works, try calling your phone company collect in the U.S. If collect calls are also blocked, call from a pay phone in the hotel lobby. Before you go, **find out the local access codes** for your destinations.

For any international call, you must first dial 00, then the country code (1 for the U.S. and Canada, 44 for England). For long-distance calls it's best to avoid the kiosk and hotel phones and use the metered phones at the OTE offices or buy a calling card.

OPERATORS & INFORMATION

There are **English-speaking operators** on the International Exchange (☎ 161 and 162), and recorded **instructions** in English, French, and German for making direct international calls on ☎ 169.

TIPPING

How much to tip in Greece, especially at restaurants, is confusing. By law a 15% service charge is figured into the price of a meal (menus sometimes list entrées with and without service, to let you know their net cost— not to imply you have a choice of how much to pay), so, technically, you don't have to leave any additional tip. If the service was poor or the waiter rude (very unlikely), you are not obligated to do so, but if the service was good, it's customary to reward it by leaving 10% more. For taxis, round up the fare to the nearest 50 dr.

The appropriate tip for maid service at your hotel will depend, of course, on the quality of the service, the length of your stay, and the quality of the hotel. A service charge is included in the price of the room, but you might consider leaving an additional 200 dr. per person per night, or more for an extended stay. Porters, found only at the more expensive hotels, should get 100 dr.–200 dr. per bag, and hatcheck persons would like the same amount. For rest-room attendants 100 dr. is appropriate. On cruises, cabin and dining-room stewards get about 500 dr. a day; guides receive about the same.

TOUR OPERATORS

A package or tour to Greece can make your vacation less expensive and more hassle free. Firms that sell tours and packages reserve airline seats, hotel rooms, and rental cars in bulk and pass some of the savings on to you. In addition, the best operators have local representatives available to help you at your destination.

A GOOD DEAL?

The more your package or tour includes, the better you can predict the ultimate cost of your vacation. Make sure you know exactly what is covered, and **beware of hidden costs.** Are taxes, tips, and service charges included? Transfers and baggage handling? Entertainment and excursions? These can add up.

Most packages and tours are rated deluxe, first-class superior, first class, tourist, or budget. The key difference is usually accommodations. If the package or tour you are considering is priced lower than in your wildest dreams, **be skeptical.** Also, **make sure your travel agent knows the accommodations** and other services. Ask about the hotel's location, room size, beds, and whether it has a pool, or room service, or programs for children, if these matter. Has your agent been there in person or sent others you can contact?

BUYER BEWARE

Each year a number of consumers are stranded or lose their money when operators—even very large ones with excellent reputations— go out of business. To avoid becoming one of them, take the time to **check out the operator**—find out how long the company has been in business and ask several agents about its reputation. Next, **don't book unless the firm has a consumer-protection program.** Members of the USTOA and the NTA are required to set aside funds for the sole purpose of covering your payments and travel arrangements in case of default. Nonmember operators may instead carry insurance; look for the details in the operator's brochure— and for the name of an underwriter with a solid reputation. Note: When it comes to tour operators, **don't trust escrow accounts.** Although there are laws governing those of charter-flight operators, no governmental body prevents tour operators from raiding the till.

Next, **contact your local Better Business Bureau and the attorney general's offices** in both your own state and the operator's; have any complaints been filed? Finally, **pay with a major credit card.** Then you can cancel payment, provided that you can document your complaint. Always **consider trip-cancellation insurance** (☞ Insurance, *above*).

BIG VS. SMALL➤ Operators that handle several hundred thousand travelers per year can use their purchasing power to give you a good price. Their high volume may also indicate financial stability. But some small companies provide more personalized service; because they tend to specialize, they may also be more knowledgeable about a given area.

USING AN AGENT

Travel agents are excellent resources. In fact, large operators accept bookings made only through travel agents. But it's good to **collect brochures from several agencies** because some agents' suggestions may be skewed by promotional relationships with tour and package firms that reward them for volume sales. If you have a special interest, **find an agent with expertise in that area;** ASTA can provide leads in the U.S. (Don't rely solely on your agent, though; agents may be unaware of small-niche operators, and some special-interest travel companies only sell direct.)

SINGLE TRAVELERS

Prices are usually quoted per person, based on two sharing a room. If traveling solo, you may be required to pay the full double-occupancy rate. Some operators eliminate this surcharge if you agree to be matched up with a roommate of the same sex, even if one is not found by departure time.

TRAIN TRAVEL

Fares are reasonable, and trains offer a good, though slow, alternative to long drives or bus rides (there are IC express trains from Athens to Thessaloniki and Patras). The main line running north from Athens divides into three lines at Thessaloniki, continuing on to Belgrade, Istanbul, and Bulgaria. The Pelopon-

nese in the south is served by a narrow-gauge line dividing at Corinth into the Mycenae-Argos route and Patras-Olympia-Kalamata. The leisurely Peloponnesian train is a pleasant way to see southern Greece, but the Patras–Athens leg can be crowded during the high season because of tourists arriving in Patras from Italy. The assigned seating of first class may be a good idea at such times. The Greek Railway Organization (OSE) has two stations in Athens, side by side, off Deliyianni Street west of Omonia Square. Trains from the north and international trains use **Stathmos Larissis** (☏ 01/823–7741). Take Trolley 1 from the terminal to Omonia square. Trains from the Peloponnese use **Stathmos Peloponnisou** (☏ 01/513–1601) next door. To Omonia and Syntagma squares, take Bus 57.

DISCOUNT PASSES

Greece is one of 17 countries in which you can **use EurailPasses,** which provide unlimited first-class rail travel, in all of the participating countries, for the duration of the pass. If you plan to rack up the miles, get a standard pass. These are available for 15 days ($522), 21 days ($678), one month ($838), two months ($1,148), and 3 months ($1,468).

If Greece is your only destination in Europe, **consider purchasing a Greek Flexipass,** which allows three or five days of travel within a one-month period. Prices

are $86 and $120 for first-class travel; no second-class option is offered. If you plan to visit one of the Greek Islands, **look into a Rail 'N Fly combination pass,** which includes a one-way flight to any Greek Island served by Olympic Airways. Prices are $163 in first class and $142 in second class. Greek Flexipasses are also offered in children's versions and with hotel-and-sightseeing packages.

FROM THE U.K.

There are two main routes to Greece by train from the United Kingdom: the overland route via Munich, Salzburg, Ljubljana, and Zagreb has resumed operation; it is more pleasant to travel through Italy, then go by ferry from Brindisi to Patras in the Peloponnese. In high summer, catch the train from London's Victoria Station to Dover for the crossing to Calais and the connecting service to Paris Gare du Nord. From there, transfer to the Gare de Lyon for the train that runs via Switzerland to Milan. Switch there and travel through to Brindisi Maritime station, where you connect with the ferry to Patras (17 hrs.), and arrive the following day. From Patras there is bus and train service to Athens (total time London–Athens 2½ days). For planning your rail journey to Greece the Thomas Cook European Timetable is essential. It is available in the United Kingdom from Thomas Cook,

THE GOLD GUIDE / SMART TRAVEL TIPS

Timetable Publishing Office (✉ Box 36, Thorpe Wood, Peterborough, Cambridgeshire PE3 6SB); in the U.S. from Forsyth Travel Library (✉ Box 2975, Shawnee Mission, KS, 66201–1375, ☎ 800/307–7984). For train information, call Rail Europe (☎ 914/682–5172).

TRAVEL GEAR

Travel catalogs specialize in useful items that can **save space when packing** and make life on the road more convenient. Compact alarm clocks, travel irons, travel wallets, and personal-care kits are among the most common items you'll find. They also carry dual-voltage appliances, currency converters and foreign-language phrase books. Some catalogs even carry miniature coffeemakers and water purifiers.

U

U.S. GOVERNMENT

The U.S. government can be an excellent source of travel information. Some of this is free and some is available for a nominal charge. When planning your trip, **find out what government materials are available.** For just a couple of dollars, you can get a variety of publications from the Consumer Information Center in Pueblo, Colorado. Free consumer information also is available from individual government agencies, such as the

Department of Transportation or the U.S. Customs Service. For specific titles, *see* the appropriate publications entry in Important Contacts A to Z, *above.*

W

WHEN TO TOUR

The best time to visit Greece is late spring and early fall. In May and June the days are warm, even hot, but dry, and the sea water has been warmed by the sun. The evenings, which seem endless, are pleasant enough to dine alfresco. For sightseeing, exploring the cities or countryside, or hitting the beach, this is the time. Greece is relatively tourist free in the spring, so if you don't like crowds, and the beach and swimming aren't high on your agenda, April and early May are a good time to tour the country. Carnavali, just before Lent, and Greek Easter, with its religious processions, lambs, and red eggs, are the highlights of the season.

September and October are a good alternative to spring and early summer. Things begin to shut down in November, however, and the winter chill and rains begin. Winter in Greece is deceptive. Any given day may not be very cold. Except in the mountains, snow is uncommon in Athens and to the south. But the cold is persistent, and the level of heating visitors may be accustomed to is not usual in Greece. Over the course

of a few days you will feel chilled to the bone. Transportation to the islands is limited in winter, and many hotels outside large cities are closed until the beginning of April. Unless you are going to Greece in pursuit of winter sports, try a different season.

Toward the end of July and through August the temperatures climb, pushing the 100°F (38°C) mark. In the south a dry, hot wind may blow across the Mediterranean from the coast of Africa. The air quality in Athens, which is surrounded on all sides by mountains (except in the direction of the harbor and oil refineries of Piraeus), can be unhealthy on especially hot days, and air-conditioning is far from ubiquitous. Coincident with these unfortunate climatic conditions is the peak of the tourist season. In August you should flee Athens as soon as possible and head off the beaten path.

CLIMATE

Greece enjoys a typical Mediterranean climate: hot, dry summers and cool, wet winters. The average high and low temperatures for Athens and Heraklion (Crete) and average temperatures for Thessaloniki and Northern Greece are presented below. Note that although *average* temperatures in the north and the south may not be too dissimilar, the temperature on a given day can differ substantially.

Climate in Greece

ATHENS

Jan.	52F	13C	May	77F	25C	Sept.	84F	29C
	43	6		61	16		66	19
Feb.	57F	14C	June	86F	30C	Oct.	75F	24C
	45	7		68	20		59	15
Mar.	61F	16C	July	91F	33C	Nov.	66F	19C
	46	8		73	23		54	12
Apr.	68F	20C	Aug.	91F	33C	Dec.	59F	15C
	52	11		73	23		46	8

HERAKLION

Jan.	61F	16C	May	73F	23C	Sept.	81F	27C
	48	9		59	15		66	19
Feb.	61F	16C	June	81F	27C	Oct.	75F	24C
	48	9		66	19		63	17
Mar.	63F	17C	July	84F	29C	Nov.	70F	21C
	50	10		72	22		57	14
Apr.	68F	20C	Aug.	84F	29C	Dec.	64F	18C
	54	12		72	22		52	11

THESSALONIKI AND NORTHERN GREECE

Jan.	45F	8C	May	74F	24C	Sept.	80F	27C
Feb.	51F	11C	June	86F	30C	Oct.	69F	21C
Mar.	54F	13C	July	90F	32C	Nov.	58F	15C
Apr.	65F	19C	Aug.	90F	32C	Dec.	50F	10C

THE GOLD GUIDE / SMART TRAVEL TIPS

1 Destination: Greece

GREECE: A BRIEF HISTORY

Mighty indeed are the marks and monuments of our empire which we have left. Future ages will wonder at us, as the present age wonders at us now. . . . For our adventurous spirit has forced an entry into every sea and into every land; and everywhere we have left behind us everlasting memorials of good done to our friends or suffering inflicted on our enemies.

–Thucydides, *The Peloponnesian War,*
Pericles's funeral oration

Greece is a bleak, unsmiling desert, without agriculture, manufactures, or commerce apparently. What supports its poverty-stricken people or its government is a mystery. I suppose that ancient Greece and modern Greece compared furnish the most extravagant contrast to be found in history.

–Mark Twain, *The Innocents Abroad*

WELCOME TO GREECE. And please forgive my trotting out a couple of quotations, but you have to keep in mind that the ancient civilization and the modern nation are two very different things. In the world of today the legacy of classical Greece must be at times a burden to this small country, and if you get off the airplane expecting to step into the Athens of Pericles, you will be disappointed. A yellow taxi, not a chariot, will drive you into the city by way of a traffic-choked road, past bright white buildings of stuccoed concrete instead of marble. Although there are ruins that evoke Homer, Sophocles, Plato, and the rest, and secluded beaches and traditional whitewashed houses, today's Greeks are not just the cut-rate descendants of a noble people living in the ruined halls of their ancestors—modern Greece is a vital, living nation.

Officially called the Hellenic Republic, the country is inhabited by about 10 million people living in an area of about 133,000 square km, or 51,000 square mi (a bit larger than Pennsylvania). The southernmost part of the Balkan Peninsula,

Greece is bounded by the Ionian, Aegean, and Mediterranean seas. The northern border, from west to east, is shared with Albania, the disintegrated remains of Yugoslavia, Bulgaria, and Turkey. Nearly 80% of the land is mountainous, with Olympus the highest peak, at 2,918 meters (9,570 feet), and no spot in Greece is more than 115 km (70 mi) from the coast. Many think this combination of rugged terrain and proximity to the sea gave rise to the independent nature of the people; others feel Greeks would be independent-minded regardless of geography.

The Mediterranean climate brings hot, dry summers and cold, rainy winters. May counts as the first day of summer, and from June through September it doesn't rain—like *Camelot,* but the Greek beaches are better than those in England. Barometric lows over the Mediterranean in summer attract winds from the Sahara, notably the sirocco, which blows in hot and dry with reddish-yellow dust. More common is the *meltemi* (a cooling wind from northern Europe that picks up in summer).

The ancient forests that once covered Greece are long gone—for construction of ships and buildings, for fuel to heat public baths and pottery kilns, and to smelt ore for the likes of the silver mines at Lavrion. Today Greece has vegetation characteristic of the Mediterranean: beginning at sea level the lower mountain slopes are covered in evergreen Aleppo pines and live oaks, with plane trees and willows along streams. Where this forest has been removed the distinctive maquis—a dense collection of shrubs, largely such broad-leaved evergreens as holm and kermes oaks, junipers, laurel, myrtle, and rosemary—takes over. But even maquis can be killed off by browsing sheep and goats, and then an even tougher group of spiny, low-lying shrubs, known as *phrygana* (or "kindling," because it produces only small sticks), moves in. It consists of thyme, basil, garlic, hyssop, lavender, oregano, rosemary, rue, sage, and savory—as aromatic a plant community as one could hope for. If you walk into a Greek grocery store and ask for dried oregano you'll get a look that means "poor child, must be touched," because the landscape is covered by fresh oregano.

Especially in northern Greece, above the evergreen forest and its maquis and phrygana replacements, there's a belt of deciduous oak, elm, beech, chestnut, ash, and hornbeam. Still higher grows a coniferous forest of pines, silver fir, cedars, and junipers, and on the highest peaks, above the tree line, you even find an alpine tundra of dwarfed flowering plants and lichens.

Modern Greece was born during World War II and its aftermath, the civil war between communist (EAM–ELAS) and royalist (EDES) forces, which lasted until late 1949. After the civil war a constitutional monarchy was re-established, and the country gradually rebuilt. In 1965 Constantine II succeeded to the throne. In 1967 rightist army officers, headed by George Papadopoulos, staged a successful coup; Constantine went into exile; and the junta abolished the monarchy in 1973. In a second coup general Phaedon Gizikis ousted Papadopoulos, in late 1973. After his failure to annex Cyprus, and the subsequent Turkish invasion of the island in 1974 (when Greek Cypriots were dispossessed and the island divided), Gizikis stepped down voluntarily, and civilian government was restored. At the end of that year voters rejected a return of the monarchy and Constantine remained in exile.

Since then the government has been in the hands of either the conservative New Democracy (ND) party or the Panhellenic Socialists (PASOK). PASOK, in power since 1981, began slipping in popularity in 1988, as Prime Minister Andreas Papandreou was caught up in sex and corruption scandals. ND made common cause with an alliance of leftist parties, including the communists (KKE), to form a coalition government. Elections in 1989 were inconclusive, but, in April 1990, ND won a slim majority and formed a government under Prime Minister Constantine Mitsotakis. Popular discontent with economic conditions and the defection of the foreign minister led to elections in October 1993, in which Andreas Papandreou (acquitted of corruption in 1992) and the PASOK party emerged winners. (Shortly afterward, Mitsotakis was charged with, among other offenses, pilfering antiquities for his own collection.)

Relations with Turkey have deteriorated considerably over the past year. In January of 1996 the two countries came close to war over possession of a tiny Aegean islet, Imia. Both Greece and Turkey were struggling with new political leaders fearful of appearing weak to their electorate. In August the Turkish government laid claim to 100 islands in the Aegean, a claim Greece disputes.

Cyprus continues to be a sore point. In 1990, local politicians called for autonomy for northeastern Greece, which has a substantial Turkish minority. Cyprus remains the primary barrier to better relations: No other nation has recognized the separate government for northern Cyprus set up by the Turks, and United Nations–sponsored talks on the Cyprus question have been unproductive.

In the postcommunist era, Greece sought to be the regional leader and intermediary between the EU and the Balkan countries, signing trade and travel agreements with Albania in 1988. Since then, thousands of Albanian refugees have flooded Greece (as have thousands of Romanians, Bulgars, and Gypsies).

Greek fears led the government to ignore a United Nations embargo against Serbia, creating considerable friction with the United States, the EU, and its Balkan neighbors. In 1993 Greece acted to defuse regional tensions by entering into treaties with Bulgaria and with Hungary, and it also relented somewhat concerning the inclusion of Skopje/Macedonia in the United Nations, provided the country be recognized only as "The Former Yugoslav Republic of Macedonia." Greece continued its demand that Skopje/Macedonia give up the use (on its flag) of the 16-point star of Vergina, the symbol of the royal house of ancient Macedonia. This ancient emblem, often called the sun, embossed on the gold larnax from the tomb of Philip II at Vergina, also appears on the 100 drachma coin, along with a portrait of Alexander the Great. Greece continues to feud with the Former Yugoslav Republic of Macedonia over the name of the new country. The new government in Skopje wants Macedonia to be in its name, but Greece fears that it would press claims to Greek Macedonia if it were allowed to do so. Serbia has exacerbated the problem by recognizing the new state as Macedonia, which is largely viewed as a concession owed because of Skopje's support of Serbia during the Bosnian War.

Greece was plunged into public mourning in June of 1996 when former Prime Minister Andreas Papandreou passed away. The ailing leader had clung to power in the fall of 1995, even while he was in the Onassis Cardiac Surgery Center (where he stayed for 123 days). Costas Simitis became leader and won a vote of confidence shortly after Papandreou's death when he was elected to the position of PASOK party president, a position that Papandreou never relinquished.

–Mark J. Rose

Mark Rose received his Ph.D. in Classical Archaeology from Indiana University, is managing editor of *Archaeology Magazine* in New York and visits Greece regularly.

WHAT'S WHERE

Athens

Voyagers touch down in Athens, the stronghold of ancient Greece. Many stay a while to immerse themselves in the hectic vibrancy; others head north and northwest toward the Balkan peninsula, southwest to the rugged Peloponnese, or to the idyllic islands scattered willy-nilly in the surrounding azure Mediterranean waters of the Aegean and Ionian seas. Athens today is a paradox of the old versus the new; for example, after exploring the evocative ancient Acropolis, you may climb Pnyx hill and view a post-sunset sound and light spectacle cast upon the sacred vestiges. Explore its patchwork of neighborhoods—from ancient Athens to quaint Plaka to ritzy Kolonaki—to truly get a sense of the history of this gregarious city, its people, and what lies beyond the ubiquitous modern concrete facades.

Excursions from Athens

Athens lies in a basin defined by three mountain masses: Mt. Hymettos to the east, Mt. Parnis and Mt. Aigaleo to the west, and Mt. Pendeli to the north. East of Mt. Hymettos unfold the gently undulating hills of the Mesogeion. Scattered among and beyond these ranges are engaging sites and villages. Due west is Delphi, where the priestesses of antiquity uttered their enigmatic prophecies. Athenians, Europeans, and far-flung travelers alike are drawn to the quirky Saronic Gulf Islands of Aegina, Poros, Hydra, and Spetses. The famous Marathon and monasteries such as Daphni lay just beyond the forbidding mountains guarding the passes into Athens.

Northern Sporades and Evia

Strung from Mt. Pelion to the center of the Aegean, the Northern Sporades are distinct in character: tourist-addled Skiathos is closest to the mainland; due east is Skopelos, marked with dense pines, scenic villages, and lovely beaches. Farther east is rugged Alonnisos, the least progressed, and a jumping-off point for the uninhabited islands. Wild-nature lovers behold Skyros as the jewel of the isles for its remoteness, myth, and stark beauty. Evia almost touches the mainland, its vast coastline dotted with fishing villages, beaches, and occasional sites.

Epirus and Thessaly

The region consists of two areas: the mountainous province of Epirus, bordered by Albania and the Ionian Sea, with the capital Ioannina to the west. Marking the threshold between Epirus and Thessaly is Metsovo, just beyond the lofty Katara Pass, which threads through the breathtaking Mt. Pindos range. At the western edge is the agricultural Thessalian plain, where the monasteries of Meteora seemingly float in midair, built atop dizzying pinnacles that tower over the town of Kalambaka.

Northern Greece

The region we call Northern Greece, comprising Macedonia to the west and Thrace to the east, covers the Balkan frontier from Albania to Bulgaria, and also touches Turkey. It is both a meeting point and a crossroads between Europe, the Mediterranean, and Asia—imbued with sights, sounds, and colors of a range of different cultures, their interaction telling of successful commingling and fierce discord.

Corfu

Northwesterly Corfu is an island unto itself with a distinct European feel, its outline aptly mimicking a miniature Italy.

Corfu's strategic presence in the northern Ionian Sea at the entrance to the Adriatic shaped its ancient history. Today isolated beaches, stylish restaurants, and tony resorts dot its landscape of serendipitous beauty.

Northern Peloponnese

Greece blessed the Northern Peloponnese—among its jewels Mycenae, Nauplion, and Olympia—with natural beauty and the mysteries of forgotten civilizations. Separated from the north by a narrow isthmus, the Northern Peloponnese comprises the Argive peninsula, jutting into the Aegean, and runs westward past the isthmus and along the Gulf of Corinth to the Adriatic coast.

Southern Peloponnese

The Southern Peloponnese is divided into regions established by the ancients— Messinia in the southwest, Laconia in the southeast, and Arcadia to the north. Massive mountain ranges sweep down the fingers of the peninsula. The beaches are some of the finest and least developed in Greece, some giving way to limestone caves. Tower houses jutting from the craggy landscape are spooky reminders of the clan feuds of centuries past.

The Cyclades

The Cyclades comprise a quintessential, pristine Mediterranean archipelago, with ancient sites, droves of vineyards and olive trees, and stark whitewashed cubist houses, all seemingly crystallized in a backdrop of lapis lazuli. The six major stars in this constellation of islands in the central Aegean Sea—Andros, Mykonos, Naxos, Paros, Tinos, and Santorini—are well visited, but still cast a magnificent fusion of sunlight, stone, and sparkling aqua sea. Plus, they promise culture and flaunt hedonism: ancient sites, Byzantine castles and museums, lively nightlife, shopping, dining, and beaches plain and fancy.

Crete

To Greeks, Crete is the Megalonissi, the Great Island, where a sophisticated culture flourished 5,000 years ago, though its location in the eastern Mediterranean 175 km (108½ mi) from Athens did not discourage invasions from the mainland in ancient times. In all of Crete, you'll find the most development on the north shore, and for the most part the southern coast remains blessedly unspoiled. Western Crete is especially rugged, with inland mountains and the rough southern shoreline; Hania and Rethymnon, mysterious old cities that trace their roots to the Arab and Venetian worlds, are found here.

Rhodes and the Dodecanese

The Dodecanese (Twelve Islands) are the easternmost holdings of Greece, wrapped around the shores of Turkey and Asia Minor. Romans, Crusaders, Turks, and Venetians have left their architectural mark here, but most likely to hypnotize the visitor are the landscape—from the rugged mountains of Patmos to the verdant fields of Kos and lush hillsides of Rhodes—and a way of life that, despite invasions of armies and sunseekers—remains essentially and delightfully Greek.

The Northern Islands

Each of these far-flung Aegean islands bordering Asia Minor is distinct: Chios is extraordinary for its architecture; Lesbos, to the north, is dappled with mineral springs and a petrified forest; northernmost is volcanic Limnos; and Samos, land of wine and honey, is farthest south.

PLEASURES AND PASTIMES

Beaches

More than 3,200 km (2,000 mi) of Greece's coastline qualify as bathing beaches. Keep in mind, however, that many of these are in remote areas or are cobble beaches, fine for swimming but not so good for sunning. On the other hand, there are many beautiful beaches, such as Kyllini Loutras on the western coast, the black volcanic sand beach at Perissa on Santorini, and Vai on the northeast coast of Crete. Most beaches are clean, except those adjacent to major urban centers—but you don't want to swim in the waters off Piraeus, anyway.

Dining

Breakfast ends at about 10, and lunch is usually between 1:30 and 3:30, after which restaurants close for the afternoon. Dinner starts late; 8 is on the early side. Breakfast in Greece is pretty light. Hotels will ply you with a Nescafé-and-bread Continental breakfast, but you might try a "toast," a sort of dry grilled-cheese sandwich (a "mixed toast" if it has a paper-thin ham slice added), or a sesame-coated bread ring sold by street vendors in the cities. Local bakeries may offer fresh doughnuts in the morning. For lunch, heavyweight meat-and-potato dishes can be had, but you might prefer a real Greek salad (no lettuce, a slice of feta with a pinch of oregano, and ripe tomatoes) or souvlaki or grilled chicken from a taverna.

The hour or so before restaurants open for dinner is a pleasant time to have an ouzo or glass of wine and try Greek hors d'oeuvres, called *mezedes*. As the sun sets over the Aegean, seek out a seaside ouzeri. It's the perfect setting for conversation or postcard writing. Dinner is the main meal of the day, and there's plenty of food. Starters include *taramosalata* (a dip or spread made from fish roe) and *melitzanosalata* (made from smoked eggplant, lemon, oil, and garlic), along with the well-known yogurt, cucumber, and garlic *tzatziki*.

On menus all over Greece you'll run into three categories of staple entrée dishes: there's *magirefta* (food that has been cooked in the oven in advance and left in the pan all day, usually served at room temperature)—like moussaka, *pastitsio* (a baked dish of minced lamb and macaroni), or *gemista* (stuffed tomatoes or peppers, which usually has some ground lamb). Then there are *tisoras* (grills), with a subcategory called *stakarvouna* (meaning "of the hour"), food that is cooked on the coals and served immediately—like chops or steak. And last, there is fish, of all kinds, which is outstanding (look for gilt-head bream, or *tsipoura*).

Ouzo, a clear licorice-flavored drink, and brandy are the national aperitifs of Greece. Served in small glasses and diluted with water (which turns the liqueur milky white), ouzo is usually enjoyed on summer evenings and should be lingered over. Try a tiny sip undiluted first, and ask for mezedes, which might include anything from tomato slices, olives, and cheese to shrimp or sausage. Give the stale crackers that accompany ouzo at outdoor cafés to the sparrows flitting around your feet. In winter, people usually ask for brandy: Botrys and the higher-grade Metaxa are both good, and you might also like the *mavrodaphne* (a heavy dessert wine).

Greek wine is relatively inexpensive. Restaurants and tavernas often sell locally produced *kokkino* (red) and *aspro* (white) table wine from the barrel; many of them, purchased by the half-kilogram or kilogram, are perfectly good wines. For bottled wine, look for Hymettos from Attica, Boutari or Tsantalis from Naousa in Macedonia, Carras Estate from Chalkidiki, and red wines from Nemea in the Peloponnese. There are many others. Enthusiasts should consult Miles Lambert-Gocs's comprehensive *The Wines of Greece* (Faber and Faber, London, 1990) for a history of modern wine-making in Greece and for descriptions of regional wines. For additional information on Greek wines and wineries contact the **Federation of Greek Wine and Spirits Industries** (✉ 15A Xenofonto, Athens, ☎ 01/322–6053) or visit the **Central Union of Vine and Wine Cooperatives of Greece** store (✉ L. Riancourt St. at Panormou, Athens, ☎ 01/692–3102, ⊘ Wed.–Mon. 8–2:30, Tues. 5–8).

The origins of retsina, the piney, aromatic, resinated wine considered Greece's *vin du pays,* are uncertain. According to ancient authors, resin was one of many ingredients added to wine to prevent it from turning to vinegar, but the substance may initially have been used to seal wine containers. Whatever the original intent, the results can be splendid. Give retsina a chance; don't take one sip, make a face, then declare you don't like it. Perhaps you've read or been told that retsina is an acquired taste. This isn't true: most people like it immediately. Besides, wouldn't it be fun to drink retsina drawn from the barrel while eating a traditional meal on a late summer's evening in Greece? If retsina out of the barrel isn't available, or if you feel safer with the bottled version, try Achaia Clauss, Thebes, Botrys, Cambas, Kourtakis, Marko, or Pikermi. Have it unchilled with pastitsio, moussaka, or grilled chicken, lamb, or souvlaki.

Outdoor Activities and Sports

Once content to put on weight and slide into middle age without a fight, Greeks are now on the fitness trail. Gymnasiums, aerobics studios, and martial-arts schools can be found in cities and larger towns. Soccer and basketball are kings of the spectator sports in Greece, and the World Cup brings the country to a standstill. Water sports, skiing, and mountaineering are gaining in popularity. The country offers plenty of unspoiled, challenging terrain for serious hiking and mountaineering.

Shopping

Many of the goods tourists purchase in Greece are inspired by the country's ancient civilization. Reproductions of early bronzes, Cycladic figurines, and Geometric, Corinthian, and Athenian vase paintings are ubiquitous. Some are poorly made and some feature rude subjects, but others are charming and even of museum quality.

Objects made of the fragrant olive wood—from worry beads to bowls and sculptures—can be very attractive. Wooden bread stamps and hand guards used in harvesting grain are among the more easily found items of Greek folk culture. Old jewelry and textiles, which are getting rather expensive, can still be a good deal and an adventure to track down.

Leather bags and sandals and heavy wool sweaters are popular; some may be good buys, but some may soon fall apart. Take your time and inspect the seams and stitches before buying. Lightweight sundresses may look wonderful on the hanger in a store, but they're often made of flimsy fabrics—beware their transparency in the bright Greek sunlight.

NEW AND NOTEWORTHY

Named the Cultural Capital of Europe in 1997, **Thessaloniki** is abuzz with museum openings, important international exhibitions, and arts events. Athens was the first to carry this EU title in 1994.

Though it claimed that it would never seek to host the **Olympic Games** again after their humiliating defeat to Atlanta, Athens has decided to put in a bid for the 2004 Summer Olympics. Its 1996 bid was marred by serious public relations and infrastructure problems.

The government a... ing to speed up **rest**... **nian Acropolis;** at the p... take another 35–40 years... Greek labor laws are blamed ... ing the progress of the restoration, is already 40% complete, but the resto... tion is very costly: 4.2 million dollars an... nually. The Committee for Conservation of the Acropolis Monuments is working on the Propylae, Temple of Athena Nike, and the north face of the Parthenon.

UNESCO Director General Federico Mayor will cooperate with the Melina Mercouri Foundation in the effort to restore the **Parthenon Marbles** to Greece. A majority of European Parliament members—269—signed a declaration for their return from the British Museum. In a television call-in show the British public overwhelmingly supported the view that they should be returned. Those working for their return are hoping that they will be returned by the year 2001, which is the 200th anniversary of their theft.

Despite initial enthusiasm the Greek government is wavering on its commitment to allow **casinos** in the country. They've canceled plans to build one in Athens, and are trying to renegotiate their contract with Club Hotels, which has been operating a very lucrative casino in Loutraki, just outside of Athens. Plans for casinos in Rhodes, Syros, and Patras are being reconsidered.

Athens is trying to improve its standing and reputation with tourists with new **tourist information kiosks.** The first one opened in Syntagma Square and the government is reporting that it has been extremely popular (55,000 visits in its first month).

Greece is enjoying an **economic upsurge** under the guidance of popular National Economy Minister Yannos Papantoniou. The OECD predicts growth over the next few years, noting that the Greek economy is growing faster than that of its EU partners.

Athens and Sparta signed a peace treaty on March 12th, 1996, officially bringing to an end the **Peloponnesian War.** Perhaps better late than never, as they say.

...d archaeologists are try-
...ration on the Athe-
...sent rate, it will
...o complete.
...r imped-
...which
...ra-

7

...t makes
... fun and
...rs think.
...iance your
...ls, refer to

Ancient Sites

★**Ancient Akrotiri, Santorini.** In the 1860s, in the course of quarrying tephra, or volcanic ash, the remains of an ancient town were discovered, frozen in time by layers of pumice that buried it at the time of the eruption, 3,600 years ago, long before Pompeii's disaster.

★**Delphi, Central Greece.** One of the most popular sites in Greece, preserved just as it was in antiquity. Follow the sacred way taken by ancient pilgrims seeking prophecies and contemplate the remnants of their offerings to the god Apollo.

★**Mystras, Laconia.** At the sunset of the dying Byzantine Empire a brief burst of renaissance lit up the Eastern Mediterranean, and today the ruins of the sprawling city it left behind engage the visitor as thoroughly as the intellectuals of Mystras enraptured the Greeks.

★**Parthenon on the Acropolis, Athens.** With its stark beauty, shimmering golden-white on the city's horizon, this architecturally sophisticated temple is a testament to the Golden Age of Greece.

★**Temple of Poseidon at Sounion.** The view from the summit is spectacular. Particularly in the slanting light of the late afternoon sun, the land masses to the west stand out in sharp profile: the bulk of Aegina backed by the mountains of the Peloponnese.

★**Theater at Epidauros.** The best-preserved ancient Greek theater in the world is still in use. Whether you're there in the day, or there for a summer show, you're sure to be awed by how seriously the Greeks took drama.

★**Tower of the Winds in Roman Agora, Athens.** The delightful octagonal water clock has been keeping time since the 1st century BC. Also a sundial and weather vane, it was topped by a bronze Triton pointing to expressive reliefs that personify the eight winds.

Hotels

★**Akti Myrina Bungalows, Limnos.** Powerfully commanding a fortified hill, this complex with wood and stone chalets is a destination in itself; you will return, as most do. $$$$

★**Elounda Mare, near Elounda, Crete.** This hotel, a luxurious Relais & Chateau property on the Mirabello Gulf, rivals the best in the world. Stunning design, superlative service, private villas and pools, and extensive wine lists are among the luxurious details. $$$$

★**Atlantis Villas, Santorini.** Each "villa" is actually built inside a cave in Oia's cliff face, one of the most unusual and dramatic places to stay in the world. Balconies have an epic view, 183 meters (600 feet) up, across the magnificent caldera. $$$–$$$$

★**Epaminondas, Andros.** Cool, handsome interiors, ensconced in marble and traditional details, promote relaxing. Favorite pastimes: a midnight dip in the freshwater pool and gazing at Batsi Bay from the huge balconies. $$–$$$

★**Malvasia, Monemvassia.** A fairy tale–like old tower in a living Byzantine town offers an unparalleled view into a forgotten time, while you take in gorgeous surroundings. $

Museums

★**Archaeological Museum, Olympia.** Some of the most impressive pieces of military equipment were uncovered at Olympia, placed there by victorious athletes in honor of the gods who brought them victory.

★**Archaeological Museum, Thessaloniki.** Inside this unassuming structure is a stunning collection of artifacts and treasures attributed to Philip of Macedon, including a brilliant gold funerary box embossed with the 16-point Macedonian sun and a legendary skull.

★**Goulandris Cycladic Museum, Athens.** A sure cure for museum burnout, this outstanding collection spans the Cycladic civilization (3000–2000 BC), dominated by the slender marble figurines that millennia later inspired artists like Picasso.

★**Peloponnesian Folklore Foundation Museum, Nauplion.** This exemplary small museum focuses on textiles. In 1981, it won

the EC's Museum of the Year award for its displays.

Picturesque Villages, Towns, and Neighborhoods

★**Agiassos, Lesbos.** Nestled at the foot of Mt. Olympus in a remote wooded valley, this special village is marked with gray stone houses, cobblestone lanes, a medieval castle, and shops offering local wood handicrafts.

★**Anafiotika quarter of Plaka, Athens.** Nestled below the Acropolis on land the Delphic Oracle once declared sacred, this serene "island village," with its tiny churches and bougainvillea-framed houses, is a blissful contrast to the cacophony of the modern city.

★**Monemvassia.** Part ancient site, part living town, Monemvassia has been called the Greek Gibraltar. Built on a rock jutting out from the Southern Peloponnese, its jumble of ruins next to shops and old churches disorients in a delightful way.

★**Oia, Santorini.** Oia is reputed to be the most beautiful settlement in the Aegean, straddling the wondrous caldera: a crescent of cliffs, striated in black, pink, brown, white, and pale green, rising 335 meters (1,100 feet). Here you will find the cubical white houses you've dreamed of, and a sunset that is unsurpassed.

★**Pirgi, Chios.** One of the few villages that once prospered from mastic production, in this case for gum used by the odalisques of Ottoman harems, Pirgi is lined with tiny arched streets with houses adorned with the lavish Italianate *xysta* design, and more than 50 churches.

Restaurants

★**Bajazzo, Athens.** Splurge with no regrets at what may be Greece's best restaurant, where the chef experiments with wildly imaginative creations for an unforgettable culinary experience. *$$$$*

★**Cava D'Oro, Rethymnon.** Lobster and a panoply of innovative fresh fish are served amid the stylish grace of the high, wood-paneled dining room, once a medieval storeroom, at one of Crete's best restaurants. *$$$*

★**Chez Cat'rine, Mykonos.** You will savor exquisite French cuisine and formality amid a mélange of Cycladic and château ambiance. Just one tantalizing *amuse-gueule* is baby squid stuffed with rice and Greek mountain spices. *$$$*

★**Ta Kioupia, outside Rhodes Town.** The quality of variety of the dishes are as exceptional as the linen-, fine china-, and crystal-appointed tables. Elegance reigns among white stucco, exposed beams, and antique farm tools. *$$$*

★**Casa la Mounte Tirotaverna, Epirus.** The chef has based the menu around Metsovo's delightful, expensive smoked cheese; generous helpings go in everything from highly recommended baked pasta to the freshly made pizza. *$$*

Stellar Views

★**Katara Pass, Metsovo.** Greece's highest mountain pass traverses the border between Thessaly and Epirus; descend through the mountains with the sun, taking in the peaceful ravine below.

★**Mega Spileo, Zakhlorou.** Ascend the towering pinnacles and precipitous rock walls of the Northern Peloponnese's Vouraikos Gorge in a diminutive train, and stop to take a hike to this 4th-century monastery through evergreen oak, cypress, and fir, with panoramic views.

★**Molyvos castle on Lesbos at dawn.** The illuminated mountains of Asia Minor seem to shoot brilliant hues into the sky, juxtaposed by a shimmering sea and red-tile rooms below.

★**Watching the sunset from Mt. Lycabettus, Athens.** On a clear day, the view from the top is the finest in Athens, stretching across the Attica basin, all the way to Piraeus and Aegina and Poros. Watch the sunset and then turn in the other direction to see the moon rise over violet-crowned Mt. Hymettos.

FESTIVALS AND SEASONAL EVENTS

The Greek calendar is filled with religious celebrations, cultural festivals, and civic occasions. Those events with roots in Byzantine Greece are especially intriguing, as they combine religious belief and national pride in a way unfamiliar to most Americans. Shops may close early for local or national celebrations, and hotels may be booked during major events (such as Carnavali at Patras). Verify the dates of events with the Greek National Tourist Organization (GNTO or EOT; ✉ Festivals Box Office, 4 Stadiou St., Athens, ☎ 01/322–1459 or 01/322–3111 ext. 240). Public holidays for 1997 are January 1 (New Year's Day), January 6 (Epiphany), March 10 (Clean Monday, first day of Lent), March 25 (Feast of the Annunciation and Independence Day), April 25, 26, 27 (Good Friday, Holy Saturday, and Orthodox Easter), May 1 (Labor Day and Flower Festival), June 12 (Whit Monday), August 15 (Dormition of the Holy Virgin), October 28 (national holiday), December 25–26 (Christmas Day and Boxing Day).

WINTER

DEC. 31➤ **New Year's Eve** is the occasion for carol singing by children and the exchange of gifts. On the island of Chios the day is marked by a con-test for the best model boat.

JAN. 1➤ The **Feast of Saint Basil** marks the beginning of the New Year. A special cake, the *Vassilopita,* is baked with a coin in it, which brings good luck to the finder.

JAN. 6➤ **Epiphany,** the day for blessing the waters, is the occasion for an official ceremony at Athens's harbor, Piraeus. Elsewhere, crosses are immersed in seas, lakes, and rivers.

JAN. 8➤ **Gynaecocracy,** in northeastern Greece, reverses the traditional roles of men and women: In the area around Serres, Kilkis, Xanthi, and Komotini, women spend the day at the cafés while the men do the housekeeping until evening.

FEB. 23–MAR. 9➤ **Carnavali,** like Mardi Gras, celebrates the period before the beginning of Lent. The evenings are marked by parades, music, and dancing, and costumes are required. Towns and islands known to celebrate Carnavali in style are Patras, Naousa, Veria, Kozani, Zante, Skyros, Xanthi, Mesta and Olimbi on Chios; Galaxidi, Thebes, Poligiros, Thimiana, Lamia, Cefallonia, Messini, Soho, Serres, and Agiassos on Lesbos; Karpathos, Heraklion and Rethymnon on Crete; Amfissa, Efxinoupolis, and Ayia Anna on Evia.

MAR. 25➤ **Independence Day** commemorates the call for independence in 1821 by Germanos, the Metropolitan of Patras, which began the uprising in the Peloponnese that eventually freed Greece from Ottoman rule. Today it is marked by parades of the armed forces, especially in Athens.

SPRING

APR. 25–27, 1997; APR. 17–19, 1998➤ **Good Friday, Holy Saturday,** and **Easter Sunday** are the most sacred days on the Orthodox calendar. The traditional candlelight funeral processions staged throughout the country on Good Friday are very powerful to watch. Not only do they attest to the strength of the participants' faith, but they link modern Greece with its Byzantine roots, and the soldiers carrying the coffins illustrate the ties between church and government. Processions to churches on the night of Holy Saturday are a memorable sight. Following the midnight ceremony of the Resurrection, the congregations head homeward to feast, with the traditional red-dyed eggs and *mayiritsa* soup. More red-dyed eggs and roast lamb highlight the feasting on Easter Sunday. Seeing the rituals of Holy Week makes you understand the depth of meaning that the Easter greeting *Christos aneste,* "Christ is risen," and its response *Alithos aneste,* "He has indeed risen," has for most Greeks.

APR. 23➤ The **Feast of Saint George** is a day for horse racing at Kaliopi on Limnos and at Pili on Kos. On Crete, a three-day-long feast begins at Arachova, near Delphi, while at Assi Gonia, near Hania, a sheep-shearing contest follows the religious fiesta.

MAY–SEPT.➤ **Folk dancing** is performed at the amphitheater on Filopappou Hill in Athens.

MAY 21–23➤ The **Anastenaria,** a traditional fire-walking ritual with pagan roots and a Byzantine overlay, is performed in Ayia Eleni near Ayia Serres, and in Langada near Thessaloniki, where villagers dance on live embers while clasping icons of Saint Constantine and Saint Helen.

SUMMER

JUNE–SEPT.➤ The **Athens Festival** presents ancient dramas, operas, music, and ballet performed by nationally and internationally famous artists, in the 2nd-century Odeon of Herodes Atticus on the south slope of the Acropolis.

JUNE–OCT.➤ **Folk-dancing** performances are held in the theater in the old town of Rhodes on that island.

MID-JUNE–LATE AUG.➤ **Lycabettus Theater** presents a variety of performances in the amphitheater on Lycabettus Hill overlooking Athens.

LATE JUNE–EARLY JULY➤ Coastal towns honor the Greek navy with the celebrations of **Navy Week.** Fishermen at Plomari on Lesbos and Agria near Volos stage festivals, and at Volos the last day of Navy Week is marked by a reenactment of the mythical voyage of the ship *Argo,* with its crew led by Jason in search of the Golden Fleece.

JULY–SEPT. WEEKENDS➤ The **Epidauros Festival,** world-renowned for the excellence of the performances, is held in the ancient theater, known for its superb acoustics. Watching a classical comedy or tragedy in this peaceful rural setting sends chills down your spine—twilight falls, the audience quiets, and a play first performed 2,500 years ago begins. The **Dodoni, Philippi,** and **Thassos festivals,** like the better-known one at Epidauros,

stage classical dramas in ancient theaters.

AUG.➤ The **Epirotika Festival** in Ioannina, Epirus, celebrates Epirotikan authors and artists with exhibitions, theatrical performances, and concerts. At the **Olympus Festival,** a series of cultural events is held at the village of Litochoro near Olympus, in the well-preserved Frankish castle of Platamona. The **Hippokrateia Festival** on the island of Kos honors the father of medicine, a native son. Events include performances of ancient dramas and music, a flower show, and a costumed reenactment of the first swearing of the Hippocratic oath.

AUG.–SEPT.➤ At the **Aeschilia** festival, ancient dramas are staged at the archaeological site of Eleusis near Athens.

AUTUMN

SEPT.–OCT.➤ Following Thessaloniki's International Trade Fair in September come the **Festival of Popular Song,** the **Film Festival,** and the **Demetria Festival,** with theater, concerts, ballet, and opera.

2 Athens

To discover Athens's pockets of beauty amid the sprawl of concrete, stroll the city's neighborhoods, from the elegant suburb of Kifissia to the hilly quarter of working-class Piraeus. This metropolis of more than 4 million people is the epitome of all that is Greek, thriving on the confluence of tradition and modernity, east and west.

By B.
Samantha
Stenzel

Updated
by Toula
Bogdanos

I WOULD URGE THAT YOU FIX YOUR EYES on the greatness of Athens as she really is and fall in love with her. . . ." These are the words (as reported by Thucydides) of Pericles, the mastermind of Greece's Golden Age, in his oration for the dead of the Peloponnesian war. In 1185, Michael Akominatos, archbishop of the city, wrote otherwise: "You cannot look upon Athens without tears. . . . She has lost the very form, appearance, and character of a city." Today, after another 800 years, the cleric's description is even more apt. Residents and visitors alike note the city's faults: the murky brown pollution cloud known as the *nefos,* the overcrowding, the traffic jams with their stench and din, and the characterless cement apartment blocks. When Athens became the capital in 1834, it was a marshy village of about 6,000 people, and today it is home to 4 million (about 40% of Greece's population) and covers 689 sq km (165 sq mi).

Life in this temperate climate is played out on street corners and balconies from early morning until very late at night. This high visibility combined with the basically nonviolent nature of the Greeks accounts for the low crime rate, which compares favorably with that of other European capitals. Although the look of the city's housing belies the substantial wealth of some of its inhabitants, slums do not exist here. As in any large city, if you exercise normal caution, such as carrying your money safely and avoiding lonely walks late at night, your chances of running into trouble are very slim. You are in more danger of being hit by a careless driver while crossing the street than of being mugged.

Although Athens may seem like one huge city, it is really a series of small villages strung together. Most of the major historic sites are within the central area; it is possible to see them on foot. When you (inevitably) wander off your planned route into less touristy areas, take the opportunity to explore. You will often discover pockets of incomparable charm, in refreshing contrast to the dreary repetition of the modern facades.

Take a break from gazing at the monuments from previous generations and settle into a shady café to observe today's Athens and the Athenians in their element. They are lively and expressive, their hands fiddling with worry beads or gesturing excitedly; earthy and fun-loving, occasionally irritating, even overbearing—they are very rarely boring. While often expansively friendly, they are aggressive and stubborn when feeling threatened, and they're also insatiably curious. You'll probably be asked direct questions about your personal affairs that might be considered rude at home; keep your sense of humor and parry with your own queries if you wish.

Athens is an intriguing crossroads, with both the city and its inhabitants blending elements of Middle Eastern and Western cultures. But underneath the confusion and modern clutter lies a palpable Mediterranean warmth that with a little encouragement will envelop you.

Pleasures and Pastimes

Cafés

On any street corner, at any time of day, you will see Athenians practicing the fine art of "hanging out," sipping their coffees, debating the latest political fiasco, watching the world go by. Walking in the city may seem difficult at times because of cars parked on the sidewalk, uneven pavements, and the ongoing Metro works, but there is no shortage of squares, *kafenia* (traditional Greek coffeehouses), trendy cafés, and makeshift arrangements—two tables set up outside a dairy store—where you can sit for hours with an ouzo or frappé, the ubiquitous summer refreshment: instant Nescafé shaken with ice water and served with milk and sugar.

Dining

For bargain dining, stick to Greek cuisine and avoid the most touristy areas. If you're not on a budget, the foreign restaurants now offer dishes of a world-class standard, with prices that you would expect in any European capital.

Nightlife

Athens is a sociable, late-night town where people love to see and be seen, and the action goes on until morning: Even at 3 AM *platias* (central squares) and streets are crowded with revelers. Options range from *rembetika* (Asia Minor blues from the 1920s) clubs to bouzoukia to seaside bars blasting rave or rock. Neither high inflation, frozen wage scales, and changing bar curfews nor a government campaign to get people to pay their taxes seems to slow the social life—clubs and restaurants are usually packed.

EXPLORING ATHENS

Although Athens covers a huge area, the major landmarks of the ancient Greek, Roman, and Byzantine periods are conveniently close to the modern city center. You can easily stroll from the Acropolis to the other sites, taking time to browse in shops and relax in cafés and tavernas along the way. The center of modern Athens is small, stretching from the Acropolis to Mt. Lycabettus, crowned by the small white chapel of Ayios Georgios. The layout is simple: Three parallel streets—Stadiou, Eleftheriou Venizelou (familiarly known as Panepistimiou), and Acadimias—link two main squares—Syntagma (Constitution) and Omonia (Concord). Try to wander off this beaten tourist track: Seeing the Athenian butchers in the Central Market sleeping on their cold marble slabs during the heat of the afternoon siesta may give you more of a feel for the city than seeing hundreds of fallen columns.

From many quarters of the city one can glimpse "the glory that was Greece" in the form of the Acropolis looming above the horizon, but only by actually climbing that rocky precipice can you feel the impact of the ancient settlement. The Acropolis and Filopappou, two craggy hills sitting side by side; the ancient Agora (marketplace); and Kerameikos, the first cemetery, form the core ancient and Roman Athens. In the National Archaeological Museum is a vast array of artifacts illustrating the many millennia of Greek civilization; smaller museums such as the Cycladic and the Byzantine illuminate the history of particular regions or periods.

The city's Asian character after the 400-year rule under the Ottoman Empire is still evident in Monastiraki, the flea market area nestled at the foot of the Acropolis. Strolling through Plaka, a delightful area of tranquil streets lined with renovated mansions, you will get the flavor of the 19th century's gracious lifestyle. The narrow lanes with tiny churches and the whitewashed, bougainvillea-framed houses of Anafiotika, a section of Plaka, are reminiscent of an island village. Formerly run-down old quarters, such as Thission, a popular nightlife area with its string of new bars, and Psirri are now in the process of gentrification, although they still retain much of their original charm, as does the colorful produce and meat market on Athinas. The area around Constitution Square, the tourist hub, and Concord Square, the commercial heart of the city about ½ mi northwest, is distinctly European, having been designed by the court architects of King Otho, a Bavarian. The most modern neighborhood, the ritzy, chic Kolonaki with its smart shops and bistros, is nestled at the foot of Mt. Lycabettus, Athens's highest hill (277 meters/909 feet). Each of Athens's outlying suburbs has a distinctive character: In the north is the wealthy, tree-lined Kifissia, once a summer resort for aristocratic Athenians, and in the south is down-to-earth Piraeus, with its bustling harbors and Saronic Gulf views.

Except for August and major holidays, when Athenians migrate to their ancestral villages outside of Athens, the streets are crowded. The best times to visit are late fall and spring when you can avoid the oppressive heat and the hordes of package tourists at major archaeological sites; you can also enjoy the bustling "winter" nightlife in the center, because after June many restaurants and clubs shut down or relocate to the seaside. Holy Week of the Orthodox Easter, at the end of April, affords visitors the chance to observe Greece's most sacred holiday, including mournful Good Friday processions through neighborhoods with Christ's bier, and the candlelit Easter midnight service, complete with fireworks. If you must come in summer, visit the sights in the early morning, then—as do Greeks—take a nap or a leisurely lunch before continuing your explorations after 5 PM, when several museums and sites are still open.

Admission to almost all museums and archaeological sites is free on Sunday from mid-November through March. Entrance is usually free every day for European Union (EU) students, half off for students from other countries, and about a third off for senior citizens. In summer, opening hours depend on available personnel, but throughout the year, arrive at least 30 minutes before official closing times to ensure a ticket. For museums, the months constituting the winter season change each year, but winter season is generally from October to April. Taking flash photos is strictly forbidden in museums.

The best time to explore churches is during mass, especially on Sunday. Otherwise, hours are not set in stone; try from about 8 AM to noon and 5:30 PM to 7:30 PM on any day, unless where noted. For walking in Athens, try to avoid the city's two rush hours, between 2 and 3 PM and again around 8:30 PM. On Monday and Saturday afternoons and on Sunday roads have the least traffic.

Great Itineraries

The temptation, especially for visitors on their way to the islands, is to get through the city as quickly as possible. This, however, is a mistake. To fully experience Athens is to understand the essence of Greece: ancient monuments surviving in a sea of cement, startling beauty amid the squalor, tradition, and modernity—a smartly dressed lawyer chatting on her mobile phone as she maneuvers around a priest in flowing robes waiting for the trolley. Locals depend upon humor and flexibility to deal with the chaos; visitors should do the same. The rewards are immense for those who take the time to catch the purple light of sundown on Mt. Hymettus, light a candle in a Byzantine church amid heavy incense and black-shrouded grandmas while teens outside argue vociferously about soccer, or breathe in the tangy sea air while enjoying a Greek coffee after a night at the coastal clubs.

IF YOU HAVE 1 DAY

Pay homage to Athens's most impressive legacy, the **Acropolis,** early in the morning, then descend through **Anafiotika,** the closest thing you'll find to an island village. Explore the 19th-century quarter of **Plaka,** with its neoclassical houses, and stop for lunch at one of its many tavernas. Do a little bargaining with the merchants in the old Turkish bazaar around

Monastiraki Square. Spend a couple of hours in the afternoon marveling at the stunning collection of antiquities in the **National Archaeological Museum,** then pass by **Constitution Square** to see the changing of the brightly costumed Evzone guards in front of the Tomb of the Unknown Soldier. You can then window-shop or people-watch in the tony neighborhood of **Kolonaki.** Nearby, take the funicular up to **Mt. Lycabettus** for the sunset before enjoying a show at the **Roman theater of Herod Atticus,** followed by dinner in the lively nightlife district of **Thission.**

IF YOU HAVE 3 DAYS

After a morning tour of the **Acropolis,** with a stop at the **Acropolis Museum** to view sculptures found on the site, pause on your descent at **Areopagus,** the ancient supreme court; the view is excellent. Continue through **Anafiotika** and **Plaka,** making sure to stop at the **Greek Folk Art Museum,** the **Roman Agora,** with its Tower of the Winds, an enchanting water clock from the 1st century BC, and the **Little Mitropolis church** on the outskirts of the quarter. After a late lunch, detour to **Hadrian's Arch** and the **Temple of Olympian Zeus,** Athens's most important Roman monuments. In **Constitution Square,** watch the changing of the Evzone guards, then head to **Kolonaki,** followed by an ouzo on the side of **Mt. Lycabettus** at I Prasini Tenta, with its splendid panorama of the Acropolis and the sea. Dine in a local taverna, perhaps in a neighborhood near the **Panathenaic Stadium,** which is lit at night. This Roman arena was reconstructed for the first modern Olympics in 1896. On day two, visit the cradle of democracy, the **ancient Agora,** with Greece's best preserved temple, the Hephaistion. Explore the **Monastiraki area,** including the tiny Byzantine chapel of **Kapnikarea,** which stands in the middle of a busy street. In Monastiraki you can snack on the city's best souvlaki, then hop the metro to **Piraeus** to explore its neighborhoods and feast on fish in Mikrolimano Harbor. On the third day, start early for the **National Archaeological Museum,** breaking for lunch in one of the city's *mezedopolia* (places that sell mezes) such as Apotsos. Swing through the city center, past the **Old University complex,** a vestige of King Otho's reign, to the **Cycladic Museum** in Kolonaki, with the curious figurines that inspired artists such as Modigliani and Picasso. Stroll through the **National Gardens,** and have a coffee in the romantic setting of To Kafenedaki café. Complete the evening with a show at **Herod Atticus,** a movie at a *therina* (open-air cinema), or a concert at the Megaron Symphony Hall in winter.

IF YOU HAVE 5 DAYS

Spend your first three days as detailed above. On the fourth, see the **Byzantine museum,** which houses Christian art from the 4th to the 19th centuries, including masterful icons and the reconstructions of Greek Orthodox churches; then take a taxi (or bus 224 followed by a 30-minute walk) to the peaceful Byzantine monastery of **Kaisariani** on the foothills of Mt. Hymettus. Here you can enjoy a picnic lunch with your Acropolis view. In the evening, splurge at Bajazzo, Athens's best haute-cuisine restaurant, then dance the *tsifteteli* (the Greek version of a belly dance) to Asia Minor blues in a rembetika club, or, if it's summer, visit the coastal stretch toward the airport, where the irrepressible bars stay open until dawn. On the last day, elbow your way through the boisterous **Central Market,** then cut through the old, fairly intact neighborhood of **Psirri** to **Kerameikos,** Athens's ancient cemetery. After lunch in **Thission,** for a complete change from the urban pace take the metro to the lovely suburb of **Kifissia** and view the grand homes by horse-drawn carriage, shop, or relax in the many cafés. As an alternative, you may want to catch a bus near the Zappion hall entrance of the National Gardens to one of the government-run beaches in Varkiza, Vouliagmeni, or Voula.

The Acropolis, Filopappou, and Environs

The Acropolis, or "High City," is a true testament to the Golden Age of Greece, from 461 to 429 BC, that magical period at the height of the Athenian statesman Pericles' influence when the intellectual and artistic life of Athens flowered. Archaeological evidence has shown that the flat-top limestone outcrop, 156 meters (512 feet) high, attracted settlers in as early as Neolithic times because of its defensible position and its natural springs. It is believed to have been continuously inhabited throughout the Bronze Age and since.

Over the years the Acropolis buildings have been damaged by war and unscrupulously transformed: on the site now are a Florentine palace, a mosque, a Turkish harem, and a brothel. The site is now undergoing conservation as part of an ambitious 20-year rescue plan launched in 1983 by Greek architects with international support. Despite the ongoing restoration works, the monument described by the French poet Lamartine as "the most perfect poem in stone" will not disappoint you. A visit to the Acropolis can evoke the presence of ancient heroes and the gods once worshiped here. See the buildings first and save the museum for last; the overall setting will give the statues and friezes more meaning. The "Acropolis" neighborhood includes fine neoclassical buildings lining its main street, Dionyssiou Areopagitou, the centuries-old theaters of Odeon of Herod Atticus and Dionyssos, and the newest museum in Greece, the Ilias LALAoUNIS Jewelry Museum. Nearby is Filopappou, a pine-clad summit that offers a respite from the heat with its several minor sites and the tiny, rustic church of Ayios Dimitrios Loumbardiaris.

A Good Walk

Numbers in the text correspond to numbers in the margin and on the Exploring Ancient Athens, Exploring Athens, and Exploring Piraeus maps.

★ If you see nothing else, you must visit the **Acropolis** ①. Even jaded Athenians, when overwhelmed by the city, need only lift their eyes to this great monument to feel renewed. Wear a hat for protection from the sun and low-heel, rubber-sole shoes, as the marble on the Acropolis steps and near the other monuments is very slippery. Take a taxi or Bus 230 to Dionyssiou Areopagitou, which winds around the Acropolis to its entrance at the Beulé Gate. Buildings include the architecturally complex Erechtheion temple, most sacred of the shrines of the Acropolis, and the Parthenon, which dominates the Acropolis and, indeed, the city skyline: it is the most architecturally sophisticated temple of its period. Time and neglect have given the marble pillars their golden-white shine, and the beauty of the building is all the more stark and striking. Even with summer's hordes wandering around the ruins, you will still feel a sense of wonder.

While on the outcrop, pause at the edge of the southern fortifications where, on a clear day, you can see the coastline toward Sounion and the Saronic Gulf islands of Aegina and Salamina. Be sure to leave
★ enough time for the **Acropolis Museum** ②, which houses some superb sculptures from the Acropolis, including the Caryatids and a large collection of colored *korai* (statues of women dedicated to the goddess Athena). As you exit the gate, detour right before descending to **Areopagus** ③, the ancient supreme court, from which St. Paul later preached to the Athenians.

Cross Dionyssiou Areopagitou to **Filopappou** ⑤, but before climbing the summit, via the marble road or the footpaths crisscrossing the hill, stop at tiny **Ayios Dimitrios Loumbardiaris** ④ church, and then for a cof-

fee at the tourist pavilion. Descend Dionyssiou Areopagitou, past the
Odeon of Herod Atticus ⑥ and the Hellenistic **theater of Dionyssos** ⑦.
Nearby is the **Ilias LALAoUNIS Jewelry Museum** ⑧, with more than 3,000
pieces and a workshop where visitors can observe ancient techniques
still used today. Off the main boulevard on Makriyianni, for those who
have the time and the interest, is the **Center for Acropolis Studies** ⑨, with
exhibits on the great monument and its restoration.

TIMING

The earlier you start out the better, but an alternative in summer is to
visit the Acropolis at about 4 PM, when the light is best for photographs.
Depending on the crowds waiting to get in to the Acropolis, the walk
takes about four hours, including two at the Acropolis Museum. Once
a month in summer, the site opens from about 9 PM to midnight so you
can enjoy the spectacle of the full moon rising and casting long shadows over the Parthenon. The Ilias LALAoUNIS Jewelry Museum is closed
Tuesday, so you may want to take this tour another day.

Sights to See

★ ❶ **Acropolis.** Foundations for a grand new temple honoring the city's patron, goddess Athena, were laid after the victory at Marathon in 490
BC, but were destroyed by Persians in 480–79 BC. After a 30-year building moratorium, ended by the peace treaty at Susa in 448 BC, Pericles
undertook the ambitious project of reconstructing it on a monumental scale. This extraordinary Athenian general is an enigmatic figure,
considered by some scholars to be the brilliant architect of the destiny
of Greece at its height, and by others a megalomaniac who bankrupted
the coffers of an empire and an elitist who catered to the privileged
few at the expense of the masses.

The appearance of the buildings that comprised the major portion of
the Acropolis was largely unaltered until AD 52, when the Roman
Claudius embellished the entrance with a typically flamboyant staircase. In the 2nd century Hadrian had his turn at decorating many shrines,
and in 529 Justinian closed the philosophical schools in the city, emphasizing the defensive character of the citadel, and changing the temples into Christian churches.

Visitors enter through the **Beulé Gate,** a late Roman structure named
for the French archaeologist Ernest Beulé, who discovered it in 1852.
Made of marble fragments from destroyed monuments, it has an inscription above the lintel dated 320 BC, dedicated by "Nikias son of
Nikodemos of Xypete," who had apparently won a musical competition. Before Roman times, the entrance to the Acropolis was a steep
processional ramp below the Temple of Athena Nike. This Sacred
Way was used every fourth year for the Panathenaic Procession, a spectacle that ended the festival celebrating Athena's remarkable birth (she
sprang from the head of her father Zeus), which included chariot
races, athletic and musical competitions, and poetry recitals. Toward
the end of July, all strata of Athenian society gathered at the Dipylon
Gate of Kerameikos and followed a sacred ship wheeled up to the summit. The ship was anchored at the rocky outcrop below Areopagus,
just northwest of the Acropolis.

The **Propylaea** is a typical ancient gate, an imposing structure designed
to instill proper reverence in worshipers as they leave the temporal world
to enter the spiritual world of the sanctuary, for this was the main function of the Acropolis. Planned by Pericles, it was the masterwork of
the architect Mnesicles. It was to have been the grandest secular building in Greece, the same size as the Parthenon. Construction was suspended because of the Peloponnesian War, and it was never finished.

The Propylaea was used as a garrison during the Turkish period; in 1656, a powder magazine there was struck by lightning, causing much damage, and the Propylaea was again damaged during the Venetian siege under Morosini in 1687.

The Propylaea shows the first use of both Doric and Ionic columns together, a style that can be called Attic. Six of the sturdier fluted Doric columns made from Pentelic marble correspond with the gateways of the portal. Processions with priests, chariots, and sacrificial animals entered via a marble ramp in the center, now protected by a wooden stairway; ordinary visitors on foot had to enter via the side doors.

The slender Ionic columns (⅔ the diameter of the Doric) had elegant capitals, some of which have been restored, along with a section of the famed paneled ceiling, originally decorated with gold eight-pointed stars on a blue background. The well-preserved north wing housed the Pinakotheke, or art gallery, specializing in paintings of scenes from Homer's epics and mythological tableaux on wooden plaques. Connected to it was a lounge with 17 couches arranged around the walls so that weary visitors could take a siesta. The south wing was a decorative portico (row of columns). The view from the inner porch of the Propylaea is stunning: The Parthenon is suddenly revealed in full glory, framed by the columns.

The all-marble **Temple of Athena Nike** on the bastion, built about 425–24 BC, has four Ionic columns on both a front and a rear porch. Pausanias called this the Temple of Nike Apteros, or Wingless Victory, for "in Athens they believe Victory will stay with them forever because she has no wings." The figures of the wingless Nikes (maidens attendant on Athena), on marble slabs from the parapet, can be seen now in the Acropolis Museum. Only the badly weathered figures on the east frieze, all now headless including Athena, are originals. The other sections, depicting battle scenes with Greeks fighting the Boeotians and Persians, are cement copies of those in the British Museum. It was from this platform that, according to Pausanias, the 2nd-century traveler and geographer, the distraught King Aegeus met his end. He leapt to his death when in the distance he saw the black sails on his son Theseus's boat returning from Crete and thought him dead. Theseus, succeeding his father, became a legendary national hero of Athens and united the different villages.

At the loftiest point of the Acropolis is the **Parthenon,** the architectural masterpiece conceived by Pericles and executed between 447 and 438 BC by the brilliant sculptor Pheidias, who supervised the architects Iktinos and Callicrates in its construction. Although dedicated to the goddess Athena (the name Parthenon comes from the Athena Parthenos, or the virgin Athena) and inaugurated at the Panathenaia Festival of 438 BC, the Parthenon was primarily the treasury of the Delian League. For the populace, the Erechtheion remained Athena's sanctified holy place.

Though the structure of the Parthenon is marble, the inner ceilings and doors were made of wood. The original building was ornate, covered with a tile roof, decorated with statuary and marble friezes, and so brightly painted that the people protested, "We are gilding and adorning our city like a wanton woman" (Plutarch). Pheidias himself may have sculpted some of the exquisite, brightly painted metopes, but most were done by other artists under his guidance. The only ones remaining in situ show scenes of battle: Athenians versus Amazons, and gods and goddesses against giants. One of the most evocative friezes, depicting the procession of the Panathenaia, was 159 meters (524 feet) long, an extraordinary parade of 400 people including maidens, magistrates, horse-

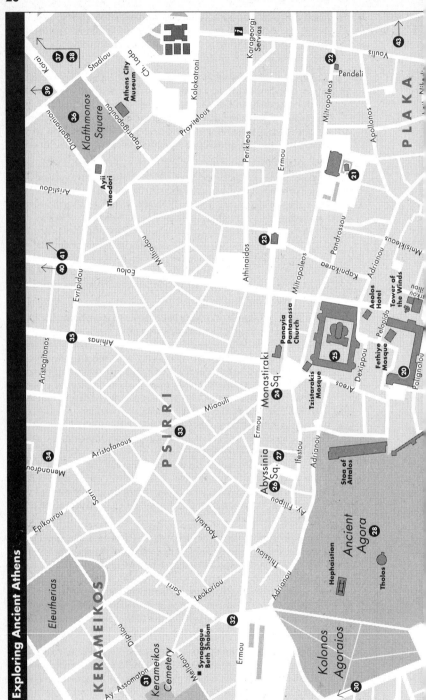

Exploring Ancient Athens

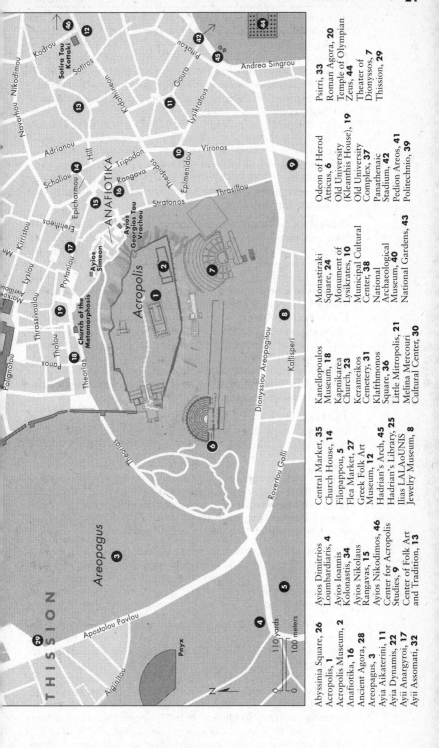

Abyssinia Square, **26**
Acropolis, **1**
Acropolis Museum, **2**
Anafiotika, **16**
Ancient Agora, **28**
Areopagus, **3**
Ayia Aikaterini, **11**
Ayia Dynamis, **22**
Ayii Anargyroi, **17**
Ayii Assomati, **32**

Ayios Dimitrios
Loumbardiaris, **4**
Ayios Ioannis
Kolonastis, **34**
Ayios Nikolaus
Rangavas, **15**
Ayios Nikodimos, **46**
Center for Acropolis
Studies, **9**
Center of Folk Art
and Tradition, **13**

Central Market, **35**
Church House, **14**
Filopappou, **5**
Flea Market, **27**
Greek Folk Art
Museum, **12**
Hadrian's Arch, **45**
Hadrian's Library, **25**
Ilias LALAoUNIS
Jewelry Museum, **8**

Kanellopoulos
Museum, **18**
Kapnikarea
Church, **23**
Kerameikos
Cemetery, **31**
Klafthmonos
Square, **36**
Little Mitropolis, **21**
Melina Mercouri
Cultural Center, **30**

Monastiraki
Square, **24**
Monument of
Lysikrates, **10**
Municipal Cultural
Center, **38**
National
Archaeological
Museum, **40**
National Gardens, **43**

Odeon of Herod
Atticus, **6**
Old University
(Kleanthis House), **19**
Old University
Complex, **37**
Panathenaic
Stadium, **42**
Pedion Areos, **41**
Politechnio, **39**

Psirri, **33**
Roman Agora, **20**
Temple of Olympian
Zeus, **44**
Theater of
Dionyssos, **7**
Thission, **29**

men, musicians, and 200 animals. To show ordinary mortals, at a time when almost all sculpture was of mythological or battle scenes, was lively and daring. About 50 of the best-preserved pieces, adamantly called the "Parthenon marbles" by Greeks but known as the "Elgin marbles" by most everyone else, are in the British Museum, and a few others can be seen in the Acropolis Museum. In the first decade of the 19th century, during the time of the Ottoman Empire, Lord Elgin, British Ambassador in Constantinople, was given permission by the Sultan Selim III to remove stones with inscriptions from the Acropolis; he took this as license to dismantle shiploads of sculptures. It remains a highly controversial issue to this day: On one side, many argue that the marbles would have been destroyed if left on site; on the other side, a spirited campaign spearheaded by the late Melina Mercouri, the actor-turned-politician, aims to have them returned to Greece where they can be appreciated in their original context.

Pheidias's most awesome contribution to the Parthenon was the 39-foot-high statue of Athena that stood in the inner chamber of the sanctuary. It was made on a wooden frame, with ivory for the flesh and more than a ton of gold for the ankle-length tunic, helmet, spear, and shield. The alleged theft of some of this gold (some say the ivory) was the basis of charges against Pheidias, who is said to have cleared his name by removing it from the statue and having it weighed to prove it all was there. After the Christian emperor Thesodosius II closed all pagan sanctuaries in AD 435, the statue seems to have disappeared. The Parthenon was later converted into a church, but the basic structure was intact until the Venetian siege of Athens in the 17th century, when Morosini's artillery hit a powder magazine, causing a fire that burned for two days. Many of the 46 columns were destroyed, along with the roof and most of the interior.

The **Erechtheion** is a distinctive structure built on uneven ground. Completed in 406 BC, it was divided into two Ionic sanctuaries, the eastern one containing an olive-wood statue of Athena Polias, protectress of the city, and the western one dedicated to Poseidon-Erechtheus.

In the contest between Athena and Poseidon for divine patronage of the city, the sea god dramatically plunged his trident into the rock next to the Erechtheion and produced a spring of water. Athena more prudently created an olive tree, the main staple of Greek society. The panel of judges declared her the winner, and the city was named Athena.

A gnarled olive tree outside the west wall was planted where Athena's once grew, and marks said to be from Poseidon's trident can be seen on a rock wedged in a hole near the north porch. His gift should not be slighted, for the continual springs of the Acropolis have made habitation possible from earliest times, as well as watering the olive trees.

The most endearing feature of the Erechtheion, which has recently undergone extensive repair, is the south portico, facing the Parthenon, known as the **Caryatid Porch.** It is supported on the heads of six strapping but shapely maidens (Caryatids) wearing delicately draped Ionian garments, their folds perfectly aligned to resemble flutes on columns. What you look at today are copies. Except for the Caryatid dismantled by Lord Elgin, now in the British museum, the originals were removed to the Acropolis Museum in 1977 to protect them from erosion caused by air pollution. ⊠ *Dionyssiou Areopagitou,* ☎ *01/321–0219.* ▨ *2,000 dr., joint ticket for Acropolis and Acropolis Museum.* ⊙ *Weekdays 8–6:30 (winter 8–4), weekends 8–3.*

★ ❷ **Acropolis Museum.** Unobtrusively snuggled in the southeast corner of the Acropolis site, the museum has nine rooms filled with the sculptures found on the Acropolis plus the votive offerings to Athena. The displays are well executed, but the English labeling is sketchy.

In Room I, the anguished expression of a calf being devoured by a lioness in a poros-stone pediment of the 6th century BC brings to mind Picasso's *Guernica*. Room II contains the charismatic *Calf-Bearer,* an early Archaic work showing a man named Rhombos carrying on his shoulders a calf intended to be sacrificed. A porous-stone pediment of the Archaic temple of Athena shows Heracles fighting against the triton and on the right side the rather scholarly looking "three-headed demon," bearing traces of the original red and black embellishment.

The most notable displays of the museum are sculptures from the Archaic and Classical periods, pieces of unique appeal, including, in Room IV, the *Horseman* and the compelling *Hound.* In Rooms IV and V, take a good look at the exquisite korai, with fascinating details of hair, clothing, and jewelry of the Archaic period. Room V also has striking pedimental figures from the Old Temple of Athena (525 BC), depicting the battle between Athena and the Giants.

In Room VI is the 5th-century BC relief, *Mourning Athena,* a fine example of the severe style favored in the Classical period.

In Room VIII, a superbly rendered slab from the eastern side of the Acropolis represents the seated Poseidon, Artemis, and Apollo (No. 856). Incomparably graceful movement is suggested in *Nike Unlacing Her Sandal* (No. 973), taken from the parapet of the Temple of Athena Nike. In a dimly lit air-conditioned glass case in Room IX are four of the badly damaged original Caryatids. ⊠ *Acropolis,* ☎ *01/323–6665.* 🎫 *2,000 dr., joint ticket for Acropolis and Acropolis Museum.* ☉ *Mon. 11:30–6:30 (winter 10:30–4:30), Tues.–Fri. 8–6:30 (winter 8–4:30), weekends 8:30–3.*

❸ Areopagus. From this limestone "Hill of Ares," sure-footed visitors have a good view of the Propylaea, the ancient Agora below, and the modern metropolis to the northwest. This was once Athens's supreme judicial court, and legend says that Orestes was tried here for the murder of his mother, Clytemnestra. From the outcrop Saint Paul delivered such a moving sermon on the "Unknown God" that he converted the senator Dionysius, who became the first bishop of Athens. Some of Saint Paul's words (Acts 17:22–34) are written in Greek on a bronze plaque at the foot of the hill. ⊠ *Outside the Acropolis's entrance.*

❹ Ayios Dimitrios Loumbardiaris. A delightful grove encloses the church, which derives its name from *loumbarda* (cannon). Here in 1656 on St. Dimitrios' Day, as is told in a text posted on the church, the congregation was gathered, while on the Acropolis a Turkish garrison commander readied the cannons of the Propylaea to open fire during the final Te Deum. The moment it started, a bolt of lightning struck the cannons, blowing up the Propylaea and killing the commander and many of his men. The stone church contains many icons and has an old-fashioned wood ceiling and roof. ⊠ *Filopappou hill.*

NEED A BREAK?
The little **Tourist Pavilion** (⊠ Filopappou hill, ☎ 01/923–1665) is a blissful oasis far from the bustle of the archaeological sites and the streets. It is beautifully landscaped, shaded by overhanging pines, and the background music is provided by chirping birds. It serves drinks, snacks, and a few hot plates; it is open daily from 9 to 1.

❾ Center for Acropolis Studies. The spacious, sunny ground floor is devoted to casts of sculptures of lounging gods and friezes of heroes battling giants or centaurs that were once (or still are) on the Acropolis.

The most notable are copies of the much-touted Elgin Marbles, presented as a consolation gift to Greece in 1846 (the British government kept the originals). On the second floor an exhibit of photos and drawings illustrates details of the painstaking restoration; models of the new Acropolis museum to be built nearby are also on display. Don't miss the terra-cotta antefixes, the ornaments at the termination of the roofing tiles, invented by the classical Greeks. On one the elegant bright-on-dark abstract design is offset by a naughty gorgon with bulging black eyes sticking out his cherry-colored tongue. ⊠ *Makriyianni 2–4,* ☏ *01/923–9381.* ⊡ *Free.* ⊙ *Daily 9–2:45.*

OFF THE
BEATEN PATH
DIAVLOS MUSIC HOUSE – Bring kids to this renovated neoclassical building, where popular Greek folksinger Mariza Koch gives special performances for children and their families, featuring a musical tour through Greece. ⊠ *Drakou 9 off Syngrou, Koukaki,* ☏ *01/923–9588.* ⊡ *1,500 dr.* ⊙ *Weekdays 10:30–noon during school year.*

❺ Filopappou. The summit's three hills include **Lofos Mouseion** (Hill of the Muses), on which stands the strange **Monument of Filopappus,** a Syrian prince. He was such a generous benefactor, the people considered him a distinguished Athenian. The marble monument is a tomb decorated by a frieze showing Filopappus driving his chariot. From here, the view of the Parthenon, stunning at night when lit, is probably one of the best-known. On the second hill, called **Pnyx** (meaning "crowded"), the general assembly met during the time of Pericles. Gathering the quorum of 5,000 citizens necessary to take a vote was not always easy. Archers armed with red paint were sent out to dab it on vote-dodgers; the offenders were then fined. Farther north is the **Hill of the Nymphs** with a 19th-century observatory, open to the public on the last Friday of each month.

☺ ❽ Ilias LALAoUNIS Jewelry Museum. Opened in late 1994, the museum houses the creations of its founder, the internationally renowned artist Ilias Lalaounis, but it also operates as a study center. The 45 collections include exhibits such as the "Golden Dawn of Art" (Paleolithic and Neolithic periods), "Jewelry Inspired by 12 Civilizations," and "Nature, Technology and Biology." Temporary exhibitions showcase pieces from other museums around the world. In the workshop, craftspeople demonstrate ancient and modern techniques such as chain weaving and hammering for visitors, who may also use the library. During the academic year the museum can arrange educational programs in English for groups of children, and it plans to set up child care in summer for visiting parents. The museum is the first in Greece to be designed to meet the needs of visitors with disabilities. The founder also has three stores (☞ Shopping, *below*). ⊠ *Kallisperi 12, Acropolis,* ☏ *01/922–1044.* ⊡ *800 dr., free on Wed. after 3 PM.* ⊙ *Mon. and Wed. 9–9, Thurs.–Sat. 9–3, Sun. 10–3.*

❻ Odeon of Herod Atticus. This hauntingly beautiful theater was dedicated by an affluent benefactor and built Greek-style into the hillside, but with typically Roman arches in its three-story stage building and barrel-vaulted entrances. The circular orchestra has now become a semicircle, and the long-vanished cedar roof probably covered only the stage and dressing rooms, not the 34 rows of seats. The theater, which holds 5,000, was restored and reopened in 1955 for the Athens Festival and is now open only to ticket-holders a couple hours before summer performances. Contact the Athens Festival box office for ticket information (☞ Nightlife and the Arts, *below*). ⊠ *Dionyssiou Areopagitou, across the street from Propylaion.*

❼ Theater of Dionyssos. Dating from about 330 BC when it was built for 15,000 spectators, the theater once had an orchestra section made of dirt, trodden by actors during performances, and a large altar of Dionyssos. Most of the upper rows have been destroyed, but the lower levels, with labeled chairs for priests and dignitaries, remain. The fantastic throne in the center was reserved for the priest of Dionyssos: It is adorned by regal lions' paws, and the back is carved with reliefs of satyrs and griffins. ⊠ *Dionyssiou Areopagitou, across from Mitsaion,* ☎ *01/322–4625.* ☑ *500 dr.* ۞ *Daily 8:30–sunset (winter 8:30–3).*

Plaka and Anafiotika

Plaka has been inhabited since prehistoric times but the neighborhood imparts the flavor of 19th-century Athens, with Byzantine accents provided by churches. During the 1950s and '60s, the area became garish with neon as nightclubs moved in and residents moved out, but residents, architects, and academicians joined forces in the early 1980s to transform a decaying neighborhood. Noisy discos and tacky pensions were closed, streets were changed into pedestrian zones, and old buildings were well restored. At night the area is still crowded with merrymakers visiting the old tavernas, which feature traditional music and dancing, many with rooftops facing the Acropolis. If you keep off the main tourist shopping streets of Kidathineon and Adrianou, you will be amazed at how peaceful the area can be, even in the height of the summer. Above Plaka is Anafiotika, built on winding lanes that climb up the slopes of the Acropolis, its upper reaches resembling a tranquil village. In Classical times it was abandoned because the Delphic Oracle claimed it as sacred ground. The buildings here were constructed by masons from Anafi island, who came to find work in the rapidly expanding Athens of the 1830s and 1840s. They took over this area, whose rocky terrain was similar to Anafi's, building their homes illegally during the night. Ethiopians who had arrived during the Ottoman period and stayed on after independence lived higher up, in caves, on the northern slopes of the Acropolis.

A Good Walk

After the Acropolis, the historical quarter of Plaka is the next mustsee. Take time to explore streets such as Flessa, Kirristou, Diogenis, and Erechtheos, where old mansions are being renovated. Begin your stroll on Lysikratous, across from Hadrian's Arch, which leads northwest to a square with the **Monument of Lysikrates** ⑩, one of the few remaining supports (334 BC) for tripods awarded to the producer of the best play in the ancient Dionyssia festival; off the square on Galanou and Goura is the pretty **Ayia Aikaterini church** ⑪. Take Herefondos to Plaka's central square, Filomoussou Eterias (or Platia Kidathineon), a great place to people-watch.

Up Kidathineon is the **Greek Folk Art Museum** ⑫, with a rich collection ranging from 1650 to the present, including works by the beloved naive artist Theophilos. Across from the museum is the 11th- to 12th-century church of **Sotira Tou Kottaki,** set in a tidy garden with a fountain that was the main source of water for the neighborhood until after Turkish times. Around the corner on Hatzimichali Aggelou is the **Center of Folk Art and Tradition** ⑬. Continue west to the end of that street, crossing Adrianou to Hill, then right on Epimarchou and the striking **Church House** ⑭ (on the corner of Scholeiou), once a Turkish police post and the headquarters for Richard Church, who led Greek forces in the War of Independence.

At the top of Epimarchou is **Ayios Nikolaos Rangavas** ⑮, an 11th-century church built with fragments of ancient columns. The church

★   marks the edge of the **Anafiotika quarter** ⑯, a village smack dab in the middle of the metropolis: its upper street, Stratonos, is lined with cottages, lovely murals painted on the stones, and a few little shops. Wind your way through the narrow lanes below Stratonos, visiting the churches **Ayios Georgios tou Vrachou, Ayios Simeon,** and **Metamorphosis Sotiros.** Another interesting church is **Ayii Anargyroi** ⑰, at the top of Erechtheos, an 8th-century chapel that according to legend was built by Empress Irene. From the church, make your way to Theorias, which parallels the ancient *peripatos* (public roadway) that ran around the Acropolis. The collection at the **Kanellopoulos Museum** ⑱ spans Athens's history; nearby on Panos is the **Old University** ⑲, the city's first higher-learning institution.

★   Walk down Panos to the **Roman Agora** ⑳, which includes the **Tower of the Winds** and the **Fethiye Mosque.** On your way back to Constitution Square, cut across Mitropolis (Cathedral) Square to the 12th-century
★   Byzantine church known as **Little Mitropolis** ㉑, its outer walls covered with reliefs. Closer to Constitution Square, on the corner of Pendelis and Mitropoleos, is the curious sight of **Ayia Dynamis** ㉒, a chapel peering out from between the cement columns of a Ministry building.

TIMING

Plaka is a delight any time of day, liveliest in the early evening or Sunday afternoon when locals congregate at its outdoor cafés and *ouzeris* (informal eateries to enjoy mezes and ouzo). Perhaps the best time to explore Anafiotika is just before sunset, when the haze is reduced and you can catch great views of the city. If you want to visit the museums (open until 3 PM) or the churches (open from 8 AM to noon and sometimes from 5 to 7 PM), begin as early as possible. For planning ahead, note that some of the museums are closed Monday (Center of Folk Art and Tradition, the Greek Folk Art Museum, the Roman Agora, and the Kanellopoulos Museum), and the Old University (Kleanthis House) is closed weekends. The walk, with leisurely stops at one or two museums, and time for a coffee, takes about three hours. During Carnival in February, costumed Athenians gather in Plaka for a stroll through the quarter, bopping each other with plastic clubs, showering confetti, and spraying foam at passersby: beware!

Sights to See

★ ☺ ⑯   **Anafiotika.** In the shadow of the Acropolis, this is the closest thing to a Cycladic village one will find in Athens. Still populated by many descendants of the original Anafi islanders who settled here, Anafiotika is an enchanting area of simple stone houses, nestled right into the bedrock, some changed little over the years, others stunningly restored. Cascades of bougainvillea and pots of geraniums and marigolds enliven the balconies and rooftops, and the serenity is a blissful contrast to the cacophony of modern Athens. You seldom see the residents—only a line of washing hung out to dry, the lace curtains on the tiny houses, or the curl of smoke from a wood-burning fireplace indicate human presence. Perched on the bedrock of the Acropolis is **Ayios Georgios tou Vrachou** (St. George of the Rock), which marks the southeast edge of the district. One of the most beautiful churches of Athens, it is still in use today. **Ayios Simeon,** a neoclassical church built in 1847 by the settlers, marks the western boundary and contains a copy of a famous miracle-working icon from Anafi, Our Lady of the Reeds. The **Church of the Metamorphosis Sotiros** (Transfiguration), a high-dome 14th-century stone chapel, has a grotto carved into the Acropolis at the rear. For those with children, there is a small playground at Stratonos and Vironos. ⊠ *On northeast slope of Acropolis rock.*

⓫ Ayia Aikaterini. Built in the late 11th–early 12th centuries and enlarged in 1927, the church took its name in 1769, when it was acquired by the Monastery of Saint Catherine in the Sinai. It is cruciform, with a dome resting on a drum supported by four interior columns; the large courtyard and garden make it popular for baptisms and weddings. ☒ *Off sq. on Galanou and Goura, Herefondos, 14,* ☎ *01/322–8974.*

㉒ Ayia Dynamis. The "Divine Power" chapel, topped by a dainty arch and bell, peeks out between the cement columns of the modern Ministry of Education and Religion. Named for the Virgin Mary's supposed power to help childless women conceive, its romantic history makes it worth mentioning. A Greek named Mastropavlis made cartridges here for the Turkish garrison, which had turned the church into a munitions works. Unbeknownst to them, he also made ammunition for Greek revolutionaries, which was smuggled out by a courageous washerwoman. These were the first bullets fired at the Turks on the Acropolis when the War of Independence broke out. ☒ *On corner of Pendelis and Mitropoleos.*

⓱ Ayii Anargyroi. According to legend, the church, also known as Metochion Panagiou Tafou, was built in the late 8th century by the Empress Irene, once an Athenian orphan. She ruled Byzantium alone after the death of her husband. The Church of the Holy Sepulchre at Jerusalem, needing a base in Athens, acquired it in the 1700s and continues to occupy it today. The church has a gingerbread-like exterior, a delightful little garden containing fragments of ancient ruins, and a well that was used as a hiding place in troubled times. ☒ *Top of stairs where Erechtheos meets Pritaniou.*

⓯ Ayios Nikolaos Rangavas. On the southeast side of this 11th-century Byzantine parish church, you can see fragments of ancient columns and capitals incorporated into its walls, an example of the pragmatic recycling of the time. It is above the stairs off Prytaneion, named after the center of the ancient city where a sacred flame was kept burning. ☒ *Pritaniou 1, at top of Epimarchou,* ☎ *01/322–8193.*

⓭ Center of Folk Art and Tradition. Exhibits in this comfortable family mansion of folklorist Angeliki Hatzimichali include detailed costumes, ceramic plates from Skyros, handwoven fabrics and embroideries, and family portraits. ☒ *Hatzimichali Aggelou 6,* ☎ *01/324–3972 and 01/324–3987.* ☒ *Free.* ☉ *Tues.–Fri. 9–1 and 5–9, weekends 9–1.*

NEED A BREAK?

Off Plaka's main square, visit the **De Profundis Tea Room** (☒ Hatzimichali Aggelou 1, ☎ 01/323-1764), in an old mansion, for pastries and a large variety of teas; it is closed from late June through August. **Byzantino** (☒ Kidathineon 18, ☎ 01/322-9636) is directly on the square—great for people-watching and a good, reasonably priced bite to eat. Go around the corner to **Glikis** (☒ Aggelou Geronta 2, ☎ 01/332-3925) for an inexpensive Greek coffee or ouzo and a *mikri pikilia* (a small plate of appetizers, including cheese, sausage, olives, and dips).

⓮ Church House. The striking abandoned tower house with tiny windows, thick stone walls, and a tall chimney bears traces of its past glory. Probably dating from the 18th century and used as a Turkish police post, it became the fortress of Richard Church, Commander-in-Chief of the Greek forces during the War of Independence. After the liberation, historian George Finlay, a veteran of the war, and his wife lived here for half a century, while he wrote his many volumes of Greek history, including what is considered the definitive work on the War of Independence. ☒ *Corner of Epimarchou and Scholeiou.*

Greek Folk Art Museum. Run by the Ministry of Culture, the collection includes examples of folk art from 1650 to the present, with especially interesting embroideries, stone and wood carvings, carnival costumes, and *Karaghiozis* (shadow player figures). Don't miss the room of uniquely fanciful landscapes and historical portraits by naive painter Theophilos Hatzimichalis, from Mytilini, one of the most beloved Greek artists. Children who can understand Greek may tour the museum and then attend a workshop, where they learn to make traditional handicrafts, but if you bring a group of English-speaking youngsters, the museum will make special arrangements. ⊠ *Kidathineon 17,* ☎ *01/322–9031, 01/323–9813 for educational program.* ☑ *300 dr.* ⊙ *Tues.–Sun. 10–2.*

Kanellopoulos Museum. The stately Michaleas Mansion, built in 1884 and recently renovated, showcases the Kanellopoulos' family collection, spanning Athens history from the 3rd century BC to the 19th century, with especially fine Byzantine icons, jewelry, and Mycenaean and Geometric vases and bronzes. Note the painted ceiling gracing the first floor. ⊠ *Theorias and Panos,* ☎ *01/321–2313.* ☑ *500 dr.* ⊙ *Tues.–Sun. 8:30–3.*

NEED A BREAK?
Pause for a cool drink at the **Nefeli Café Restaurant** (⊠ Panos 24, ☎ 01/321-2475), a large complex with an idyllic outdoor café shaded by smart awnings and draped with grapevines. It's perched just below the Acropolis cliffs, looking down on Ayia Anna church. Or go around the corner to less upscale **Cafe Dioscouri** (⊠ Dioscouron and Mitroou, ☎ 01/321-9607), which lines the pedestrian zone by the same name and has a view of the Hephaistion temple.

★ **Little Mitropolis.** This church snuggles up to the pompous **Mitropolis** (⊠ On the northern edge of Plaka), the ornate Cathedral of Athens. Also called Panayia Gorgoepikoos (the Virgin Who Answers Prayers Quickly), Little Metropolis dates to the 12th century, and its most interesting features are its outer walls, covered with reliefs dating from the Classical to the Byzantine periods. Reliefs of figures and fanciful zodiac signs decorate slabs set above the entrance. Most of the paintings inside were destroyed, but the famous 13th- to 14th-century Virgin, said to perform miracles, remains. If you would like to follow Greek custom and light an amber beeswax candle for yourself and someone you love, drop the price of the candle in the slot. ⊠ *Cathedral Square.*

★ **Monument of Lysikrates.** One of the least known Athenian sights, this monument was built by a *choregos* (producer) as the support for the tripod he won for sponsoring the best play at the Theater of Dionyssos. It dates to 335 BC–334 BC. Six of the earliest Corinthian columns are arranged in a circle on a square base, topped by a marble dome from which rise acanthus leaves. In the 17th century the monument was incorporated into a Capuchin monastery (it was known then as the Lantern of Demosthenes because it was incorrectly believed to be where the famous orator practiced reciting his speeches with pebbles in his mouth to overcome his stutter). ⊠ *Lysikratous and Heresondos.*

Old University or Kleanthis House. King Otho's top architect, Kleanthis, lived here, and from 1837 to 1841, this was the first seat of the new University of Athens. Private benefactors have restored the building and opened a museum of university memorabilia. ⊠ *Tholou 5,* ☎ *01/324–0861.* ☑ *Free.* ⊙ *Mon. and Wed. 5–9 (winter 2:30–7); Tues., Thurs., and Fri. 9:30–2:30.*

Roman Agora. The Roman market served as the city's commercial center during the 1st century BC to the 4th century AD. The large rectangular courtyard had a peristyle that provided shade for the arcades of shops. Its most notable feature is the **Gate of Athena Archegetis**, completed around AD 2; the inscription records that it was erected with funds from Julius Caesar and Augustus. Halfway up one solitary square pillar behind the gate's north side an edict inscribed by Hadrian regulates the sale of oil. On the north side of the Roman Agora stands one of the few remains of the Turkish occupation, the **Fethiye (Victory) Mosque**. The eerily beautiful mosque was built in the late 15th century on the site of a Christian church to celebrate the Turkish conquest of Athens and was dedicated by Mehmet II (the Conqueror). The mosque was converted in the 17th century to a Roman Catholic church and is now used as a storehouse, closed to the public. Three steps in the right-hand corner of the porch lead to the base of the minaret, the rest of which

★ has disappeared. The octagonal **Tower of the Winds (Aerides)** is the most appealing and well-preserved of the Roman monuments of Athens, keeping time since the 1st century BC. It was originally a sundial, water clock, and weather vane topped by a bronze Triton with a metal rod in his hand, which pointed in the direction of the wind. Expressive reliefs around the octagonal tower personify the eight winds, called *Oi Aerides* (the Windy Ones) by Athenians. Note the north wind, Boreas, depicted as an old man blowing on a conch. ✉ *Pelopida and Eolou,* ☎ *01/324–5220.* 🎫 *600 dr.* ☉ *Tues.–Sun. 8:30–3.*

Ancient Agora, Monastiraki, and Thission

The ancient Agora was once the focal point of community life in ancient Athens, the place where Socrates met with his students, while merchants squabbled over the price of olive oil. It was here that the Assembly first met before it moved to the Pnyx, and the locals gathered to talk about current events. The Agora first became important under Solon (6th century BC), who founded Athenian democracy; construction continued for almost a millennium. Today, the site's sprawling confusion of stones, slabs, and foundations is dominated by the best-preserved Doric temple in Greece, the Hephaistion, built during the 5th century BC, and the impressive reconstructed Stoa of Attalos II, which houses the Museum of the Agora Excavations. You can still experience the sights and sounds of the marketplace in Monastiraki, the former Turkish bazaar area, which retains vestiges of Orientalism from the 400-year period when Greece was subject to the Ottoman Empire. On the opposite side of the Agora is another meeting place of sorts: Thission, a former red-light district complete with a hat factory, that in the last few years has become one of the most sought-after residential neighborhoods and a popular nightspot, with new bars and cafés springing up weekly.

A Good Walk

Approach Monastiraki from Ermou: in the middle of the Kapnikareas intersection is striking **Kapnikarea Church** ㉓. Take a left, past Number 49, and turn right on Pandrossou, a main shopping street that leads to **Monastiraki Square** ㉔, graced by the **Tzistarakis Mosque** and **Panayia Pantassa church**, exemplifying the East-West paradox that characterizes Athens. Unfortunately, as in many parts of the city, the square is marred by metro construction. Walk up Areos, which during the Ottoman Empire was the Lower Bazaar, roofed and covered with vines. On the corner of Eolou, you'll pass a nicely restored Othonian building, the former Aeolos Hotel, built in 1837 just after Athens was made capital of Greece. Advertisements boasted that it offered all European conveniences including beds, at a time when guests in public lodging usually brought their blankets and slept on the floor. This area was the edge of the Upper Bazaar. You will arrive at what remains of

Hadrian's Library ㉕, built in AD 132 and the intellectual center of its time. Return to the square and head west on Ifestou to **Abyssinia Square** ㉖, where junk dealers and antiques merchants gather; it's the perfect place to see a side of the city that is vanishing. It is also the heart of Sunday's rambunctious **flea market** ㉗.

★ After browsing the stalls, enter the **ancient Agora** ㉘ at the corner of Kinetou and Adrianou (the latter runs parallel to Ifestou). Be sure to visit the site's **Museum of Agora Excavations,** which offers a fascinating glimpse of everyday life in the ancient city. Exit at the site's opposite end onto Dionyssiou Areopagitou, crossing the boulevard to the **Thission** ㉙ quarter, a lively area with neoclassical homes overlooking trendy cafés. At the **Melina Mercouri Cultural Center** ㉚, exhibits recreate the streets of Athens during different epochs.

Those who want to escape Athens for a while should board the metro at the Thission station (at the end of Dionyssiou Areopagitou) to the
★ northern suburb of **Kifissia,** once a summer resort for wealthy Athenians, evident in its tree-lined boulevards and grand villas.

TIMING

Monastiraki is at its best on Sunday morning when the flea market is in full swing. The ancient Agora is closed Monday; it offers little shade, so in summer it's better to visit the site in early morning or late afternoon. Late-afternoon visits are strongly encouraged, as you can stay to ease into Thission's café scene. Assuming you visit the Agora for about two hours, including a visit to the Museum of Agora Excavations, the walk lasts about four hours. You can spend an entire afternoon or evening in Kifissia. The trip takes about 35 minutes each way; the last train leaves Kifissia for Athens around midnight.

Sights to See

㉖ **Abyssinia Square.** All day long, the square bustles with activity, with shop owners refinishing furniture and rearranging the bric-a-brac in their stalls. Weekend mornings, dealers flock from all over Greece to peddle an incredible array of goods, from old toasters to exquisite icons, while street musicians stroll amid the café tables, jostling their accordions and singing ballads of love and loss. ⊠ *Entrance off Ermou, between Normanou and Kinetou.*

NEED A BREAK?   After you've haggled and won, enjoy a well-deserved libation or snack at the wine bar **Oinothiki** (⊠ Abyssinias Sq. 3, ☎ 01/321–5465), with exceptional mezes and a large selection of domestic wines from small producers.

★ ㉘ **Ancient Agora.** This marketplace was the hub of ancient Athens. Besides administrative buildings, it was surrounded by the schools, theaters, workshops, houses, stores, and market stalls of a thriving town. Now carefully landscaped, it is scattered with Hellenistic and Roman fragments and ruins.

Prominent on the grounds is the **Stoa of Attalos,** a two-story building, now a museum, designed as a retail complex and erected in the 2nd century BC by Attalos, a king of Pergamum. The reconstruction in 1953–56 (funded by private American donors) used Pentelic marble and creamy limestone from the original structure. The colonnade, designed for promenades, is protected from the blistering sun and cooled by breezes. The most notable sculptures, of historical and mythological figures from the 3rd and 4th centuries BC, are at ground level outside the museum. In the exhibition hall, chronological displays of pottery and objects from everyday life (note the child's terra-cotta potty) demonstrate the continual settlement of the area from Neolithic times. There are such toys as knucklebones and miniature theatrical masks carved from bone (case 50); a *klepsydra* (a terra-cotta water clock designed to measure the time allowed for pleadings in court) and bronze voting discs (cases 26–28); and, in case 38, bits of *ostraka* (pottery shards used in secret ballots to recommend banishment), from which the word "ostracism" comes. Among the famous candidates for a 10-year banishment, considered a fate worse than death, were Themistocles, Kimon, and even Pericles, who had his fair share of enemies. On the back wall are two segments of well-preserved Byzantine mosaics from the floors of the house.

Take a walk around the site and speculate on the location of Simon the Cobbler's house and shop, which was a meeting place for Socrates and his pupils. The carefully landscaped grounds display a number of plants known in antiquity, such as almond, myrtle, and pomegranate. Standing in the center, you have a glorious view up to the Acropolis, which on a clear day is given a mellow glow by the famous Attic light.

On a mound in the northwest corner of the grounds stands the best preserved extant Doric temple, the **Hephaistion,** sometimes called the Thission because of friezes showing the exploits of Theseus. Like the other monuments, it is roped off, but you can walk around it to admire its 34 columns. It was originally dedicated to Hephaistos, god of metalworkers; metal workshops still exist in this area near Ifestou. The temple was converted to Christian use in the 7th century; the last services held here were a Te Deum in 1834, to celebrate King Otho's arrival, and a centenary Te Deum in 1934.

Behind the temple, paths lead to the northwest slope of the **Kolonos Agoraios,** an area dotted with archaeological ruins half hidden in deep undergrowth, where you can sit on a bench and contemplate the scene that Englishman Edward Dodwell saw in the early 19th century, when he came to sketch antiquities. ⊠ *Three entrances: from Monastiraki on Adrianou; from Thission on Apostolou Pavlou; and descending from Acropolis on Ayios Apostoli,* ☎ *01/321–0185.* ⌧ *1,200 dr.* ☉ *Tues.–Sun. 8:30–3.*

㉗ Flea market. For Athenians all the world's a stage. Watching the interplay between Greeks, complete with wildly gesturing hands and dramatic facial expressions, will provide hours of entertainment. The Sunday morning market is a fitting setting in which to see lively haggling, and a fine destination in itself. Music blares from the carts pushing bootleg cassettes, mingling with the twang of a bouzouki a prospective buyer is strumming. Peddlers shout their wares: everything's for sale, from gramophone needles to old matchboxes, from nose rings sold by young nomads to lacquered eggs and cool white linens from the Pontian Greeks from the former USSR. Haggle no matter how low the price. ⊠ *Along Ifestou, Kynetou, and Adrianou.*

㉕ Hadrian's Library. Built in AD 132, it is closed to the public, but you can easily see the remains of this public building (122 meters/400 feet by 71 meters/270 feet). The east wall is supported by six attached Corinthian columns, and Pausanias mentions "one hundred splendid columns of Phrygian marble," which apparently enclosed a cloistered court with a garden and pool. On the east side was the library itself, the intellectual center of its age, decorated with statues and murals under an alabaster and gold ceiling. Other areas were used for lectures and classes. On the west wall are traces of a fresco showing the outline of the Byzantine Ayios Assomati, which stood next to it. ⊠ *Areos and Dexippou.*

㉓ Kapnikarea Church. It's said that the chapel was named for the *kapnikarious* (men who during the Byzantine period taxed residents for smoke coming from their chimneys); emanating smoke meant wealth enough to burn possessions. The building is really two adjoining chapels, one a cruciform structure of the 11th century, and the other a handsome building of typical Byzantine raised brickwork, with a dome supported by four Roman columns. The latter was carefully restored by the University of Athens, of which it is now the official church. A prominent modern mosaic of the Virgin and Child adorns the west entrance, and inside are colorful frescoes. ⊠ *In middle of intersection at Kapnikareas and Ermou,* ☎ *01/322–4462.*

㉚ Melina Mercouri Cultural Center. Installed in the old Poulopoulos hat factory (built 1886), the center offers a rare glimpse of Athens during the last centuries and a chance to experience the atmosphere of the city's lost neighborhoods. Several rooms are being reconstructed to resemble city streets from different eras, complete with houses, storefronts, and everyday objects once used. The center also organizes lectures, seminars, and art exhibits. ⊠ *Irakleidon 66,* ☎ *01/345–2150 and 01/362–1601.* ▣ *Free.* ☉ *Mon.–Sat. 9–1 and 5–9, Sun. 9–1. Closed July 10–Aug.*

㉔ Monastiraki Square. The square takes its name from **Panayia Pantanassa Church,** commonly called Monastiraki (Little Monastery) because of its smallness. It once flourished as an extensive convent, perhaps dating to the 10th century. The nuns took in poor people, who earned their keep weaving the thick textiles known as *abas.* The convent's basic basilica form, now recessed a few steps below street level, has been altered through a poor restoration in 1911, when the bell tower was added. The square's focal point, the **Tzistarakis Mosque** (1759) houses the **Museum of Traditional Greek Ceramics.** The collection is beautifully designed, with the exhibits properly lit and labeled. The mihrab (niche facing Mecca) is of delicate pastel stone. ⊠ *Just south of intersection of Ermou and Athinas,* ☎ *01/324–2066.* ▣ *Museum: 500 dr.* ☉ *Museum: Wed.–Mon. 9:30–2:30.*

NEED A
BREAK?

On Mitropoleos just off Monastiraki Square you'll find a handful of places selling souvlaki, grilled meat rolled in a pita with onions, *tzatziki* (yogurt-garlic dip), and tomatoes—the best bargain in Athens. Your choices include **Thanassis** (⊠ 69 Mitropoleos, ☎ 01/324–4705), which is always crowded with Greeks, and **Savvas** (⊠ 86 Mitropoleos, ☎ 01/321–3201), which also serves gyros, sandwiches of spicy spit-roasted meat, to patrons who can eat across the road in a small umbrella-shaded square.

㉙ Thission. Whether you want to enjoy a bite to eat in a turn-of-the-century ouzeri, listen to hard rock in a bar that was once the Royal Stables, or sit down to a late supper after a show at the Herod Atticus, you will enjoy this vibrant neighborhood, which in the last few years has become one of Athens's popular gathering places, rivaling upscale Kolonaki Square. The main strip is the area in front of the ancient Agora entrance and the Akamantos pedestrian zone, which is lined with cafés that are cozy in winter and have outdoor tables in summer. The rest of the neighborhood is quiet, an odd mix of ma-and-pop stores and dilapidated houses that are now slowly being renovated. ⊠ *West of ancient Agora, Apostolou Pavlou, and Akamantos.*

NEED A
BREAK?

It's a great concept: an old-style kafenion complete with ouzo, Greek coffee, and *tavli* (backgammon games) for customers, but with 1990s decor, designer lighting, and foreign music. No wonder most people rolling the dice at **Kafenion Thission** (⊠ Akamantos 2, ☎ 01/347–

3133) are not elderly gents but the under-40 set, who, when the weather warms up, spill out onto the sidewalk. At night, Kafenion becomes a bar.

OFF THE
BEATEN PATH

KIFISSIA – For a superbly peaceful afternoon, hop on the metro heading to this northern suburb, a summer resort for aristocratic Athenians at the turn of the century. The streets north of the Kifissia station, with their verdant landscaping and ostentatious villas, evoke another, gentler era. Especially rewarding are Dragoumi, Tatoi, Rangavi, Pan, Tsaldari, Amalias, and Strofiliou streets. After exploring the area, head east from the station through Alsos Kifissias park, crossing Kifissias to Kassavetis, where young people flock to the many cafés. Be sure to stop for a *rizogalo* (rice pudding) at Varsos (⊠ Kassavetis 5, ☎ 01/801–2472 and 01/801–2473), a Kifissia institution. If you have children, you may want to detour left at Levidou to the Goulandris Natural History Museum (⊠ Levidou 13, ☎ 01/808–6405) for its displays of animal and plant life, fossils, and reconstructed prehistoric animals; it's closed July 20– Aug. 15. Kassavetis becomes Kolokotronis, which ends at shady Kefalari Square, where decorated horse-drawn carriages await to take you on a ride through the cool, quiet roads.

Kerameikos, Psirri, and Central Athens

Archaeology buffs will want to visit Kerameikos, the main cemetery in ancient Athens until Sulla destroyed the city in 86 BC. The name is associated with the modern word "ceramic": in the 12th century BC it was a district of potters who used the abundant clay from the languid Iridanos River to make the funerary urns and grave decorations. It contains the foundations of two ancient monuments: the Dipylon Gate where visitors entered the city, and the Sacred Gate used for both the pilgrimage to the Eleusinian rites and for the Panathenaic procession in which the tunic for the statue of Athena was carted to the Acropolis. The area outside Kerameikos was populated by Turkish gypsies before the War of Independence and then by Athens's Jewish community. The shops of the leading families, including the Cohens, Levis, and Camkhis, ran along Ermou; on Melidoni stands the Synagogue Beth Shalom, where people still worship. Nearby Psirri, one of the city's oldest neighborhoods, is rather ramshackle. Although it is now being renovated, destined to become another "in" spot like Thission, Psirri affords visitors a different view of the city.

Downtown Athens is not for the fainthearted; it's an interesting combination of the squalid and the grand: The cavernous, chaotic Central Market, which replaced the Bazaar when it burned down in 1885, is just 10 minutes from the elegant, neoclassical Old University Complex. Farther north is the stately National Archaeological Museum, one of the most exciting collections of Greek antiquities in the world.

A Good Walk

Those interested in archaeology should begin at **Kerameikos Cemetery** ㉛, where ancient Athens's famous were buried. Continue east on Ermou to the intersection with Ayios Assomaton, where the 11th-century church of **Ayii Assomati** ㉜ stands. The quirky, run-down neighborhood of **Psirri** ㉝, in the early stages of gentrification, starts here. Take some time to explore its narrow streets, eventually making your way to Evripidou and the oddest church in Athens, **Ayios Ioannis Kolonastis** ㉞, at the intersection with Menandrou.

Continue east on Evripidou, lined with aromatic shops selling herbs, nuts, olive-oil soap, and household items, until you reach the **Central Market** ㉟

34

Exploring Athens

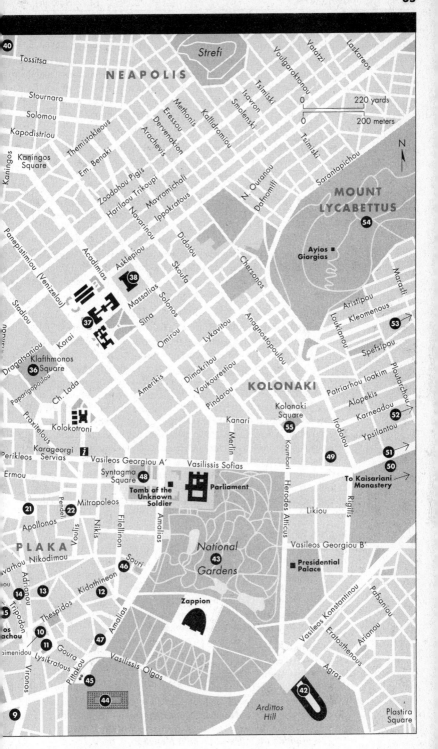

40

Tossitsa

NEAPOLIS

Strefi

Stournara

Solomou

Kapodistriou

Kaningos
Square

Kaningos

Themistokleous

Em. Benaki

Zoodohou Pigis

Harilaou Trikoupi

Navarinou

Methonis

Eressou

Dervenakion

Arachevis

Mavromichali

Ippokratous

Didotou

Skouta

Kallidromiou

Smolenski

Isavron

Tsimiski

Voulgaroktonou

Vatatzi

Laskareos

N. Ouranou

Dafnomili

Chesonos

Sarantapichou

**MOUNT
LYCABETTUS**

54

Ayios ■
Giorgias

Marasli

Aristipou

Loukianou

Kleomenous

53

Spetsipou

Ploutarchou

Patriarhou Ioakim

Alopekis

Karneadou

52

Irodotou

Ypsilantou

51

50

**To Kaisariani
Monastery**

Panepistimiou (Venizelou)

Stadiou

Akadimias

Asklepiou

38

Massalias

Sina

Solonos

Omirou

Lykavitou

Anagnostopoulou

Dimokritou

Voukourestiou

Pindarou

Amerikis

37

Korai

Dragatsaniou

Papariqopoulou

Klafthmonos
Square

36

Ch. Lada

Kolokotroni

Praxitelous

Karageorgi
Servias

Perikleos

Ermou

i

Kanari

Merlin

Koumbari

KOLONAKI

Kolonaki
Square

55

Herodes Atticus

49

Likiou

Rigilis

Vasileos Georgiou A'

Vasilissis Sofias

Syntagma
Square

48

Mitropoleos

21

22

Apollonos

Nikis

Filellinon

Amalias

PLAKA

Nikodimou

Adrianou

13

14

Tripodon

15

Thespidos

Kidathineon

12

Souri

46

Vironos

Lysikratous

Pittakou

Goura

10

11

47

Amalias

Vasilissis Olgas

45

44

9

**Tomb of the
Unknown
Soldier**

■

Parliament

*National
Gardens*

43

Zappion

**Presidential
Palace** ■

Vasileos Georgiou B'

Vasileos Konstantinou

Eratosthenous

Patsaniou

Arianou

Agras

42

*Ardittos
Hill*

Plastira
Square

0 ____ 220 yards
0 ____ 200 meters

N

on the corner of Athinas. Hectic, crowded Athinas stretches from Concord Square to Monastiraki, replete with everything from canaries to garlic braids, but it is the 19th-century meat and fish market that is the most entertaining. Evripidou ends at **Klafthmonos Square** ㊱ and what is perhaps the oldest church in Athens, **Ayii Theodori.** Cross Stadiou, walking up the Korai pedestrian zone, past the cranes and makeshift walls of the metro works to the **Old University complex** ㊲ on Panepistimiou. Behind the three grand buildings is the **Municipal Cultural Center** ㊳, which hosts interesting exhibitions and has a theater museum.

★ Cut through the student neighborhood of Exarchia or take Trolley 2, 4, or 11 from Panepistimiou to the **Politechnio** ㊴, a national symbol of student resistance, and the **National Archaeological Museum** ㊵. The museum includes sensational archaeological finds made by Heinrich Schliemann at Mycenae and 16th-century BC frescoes from the Akrotiri ruins on Santorini. Athens's other main square, Concord, is to the west, but it's not really worth the detour owing to the ongoing metro construction. It has been spruced up with a new fountain, palm trees, and a jagged glass sculpture representing a runner, now moved to the Athens Hilton. Two blocks up from the museum at the intersection of Oktovriou (Patission) and Leoforos Alexandras is Athens's largest park, **Pedion Areos** ㊶, which provides visual relief from the urban sprawl.

TIMING

Weekday mornings are the best time to take this approximately 5-hour walk: the museums will be open and the Central Market, which is closed Saturday afternoon and Sunday, bustles with pensioners picking over the produce and Athenian housewives exchanging news with the fishmonger. You'll also get a better sense of Psirri as a neighborhood then, although the area is liveliest Sunday afternoon, when Athenians tend to congregate in its new bars. Try to visit the National Archaeological Museum after lunch, when most tour groups have departed. Look at a floor plan to organize your plan of attack; the collection is too huge to cover comfortably in one stretch. If you hang on to your admission ticket, you can take a break at the pleasant garden café in front of the museum. Many of the sites are closed on the weekends. The National Archaeological Museum and the Kerameikos Cemetery are closed on Monday; the Vouros-Eftaxias Athens City Museum is closed on Tuesday and Sunday—plan accordingly.

Sights to See

㉜ **Ayii Assomati.** Named after the Bodiless Angels, the church dates to the 11th century. It was poorly rebuilt in 1880 but properly restored in 1959. It is in the form of a Greek cross, with a hexagonal dome and impressive exterior stonework. Some fragments of frescoes inside are probably from the 17th century, but art historians dispute the claim that an oil painting to the left of the entrance is by El Greco. ⊠ *At intersection of Ermou and Ayios Assomaton.*

㉞ **Ayios Ioannis Kolonastis.** Saint John of the Column is the most peculiar church in Athens. A Corinthian column, probably from a gymnasium dedicated to Apollo, protrudes from the tiled rooftop of the little one-sided basilica built around it in AD 565, and people with a high fever still come here to perform "curative" rituals that involve tying a colored thread to the column and saying a special prayer. Mosaic floors that were unearthed here were probably part of an ancient temple to Asklepeios. ⊠ *72 Evripidou (at intersection with Menandrou, behind sq.).*

㉟ **Central Market.** The market runs along Athinas: On one side are open-air stalls selling fruit and vegetables at the best prices in town, although wily merchants may slip overripe items into your bag. At the corner of Armodiou, shops stock live poultry and rabbits. Across the street, in the huge covered market built in 1870, the surrealistic composition of suspended carcasses and shimmering fish on marble counters emits a pungent odor that is overwhelming on hot days. The shops at the north end of the market, to the right on Sofokleous, sell the best cheese, olives, halvah, bread, and cold cuts, including *pastourma* (Mediterranean pastrami), available in Athens. ⊠ *Athinas.* ✆ *Closed Sat. afternoon and Sun.*

NEED A BREAK?	"If you don't behave, I won't take you to **Krinos**" (⊠ Eolou 87, ☎ 01/321–6852), mothers in the Central Market used to warn unruly offspring. The draw: *loukoumades* (an irresistible, doughnutlike fritter sprinkled with cinnamon and drizzled with a honeyed syrup based on a Smyrna recipe) that the shop has been serving since it opened its doors in the 1920s. The shop is closed Sunday.

③① Kerameikos Cemetery. From the entrance of ancient Athens's cemetery, you can still see remains of the **Makra Teixoi** (Long Walls of Themistocles), which ran to Piraeus, and the largest gate in the ancient world, the **Dipylon Gate** where visitors entered Athens. Here was also the **Sacred Gate,** used by pilgrims headed to the mysterious rites in Eleusis and those who participated in the Panathenaic procession, which followed the Sacred Way. Between the two gates are the foundations of the **Pompeion,** from where the Panathenaic procession began. It is said the courtyard was large enough to fit the ship on which the huge peplum dedicated to Athena was hung. On the **Street of Tombs,** which branches off the Sacred Way, plots were reserved for affluent Athenians. A number of the distinctive *stelae* (funerary monuments) remain, including a replica of the marble relief of Dexilios, a knight who died in the war against Corinth (394 BC), shown on horseback getting ready to spear a fallen foe. From the terrace near the tombs, Pericles gave his famous speech honoring those who died in the early years of the Peloponnesian War, thus persuading many to sign up for a campaign that ultimately wiped out thousands of Athenians. To the left of the site's entrance is the **Oberlaender Museum,** whose four rooms contain sculpture, terra-cotta figures, and some striking red-and-black-figured pottery. The extensive grounds are marshy in some spots, and in spring frogs exuberantly croak their mating songs near magnificent stands of lilies. ⊠ *Ermou 148 or Pireos 91,* ☎ *01/346–3552.* 🎟 *600 dr. for site and museum.* ✆ *Tues.–Sun. 8:30–3.*

③⑥ Klafthmonos Square. Public servants from the surrounding ministries lamented loudly here after being dismissed; hence, its name, the Square of Wailing. Behind the square at the corner of Evripidou and Aristidou is **Ayii Theodori,** a lovely mid-11th-century cruciform church, probably the oldest in Athens. The **Vouros-Eftaxias Athens City Museum,** across from the square, was home to teenage King Otho and his bride Amalia for seven years while they were waiting for the royal palace to be completed. In a sub-basement you can see a segment of the ancient city walls. A Throne Room still exists, and on the ground floor a model of Athens in 1842 shows how sparsely populated the new capital was. The first floor displays paintings by European artists who came to Athens, such as Edward Lear, Gasparini, and Dodwell. ⊠ *Off Stadiou, between Paparigoupoulou and Dragatsaniou. Museum:* ⊠ *Paparigoupoulou 7,* ☎ *01/323–0168.* 🎟 *400 dr.* ✆ *Mon., Wed., Fri., Sat. 9–1:30.*

③⑧ Municipal Cultural Center. Originally the city hospital, the center is now used for lectures and exhibits. In front stands the only known surviving statue of Pericles, a fine work in Parian marble by Heinrich Faltermeier, showing Pericles with sturdy legs and the helmet he always wore because his head was, it's said, slightly deformed—which explains his nickname, Onion Head. Almost directly across Acadimias, facing Pericles, is a much smaller and less-skillful bust of Aspasia, the cultured courtesan who was his beloved companion and mother of his son. On the lower level is the cozy **Hellenic Theater Museum and Study Center.** It features dressing rooms and costumes of Greek stage and screen stars plus posters, playbills, and other memorabilia. ⊠ *Acadimias 50,* ☎ *01/362–1601.* ⊘ *Free.* ⊘ *Tues.–Sun. 9–1. Theater museum:* ☎ *01/362–9430.* ⊠ *500 dr.* ⊘ *Weekdays 9–2:30.*

NEED A
BREAK?

The spacious **Athinaiko Kafenio** (⊠ Acadimias 50, in back of the Municipal Cultural Center, ☎ 01/361–6879), in the same building as the Municipal Cultural Center, beckons, offering good coffees, drinks, and tempting sweets, with both indoor and shady outdoor seating. The area east of the center is packed with student cafés; a popular venue is the cozy **Gallerie Amsterdam** (⊠ Sina 21 and Skoufa, ☎ 01/361–9593), in a converted old house with closely set tables and a tiny gallery that's a favorite among couples. The café is closed July through August.

★ ④⓪ **National Archaeological Museum.** The collection extends from Neolithic to Roman times; unfortunately, both the Greek and English labeling is woefully inadequate. Sculpture is on the ground floor, ceramics on the first floor, ceramics and **frescoes from Santorini** on the upper level of the first floor. These outstanding frescoes, delightful re-creations of daily life in Minoan Santorini, should not be missed. They are scheduled to be sent back to Santorini on completion of the long-awaited museum there.

The most celebrated finds are in the central **Hall of Mycenaean Antiquities,** Room 4, the stunning gold treasures from Schliemann's excavations of Mycenae in 1876: the funeral mask of a bearded king once thought to be the image of Agamemnon but now believed to be much older, from about the 15th century BC; a splendid silver bull's-head libation cup; and the 15th-century BC Vaphio Goblets, masterworks in embossed gold. Mycenaeans were famed for their miniature carving, and an exquisite example is the ivory statuette of two curvaceous mother goddesses with a child nestled on their laps.

Rooms 7–14 contain Geometric and Archaic art (10th–6th centuries BC), and Rooms 11–14 have kouroi and funerary stelae, among them the stelae of the warrior Aristion signed by Aristokles, and the unusual *Running Hoplite.*

Rooms 15–21 focus on Classical art (5th–3rd centuries BC). Be sure to see the bareback *Jockey of Artemision,* a 2nd-century BC Hellenistic bronze salvaged from the sea; from the same excavation, the bronze *Artemision Poseidon* (some say Zeus), poised and ready to fling a trident (or thunderbolt?); and the *Varvakion Athena,* a marble version of the goddess ¹⁄₁₂ the size of Pheidias's gigantic gold-and-ivory cult statue that stood in the Parthenon.

Room 28 displays funerary architecture: the spirited 2nd-century relief of a rearing stallion held by a black groom, which exemplifies the transition from Classical to Hellenistic style. Room 30 holds the famous humorous marble group of a nude *Aphrodite* getting ready to slap an advancing Pan with a sandal, while Eros floats overhead and grasps one of Pan's horns. ⊠ *28 Patission 44,* ☎ *01/821–7717.* ⊠ *2,000 dr.* ⊘ *Mon. 12:30–7 (winter 11–5), Tues.–Fri. 8–7 (winter 8–5), weekends 8:30–3.*

③⑦ **Old University complex.** These three dramatic buildings belong to the University of Athens, designed by the Hansen Brothers in the period after independence and built of white Pentelic marble, with tall columns and decorative friezes. In the center is the **Senate House** of the university; on the right is the **Academy,** flanked by two slim columns topped by statues of Athena and Apollo; and on the left is the **National Library,** containing 500,000 books and 3,000 manuscripts. ✉ *Panepistimiou 28,* ☎ *01/360–0207 and 01/360–0209.*

👆 ❹❶ **Pedion Areos.** Athens's largest park is open 24 hours a day. Statues of war heroes from the 1821 revolution dot the many walkways and hidden corners, and during the summer a small theater and cultural center stage performances. The park was named for Ares, the god of war, because it was once a firing range. It extends all the way to the **Courts,** where at night several ouzeris are packed with Athenians taking advantage of the cool forest air. There are three **playgrounds**: two near the central entrance and one off Evelpidon. A small train for youngsters traverses the park throughout the day; tickets are 500 dr. ✉ *Main entrance at Patission and Leoforos Alexandras,* ☎ *01/821–2239.*

❸❾ **Politechnio.** In late 1973 students occupied this University of Athens building to protest the junta, broadcasting calls for resistance. Many Greeks disobeyed military orders and showed support by smuggling in supplies. On the night of November 16 snipers were ordered to fire into the courtyards while tanks rammed the gates: no one knows how many students were killed because they were secretly buried in mass graves. The public was outraged, and less then a year later, the junta fell. Every year on November 17 students still march from the Politechnio to the embassy of the United States, which supported the dictatorship, and throughout the year it is the site for student unrest. ✉ *Panepistimiou 42,* ☎ *01/369–1111.* 🕙 *Weekdays 8–3.*

❸❸ **Psirri.** The district has many buildings older than those in Plaka, though until lately it has always been less fashionable. Peek over the wrought-iron gates of the old houses on the narrow side streets between Ermou and Kerameikou, a street north of Kerameikos Cemetery, to see the charming courtyards with long, low buildings whose many small rooms were rented out to different families. The streets are quiet, too narrow for most cars. This was the setting for a number of popular Greek novels around the turn of the century and is now a mercantile area with small workshops supplying leather and glassware to retail shops. Similar to New York City's Tribeca, it has been targeted by developers eager to renovate, resulting in a flurry of building and signs of gentrification since the mid-'90s. You will not spot trendy clubs where young Athenians dance on the tables to popular Greek music. ✉ *Just north of Monastiraki, between Ermou, Athinas, and Evripidou.*

NEED A BREAK? Especially late on weekend afternoons, Athenians, be it couples from Kolonaki or elderly women from Patissia, head for **Taki 13** (✉ Taki 13, ☎ 01/325-4707) for its unusual mezes and live Greek music. In summer, although the shaded courtyard stays open, Taki 13 operates only in the evenings when the city cools off.

Constitution Square, National Gardens, and Kolonaki

Sooner or later, everyone passes through Constitution Square. Unfortunately, even after several beautification campaigns, the square is rather nondescript, surrounded by fast-food restaurants and metro construction. However, the area has several sights spanning Athens's history from the Roman period (Temple of Olympian Zeus) to King Otho's reign after the War of Independence in 1821 (the National Gardens and Parliament). Neighboring Kolonaki, the chic shopping district and one of the most fashionable residential areas, occupies the lower slopes of Mt. Lycabettus. Besides its several museums, you will enjoy window-shopping and people-watching, since cafés are busy from early morning to dawn.

A Good Walk

Begin at the site of the first modern Olympics (1896), the **Panathenaic Stadium** ㊷ on Vassileos Konstantinou. You may want to detour right onto Herod Atticus, which leads to the **Presidential Palace,** used by Greece's kings after the restoration of 1935 and now by the head of state. Across the street from the Stadium are the **National Gardens** ㊸, a pet project of Queen Amalia. Bear right, past the neoclassical **Zappion hall,** where you exit onto Vasilissis Olgas, dominated by the **Temple of Olympian Zeus** ㊹, built by Emperor Hadrian in AD 132, and around the corner on Amalias, **Hadrian's Arch** ㊺, which marks the spot where the ancient city ended and Hadrian's Athens began.

Off Amalias is the large Russian Orthodox church of **Ayios Nikodimos** ㊻, and the **Jewish Museum** ㊼, which details the history of one of Greece's decimated communities. Amalias also passes above **Constitution Square** ㊽ in front of the **Parliament** and the **Tomb of the Unknown Soldier,** guarded by massive Evzones. Proceed up Vasilissis Sofias (often
★ indicated as Eleftheriou Venizelou on maps) to the delightful **Goulandris Cycladic Museum** ㊾, with nearly 100 exhibits of the Cycladic civilization (3000–2000 BC). A few blocks up Vasilissis Sofias, the
★ **Byzantine Museum** ㊿, housed in an 1848 mansion built by an eccentric French aristocrat, features a unique collection of icons.

Five minutes east of the museum is the **Ethniki Pinakothiki** �51 (National Gallery of Art), worth a visit more for its special exhibits than for its uninspiring permanent collection. Turn off Vasilissis Sofias onto Gennadiou, passing the 12th-century **Moni Petraki** ㊾2, to **Gennadius Library** ㊾3, one of the greatest collections on Greek subjects. Go left on Souidias (which becomes Spefsipou), where at Ploutarchou, steps as-
★ cend to the funicular to the top of **Mt. Lycabettus** ㊾4, three times the height of the Acropolis. The view from the top—pollution permitting—is the finest in Athens. You can see all the Attica basin, the harbor, and the islands of Aegina and Poros laid out before you. Minibus 60 from Kolonaki Square also drops you at the funicular station. Walk or ride back to **Kolonaki Square** ㊾5, which, especially on Saturday at noon, is crammed with chattering crowds who relax on the café-lined pedestrian zone or shop the designer boutiques.

TIMING

Because most of the museums close around 3 PM, as do shops on Monday, Wednesday, and Saturday, plan your walk for mid-morning. The walk takes about 4 hours, but you may want to extend this to visit Mt. Lycabettus in the late afternoon, when the light is best for the view. Kaisariani monastery stays open until about 2:30, but you can hike through the wooded grounds until sunset. Many of the sites are closed Saturday, Sunday, or Monday; the National Gallery of Art is closed Tuesday, so you should plan to go another day if you want to see everything.

Sights to See

㊻ **Ayios Nikodimos.** In 1780 the notoriously brutal Hadji Ali Haseki pulled down this 11th-century chapel of a convent and used the stone for a defense wall around Athens. The church was sold to the Russian government, who in 1852–56 modified it into a larger, cruciform building with a distinctive terra-cotta frieze; the separate tower was built to hold a massive bell donated by Tsar Alexander II. Note the displays of ornate Russian embroidery and the bright blues of the Pantocrator overhead. The female chanters of this Russian Orthodox church are renowned. ⊠ *Fillelinon 21,* ☎ *01/323–1090.*

★ ⑳ **Byzantine Museum.** The only museum in Europe concentrating exclusively on Byzantine art, this is housed in the mansion of the Duchess of Plaisance, built from 1840 to 1848 by Kleanthis. Rooms are arranged to look like Greek churches of different eras, and the upper floor contains mostly icons, many quite valuable. Much of the museum is still closed for restoration. ⊠ *Vasilissis Sofias 22,* ☎ *01/721–1027.* ☞ *500 dr. during restoration.* ☉ *Tues.–Sun. 8:30–3.*

OFF THE BEATEN PATH **MONASTERY OF KAISARIANI** – For an exceptional trek outside central Athens, head to the slopes of Mt. Hymettus, where you'll find one of the city's most evocative Byzantine remains. The well-restored 11th-century church, built on the site of a sanctuary of Aphrodite, has some beautiful frescoes dating from the 17th century (☞ Attica *in* Chapter 3). Nearby is a ruined basilica and a picnic site with a superb view of the Acropolis and Piraeus. Take a taxi or Bus 224 from in front of the Byzantine Museum for 6 km (4 mi) east of central Athens to the terminal in the working-class suburb of Kaisariani. The monastery is an additional 30-minute walk along the paved road that climbs Mt. Hymettus. ⊠ *The mountain road starting at Ethniki Antistaseos,* ☎ *01/723–6619.* ☞ *800 dr.* ☉ *Tues.–Sun. 8:30–2:50.*

⑤ **Ethniki Pinakothiki (National Gallery of Art).** The permanent collections of Greek painting and sculpture of the 19th and 20th centuries, including the work of naive artist Theophilos, have made way for long-running international exhibits. ⊠ *Vassileous Konstandinou 50,* ☎ *01/721–1010.* ☞ *Free, except for special exhibits.* ☉ *Wed.–Sun. 9–3.*

OFF THE BEATEN PATH **HELLENIC CHILDREN'S MUSEUM** – Children ages 4–12 can join trips organized by the museum to places such as a gasworks, the Acropolis, and the Train Museum; the museum also offers occasional workshops in crafts such as mask-making. The museum provides a children's pamphlet in English on the National Archaeological Museum (other pamphlets are being written). Near the museum is a playground (⊠ In a large wooded park [Alsos Syngrou], behind Ayios Haralambos Church on Dragoumis). ⊠ *Dimitressa 7–9,* ☎ *01/729–0202.* ☉ *Weekdays 9–1.*

㊚ **Gennadius Library.** Opened in 1926, the library contains a superb collection of material on Greek subjects. Besides the 24,000 volumes bequeathed by John Gennadius, the founder, there are many rare books, some of Lord Byron's belongings, and interesting paintings; for example, watercolors of Greece by Edward Lear. The library facade is imposing, a portico of Ionic columns in front of a brilliantly colored neoclassical facade. ⊠ *Souidias 61,* ☎ *01/721–0536.* ☉ *Mon., Tues., and Fri. 9–5; Wed.–Thurs. 9–8; Sat. 9–2. Closed mid-Aug–mid-Sept.*

★ ㊾ **Goulandris Cycladic Museum.** A wing opened in 1994 in the gorgeous Stathatos Mansion, where special exhibits are held. The museum has an outstanding collection dating from the Bronze Age, with especially notable slender marble figurines, the primitive Cycladic form of the Great Earth Mother. ⊠ *Neofitou Douka 4 and Irodotou 1,* ☎ *01/722–8321 through 8323.* ☞ *400 dr.* ☉ *Weekdays 10–4, Sat. 10–3.*

㊺ **Hadrian's Arch.** The marble gateway built in AD 131 with Corinthian details was intended to honor Hadrian and separate the ancient and imperial sections of Athens. On the side facing the Acropolis an inscription reads THIS IS ATHENS, THE ANCIENT CITY OF THESEUS, but the side facing the Temple of Olympian Zeus proclaims, THIS IS THE CITY

OF HADRIAN AND NOT OF THESEUS. ⊠ *Amalias and Dionyssiou Are-opagitou.*

47 Jewish Museum. The museum's vivid memorabilia tells the story of the Jews in Greece, as far back as the 3rd century BC in Thessaloniki. Eighty-seven percent of the Greek Jews were killed during the Holocaust, and only 5,000 remain in Greece today. Religious artifacts, costumes, embroideries, and photos are well organized according to periods and themes. One room contains an actual synagogue, moved from Patras, since there were no more Jews in that city. The museum will eventually relocate to new accommodations at Nikis 39, but for now it's on the third floor of a handsome art deco building with a Parisian-style lift enclosed in intricate wrought iron. ⊠ *Amalias 36,* ☎ *01/323–1577 or 01/322–5582.* ◲ *Free; ring bell.* ⊙ *Sun.–Fri. 10–1.*

☝ 55 Kolonaki Square. When Athenians say *pame platia* (let's go to the square), there's no confusion about where they're supposed to meet. They don't actually go to the square, officially called Filikis Eterias, but to the Tsakalof pedestrian zone. They congregate here for a quick coffee before work, after a hard day of shopping, or to pick up foreign newspapers at the all-night **kiosk.** On the lower side of the square is the **British Council Library** (⊠ Kolonaki Sq. 17, ☎ 01/364–5768), which has many children's books and a table at which children can sit and read. ⊠ *Where Patriarchou Ioakeim and Canari meet.* ⊙ *Library: Tues.–Fri. 10–1:30 and Tues.–Thurs. 5:30–8, reduced hours June–July. Closed Aug.*

NEED A BREAK?   Enjoy a cappuccino and an Italian sweet standing at **Da Capo** (⊠ Tsakalof and Kolonaki Sq., ☎ 01/360–2497), frequented by young trendsetters. Or you can walk to **Dexameni** (⊠ Deinokratous and Xanthippou, Dexameni Sq., ☎ 01/729–2578), a favorite because its tables line either side of a tree-shaded lane, and it's an ideal spot for people-watching.

52 Moni Petraki. Tucked into a sweet little park at Iassou, this church was built in the 12th century and decorated with paintings by Yiorgios Markos in the 18th century. ⊠ *Off Moni Petraki,* ☎ *01/721–2402.*

★ 54 Mt. Lycabettus. Myth claims that Athens's highest hill came to be when Athena removed a piece of Mt. Penteli, intending to boost the height of her temple on the Acropolis. En route, a crone brought her bad tidings, and the flustered goddess dropped the rock in the middle of the city. A steeply inclined *teleferique* (funicular) takes visitors to the summit, crowned by whitewashed **Ayios Georgios** chapel with a bell tower donated by Queen Olga. On the side of the hill, near the I Prasini Tenta café, there is a small shrine to **Ayios Isidoros** built into a cave. It was here that in 1859 students prayed for those fighting against the Austrians, French, and Sardinians with whom King Otho had allied. From Mt. Lycabettus you can watch the sunset and then turn in the other direction to see the moon rise over "violet-crowned" Hymettus, as the lights of Athens blink on all over the city. ⊠ *Funicular at Aristippou and Ploutarchou,* ☎ *01/722–7065.* ⊙ *Fri.–Wed. 8:45 AM–midnight, Thurs. 10:30 AM–midnight.* ◲ *800 dr. round-trip, 400 dr. one-way.*

NEED A BREAK?   The pricey **Café Dionysos** (⊠ On the top of Mt. Lycabettus) has drinks and a full menu, but you'll get a better deal at **I Prasini Tenta** (The Green Awning; ⊠ 5 min down road that descends Mt. Lycabettus, turn left at fork, ☎ 01/361-9447), an outdoor café where you can savor an ouzo and appetizers such as mushrooms stuffed with four cheeses with your Acropolis view.

🕃 ❹ **National Gardens.** When you can't take the city noise anymore, step into this oasis completed in 1860 as part of Otho and Amalia's royal holdings. Here old men on the benches argue politics, policemen take their coffee break, and animal lovers feed the stray cats that roam among the more than 500 species of trees and plants, many labeled. At the east end is the neoclassical **Zappion hall,** built in 1888 and used for major political and cultural events: it was here that Greece signed its entrance into the EC. At night, a café attracts large crowds who pass the time gossiping and nibbling on pastries and ice cream. There is a **playground** (⊠ Off Vasilissis Olgas) near the bus terminal. Youngsters aged 5–15 may settle into a good book at the **Children's Library** (☎ 01/323–6503, ☉ Tues.–Sat. 8:30–2:30), a rustic vine-covered stone cottage in a tranquil corner of the garden; it's closed in August. Of its 4,000 books, 60 are in English and French. It also has games and puzzles (some in English), a chess set, dominoes, crayons, and coloring books. Albums, including a large selection of classical music, can be played on the turntable. ⊠ *East of Amalias, between Vasilissis Olgas and Vasilissis Sofias,* ☎ *01/721–5019.* ☉ *Daily sunrise to sunset.*

NEED A BREAK? | If you prefer a quiet setting with no traffic, visit the romantic café **Kafenedaki** (⊠ In the National Gardens), sometimes called Kipos, with wrought-iron chairs and tables nestled under flowering vines next to a cozy stone cottage for cool weather. The café is just inside the park's Herodou Attikou entrance (near Lykeiou). The menu is limited to a *poikilia* (variety) of mezes, grilled "toast" (with ham and cheese), ice cream, apple pie, and drinks.

❷ **Panathenaic Stadium.** Constructed by Lykourgus from 330 BC to 329 BC and used intermittently for Roman spectacles, it was reseated for the Panathenaic Games of AD 144 by Roman citizen Herod Atticus of Marathon, a magistrate, senator, and wealthy patron of Athens. The stadium later fell into ruin, and its marble was quarried for other buildings. By the mid-18th century, when it was painted by French artist Le Roy, it was little more than a wheat field with scant remains and was later the midnight site of the secret rites of the witches of Athens. A blinding-white marble reconstruction of the ancient Roman stadium was rebuilt for the first modern Olympics, in April of 1896, and is now used mainly for an occasional concert and the finish of the annual marathon; it seats 80,000 spectators. ⊠ *Vassileos Konstantinou, across from National Gardens.* ☉ *Daily 9–2 but can be viewed in its entirety without entering.*

OFF THE BEATEN PATH | **FIRST CEMETERY** – This is Athens's equivalent of Paris's Père-Lachaise, but it is whitewashed and cheerful rather than gloomy and Gothic. The graves are surrounded by well-tended gardens and decorated with small photographs of the departed, and doves coo perpetually from the stately cypress trees. The main entrance off Anapafseos leads to an open-air museum of mind-boggling funerary architecture, including the imposing temple of Heinrich Schliemann, high on a bluff, and the touching marble *Sleeping Maiden* statue on the grave of Sophia Afendaki. In 1994 the film star and politician Melina Mercouri was buried here, as was the popular, controversial former prime minister Andreas Papandreou in 1996. ⊠ *Anapafseos and Trivonianou, near Panathenaic Stadium,* ☎ *01/923–6118.* ☉ *Daily 7:30–7 (winter 7:30–5).*

❹ **Syntagma (Constitution) Square.** At the top of the square stands **Parliament,** formerly the royal palace, completed in 1838 for the new monarchy. Here you can watch the **changing of the Evzone guard** at the **Tomb of the Unknown Soldier,** which happens every day at different times, except on Sunday, when it is scheduled for 11:25 AM. The bas relief of a dying soldier is modeled after a sculpture on the Temple of Aphaia in Aegina, and the text is from the funeral oration said to have been given by Pericles. On Sunday the honor guard of tall young men don their dress wear—a short white *foustanella* (kilt) with 400 neat pleats, one for each year of the Ottoman occupation, and red shoes with pompons—and still manage to look brawny rather than silly. A band accompanies a large troop of them in a memorable ceremony that begins at 11 AM from the barracks and ends in front of Parliament 15 minutes later. Every day, a group of the Evzones raise the Greek flag on the Acropolis and return to take it down at closing time. ⊠ *Where Vasilissis Sofias becomes Panepistimiou.*

NEED A   Since 1910, **Ariston** (⊠ Voulis 10, ☎ 01/323–4203) has been turning
BREAK?   out the city's best *tiropites* (cheese pies); these are a little more piquant
           than usual and have a thicker phyllo. Avoid the tasteless variety often
           sold on the street and make a pit stop here for the real thing.

🏛 **Temple of Olympian Zeus.** Begun in the 6th century BC, it was completed in AD 132 by Hadrian, who also built one huge gold-and-ivory statue of Zeus for the inner chamber and another, only slightly smaller, of himself. Only 15 of the original Corinthian columns remain, but standing next to them inspires a sense of awe at their bulk, which is softened by the graceful carving of the acanthus-leaf capitals. The clearly defined segments of a column blown down in 1852 give you an idea of the method used in its construction. The site is floodlighted in summer, a majestic scene when you round the bend from Syngrou. On the outskirts of the site to the north are remains of houses, the city walls, and a Roman bath. ⊠ *Vasilissis Olgas 1,* ☎ *01/922–6330.* 🎟 *500 dr.* 🕙 *Tues.–Sun. 8:30–3.*

Piraeus

The port of Athens, 11 km (7 mi) southwest of the center, is a city in its own right (third-largest after Athens and Thessaloniki), with a population including suburbs of about 500,000. To those who remember the film *Never on Sunday,* the name Piraeus evokes images of earthy waterfront cafés frequented by free-spirited sailors and hookers, though many Athenians regard Piraeus (except for Mikrolimano or Kastella) as merely low class. Neither image is correct: the restoration of older buildings and the addition of shopping centers and cafés have brought about a rejuvenation of community pride. Piraeus caters more to Greek families and young singles than to the rough-and-tumble crowd, and living in some parts of it carries a certain cachet these days. Also, the air pollution, noise level, and temperatures are considerably lower than they are in inner Athens.

Piraeus, in ancient times an island surrounded by marshes, was settled by the Minyans, a warlike, seafaring people who built a temple to Artemis Munychia on the hill now known as Kastella. At first the Athenians docked their triremes at Phaleron (where Theseus set off on his journey to Crete), but around 493 BC Themistocles persuaded them to use Piraeus and built the Long Walls, from Kastella to Athens. Piraeus was razed by the Roman general Sulla in 86 BC and afterward remained virtually uninhabited.

In 1834, after gaining independence from the Turks, the government offered land on favorable terms to rebuild Piraeus (at that point a mere wilderness), and it was resettled by islanders from other parts of Greece. The first factory was founded by Hydriots in 1847, and by the turn of the century there were 76 steam-powered factories. After the 1920s Piraeus developed as the economic center, while Athens maintained the cultural sphere. In the years following 1922, refugees from Asia Minor swelled the population, bringing with them rembetika music.

A Good Walk

The fastest and cheapest way to get to Piraeus from central Athens is to take the electric train (about 25 minutes from Concord Sq.). The metro station is just off Akti Kallimasioti on the main harbor. For those who don't have much time, take Bus 904, 905, or 909 opposite the Piraeus station directly to the Archaeological Museum rather than walking there; get off at the Fillelinon stop. If it's Sunday, detour a few blocks north of the metro to the **flea market** 56, at the intersection of Mavromichali and Drapatsianou. If walking, turn left when exiting the metro, following Akti Kallimasioti to Akti Poseidonos. South of here is the Customs House and Port Authority, through which one passes to board boats going to other countries, and a modern exhibition center, where the Poseidonia Shipping Exhibition is held in June in connection with a biannual Nautical Week. Continuing on Akti Poseidonos, turn onto Vasileos Georgiou A', which passes the splendid 800-seat **Municipal Theater** 57 near Korai Square. Head south on Hroon Polytechneiou, cutting through Terpsithea Square, and then go east on Harilaou Trikoupi to the remodeled **Archaeological Museum** 58, with rare finds such as the Piraeus Kouros, a cult statue of Apollo from the 6th century BC. The street ends at the harbor of **Pasalimani** 59 (Zea Marina). To the west is the coastal road Akti Themistokleous, whose lantern-lined stretch offers good views and reasonably priced seafood restaurants. Incorporated into the foundation of the **Naval Museum** 60, also on the road, are the original Long Walls. To the east is the pretty, crescent-shape harbor of **Mikrolimano** 61, famed for its more than 20 seafood restaurants (you can take a bus from the Fillelinon stop near the archaeological museum to Palio Faliro station if you don't want to walk). Mikrolimano has lost favor with some Athenians because the harbor suffers from pollution, but the delightful atmosphere remains intact, and the harbor is crowded with yachts.

Above Mikrolimano is charming **Kastella** 62, terraces of 19th-century houses tucked up against the sloping hillside—an ideal spot for a walk before dinner on the harbor or a show at its **Veakio Theater.** A short walk north of Mikrolimano brings you to the **Peace and Friendship Stadium,** nicknamed the Shoe because of its distinctive shape. Wrestling matches and other sporting events, concerts, and exhibitions are held here. From its metro station (Neo Faliro), you can return to Athens.

TIMING

On a day trip to Piraeus you can see the main sights, explore the neighborhoods around its three harbors, and have a seafood meal before returning to Athens. If you are taking an early-morning ferry or seeing a performance at the Veakio Theater, it makes good sense to stay in one of the seaside hotels. Note—particularly if you crave tacky ashtrays and tchotchkes—that the flea market is held only on Sunday, the Archaeological Museum is closed Monday, and the Municipal Theater is closed weekends.

Sights to See

★ 58 **Archaeological Museum.** Besides an admirable collection of funerary stelae, urns, monuments, and korai, the museum's prize exhibits, found in a sewage drain in 1959, include the exquisitely made **Piraeus Kouros** (probably a cult statue of Apollo from the 6th century BC, and therefore the oldest known hollow-cast bronze statue); a 4th-century bronze of a pensive Athena, wearing a helmet decorated with griffins and owls;

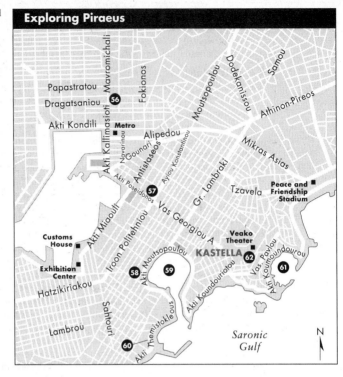

Exploring Piraeus

and two bronze versions of Artemis. ⊠ *Harilaou Trikoupi 31,* ☎ *01/452–1598.* ▦ *500 dr.* ⊙ *Tues.–Sun. 8:30–3.*

56 **Flea market.** On Sunday outdoor stalls overflow with household items, electronic goods, and offbeat videocassettes—all of more appeal to residents than tourists, although a few collectible white elephants emerge from the kitsch. On Navarinou, parallel to Akti Kallimasioti, there's another market selling cheese, cold cuts, dried fruit, bread, and nuts. It's good to buy provisions before taking a ferry because the snack bars on board often have just a few items at high prices. ⊠ *At intersection of Mavromichali and Drapatsaniou.* ⊙ *Sun. 8–2.*

62 **Kastella.** This neighborhood behind Mikrolimano Harbor retains the charm of a bygone era, its neoclassical houses skillfully restored. On the hill the **Veakio Theater** (⊠ Idis on Lofos Prof. Ilias, ☎ 01/412–5498) has an interesting festival July through September, featuring visiting dance troupes, plays, and concerts. ⊠ *Behind Mikrolimano.*

★ **61** **Mikrolimano.** The most touristy part of Piraeus, this graceful small harbor is known to old-timers as **Turkolimano.** Sitting under the awnings by the sea and watching the water and the gaily painted fishing boats is the next best thing to hopping on a ferry boat and going to an island. During high season, it is a good idea to have lunch here, as most of the many restaurants lining the harbor are packed in the evening. The hawkers in front of the restaurants are entertaining, but they can be aggressive. Don't be afraid to ask to see the prices on the menu or go to look at the fish stored in iced compartments. Be sure to specify how large a portion you want, and find out its price in advance. ⊠ *Akti Koumoudourou.*

OFF THE
BEATEN PATH

LUNA PARKS – Kids love these small, movable amusement parks, which are usually set up in parks every day, all over the city. They mostly have merry-go-rounds, Ferris wheels, and bumper cars; some have roller coasters. If you hop on the metro at Neo Faliro and get off one stop north at Moschato, your children can enjoy a Punch and Judy–type shadow show starring Karaghiozis (the Black Eye), a character developed in Asia Minor and brought over to Greece. One such performance you can count on is The Athanasiou Brothers, held every Sunday at 11:30 AM, from October to May at the Moschato Theater (✉ Metamorphosis Sq., next to the Neo Faliro metro station, ☎ 01/413–1226 or 01/481–6276); the cost is 700 dr. A free workshop in the same complex is given on Saturday from 12 to 3:30, during which children can get a closer look at the painted-leather figures used in performances and learn to make their own puppets.

57 **Municipal Theater.** The 800-seat theater was modeled after the Opéra Comique in Paris and finished in 1895. In the same building is the **Panos Aravantinos Decor Museum,** which displays sketches and models of the artist's theatrical sets. ✉ *Theater and museum: Ayios Konstantinou 2,* ☎ *01/412–2339.* ⊠ *Free.* ⊘ *Mon., Tues., and Wed. 4–8; Thurs. and Fri. 9–2. Closed Aug.*

NEED A
BREAK?

Stop in at the pastry shop **Harami** (✉ Konstantinou Palaiologou 13, ☎ 01/417–6080 and 01/412–6302) to snag a few pieces of their famous creations dubbed "per mar": biscuits filled with pastry cream and nuts, dipped in liqueur and covered with chocolate. You can enjoy your treat in nearby **Terpsithea Square.**

60 **Naval Museum.** The 13,000 items on display include scale models and actual sections of triremes and famous boats, Byzantine flags, figureheads, documents, and uniforms. A section of the **Long Walls** is incorporated into the museum's foundation, and other well-preserved segments run along Akti Themistokleous, south of Zea Marina. ✉ *Akti Themistokleous at Freattida,* ☎ *01/451–6822.* ⊠ *400 dr.* ⊘ *Tues.–Sat. 9–2:30, Sun. 9–1.*

59 **Pasalimani (Zea Marina).** The small harbor has a new marina, complete with shops and all yachting facilities, with berths for more than 400 boats. The surrounding area has been rejuvenated, with the addition of many enticing cafés and pubs. There's Greek National Tourist Organization (GNTO or EOT) office with maps, brochures, and timetables on the west side of the harbor close to the departure point for Saronic Gulf Islands hydrofoils.

DINING

Whether you sample octopus and ouzo near the sea, roasted goat in a turn-of-the-century taverna, or nouvelle cuisine in Athens's newest restaurants, dining in the city is as relaxing as it is everywhere else in Greece: waiters never rush you, reservations are seldom necessary, and no matter how tight the space, the establishment can always make room for another table.

Forgo the ubiquitous moussaka, and opt instead for house and regional specialties, and don't hesitate to try the barrel wine, inexpensive and often quite good. If you can't read the menu, just go back to the kitchen and point at what looks most appealing. This is also a good idea in tavernas, where not everything on the menu may be available when you order. Most places serve at least until midnight.

CATEGORY	COST*
$$$$	over 12,000 dr.
$$$	8,000 dr.–12,000 dr.
$$	4,500 dr.–8,000 dr.
$	under 4,500 dr.

per person for a 3-course meal, including service and tax, but excluding drinks.

In the last three weeks of August, when the city empties out and most residents head for the seaside, more than 75% of the restaurants and tavernas popular among Greeks close, though hotel restaurants, seafood restaurants in Mikrolimano, and tavernas in Plaka usually remain open.

Eating Places

Eating places fall into several categories. **Greek** and **foreign restaurants** offer a more sophisticated selection of dishes than do tavernas, and they often serve some international dishes, too. A few years ago the category of **haute cuisine** would not have existed, but Athens now has restaurants—including those specializing in foreign cuisine—of international standard, in both preparation and presentation. Truly authentic **tavernas** have wicker chairs that inevitably pinch your bottom, checkered tablecloths covered with butcher paper, wobbly tables that need coins under one leg, and wine from the barrel served in little metal carafes. If a place looks inviting and is filled with Greeks, give it a try. **Ouzeri,** sometimes called **mezedopolia,** are friendly little publike establishments that serve tidbits for you to nibble on while sipping ouzo. **Greek fast-food** and **seafood** spots offer a change of pace, and a break to your wallet.

What to Wear

As in most cosmopolitan cities, dress varies from casual to fancy, according to the establishment. Although Athens is informal and none of the restaurants listed here requires a jacket or tie, you'll feel more comfortable wearing them in the more expensive places (as noted). Conservative casual dress (not halter tops or shorts) is acceptable at most establishments.

Fast Food

The souvlaki joints in Monastiraki (☞ Exploring Athens, *above*) provide a satisfying and cheap snack. The souvlaki chain **Loxandra** (⊠ Ermou 2, Constitution Sq., ☎ 01/331–2212) has branches throughout the city; especially good is the chicken Loxandra, a roasted breast served in a homemade pita. Night owls looking for a snack will probably find something to their liking at **Everest Fast Food** (⊠ Tsakalof and Pindarou, Kolonaki, ☎ 01/361–3477; ⊠ Concord Sq. 18, ☎ 01/324–2329), with a wide menu, including various pites (pies) with meat, spinach, and cheese fillings; pastries; and toast, or sandwiches you stuff with as many ingredients as you can handle. Order first, then pay, bringing your receipt to pick up the food. After 2 AM there's always a crowd standing outside.

Neon (⊠ Concord Sq. and Dorou, ☎ 01/522–3201), a remodeled cafeteria in a stunning 1920s building that's open until at least 2 AM, was so popular that other branches immediately appeared at Tsakalof 6, Kolonaki; Mitropoleos 3, Constitution Square; and G. Lambrakis 156, Zea Marina. The vast selection ranges from salad-bar fare, pasta, and meat dishes to sandwiches, ice cream, and other desserts, and prices are moderate.

If you *must* placate the children in American terms, there are local **McDonald's, Wendy's, Taco Time,** and **Pizza Huts,** as well as **Goody's,** a Greek chain that serves good, inexpensive burgers.

Foreign

$$$$ ✕ **Kona Kai.** A setting of tropical luxury and almost 60 Polynesian dishes make one feel pampered. Choosing from the Royal Luau menu is an easy way to sample a cross section of sumptuous fare, or try something from the Japanese *teppanyaki* menu, prepared in front of you at tables for 24. Memorable dishes include the shrimp with Kenya beans and red curry sauce, the mango beef, and for dessert, chocolate cake laced with Kahlúa and topped with chocolate sauce and strawberries. ⊠ *Ledra Marriott Hotel, Syngrou 115, near Neos Kosmos,* ☎ *01/934–7711. AE, DC, MC, V. Closed Sun. and mid-Aug. No lunch.*

$$$ ✕ **Boschetto.** Set in the Evangelismos park, Boschetto pampers diners with a soothing view, an expert maître d', and creative Italian nouvelle cuisine: You'll forget you're in the center of Athens. The specialty here is fresh pasta dishes such as tagliatelle with fresh squid and zucchini; ravioli with spinach, *anthotiro* (a creamy Greek cheese), foie gras, and poppy seeds; and penne with pecorino and artichokes. Popular entrées are beef fillet with rosemary, green peppers, and garlic or with black truffles and red wine. There are a few Italian wines on the list; surprisingly good is Boschetto's grappa. The tables tend to be close together and some are ill-placed; try to reserve near the window looking out on the park. In summer, the courtyard is open. ⊠ *Alsos Evangelismos, near the Hilton,* ☎ *01/721–0893. Reservations essential. AE, V. Closed Sun. and 2 wks. in Aug. No lunch winter.*

$$$ ✕ **Far East.** Many Chinese restaurants in Athens tend to be overpriced yet mediocre. If you must indulge, though, you can't go wrong here. At both branches the decor (birdcages, aquarium) and the service (waitresses in vermilion sheaths) are a cut above that at other establishments. Choose from the more than 100 items—hot-and-sour vegetable soup, crab and cheese wontons, cashew shrimp, and almond chicken—all somewhat authentic and good. The restaurants also serve some Korean dishes, such as kimchee, or spicy cabbage, and Japanese sushi and sashimi. On Sunday the Kefalari restaurant hosts a reasonably priced breakfast buffet. For dessert, there's the ubiquitous fried banana served with ice cream. ⊠ *Stadiou 7, just off Constitution Sq.,* ☎ *01/323–4996/7;* ⊠ *Deligianni 54, Kefalari,* ☎ *01/623–3140 through 3144. AE, DC, MC, V.*

$$$ ✕ **Melrose.** An anomaly in the student neighborhood of Exarchia, this restaurant has had great success with its "Pacific Rim" cuisine. Its understated style punctuated with modern art is the work of Yiannis Tsanaklidis; his brother Aris, a former chef in Beverly Hills and Maui, runs the kitchen. Delight your palate with choices ranging from chicken fajitas to duck breast with wild rice and kumquats to salmon seared and served with *ponzu* (Japanese saki-soy-scallion sauce). The Kaesaki plate includes swordfish carpaccio, shrimp *kinzu* (with a tart citrus-lemongrass-ginger sauce), and fish paté with Vietnamese fish sauce. Service is impeccable: if your delectable chocolate soufflé is the slightest bit deflated, they'll bake you another one. In summer, the restaurant moves to Glyfada. ⊠ *Zosimadou 16, at the top of the stairs off Kallidromiou 68, Exarchia,* ☎ *01/825–1627. AE, V. Closed Sun. and Aug. No lunch.*

$$$ ✕ **Prunier.** This cozy French bistro accented with copper utensils, antiques, and tasteful art nouveau exudes romance. The repertoire is solid French standards such as coq au vin and snails bourguignonne and original concoctions like quail *salmnis* (with oregano and lemon) and *delice des amoureux* (sautéed seafood laced with cognac in a vol-auvent). ✉ *Ipsilantou 63, Kolonaki,* ☎ *01/722–7379. Reservations essential. AE, D, MC, V. Closed Sun. and Aug. No lunch.*

$$$ ✕ **White Elephant.** The Polynesian food at this restaurant rivals that
★   at Kona Kai; also served are some Chinese and Indian dishes. You'll
find fresh lobster, perhaps Szechuan style, as well as Phuket fish,
sautéed sea bass in ginger and bean sauce, and piquant Thai shrimp.
Meat dishes include zesty seared barbecued pork, coconut chicken, spicy
Mandarin beef, and tea-smoked duck with hoisin and oyster sauce,
wrapped in pancakes. ✉ *Andromeda Hotel, Timoleontos Vassou 22,
near American Embassy,* ☎ *01/643–7302. Reservations essential. AE,
DC, MC, V. Closed Sun. and July–Aug. No lunch.*

$$ ✕ **Famagusta.** The Mediterranean and Middle East have both influ-
★   enced Cypriot cuisine, resulting in the tasty assortment of mezes. Fam-
agusta is romantic, with candlelit tables and Cypriot handicrafts:
baskets, colorful weavings, and ceramics. A guitarist and a bouzouki
player discreetly sing Greek and Cypriot favorites, and later the dance
floor is packed. The *seftalia* (minced meat wrapped in suet), *ofton* (lamb
in pastry cooked in a ceramic dish), tabbouleh salad with cracked wheat,
and *lounza* (a thick smoked pork fillet spiced with coriander) are some
recommended treats. ✉ *Zagoras 8 (end of Michalachopoulou), Am-
belokopi,* ☎ *01/778–5229. DC, MC. No lunch.*

$$ ✕ **Michiko.** This reliable favorite, set in a gracious Plaka mansion with
a garden shaded by a giant fig tree, has been around for more than 20
years, serving decorative, meticulously prepared Japanese dishes. An
authentic sushi and sashimi bar has its own chef. Special menus offer
a sampling of some of the best dishes. ✉ *Kidathineon 27, Plaka,* ☎
01/322–0980. AE, DC, MC, V. Closed Sun. No lunch Sat.

Greek

$$–$$$ ✕ **Vitrina.** It's obvious this progressive, highly stylized restaurant is the
★   new creation of a fashion photographer—from the stenciled bread bas-
kets to the tiny lights shimmering among a jumble of branches. More
food for thought: fragrant bread arrives with both an olive-anchovy-
caper spread and cumin-sunflower seed spread. The combinations are
bold: crayfish with coffee and coriander, beef filet sautéed in mastic and
Vizanto wine sauce. What's more, the Aegean-inspired cooking is light,
without much fat. Try the chicken filled with eggplant, dill, and thyme
in a buttermilk sauce, or one of the best dishes, lamb with whole mush-
rooms and red peppers in a sweet-sour port sauce. If it's in season, sam-
ple the delicate chestnut mousse; always good is the chocolate cake with
vanilla cream and gooseberry sauce. The logically priced wine list fea-
tures small producers, especially from Santorini. Seating upstairs is
best; downstairs is a bit claustrophobic. ✉ *Navarchou Apostoli 7 (off
Ermou), Psirri,* ☎ *01/321–1200. Reservations essential. No credit
cards. Closed Mon. and Aug. No lunch Mon.–Sat. No dinner Sun.*

$$ ✕ **Ideal.** The original Ideal burned down after almost 70 years, and
its art deco protégé is in bright contrast. The oldest restaurant in the
city center, it has a following for the quality and variety of its more
than 20 daily specials such as mussel souvlaki and leek croquettes. Best
bets on the regular menu are the piquant mincemeat kebab, the juicy
baby lamb wrapped in phyllo, and the Smyrnaika *tsoutsoukakia* (spicy
sausage patties liberally seasoned with cinnamon) spiced with ouzo and
rosemary. The service is fast but fastidious, and almost everyone speaks
English. ✉ *Panepistimiou 46, Omonia,* ☎ *01/330–3000. AE, DC, MC,
V. Closed Sun.*

$ ✕ **Pandelis.** The proprietor and chef's grandfather owned the leg-
endary Pandelis in Istanbul, and this one is a real find: the tables are
set among greenery on a quiet side street and the waiters are courte-

ous and helpful. Among the entrées are eggplant with garlic and tomato named *Imam Bayildi* (the cleric fainted)—presumably because the dish was so delicious—and the pièce de résistance: *yaourtlu kebab* (skewered lamb and beef with a zesty yogurt sauce). Try *kavuk gogsu* (an unusual chicken-based dessert pudding). ⊠ *Naiadon 96, Palio Faliro,* ☎ *01/982–5512. DC, MC. No lunch weekdays. No dinner Sun.*

Haute Cuisine

$$$$ ✕ **Bajazzo.** If you have only one big splurge in Athens, have it here, one
★ of the finest restaurants anywhere. The main dining room is a joyful explosion of scents and colors, and the menu constantly changes as Chef Klaus Feuerbach experiments with wildly imaginative creations. Dishes are brought to your table for your inspection: appetizers may include a heavenly seafood bisque or porcini mushrooms and pine nuts layered in crepes and served with basil sauce. Also delectable are the beef fillets layered with foie gras and served with cognac-cream sauce; the sole with smoked salmon mousse, mascarpone cheese, and chive sauce; and duck breast with *crème de bananes* (banana liqueur). Leave room for dessert: various stunning chocolate masterpieces or lighter fruit dishes such as pears stewed in *mavrodaphne* (a sweet red wine) with herb ice cream. ⊠ *Anapafseos 14, Mets,* ☎ *01/921–3013. Reservations essential; for lunch, you must call one day before. AE, DC, V. Closed Sun.*

$$$$ ✕ **Rose.** Though slightly out of the way for visitors, this bar and restaurant has become a favorite among Greek yuppies—media stars, political consultants, and young entrepreneurs. Despite the occasionally indifferent service, the food is excellent—shrimp carpaccio, quail stuffed with foie gras, salmon in pastry with champagne sauce. For dessert, opt for the white- and dark-chocolate mousse. ⊠ *Kifissias 227, in the Anavrita shopping center, Maroussi,* ☎ *01/612–3051 through 3053. Reservations essential. AE, DC, V. Closed Sun. No lunch.*

$$$ ✕ **Symposio.** This restored 1920s house near the Herod Atticus theater has a spacious garden and a cheerful front bar now a late-night gathering place for the Athens intelligentsia. Symposio blends the familiar with the new in unexpected ways. Pasta with Metsovone cheese, fillets of St. Peter fish with saffron, breast of duck with cassis or mango sauce, and prawns and caviar with vodka dressing are some of the best dishes that may be offered. Desserts include American cheesecake (hard to find in Greece) and *negraki* (chocolate cake made with rum and raisins and served with hot chocolate sauce). ⊠ *Erechthiou 46, Makriyanni,* ☎ *01/922–5321, reservations 01/996–0501. AE, DC, MC, V. Closed Sun., Greek Easter, and 2nd wk. of Aug. No lunch.*

Ouzeri

$$ ✕ **Apotsos.** This folksy, old ouzeri with bentwood chairs, old posters, and early calendars is reminiscent of the '30s. Full of talkative journalists and politicians, it's lively and crowded, and the food is almost secondary. *Saganaki* (fried cheese) and *gigantes* (broad beans in tomato sauce) are typical. Get there early; it closes at 5. ⊠ *Panepistimiou 10, in arcade, Constitution Sq.,* ☎ *01/363–7046. No credit cards. Closed Sun. and 2 wks in Aug. No dinner.*

$$ ✕ **Athinaikon.** This renowned establishment moved here after almost
★ 60 years near the law courts, and it is still a favorite of attorneys and local office workers. The decor is no-nonsense ouzeri, with rectangular marble tables, dark wood, and framed memorabilia. Abide by the classic specialties: crisp shrimp croquettes, swordfish souvlaki with bay leaves and a light mustard sauce, and *ameletita* (sautéed testicles). A favorite new dish is *patsage* (dried, spiced meat called pastourmas wrapped in phyllo with cheese and tomato). All go well with the light

barrel red. ⊠ *Themistokleous 2, Omonia,* ☎ *01/383–8485. No credit cards. Closed Sun. and Aug.*

$$ ✕ **Kafenio.** A Kolonaki institution, this ouzeri is slightly fancier than the norm, with cloth napkins and a handsome dark wood interior. The menu is enormous, with many unusual creations. The tender marinated octopus, fried eggplant, and the onion pie are good choices. ⊠ *Loukianou 26, Kolonaki,* ☎ *01/722–9056. No credit cards. Closed Sun. and Aug.*

$$ ✕ **Ta Tria Tetarta.** There's something dollhouse-like about this tri-level
★   stone and wood interior with nooks and crannies, a fireplace, and Greek knickknacks. The appetizers served here are usually hard to find: spicy feta sprinkled with red pepper and roasted in foil, cheese bread, skewered *seftalies* (a tasty mix of lamb liver bits and onions wrapped in intestines), seafood pie, and Turkish favorites such as yogurt and sausage salad. ⊠ *Oikonomou 25, Exarchia,* ☎ *01/823–0560. No credit cards. Closed Aug.*

$ ✕ **Salamandra.** In this bi-level house, the seating is at wooden tables in comfy nooks, with a fireplace lit downstairs in winter, and air-conditioning in summer. Salamandra has a reputation for well-prepared mezes (more than 60), like the *tsirosalata,* (tiny fish marinated in vinegar), eggplant croquettes, and *haloumi* (fried mild Cypriot cheese). Draft beer and barrel wine are available. ⊠ *Mantzarou 3, Kolonaki,* ☎ *01/361–7927. V. Closed Sun. in winter; in summer, closed dinner, weekends, and Aug. 10–20.*

$ ✕ **To Karafaki.** Relax in this traditional mezedopolio, housed in a neoclassical building with marble tables, rush chairs, and lace curtains. The variety of dishes include vegetable croquettes, stuffed eggplant roll, onion pie, and Cypriot *flogeres* ("flutes" of ham and melted cheese). ⊠ *Moustoxidi 19, Pedion Areos,* ☎ *01/641–0192. No credit cards. Closed Sun. and June–Sept. No lunch.*

Seafood

$$$ ✕ **Fourtouna.** This restaurant excels in fresh seafood, and it's no surprise to see the handsome dining rooms in this restored 1930s house perpetually crammed. A wood boat in the front hall is a buffet area, displaying the main dishes. The splendid *karavides* (crayfish), grilled or steamed, are tender-sweet morsels served simply with a butter sauce and lemon. *Thalassina* (fluted clamlike shellfish) are a rare treat. The barreled white wine from an Attic village has a fine bouquet, and there are excellent small Greek wine producers on the list. ⊠ *Anapiron Polemou 22, Kolonaki,* ☎ *01/722–1282. Reservations essential for dinner. DC, V. Closed Sun. (except in winter, when they open for dinner) and Aug. No lunch Mon.–Sat.*

$$$ ✕ **Kaldera.** Dedicated to island dishes not found at most tavernas, this restaurant brings back fond memories to those who love the Greek islands. Although technically a mezedopolio (with about 45 starters), it serves very good, reasonably priced seafood. Amid the blue and white decor and ship pictures, diners can indulge in such specialties as the Mytilini plate, 12 kinds of fish fried with fresh tomato sauce and doused with Ricard and wine, *gavros* (fresh anchovy) marinated in vinegar from Salamina, and steaming hot mussels in mustard sauce from Skopelos. That's just for starters; if you can manage an entrée, try the *makaronada thalassina* (al dente pasta with crab, shrimp, and mussels) or any of the fresh catch, straight from the Aegean (many of today's fish are cultivated): sargus, sole, sea bream, and monkfish. The wine list, though limited, features island wines. If you need help making a selection, the waiters are happy to make recommendations. ⊠ *Leoforos Poseidonos 54, Palio Faliro,* ☎ *01/982–9647. AE, DC, MC, V.*

$$–$$$ ✕ **Kollias.** The restaurant's terrace, with pots of geraniums and jasmine, evokes Athens in the 60s. Friendly owner Tassos Kollias has a way with seafood, often creating his own dishes that range from the humble to the aristocratic, from marinated gavros to lobster with tomato, basil, cardamom, and pasta. Try the grilled scorpion fish flavored with mastic, the flambéed mackerel, or mussels stuffed with rice, grapes, and pine nuts. Besides piping-hot tomato and other vegetable croquettes, there are large mixed salads with white beets, arugula, lettuce, parsley, caper leaves, endive, and radishes. A fitting end to such a meal are the loukoumades, best with the kumquat liqueur. If you have trouble getting to the area, the owner will arrange for a taxi to pick you up. ✉ *Stratigou Plastira 3, Tabouria, Piraeus,* ☎ *01/462–9620. Reservations essential on weekends. AE, DC, MC, V. Closed Sun. and 3 wks. in Aug. No lunch May–Sept.*

$$–$$$ ✕ **Mavri Gida (Black Goat).** Also known as Kavos, this restaurant is one of few in the Mikrolimano area with a Greek clientele. It has a wide selection of such fresh fish and seafood as *barbouni* (red mullet), *lithrini* (sea bream), and calamari. Since grade-A fish and lobster are expensive, it's a good idea to make your choice from the refrigerated compartments, then have it weighed, so you'll know the exact price in advance. Specialties include a thick seafood crepe, conch with various shellfish, and *garides yiouvetsi* (shrimp baked in a casserole with feta, tomato sauce, and tiny noodles called *kritharakia*). Game—wild pig and deer—is also served. ✉ *Akti Koumoundourou 64, Piraeus,* ☎ *01/422–0691. AE, DC, MC, V.*

$$–$$$ ✕ **Varoulko.** Although the restaurant has moved to larger quarters with
★ a courtyard, it often still has a line of customers waiting outside to sample Lefteris Lazarou's acclaimed version of the humble monkfish. It's the only whole fish he serves, and he does it grilled, á la crème, and most popularly, steamed with vegetables. If you don't like monkfish, the chef and owner has a mouth-watering array of other seafood dishes: *skaltsouni* (pastry stuffed with fresh shrimp and crab), smoked swordfish, baby squid with pesto, and lobster with wild rice, celery, and champagne sauce. The dessert menu changes often, with various tortes and Greek-style apple pie. ✉ *Deligeorgi 14, Piraeus,* ☎ *01/411–2043. Reservations essential 2 days in advance. AE, V. Closed Sun. and Aug. 10–Sept. 10. No lunch.*

$$ ✕ **Botsaris.** Tucked away in a residential area, this bustling corner restaurant is a welcome alternative to the usual pricey seafood spots. Try grilled octopus, fish soup with large chunks of seafood and shrimp, or one of many fresh catches—red mullet, sea bream, and grouper. Service is friendly and prompt. ✉ *Zisimopoulou 24, Palio Faliro,* ☎ *01/941–3022. AE, DC, V. Closed 2 wks in Aug. No lunch Mon.–Sat. No dinner Sun.*

Tavernas

$$ ✕ **Kostoyannis.** If you're looking for authenticity, this is the place to go. One of the oldest and most popular tavernas in the area, it has an impressively wide range of Greek dishes—including shrimp salads, stuffed mussels, rabbit *stifado* (a baked stew of meat, white wine, garlic, cinnamon, and spices), and sautéed sweetbreads. ✉ *Zaimi 37, Pedion Areos, behind the Archaeological Museum,* ☎ *01/821–2496. No credit cards. Closed Sun. and mid-July–mid-Aug. No lunch.*

$$ ✕ **Manessis.** One of the best of the old-time haunts, Manessis is a homey garden in summer and several rooms of a little house in winter. A waiter brings you a long wooden tray with appetizers to choose from, including smoked herring, sausage, which he'll fry right at the table, and black-eyed peas. Specialties include Zakinthos-style veal, shrimp saganaki,

Athens Dining and Lodging

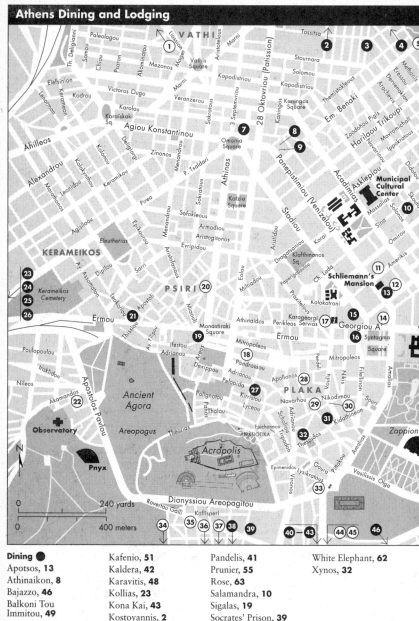

Dining ●

Apotsos, **13**
Athinaikon, **8**
Bajazzo, **46**
Balkoni Tou
Immitou, **49**
Boschetto, **59**
Botsaris, **40**
Everest Fast Food, **52**
Famagusta, **60**
Far East, **15**
Fourtouna, **58**
Ideal, **9**

Kafenio, **51**
Kaldera, **42**
Karavitis, **48**
Kollias, **23**
Kona Kai, **43**
Kostoyannis, **2**
Loxandra, **16**
Manessis, **47**
Mavri Gida, **24**
Melrose, **4**
Michiko, **31**
Neon, **7**
O Platanos, **27**

Pandelis, **41**
Prunier, **55**
Rose, **63**
Salamandra, **10**
Sigalas, **19**
Socrates' Prison, **39**
Symposio, **38**
TaTria Tetarta, **3**
To Karafaki, **6**
Varoulko, **25**
Vasilenas, **26**
Vitrina, **21**
Vlassis, **50**

White Elephant, **62**
Xynos, **32**

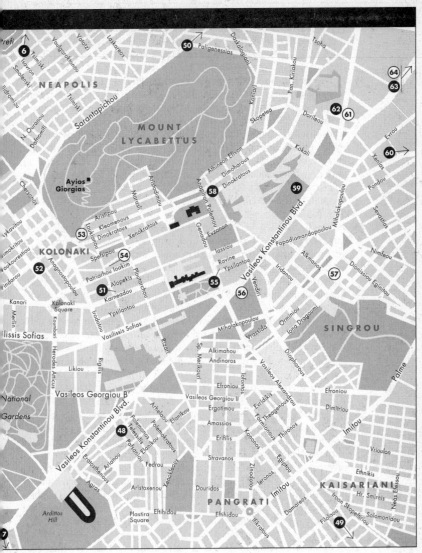

Lodging ○
Acropolis House, **30**
Acropolis View, **35**
Andromeda Athens
Hotel, **61**
Aphrodite Hotel, **28**
Art Gallery
Pension, **36**
Astor, **17**
Athenaeum
Inter-Continental, **45**
Athenian Inn, **54**
Athens Gate, **33**

Athens Hilton, **56**
Attalos Hotel, **20**
Austria, **34**
Electra Palace, **29**
Erechtheon, **22**
Grande Bretagne, **14**
Holiday Inn, **57**
Ledra Marriott, **44**
Lycabette, **12**
Marble House, **37**
Novotel Athenes, **1**
Orion and
Dryades, **5**

Plaka Hotel, **18**
President, **64**
St. George
Lycabettus, **53**
XEN (YWCA,) **11**

gardoumba (spit-roasted innards and meat), swordfish, and chicken souvlaki. The owner has added more vegetarian dishes like falafel, hummus, and tabbouleh; sweets, include *hasissame* (ice cream served on a cake soaked in syrup). ✉ *Markou Moussourou 3, Mets,* ☎ *01/922–7684. No credit cards. Closed 2 wks in Aug. No lunch.*

$$ ✕ **Socrates' Prison.** At this taverna near the Herod Atticus theater, you will often hobnob with actors. Tables are street-side in summer; but sit inside for quiet conversation. In cooler months, the action moves to the cozy room upstairs with a fireplace. Amiable owner Socrates—whose motto is "I never take a dish away; I just keep adding new ones"—makes many unusual dishes, including his own special salad with dill, carrots, olives, and eggs; spicy stuffed pita bread; *bourekaki* (fritters) with eggplant, parsley, and onion; zucchini with ham and bacon topped with béchamel; and pork rolls stuffed with carrots and celery in lemon sauce. ✉ *Mitseon 20, Makriyanni,* ☎ *01/922–3434. AE, V. Closed Sun. No lunch.*

$$ ✕ **Vlassis.** Relying on traditional recipes from Thrace, Roumeli, Thes-
★   saly, and the islands, the cooks here whip up Greek home cooking in generous portions that more than make up for the daunting noise level. The best way to sample as much as possible is to order several appetizers for a meal (there are more than 20, all reasonably priced). Essentials include the spicy cheese salad, marinated eggplant, *pastitsio* (a casserole of pasta, meat and cheese with seasonings and cinnamon) with bits of liver, and the octopus stifado, tender and sweet with lots of onions. Also good are the kebabs, seftalies, oven-baked pork, and *katsiki ladorigani* (goat with oil and oregano). Fresh fish is also served, and for dessert, the *galaktobouriko* (custard in phyllo) is delicious. In summer, the restaurant moves to Mt. Athos in northern Greece. ✉ *Armatolon and Klefton 20, Ambelokipi,* ☎ *01/642–5337. Reservations essential. DC, MC, V. Closed Sun. and July–Sept. No lunch.*

$$ ✕ **Xynos.** Stepping into the courtyard of this Plaka taverna is like entering a time warp: Athens in the '50s. According to loyal customers, nothing's changed much since then, including the excellent food. Start with the classic appetizer of stuffed grape leaves, then move on to the taverna's forte–cooked dishes such as lamb yiouvetsi, livers with sweetbreads in vinegar and oregano, and tsoutsoukakia. In summer, tables move outside; year-round, roving musicians charm the crowd as they croon ballads of yesteryear. ✉ *Aggelou Geronda 4, Plaka (entrance down the walkway next to Glikis kafenion),* ☎ *01/322–1065. No credit cards. Closed weekends and part of July. No lunch.*

$ ✕ **Balkoni Tou Immitou.** This large, unpretentious place has a huge balcony on a hill, with panoramic views of the Saronic Gulf islands. It's known to few tourists, though the waiters speak some English. The extensive menu covers the standards, plus quail, partridge, and rabbit stew, and gardoumba, which tastes much better than it looks. ✉ *Pavlou Mela 13, Karea (take Bus 203 from Acadimias to Byzantio stop),* ☎ *01/764–0240. No credit cards. No lunch except holidays and Sun.*

$ ✕ **Karavitis.** In this neighborhood favorite near the Panathenaic Stadium,
★   the winter dining room is insulated with huge wine casks, and in summer there's garden seating; get there early so you don't end up at the noisy sidewalk tables. The classic Greek cuisine is well prepared, including pungent tzatziki, *bekri meze* (lamb chunks in spicy red sauce), and *stamnaki* (beef baked in a clay pot). ✉ *Arktinou 35 and Pausaniou 4, Pangrati,* ☎ *01/721–5155. No credit cards. Closed Greek Easter. No lunch.*

$ ✕ **O Platanos.** Set on a picturesque corner, this is one of the oldest tav-
★   ernas in Plaka, and it's a welcome sight compared with the many overpriced tourist traps in the area. It has a shady courtyard for outdoor dining. Don't miss the oven-baked potatoes, roasted lamb, and the exceptionally cheap but delicious barrel retsina. Although not much En-

glish is spoken, the staff is extremely friendly; you can always go back to the kitchen and point to what you want. ⊠ *Diogenous 4, Plaka,* ☎ *01/322–0666. No credit cards. Closed Sun.*

$ ✕ **Sigalas.** Run by the Bairaktaris family for more than a century, this
★ is the best place to eat in Monastiraki Square. After admiring the painted wine barrels and black-and-white snapshots of Greek film stars, go to the window case to view the day's *magirefta* (stove-top cooked dish, usually made earlier)—beef *kokkinisto* (stew with red sauce), tsoutsoukakia spiked with cloves—or sample the gyro platter. Appetizers include small cheese pies with sesame seeds, tender mountain greens, and fried zucchini with a garlicky dip. ⊠ *Monastiraki Sq. 2,* ☎ *01/321–3036. No credit cards.*

$ ✕ **Vasilenas.** Longtime residents and frequent visitors rejoice in this precious vestige of the good old days, a family-run taverna that is probably as good a bargain now as it was 60 years ago. The decor is minimal; in summer the operation moves to the upper terrace. Come here ravenously hungry with friends, so you can do justice to the set menu of 16 dishes, brought at a steady stream to your table. Zesty shrimp yiouvetsi and prawn croquettes are two standouts, as is the dessert called *tiganites* (a sort of fried bread filled with walnuts). ⊠ *Etolikou 72, Ayia Sophia, Piraeus,* ☎ *01/461–2457. Reservations essential for groups and on weekends. No credit cards. Closed Sun. and part of Aug. No lunch.*

LODGING

Athens has true luxury hotels and many in the budget range, but a shortage of middle-rank family-style hotels. Staying in a seaside suburb or in Piraeus is a good way to beat the heat and smog of the city center in summer, although the traveling time and expense are a deterrent.

Greek hotels are classified as Luxury (L) and A–E. Within each category, which is set by the government, quality varies greatly, but prices usually don't. Still, you may come across an A-class hotel that charges less than a B-class, depending on facilities. Some of the older hotels in Plaka and near Omonia are comfortable and clean, their charm inherent in their age. But along with charm may come leaking plumbing and sagging mattresses—take a good look at the room. The thick stone walls of neoclassical buildings keep them cool in the summer, but few of the budget hotels have central heating, and it can be devilishly cold in the winter, especially in the $$ and $$$ categories; also, don't assume all rooms have TVs. All hotels in the $$$$ and $$$ categories have air-conditioning; those in the lower-price categories that have air-conditioning are indicated. A buffet breakfast is often served, which includes cold cuts and cheese, even poached eggs and other meat, but nothing cooked to order. The cost is not included unless noted.

CATEGORY	COST*
$$$$	over 40,000 dr.
$$$	23,000 dr.–40,000 dr.
$$	15,000 dr.–23,000 dr.
$	under 15,000 dr.

All prices are for a standard double room, including tax and service, in high season.

Athens

$$$$ 🏨 **Andromeda Athens Hotel.** Athens's newest luxury hotel caters to business travelers with a mixture of deluxe rooms, studios, suites, and penthouses. The spacious rooms have a salmon color scheme with quilted headboards, wall-to-wall carpeting, and TV (computers and fax ma-

chines are available on request). The hotel is on a quiet street, and the bedrooms have double-glazed windows. The White Elephant Polynesian restaurant is one of the city's best. If you are Greek, please note that though you may not get first dibs on the rooms, the price drops by half. Also available is a limo service. ✉ *Timoleondos Vassou 22, Mavili Sq., near the U.S. Embassy, 11521,* ☎ *01/643–7302 through 01/643–7304,* FAX *01/646–6361. 30 rooms with bath, 4 suites and penthouses. 2 restaurants, minibars, business services, meeting rooms, airport shuttle. AE, DC, MC, V.*

$$$$ 🏨 **Athenaeum Inter-Continental.** One of Athens's most posh hotels, it has a marble atrium lobby with a central fountain, mirrored planters, and a private art collection. The rooms are very spacious, with sitting areas, marble bathrooms, and thick carpeting. A planned executive floor is under renovation. The Kublai Khan restaurant is known city-wide for its Far Eastern cuisine, including Mongolian barbecue. In the morning a shuttle takes guests to the airport, and then until 9:30 PM it travels hourly between the hotel and Constitution Square, 15 minutes away. ✉ *89–93 Syngrou Ave., near Neos Kosmos, 11745,* ☎ *01/902–3666,* FAX *01/924–3000. 520 rooms with bath, 38 suites. 3 restaurants, 2 bars, pool, health club, shops, business services, convention center, meeting rooms. AE, DC, MC, V.*

$$$$ 🏨 **Athens Hilton.** A 200-year-old olive tree with a Turkish cannonball lodged in its branches adds an earthy touch to the glamorous entrance, with its multilevel lobby of variegated marble. Opened in 1963, this is still one of the top hotels in the city, giving an impression of calm confidence amid the comings and goings of various conventions, banquets, and meetings. The spacious rooms have a subdued color scheme and carpeting; double-glazed windows and thick curtains buffer the street noise. The huge balconies face either the Acropolis or Mt. Hymettus. The executive floor has private check-in and check-out, a private lounge, and business facilities. The Byzantine Café serves a Sunday brunch, a rarity in Athenian restaurants. ✉ *Vasilissis Sofias 46, Hilton, 11528,* ☎ *01/725–0201 and 01/725–0301,* FAX *01/725–3110. 434 rooms with bath, 19 suites (3 with hot tubs). 3 restaurants, 2 bars, pool, massage, sauna, shops, business services, convention center, meeting rooms. AE, DC, MC, V.*

$$$$ 🏨 **Grande Bretagne.** Built in 1842, the GB is an Athens landmark, and
★ its guest list over the years has matched its colorful history. During World War II, it was headquarters of the Greek, German, and British forces, in turn, and when Churchill was visiting on Christmas Eve 1944, a plot to blow up the hotel from the sewers was foiled. The hotel's marble lobby is graced with antiques, plush sofas, Oriental rugs, tapestries, and ornate chandeliers. The most coveted rooms are the Syntagma rooms, with Acropolis views and huge balconies facing the square, but the ones overlooking the courtyard are quieter. Lounge areas on each floor have velvet couches, antiques, and etchings; the ceilings are so high that corridors seem like tall tunnels. Afternoon tea is served in the Winter Garden, and in the GB Corner (not particularly known for its food) you can sometimes catch a glimpse of politicians taking a break from Parliament. Continental breakfast is included in the rate. ✉ *Vasileos Georgiou A' 1, Syntagma Sq., 10563,* ☎ *01/331–4444,* FAX *01/322–8034. 341 rooms with bath, 23 suites. Restaurant, 2 bars, business services, meeting rooms. AE, DC, MC, V.*

$$$$ 🏨 **Holiday Inn.** This favorite among businesspeople was completely refurbished in 1996, and the lobby is quite striking, with a glass-enclosed shopping arcade, a coffee shop, and a monolithic sculpture in the center. The light, modern rooms now have voice mail, satellite TV, and video, as well as double-glazed windows; those on the fifth and sixth floors are quieter. The rooftop pool has a pleasant garden with a cozy

bar. ⊠ *Michalakopoulou 50, Ilisia, 11528,* ☎ *01/724–8322 through 8329,* FAX *01/724–8187. 190 rooms with bath, 4 suites. Restaurant, bar, pool, meeting rooms. AE, DC, MC, V.*

$$$$ 🏨 **Ledra Marriott.** The Ledra has earned a reputation as one of the most efficient and attractive hotels in this chain. The lobby piano bar sits below a spectacular 1,000-crystal chandelier; Kona Kai, the Polynesian restaurant, is excellent; and the Zephyros Café has a bountiful Sunday brunch. The rooftop pool has a view of the Acropolis that is breathtaking at sunset. The pastel rooms have vast closet space and armchairs, and some have views of the Acropolis. The Executive Level offers fax and secretarial services and a private dining area. Shuttles run hourly to and from Constitution Square. ⊠ *Syngrou 115, near Neos Kosmos 11745,* ☎ *01/934–7711,* FAX *01/935–8603. 258 rooms with bath, 1 presidential suite. 3 restaurants, 3 bars, pool, shops, business services, meeting rooms. AE, DC, MC, V.*

$$$$ 🏨 **St. George Lycabettus.** This hotel, in a great location on the wooded slopes of Mt. Lycabettus in upscale Kolonaki, has a splendid view. Getting there, however, involves a steep, short walk or a ride up (remember: taxis are inexpensive). There are sumptuous rooms and suites, and in late 1995 the hotel opened the decadent Maria Christina presidential suite, inaugurated by the Duchess of Kent. The hotel has an attractive ground-floor bistro and its trump card, Le Grand Balcon, a rooftop restaurant with good food and a panoramic view. Continental breakfast is included in the price. ⊠ *Kleomenous 2, Kolonaki, 10675,* ☎ *01/729–0711,* FAX *01/729–0439. 162 rooms with bath, 5 suites. 2 restaurants, bar, pool. AE, DC, MC, V.*

$$$ 🏨 **Athens Gate.** This hotel, now a Best Western, is a bargain, but many have complained about malfunctioning air-conditioners and noise. The lobby now has couches in muted hues, apricot rugs, and sleek glass-and-chrome tables. From the front rooms you see the Temple of Olympian Zeus, from the back rooms above the fifth floor, the Acropolis. Some rooms need refurbishment. The good buffet breakfast is included in the price, and the bar and restaurant on the breezy rooftop has a generous buffet table. There's also a roof garden. ⊠ *Syngrou 10, Syntagma, 11743,* ☎ *01/923–8302 through 8304,* FAX *01/923–7493. 104 rooms with bath. Restaurant, bar, minibars. AE, DC, MC, V.*

$$$ 🏨 **Electra Palace.** At the edge of Plaka, this hotel has cozy rooms done in warm hues, complete with balconies—for comparatively low prices. All rooms were recently renovated. Keep in mind that rooms from the fifth floor up are smaller but have larger balconies; the top floor has wonderful views facing either the Acropolis or Mt. Lycabettus. The staff is helpful, the American breakfast (included in the price) is abundant, and best of all, you can spend hours by the rooftop pool, sipping a cool drink and gazing at the Parthenon. ⊠ *Nikodimou 18, Plaka, 10557,* ☎ *01/324–1410,* FAX *01/324–1875. 101 rooms with bath, 5 suites. Restaurant, bar (summer), pool, meeting rooms. AE, DC, MC, V.*

$$$ 🏨 **Novotel Athenes.** Though not central, this hotel is just a 10-minute walk to the rail station and the National Archaeological Museum. One of the city's better values, it has an elegant lobby and tranquil rooms with sofas. The rooftop pool with Acropolis views is beside the hotel's Greek restaurant. ⊠ *M. Voda 4–8, Vathis Sq., 10439,* ☎ *01/825–0422,* FAX *01/883–7816. 190 rooms with bath, 5 suites. 2 restaurants, bar, minibars, pool. AE, DC, MC, V.*

$$ ★ 🏨 **Acropolis View.** This hotel in a quiet neighborhood below the Acropolis has a roof garden and pleasant rooms, half with Parthenon views. An American breakfast (cornflakes, eggs, ham, and cheese) is included in the price. The staff in the homey lobby is efficient and friendly, and major sights lie just a stone's throw away. ⊠ *Webster 10, Acropolis,*

11742, ☎ 01/921–7303 through 7305, ⨎ 01/923–0705. *32 rooms with bath. Bar, air-conditioning. AE, MC, V.*

$$ ⛫ **Astor.** A good choice for those who want to stay near Constitution Square, the Astor is convenient, with amenities, such as TVs, usually found at more expensive places. The rooms have modern furniture; request one above the fifth floor for a memorable view of the Acropolis, which may also be taken in from the roof garden where guests enjoy their (included) Continental breakfast. ⊠ *Karageorgi Servias 16, Syntagma, 10562,* ☎ *01/325–5111,* ⨎ *01/325–5115. 131 rooms with bath. Restaurant, bar, air-conditioning, room service. AE, DC, V.*

$$ ⛫ **Athenian Inn.** The best things about this hotel, with its flowering
★ plants, white stucco walls, dark beams, terra-cotta tile floors, and watercolors of Greek scenes, are its location in the heart of Kolonaki and that it is quiet. Opened more than 20 years ago, it has a loyal clientele of return visitors, so you must book well ahead. The lounge and breakfast room has an open fireplace, and Continental buffet breakfast is included in the price. Guest rooms have modern bathrooms, carpeting, radios, and traditional Greek spreads on the wood-frame beds; the upper rooms in front have balconies, some with a view of Mt. Lycabettus. The street has little traffic, but there's occasional loud conversation at the popular Ratka restaurant nearby. ⊠ *Haritos 22, Kolonaki, 10675,* ☎ *01/723–8097, 01/723–9552, or 01/721–8756,* ⨎ *01/724–2268. 28 rooms with bath. Bar, air-conditioning. AE, DC, V.*

$$ ⛫ **Austria.** This small, unpretentious hotel is on Filopappou Hill, opposite the Acropolis, ideal as a base for wandering around the heart of ancient Athens. It has no restaurant, but it is at the low end of the moderate category and is well worth considering. Continental breakfast (included in the price) is not mandatory; without it, deduct 700 dr. per person. ⊠ *Mouson 7, Filopappou, 11742,* ☎ *01/923–5151 or 01/922–0777,* ⨎ *01/924–7350. 37 rooms with bath. Breakfast room, air-conditioning. AE, DC, MC, V.*

$$ ⛫ **Lycabette.** This convenient hotel at the edge of Kolonaki has a gregarious atmosphere and pleasant service, but the "pedestrian" street is sometimes filled with motorbikes. The comfortable rooms all have balconies (those overlooking Acadimias are smaller), and about 10 now have TVs. The lobby is cheerful, and the optional Continental breakfast is served in a pretty breakfast room. ⊠ *Valaoritou 6, Syntagma, 10671,* ☎ *01/363–3514 through 3517,* ⨎ *01/363–3518. 39 rooms with bath. Restaurant-cafeteria, tea shop, air-conditioning. AE, DC, MC, V.*

$$ ⛫ **Plaka Hotel.** Close to many sights and the Monastiraki Square metro, this hotel has a roof garden with a view to the Parthenon. Double-glazed windows cut down the noise; the highest floors are the quietest. All rooms have TV and are simply furnished; those in back from the fifth floor up have the best Acropolis views. ⊠ *Kapnikareas 7, Plaka, 10556,* ☎ *01/322–2096 through 2098,* ⨎ *01/322–2412. 67 rooms with bath. Air-conditioning. AE, DC, MC, V.*

$$ ⛫ **President.** Perhaps the most inexpensive A-class hotel in Athens, the President is a favorite of athletic teams and tourist groups. The staff is professional; the rooms, though unexceptional, are quiet and have city views (the Acropolis is visible from the sixth floor up), and there's a rooftop pool in summer. Continental breakfast is included in the price. Taxis stop often at the hotel, and there are trolley and bus stops nearby for the 20-minute journey to Constitution Square. ⊠ *Kifissias 43, Ambelokipi, 11523,* ☎ *01/692–4600,* ⨎ *01/692–4968. 513 rooms with bath. Restaurant, piano bar, air-conditioning, pool (summer), meeting rooms. AE, DC, MC, V.*

$ ⛫ **Acropolis House.** This landmark family-run villa on the edge of Plaka is frequented by visiting students and faculty. Check out the belle époque accents—such as the painting behind the reception desk. The rooms are clean, usually with new spreads and curtains. It may be somewhat cluttered, and the wallpaper decrepit, but this makes it all the more endearing—and the friendly atmosphere more than compensates. ⊠ *Kodrou 6–8, Plaka, 10558,* ☎ *01/322–2344 or 01/322–6241,* FAX *01/324–4143. 23 rooms, 20 with bath. V.*

$ ⊞ **Aphrodite Hotel.** This hotel near Syntagma is an excellent value, and it includes a buffet breakfast. Rooms are quiet and tidy, with spare furnishings and all the amenities of more costly hotels; the staff's even helpful. Don't be put off by its cold-looking entrance: the gleaming white marble lobby ends with a bar where guests relax in the evenings. ⊠ *Apollonos 21, Syntagma, 10557,* ☎ *01/323–4357 through 4359,* FAX *01/322–5244. 84 rooms. Bar, air-conditioning. AE, DC, MC, V.*

$ ⊞ **Art Gallery Pension.** On a quiet side street near the Acropolis, this
★ friendly place, much prized by visiting students and single travelers, draws a congenial crowd. The handsome house has an old-fashioned look, with family paintings on the muted white walls, earth-tone spreads on the comfortable beds, hardwood floors, and overhead fans. Many rooms have balconies with views of the Acropolis. ⊠ *Erechthiou 5, Koukaki, 11742,* ☎ *01/923–8376 or 01/923–1933,* FAX *01/923–3025. 21 rooms with bath, 2 suites. Bar. No credit cards. Closed Nov.–Feb.*

$ ⊞ **Attalos Hotel.** The market area, where you'll find the Attalos, is full of life and color by day, but deserted at night. The pleasant hotel is well run by its friendly owner, Kostas Zisis, who goes out of his way for guests. The rooms are large; many have an exceptionally fine view of the Acropolis and Mt. Lycabettus. Try to get one on the fifth or sixth floor and in the rear, where the street noise is reduced, though the double-glazed windows and air-conditioning usually deaden the noise. ⊠ *Athinas 29, Monastiraki, 10554,* ☎ *01/321–2801 through 2803,* FAX *01/324–3124. 80 rooms with bath. Bar, air-conditioning. V.*

$ ⊞ **Erechtheon.** This fairly quiet hotel off busy Apostolou Pavlou is convenient to ancient Athens and perfect for partaking in the area's lively nightlife. The rooms are air-conditioned, most have balconies, and all doubles have a view of the Acropolis. If you like, breakfast can be served in your room. ⊠ *Flamarion 8, Thission, 11851,* ☎ *01/345–9606 or 01/345–9626,* FAX *01/346–2756. 22 rooms with bath. Breakfast room, air-conditioning. AE, MC, V.*

$ ⊞ **Marble House.** This popular pension, in a cul-de-sac about a 15-minute walk from the Acropolis, has a steady, satisfied clientele—even in winter, when it offers low monthly and weekly rates. Rooms are clean and quiet, with ceiling fans and basic furniture. The international staff is always willing to help out, and the courtyard is a fine place to relax. Take Trolleys 1, 5, or 9 from Syntagma and get off at the Zinni stop. ⊠ *A. Zinni 35, Koukaki, 11741,* ☎ *01/923–4058 or 01/922–6461. 16 rooms, 11 with bath. Breakfast room. No credit cards.*

$ ⊞ **Orion and Dryades.** These two hotels in a residential area across from the park on craggy Lofos Strefis are often booked by local fashion agencies, who house their models there. Orion is the humbler, with smaller rooms and shared baths between two rooms; its third-floor roof garden serves as the breakfast area for both hotels. Each hotel has a kitchen guests may use, and most rooms have balconies. For those who don't want to go far for dinner, the park has several inexpensive ouzeris open in summer. The atmosphere is congenial, the help very friendly, and the hotels attract a young, lively crowd. ⊠ *Emmanuel Benaki 105, Lofos Strefi, 11473,* ☎ *01/330–2387, 01/330–2388, 01/382–0191, 01/382–7116, and 01/382–7362,* FAX *01/380–5193. Orion: 20 rooms share bath. Dryades: 15 rooms with bath. No credit cards.*

$ ⊞ **XEN (YWCA).** This centrally located budget (7,000 dr. and under) choice for women (and occasionally their young children) has rooms with a communal bathroom, although three doubles and one single have private baths. The marble floors have rugs in winter; sheets and blankets are provided. The rooms are not air-conditioned, but those at the back are cooler and quieter. Some meals are available in the cafeteria. ✉ *Amerikis 11, Syntagma, 10672,* ☎ *01/362–4291 through 4293,* FAX *01/362–2400. 26 rooms share bath, 4 with bath. Cafeteria, laundry facilities. No credit cards.*

Piraeus

$$ 🏨 **Castella Hotel.** Beautifully located on the hill above Mikrolimano, the rooms here are fairly large and pleasant, with TVs; some rooms on high levels have a sea view. The spacious roof garden is landscaped with flowering plants and has a splendid view of Mikrolimano and the yacht club. ✉ *Vassileos Pavlos 75, Kastella, 18533,* ☎ *01/411–4735,* FAX *01/417–5716. 32 rooms with bath. Restaurant, bar, air-conditioning. AE, DC, MC, V.*

$$ 🏨 **Mistral Hotel.** This pleasant Piraeus hotel is quite suitable for fami-
★ lies. The rooms are attractive, and many have balconies. The price includes Continental buffet breakfast. The furniture is modern wood, and there are marble-top tables, blue spreads and curtains, and tile floors. A pool is expected to be completed eventually, which is anybody's guess in Greece. ✉ *Vassileos Pavlos 105, Kastella, 18533,* ☎ *01/412–1425, 01/412–6589, 01/411–5887;* FAX *01/412–2096. 74 rooms with bath. Restaurant, bar, cafeteria, air-conditioning, meeting room. AE, MC, V.*

$$ 🏨 **Scorpios.** The view of the Makra Teixoi is the draw at this little hotel in Piraiki, not far from Zea Marina. At the low end of the moderate range, the rooms are small but attractive, with fans, wood furniture, and brown decor; the balconies in front have fine views of the harbor and ancient walls. The lounge and living room are cooled by a fresh sea breeze and overlook Mikrolimano and the Saronic Gulf. ✉ *Akti Themistokleous 156, Piraiki, 18539,* ☎ *01/451–2172,* FAX *01/452–4751. 24 rooms with bath. Breakfast room. AE, MC, V.*

NIGHTLIFE AND THE ARTS

The weekly magazines *Athenscope* (in English), *DownTown,* and *Athinorama* (both in Greek) cover current performances, gallery openings, and films, as do the English-language newspapers, *Hellenic Times,* a weekly, and *Athens News,* a daily.

Nightlife

Bars

Bars are the staple of Greek nightlife, with new establishments opening every week. In summer, many of the most popular spots, especially dance clubs, move to the coastal road; check with your hotel first. Most bars stay open until 3 AM, although the government keeps trying to shut them down earlier. Drinks are rather steep (from 1,700–2,000 dr.) and often there is a surcharge on weekend nights. Imbibing too much, especially by women, is frowned upon. Most clubs and bars do not take credit cards for drinks.

According to Greeks, to avoid a hangover go to **To Monastiri,** a taverna in the central meat market on Athinas (☎ 01/324–0773 or 01/324–0693), for *patsas* (a murky tripe soup), which is said to be infallible.

Art Café (✉ Vassileos Pavlou 61, Kastella, ☎ 01/413–7896) is a bar-restaurant in a restored old Piraeus mansion, with high ceilings, low lighting, art objects, and traditional furniture. The music is eclectic, the food—maybe shrimp with lemon and capers or chicken in orange sauce—is good, and the view of Mikrolimano from the window seats is lovely.

Balthazar (⊠ Tsoha 27, Ambelokipi, ☎ 01/644–1215 or 01/645–2278) is a bar-restaurant in a neoclassical house, with a lush garden courtyard where Athenians of all ages come to escape the summer heat.

One of the best-natured, easygoing bars where clubgoers are not too cool to have fun is **Folie** (⊠ Eslin 4, Ambelokipi, ☎ 01/646–9852), which plays reggae on Monday, Brazilian on Wednesday, and hip-hop on Thursday. When it's packed, people go next door to the **Folie Cafe** to wait for the crowd to subside.

Few Athenians don't know the **Green Door** (⊠ Kallidromiou 52, Exarchia, ☎ 01/383–9159), a transformed two-story home in the student neighborhood of Exarchia. Summers you can sit on the veranda tables; the rest of the year, most of the dedicated clientele cram into the dark wood-and-stone interior to listen to predominantly rock music.

To enjoy Greek *kefi* (high spirits) without the formalities of a big bouzouki club, visit **Karpouzi** (⊠ Politechniou and 34ou Syntagmatos, Piraeus, ☎ 01/412–6074), especially on a Sunday afternoon, when DJs spin Greek music and the audience inevitably dances on the tabletops.

Of the many new bars for the under-40 crowd, **Lobby** (⊠ Ermou 110 and Avliton 6–8, Psirri, ☎ 01/323–6975) is visually the most interesting, an ode to kitsch, with rooms dedicated to modern figures (Mickey Mouse, Andy Warhol, Madonna, Philippe Starck, etc.) and decorated as a boardroom, classroom, and a bedroom (complete with bed and fake-fur pillows). There are several dance floors featuring Greek, trance, mainstream, and happy-house music.

Gregarious **Memphis Booze** (⊠ Ventiri 5, Ilisia, behind the Hilton, ☎ 01/722–4104) is an Athens classic, where the good-natured crowds listen to rock, jazz, blues, and occasional live music.

On the bar scene for more than a decade, **No Name** (⊠ Orminiou 6, Ilisia, ☎ 01/722–2941) continues to be popular for its generous bartenders, eclectic music (funk, rock, and some modern), and lively revelers.

Relaxed, with low-key music, and set in the park next to the American Embassy, **Parko** (⊠ Eleftherias Park, Ilisia, ☎ 01/722–3784) is a favorite among couples, journalists, and artists who come to get away from the city's bustle and heat.

All ages will feel comfortable at **Stavlos** (⊠ Irakleidon 10, Thission, ☎ 01/345–2502 and 01/346–7206), in what used to be the Royal Stables. Sit in the courtyard or the brick-walled restaurant for a snack like Cretan *kaltsounia* (like a calzone) or dance in the long bar, which usually features rock and soul. Stavlos often hosts art exhibits, film screenings, live jazz, and other "happenings," as the Greeks call them, on Sunday.

Strofilia (⊠ Karitsi Sq. 7, ☎ 01/323–4803), one of Athens's few wine bars, is a comfortable hangout, with more than 50 Greek wines to sip, many from small producers; about 20 are offered by the glass. It closes May through August.

Bouzoukia

Many tourists think Greek social life centers around large clubs where live bouzouki music is played and patrons get their kicks by smashing up the plates. This practice, called *spasta*, is now prohibited. A few clubs provide specially made light plates that are harmless when smashed. More often flowers are sold for showering your companions when they take to the dance floor. An upscale form of bouzoukia is found near the airport, where top entertainers deservedly command top prices. Be aware that the food tends to be overpriced and often second rate. There is a per person minimum or a prix-fixe menu; a bottle of whiskey costs about 27,000 dr., a drink, 3,000 dr.

Currently the "in" place with Athenians who want to hear Greece's most famous singers, such as Iannis Parios and Katerina Kouka, is **Diogenis Palace** (⊠ Syngrou 259, Nea Smyrni, ☎ 01/942–4267 and 01/941–7602). Decadence reigns at **Posidonio** (⊠ Posidonios 18, Elliniko, ☎ 01/894–1033), where Greeks dance the seductive tsifteteli with enthusiasm and order flower vendors to shower gardenias on their favorite singers.

Dance Clubs

Dance clubs come and go every year, and most move around town, depending on the season. Currently popular among young Athenians, who swarm the dance floors for everything from house to Greek pop tunes, are **Amfiteatro** (⊠ Vasileos Georgiou B' 58, Alimos, ☎ 01/894–4538), **Theatro** (⊠ Leoforos Posidonios, Palio Faliro, ☎ 01/983–6298), and **Up 'N High–Aerodromio** (⊠ Pergamou 25, Glyfada, ☎ 01/965–0879).

The crowd at **Wild Rose** (⊠ Panepistimiou 10 in the arcade, Syntagma, ☎ 01/364–2160 and 01/363–3087, ⊠ Kiprou 64, Glyfada, ⊠ 01/894–7085 in summer) is older, and studded with celebrities and Beautiful People. The music is eclectic (rock, soul, rave, and "future sound").

Jazz Clubs

Do not expect a flourishing jazz scene in Greece, as the expense of importing foreign entertainment outweighs the interest. Tickets to the limited shows can be purchased at the venues or major record stores.

Known as the venue for noteworthy groups, especially European ones, is the casual **Half Note** (⊠ Trivonianou 17, Mets, ☎ 01/923–2460 or 01/921–3310); this is the place for serious jazz fans. **Parafono** (⊠ Asklippiou 130, Exarchia, ☎ 01/644–6512) has live jazz and blues nightly. Occasionally in winter big-name jazz groups appear at **Pallas** (⊠ Voukourestiou 1, Syntagma, ☎ 01/323–4434). The smaller, informal **Rodon** (⊠ Marni 24, Vathis Sq. near the Archaeological Museum, ☎ 01/524–7427) also attracts some important gigs come winter.

Live-Music Bars

A small bar with few tables, **Cafe Asante** (⊠ Damareos 78, Pangrati, ☎ 01/726–01021) hosts ethnic music groups (Afro-Cuban, Indian, Peruvian); be sure to order potent *rakomelo* (raki with honey). Named after an important Mayan city, with decor to match, **Palenque Club** (⊠ Farantaton 41, Ambelokipi, ☎ 01/748–7548 and 01/771—8090) also features musicians from around the world (Peru, Brazil, even some Greek groups) several times a week. Rock fans should check the listings for **Rodon** (⊠ Marni 24, Vathis Sq., ☎ 01/524–7427); blue jeans and anything black are the usual attire. For a less energetic evening, try **Cafe Parastasi** (⊠ Valtetsiou 15 and Ippokratous, Exarchia, ☎ 01/645–0166), which often organizes musical evenings, usually acoustic, along with poetry readings.

Plaka Tavernas with Music

Klimataria (⊠ Klepsidras 5, ☎ 01/324–1809), an authentic century-old taverna with music, is in an old house without a roof. It features a guitarist and an accordion player who play sing-along favorites much appreciated by the largely Greek audience. This slice of old-style Greek entertainment is surprisingly reasonable.

Palea Taverna Kritikou (⊠ Mnisikleous 24, ☎ 01/322–2809) specializes in distinctive Cretan music featuring the *lyra* (a bowed instrument) and a spirited dance group wearing authentic costumes. This is a good way to see regional dancing.

Yeros tou Morea (✉ Mnisikleous 27, ☎ 01/322–1753), a vine-draped outdoor club that has stood for almost 150 years at the top of a steep pedestrian street, features pleasant popular Greek music (guitar, bouzouki, and accordion) and satisfactory food.

Stamatopoulou Palia Plakiotiki Taverna (✉ Lysiou 26, ☎ 01/322–8722) is in a converted 1822 Plaka house and is where you'll find good food and an acoustic band of three guitars and bouzouki playing old Athenian songs. In summer the show moves to a cool garden. Greeks will often get up and dance, beckoning you to join them, so don't be shy.

Rembetika Clubs

Rembetika, the blues sung by Asia Minor refugees who came to Greece in the 1920s, still enraptures clubgoers. At these thriving clubs, you can catch a glimpse of Greek social life and even join the dances (but remember, it is considered extremely rude to interrupt a solo dance). Most of the clubs are closed in the summer, so call in advance. They have reasonable prices for an evening of live entertainment, but the food is often expensive and unexceptional; it's wise to order a fruit platter or a bottle of wine.

Anifori (✉ Vasileos Georgiou A' 47, Piraeus, ☎ 01/411–5819) is a friendly club popular with young people that plays both rembetika and *dimotika* (Greek folk music). It is closed Monday through Thursday.

Douzeni (✉ Makriyianni 8, Makriyianni, ☎ 01/922–7597 and 01/921–9427) features Bobis Goles, a grave-voiced entertainer who's one of the best of the bouzouki players; it's closed Sunday.

Ennea Ogdoa (✉ Leoforos Alexandras 40, Pedion Areos, ☎ 01/823–5841 and 01/882–1095) usually plays Greek popular music but occasionally features the "forbidden" rembetika, in which lyrics refer to hashish, popular with the original rembetes. The band starts off slowly, but by 1 AM, they're wailing to a packed dance floor. The club is closed Sunday.

Frankosyriani (✉ Arachovis 57, Exarchia, ☎ 01/380–0693) is run by dedicated musician Nikos Argyropoulos, with a group specializing in the songs of Markos Vamvakaris, a rembetika great. Doors are shut on Tuesday and Wednesday.

Stoa Athanaton (✉ Sofokleous 19, Central Market, ☎ 01/321–4362), in a renovated warehouse right in the Central Market, is a joy. The authentic music is enhanced by an infectious, devil-may-care mood and the enthusiastic participation of the audience. The small dance floor is jammed; the food is delicious and reasonable, but liquor is expensive. Reservations are essential for evenings; the club is closed Sunday.

The Arts

Athens Festival and Other Shows

The city's primary artistic event, the **Athens Festival,** in Herod Atticus from June through September, draws performers such as Pavarotti and Diana Ross; such dance troupes as the Royal London Ballet and Maurice Béjart; symphony orchestras; and local groups doing ancient Greek drama. It is a delightful setting, the Roman arches a stunning backdrop for the performers, but the upper-level seats have no cushions, so bring one, along with a light wrap. Tickets sell out quickly for popular shows; they are available from the **Festival box office** (✉ In the arcade at Stadiou 4, ☎ 01/322–1459). Prices vary from about 2,000 dr. to as high as 20,000 dr. for the big names.

Other Festival events are held at the more intimate **Lycabettus Theater** (✉ At the top of Mt. Lycabettus, ☎ Athens Festival: 01/322–1459, ☎ Box office: 01/722–7233), set on a pinnacle of Mt. Lycabettus, with wooden bleachers and a glorious view. The specialty here is popular concerts, with such performers as B.B. King, Bob Dylan, and Paco de Lucia. Bus 23 gets you only to the bottom of the hill, and taxi drivers often won't drive to the top. Buy a one-way ticket on the funicular and walk about 10 minutes to the theater.

Every evening from April through October, **Sound and Light Spectacles** casts dramatic lighting upon the Acropolis along with a brief recorded history. The English-language version is at 9 PM. Seating is on the **Pnyx hill** opposite the Acropolis, a great place to view the sunset before the show. Tickets are sold at the **box office of the Pnyx** (⊠ West of the Acropolis, Dionyssiou Areopagitou, ☎ 01/922–6210) before shows; tickets cost 1,200 dr. and the box office opens at 8:20 PM.

The **Dora Stratou Group,** a young, spirited dance troupe, is well worth seeing. They perform a fine selection of **Greek folk dances** from all regions, as well as from Cyprus, in eye-catching authentic costumes. Performances are held daily from mid-May through mid-September at 10:15 PM; Wednesday and Sunday there are additional shows at 8:15 PM at the **Filopappou Theater** (⊠ Arakinthou and Voutie, near the Pnyx, ☎ Office: 01/324–4395, FAX 01/324–6921; ☎ Theater: 01/921–4650). Tickets range from 2,500 to 3,000 dr. and can be purchased at the box office before the show.

Concerts and Operas

Concerts and operas are given September through June at the Megaron by Greek and world-class international orchestras. Information and tickets are available from the **Megaron Athens Concert Hall** (⊠ Vasilissis Sofias and Kokkali, ☎ 01/728–2333), next to the U.S. Embassy. Prices range from 2,500 dr. to 20,000 dr. Tickets go on sale a few weeks in advance but many events sell out within hours. On the first day of sales, tickets can be purchased by cash or credit card only in person at the Megaron; sales begin at 8 AM, but try to arrive an hour before. From the second day on, remaining tickets may be purchased by phone or in person from the **Megaron's downtown box office** (⊠ In the arcade at Stadiou 4).

Film

Films are shown in original-language versions with subtitles (except for major animated films), a definite boon for foreigners. Check the *Athenscope* or the *Athens News* for programs, schedules, and addresses and phone numbers of theaters (including those of the Hellenic-American Union and the British Council, which both screen films free).

Best bets are the **downtown theaters,** mostly near Syntagma, which have the best equipment and most comfortable seats. Try **Astor** (⊠ Stadiou 28, ☎ 01/323–1297); **Apollon Renault** (⊠ Stadiou 19, ☎ 01/323–6811); **Attikon Renault** (⊠ Stadiou 19, ☎ 01/322–8221); and **Ideal** (⊠ Panepistimiou 46, near Omonia Sq., ☎ 01/362–6720).

Unless theaters have air-conditioning, most close from June–September, giving way to *therina* (outdoor cinemas), a charming, uniquely Greek entertainment that supposedly ranks second to the Acropolis as an Athens attraction. About 40 therina operate in vine-covered empty lots and on rooftops with customers sitting on lawn chairs, or in traditional theaters with roofs or walls that open. A disadvantage is the mandatory low sound level at the second screening, so audiences have to resort to lip reading, especially a drag at comedies, when the laughter drowns out the lines. Screenings are listed in English in the *Athenscope, Greek Times,* and *Athens News.* Some of the best theaters include: **Cine Paris** (⊠ Kidathineon 22, Plaka, ☎ 01/322–2071); **Thisio** (⊠ Apostolou Pavlou 7, ☎ 01/342–0864); **Athinaia** (⊠ Haritos 50, Kolonaki, ☎ 01/721–5717), which has good toasted sandwiches and imported beer; **Vox** (⊠ Exarchia Sq., ☎ 01/330–1020); **Amaryllis** (⊠ Ayios Ioannou 2, Ayia

Paraskevi, ☎ 01/639–6315), which serves mezes at little tables; and **Zephyros** (✉ Troon 36, Thission, ☎ 01/346–2677), known for its art films.

Galleries

A pleasant way to get a feel for contemporary Athenian life and get acquainted with leading figures on the arts scenes (ideally through conversation) is to attend the opening nights of exhibits. Many of the galleries close in July and August. Information in English about shows and opening dates appears in *The Athenian*, the *Greek Times*, and the *Athens News*.

Galleries that hang the more interesting work include **Epoches** (✉ Kifissias 263, Kifissia, ☎ 01/808–3645); **Gallery 7** (✉ Zalakosta 7, ☎ 01/361–2050); **Ileana Tounda** (✉ Armatolon and Klefton 48, ☎ 01/643–9466); **Nees Morphes** (✉ Valaoritou 9, ☎ 01/361–6165); **Rebecca Camkhi** (✉ Sofokleous 23, ☎ 01/321–0448); **Zoumboulakis** (✉ Kolonaki Sq., 20, ☎ 01/360–8278); and **Zygos** (✉ Vasilissis Sofias 65, ☎ 01/722–9272).

OUTDOOR ACTIVITIES AND SPORTS

Beaches and Beach Volleyball

Volleyball games open to the public begin in July at Palio Faliro, Skinies, and Palaia Fokaia beaches.

The beaches at **Palio Faliro** and **Piraeus** have signs to warn you of the high levels of pollution. Believe them. The **Greek National Tourist Organization** (GNTO or EOT; ☞ Visitor Information *in* Athens A to Z, *below*) can give you a list of their beaches, which have snack bars and beach umbrellas, chairs, dressing rooms, and sports equipment for rent, and occasionally windsurfing and waterskiing lessons.

The main **beaches close to Athens** are found at the shoreline in the regions by the same name: Alimos (☎ 01/982–7064); **Porto Rafti** (☎ 0299/72572); **Voula** (1st beach: ☎ 01/895–1646; 2nd beach: ☎ 01/895–9569); **Vouliagmeni** (☎ 01/896–0906); and **Varkiza** (☎ 01/897–2102). Vouliagmeni Lake (☎ 01/896–2351 and 01/896–0341), whose spring-fed waters are reputed to have curative powers, is popular with older Greeks. A number of nice tavernas line the sandy shoreline.

Golf

Glyfada Golf Course (✉ Glyfada, ☎ 01/894–6820) has 18 holes, locker rooms, a restaurant, and a bar, all open to the public.

Health Clubs

Health clubs abound these days, and you'll have little problem finding one near your hotel. The Athens Hilton, Inter-Continental, and Caravel hotels have excellent facilities with saunas and pools that can be used by the general public for a fee.

Hiking and Mountain Biking

The **Greek Federation of Mountaineering Associations** (✉ Milioni 5, Kolonaki, ☎ 01/364–5904) supplies details on mountain paths and refuges and has contact numbers for local hiking groups. One local hiking group to try is **Alpine Club of Aharnon** (✉ Filadelfias 126, Aharnes, ☎ 01/246–1528). The **Alpine Club of Athens** (✉ Kapnikareas Sq. 2, Center, ☎ 01/321–2355 and 01/321–2429) arranges hikes throughout the month, as well as adventure camps for children in summer.

Trips in and around Athens are often offered by specialist travel agencies. Try **Trekking Hellas** (✉ Fillelinon 7, Syntagma, 10577, ☎ 01/325–0317 or 01/325–0853) for trips. **Ev Zin** (✉ Syngrou 132, near Olympic Airways office, ☎ 01/923–0263 and 01/921–6285) offers trips and also organizes kayaking, rafting, mountain biking, and camping trips for youngsters.

Horse Racing

Racing is held at the **Syngrou–Delta Faliro** racetrack in Tsitsifies Monday, Wednesday, and Friday 4–8:30.

Horseback Riding

Most riding centers are closed on Monday; be sure to call ahead of time to make arrangements. The helpful **Greek Equestrian Federation** (✉ Messinias 55, Agia Paraskevi, ☎ 01/652–8139) can assist you in locating the closest riding club.

Try the **Athletic Riding Club of Ekali** (✉ Irakliou 6, Anoixi, Ekali, ☎ 01/813–5773 and 01/622–9773); **Hellenic Riding Club** (✉ Paradissou 18, Paradissos Amaroussiou, ☎ 01/681–2506); or the **Riding Club of Parnitha** (✉ Parnitha, ☎ 01/246–5559).

Parachuting and Hang Gliding

The oldest parachuting school in Athens, **Ikarus Aero Centre** (✉ Theofrastou 3, Pangrati, ☎ 01/701–8330 and 01/701–7014), has been urging people to make the jump since 1983. They also run package hang-gliding vacations about 65 km (42 mi) north of Athens in Plateas Boeitias (☎ 0262/97498).

Rafting and Kayaking

Alpine Club (✉ Michalakopoulou 39, Ilisia, ☎ 01/721–2773) organizes trips—including transportation, guides, and equipment—to nearby rivers and will make special arrangements for groups.

Sailing and Windsurfing

The **Greek Sailing Federation** (✉ Leoforos Posidonios, 51, Moschato, ☎ 01/930–4826 and 01/930–4822) can recommend clubs and places to windsurf, sail, and take lessons.

Many sailing clubs in the area give lessons and information. **Vouliagmenis Sailing Club** (✉ Laimos Vouliagmenis, ☎ 01/896–2142) sails out of Vouliagmenis Bay, 20 km (12½ mi) south out of Athens. **Piraeus Sailing Club** (✉ Mikrolimano, ☎ 01/417–7636) provides lessons. For children's sailing lessons only, contact **Alimos Sailing Club** (✉ Loutra Alimou, off Leoforos Poseidonos, ☎ 01/983–8358). Sailing and windsurfing lessons, plus equipment, are available at the **Varkiza Sailing Club** (✉ Leoforos Poseidonos in Vari Bay, ☎ 01/897–4305).

Scuba Diving

Scuba diving is heavily restricted, to protect underwater artifacts. A travel agent can direct you to a supervised diving trip, or you can call the **Greek Diving Center** (✉ Vassileos Pavlou 26, Kastella, ☎ 01/412–1708), which offers lessons up to the instructor's level, rents equipment, and organizes one- to two-day diving excursions on weekends. For those who want an introduction to the sport, **Scuba Diving Club of Vouliagmeni** (✉ Leoforos Poseidonos behind Albatross candy shop, Ormos Vouliagmeni, ☎ 01/696–4609) runs a one-day orientation called Discover Scuba, where you learn basic theory and then dive with an instructor. The 18-year-old center, which is one of the few directly on the sea (visitors can just show up with a towel), also offers regular diving courses, equipment, boat rentals with guides for expeditions, and water sports. Call a few days ahead for reservations.

Skiing

The **Greek Ski Federation** (✉ Karageorgis Servias 7, 8th Floor, Syntagma, ☎ 01/323–0182) can give you a bilingual brochure with addresses for other ski centers as well as mountain refuges.

Ski Centre Parnassos (☎ 0234/22–689, 0234/22–693, and 0234/22–694) is reputedly the best resort close to Athens (about a 3-hour drive).

Tennis

The **Hellenic Tennis Federation** (✉ Olympic Stadium offices, Kalogreza, ☎ 01/685–2511 and 01/685–2512) can give you information on the nearest tennis clubs that rent courts by the hour; several are near the EOT beaches.

SHOPPING

The main shopping districts are in the area bounded by Syntagma, Monastiraki, Omonia, and Kolonaki. One of the main hurdles is figuring out when shops in Athens are open—there always seems to be some bill in parliament to change the hours. In general, stores are open Monday, Wednesday, and Saturday 9–3, Tuesday, Thursday, and Friday 9–2 and 5:30–8. In summer they often stay open until 8:30 or 9.

The **souvenir shops** in Plaka are usually open from early morning until the last tourist leaves. *Periptera,* the Greek version of a convenience store, are set up by the government to provide employment for veterans. Many of them have public phones, some metered for long-distance calls. Those in central squares are often open until very late, and occasionally are open around the clock.

The **flea market** centered on Pandrossou and Ifestou in Monastiraki operates on Sunday mornings and has practically everything, from secondhand guitars to Russian vodka (☞ Ancient Agora, Monastiraki, and Thission *in* Exploring Athens, *above*). **Ifestou,** where coppersmiths have their shops, is more interesting on a weekday—and you can pick up copper wine jugs, candlesticks, cookware, and more for next to nothing.

Antiques and Icons

Antiques and older wares are in vogue now, so these items have naturally soared in price. Shops on Pandrossou sell small antiques and icons, but keep in mind that many of these are fakes, and you must have government permission to export genuine objects from the Greek, Roman, or Byzantine periods.

The **Benaki Museum gift shop** (✉ Koumbari and Vasilissis Sofias, Kolonaki, ☎ 01/362–7367) has excellent copies of Greek icons at fair prices.

Martinos (✉ Pandrossou 50, Monastiraki, ☎ 01/321–2414 and 01/321–3110) should be the destination for serious antiques collectors.

Motakis (✉ Abyssinia Sq. 3, in the basement, Monastiraki, ☎ 01/321–9005), run by the same family for more than 90 years, is a *palaiopolio* (junk dealer), and it sells antiques, beautiful old objects, or that fabulous old trident you simply cannot live without.

At **Nasiotis** (✉ Ifestou 24, Monastiraki, ☎ 01/321–2369), with a little perseverance, you can make some interesting finds in this huge basement stacked with books: engravings, old magazines, first editions.

Clothing

Greece is known for its well-made shoes (✉ most shops are around Ermou and in Kolonaki), its furs (✉ Mitropoleos near Syntagma), and its durable leather items (✉ Pandrossou in Monastiraki). Fishermen's caps—always a good present—have now surfaced at high prices across the United States (triple the Athens price), as have the natural wool undershirts and hand-knit sweaters worn by fishermen; all can be found in many Plaka shops.

Stavros Melissinos (✉ Pandrossou 89, Monastiraki, ☎ 01/321–9247), a legendary poet and gentle soul, sends many tourists packing with his handmade sandals. The Beatles once visited his shop. He also makes handsome boots.

Voula Mitsakou (✉ Mitropoleos 7, Syntagma, ☎ 01/322–8561) is the best place to shop for furs near Syntagma. "Politically correct" is an unknown phrase in Greece, and although business has been affected by the anti-fur campaign, Mitropoleos is lined with shops selling everything from pieced-together stoles to full-length minks, often from the northern city of Kastoria.

Coins and Stamps

Check out **Pylarinos** (✉ Stadiou 6, Syntagma, ☎ 01/321–0577) for an eclectic coin and stamp collection.

Gold Coin Jewelry (✉ Stadiou 17, Syntagma, ☎ 01/322–9004) is known for its decorative copies of ancient Greek coins.

Gifts

Athens has great gifts, particularly handmade crafts. Better tourist shops sell copies of traditional Greek jewelry, silver filigree, enamel, Skyrian pottery, onyx ashtrays and dishes, woven bags, attractive rugs (including flokati, or shaggy goat wool rugs, often brightly colored), and little blue-and-white pendants designed as amulets to ward off the *mati* (evil eye).

An inexpensive but unusual gift is a string of *koboloi* (worry beads) in plastic, wood, or stone. You can pick them up very cheaply in Monastiraki or look in antiques shops for more expensive versions, with amber or black onyx beads. Reasonably priced natural sponges from Kalymnos also make good presents. Look for those that are unbleached, since the lighter ones tend to fall apart quickly. They're usually sold in front of the National Bank on Syntagma and in Plaka souvenir shops. The price is set by the government, so don't bother to bargain.

George Goutis (✉ Pandrossou 40, Monastiraki, ☎ 01/321–3212 and 01/321–3044) is one of the more interesting stores on Pandrossou; it has a satisfying assortment of jewelry, costumes, embroidery, and Karaghiozi shadow puppets.

At **Riza** (✉ Voukourestiou 35 and Skoufa, Kolonaki, ☎ 01/361–1157 and 01/360–0704) you can pick up wonderful lace in romantic designs, often handmade. The shop also carries unusual material at good prices, and decorative items like handblown glass bowls and brass candlesticks.

Mati (✉ Voukourestiou 20, Syntagma, ☎ 01/362–6238) has finely designed amulets, for protection against the evil eye, and an unusual collection of monastery lamps and candlesticks make excellent gifts.

Karamichos Mazaraki (✉ Voulis 31–33, Syntagma, ☎ 01/323–9428) offers a large selection of flokatis and will insure your purchases and mail them to your home.

At **Panigiri** (✉ Kleomenous 23–25, Kolonaki, ☎ 01/722–5369), open for almost 20 years, Nelli Iatropoulou has been making playful wooden ships from tankers to dinghies, each unique and carved from the wood of old ships.

Karoukis (✉ Skoufa 25, Kolonaki, ☎ 01/361–1012) carries all kinds of miniatures, and if you browse long enough, he's likely to brew you a Greek coffee.

Centuries-old **Ilias Kokkonis** (✉ Stoa Arsakeiou 8, Omonia, ☎ 01/322–1189 and 01/322–6355; ✉ Kifissias 264, Halandri, ☎ 01/689–1491 and 01/683–4708) most certainly stocks any flag you've hankered over—large or small, from any country.

Handicrafts

The **National Welfare Organization** (✉ Vasilissis Sofias 135, ☎ 01/646–0603; ✉ Ipatias 6 and Apollonos, Plaka, ☎ 01/325–0524), relying on craftspeople throughout Greece, carries fine examples of folk crafts: stunning handwoven carpets, flat-weave kilims, and tapestries from original designs, as well as hand-embroidered tablecloths and wall decorations. Napkins and place mats, ceramics, and embroidered pillowcases make handsome presents, and the shaggy woolen flokati rugs can be found here, too.

The **Center of Hellenic Tradition** (✉ Entrances on Mitropoleos 59 or Pandrossou 36, Monastiraki, ☎ 01/324–6746, café 01/321–3842) is an outlet for quality handicrafts; here you can take a break from shopping in its wonderful Oraia Ellada café, in clear view of the Parthenon.

Yiannis Komboyannis (✉ Diagora 4, Pangrati, ☎ 01/752–1539) sells gaily colored Skyrian pottery, including delightful fish plates, and more modern pieces from his workshop. You won't find him in his shop in summer, when he runs a ceramics school on Skyros.

At **Studio Kostas Sokaras** (✉ Adrianou 25, Plaka, ☎ 01/321–6826) you can buy handmade Karaghiozi puppets and other unusual items.

EOMMEX (✉ Mitropoleos 9, Syntagma, ☎ 01/323–0408), the Greek cooperative, operates a showroom with beautiful rugs made on wooden frames from more than 30 weavers around the country.

At the gracious **P. Serafetinidis** (✉ Haritos 29, Kolonaki, ☎ 01/721–4186; ✉ Parnassou 7, Karitsi Sq., ☎ 01/322–5207) enjoy the stunning colors and patterns of rare rugs and kilims from Persia, the Caucus, and Turkey.

Jewelry

Prices are much lower for gold and silver in Greece than in many Western countries, and jewelry is of high quality. Many shops in Plaka carry original pieces available at a good price if you bargain hard enough (a prerequisite).

For those with more expensive tastes, the Voukourestiou pedestrian mall off Constitution Square has a number of the city's leading jewelry shops: **PentheRoudakiS** (✉ No. 19 Voukourestiou, ☎ 01/361–3187) has classic designs. **Xanthopoulos** (✉ No. 4 Voukourestiou, ☎ 01/322–6856) has traditional gold, silver, and jewels. The baubles at **J. Vourakis & Fils** (✉ No. 8 Voukourestiou, ☎ 01/323–1258) will put a twinkle in your eye.

At **Ahtida** (✉ Solonos 97, Kolonaki, ☎ 01/360–6331) you'll find original designs by Athenian artists, as well as antique jewelry.

LALAoUNIS (✉ Panepistimiou 6, Syntagma, ☎ 01/362–4354 and 01/361–1371; ✉ The Athens Tower, Sinopis 2, ☎ 01/770–0000; and the Athens Hilton ✉ Vasilissis Sofias 46, ☎ 01/725–0201), the world-famous Greek jeweler, is always experimenting with designs, taking ideas from nature, biology, and ancient Greek pieces.

La Chrysoteque Zolotas (✉ Panepistimiou 10, Syntagma, ☎ 01/361–3782), Lalaounis's main competitor, is noted for its superb museum copies.

Other finely rendered copies of classical jewelry can be found at the **Benaki Museum gift shop** (✉ Koumbari and Vasilissis Sofias, Kolonaki, ☎ 01/362–7367). The **Goulandris Cycladic Museum** (✉ Neofitou Douka 4, Kolonaki, ☎ 01/724–9706) sells exceptional modern versions of classic jewelry designs as well.

Local Delicacies

Try the central market on Athinas for tasty local foods to bring back: packaged dried figs, packaged pistachios, *pastelli* (sesame seed and honey candy), and canned olives.

Brothers (Afoi.) Hatzigeorgiou (✉ Evripidou 37, Central Market area, ☎ 01/325–0434), founded in 1935, is an assault on the senses, with bags of Greek herbs and spices from around the world.

Bachar (✉ Evripidou 31, Central Market area, ☎ 01/321–7225), one of the many spice shops lining Evripidou, carries aromatic and pharmaceutical herbs.

Katsarou (✉ Liossion 89, near Stathmos Larissis train station, ☎ 01/821–1767) tempts ouzo lovers with rock-bottom prices, as well as competitively priced brandies and *kokkinelli* (resinated red wine).

ATHENS A TO Z

Arriving and Departing

By Bus

Travel by bus is inexpensive, usually comfortable, and relatively fast. The journey from Athens to Thessaloniki takes roughly the same time as the train, though the IC express covers the distance 1¼ hours faster. To the Peloponnese, however, buses are speedier than trains. Information and timetables are available at tourist information offices. Make reservations at least one day before your planned trip, earlier for holiday weekends.

Terminal A (✉ At Kifissou 100, ☎ 01/512–4910) is the arrival and departure point for bus lines that serve parts of northern Greece, including Thessaloniki, Epirus, and Macedonia, and the Peloponnese destinations of Epidaurus, Mycenae, and Corinth. Each has its own phone number; EOT offices distribute a list. **Terminal B** (☎ 01/831–7153), serving Evia, eastern, and central Greece, including Delphi, is behind Liossion 260, in a remote area northwest of Concord Square near the Tris Yefiris (Three Bridges) district. Tickets for these buses are sold only at this terminal, so you should call to book seats well in advance during high season or holidays.

From Terminal A, take Bus 51 to Concord Square; from Terminal B, take Bus 24 downtown. To get to the stations, catch Bus 51 at Zinonos and Menandrou off Concord Square (for Terminal A) and Bus 24 on Amalias in front of the National Gardens (Terminal B). International buses drop their passengers off on the street, usually in the Concord or Constitution Square areas or at the Peleponnisos train station.

By Car

The main highways going north and south link up in Athens and both are called *Ethniki Odos* (the National Road). At the city limits, signs in English clearly mark the way to both Constitution Square and Concord Square in the town center. Leaving Athens, routes to the National Road are well marked; signs usually name Lamia for points north and Corinth or Patras for points southwest. On the road map distributed by the EOT (☞ *below*), the National Roads are yellow and are marked by European road numbers, although these are not used on the roads themselves. Beware: the highways are very slick when wet, and there are many fatal accidents. Avoid driving in rain and on days preceding or following major holidays; Greece's car-accident rate, one of the highest in the EU, escalates wildly during the mass migrations to and from the city. The speed limit is 120 kph (74 mph) on the National Road, 90 kph (54 mph) outside urban areas. From Athens to Thessaloniki, the distance is 515 km (309 mi); to Kalamata, 257 km (154 mi); to Corinth, 84 km (50 mi); to Lamia, 214 km (128 mi); to Patras, 218 km (131 mi); to Igoumenitsa, 472 km (283 mi).

By Plane

Athens's **Ellinikon Airport** (⊠ Vasileos Georgiou B', West Terminal: ☎ 01/969–9111; East Terminal: ☎ 01/969–4111) is between Alimos and Glyfada on the southwest coast of Attica, about 10 km (6 mi) from the city center. Olympic Airways (⊠ Syngrou 96, ☎ 01/966–6666) has service between Athens and several cities and islands. Reservations can be made by telephone daily from 7:30 AM to 9:30 PM. All domestic and international Olympic Airways flights depart from the West Terminal (☎ Arrival and departure information: 01/936–3363 through 3367). Other airlines use the East Terminal (☎ 01/969–4466 or 01/969–4467). In summer charter flights are available: American based (☎ 01/969–4686); others (☎ 01/969–4240).

For travel to and from the airport, yellow-and-blue double-decker express **buses** connect the two airport terminals, Constitution Square, Concord Square, and Piraeus. Between the terminals and Athens, the express Bus 91 runs every 35 minutes 7 AM–12:30 AM. You can catch the bus to the airport on Constitution Square or off Concord Square on Stadiou. From the terminals to Karaiskaki Square in Piraeus, the express Bus 19 runs hourly 7 AM–11:10 PM. The night express buses for both lines leave at irregular intervals; ask for a schedule from an EOT office (☞ *below*). The fare is 160 dr., 200 dr. after 11:30 PM.

It's easier to take a **taxi** from the airport stands: about 1,800 dr. to Piraeus; 1000 dr. between terminals; 1,600 dr. to the center. The price goes up by about two-thirds between midnight and 5 AM. If you want to arrive at your hotel in style, **Yiannis Yiannakopoulos Limousines** (☎ 094/316–798) will pick you up at the airport and drop you at your hotel or vice versa for 12,000 dr.

By Ship

Cruise ships and ferries to and from the Aegean islands dock at **Piraeus** (⊠ Port Authority, Akti Mouli, ☎ 01/422–6000 or 01/451–1311), the main port, 10 km (6 mi) southwest of Athens. Ships for the Ionian islands sail from ports nearer to them, such as **Patras** and **Igoumenitsa**. Connections from Piraeus to the main island groups are good, connections from main islands to smaller ones within a group less so, and services between islands of different groups or areas—such as Rhodes and Crete—are less frequent. Travel agents (☞ *below*) and ship offices in Athens and Piraeus have details. Timetables change very frequently, and boats may be delayed by weather conditions, so your plans should be flexible. Buy your tickets two or three days in advance, especially if you are traveling in summer or taking a car. Reserve your return journey or continuation soon after you arrive.

From Piraeus, the quickest way to get into town center, if you are traveling light, is to walk to the metro station and take an electric train to Concord Square, a trip of about 25 minutes (100 dr.). Those arriving by hydrofoil at the smaller **Zea Marina Harbor** should take Bus 905 or Trolley 20 to the metro station. Alternatively, you can take a taxi (if you find one), which may take longer owing to traffic, and will cost around 1,300 dr.

The other main port is **Rafina** (⊠ Port, Port Authority, ☎ 0294/22300), on the eastern coast of Attica, where boats to and from Evia and some of the closer Cyclades dock. Orange KTEL buses (☎ 01/821–0872) make the trip to Athens every half hour until about 10 PM; they leave from the station slightly up the hill from the port and the fare is 400 dr. The trip takes about one hour. It is difficult to find taxis to take you to Athens (about 5,000 dr.).

By Train

Greek trains have a well-earned reputation for being slow and for having a limited network. The main line runs north from Athens to the former Yugoslavia, dividing into three lines at Thessaloniki. The main line continues on to Belgrade, a second line goes east to the Turkish border and Istanbul, and a third line heads northeast to Bulgaria. The Peloponnese in the south is served by a narrow-gauge line dividing at Corinth into the Mycenae–Argos route and Patras–Olympia–Kalamata.

The **Greek Railway Organization (OSE)** has two stations in Athens, side by side: trains from the north and international trains arrive at, and depart from, **Stathmos Larissis** (✉ Between Diliyianni and Leoforos Konstantinoupoleos, ☎ 01/823–7741). Take Trolley 1 from the terminal to Omonia Square; trains from the Peloponnese use the quaint **Stathmos Peloponnisou** (✉ Between Diliyianni and Leoforos Konstantinoupoleos, ☎ 01/513–1601) next door. The café continues the station's striking art-nouveau motif, from its burgundy ceiling with ornate moldings and antique crystal–teardrop chandelier to its original bronze gas lamps. Both stations have left-luggage service and snack bars.

OSE buses (☎ 01/513–5768 or 01/513–5769) for Albania, Bulgaria, and Turkey also leave from Stathmos Peloponnisou station. To Omonia and Syntagma squares, take Bus 57.

The **IC express service** from the north is fast and reliable (Thessaloniki–Athens takes 6 hours). Express service has also begun on the Athens–Patras line (about 4 hours). On any train, it is best to travel first class, with a reserved seat, as the difference between the first-class and tourist coaches can be vast: without a seat reservation you could end up standing or crouched among the baggage.

Since the station phones are almost always busy and agents often don't speak English, it's easier to get information and tickets at a railway office downtown (✉ Karolou 1, near Concord Sq., ☎ 01/524–0646 through 0648; ✉ Sina 6, ☎ 01/362–4402 through 4406; ✉ Filellinon 17, near Syntagma Sq., ☎ 01/323–6747 and 01/323–6273). You may also call (☎ 145) for a recorded departure timetable, in Greek, of trains within Greece; call (☎ 147) for information on trains to Europe and Russia.

Getting Around

Many of the sights you'll want to see, and most of the hotels, cafés, and restaurants, are within a fairly small central area. It's easy to walk everywhere.

The price of public transportation has risen steeply in the last couple of years, but it is still less than that in western European capitals. Riding during rush hours is definitely not recommended. Upon boarding, validate your ticket in the orange canceling machines at the front and back of buses and trolleys and in the stations of the electric trains. Keep your tickets until you reach your destination, as inspectors occasionally pop up to check that they have been canceled and validated. They are strict about fining offenders, including tourists.

The **Organization for Urban Public Transportation** (✉ Metsovou 15, ☎ 185 or 01/883–6076), open Monday to Friday 8 to 2:30, one block north of the National Archaeological Museum, answers questions about routes (usually only in Greek) and distributes maps with street names in Greek.

By Bus and Trolley

Main bus stations are at Vasilissis Olgas next to Zappion hall, at Acadimias and Sina and at Kaningos Square. Bus and trolley tickets cost 75 dr. You may continue from a trunk line (A1–A16) to a connecting bus on the same ticket, and the mini "shopping" buses that serve the downtown historical triangle are free. No transfers are issued; monthly passes are available. Tickets are sold in special booths at bus terminals and at selected *periptera* (street kiosks). Buses run from the center to all suburbs and suburban beaches from 5 AM–midnight, and major routes have infrequent owl service. For suburbs farther north than central Kifissia, you have to change at Kifissia.

KTEL orange buses provide efficient bus service throughout the Attica basin. Most buses to the east Attica coast, including those for **Sounion** (☎ 01/823–0179), fare 1,050 dr., and **Marathon** (☎ 01/821–0872), fare 650 dr., leave from the KTEL terminal, ✉ *Platia Aigyptou at corner of Mavromateon and Leoforos Alexandras.*

By Car

Driving in Athens is not recommended unless you have nerves of steel. Red traffic lights are frequently ignored, and it is not unusual to see motorists passing on hills and while rounding corners. Driving is on the right, and although the vehicle on the right has the right-of-way, don't expect this or any other driving rule to be obeyed. The speed limit is 50 kph (31 mph) in town. Seat belts are compulsory, as are helmets for motorcyclists, though many natives ignore the laws. In downtown Athens do not drive in the bus lanes marked by a yellow divider.

Unless you are a citizen of an EC country, you must have an international driver's license. The **Automobile and Touring Club of Greece** or ELPA (✉ Athens Tower, Messoghion 2–4, ☎ 01/748–8800; in an emergency, ☎ 104) no longer issues these, so non-EC members should arrange for a license through their local automobile association. ELPA can help with tourist information for drivers (☎ 174), and they assist tourists with breakdowns free of charge if they belong to AAA or to ELPA; otherwise, there is a charge.

Downtown **parking spaces** are hard to find—you can pay to use one of the few temporary parking areas set up in vacant lots, but you're better off leaving your car in the hotel garage and walking or taking a cab. Gas pumps and service stations are everywhere, and lead-free gas is widely available. Be aware that many stations close at 7 PM.

By Subway

The one partially underground electric train line stretches from Piraeus to Kifissia, northeast of the city's center, with 20 stops in between. It was constructed in 1868, one of the earliest in Europe, and electrified in 1904. It is limited but functions well and is very safe, even late at night. The trains run 5 AM–midnight and the fare is 75 dr. or 100 dr. depending on the distance. There are no special fares or day tickets for visitors. Validate your ticket by stamping it in the orange machines at the entrance to the platforms.

By Taxi

Taxi rates are still affordable compared to fares in other European capitals. It seems paradoxical that more than 17,000 taxis are on the streets of Athens, yet during peak hours it's impossible to find an empty one. A taxi driver may pass you up because it's not his day to enter the center of Athens. Taxis with passengers often operate unofficially on the jitney system, indicating willingness to pick up others by blinking their headlights. Would-be passengers shout their destination as the driver cruises past.

Radio taxis can be booked by your hotel (a good idea when taking an early morning flight) with a surcharge of 300 dr. for immediate response and 400 dr. for an appointment to come later. Some radio-taxi companies are **Aris** (☎ 01/346–7137 or 01/346–7102); **Ermis** (☎ 01/411–5200); **Enotita** (☎ 01/645–9000); **Kifissia** (☎ 01/801–8820 or 01/801–2270); **Kosmos** (☎ 01/420–7244, 01/420–7261, or 01/420–7247); **Parthenon** (☎ 01/581–1809); and **Piraeus I** (☎ 01/413–5888 or 01/418–2333).

Most taxi drivers are honest and hardworking, but a few con artists infiltrate the ranks at the airports and near popular restaurants and clubs frequented by foreigners. Make sure the driver turns on the meter and that the rate listed in the lower corner is 1, the normal rate before midnight. Don't be alarmed if your driver picks up other passengers (although protocol indicates he should ask your permission first). Each passenger pays full fare for the distance he or she has traveled.

The fare begins at 200 dr., and even if you join other passengers, you must add this charge to the final amount: note the fare on the meter when you get in an occupied taxi. The rate is 58 dr. per km, 113 dr. between midnight and 5 AM. Surcharges are made for holidays (100 dr.), fares from, not to, the airport (300 dr.); fares from ports, railway stations, and bus terminals (160 dr.); and for each bag weighing more than 10 kilograms (55 dr.). Waiting time is 2,000 dr. per hour.

Taxi drivers know the major central hotels, but if your hotel is less well known, show the driver the address written in Greek and make note of the phone number and if possible a nearby landmark. If all else fails, the driver can call from a periptero. Athens has thousands of short side streets, and few taxi drivers have maps. If your driver gets lost despite all precautions, use the time to practice answering personal questions gracefully.

Contacts and Resources

Doctors and Dentists
Most hotels will call a **doctor** for you. You can also call your embassy. For a doctor on call 2 PM–7 AM on Sunday and holidays (☎ 105 in Greek). For a **dentist,** check with your hotel, embassy, or the tourist police.

Embassies
United States: Vasilissis Sofias 91, ☎ 01/721–2951. **Canada:** Gennadiou 4, ☎ 01/725–4011. **United Kingdom:** Ploutarchou 1, ☎ 01/723–6211.

Emergencies and Hospitals
For auto accidents call the **city police** (☎ 100). **Tourist police** (☎ 171). **Fire** (☎ 199). **Ambulance,** though a taxi is often faster (☎ 166).

Not all hospitals are open nightly; dial (☎ 106 in Greek) or check the English-language *Athens News,* which lists emergency hospitals daily.

KAT Hospital (✉ Nikis 2, Kifissia, ☎ 01/801–4411 for accidents); **Asklepion Hospital** (✉ Vassileos Pavlou 1, Voula, ☎ 01/895–8301 through 01/895–8305); **Ygeia** (✉ Er. Stavrou 4, Maroussi, ☎ 01/682–7940). Children go to **Aglaia Kyriakou Hospital** (✉ Livadias and Thivon, Goudi, ☎ 01/777–5610 and 01/778–3212) or **Ayia Sofia Hospital** (✉ Mikras Asias and Thivon, Goudi, ☎ 01/777–1811 or 01/775–8010).

English-Language Bookstores and Libraries

The Booknest (⊠ Folia Tou Bibliou, Panepistimiou 25–29, near Syntagma, ☏ 01/322–9560) has an ample selection of American authors. **Compendium** (⊠ Nikis 28, near Syntagma, ☏ 01/322–1248) has travel books, books on Greece, one of Athens's few women's-studies sections, and used books. Go to **Eleftheroudakis** for fiction, language guides, and coffee-table editions at the following locales: (⊠ Nikis 4, Syntagma Sq., ☏ 01/322–9388); a newer larger store (⊠ Panepistimiou 17, ☏ 01/331–4180); (⊠ Athens Tower, Building A, Sinopis 2, ☏ 01/770–8007); and in the Psychiko shopping center (⊠ Kifissias 294, ☏ 01/687–8350). There's also **Kauffman** (⊠ Stadiou 28, Center, ☏ 01/322–2160), for a limited selection of American fiction. Try **Pantelides** (⊠ Amerikis 9-11, Syntagma Sq., ☏ 01/362–3673). Worth a visit is **Reymondos** (⊠ Voukourestiou 18, Center, ☏ 01/364–8188).

At the Hellenic-American Union (⊠ Massalias 22, Exarchia) is the **American Library** (⊠ 4th Floor, ☏ 01/363–8114); The **Greek Library** (⊠ 7th Floor, ☏ 01/362–9886) has a section of books in English on Greek subjects. Also try the **British Council Library** (⊠ Kolonaki Sq. 17, ☏ 01/364–5768). The **Gennadius Library, American School of Classical Studies** (⊠ Soudias 61, Kolonaki, ☏ 01/721–0536) is also interesting.

Guided Tours

EXCURSIONS

Most agencies offer excursions at about the same prices, but **CHAT** (☞ *below*) is reputed to have the best service and guides. Taking a half-day trip to the breathtaking **Temple of Poseidon** at Sounion avoids the hassle of dealing with the crowded public buses or paying a great deal more for a taxi. The 6,400-dr. cost is well spent. A 1-day tour to **Delphi** with lunch costs 17,900 dr. (15,900 dr. without lunch), but the 2-day tour (29,500 dr.) is far preferable. There's also a 1-day tour to **Mycenae** and **Epidauros** (17,900 dr. with lunch). There's a 2-day tour to ancient **Corinth, Mycenae, Nauplion,** and **Epidaurus** (29,500 dr. including half-board). A 3-day tour takes in both Delphi and the stunning monasteries of **Meteora** with half-board in first-class hotels (73,000 dr.). A full-day cruise from Piraeus, visiting three nearby islands—**Aegina, Poros, and Hydra**—costs around 16,000 dr. (including buffet lunch on the ship). Athens travel agencies can also arrange a four-day **Thessaloniki** tour via plane (about 116,500 dr. not including airfare).

ORIENTATION TOURS

Many travel agencies offer 4-hour morning bus tours (8,400 dr.), including a guided tour of the Acropolis. Reservations can be made through most hotels or you can contact one of the major travel agencies (☞ *below*).

PERSONAL GUIDES

Major agencies can provide English-speaking guides. The **Association of Guides** (⊠ Apollonas 9A, ☏ 01/322–9705) provides licensed guides for individual or group tours, starting at about 22,000 dr. including taxes for a 4-hour tour of the Acropolis and its museum. It is advisable to arrange for a guide through a reliable agency; only hire one licensed by the EOT.

SPECIAL-INTEREST TOURS

Athens by Night tours, offered by all agencies, are a convenient way to see some of the evening entertainment, especially for single travelers who may not want to venture out alone. For those interested in folk dancing, there is a 4-hour evening tour (8,200 dr.) from April to October, which includes the Sound and Light Spectacle and a performance of Dora Stratou folk dances. Another evening tour follows the Sound and Light Spectacle with a **dinner show at a Plaka taverna**

(11,300 dr.). Any travel agency can arrange these tours, but go first to CHAT Tours (☞ *below*) for reliable and efficient service.

The **Amphitrion Holidays** agency (☞ *below*) specializes in educational and offbeat tours for individuals in Athens and elsewhere, including island-hopping tours and treks in the Pindos mountains.

Cruises to the four most popular islands—Mykonos, Rhodes, Crete, and Santorini—usually operate from April through October. Try any of the following agencies: Chandris Cruises (⊠ Akti Miaouli 95, Piraeus, ☎ 01/429–0300); Epirotiki (⊠ Akti Miaouli 85, Piraeus, ☎ 01/429–1000); Hydrodynamic Cruises (⊠ Xenofontos 14, Athens, ☎ 01/323–4292); Royal Cruise Lines (⊠ Akti Miaouli 1, Piraeus, ☎ 01/428–2440 or 800/227–0925 in the U.S.); or Sun Line (⊠ Iasonas 3, Piraeus, ☎ 01/452–3417 or 800/872–6400 in the U.S.). Most also have downtown Athens representatives.

For hiking tours, the **Greek Federation of Mountaineering Associations** (⊠ Milioni 5, Kolonaki, ☎ 01/364–5904) supplies details on mountain paths, refuges, and contact numbers for local clubs.

For horseback riding tours, the helpful **Greek Equestrian Federation** (⊠ Messinias 55, ☎ 01/652–8139) provides a list of Athens's riding clubs.

Late-Night Pharmacies
Call 107 for a Greek recording of pharmacies open on holidays or check the *Athens News*. Each pharmacy posts a list of establishments close by that are open during the afternoon break or late at night. A conveniently located pharmacy where English is spoken is **Marinopoulos** (⊠ Kanari 23, Kolonaki, ☎ 01/361–3053). **Thomas** (⊠ Papadiamantopoulou 6, near the Hilton Hotel and Holiday Inn, Ilissia, ☎ 01/721–6101) is another safe bet for convenience and spoken English.

Travel Agencies
American Express (⊠ Ermou 2, ☎ 01/324–4975, FAX 01/322–7893); **Amphitrion Holidays** (⊠ Karageorgi Servias 2, ☎ 01/322–8884 through 8887, FAX 01/323–0370; ⊠ Deuteras Merachias 3, Piraeus, ☎ 01/411–2045 through 2049, FAX 01/417–0742; and ⊠ Karageorgi Servias 4, ☎ 01/323–0344, FAX 01/323–1295); **CHAT Tours** (⊠ Stadiou 4, ☎ 01/322–2886, FAX 01/323–5770); **Key Tours** (⊠ Kallirois 4, ☎ 01/923–3166, FAX 01/923–2008); **Magic Bus** (⊠ Filellinon 20, ☎ 01/323–7471, FAX 01/322–0219); **Travel Plan** (⊠ Christou Lada 9, ☎ 01/323–8801 through 8804 and 01/324–0224/5, FAX 01/322–2152); and **Carolson WagonLit** (⊠ Karageorgi Servias 2, ☎ 01/324–7196, FAX 01/322–0397).

Near Omonia, try **Condor Travel** (⊠ Stadiou 43, ☎ 01/321–2453, FAX 321–4296) and **Pharos Travel and Tourism** (⊠ 18 Triti Septemvriou, ☎ 01/523–3403 and 01/523–6142, FAX 01/523–6261). In New York **Pharos Travel and Tourism** (⊠ 230 W. 31st St., ☎ 212/736–6070, FAX 212/736–3921) can help you put together an independent tour at competitive prices.

Visitor Information
There are **Greek National Tourist Organization (EOT)** offices near Constitution Square (⊠ Karageorgi Servias 2 in the National Bank of Greece, ☎ 01/322–2545); at the East Terminal of Ellinikon Airport (☎ 01/961–2722); and on the Piraeus Harbor (⊠ EOT Building, 1st Floor, Zea Marina, ☎ 01/413–5716).

The **tourist police** (⊠ Dimitrakopoulou 77, ☎ 171) can answer questions in English about transportation, steer you to an open pharmacy or doctor, and locate phone numbers of hotels and restaurants.

3 Excursions from Athens

Attica, the Saronic Gulf Islands, and Delphi

The crumbling 19th-century merchants' mansions of Aegina and Hydra, the white and periwinkle homes in the labyrinthine streets of Poros, and the ghosts of Spetsiot pirates will steal you away to the Saronic Gulf Islands. Or maybe the fame of Marathon, or the rich iconography of Daphni monastery will inspire an excursion over the forbidding mountains guarding the passes into Athens. All who land in Athens are destined sooner or later to make a pilgrimage to Delphi, where the priestesses of antiquity uttered their enigmatic prophecies.

SINCE THE FIRST MILLENNIUM BC, the story of Attica has been almost inextricably bound to that of Athens, the most powerful of the villages that lay scattered over the peninsula. By force and persuasion Athens brought these towns together, creating a unit that by the 5th century BC had become the center of an empire. For the ancient Greeks, Delphi was the center of the universe, home to Apollo and the most sacred oracle, and today it remains a principal place of pilgrimage for visitors to Greece. The Saronic Gulf Islands straddle the gulf between Athens and the Peloponnese: Aegina, the closest Saronic island to Piraeus, in ancient times was renowned for its bronze work and eventually succumbed to the power of Athens, and two millenniums later played a pivotal role in the War of Independence; tiny Poros, almost grazing the shores of the Peloponnese, was once the site of an important Temple of Poseidon, now dilapidated; proof of Hydra's and Spetses's 18th- and 19th-century prosperity through their fleet of trading ships is the stately, forbidding mansions of shipping magnates; they are now the stomping grounds of wealthy European vacationers.

By Catherine Vanderpool

Updated by Terrence Moloney and Susan Lupack

Pleasures and Pastimes

Dining

The cuisine of Attica resembles that of Athens, central Greece, and the Peloponnese. Local ingredients predominate, with fresh fish perhaps the greatest (and most expensive) delicacy. Since much of Attica's vegetation used to support herds of grazing sheep and the omnivorous goat, the meat of both animals is also a staple in many country tavernas. It is becoming increasingly difficult, particularly in areas close to Athens, to find the traditional Greek taverna with large stew pots full of the day's hot meal, or big *tapsis* (casseroles) of eggplant moussaka or *pastitsio* (a casserole of pasta, meat, and cheese with seasonings and cinnamon). Always ask to see the *kouzina* (kitchen) to look at the day's precooked dishes, or even to get a glimpse inside the pots. Informal dress is appropriate at all but the very fanciest of restaurants, and unless noted, reservations are not necessary.

CATEGORY	COST*
$$$$	over 9,000 dr.
$$$	7,000 dr.–9,000 dr.
$$	3,000 dr.–7,000 dr.
$	under 3,000 dr.

for 3-course meal, including tax, service, and usually beer or a small carafe of wine.

Lodging

Many of the hotels in Attica are resorts catering to people who commute to Athens. Many have been built recently of reinforced concrete slabs, with spindly metal balconies and diverse arrays of facilities, but the decor, which varies little from one to the next, tends to be a modern "Greek island" look: simple pine furnishings, tile floors, and, at most, a colorful bedspread. Be forewarned: some of the large hotels ask you to take half board, particularly in high season. If you know your plans ahead of time, you should book through a travel agent, who can negotiate a good price and eliminate the half-board requirement, if you wish. Delphi and Arachova, which have had recent minibooms in hotel construction, have a number of appealing small establishments, with fresh, cheerful rooms and public spaces, but elsewhere, these picturesque, cozy family-owned country inns and pensions are rare. Note also that many hotels close in late fall and reopen usually around

Easter week, except in Delphi and Arachova, where high season (with top prices) is often during ski season.

CATEGORY	COST*
$$$$	over 39,000 dr.
$$$	22,000 dr.–39,000 dr.
$$	13,000 dr.–22,000 dr.
$	under 13,000 dr.

All prices are for a standard double room, including taxes but not breakfast, in the spring and summer high season (Arachova and Delphi's high season is winter).

Nightlife

Perhaps it is the daytime heat through so many months of the year; perhaps it is an excess of energy; perhaps it is their intense sociability, unrequited during the workday; but whatever the reason, Greeks love going out at night. Traffic can be as bad at 3 AM as in the morning rush hour. Greeks also like to combine food with their entertainment and there are many ways to do it. Some nightspots emphasize the show over the cuisine, others do the opposite, and they range from the simplest taverna with a bouzouki trio to fancy nightclubs with elaborate floor shows.

For dancing, the discos at most large resort hotels are usually open to outsiders as well as guests. During the summer, many of the central Athens dancing clubs move to rented space on the coastal road; clubs and addresses change annually, so ask around or check the weekly English-language *Athenscope*. Of the islands, Hydra and Spetses offer the most sophisticated bars and discos.

Tennis

The large resort hotels have tennis courts, which are sometimes open to the public, and there are public courts on the shore opposite the airport, on Poseidonios Avenue in Voula.

Windsurfing

Most of the large seaside resort hotels rent windsurfing equipment and arrange lessons, usually for guests only. For further information, contact the Greek Windsurfing Association (☞ Contacts and Resources *in* Excursions from Athens A to Z, *below*).

Exploring Attica, the Saronic Gulf Islands, and Delphi

Athens lies in a basin defined by three mountain masses: Mt. Hymettos to the east, Mt. Parnis and Mt. Aigaleo to the west, and Mt. Pendeli to the north. East of Hymettos stretches the Mesogeion, or "middle territory," those gently undulating hills and fields laced with vineyards and dotted with olive trees, and the source of the sweet-smelling thyme, food for the bees whose hives in blue boxes were once a familiar sight along any country road. Northeast of Pendeli, between the slopes and the sea, lies the fabled plain of Marathon, its flat expanse now dotted with small agricultural communities and seaside resorts, second home to many Athenians. Attica includes such sites as the Temple of Poseidon at Sounion, and, up the coast and around the northern flank of Pendeli, the enchantingly rural archaeological site at the Amphiareion. It takes in the Fortress of Phyle, on the slopes of Parnis; the Sanctuary of Demeter and Kore at Eleusis; and the Monastery of Daphni. The Saronic Gulf Islands of Aegina, Poros, Hydra, and Spetses are popular with Athenians, owing to their proximity and pleasantness. Each offers a mix of opportunities to sightsee, relax, and enjoy contemporary Greek culture. They are all covered in separate sections below.

Great Itineraries

If you only have a few days to explore the areas around Athens, you'll probably want to stick to the most important site, which is Delphi. In a 5- or 6-day itinerary you'll be able to see Delphi, some of the major sites around Athens such as Daphni and Sounion, and maybe an island (Aegina is the closest). A 9- or 10-day trip will enable you to see all of the above, a few more sites in Attica, and the farther Saronic Gulf Islands, such as Hydra and Spetses.

IF YOU HAVE 3 DAYS

Numbers in the text correspond to numbers in the margin and on the Attica and the Saronic Gulf Islands and Delphi maps.

A 3-day trip means concentrating on the essentials so you get the most out of your time. Exploring ☒ **Delphi** ㉓–㉖ requires at least one full day, so be sure to go early in the morning (it's a 3-hour drive) or go the night before. A second could be spent visiting the principal sites of Attica, starting with ☒ **Sounion** ④, up to ☒ **Marathon** ⑧, and the **Amphiareion** ⑪. A third day offers the chance to visit ☒ **Aegina** ⑯–⑰, the Saronic Gulf Island closest to Athens.

IF YOU HAVE 6 DAYS

Attica makes the most reasonable start of a six day tour; begin by going to Poseidon's temple at ☒ **Sounion** ④, followed by a foray north to **Brauron** ⑦, ☒ **Marathon** ⑧, and either **Rhamnous Archaeological Site** ⑨ or the **Amphiareion** ⑪. A morning seeing the Sanctuary of Demeter at ancient **Eleusis** ⑮ is best succeeded by an afternoon at the Byzantine **Monastery of Daphni** ⑭. Spend your third and fourth days in and around ☒ **Delphi** ㉓–㉖, where nearby **Osios Loukas** ㉑, with its early Byzantine monastic complex, and ☒ **Arachova** ㉒, with its sophisticated cafés, offer pleasant digressions from the ancient sites. Finally, a couple of days among the Saronic Gulf Islands will round out your trip. Two days could pass very quickly on ☒ **Aegina** ⑯–⑰, but you could also see the principal sites (the **Sanctuary of Aphaia** ⑰ being the foremost) in one day, and spend a second on ☒ **Hydra** ⑲, an island whose shops, nightlife, and pace appeal to an international clientele.

IF YOU HAVE 9 DAYS

A thorough exploration of Attica, the Saronic Gulf Islands, and Delphi requires nine days. Step into ancient Greece on your first day with visits to ☒ **Sounion** ④, **Brauron** ⑦, ☒ **Marathon** ⑧, and the **Amphiareion** ⑪. On day two take a break from ancient Greece and visit the Byzantine **Monastery of Kaisariani** ①, and the Vorres museum at **Paiania** ⑥. Next day, go west from Athens to the **Monastery of Daphni** ⑭ and ancient and vast Eleusis. After three days of Attica start your journey to ☒ **Delphi** ㉓–㉖, deep in the mountains to the west of Attica. **Delphi** is one of Greece's best sites, with an excellent museum, an extensive jumble of ruins, and a restored treasury, and it can be seen in a day or two. The nearby mountain village of ☒ **Arachova** ㉒ and the harbor town of ☒ **Galaxidi** ㉗ make fabulous alternative bases for **Delphi,** especially for those eager for a taste of modern as well as ancient Greece. While in the vicinity don't forget to visit **Osios Loukas** ㉑, nestled in a secret valley. Your last three or four days will find you relishing the surprisingly varied Saronic Gulf Islands, each with their own flavor, but all sharing in the common credo that the leisurely life is better than life in the fast lane. Your island tour can begin at ☒ **Aegina** ⑯–⑰, where you can snack on the island's famous pistachios and visit the **Sanctuary of Aphaia** ⑰. A day on Aegina can only be outdone by a day on ☒ **Hydra** ⑲, where the European jet set escapes when struck by the urge to lounge in beautiful mansion hotels and putter about the island's shops, cafés, and nightclubs. Once you've wandered around

Hydra's car-free streets you may not want to go anywhere else, but ⊞ **Spetses** ⑳, too, won't allow cars (motorcycles are allowed), and it has at least as many sites scattered along her extensive shoreline and pine-forested hills.

When to Tour

As with elsewhere in Greece, services in these regions are greatly reduced during the winter, except for at Delphi and Arachova, which are refuges for skiers. The islands explode into activity during July and August, so be prepared to go head to head with the crowds and the heat.

ATTICA

Glyfada, Vouliagmeni, Sounion, Lavrion, Paiania, Brauron, Marathon, Phyle, Daphni, Eleusis

The bulk of Attica, which stretches southeast into the Aegean, lies east and north of Athens. Separated from Central Greece by mountains—Pateras, Kithairon, Pastra, and Parnis—and bordered by the sea, Attica was easily defensible. It also had several fertile plains, well watered with rivers and seasonal streams, and its coves and natural harbors encouraged the development of seafaring and trade.

Kaisariani

5½ km (3½ mi) east of Athens.

The neighborhood of Kaisariani lies on the slopes of Hymettos, the eastern "wall" of Athens, which yields the sun each morning and catches its last purple shadows at night. Denuded of its pine forests in the terrible years during World War II, the mountain has been partially reforested.

❶ A glen of pine, cypress, and plane trees fed by a copious flow of water cradles the **Monastery of Kaisariani.** A temple of Aphrodite stood on the hill just above the present-day monastery, which dates to the 11th century. The buildings surround a central court, including, besides the church, a refectory, mill, and bakery, all restored in 1956–57. Most of the frescoes are from the 17th and 18th centuries. If you have time, walk 10 minutes on the dirt path to a clearing with a picnic bench for a spectacular view of Athens, including the Acropolis and the ships in Piraeus Harbor. ✉ *5½ km (3½ mi) east of Athens,* ☎ *01/723–6619.* ✉ *500 dr.* ☉ *Tues.–Sun. 8:30–3.*

The **Moni Asteriou** (✉ 1½ km/1 mi up the hill to the end of the public road) also dates to the 11th century. The chapel of **Ayios Ioannis Theologou** (✉ 1½ km/1 mi up the hill to the end of the public road, just below Moni Asteriou) is a pleasant detour; you will enjoy another view of Athens and a closer look at—and smell of—the tiny aromatic shrubs—above all sage—that once fed the bees of Mt. Hymettos, giving that special flavor to its famous honey.

Festival

In summer, the **Pendeli Festival** offers evening performances in the courtyard of Rododafni Palace, the Duchess de Plaisance's home in Pendeli (✉ 16 km/10 mi northeast of Athens on Mount Pendeli, near the Athenian suburb of Kifissia). Built in 19th-century neo-Gothic style by the architect Kleanthes for this eccentric lady, it belonged for a time to the former Greek royal family. For information on the festival, con-

Attica and the Saronic Gulf Islands

tact the Greek National Tourist Organization (GNTO or EOT) in Athens.

Glyfada

❷ *17 km (10½ mi) southeast of Athens, 21 km (13 mi) south of Kaisariani.*

Found at this prosperous seaside resort town are the most meager of sites, and it is best used as a base from which to explore Attica. Its proximity to the airport should please those with early-morning flights and distress all others.

Beaches
Attica's eastern coast is mainly rock, with some short sandy stretches in **Glyfada** and **Voula,** which have been made public beaches. These have full facilities for a day in the sun, but the water is not very clean; whether the water is swimmable depends on pollution levels in the Saronic Gulf.

Dining and Lodging

$$$ ✕ **La Fenice.** This is the place to spend a romantic evening dining on beautifully presented, imaginative Italian food. You'll feel well taken care of the minute you enter the soothing, elegant restaurant, which also offers alfresco dining in a courtyard. Try the rigatoni with partridge ragout, crayfish in pastry, or beef filet with balsamic vinegar. If it's available, don't miss the lotus fruit sorbet. ⊠ *Zisimopoulou 10,* ☎ *01/894–9454. Reservations essential. AE, DC, V. Closed Sun. No lunch.*

$$$ ✕ **Psaropoulos.** A favorite with Athenians from way back, Psaropou-
★ los continues to serve up excellent fish in an informal, family-style setting. It is always crowded on weekends and holidays, especially at lunchtime. ⊠ *Kalamon 2,* ☎ *01/894–5677. No credit cards.*

$$ ✕ **Loxandra.** Known for home-style Greek cuisine, Loxandra also provides bouzouki-guitar accompaniment with your meal. Enjoy *magirefta* (a stove-top cooked dish, usually made earlier) such as *bourekakia* (cheese fingers in flaky pastry), *spanikopita* (spinach pie), and *yiouvetsi loxandra* (pork on a spit with miniature macaroni). Sugar lovers will get their fix from *haloum pagoto* (a sort of baklava with syrup and ice cream). ⊠ *Eleftherios Venizelou 15,* ☎ *01/963–1731. No credit cards. No lunch Sun.–Fri.*

$$ ▥ **Hotel Fenix.** For a good price, this Best Western hotel offers comfortable rooms, facilities, and proximity to the airport and the Glyfada Golf Club. Rooms with new furniture and redone bathrooms are a little bit more than the standard ones. Double-glazed windows help reduce the noise (and block stray golf balls?), although planes don't fly after midnight. ⊠ *Artemisiou 1, 16675,* ☎ *01/898–1255,* ℻ *01/894–9061. 135 rooms with bath, 3 suites. Restaurant, bar, air-conditioning, pool. AE, DC, MC, V.*

$$ ▥ **Palace Hotel.** Rooms, baths, and public spaces at the Palace are attractively contemporary. Buffet breakfast is included in the price. Although it is close to the sea (though not swimmable here), it's just 20 minutes or so from the center of Athens—a good choice for those who want a first-class city hotel out of the city. ⊠ *Vasileous Georgiou 4, 16675,* ☎ *01/894–8361,* ℻ *01/894–9061. 80 rooms with bath. Restaurant, bar, air-conditioning, pool. AE, DC, MC, V.*

Nightlife

NIGHTCLUBS

One club that draws a trendy crowd year-round is **Opera** (✉ Diadochou Pavlou 6, ☎ 01/894–6972). **Oui** (✉ disco only: Vas. Georgiou B' 33, disco and restaurant: Colosseum mall, Vas. Georgiou B' 81, ☎ 01/894–1456, 01/964–9065, or 01/894–9585) has a retro music disco and a disco and restaurant with music from the 1950s, '60s, and '70s; reserve for dinner on weekends.

Outdoor Activities and Sports

GOLF

The **Glyfada Golf Club** (✉ End of Pronois, at the east end of Athens International Airport, ☎ 01/894–6820 or 01/894–6834) has many distinguished politicians, businessmen, and members of the diplomatic community on its roster. It is open to travelers; tee times are daily, from 8 AM to just before sunset.

SAILING

Many yacht brokers charter boats and organize underwater "safaris," scuba tours, and "flotilla" cruises around the islands in small rented sailboats. **Vernicos Yachts** (✉ Diadochou Pavlou 12, Glyfada, ☎ 01/894–6981).

Vouliagmeni

❸ *25 km (15½ mi) south of Athens, 8 km (5 mi) southwest of Glyfada.*

Vouliagmeni has little to distinguish itself except as the home to many American families when the United States maintained a major base at the airfield. Much like Glyfada, today it serves the tourist as an alternative base from which to explore Attica.

Beaches

As in Glyfada, some **beaches** lie along the coastline of Vouliagmeni, but they are not always clean enough to allow swimming. Whether the water is swimmable depends on pollution levels in the Saronic Gulf.

Dining and Lodging

$$ ✗ **Imvros.** The Stamatelos family hails from Imvros, a Turkish island with many Greek inhabitants. They are obliging hosts, particularly with generous portions of everything from a crisp shrimp with olive oil, lemon, and homemade mayonnaise appetizer to fresh *lakerda* (Black Sea tuna) and *skordalia mides* (mussels served with aioli). Meat lovers should order *donner* kebab (like souvlaki). ✉ *Athinas 43, Kavouri,* ☎ *01/896–0842 or 01/896–2530. AE, V. Closed Easter.*

$$ ✗ **Panorama.** For the best food in Vouliagmeni, head to the pine-studded stretch called Kavouri. Panorama is almost impossible to get into for Sunday lunch, because it's crowded with Athenians who come feast on the large selection of fish and relax on the cool seaside terrace. Besides the fresh catch, especially good are the squid and the *garides giouvetsi* (shrimp baked in a red sauce with tiny noodles). You can also stuff yourself on a sampling of appetizers. ✉ *Iliou 4, Kavouri,* ☎ *01/895–1298. No credit cards.*

$$$$ ▦ **Margi House.** The Margi, popular for its location 100 yards from the beach, has comfortable, plainly furnished pastel-hued rooms done in "Greek modern," all with TVs. The included buffet breakfast will rev you up for a day of Attica or Athens sites. ✉ *Letous 11, 16671,* ☎ *01/896–0812 or 01/896–0061 through 0065,* ℻ *01/896–0229. 109 rooms with bath, 2 suites. Restaurant, bar, snack bar, air-conditioning, pool. AE, DC, MC, V.*

$$$ 🏨 **Armonia.** Most guest rooms in the beachside Armonia have sea views and private terraces, and all are done in impeccable Greek island style. If the sea is unswimmable during your stay, the pool offers refreshment and a section for children. Buffet breakfast is included in the price. ⊠ *Armonias 1, 16671,* ☎ *01/896–0030, 01/896–0105, 01/896–2656, or 01/896–3184,* 📠 *01/896–3698. 100 rooms with bath, 25 suites. Restaurant, 2 bars, pool. AE, DC, MC, V.*

En Route   Beyond Vouliagmeni the road threads along a rocky coastline dotted with inlets, where intrepid bathers swim off the rocks, leaving their cars in the roadside parking areas and scrambling down to the inviting coves below. If you join them, take along your snorkels, fins, and masks so you can enjoy the underwater scenery, but avoid the sea urchins. Beyond Vouliagmeni is one of the most heavily developed seacoasts in Greece; only the many tavernas proclaiming *psaria fresca* (fresh fish) remind us of the former fishing villages here.

Sounion

❹   *70 km (43½ mi) southeast of Athens, 50 km (31 mi) southeast of Vouliagmeni.*

Sounion, in addition to being the important home to the enormous Temple of Poseidon, was a seaport with a well-protected harbor, where today the beach, a hotel, and several tavernas accommodate visitors and those paying homage to the gods. Just offshore is the uninhabited islet of Patroklou, and ahead is the steep-walled promontory of Sounion itself.

Beyond the scanty remains of an ancient *propylon* (gateway) is the **Temple of Poseidon;** on your left are the remains of the *Temenos* (precinct) **of Poseidon,** on your right a **stoa** and **rooms.** The temple itself (now off limits to tourists) may have been designed just after the middle of the 5th century BC by the same architect who built the Temple of Hephaistos in the ancient Agora of Athens: The people here were considered Athenian citizens, the sanctuary was Athenian, and Poseidon occupied a position second only to Athena herself. Situated on the highest point of the acropolis, the temple was built on the site of an earlier cult to Poseidon, and two colossal statues of youths (perhaps votives to the god), carved well over a century before the temple's construction, were discovered in early excavations. Both are now in the National Museum in Athens. The remaining columns, some of which have recently been re-erected, now stand sentinel over the Aegean, visible from miles away. The view from the summit is spectacular. In the slanting light of the late-afternoon sun, the land masses to the west stand out in sharp profile: the bulk of Aegina backed by the mountains of the Peloponnese. On the land side, the slopes of the acropolis retain traces of the fortification walls. ⊠ *From promontory, pass through gate and climb rocky path that follows, roughly, the ancient approach,* ☎ *0292/39363.* 💶 *600 dr.* ☉ *Mon.–Sat. 9 AM–sunset, Sun. 10 AM–sunset.*

Beach

If you spend the morning at Sounion and have lunch on the beach below, you may also want to take a swim, although the sandy strip becomes uncomfortably crowded in summer.

Dining and Lodging

$$ ✕ **Restaurant Ilias.** Stop at this converted fisherman's shack for a selection of fresh fish, simple salads, and greens enjoyed indoors or outdoors. Fish is always expensive, so do not be surprised at the size of the bill (but it is still less than in Athens). In winter, try *barbounia* (red mullet) and remember, the shrimp is always "fresh frozen," and the

squid is fresh only in winter. ⊠ *On beach below Temple of Poseidon,* ☎ *0292/39114. No credit cards.*

$$$ 🏨 **Cape Sounion Beach.** The rooms at this self-contained complex of little bungalows are tasteful, with solid furniture and attractive Greek-island colors. All open into a garden, and most face southeast toward the Temple of Poseidon. The hotel's cove-embraced beach would be idyllic without the din of the nearby road. The obligatory half board includes American breakfast and lunch or dinner. ⊠ *Poseidonios at 67 km mark, 19500,* ☎ *0292/39391 through 0292/39394, 0292/39821 through 39825,* FAX *0292/39038;* ☎ *Athens: 01/861–7837 or 01/865–5516,* FAX *01/861–6473. 188 rooms with bath. 2 restaurants, 3 bars, cafeteria, pool, 5 tennis courts, exercise room, beach, water sports, dance club. AE, DC, MC, V. Closed Nov.–Mar.*

$$ 🏨 **Aegeon Hotel.** This hotel has seen much better days and is slowly starting to renovate piecemeal, but nothing can beat its location—much objected to by environmentalists and archaeologists—on *the* beach below the Temple of Poseidon, at the very harbor ancient ships once negotiated. Even the rooms in back, which look up the slopes flanking the acropolis, have a good view. Continental breakfast is included in the price. Be warned: The beach will be crowded in high season, and the heat may not work in the winter. ⊠ *Sounion Beach, 19500,* ☎ *0292/39200,* FAX *0292/39234. 45 rooms with bath. Restaurant, bar. No credit cards.*

Lavrion

❺   *80 km (50 mi) southeast of Athens, 10 km (6¼ mi) north of Sounion.*

Lavrion, a post-industrial town with a few remnants of belle époque architecture, is best known for its important ancient silver mines, exploited since prehistoric times, which provided the wherewithal for Athens's astounding growth. Several thousand ancient shafts have been discovered in the area, perpendicular and diagonal bores that were worked by slave labor controlled by contractors with state-granted leases. The last mines closed in the late '70s.

In Thorikos, 5 mi north of Lavrion, are the remains of the 4th-century BC **Theater of Thorikos,** (⊠ On the hill of the ancient town), built for the slaves who worked in the silver mines.

Lodging

$ 🏨 **Belle Epoque Hotel.** Not even the inhabitants of Lavrion know about this little in-town hotel in a renovated belle époque mansion. The outside is much more inviting than the inside, which now has cell-like rooms and baths, but the public areas have been lovingly decorated with the owners' collections of minerals, shells, and bric-a-brac. It is a welcome alternative to some of the high-priced resort hotels in the area. ⊠ *Pleion 23, 19500,* ☎ *0292/27130, 0292/26564, or 0292/26059. 28 rooms with bath. Bar, breakfast room, cafeteria. No credit cards.*

En Route   The road winds inland, through bare hilly country now spoiled by cement-box dwellings, past **Keratea** and **Markopoulos,** a market center of the Mesogeion, known for its wine and good-quality bread. Continuing through stands of olive trees and vineyards, the road now runs almost due west, with Mt. Hymettos hovering straight ahead.

Paiania

❻   *18 km (11 mi) east of Athens, 34 km (21 mi) northwest of Lavrion.*

The Athenian suburb of Paiania is home to a unique site to Greece: the **Vorres Museum of Greek Art,** which displays some interesting folk art and a collection of contemporary Greek works, all in buildings restored in traditional style. Mr Vorres owns, operates, and even lives in the museum. When he's not busy in his museum gallery, he wears the hat of mayor, trying to organize the citizens of Paiania. ☎ *01/664–2520 or 01/664–4771.* ✉ *300 dr.* ☉ *Weekends 10–2.*

The **Koutouki cave,** discovered in 1926, is just the right depth and darkness to awe young children into silence without frightening them. High on the eastern slopes of Hymettos, connected to Paiania village by a good paved road, the cave has been rigged with paths, lights, and sound. ✉ *Above village of Paiania,* ☎ *01/664–2910.* ✉ *500 dr.* ☉ *Daily 9–4.*

Brauron

❼ *40 km (25 mi) east of Athens, 40 km (25 mi) southeast of Paiania, via Makropoulo.*

Brauron, where the **Sanctuary of Artemis** rises on the site of an earlier shrine, lies in a waterlogged depression at the foot of a small hill. Found here are a **5th century** BC **temple** and a horseshoe-shape **stoa.** Here, the virgin huntress was worshiped as protectress of childbirth. Every four years, the Athenians celebrated the Brauronia, in which girls between ages 5 and 10 took part in arcane ceremonies, including a dance in which they were dressed as bears. The **museum** next to the site contains statues of these little girls, as well as many votive offerings. ✉ *At foot of hill near fork in road to northern Loutsa,* ☎ *0299/27020.* ✉ *400 dr.* ☉ *Tues., Wed., Sat., and Sun. 8:30–3.*

Beach

The coast road north from Brauron, which skirts an extensively (and badly) developed coastline, leads to a pleasant **beach** at Loutsa (✉ 8 km/5 mi north of Brauron), framed by a backdrop of umbrella pines and with shallow waters—perfect for small children but crowded in the summer.

OFF THE BEATEN PATH **MONASTERY OF DAOU PENDELI AND PIKERMI** – In spite of its accessibility only via the road west toward Athens from Loutsa (✉ Mt. Pendeli, about 13 km/8 mi west of Loutsa; ✉ Free; ☉ Daily about 8–3), this site preserves a certain humble charm. Monastery buffs may endeavor the cypress-lined drive to the peaceful, fortresslike monastery of Daou Pendeli, set in a glen with water and a thick stand of enormous maple trees and Aleppo pines. It's secluded in a large garden, where the fragrance of jasmine and roses mingles with the delicate scent of pines and cypresses. The unattractive apartment buildings you passed are Kallitechnoupolis, or Artists' Town, where some of Greece's notables in music and art have banded together in a joint building project. Farther west along the Athens road is the village of Pikermi, where in the last century fossils were found that show the existence in Greece of saber-tooth tigers, mammoths, miniature horses, and a dinotherium (a huge protoelephant with a downturn to the tusks).

Marathon

❽ *42 km (26 mi) northeast of Athens, 33 km (20½ mi) north of Brauron*

Today, Athenians enter the fabled plain of Marathon only to enjoy a break from Athens. But when the Athenians hoplites entered the plain in 490 BC, it was to crush a numerically superior Persian force. Some

6,400 invaders were killed fleeing to their ships, while the Athenians lost just 192 warriors. This, their proudest victory, became the stuff of Athenian legends; the hero Theseus was said to have appeared himself in aid of the Greeks, along with the god Pan.

A sign for the **Marathon Tomb** directs you to the ancient mound built over the graves of the Athenian dead and to the **Museum of Marathon,** which contains objects from excavations in the area. ⊠ *Approx. 6 km (3¾ mi) south of modern village of Marathon,* ☎ *0294/55155.* ⊡ *400 dr.* ⊙ *Tues.–Sun. 8:30–3.*

❾ The **Rhamnous archaeological site,** an isolated, romantic spot on a small promontory, overlooks the sea between continental Greece and the island of Euboia. From at least the Archaic period, Rhamnous was known for the worship of Nemesis, the great leveler, who brought down the proud and punished the arrogant. The site, excavated over many years, preserves traces of temples from the 6th and 5th centuries BC. The later temple housed the cult statue of Nemesis, envisioned as a woman, which is the only cult statue (even fragmentary) left from the High Classical period. Many fragments have turned up, including the head, which was shipped off to the British Museum before the establishment of the modern Greek state. As you wander over this usually serene, and always evocative site, you'll discover at its edge little coves where you can take a swim. ⊠ *10 km (6 mi) northeast of Marathon,* ☎ *0294/63477.* ⊡ *400 dr.* ⊙ *Daily 7–6.*

❿ **Lake Marathon** (⊠ 8 km/5½ mi west of Marathon), a man-made reservoir formed by the **Marathon Dam,** was built by an American company in 1925–31. Walk or drive across the dam (⊠ 9 km/½ mi west down a side road from the village of Ayios Stefanos) for a picnic in its cool park; you may be astonished by the sight of all that landlocked water in Greece. A replica of the Athenian Treasury from Delphi stands in the park behind the dam.

Beaches

Near Marathon, the best beach is the long, sandy stretch called **Skinies.** The coves at **Rhamnous** are delightful, but beware of sea urchins when swimming off the rocks.

Dining and Lodging

$$ ✕▥ **Golden Coast Hotel and Bungalows.** Right on the beach, the Golden Coast has the kind of simple, functional rooms and facilities that are perfect for families. Although the beach is narrow and rocky—as on most of this coast—children have a choice of two pools, and the adults can go in a third. The restaurant's food is unusually good, and buffet breakfast is included in the price. ⊠ *Marathon Beach, 19005,* ☎ *0294/57100,* ℻ *0294/57300;* ☎ *Athens: 01/362–0662. 550 rooms with bath, 254 bungalows, and 45 apartments. Restaurant, 4 bars, grill, 3 pools, miniature golf, tennis court, volleyball, water sports, dance club, meeting room. Closed Oct.–Apr. AE, DC, MC, V.*

Outdoor Activities and Sports

RUNNING

Every year in October the **Athens Open International Peace Marathon** is run over the same course taken in 490 BC by Pheidippides, when he carried to Athens the news of victory over the Persians. The 42.2-km race, open to men and women of all ages, starts in Marathon and finishes at the Olympic Stadium in Athens. There is a $10 entry fee. Apply by mail (⊠ SEGAS, Race Organizers, Syngrou 137, 17121 Athens, ☎ 01/935–9302, ℻ 01/934–2980).

En Route Approximately 10 km (6 mi) north of Ayios Stefanos the road begins the gentle climb to Kapandriti, a fast-developing country village.

Amphiareion

⑪ *49 km (30½ mi) northeast of Athens; 18 km (11 mi) north of Lake Marathon.*

Cradled in a hidden valley at a bend in the road, the **Sanctuary of Amphiareos** is a quiet, well-watered haven, blessed with green bushes and trees. It is startlingly different from the surrounding countryside, where overgrazing and development have destroyed most of the trees. Amphiareos was a mortal transformed after death into a healing divinity. In the sanctuary are the remains of a miniature **theater;** a 4th-century BC **Doric temple;** the long **stoa;** and the **Enkimiterion** (literally, "dormitory"), where patients stayed awaiting their cure. They would sacrifice a ram, then lie down wrapped in its skin, waiting for a dream, which resident priests would interpret for the prescribed cure. There is also a small **museum** containing finds from early excavations, but at press time (October, 1996) it was still closed for renovation. ⊠ *Site,* ☎ *0295/62144.* ⌨ *400 dr.* ⊘ *Weekdays 8–6, weekends and holidays 8:30–3.*

Ayia Triada

33 km (20½ mi) northwest of Athens, (not accessible from Amphiareion).

The tiny resort of Ayia Triada offers a splendid view of the plain of Athens cradled by Mt. Pendeli and Mt. Hymettos. Once the heavily wooded habitat of wolves and bears, Mt. Parnis provided fuel for the charcoal burners of Acharnes in the days before oil. There are many lovely nature walks through the Mt. Parnis massif, reachable from Ayia Triada, and its rugged heights, often snow-clad in winter, make a natural barrier dividing Attica and the lands claimed by Athens from Boeotia in central Greece.

Phyle

⑫ *31 km (19¼ mi) northwest of Athens, 2 km (1¼ mi) south of Ayia Triada.*

Evidence of Phyle's source of wealth, livestock, is everywhere: in the dozens of whole lambs, pigs, and goats strung up in front of butcher shops; in the numerous tavernas lining the main street; in the many window displays of fresh sheep yogurt.

⑬ **Moni Kleiston** (⊠ 5 km/3 mi north of Phyle), perched over a steep, densely wooded gully, dates mainly from the 17th century. The tiny, neatly maintained monastery, home still to a handful of nuns, was partially renovated in the recent past. Part of the tiny 14th-century chapel, rebuilt in the 17th century, is carved out of a cave. Across a gully, another cave, on a perilously steep slope above the rushing waters of the gorge, is full of votives placed there by nimble worshipers.

OFF THE BEATEN PATH   **FORTRESS OF PHYLE** – The road from the monastery loops back and around the flank of Mt. Parnis, climbing slowly through rugged, deserted country on the ancient road northwest to Thebes. The Athenians built several fortresses along the way, including the untended 4th-century BC Fortress of Phyle (⊠ On a high bluff just west of the road to Thebes, 13 km/8 mi north of the modern town), a dramatically beautiful site, its rugged rectangular masonry standing or scattered about the site.

Dining

$$ ✕ **To Frourio.** If you visit the fortress on a weekend, be sure to stop at "The Fort," for great, inexpensive lamb, potatoes, and salad. On cold days, you'll wish you had marshmallows for the fireplace; on warm days the outdoor terrace offers an unforgettable setting. *Note:* when it snows on Parnis, the road up here may be closed, so call before setting out. ⊠ *Several hundred feet beyond turnoff to ruins, Phyle,* ☎ *01/241–1172. Closed weekdays.*

Monastery of Daphni

⑭   *11 km (7 mi) west of Athens.*

The Monastery of Daphni, which means "laurel tree," sacred to Apollo, reminds us that his sanctuary once occupied this site. It was destroyed in AD 395 after the antipagan edicts of the Emperor Theodosius, and the Orthodox monastery was probably established in the 6th century. The church and monastery were rebuilt in the 11th century, sacked in 1205 by the Crusaders, and reoccupied by Orthodox monks only in the 16th century. Since then it has been a barracks and a lunatic asylum, and it has been restored extensively in several phases. The miraculously preserved mosaics are among the finest from the golden age of Byzantine art: powerful portraits of figures from the Old and New Testaments, images of Christ and his mother, and in the golden dome, a stern Pantokrator, "ruler of all." ⊠ *End of Iera Odos,* ☎ *01/581–1558.* ▢ *500 dr.* ☉ *Daily 8:30–3.*

Eleusis

⑮   *22 km (13½ mi) west of Athens, 11 km (7 mi) west of the Monastery of Daphni.*

The growing city of Athens co-opted the land around Eleusis, placing shipyards in the pristine gulf and steel mills and petrochemical plants along its shores. It is hard to imagine that once there stretched in every direction fields of corn and barley sacred to the goddess symbolized by the sheaf and sickle; the **sanctuary of Demeter** now lies in the new town, on the east slope and at the foot of the acropolis, which is hardly visible amid the modern buildings. The legend of Demeter and her daughter Persephone explained for the ancients the cause of the seasons and the origins of agriculture.

It was to Eleusis that Demeter traveled in search of Persephone after the girl had been kidnapped by Hades, god of the underworld. Zeus himself interceded to restore her to the distraught Demeter, but succeeded only partially, giving mother and daughter just half a year together. Nevertheless, in gratitude to King Keleos of Eleusis, who had given her refuge in her time of need, Demeter presented his son Triptolemos with wheat seeds, the knowledge of agriculture, and a winged chariot so he could spread them to mankind. Keleos built a megaron (large hall) in her honor, the first Eleusinian sanctuary.

The worship of Demeter took the form of mysterious rites, and both the Lesser and the Greater Eleusinian rituals closely linked Athens with the sanctuary. The procession for the Greater Eleusinia began and ended there, following the route of the Sacred Way. Much of what we see now in the sanctuary is of Roman construction or repair, although physical remains on the site date back to the Mycenaean period. One follows the old Sacred Way to the **Great Propylaea** (Gates) and continues on to the **Precinct of Demeter,** which was strictly off-limits on pain of death to any but the initiated. The **Telesterion,** or Temple of Demeter, now a vast open space surrounded by battered tiers of seats, was the hall of initiation. It had a roof supported by six rows of seven columns, presumably so the mysteries would be obscured, and it could accommodate 3,000 people. The **museum,** just beyond, contains an array of pottery and sculpture, particularly of the Roman period. ⊠ *Iera Odos 2,* ☎ *01/554–6019.* 🖾 *400 dr.* 🕙 *Tues.–Sun. 8:30–3.*

The Arts

FESTIVAL WITH GREEK DRAMA

Throughout the month of September, Eleusis hosts the **Aeschilia** festival with ancient Greek drama presented on the archaeological site; call the Athens EOT for details (☞ Visitor Information *in* Excursions from Athens A to Z, *below*).

OFF THE BEATEN PATH

STRAITS OF SALAMIS – It was here that the desperate and wily Athenians aided by Sparta, Corinth, and Aegina destroyed the Persian fleet. In 490 BC, the Persians had returned to exact revenge for their defeat at Marathon in 480 BC, attacking and burning the Acropolis. The Athenians, told by the Delphic oracle to protect themselves with "wooden walls," interpreted this to mean their ships. Evacuating their women and children, they drew up their wooden boats and, by a ruse, drew the Persians into a trap. So sure were the Persians of a devastating victory that Xerxes the king had set up a fine silver throne on the hill overlooking the strait to watch his troops thrash the Greeks. He witnessed instead a disaster that, even more than that at Marathon, put a definitive end to Persian ambitions in the western Aegean. Ferries leave Perama (15 km/9⅓ mi west of Athens) every half hour.

THE SARONIC GULF ISLANDS
Aegina, Poros, Hydra, Spetses

The Saronic Gulf Islands are a diverse group: Aegina's pine forests mix with groves of pistachio trees, a product for which Aegina is justly famous. Water taxis buzz to Poros, more like an islet, from the Peloponnese, carrying weary locals eager to relax on its beaches and linger in the island cafés. Hydra and Spetses are farther south and more rewarding: both ban automobiles, and though Hydra's restaurants and boutiques cater to the sophisticated European traveler, Spetses's broad forests and scattered resorts lure Greeks.

Aegina

30 km (18½ mi) south of Piraeus.

Aegina has become an inexpensive resort area primarily frequented by Athenians. By the 6th century BC, Aegina, the commercial entrepôt, had become a major art center, known in particular for bronze foundries, worked by such sculptors as Kallon, Onatas, and Anaxagoras. This powerful island, lying so close off the coast of Attica, could not fail to come into conflict with Athens. As Athens's imperial ambitions grew, Aegina became a thorn in its side. In 458 BC Athens laid siege to the city, eventually conquering the island. In the 19th century, it experienced a remarkable rebirth as an important base in the War of Independence, and it was briefly the capital of the new Greek state.

❶❻ The boats and hydrofoils dock at the main town, **Aegina town,** a busy little harbor city on the western side of the island, where a few surviving neoclassical buildings mingle with a modern cement and cinder-block sprawl. Idyllic seascapes and a few beautiful gardens make Aegina attractive; its numerous cafés and restaurants lining the harbor face a road along the water teeming with horse-and-carriage traffic, trucks, and taxis. Take a stroll around town before heading to the eastern shore. This side of the island is more fertile and less mountainous than the east side; its gardens and fields are blessed with grapes, olives, figs, almonds, and above all, the treasured pistachio trees.

As you approach from the sea, your first view of the town of Aegina takes in the sweep of the harbor, punctuated by the tiny white Chapel of **Ayios Nikolaos** (⊠ Aegina town harbor).

While conducting negotiations for Greece, Ioannis Kapodistrias, the first president of Greece, conducted meetings in the medieval **Markelon Tower** (⊠ Aegina town center).

The Aeginetans were first among the peoples of Greece to mint their own coins (often of fine silver, stamped on one face with the image of a turtle), which for generations were common tender throughout the Greek world. They created a standardized system of weights and measures, and Aegina became a major trader in grain, wine, oil, and slaves during Greece's Archaic period, her ships plying from the Black Sea to the coast of Egypt. Much of the ancient city lies under the modern, with public buildings and sanctuaries built on the promontory just north of the modern town. Still visible on this hill (known as Kolonna, or "column") is a single column of a late Archaic Temple of Apollo. The small **archaeological museum and site** on the site has a jumble of items, including Bronze Age pottery found in the excavations and a Hercules sculpture from the Temple of Apollo. Unfortunately the museum is closed because of a theft several years ago, but the site itself remains open to the public. ⊠ *Aegina town,* ☎ *0297/22248.* 🎟 *500 dr.* ⏲ *Tues.–Sun. 8:30–3.*

NEED A BREAK? On narrow Pan Irioti street behind the harbor, near the entrance of the fish market, you'll find ouzeris and tavernas—generally without an official name—where you can snack on grilled octopus, perfect with an afternoon ouzo. You'll know you're in the right place when you see elderly gents worrying their beads seated beside glistening octopus hung up to dry.

In the midst of a valley filled with gardens of pistachio, almond, and olive trees sits the **Monastery of Ayios Nektarios** (⊠ 6 km/4 mi east of Aegina town), the island's patron saint (canonized in 1961), whose relics lie in a dozen churches throughout Greece. The sprawling remains of the medieval "Old Town" or **Palaiochora** (⊠ On the rocky barren hill above the monastery, 6 km/4 mi east of Aegina town), built in the 9th century by islanders whose seaside town was the constant prey of pirates. Capital of the island until 1826, Palaiochora still has more than 20 **churches** in various stages of decay, some still in use, amid the rubble of its houses and streets.

Beaches

Aegina's beaches near town are pleasant enough, though crowded.

Dining and Lodging

$–$$ ✕ **To Maridaki.** The gracious owner will do his best to make you feel welcome at this crowded waterfront restaurant near the cathedral. In addition to the large selection of fresh fish the restaurant also serves grilled octopus and grilled meats—souvlaki, beef patties heavy on the onions, chops—and of course, standard magirefta such as pastitsio and moussaka. In summer try one of the sticky sweets, like *kaidaifi* (made from shredded wheat) for dessert. ⊠ *Paralia Aegina,* ☎ *0297/25869. No credit cards.*

$$ ⊞ **Moondy Bay Hotel.** This hotel 6 km (4 mi) outside Aegina sits next to a beach. One of the older of the "modern" hotels (built in 1967), it has simple, comfortable rooms and a relaxing setting. The price is for half-board, which in this case means breakfast and dinner. ⊠ *Moondy Bay Beach, Profitis Ilias 18010,* ☎ *0297/61222, 0297/61146,* 🖷 *0297/61147;* ☎ *Athens: 01/360–3745 or 01/360–3746. 78 rooms with bath. Restaurant, bar, air-conditioning, saltwater pool, miniature golf, tennis court, playground. V. Closed Nov.–Easter.*

$ ⊞ **Eginitiko Archontiko (Traditional Settlement).** This jewel of a pension, in a restored 19th-century mansion of neoclassical inspiration, has been host to Kapodistrias and the island's own Saint Nektarios. Care has been taken to preserve the original painted walls and ceilings, and every nook and cranny has been done in period style. The new owner provides somewhat erratic service, but she has a way with charming stories about Aegina. Its in-town location, next to the Markelos Tower, is very convenient. ⊠ *Ayiou Nicolaou and 1 Thomaidou, 18010,* ☎ *0297/24156 or 0297/24968,* 🖷 *0297/26716. 12 rooms with showers, 1 suite. AE, DC, MC, V.*

Shopping

PISTACHIO STANDS

Aegina's famous pistachios can be bought from stands along the harbor. They make excellent snacks and gifts.

Eastern Aegina

Area approximately 11 km (7 mi) east of Aegina town.

The eastern side of Aegina is rugged and sparsely inhabited, except for a former fishing hamlet now given over to tourism. The small port of **Ayia Marina** (⊠ Below the Sanctuary of Aphaia [☞ *below*], via the small paved road) has many hotels, cafés, restaurants, and a beach to accommodate visitors.

⑰ The **Sanctuary of Aphaia** perches on a promontory with superb views of Athens and Piraeus across the water. This site has been occupied by many sanctuaries to Aphaia; the ruins visible today are those of the temple built in the early 5th century BC. Aphaia was apparently a pre-Hellenic deity, whose worship eventually converged with that of Athena. The temple, one of the finest extant examples of Archaic architecture, was adorned with an exquisite group of pedimental sculptures that are now in the Munich Glyptothek. ⊠ *12 km (7 mi) east of Aegina town,* ☎ *0297/32398.* 🖻 *800 dr.* ☉ *Weekdays 8:15–7 (winter 8:15–5), weekends 8:30–3.*

Lodging

$$ ⊞ **Apollo.** Thanks to the good location on the beach at Ayia Marina, most of the rooms at this hotel have balconies and sea views. The service is satisfactory, and the many amenities are ideal for active travelers who don't want to go far. Buffet breakfast is included in the price and TVs are provided upon request. ⊠ *Ayia Marina beach, 18010,* ☎ *0297/32281 or 0297/32271 through 32274,* 🖷 *0297/32688. 107 rooms with bath. Restaurant, bar, saltwater pool, miniature golf, tennis court, Ping-Pong, waterskiing. AE, DC, MC, V. Closed Nov.–Mar.*

Poros

⑱ *21½ km (13½ mi) south of Aegina.*

The island of Poros sits due south of Aegina, separated from the Peloponnese by a narrow strait. **Poros town** (⊠ Draped over the promontory guarding the strait) has a long attractive waterfront skirting the base of the hill. In antiquity, Poros was the site of an important **Sanctuary of Poseidon,** whose scrappy **ruins** can be seen at the approximate center of the island. Many of the blocks from the temple were carried off in the 18th century to build the monastery on nearby Hydra, which you can reach by hydrofoil or ferry.

As you clear the narrow straits of Poros and head east, you will see on your left the 18th-century monastery of **Zoodochos Pighi** (Life-giving Spring; ⊠ On a pine-clad hillside just east of the town of Poros).

In case you haven't seen enough of ancient Greece yet, Poros's **archaeological museum** houses a spare collection of antiquities found on the island and at Troizen on the shore opposite. A copy of the famous Troizen Inscription referring to Themistocles and his plans before the Battle of Salamis can be found here. ⊠ *Main Plateia.* ☎ *No phone.* 🎫 *Free.* ⊙ *Tues.–Sun. 8:45–3, Sun. and holidays 9:30–2:30.*

Hydra

⑲   *28 km (17½ mi) south of Poros.*

As you round the tip of the Northern Peloponnese, before you stretches the full length of Hydra, mountainous and barren. Although there are traces of an ancient settlement, the island was sparsely inhabited until the Ottoman period. In the 16th century, its rugged slopes offered a haven for refugees from the Peloponnese during the constant wars between the Ottomans and the Venetians. The settlers turned to the sea and began building boats, and by the early 18th century, their trade routes stretched from the mainland to Asia Minor and even America. By its end, the fleet, profiting from the Napoleonic Wars, had captured much of the lucrative grain trade between the Ukraine and western Europe, earning great fortunes and much notoriety in blockade-running. After the Greek Revolution, Hydra sank into relative obscurity until well past the middle of this century, when it was discovered by outsiders; its noble port and houses have since been rescued and placed on the Council of Europe's list of protected monuments, with strict ordinances regulating construction and renovation. All motor traffic is banned from the island (except for several rather noisy garbage trucks).

Upon approaching the island, **Hydra town,** invisible at first, gradually reveals itself, with gray and white houses climbing steep slopes surrounding a nearly round harbor, looking much as it did in 1821, when Hydra was crucial in the struggle for independence.

Many of the waterfront houses, built between 1770 and 1821, consist of a rectangular basic unit two to three stories tall, with the upper floor set back to create a terrace, and most have courtyards with large subterranean cisterns. (People claim that the cisterns were also used to hide gold and treasure in the 18th and 19th centuries, and that eels were introduced to keep the water clean and drinkable.)

In the early 19th century, the tremendous surge in disposable wealth enabled shipowners to build the characteristic **archontika** ("great houses"), massive gray stone mansions facing the harbor, with forbidding, fortresslike exteriors. Good examples include the **Tsamados House** (⊠ On the harbor opposite the ferry landing); the **Tombazi House,** now the School of Fine Arts (⊠ Halfway up the west side of the harbor); the **Voulgaris (Merikles-Oikonomou) House** (⊠ On the west harbor); and the **Koundouriotes House** (⊠ Looming on the west headland). The **Monastery of the Panaghia** (⊠ Along the central section of the harbor) was built in the late 18th century partly of stone taken from the Sanctuary of Poseidon on Poros. The monastery's bell tower is a fine example of the early 19th-century marble-carving done by a guild of traveling artisans (perhaps from the island of Tinos) who left their mark all over the Aegean in this period.

Beach

Hydra has only a small one at the little harbor called **Miramare.**

Dining and Lodging

$$ ✕ **O Kipos (The Garden).** A favorite with Hydra's foreign community, O Kipos is so-called because of its shady courtyards away from the hustle of the port. The specialty is *tis oras* (grilled meats) like chicken souvlaki, *kokkoretsi* (goat cooked over a spit), lamb *exohiko* (cooked in paper with vegetables), lamb chops, and *kontosouvli* (pork grilled on a short), but fresh grilled swordfish fillet or souvlaki are also tasty. For something lighter in summer, graze on a bunch of appetizers—an excellent homemade *taramosalata* (dip made from roe), zucchini pies, and the Greek version of chicken salad. For dessert, there is homemade halvah, much better than the store-bought variety. ⊠ *Near stadium,* ☎ *0298/52329. No credit cards. Closed Nov.–Apr. No lunch.*

$$$–$$$$ 🏨 **Bratsera.** An old sponge factory was transformed into a posh,
★ unique A-class hotel with doors made out of old packing crates still bearing the "Piraeus" stamp. The service is excellent in the hotel and the restaurant, which specializes in European cuisine for a nice break from souvlaki. Try the filet mignon and take in the sophisticated scene. ⊠ *1st street to left as you leave ferry, near Flying Dolphin office,* ☎ *0298/53971, restaurant* ☎ *0298/52794,* FAX *0298/53626, 23 rooms with bath. Restaurant, bar, air-conditioning, pool, conference room. AE, DC, MC, V.*

$$$ 🏨 **Hotel Orloff.** Built in 1798 by Count Orloff, who came to Greece
★ with a Russian fleet to try and undo the Turks, this archontiko still retains the splendor of the past with the benefit of modern amenities. The heavy single shutters, which were used to protect against attack, have been preserved, and antiques—walnut furniture, paintings, and lithographs—grace the blue-and-white rooms. No two are alike; some have sitting areas, and all have views of the town or the pretty courtyard. Buffet breakfast is included. ⊠ *Rafalia 9, 18040,* ☎ *0298/52564 or 0298/52495,* FAX *0298/53532;* ☎ *Athens: 01/822–6210 or 01/823–6808,* FAX *01/825–1778. 10 rooms with bath. Bar, breakfast room. AE, DC, MC, V. Closed end Oct.–late-Mar.*

$$–$$$ 🏨 **Miranda Guest House.** Artists and art collectors alike will feel at home in this aesthetically decorated traditional Hydroit home, which now contains an art gallery that, in July and August, exhibits local and international artists. Some have balconies with sea views, and others have air-conditioning. This hotel is convenient to the port. Continental breakfast is included. ⊠ *Miaouli, 2 blocks inland from center of port, 18040,* ☎ *0298/52230,* FAX *0298/53510. 9 rooms with bath, 3 suites. MC, V. Closed Dec.–Feb.*

$$ 🏨 **Leto Hotel.** The Leto makes up for its plain, rudimentary design and furnishings with its cordial staff and central location. The narrow streets can be noisy, so ask for a room on the upper floors, away from the alleys. Buffet breakfast may be included. ⊠ *1 block inland from center of port, 18040,* ☎ *0298/52280, 0298/53385, or 0298/53386,* FAX *0298/53806. 30 rooms with shower. Bar, breakfast room, air-conditioning. No credit cards. Closed Nov.–end of Mar.*

$$ 🏨 **Miramare Beach Hotel.** This small, simple hotel is perfect for families with small children. Most rooms open directly onto the little beach, the only stretch of sand in or near the town of Hydra, which offers parasailing and has a boat-pulled rubber banana. The town is about 20 minutes away on foot, but the hotel's two boats shuttle back

and forth to the main harbor from 8 AM to 3 AM. The attached restaurant has expensive Greek and Continental food that's not particularly good, but at least it's convenient, if you are spending the day on the beach. ⊠ *Mandraki Beach, 18040,* ☎ *0298/52300,* FAX *0298/52301. 28 bungalows with bath. Restaurant, air-conditioning. No credit cards. Closed Dec.–mid-Apr.*

$$ 🏨 **Mistral Hotel.** This archontiko offers you cozy rooms in simple, traditional style; the rooms in front have panoramic views of town. It is small and fills up quickly in summer. Breakfast is included. ⊠ *Above port, 18040,* ☎ *0298/52509 or 0298/53411,* FAX *0298/53412. 18 rooms with bath (6 rooms with air-conditioning for 2,600 dr. more per day). Dining room, snack bar. MC, V. Closed Dec.–mid-Feb.*

Nightlife

DISCOS

For dancing try **Disco Kavos-Lagoudera** (⊠ On the port), **Disco Heaven** (⊠ above the west side of the harbor), and the boisterous **Fever** (⊠ Halfway between the town and the hamlet of Kaminia).

Shopping

A number of elegant shops (some of them offshoots of Athens stores) sell fashionable and amusing clothing and jewelry, though you won't save anything by shopping here.

GIFTS

One especially delightful shop with a wide assortment of goods is aptly named "What is it?": **Ti Ein Auto** (⊠ About a block uptown from the harbor, ☎ FAX *0298/52546*).

Spetses

⑳ *24 km (15 mi) southwest of Hydra.*

In the years leading up to the revolution, Hydra's great rival and ally was the island of Spetses. Lying at the entrance to the Argolic Gulf, just off the mainland, Spetses was known even in antiquity for its hospitable soil and verdant, pine-clad slopes. The pine trees on the island today, however, were planted by a Spetsiot philanthropist dedicated to restoring the beauty stripped by the ship-building industry. There are far fewer trees than there were in antiquity, but the island is still well watered, and the many prosperous Athenians who have made Spetses their second home compete for the prettiest gardens and terraces. The island shows sporadic evidence of continuous habitation through all of antiquity. From the 16th century, settlers came over from the mainland and, as on Hydra, they soon began to look to the sea, building their own boats. They became master sailors, successful merchants, and later, in the Napoleonic wars, skilled blockade runners, earning fortunes that they poured into bigger boats and bigger houses. With the outbreak of the War of Independence in 1821, the Spetsiots dedicated their best ships and brave men (and women) to the cause.

Ships meet Spetses at **Dapia,** the jetty protecting the modern harbor. Fortified with cannons dating to the War of Independence, it faces the attractive waterfront, full of outdoor cafés and restaurants. The harbormaster's offices, to the right as you face the sea, occupy a building designed in the simple two-story, center-hall architecture typical of the period and this place.

In front of a popular park is **Bouboulina's house,** where guided tours in English on this interesting heroine's life are given. Laskarina Bouboulina was the bravest of all Spetsiot revolutionaries, the daughter of a Hydriot sea captain, and the wife, then widow, of two more sea captains. Left with a considerable inheritance and nine children, she dedicated herself to increasing her already substantial fleet and fortune. On her flagship, the *Agamemnon*, the largest in the Greek fleet, she sailed into war against the Ottomans at the head of the Spetsiot ships. Her fiery temper led to her death in a family feud many years later. ⊠ *Behind Dapia, near the harbor,* ☎ *0298/72416.* 🎫 *700 dr.* ☉ *45-minute tours daily 10–1, 4:30–9, daily morning and afternoon tour in English (6 PM off-season). Closed Dec.–Feb.*

Spetses's **museum** found an unlikely home in a fine late-18th-century archontiko built in a style that could be termed Turko-Venetian. It contains articles from the period of Spetses's greatness, including Bouboulina's bones, in a room festooned with the revolutionary flag. ⊠ *Town center, south of harbor,* ☎ *0298/72994.* 🎫 *500 dr.* ☉ *Tues.–Sun. 8:30–2:30.*

The promontory is the site of the little 19th-century **Church of Ayios Mamas.** On the headland sits the **Monastery of Ayios Nikolaos** (⊠ On the road heading southeast from the Dapia), now the episcopal seat. Its lacy white-marble bell tower recalled that of Hydra's port monastery. Presently it is undergoing extensive restoration, but much of it can still be seen, as it is being restored in the plateia directly adjoining the church.

Spetses has two harbors, and the **Old Harbor** conversely slumbers in obscurity. It is dominated by the gray stone mansion of the Botassis family, one of the earliest to settle on Spetses. The Old Harbor is perfect for an afternoon or evening stroll, while you might picture it in its heyday: the walls of the mansions resounding with the noise of shipbuilding and the streets humming with the discreet whisperings of revolution and piracy.

Well-to-do Athenians would descend to the 1914 **Posidonion Hotel** (⊠ Immediately west of the Dapia, near the harbor), the scene of glamorous society parties and balls in the era between the two world wars. The hotel's public rooms have retained this marvelous, unusual elegance.

The **Anargyrios and Korgialenios School** (½ km/⅓ mi west of the Dapia), established as an English-style boarding school for the children of Greece's Anglophilic upper class, is known as the inspiration for the school in John Fowles's *The Magus.*

You may wish to walk up to **Kastelli,** the original settlement of Spetses, of which little remains but four churches: the **Panaghia** or *Koimisis tis Theotokou* (the Assumption of the Virgin Mary), from the 17th century; **Ayios Vassilis** (Saint Basil); the **Taxiarchoi** (Archangels), early 19th century; and **Ayia Triada** (Holy Trinity), late 18th century. The churches are kept locked, but ask for the property owner or the guardian, who has a key.

Beaches

Spetses's best beaches are on the south side of the island, in **Ayioi Anargyroi** and **Ayia Paraskevi.**

Dining and Lodging

$ ✕ **Lirakis.** On the roof above the Lirakis supermarket, this restaurant serves up some of the best Greek cooking in town. Watch the boats come and go while you contemplate the many magirefta such as lamb fricassee, *briam* (like ratatouille), and *yiourvelakia* (minced meat in cabbage leaves and an avgolemono sauce), or opt for a lighter Greek salad, roasted chicken, or a cheese-ham omelet. ⊠ *Harbor,* ☎ *0298/72188. No credit cards. Closed Nov.–Apr.*

$$$ ✕⊞ **Spetses Hotel.** This self-contained resort has the best of both worlds: privacy and proximity to the delightful town. The rooms are comfortable, with TVs, and some of them have a sea view. ⊠ *Spetses beach, 18050,* ☎ *0298/72602, 0298/72603, or 0298/72604,* ⴼⴰⵅ *0298/72494. 77 rooms with bath. Restaurant, 2 bars, air-conditioning, beach. MC, V. Closed Nov.–Mar.*

$$ ✕⊞ **Kastelli Hotel.** This ordinary hotel, with rooms and baths of standard shape and decor, has no frills, but you could nearly bodysurf a good wave right up to the property—and it's also close to town. Buffet breakfast is included. ⊠ *Spetses beach, 18050,* ☎ *0298/72311, 0298/72312, 0298/72313,* ⴼⴰⵅ *0298/72161. 38 rooms with bath, 41 bungalows. Restaurant, bar, 2 tennis courts. DC, MC. Closed Nov.–Easter.*

$$$ ⊞ **Hotel Posidonion.** This glorious fin-de-siècle waterfront hotel has a
★ remarkable vantage point of Spetses Harbor to the mainland opposite. The belle époque public rooms have the grace of an earlier age and an air of grandeur atypical of Greece. The high-ceiling guest rooms are more modest than the public rooms, although the windows in the front rooms frame the wonderful view. Buffet breakfast is included. ⊠ *Dapia waterfront, 18050,* ☎ *0298/72308,* ⴼⴰⵅ *0298/72208. 52 rooms with bath. Bar, breakfast room. AE, DC, V. Closed. mid-Oct.–April.*

Festivals

Spetses holds the **Anargiria** during August at the Anargyrios School: The festival includes lectures, art exhibitions, and theatrical performances. Contact the Spetses tourist police for information (☞ Visitor Information *in* Excursions from Athens A to Z, *below*).

BATTLE REENACTMENT

Spetses also puts on an enormous reenactment of a War of Independence naval battle, in the first weekend of September. Book your hotel well in advance if you wish to see this popular event.

Nightlife

DISCOS

For the latest in the disco scene on Spetses head to **Delfinia** (⊠ New harbor) and **Le Figaro** (⊠ Old harbor).

DELPHI

Arachova, Delphi, Galaxidi

The sublime ruins of Delphi will invigorate those new to the study of ancient Greece, and those who have long awaited a chance to see where the Pythian priestess uttered her cryptic prophecies. The proximity to the ski lifts on Mt. Parnassos has turned the formerly quiet mountain village of Arachova into an odd confluence of traditional Greek mountain village and Athenian cafés, while Galaxidi on the coast now caters to wealthy Athenians who have restored many of the mansions once owned by shipbuilders.

En Route   The preferred route to Delphi follows the National Road to the Thebes turnoff, at 74 km (46 mi). Take the secondary road south past Thebes and continue west through the fertile plain, now planted with cotton, to busy Levadia, capital of the nome of Boeotia.

Osios Loukas

㉑   *150 km (93 mi) northwest of Athens, 24 km (15 mi) southeast of Arachova.*

The monastic complex Osios Loukas, still inhabited by a number of monks, looms on a prominent rise above a sparsely inhabited, fertile valley. Named for a local hermit named Luke, not the Evangelist, this important monastery was founded by the emperor Romanos II in 961, in recognition apparently of the accuracy of Luke's prophecy that Crete would be liberated by an emperor named Romanos. The Katholikon dates from the early 11th century and can be compared to the Church at Daphni in the beauty of its architecture and quality of the mosaics in the narthex and in portions of the domed nave. The tomb of Osios Loukas is set in the crypt, which is covered by lively and colorful 11th-century frescoes. ⊠ *On rise above valley,* ☎ *0267/22797.* ☞ *600 dr.* ☉ *Daily 8–2 and 4–6.*

Lodging

$ ⊞ **Hotel Delphi-Panorama.** Aptly named, the Panorama has a splendid view from its perch on the highest road in town, looking out to Mt. Parnassos or the Itea Gulf. The spotless, cheerful rooms and living area make up for the nondescript furnishings, and buffet breakfast is included in the price. ⊠ *Osios Loukas 47, 33054,* ☎ *0265/82437 or 0265/82061,* ☒ *0265/82081. 20 rooms with bath. Breakfast room. MC, V. Closed weekdays Jan.–Feb., except holidays.*

En Route From Dhistomo, 8 km (5 mi) west of Osios Loukas, an alternate, less-traveled route to Delphi climbs over the plain of Desfina and descends sharply to the sea just east of Itea. This route is slightly longer but more pleasant and lets you stop in Itea for a seaside lunch. The conventional route ignores Dhistomo and continues west past the Schiste turnoff, climbing ever higher as it nears Mt. Parnassos.

Arachova

㉒ *24 km (15½ mi) northwest of Osios Loukas, 157 km (97 mi) from Athens.*

Arachova's gray-stone houses with red-tile roofs cling to the steep slopes. Mt. Parnassos, the highest mountain range in Greece after Mt. Olympos, has since 1980 been developed for skiing and is now transformed into a winter resort, which may have spoiled its pristine calm, but has brought new life and money. The sophisticated newcomers (mostly Athenians) have preserved and restored many otherwise doomed houses, and several good tavernas and cozy hotels have cropped up.

Dining and Lodging

$–$$ ✕ **Pterolakka.** This brand-new restaurant is reliable for standard Greek cuisine in a large well-lit and friendly establishment. They specialize in grilled foods and offer a tasty souvlaki. ⊠ *Delphi–Arachova Rd.,* ☎ *0267/32556. No credit cards.*

$ ✕ **Taverna P. Thasargiris (Barba Yannis).** The son of the late Barba Yannis (Uncle John) now runs this busy taverna, the first in Arachova. The gargantuan summer or winter throngs can cause occasional surliness in the staff, but the food is worth it. In a town that counted its wealth in the size of its flocks, this taverna fittingly serves standard meat dishes and, above all, lamb. Try the fried *formaella* (a mild local sheep's milk cheese), *splinendera* (a tasty mix of various sheep organs), which Greeks customers swear by, kontosouvli, and the homemade *kokkineli* (a light, non-acidic rosé), which seemingly cuts right through the cholesterol. ⊠ *56 Delphi–Arachova Rd.,* ☎ *0267/31291. No credit cards. No lunch May–Oct.*

$$$ ⊞ **Arachova Inn.** Built in 1991, most of this inn's small, efficient, blue and white guest rooms have a view of the lower town and valley. The

sitting rooms and dining area have touches of local handicrafts and rustic wood furnishings. In winter the dining room and the lounge are warmed by fireplaces; breakfast is included. ⊠ *Delphi–Arachova Rd., 32004,* ☎ *0267/31353, 0267/31497, or 0267/32195,* 𝔽𝔸𝕏 *0267/31134. 42 rooms with shower. Restaurant (tour groups of about 12 only), bar. AE, DC, MC, V.*

$ 🏨 **Apollo Inn.** This inn makes up for its crammed location in the center of town with neat pine-furnished rooms, pretty bedspreads, and lovely terraces. Be careful not to confuse this hotel with the Apollo Hotel at the other end of town. ⊠ *106 Delphi–Arachova Rd., 32004,* ☎ *0267/31057 or 0267/31540. 19 rooms with bath. Breakfast room. AE, MC, V.*

$ 🏨 **Hotel Anemolia.** At this homey hotel on a bluff above the Delphi
★ road at the western edge of Arachova, about half the guest rooms have a view of the plain of Amphissa; on a clear day you may be able to see as far as the Peloponnese. Enjoy après ski among the simple furnishings, large lobby fireplace, and country antiques. The only covered swimming pool in Arachova here is usable year-round, and buffet breakfast is included in the price. ⊠ *Delphi–Arachova Rd., 32004,* ☎ 𝔽𝔸𝕏 *0267/31640 through 31644. 52 rooms with bath. Restaurant, bar, pool, sauna, exercise room. AE, DC, MC, V.*

$ 🏨 **Parnassos.** This little family-run hotel offers a rock-bottom solution to the housing problem and is comfortable for the price. The bedrooms in the old family home are of various sizes, mostly large, with high ceilings, and neat, plain furniture. ⊠ *18 Delphi–Arachova Rd., 32004,* ☎ *0267/31307,* 𝔽𝔸𝕏 *0267/31189. 9 rooms with shared baths. Breakfast room. No credit cards.*

Outdoor Activities and Sports

HIKING

The summit of Mt. Parnassos (2,457 meters/8,061 feet) is now easily accessible, thanks to roads opened up for the ski areas. The less hardy can drive to within 45 minutes of the summit. You can also drive to the Hellenic Alpine Club's refuge at 1,890 meters (6,201 feet) to spend the night and then walk to the summit in time to catch the sunrise— the only way to climb Mt. Parnassos!

For a booklet on Greece's refuges and information on the E4 and E6 hiking trails, contact the **Greek Federation of Mountaineering Associations** in Athens (⊠ Milioni 5, ☎ 01/363–6617 or 01/364–5904). The **Greek Touring Club** (⊠ Polytechniou 12, Athens, ☎ 01/524–8600) organizes hiking trips. The **Federation of Excursion Clubs** (⊠ Dragatsaniou 4, Athens, ☎ 01/323–4107) can provide a list of Greece's hiking clubs. For guides in Arachova and detailed maps, call the **EOT** (☞ Contacts and Resources *in* Excursions from Athens A to Z, *below*).

SKIING

If you hear that the snow is good on Parnassos, go for it. Ski with the gods and the muses, just 40 minutes from Arachova, at **Kelaria** and **Fterolakas** ski centers, which have 12 lifts, including a gondola. Kelaria has more challenging runs; Fterolakas has better restaurants and beginners' slopes. Rental equipment is available at the centers and in Arachova. Contact the **Greek Skiing Federation** (⊠ Karageorgi Servias 7, ☎ 01/323–0182).

Shopping

Arachova's main street is lined with shops selling rugs and weavings; the town was known even in pre-ski days as a place to shop for handicrafts, honey, and wine.

HANDICRAFTS

The modern mass-produced bedspreads and kilim-style carpets sold today in Arachova are colorful and reasonably priced. If you poke into dark corners in the stores, you still might turn up something made of local wool, though anything that claims to be antique brings a higher price.

LOCAL SPECIALTIES

Here you'll also find delicious Parnassos honey, formaella and *hilopites* or "thousand pies" (thin homemade noodles cut into thousands of tiny squares, often served with chicken and lamb).

Delphi

189 km (117½ mi) northwest of Athens, 10 km (6¼ mi) west of Arachova.

Home to Apollo and to the most famous oracle of antiquity, Delphi is one of the most evocative and enchanting sites in Greece. Its history reaches back at least as far as the Mycenaean period, and in Homer's *Iliad* it is referred to as Pytho. At first the settlement probably was sacred to a female deity; toward the end of the Greek Dark Ages (circa 1100 BC–800 BC), the site incorporated the cult of Apollo. According to Plutarch, who was a priest of Apollo at Delphi, the oracle was discovered by chance, when a shepherd noticed that his flock went into a frenzy when it came near a certain chasm in the rock. When he approached, he also came under a spell and began to utter prophecies, as did his fellow villagers. They chose from among their number a woman to sit over the chasm on a three-footed stool and to prophesy.

Traditionally, the Pythia was a woman over 50, who, upon her anointment, gave up normal life and lived thereafter in seclusion. On oracle day, the seventh of the month, the Pythia prepared by washing in the Castalian Spring and undergoing a purification involving barley smoke and laurel leaves. If the male priests of Apollo determined the day was propitious for prophecy, she entered the Temple of Apollo to sit on the tripod, where she drank the Castalian water, chewed laurel leaves, and presumably sank into a trance. Questions presented to her received strange and garbled answers, which were then translated into verse by the priests. Those citizens who wished to consult the oracle took their place in a line that might form days in advance, and after an animal sacrifice each questioner was admitted to the Adyton. A number of the lead tablets on which questions were inscribed have been uncovered, but the official answers were inscribed only in the memories of questioners and priests. Those that have survived, from various sources, suggest the equivocal nature of these sibylline emanations: Perhaps the most famous is the answer given to King Croesus of Lydia, who asked if he should attack the Persians. "Croesus, having crossed the Halys River, will destroy a great realm," said the Pythia. Thus encouraged, he crossed it, only to find his *own* empire destroyed.

From its earliest years, Delphi was the center of the Amphictyonic League, made up of 12 tribes, including Athens and Sparta. During the 8th and 7th centuries BC, the oracle's advice played a significant role in the colonization of southern Italy and Sicily (Magna Graecia), and as the league grew in stature and significance, so did the potential for conflict over its control. In the early 6th century BC, members of the league embarked on the First Sacred War, against the town of Krisa. The town was leveled, and the plain, declared sacred to Apollo, was left uncultivated.

Beginning in 582 BC the Pythian Games became a quadrennial festival similar to that held at Olympia. Increasingly an international center,

Delphi

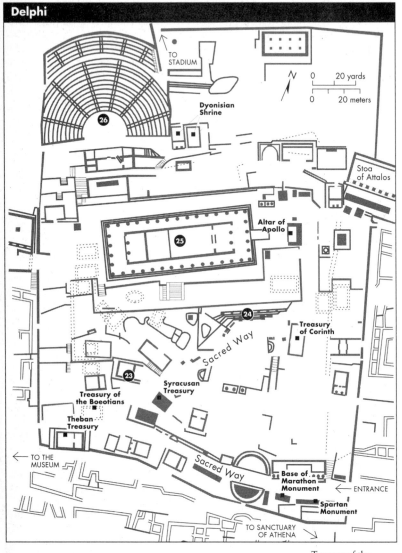

TO
STADIUM

Dyonisian
Shrine

Stoa
of Attalos

0   20 yards

0   20 meters

Altar of
Apollo

25

24

Treasury
of Corinth

Sacred Way

23

Syracusan
Treasury

**Treasury of
the Boeotians**

**Theban
Treasury**

← TO THE
MUSEUM

Sacred Way

**Base of
Marathon
Monument**

← ENTRANCE

**Spartan
Monument**

TO SANCTUARY
OF ATHENA

26

Delphi attracted supplicants from beyond the Greek mainland, including such valued clients as King Midas of Phrygia and King Croesus of Lydia, both wealthy kingdoms of Asia Minor. During this period of prosperity many cities built treasure houses at Delphi. The sanctuary was threatened during the Persian War but never attacked, and it continued to prosper, in spite of the fact that Athens and Sparta, two of its most powerful patrons, were locked in war. In 373 BC an earthquake damaged the site and destroyed the temple.

Delphi came under the influence first of Macedonia and then of the Aetolian League (290 BC–190 BC) before yielding to the Romans in 189 BC. Although the Roman general Sulla plundered Delphi in 86 BC, there were at least 500 bronze statues left to be collected by Nero in AD 66, and the site was still full of fine works of art when Pausanias visited and described it a century later. The emperor Hadrian restored many sanctuaries in Greece, including Delphi's, but within a century or two the oracle was silent (Theodosius abolished the oracle in AD 385). The town survived, but by the 7th century, after the barbarian invasions, it had become a small village known as Kastri. Probably little changed until the late 19th century, when French excavators began to uncover the site of Apollo.

The road from Arachova to Delphi is guarded by great twin cliffs, the **Phaedriades** (the Bright Ones), which glow with reflected light, particularly in late afternoon. These form the eastern gate, so to speak, of Delphi, whose **ancient ruins** lie cradled in a theatrical curve between the Phaedriades and Mt. Ayios Ilias to the west. Below Delphi the valley of the Pleistos opens into the plain of Krisa (named for a powerful 7th-century BC city) and the modern town of Chrissa, close to the floor of the plain. A sea of olive trees flows almost unbroken from the Pleistos valley to the edge of Itea, on the shore of the Gulf of Corinth.

The **Sanctuary of Athena** is just below the Arachova road before you reach the Phaedriades. The most notable among the numerous remains on the terrace is the **Tholos,** or Round Building, a graceful 4th-century BC ruin of Pentelic marble, whose purpose and dedication are unknown. Beneath the Phaedriades, in the cleft between the rocks a path leads to the **Castalian Fountain,** a spring where visitors bathed to purify themselves before approaching the sanctuary. Access to the fountain is presently restricted because of the danger of falling rocks.

On the main road, beyond the spring, is the modern entrance to the sanctuary. Passing through a **square** surrounded by late-Roman porticoes, the path leads through the main gate onto the **Sacred Way.** On its way up the hill the Sacred Way passes between building foundations and bases for votive dedications, stripped now of ornament and statue, mere scraps of what was one of the richest collections of art and treasures in antiquity. Thanks to the 2nd-century-AD writings of Pausanias, archaeologists have identified treasuries built by the Thebans, the Corinthians, the Syracusans, and others—a roster of 6th- and 5th-century BC powers.

㉓ The **Treasury of the Athenians** was built with money from the victory over the Persians at Marathon. Northeast of the treasury are the remains of the **Stoa of the Athenians** which housed, among other objects, an immense cable with which the Persian king Xerxes roped together a pontoon bridge for his army to cross the Hellespont from Asia to Europe.

㉕ The **Temple of Apollo** visible today (there were three successive temples built on the site) is that of the 4th century BC. Although ancient sources speak of a chasm within, there is no trace of that opening in the earth from which emanated trance-inducing vapors. Above the temple is the well-preserved **Theater** (which seated 5,000); it was built in the 4th century BC, restored in about 160 BC, and later was restored again by the Romans. The view from the theater is worth the climb, as is that from the **Stadium,** still farther up the mountain, at the highest point of the ancient town. Built and restored in various periods and cut partially from the living rock, the stadium underwent a final transformation under Herodes Atticus, the Athenian benefactor of the 2nd century AD. It lies cradled in a grove of pine trees, a quiet refuge removed from the sanctuary below and backed by the sheer, majestic rise of the mountain. ⊠ *Delphi site, immediately east of Delphi modern town along rd. to Arachova,* ☏ *0265/82313.* ◿ *1,200 dr.* ◷ *Weekdays 7:30–7:15, weekends and holidays 8:30–2:45.*

The **Delphi Museum** contains a wonderful collection of art and architectural sculpture, principally from the Sanctuaries of Apollo and Athena Pronoia. Among the masterpieces are a beautiful statue of Antinoos, Emperor Hadrian's favorite, and the twin statues of Kleobis and Biton, stylized representations of young brothers who were given the gift of eternal sleep by Hera, after they yoked themselves to a chariot to carry their mother to Hera's temple, and of whom it was said, "those whom the gods love die young." Dating to the first half of the 6th century BC, these statues are related to the series of *kouroi* (stylized statues of young men) in the National Museum in Athens. There are fragments of a silver-plated bull of the 6th century BC, the largest example we have from antiquity of a statue in precious metal. In the same room are the remarkable remains of a male figure executed in the chryselephantine technique, which used chrys- (gold) and *elephantine* (ivory). Also on exhibit in the Hall of the Siphnian Treasury is that building's east pediment, with scenes from the Trojan War and of the Olympic gods in battle with the Giants. In Room 11 note the family monument of nine statues, which reproduces in marble a group in bronze, at least partially by Lysippos, one of the best sculptors of the 4th century BC. The museum's chief masterpiece is the famous bronze *Charioteer,* a delicate, diminutive work, whose size is surprising if you are seeing it in person for the first time. Created in about 470 BC to commemorate the victory of a Syracusan prince in the Pythian chariot races, the statue is one of the few ancient bronzes to survive pillage and war. Its strength and quality remind us of what we have lost. ⊠ *Immediately east of Delphi modern town along rd. to Arachova,* ☏ *0265/82313.* ◿ *1,200 dr.* ◷ *Mon. noon–6:15, Tues.–Fri. 7:30–7:15, weekends and holidays 8:30–2:45.*

Dining and Lodging

$$ ✕ **Iniochos.** With turn-of-the-century touches, this *mezedopolia* (a place that serve mezes) offers some of Delphi's best eating. The large dining room has the requisite fine view, and there's an enormous veranda. You can bank on good seafood in season, as well as homemade lamb *kleftiko* (baked in a pastry shell), *hortopites* (vegetable pies), *mides saganaki* (mussels with fried cheese), and wine-stewed rooster, a regional dish. Try the house wine, a light rosé. Evening meals are accompanied by a piano and guitar duo. ⊠ *Friderikis 19,* ☏ *0265/82710, 0265/82071. AE, DC, MC, V.*

$$$ 🏨 **Hotel Vouzas.** The hotel crests the edge of a gorge and has won-
★ derful views from every room, and an intimate living room with a fireplace. It fills up on winter weekends with Athenians who come to challenge Mt. Parnassos, fortified by the buffet breakfast. ⊠ *Friderikis 1, 33054,* ☏ *0265/82232,* 🖷 *0265/82033. 59 rooms with bath. Restaurant, air-conditioning. MC, V.*

$$ ★ 🏨 **Apollo Hotel.** Owned and operated by a husband-and-wife team ("She's the decorator, I do the public relations," says he), this hotel is lovely. The cheerful rooms have light-wood furniture set off by blue quilts and striped curtains, with pretty bathroom tiles, hair dryers (a rarity in rural Greek hotels), and TVs. Many have wood balconies with black-iron railings, and a full breakfast is included. The *saloni* (living room), with traditional wall hangings and handsome furnishings, invites relaxation. ✉ *Friderikis 59B, 33054,* ☎ *0265/82580 or 0265/82244,* 🖷 *0265/82455. 21 rooms with bath. Breakfast room, bar, air-conditioning. MC, V. Closed weekdays Oct.–Mar. except Christmas and Carnival holidays.*

$$ 🏨 **Hotel Kastalia.** The Kastalia and its sisters, **Hotel Fedriades** and the brand-new **Villa Appollonia,** are owned and operated by the Maniatis family. All three have been recently rebuilt in the traditional style that has taken over Delphi and imparted an element of charm into streets that for a time looked doomed to anonymous cement-block modernism. The Kastalia's rooms are decorated with touches of red, those at the Fedriades with brown. The Appollonia's rooms are also in subdued browns, but they have the advantage of being extremely new, and thus untarnished. The views from some of the rooms and from the public rooms are spectacular, and Continental breakfast (Kastalia) or buffet breakfast (Fedriades and Appollonia) is included in the price. ✉ *Kastalia: Friderikis 13, 33054,* ☎ *0265/82205 through 82207,* 🖷 *0265/82208. 26 rooms with bath. Restaurant.* ✉ *Fedriades: Friderikis 38, 33054,* ☎ *0265/82919 or 0265/82370,* 🖷 *0265/82208. 24 rooms with bath. Bar, cafeteria.* ✉ *Appollonia: Friderikis 38, 33054,* ☎ 🖷 *0265/82325. 12 rooms with bath. Restaurant. All accept AE, DC, MC, V. All closed weekdays Nov.–Mar.*

$ 🏨 **Hotel Dolphin.** The rooms at this hotel are truly tiny, with the most modest amenities. But the warmth of the owners, who have run this pension in their former home for years, provides a singular experience. The street is noisy, however, and some rooms are better than others, so investigate before moving in. ✉ *Dimou Frangou 4, 33054,* ☎ *0265/82202. 13 rooms with bath. No credit cards.*

En Route The road west from Delphi winds down into the Sacred Plain, passing the modern village of Chryssa and leading through olive groves to the seaside port of Itea, which takes its name from the *ites* (willows) that used to stretch down to the sea.

Galaxidi

㉗ *17½ km (11 mi) southwest of Itea.*

The harbor town of Galaxidi has preserved traces of classical masonry, but enjoyed its heyday in the 19th century, thanks to shipbuilding and a thriving mercantile economy. After the invention of steamships, the town faded until its recent discovery by outsiders, who appreciated the sea captains' fine houses and the idyllic atmosphere. Now a historical monument, Galaxidi is undergoing renovation and restoration. If you are a shore person rather than a mountain person, Galaxidi is a good alternative to Delphi as a base. It's rewarding to stroll the narrow streets, there are places to swim nearby, and you'll find several tavernas on the harbor, though the food doesn't always live up to the environment.

Dining and Lodging

$$ ✕ **Porto.** This new and popular restaurant is one of many near the harbor that, unsurprisingly, specializes in fish. It is fun and friendly, and there are always plenty of locals huddled around the outdoor tables sampling *kalamaria* and *valanari* (tiny fried fish). ✉ *53 Akte Eanthes, near end of harbor,* ☎ *0265/41182. No credit cards.*

$$ ✕ **To Derveni.** The tiny main port of Galaxidi is lined with restaurants, bars, and cafés, but perhaps the best food in town can be found a few blocks inland, at To Derveni. The restaurant has a big covered garden for outdoor dining and serves a range of excellent standard taverna fare, such as stuffed tomatoes and grape leaves, grilled meats, and a local specialty, *avgopita* (egg pie). The service is good and the staff pleasant. ⊠ *Gourgouris St. next to old school,* ☎ *0265/41177. No credit cards. Closed Oct.–May.*

$$ 🏨 **Galaxa Hotel.** Opened in 1989 in a 200-year-old archontiko by the nice, professional Emanuel Papilaris, the Galaxa has simple rooms with museum prints and ship models. Most have a view to the sea, but if yours hasn't, you have an excuse to sidle up to the terrace bar. The restaurant (only open to guests) has good food: *pites* (savory pies) with homemade phyllo, baked *gavros* (a sort of anchovy), mussels, and other shellfish. ⊠ *Eleftherias 8, near Kennedy Rd., 33052,* ☎ *0265/41620 or 0265/41625,* 𝔽𝔸𝕏 *0265/42053. 10 rooms with bath. Restaurant, bar, air-conditioning. AE, DC, MC, V.*

$ 🏨 **Hotel Galaxidi.** The Galaxidi lies just two blocks from the busy port. Although the building is entirely modern, it has taken its style, outside and in, from the traditional Galaxidi captains' houses. The rooms are small but bright, with color TVs, and they open onto balconies with views of narrow streets lined with traditional Galaxidi houses. ⊠ *Sigrou 11, 33052,* ☎ *0265/41850 or 0265/41851,* 𝔽𝔸𝕏 *0265/41126. 22 rooms with bath. Breakfast room, air-conditioning, minibars, refrigerators. No credit cards.*

$ 🏨 **Pension Ganimede.** One of the few truly comfortable bed-and-breakfasts in all of Greece, the owner-manager Brunello Perocco has taken full advantage of the elegant spaces provided by a typical 19th-century Galaxidi mansion. Best of all is having breakfast in the shade of the lush garden, accompanied by the owner's gentle multilingual humor. Book ahead in high season; the few rooms go fast. ⊠ *Gourgouris 20, 33052,* ☎ *0265/41328. 11 rooms with bath. Breakfast room. No credit cards. Closed Nov.–Dec. 15.*

NEED A BREAK?

For an evening drink in summer, try the **Omilo** (⊠ Old Yacht Club, ☎ 0265/42110, 𝔽𝔸𝕏 0265/42298), at the entrance to the main harbor. The few chairs and tables on a little beach make a simple setting, and one of the best bartenders in town provides exceptional service. The view is unforgettable, especially at sunset: the Gulf of Itea stretches before you and the peaks of Parnassos tower in the background, with the little gray houses of Delphi clustered on its slopes. You can swim off the beach here, and midnight dips are encouraged.

EXCURSIONS FROM ATHENS A TO Z

Arriving and Departing

☞ Athens A to Z *in* Chapter 2.

Getting Around

By Bus

If you are not renting a car, the next most efficient mode of travel (as usual in Greece) is the KTEL bus system. An extensive network of public buses serves all points in **Attica** from Athens, and local buses connect the smaller towns and villages at least daily. Buses leave frequently from 2 stations: (⊠ 29 Mavromateon, ☎ 01/821–0872; ⊠ 14 Mavromateon, ☎ 01/823–0179). To **Delphi,** there are five departures per day (six on Sunday, about 3 hrs) from 260 Liossion (☎ 01/831–7096), beginning at 7:30 AM.

By Car

Points in Attica can be reached from the main Thessaloniki–Athens highway without ever having to go into Athens itself. From the Peloponnese, you can drive east via Corinth to Athens, or from Patras, take the Rion–Antirion ferry and the coast road, visiting Delphi first. Most of the roads are two-lane secondary arteries; a few of them (notably from Athens to Delphi and Itea and to Sounion) have been recently upgraded, are very good, and often spectacularly scenic. Expect heavy traffic to Delphi in summer and ski season, and to and from Athens on weekends. Cars are not allowed on Hydra and Spetses.

By Ferry

The islands of Poros and Spetses are so close to the Peloponnese mainland that you can drive there, park, and ferry across the channel in any of a number of caïques (price negotiable), but to get to them from Athens or to visit the other Saronic Gulf Islands, you must take to the sea in a ship.

The **Argosaronikos Line** will take you (and your car) from the main port in Piraeus to Aegina (1½ hours) and Poros (3 hours, 40 minutes), or you alone to Hydra (4 hours, 10 minutes) and Spetses (5 hours, 25 minutes). There are approximately a half-dozen departures per day, and fares range from 1,500 dr. per person for Aegina to 3,000 dr. for Spetses. Car rates are usually four times the passenger rate. These ferries are the leisurely—meaning *very* slow—and cheap way to travel.

Most people now prefer the speedier **Flying Dolphins** (☎ 01/428–0001, no cars carried), hydrofoils that depart from the harbor of Zea, also in Piraeus. There are about a half-dozen departures daily, and it is advisable to make reservations ahead of time—they book up quickly. The cost ranges from 3,154 dr. for Aegina to 5,375 dr. for Spetses. You can also reserve through a travel agent.

Contacts and Resources

Car Rentals

Most international agencies have offices in Athens and desks at the airport.

Avis (✉ 46–48 Amalias, ☎ 01/322–4951 through 4957; ✉ West Terminal, ☎ 01/981–4410; ✉ East Terminal, ☎ 01/995–3440; ✉ Athens Hilton, ☎ 01/725–0200, ✉ Akti Miaouli (Piraeus), ☎ 01/428–0218 or 01/452–0639). **Budget** (✉ Syngrou 8, ☎ 01/921–4771 through 4773; ✉ West Terminal, ☎ 01/922–2442; ✉ East Terminal, ☎ 01/961–3634). **Hertz** (✉ Syngrou 12, ☎ 01/922–0102 through 0104; ✉ Vas. Sofias 71, ☎ 01/724–7071 or 01/722–7391; ✉ West Terminal, ☎ 01/981–3701; ✉ East Terminal, ☎ 01/961–3625 or 01/961–3530). **Europcar-Interrent** (✉ Syngrou 4, ☎ 01/921–5788 or 01/921–5789; ✉ West Terminal, ☎ 01/982–9565; ✉ East Terminal, ☎ 01/961–3424). **Thrifty** (✉ Syngrou 24, ☎ 01/922–1211 through 1213).

Emergencies

Tourist Police: Attica (☎ 171); Delphi (☎ 0265/82222); Aegina (☎ 0297/22100); Poros (☎ 0298/22462); Hydra (☎ 0298/52205); Spetses (☎ 0298/73100).

Guided Tours

A cruise through the Saronic Gulf islands on the **Saronic Star** (☎ 01/323–5472) usually departs from the Trocadero in Palio Faliro about 8:30 AM and touches in at Poros, Hydra, and Aegina before returning about 7:30 PM. The tours can include pickup at your hotel in Athens, a visit to the Temple of Aphaia at Aegina, a beach stop, and buffet lunch at an Aegina hotel (13,800 dr. for cruise, about another 6,000 dr. for the optional trip to the temple). It is best to book through a travel agency.

Moped Rentals

On the islands of Aegina and Spetses, many people rent scooters, mopeds, and bicycles from shops along the harbor, but extreme caution is advised: The equipment may not be in good condition, roads can be narrow and treacherous, and many drivers scorn your safety. Wear a helmet, and drive defensively.

Outdoor Activities and Sports

HIKING

Greek Federation of Mountaineering Associations in Athens (⊠ Milioni 5, ☎ 01/363–6617 or 01/364–5904). **Greek Touring Club** (⊠ Polytechniou 12, Athens, ☎ 01/524–8600). **Federation of Excursion Clubs** (⊠ Dragatsaniou 4, Athens, ☎ 01/323–4107).

RUNNING

Athens Open International Peace Marathon (⊠ SEGAS, Race Organizers, Syngrou 137, 17121 Athens, ☎ 01/935–9302, FAX 01/934–2980).

SKIING

Greek Skiing Federation (⊠ Karageorgi Servias 7, ☎ 01/323–0182).

WINDSURFING

Greek Windsurfing Association (⊠ Fillelinon 7, ☎ 01/323–3696 or 01/323–0068).

Visitor Information

Tourist office: Delphi (⊠ Friderikis 12, ☎ 0265/82900); Aegina (⊠ Town Hall, ☎ 0297/22220); Arachova (winter only; ⊠ Delphi–Arachova Rd., ☎ 0267/31692).

Tourist Police: Attica (☎ 171); Delphi (☎ 0265/82222); Aegina (☎ 0297/22100); Poros (☎ 0298/22462); Hydra (☎ 0298/52205); Spetses (☎ 0298/73100).

Greek National Tourist Organization (GNTO or EOT): Athens (⊠ Near Syntagma Sq., Karageorgi Servias 2 in the National Bank of Greece, ☎ 01/322–2545).

4 The Northern Sporades

Skiathos, Skopelos, Alonnisos, Skyros, and Evia

Island-hopping the Northern Sporades, strung from Mt. Pelion to the center of the Aegean, promises quintessential Greek-island pleasures: boat journeys, pretty harbors, hillside towns, deserted beaches, screaming nightlife. Many tourists don't make it beyond Skiathos, but the charm of the Sporades is found on the quieter islands, where the pace of life is slower, the outside world more distant.

By Diana Farr
Louis

Updated by
Michael Boyd

LIKE EMERALD BEADS SCATTERED ON SAPPHIRE velvet, the verdant Northern Sporades islands of Skiathos, Skopelos, and Alonnisos, and a nearby host of tiny, uninhabited islets—resplendent with pines, fruit trees, and olives, and marked with sloping, slate roofs and wooden balconies—strongly resemble the Pelion peninsula to which they were once attached. Only on Skyros, farther out in the Aegean, will you see the windswept, treeless landscape, or the cubistlike architecture of the Cyclades. Sitting by itself east of Evia, Skyros is neither geographically nor historically related to the other Sporades, though in recent years, the hydrofoils skimming between the islands, Evia, and the mainland have made them closer than ever before. Evia itself, Greece's second-largest island (after Crete), presents a curious mix of mainland and island culture. It is a favorite of Athenian sun-seekers.

The Sporades have changed hands constantly throughout history, and wars, plunder, and earthquakes have eliminated all but the strongest ancient walls. A few castles and monasteries remain, but these islands are now geared more for fun than for sightseeing. Skiathos, closest to the mainland and the first to be discovered, is the most touristy—to the point of overkill—with a diverse social scene, international restaurants, English pubs, and luxury hotels. Less-developed Skopelos has several lovely villages to explore by day—its main town is said to be the most beautiful of the Sporades—though far fewer beaches and nightlife.

Owing to natural disasters, the second half of the 20th century has been hard on Alonnisos, which is only beginning to recover. Once called Evoinos (Goodwine), in 1950 its grapevines suffered a plague of phylloxera that destroyed most of them virtually overnight and, 15 years later, an earthquake ruined the lovely hilltop capital. Still, its scenery is so stunning that nature lovers flock there in increasing numbers. Skyros, late to attract tourists, is the least traveled of the Sporades. Yet those who discover its well-preserved traditions, its arcane rabbit warren of a town, and its expansive beaches come back year after year.

Pleasures and Pastimes

Beaches

The Sporades boast a huge number of beaches, and Skiathos's Koukounaries is said to be the best beach in Greece. Beaches here suit every taste—from those crowded with people, bars, water sports, and music to secluded coves only accessible by boat; and of course, nude beaches can be found on each island.

Dining

Eating can be a real pleasure in the Sporades, whether in a simple taverna or a fancier restaurant. There are immense numbers of eating places on all the islands, and fast-food joints abound. Great views and good cooking are rarely found together. Few of the many places touted as charming on the waterfront serve exceptional food, and prices are apt to decrease the farther you get from views or water.

Local dishes are normally not found on menus, but Alonnisos and Skyros especially are noted for spiny lobster. Keep in mind that fresh fish and lobster invariably raise the price considerably. You'll find ordering several *mezedes* (starters) rather than a first and second course a tasty and popular option. Desserts are rarely served at tavernas. Almost all restaurants have outside seating; dress at most is casual. Sadly, only on Skyros will you find barrel wine; the small amount produced elsewhere is savored at home.

CATEGORY	COST (ALL ISLANDS)*
$$$$	over 6,000 dr.
$$$	3,200–6,000 dr.
$$	2,200–3,200 dr.
$	under 2,200 dr.

per person for about two appetizers, salad, and main course, including service and tax, but not drinks.

Festivals

Of tremendous interest are the pre-Lenten Carnival traditions on Skyros. The Skyrian revelry relates to pre-Christian fertility rites. They are performed by bands of young men dressed as old men, maidens, or "Europeans," who roam the streets teasing and tormenting onlookers with ribald songs and clanging bells. The "old men" wear an elaborate shepherd's outfit, with a mask made of the hide of a baby goat and a belt from which dangle as many as 40 sheep bells. Their costumes and antics are famous throughout Greece.

The Skopelos Municipality sponsors a series of cultural events in late August, with the last day a celebration of the plum harvest (☞ Visitor Information *in* The Northern Sporades A to Z, *below*). The pre-Lenten Carnival traditions of Skopelos, although not as exotic as those of Skyros, parody the expulsion of the once-terrifying Barbary pirates.

On Skyros on August 15 **Panayia** (the festival of the Virgin) is celebrated on the beach at Magazia, where children race on the island's domesticated small ponies, similar to Shetland ponies.

Hiking

All of the islands are wonderful for walkers, especially in spring, when Greece's wildflowers are unsurpassed. Some of the monasteries and more remote refuges are only accessible on foot. You can buy walkers' maps in the souvenir shops.

Lodging

Skopelos has a good amount of hotels and Skiathos a huge number; there are not many hotels on Alonnisos, and Skyros has even fewer. Most hotels close for winter, as noted in their individual listings; reservations are a good idea, unless you are looking for a private room. The best bet, especially for those on a budget, is to rent a converted room in a private house—look for the Greek National Tourist Organization (GNTO or EOT) license displayed in windows. Landladies meet incoming boats to offer rooms; negotiate over the price and ask about the island location. At the height of summer, island-hopping without reservations might be risky, however.

In Skyros most people rent rooms in town or along the beach at Magazia and Molos. Accommodations are basic and televisions are not standard. You must choose between being near either the sea or the town's bars and eateries. The average room cost in August is about 8,000 dr. In Skiathos, tourists are increasingly renting apartments, villas, and minivillas with kitchen facilities. Contact the local island travel agents to discuss the range of possibilities.

The hotels recommended here vary from simple, clean family-run pensions to large, impersonal, self-contained resorts. You can expect air-conditioning in $$$ and $$$$ hotels, and buffet breakfast is usually included in the rate everywhere. Rates fluctuate considerably from season to season; the August prices listed in the lodging chart below may drop by more than half between October and May. You should always negotiate off-season.

CATEGORY	COST (ALL ISLANDS)*
$$$$	over 25,000 dr.
$$$	17,000–25,000 dr.
$$	11,000–17,000 dr.
$	under 11,000 dr.

for a standard double room for two, including breakfast, service, and tax.

Nature Cruises

The islands around Alonnisos are the gateway to the National Marine Park, which comprises all the islands in the vicinity, some of which are off-limits to all visitors. Found here is one of the last preserves of the endangered monk seal. Nature lovers can explore their appreciation with such excursions as the caïque cruise, run by a marine biologist, from Skopelos to Psathoura and Kyra Panayia in the National Marine Park.

Sailing

Because of their many protected coves, the Northern Sporades (excluding Skyros) are ideal for yachting, especially the uninhabited islands. Mooring can be arranged at the ports at each island.

Shopping

Alonnisos excepted, all the Sporades have a lot to offer shoppers, especially local crafts. Crafts stores on Skiathos and Skopelos also sell goods from other islands and the mainland, including attractive pottery, kilims, antiques, and embroideries. Skopelos seems to have the most imaginative and tempting range of shops and boutiques; on Skiathos, beautiful modern jewelry can be found in its boutiques. On Skyros, mostly free of boutiques, shops feature the island's traditional hand-painted ceramics.

Windsurfing

Windsurfing equipment can be rented in Skyros on the beach between Magazia and Molos; on Skopelos at Stafilos, Panormos, and Milia; on Skiathos at Koukounaries and many other beaches along the main coast road.

Exploring the Northern Sporades

Each of the Northern Sporades has a distinct character. Tourist-ridden, developed Skiathos is closest to the mainland; due east is Skopelos, covered with dense pines, where you can enjoy scenic villages and lovely beaches. Farther east in the Aegean is rugged Alonnisos, the least progressive of the islands. Skyros, southeast of the other islands, is the most remote, filled with myth; it is often difficult to get to Skyros from the other Sporades without a mainland stop. There are a number of uninhabited islands that can be visited by boat. Evia, almost touching the mainland, with ancient sites and fishing villages, is a vast, elongated strip of coast with plenty of beaches.

Great Itineraries

If you are taking it easy and want to relax, you can generally just jump on a caïque and island-hop as you choose. If you want to see or do something in particular, however, it is best to plan your schedule in advance, because with limited time, you might find you can't get to each thing you want to see. Flying Dolphin hydrofoils and Olympic Airways timetables are available from travel agents; for regular boats, consult the EOT in Athens (☞ Visitor Information *in* The Northern Sporades A to Z, *below*).

You could get around Skiathos, Skopelos, and Alonnisos in three days, but to enjoy the relaxed nature of the islands, stay on one. The trip between these three and Skyros requires advance planning and more time; at press time (October, 1996) there was only one Flying Dolphin hydrofoil per week. Ten days would be more than enough to see all the islands and still maintain a degree of relaxation.

IF YOU HAVE 3 DAYS
Numbers in the text correspond to numbers in the margin and on The Northern Sporades map.

Inveterate island-hoppers will spend one night on each of the three main islands. Otherwise, choose an island and stay there for three days. On ⊞ **Skiathos** ①–⑩, by day take in the beautiful, crowded beaches and a museum or perhaps **Evangelistria monastery** ⑫, and at night join the night owls at a taverna or restaurant, and then a bustling nightclub. Day people should stay on ⊞ **Skopelos** ⑪–㉓ to explore the numerous monasteries and churches. ⊞ **Skyros** ㉘–㉝ is ideal for those seeking a slower pace. If you want to escape civilization as much as possible, head for ⊞ **Alonnisos** ㉔–㉗.

IF YOU HAVE 5 DAYS
Spend a few relaxing days on ⊞ **Skyros** ㉘–㉝ and take a day to explore Evia. Alternatively, base yourself in the main group of Skiathos, Skopelos, and Alonnisos. Spend a day on **Skiathos** ①–⑩, then head for ⊞ **Skopelos** ⑪–㉓ and stay there for 4 nights. You can take a short day cruise to see **Alonnisos** ㉔–㉗ and some of the uninhabited islands, with deserted beaches, ancient monasteries, and wildlife reserves.

IF YOU HAVE 10 DAYS
A longish period of time is necessary for a relaxed exploration of the Sporades. Start in Evia and visit **Halkidha** and **Eretria** before heading to **Kimi** for the boat to ⊞ **Skyros** ㉘–㉝. Spend a few days on **Skyros** and plan ahead so that you can catch the weekly Flying Dolphin to ⊞ **Alonnisos** ㉔–㉗. You might not stay on **Alonnisos,** especially if you visit it as part of a cruise from **Skopelos** ⑪–㉓. Stay awhile on **Skopelos** and perhaps rent a car to explore the island. Spend your last couple of days on ⊞ **Skiathos** ①–⑩; from here you might leave time to go on to **Volos** and **Pelion** on the mainland.

When to Tour
Most hotels, rooms, and restaurants are closed in winter; if you go November through March, book everything in advance and leave no planning to chance. The same advice applies to the month of August, when everything is open but overcrowded.

SKIATHOS

The wooded island of Skiathos covers an area of only 42 sq km (16 sq mi), but it boasts some 60 beaches. Many tourists flock here, attracted by promises of sun, sea, sand, and a swinging partying—and these are delivered.

In winter most of the island's 5,000 or so inhabitants live in its only town, Skiathos, built after the War of Independence on the site of the colony founded in the 8th century BC by the Euboean city-state of Chalkis. Like Skopelos and Alonnisos, Skiathos was on good terms with the Athenians, prized by the Macedonians, and treated gently by the Romans. Saracen and Slav raids left it virtually deserted during the early Middle Ages, but it started to prosper during the later Byzantine years. When the Crusaders deposed their fellow Christians from the throne of Constantinople in 1204, Skiathos and the other Sporades became the fief of the Ghisi, knights of Venice. One of their first acts was to fortify the hills behind the islet separating the two bays of Skiathos Harbor. Now connected to the shore, this former islet, the Bourtzi, still has a few stout walls and buttresses shaded by some graceful pine trees. The rest of the fort was blown up in 1660, when Morosini (who also blew the roof off the Parthenon) tried to oust the Turks from it.

Skiathos Town

❶ *8 km (5 mi) east of Troullos.*

Though picturesque from a distance, Skiathos town has few buildings of any distinction. Many traditional houses were burned by the Germans in 1944, and postwar development has pushed up ugly cement apartments between the pleasantly squat, red-roof older houses. But magenta bougainvilleas, sweet jasmine, and the casual charm of brightly painted balconies and shutters camouflage most of the eyesores as you wander through the narrow lanes and climb up the steep steps that serve as streets. Almost all the activity is either on the waterfront or on Papadiamantis street, the main drag: banks, travel agents, telephones, post office, police and tourist police stations, plus myriad cafés, fast-food joints, porno postcard stands, tacky souvenir shops, tasteful jewelry stores, and rent-a-car and bike establishments. More shops, bars, and restaurants line the side streets, where you will also spot the occasional modest hotel and rooms-to-rent signs.

A **museum** devoted to Alexandros Papadiamantis (1851–1911), one of Greece's finest novelists, stands near the entrance to the street named after him. Three humble rooms with his bed, the low, narrow divan where he died, some photos, and a few personal belongings are all that is exhibited, but the case with his pen, inkwell, and pot of sand for blotting recall times past. For further understanding, try to find a translation of his most famous novel, *The Murderess.* ✉ *In small platia to right of Papadiamantis at fork in rd.,* ☎ *0427/23843.* 🖃 *250 dr.* 🕐 *Tues.–Sun. 9:30–1, 4–6.*

West of the waterfront, or **Bourtzi,** is the fishing port and the dock from which the caïques depart for round-the-island trips and the beaches. The sidewalk is filled with cafés and ouzeris catering more to people-watchers than gourmets. At the far end of the port, beginning at the square around the 1846 church of Trion Hierarchon, fancier restaurants spread out under awnings overlooking the sea. A few gourmet restaurants are hidden on back streets in this neighborhood, many of them foreign. The east side of the port, past the Bourtzi, where the larger boats and Flying Dolphins dock, is not as picturesque. The little church and clock tower of Ayios Nikolaos watch over it from a hill reached by steps so steep, they're almost perpendicular to the earth.

NEED A BREAK?   On the Bourtzi's steep hill, with the church and clock tower of Ayios Nikolaos, is **The Final Step** (✉ Bourtzi, on the hill), a café at which you can catch your breath and admire the view over a snack or a drink.

Beaches

Since the arrival of English expatriates in the early 1960s, the beautiful piney 14-km (9-mi) stretch of coast running south of town to Koukounaries has become almost one continuous ribbon of villas, hotels, and tavernas. This development is a real blight on the landscape. One beach succeeds another, and the asphalted coast road carries a continual stream of cars, buses, motorbikes, and pedestrians dipping from beach to beach, like frenzied bees sampling pollen-laden flowers. To access most beaches, you must take a little, usually unpaved, lane

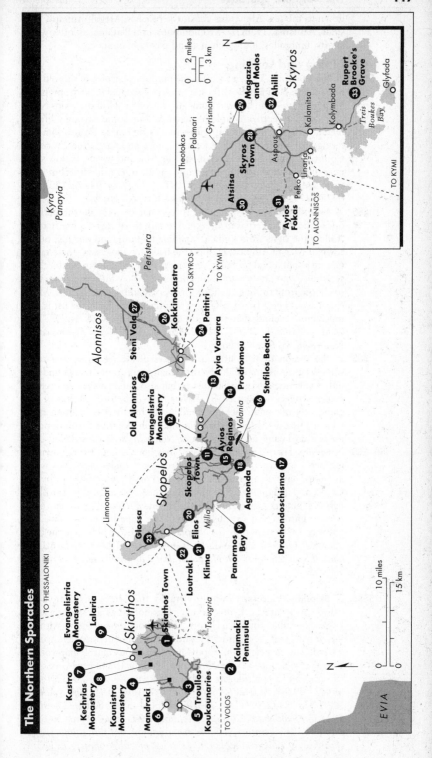

The Northern Sporades

EVIA

TO THESSALONIKI

Skiathos

Evangelistria Monastery
Lalaria
Kastro
Kechrias Monastery
Kounistra Monastery
Mandraki
Koukounaries
Troullos
Kalamaki Peninsula
Skiathos Town
TO VOLOS
Tsougria

Limnonari
Glossa
Skopelos
Elios
Loutraki
Klima
Panormos Bay
Skopelos Town
Milia
Agnonda
Drachondoschisma
Stafilos Beach
Ayia Varvara
Ayios Reginos
Valania
Prodromou
Evangelistria Monastery
Old Alonnisos

Alonnisos
Steni Vala
Kokkinokastro
Patitiri
TO SKYROS
TO KYMI

Peristera

Kyra Panayia

0   10 miles
0   15 km

N

Skyros

0   2 miles
0   3 km

N

Theotokos
Palamari
Gyrismata
Magazia and Molos
Ahilli
Atsitsa
Skyros Town
Aspous
Kalamitsa
Kolymbada
Rupert Brooke's Grave
Glyfada
Treis Boukes Bay
Pefko
Linaria
Ayios Fokas
TO ALONNISOS
TO KYMI

down to the sea. Along this coast, the beaches, **Megali Ammos, Vas-silias, Achladia, Tzaneria, Vromolimnos,** and **Platania,** all offer water sports, umbrellas, lounge chairs, and plenty of company.

Dining and Lodging

$$$$ ✕ **The Windmill.** The views from the outdoor platform of this old mill turned elegant international restaurant are spectacular, but be prepared to climb up to—and descend from—the top of the hill above Ayios Niko-laos. Here a Scottish couple has created an eclectic, strongly French menu, with traditional meat-with-sauce dishes; there are also some of-ferings for vegetarians. For dessert, most popular is the chocolate Cointreau fondue, into which diners dip fruit and sweets. Follow signs near the clock tower; the restaurant is at the top of the short but steep staircase. ⊠ *Skiathos town,* ☎ *0427/21223 or 0427/21224,* ℻ *0427/21791. V. Closed mid-Oct.–mid-May. No lunch.*

$$$ ✕ **Asprolithos.** Superb food and professional service make this perhaps
★   one of the best tavernas in Greece. Actually, there are two: one in town (follow the signs from Odhos Papadhiamndiou), and one just out of town at Megali Ammos. Despite the backstreet location, these taver-nas are popular and probably very busy. They are not paper-tablecloth, set-your-own-cutlery establishments, and it may take you some time to choose from the huge menu with overwhelming descriptions. Much easier would be a list of what's not on the menu. The wine list is also much more exciting than the norm. ⊠ *Skiathos town,* ☎ *0427/23110;* ⊠ *Megali Ammos,* ☎ *0427/22702. AE, MC, D, V. Megali Ammos closed Nov.–Apr. No lunch at both.*

$$$ ✕ **The Lemon Tree.** If, after a few days of local cuisine, you crave something more unusual, try this small restaurant. You'll find not only a selection of vegetarian dishes, but also Indian dishes—extremely rare in Greece—prepared by a chef from Bradford, capital of En-gland's Asian community. It's small inside, but there is a garden at the rear. It's just off Odhos Papadhiamndiou in Skiathos town, opposite the National Bank. ⊠ *Skiathos town. No credit cards. Closed Nov.–Apr.*

$$–$$$ ✕ **Family.** There's nothing really homey here, except for the owner's mother's baklava. The tables, on three levels under capacious white awnings, have a superb view of the harbor. The cuisine is primarily Greek, and imaginative. The miniature cheese pie and cabbage roll ap-petizers, among others, are delightful, and there are many more ex-pensive entrées and various desserts. The wine list is extensive. It's halfway up the steps to Ayios Nikolaos clock tower, hidden in the back alleys. ⊠ *Ouranitsa St., Skiathos town,* ☎ *0427/21439. AE, MC, V. Closed Sept. 26–May 19. No lunch, but will usually serve on request anyway.*

$$$$ 🏠 **Skiathos Princess.** Covering virtually the whole of Platania Bay below Ayia Paraskevi, this luxury-class hotel has all the amenities you'd expect but not much charm. The air-conditioned rooms with pa-tios or balconies are comfortable and private, built in three tiers around a lawn. The carpeted pink rooms have luxurious marble bathrooms. There's also a money-exchange service, *kafenion* (traditional Greek cof-fehouse), and a poolside bar. ⊠ *Ayia Paraskevi 37002,* ☎ *0427/49226 or 0427/49369,* ℻ *0427/49666. Athens:* ⊠ *Amalias 42, 10558 Athina,* ☎ *01/324–2152, 01/324–2153, and 01/324–5963,* ℻ *01/323–3667. 132 rooms with bath, 27 suites. Restaurant, 2 tavernas, 2 bars, in-room safes, minirefrigerators, 2 pools, beauty salon, hot tub, sauna, water-skiing, shop, playground, laundry service, meeting rooms. AE, DC, V. Closed Nov.–Apr.*

$$ 🏠 **Bourtzi and Pothos.** If you want to be near the action and have your
★   peace and quiet too, then either of these hotels under the same man-

agement is for you. Both are no-frills and spotlessly clean, with rooms that look onto a pleasant green garden and courtyard untouched by the bustle on nearby Papadiamantis. The furniture is simple but functional, the staff warm and conscientious. Bourtzi is two or three streets farther from the waterfront than Pothos. ⊠ *Skiathos town 37002,* ☎ *0427/22694 or 0427/21304,* FAX *0427/23243. Pothos: 22 rooms with shower; Bourtzi: 23 rooms with shower. Minirefrigerators. AE, DC, MC, V. Closed Nov.–Apr.*

$ 🏠 **Pension Danaos.** A first choice for budget travelers, this hotel is centrally located. Rooms are airy and clean, most with balconies, and there is even a roof garden. Despite the decent facilities, including TVs, these rooms are among the cheapest in Skiathos, except during August. ⊠ *Skiathos town (just off Odhos Papadhiandi) 37002.* ☎ *0427/22834. 16 rooms with shower. Refrigerators. No credit cards.*

Nightlife

Skiathos is a night owl's dream come true. There are bars for all tastes, from pubs with draft beer run by Brits to quintessential Greek bouzouki joints.

MUSIC AND NIGHTCLUBS

Among the perennial favorites are **La Piscine;** its disco has live music from 9:30 to midnight and a DJ afterward. This entertainment emporium, open all day and almost all night at the height of the season, has four bars, video games, outdoor dancing, and an ample swimming pool. For oldies but goodies, try the **Kentavros** music bar. For heavy rock, **Café Santan** is the place. **Borzoi,** the oldest club in Skiathos, is decorated like a folk art museum and has a tiny dance floor, too. Popular **Remezzo** (⊠ Near the old shipyards) airs a blend of old and new music at the water's edge. And that's just scratching the surface.

Outdoor Activities and Sports

FISHING

Overfishing and such scurrilous practices as dynamiting and bottom trawling have greatly diminished the once abundant resources of the Northern Sporades. It is now illegal to fish with scuba equipment. You can hire fishing boats to go fishing; look for signs on the boats at the ports.

HIKING

In Skiathos, a Dutch couple takes people on nature walks; check with **Mare Nostrum Travel** (☞ Contacts and Resources *in* The Northern Sporades A to Z, *below*).

SAILING

The **Yachting Club** (⊠ Skiathos town, ☎ 094/505426) organizes daily and moonlight cruises, two-day trips to Planitis, and special charters.

SCUBA DIVING

Skiathos is the only island with a scuba diving school, the **Dolphin Diving Center** (⊠ Porto Nostos Beach, ☎ 0427/21599, FAX 0427/22525).

Shopping

ANTIQUES AND CRAFTS

The **Archipelago** (⊠ Near Papadiamantis museum, ☎ 0427/22163) is by far the most stunning shop on the island. Browse here among the antiques, pottery, jewelry made from fossils, and embroideries. Archipelago also has a stylish **boutique** (⊠ Waterfront, ☎ 0427/21681). **Galerie Varsakis** (⊠ Trion Hierarchon Sq., ☎ 0427/22255), another fabulous antiques store, has kilims, embroideries, jewelry, and hundreds of other objects, set off by the proprietor's unusual surrealistic paintings.

CLOTHING

Zoe (✉ Across from square, ☎ 0427/22865) has attractive women's clothing.

JEWELRY

Seraïna (✉ Near Papadiamantis museum, ☎ 0427/22039) has jewelry and unusually eclectic tourist junk. **Simos** (✉ Waterfront, opposite the excursion caïques, ☎ 0427/22916) has unique silver and gold designs. **G&P Papapanagiotakis** (✉ Waterfront, opposite the caïques, ☎ 0427/21056) also has fine gold and silver. The jewelry creations at **Pan** (✉ Waterfront, ☎ 0427/23347) are the most imaginatively displayed.

OFF THE BEATEN PATH

PELION – Jason and the Argonauts are said to have embarked from Pelion, the mountainous peninsula west of Skiathos, on the mainland. Mt. Pelion, thickly wooded with pine, cypress, chestnut, and fruit trees, was the home of the legendary centaurs; its striking, mythical beauty is still preserved. Modern **Volos,** at the northwestern tip of the peninsula, has a waterfront esplanade and a splendid archaeological museum. As you leave Volos along the serpentine roads, you'll ascend into the cooler mountains, and the views over Volos Bay are spectacular. Some roads wind down to exquisite, white-sand or round-stone beaches, such as Horefto and Milopotamos. Nestled among the forests are delightful villages—**Makrynitsa, Tsangarades, Milies,** and **Vyzitsa**—built around plane tree–shaded squares and adorned with splashing fountains. Pelion is also noted for its churches, autumn foliage, and winter skiing. To get to Pelion by car, take the 3-hour ferry from Skiathos town to Volos; you can also board the hydrofoil and rent a car in Pelion.

Northeastern Coast

Just north of Skiathos town.

On the water's edge north of Skiathos town are a string of restaurants and nightclubs, the beached hulks of some caïques at the old shipyards, a small lagoon, and the airport runway. The countryside starts at lush Cape Pounda at the end of the peninsula that embraces Skiathos Harbor.

Kalamaki Peninsula

❷ *6 km (3¾ mi) south of Skiathos town.*

The one slightly less-developed area on the south coast is the Kalamaki peninsula, where the British built their first villas. Some are available for rent in summer, many above tiny, unfrequented coves.

Lodging

$$$–$$$$ 🏠 **Atrium.** The architect of this hotel possessed an unusual sensitivity to the island's scenery. Its stone and pale ocher walls, aged terra-cotta floor tiles, and sloping roofs fulfill its claim to resemble "a Mt. Athos monastery." There's nothing monastic, however, about its squashy white leather sofas, mellow antiques, cozy nooks for conversation, TV room, backgammon, pool bar, or view. The hotel's top floor has its pool and taverna, the quiet, air-conditioned rooms below are welcoming, with dark-green wooden furniture, apricot bedspreads, and matching curtains. Ask for a room with a view of the sea, and put on your hiking boots for the climb up from the beach at Ayia Paraskevi. ✉ *Platanias 37002,* ☎ *0427/49345, 0427/49376.* FAX *0427/49376. 75 rooms with bath, 6 suites. Restaurant, bar, bar, pool, exercise room, Ping-Pong, shop, billiards. AE, DC, MC, V. Closed mid-Oct.–Apr.*

$$$–$$$$ 🏨 **Nostos.** This large four-story hotel stretches from the top of a hill across from the Kalamaki peninsula down to its beach. Several one-room bungalows are scattered along the pine-covered slope down to the beach. Though the big common rooms, done in a rustic Pelion style, are rather impersonal and the maintenance a bit lax, this hotel has remained popular since it opened in 1972. The rooms are simple, with colorful striped bedspreads; the view from their balconies is splendid. It has a bus to ferry people up and down, or you can walk for a bit of exercise. There's also a diving school, pool bar, and beach taverna for aquatic diversion. ⊠ *Tzaneria 37002,* ☎ *0427/22520 through 22524,* 𝖥𝖠𝖷 *0427/22525. 170 rooms and bungalows with bath, 5 suites. Restaurant, 2 tavernas, 2 bars, mini-refrigerators, pool, tennis court, water-skiing. AE, DC, MC, V. Closed Nov.–Apr.*

$$$–$$$$ 🏨 **Plaza.** Just 100 meters (328 feet) from Kanapitsa Bay, this ultra-modern hotel is set against a green hillside, its rooms arranged in staggered wings for privacy. Both the lobby and the rooms are decorated in cool tones of gray, aqua, and pink; the furniture is comfortable contemporary and carpeting covers the floors, adding a luxurious note. Rooms have large beds and generous balconies. Since the hotel opened in 1989, the garden has grown, softening the stark white facade, honeycombed with arches. There's also a roof garden, money exchange, and pool bar. ⊠ *Kanapitsa 37002,* ☎ *0427/21971 through 21974,* 𝖥𝖠𝖷 *0427/22109. Athens:* ⊠ *69 Vassilis Giorgiou, 16675 Athina,* ☎ *01/967/0393,* 𝖥𝖠𝖷 *01/896/2285. 79 rooms with bath, 2 suites. Restaurant, 2 bars, minibars, pool, 2 tennis courts, Ping-Pong, volleyball, sea parachuting, windsurfing, waterskiing, shop, billiards, playground. MC, V. Closed Nov.–Apr.*

Troullos

❸ *8 km (5 mi) west of Skiathos town, 4 km (2½ mi) west of Kalamaki peninsula.*

On the coast road west of Kalamaki peninsula are Troullos and an even smaller village at Troullos Bay, a resort for visitors to Koukounaries who want to get away from it all.

The dirt road north of Troullos leads to beaches and also branches off
❹ to the small and now deserted **Kounistra Monastery,** 4 km (2½ mi) north of Troullos. It was built in the late 17th century on the spot where a miraculous icon of the Virgin was found swinging from a pine tree. The icon spends most of the year in the church of Trion Hierarchon, in town, but on November 20, the townspeople parade with it to its former home for the celebration of the Presentation of the Virgin the following day. The interior of the monastery church has been blackened by fire and its frescoes (1741) are hard to see.

Beaches

❺ Though **Koukounaries** (⊠ 12 km/8 mi west of Skiathos town, and 4 km/2½ mi northwest of Troullos), with golden sands framed by umbrella pines, has been much touted as Greece's most exquisite beach, most of the photos displaying it must either have been taken a long time ago or on a brilliant winter's day. All summer it is so packed with umbrellas, beach chairs, and blistering tourists that you can hardly see the sand. The beach can only be reached from its ends, as a lagoon separates it from the hinterland.

Around the island's western tip are a few more **beaches facing Pelion** (⊠ 13 km/8 mi west of Skiathos town, and 1 km/½ mi west of Koukounaries beach), which looms close. These are **Big and Little Banana,** officially known as **Krassas,** and **Ayia Eleni.** The former are nudist beaches, and topless is definitely in vogue everywhere.

❻ You'll find more privacy but less organization at some of the more remote beaches. **Mandraki** (⊠ 5 km/3 mi west of Troullos Bay and 12 km [8 mi] west of Skiathos town), for example, is a 25-minute walk. Sometimes called Xerxes' Harbor, this is where the Persian king stopped on his way to ultimate defeat at the battles of Artemisium and Salamis. The reefs opposite are the site of a monument said to have been erected by him as a warning to ships, the first such marker known in history.

Megalos Aselinos and **Mikros Aselinos** beaches (⊠ About 8 km/5 mi west of Skiathos town and 7 km/4 mi north of Troullos), north of Mandraki beach, can be reached by car or bike. Except for a ramshackle taverna, there is nothing here but broad sands and, at times, locals donning big hair rollers.

Lodging

$$–$$$ 🏨 **Troullos Bay.** This attractive, homey beachfront hotel invites reading, chatting, and relaxation around the lobby's fireplace—although it's never lit—and soft-cushioned bamboo armchairs. Bedrooms have dark wooden beds with striped duvets, tile floors, and colorful prints. Most rooms have sea views. The restaurant, also with bamboo chairs with chintz pillows, opens onto the lawn that separates the hotel from the sand. ⊠ *Troullos Bay 37002,* ☎ *0427/49390, 0427/49391, or 0427/21223,* 🆉 *0427/21791. 43 rooms with shower, 6 duplex suites (4 beds in each). Restaurant, bar. V. Closed Nov.–Apr.*

Outdoor Activities and Sports

HORSEBACK RIDING

Skiathos's **Pinewood Riding Centre** (⊠ On the road to Aselinos Beach) conducts lessons, mountain trail outings, and all-day excursions for beginners and experienced riders.

Kastro

❼ *5 km (3 mi) north of Skiathos town.*

A caïque will bring you to Kastro, perched on a forbidding promontory high above the water; you can also take the 3-hour walk from Skiathos town (☞ *below*). Skiathians founded this town in the 16th century when they fled from the pirates and the turmoil on the coast to security on this remote cliff—staying until 1829. Its landward side was additionally protected by a moat and drawbridge, and inside the stout walls they erected 300 houses and 30 churches, of which only three still stand. They must have prayed often for deliverance from the sieges that left them close to starvation. This cramped, windswept colony, deserted for so many years, bears no resemblance to the rest of fun-filled Skiathos of today, but it played a role during World War II. Brave Skiathians, especially a fearless woman called Kaliarina, hid Allied soldiers here until they could escape to Turkey or Egypt. After the Nazis caught her, they sent Kaliarina to a concentration camp and torched the town in retaliation.

❽ Four kilometers (2½ miles) southwest of Kastro is the deserted **monastery of Kechrias.** Be warned: The road to Kechrias and the beach below should only be attempted with a four-wheel-drive vehicle.

Outdoor Activities and Sports

HIKING

If you like to hike, leave the boat at Kastro and walk back to town to Skiathos through the orchards, fields, and forests of the interior. The walk takes about three hours; the paths are well-marked and are downhill most of the way.

Lalaria

9 *7 km (4 ⅓ mi) north of Skiathos town.*

Though more and more roads are being carved out of the pine forests, some key spots can only be reached by caïque. Chief among them is much photographed Lalaria, on the north coast, whose polished white stones are flanked by a majestic rocky promontory forming an arch. In the same area are three lovely grottoes, the *Skoteini* (**Dark**) **Cave,** the *Galazia* (**Azure**) **Cave,** and the *Halkini* (**Copper**) **Cave.** If caïque-hopping, you'll stop an hour or two here to swim and frolic.

10 When the island's best-known monastery, **Evangelistria,** was dedicated in the late 18th century to the Annunciation of the Virgin by monks from Mt. Athos, it had an enormous influence on island life. Not only did it encourage education, it gave a base to the revolutionaries, who pledged an oath to freedom and first hoisted the blue and white flag of Greece here in 1807. The monastery is surrounded by a high wall designed to keep pirates out; today, encloses a ruined refectory kitchen, the cells, a small museum library, and a magnificent church with three domes. It's about a 10-minute drive from town. ⊠ *5 km (3 mi) north of Skiathos town, 2 km (1¼ mi) south of Lalaria.* ☉ *Daily 9–5.*

NEED A BREAK? — Just south of Evangelistria monastery, the dirt road veers off toward the north and northwest of the island. For a quick repast, take this route; about a mile farther on, an enterprising soul has set up a café and snack bar, **Platanos** (⊠ On route south of Evangelistria monastery), where you can stare at the astounding view for as long as you want.

SKOPELOS

Second largest of the Sporades is triangular Skopelos, which means a sharp rock or a reef—a fitting description for the terrain on its northern shore. Most of its 122 sq km (47 sq mi), up to its highest peak on Mt. Delfi, at 666 meters (2,184 feet), are covered with dense pine forests, olive groves, and orchards. On the south coast, where most of the villages are, pines line the white beaches, casting jade shadows on the turquoise water.

Legend has it that Skopelos was settled by Peparethos and Staphylos, colonists from Minoan Crete, said to be the sons of Dionysos and Ariadne, King Minos's daughter. They brought with them the lore of the grape and the olive. The island was called Peparethos until Hellenistic times, and its most popular beach still bears the name Stafilos.

Skopelos Town

11 *11 km (7 mi) southeast of Loutraki.*

Skopelos town, the administrative center of the Sporades, overlooks a bay on the north coast, on a steep hill below scant vestiges of the ancient acropolis and medieval castle. Three- and four-story houses, rising virtually straight up the hillside, are reached by flagstone steps, where women sit chatting and knitting by their doorways. The white houses look prosperous and well tended, their facades enlivened by brightly painted or brown timber balconies, doors, shutters, flamboyant vines, and potted plants. Interspersed among their red-tile roofs are several still covered with the traditional gray slate—too heavy and expensive to be used often nowadays.

For a glimpse of the interior of a Skopelan house, visit the **Folk Art Museum** (⊠ Skopelos town), a 19th-century mansion with period furniture, traditional tools, and an example of an elaborate festive women's costume. It is open July and August.

To get an idea of what life is like off the waterfront, gear your legs for a breath-snatching climb up the almost perpendicular steps in Skopelos town, at the sea wall. You will encounter many **churches** as you go. The uppermost, the 11th-century **Ayios Athanasios,** was built on a 9th-century foundation. At the top you'll be standing within the walls of the 13th-century castle, erected by the Venetian Ghisi lords who held all the Sporades as their fief. It in turn rests upon polygonal masonry of the 5th century BC, as this was the site of one of the island's three ancient acropolises. Once you've admired the view and the stamina of the old women negotiating the steps like mountain goats, wind your way back down the sea wall steps by any route you choose. Wherever you turn, you'll probably spy a church; Skopelos claims some 360, of which 123 are in the town alone. Unfortunately, most of them seem to be curiously locked, though you'll nevertheless be taken with their exteriors—some incorporating ancient artifacts, Byzantine plates, or early Christian elements—and their slate-capped domes.

A few of Skopelos's 40 monasteries are perched on the mountainside opposite the town. Some are deserted, but others are in operation and welcome visitors (dress appropriately: no bare legs or arms; women must wear skirts). You can drive or go by bike, but even with just a

⑫ good walking guide, you can visit them all in a few hours. One is **Evangelistria Monastery** (⊠ On the mountainside opposite Skopelos town, 1½ km/1 mi northeast), founded in 1676 and completely rebuilt in 1712. It contains no frescoes, but it is justly proud of its intricately carved iconostasis and an early icon of the Virgin with Child, said to be miraculous.

⑬ Following the signs east of Skopelos town will bring you first to **Ayia Varvara** (⊠ East of Skopelos town), empty behind fortresslike walls. The **Metamorphosis tou Sotera,** the oldest monastery on the island (circa

⑭ 1600), is open only on August 6. The **Prodromou** (Forerunner), dedicated to St. John the Baptist, now operates as a convent, and is found 2½ km (1½ mi) east of Skopelos town. Besides being of unusual design, its church contains some outstanding 14th-century triptychs, an enamel tile floor, and an iconostasis spanning four centuries (half carved in the 14th, half in the 18th).

⑮ About 2 km (1¼ mi) south of Skopelos town, the **Ayios Reginos** monastery, the namesake of the island's patron saint, is disappointingly modern. It stands on the site of a series of churches, the first of which was erected where the saint was buried in AD 362. Bits and pieces of the earlier churches lie about the courtyard or have been set into the walls of the present structure. St. Reginos's main claim to sanctity, apart from numerous good works, seems to have been ridding the island of a fearsome dragon. Notwithstanding, Reginos was martyred under Julian the Apostate and beheaded.

Beaches

Scattered farms and tavernas, houses with rooms for rent, and one or

⑯ two nice hotels line the road to **Stafilos Beach** (⊠ 8 km/5 mi southeast of Skopelos town), the closest to town and therefore the most crowded. Prehistoric walls, a watchtower, and particularly an unplundered grave suggest that this was the site of an important prehistoric settlement. **Valania** (⊠ East of Stafilos Beach), reachable by footpath, takes its name from the *valanium* (Roman bath) that once stood here, which has since disintegrated under the waves.

Dining and Lodging

Most shops and eateries are announced by hand-painted traditional signs, part of the town council's effort to keep the honky-tonk element out of Skopelos. In 1992, it established **Demotiko Kafenion** (⊠ On the waterfront), a traditional Municipal Café where the locals, pensioners especially, can gather without being turned off by the glossy menus and bamboo armchairs designed to entice tourists. It is fairly cheap, and by no means off-limits to visitors, if they can find a seat.

$$ ✕ **Alexander.** When you've had enough of the waterfront, follow the signs up from the Emboriki Bank to this little garden restaurant. Here, none of the main dishes are prefab; your order is cooked for you. Especially recommended are *orektika* (appetizers) such as fried eggplant or zucchini, served with *tzatziki* (garlic and yogurt dip) or *tirosalata* (cheese dip). After these you might not have room for the main courses! ⊠ *Odhos Manolaki,* ☎ *0424/22324. MC, V. Closed Nov.–Mar. No lunch.*

$$ ✕ **Perivoli.** This is where the locals go to get away from the crowds and to undoubtedly enjoy the owner's cooking—traditional Greek prepared with a finesse rarely encountered—and his beautiful candlelit garden. *Dolmades* (stuffed cabbage leaves), *stamna* (lamb stew with cheese in an earthenware pot), and *tsoutzoukakia* (cumin-flavored meatballs in tomato sauce) are some of the unsurpassed entrées. Follow the signs up from Platanos (a.k.a. Souvlaki) Square. You may find it crowded. ⊠ *Skopelos town,* ☎ *0424/23758. Reservations essential in Aug. No credit cards. Closed Oct. 1–May 31. No lunch.*

$ ✕ **Molos.** This is the best of the cluster of tavernas near the ferry dock, serving excellent orektika and precooked dishes. Exceptional is the Melintzanes Imam, eggplant in a rich sauce, that might just make you swoon, as did the Turkish Sultan to whom it was first served. It's one of the few places open for lunch. ⊠ *Waterfront,* ☎ *0424/22551. No credit cards. Closed Nov. 1–May 25.*

$ ✕ **Spiros.** This is everybody's favorite waterfront taverna, where you can't go wrong—the food is always fresh and well prepared. Aside from the usual starters and meat dishes, the specialty here is salads—10 or 12 different ones are served every night. Atmosphere is the strong point here, but the service and food make it an excellent value. ⊠ *On waterfront, Skopelos town,* ☎ *0424/23146. No credit cards. Closed Nov.–Mar. No lunch.*

$$$–$$$$ ▥ **Skopelos Village.** This is really a group of bungalows on the water, each with a balcony or a patch of lawn, kitchen, large bedroom(s), and a living room; they sleep from two to six people. The decor is traditional northern Greek, with a large, built-in corner hearth, although it's doubtful you'll use it in summer. The surroundings are pleasantly landscaped and quiet. Children will enjoy the pool and playground, parents the congenial bar and taverna and the housekeeping service. Don't confuse this place with Sunrise Village next door. It is about a 15-minute walk from the town center. ⊠ *Skopelos town 37003,* ☎ *0424/22517,* ℻ *0424/22958. 36 bungalows with shower. Bar, pool, playground. No credit cards. Closed Nov.–Apr.*

$$$ ▥ **Alkistis.** Amid a sea of olive trees stand four buildings of cheerful air-conditioned apartments with kitchenettes, housekeeping, and a pool bar. The exteriors are pastel contemporary, but the lounges and dining terraces are more traditional, though airy and bright. It's 1 mi out of town on the road to Stafilos Beach. Geared toward families or

couples with cars, it makes an agreeable alternative to a beach or town hotel. ⊠ *Skopelos town 37003,* ☎ *0424/23006 through 23009,* FAX *0424/22116. Athens:* ☎ *01/682–3129. 25 apartments with bath. Restaurant, 2 bars, pool, wading pool, playground. No credit cards. Closed mid-Oct.–mid-May.*

$$–$$$ ⚓ **Dionysos.** Although it's right in town, everything about this hotel
★ is spacious: from the umbrellas that shade the bamboo chairs on the terrace and the lobby with embroidered curtains, to the air-conditioned rooms with a view of the hills, and the pool (with a pool bar, of course). The rooms, with brown woodwork, slate floors, and rustic-style furniture, are all kept spotlessly clean. The intelligent design and traditional decor help it to blend in with its older neighbors. ⊠ *Skopelos town 37003,* ☎ *0424/23210 through 23215,* FAX *0424/22954. 52 rooms with bath. Restaurant, 2 bars, pool. DC, MC, V. Closed Nov.–mid-Apr.*

$–$$ ⚓ **Pension Sotos.** People choose this small, cozy, remodeled family house on the waterfront because it's near the action, inexpensive, and extremely casual. The tiny rooms look onto one of the hotel's two courtyard terraces, where guests can bring their own food and are welcome to use the kitchen and refrigerator. It's not very private, but it's fun. It's one block from the Emboriki Bank, next to Ecstasy Café. ⊠ *Skopelos town 37003,* ☎ *0424/22549,* FAX *0424/23668. 12 rooms with shower. No credit cards. Closed Oct.–Apr.*

Outdoor Activities and Sports

NATURE CRUISES

A big caïque captained by a marine biologist makes 2-day weekend cruises from Skopelos to Psathoura and Kyra Panayia in the National Marine Park. Videos, slides, binoculars, snorkeling equipment, underwater cameras, and hydrophones to record dolphin signals make the trip educational and fun. The trip costs 40,000 dr.; make reservations at Madro Travel (☞ Contacts and Resources *in* The Northern Sporades A to Z, *below*).

Nightlife

BARS AND DISCOS

Nightlife on Skopelos is more sedate than it is on Skiathos. There is a smattering of cozy bars playing music of all kinds, and there is at least one disco, which changes each year (look for advertisements).

BOUZOUKI CLUB

Meintani (⊠ Skopelos town), a traditional Greek bouzouki club, stages performances in a beautifully converted olive-oil factory.

OUZERI

At **Anatoli** (⊠ In the Old Kastro), an ouzeri, the proprietor strums his bouzouki and sings *rembetika* (blues) without benefit of microphone. Sometimes, other musicians join in.

Shopping

The town's tiny shops are tucked into a few streets behind the central part of the waterfront.

CLOTHING

Try **Riska** (☎ 0424/23339) for children's clothing. **Phaedra** (☎ 0424/23806) specializes in imaginative clothing from Greece, Italy, and Bali.

LOCAL CRAFTS

One of the most alluring shops is **Archipelago** (☎ 0424/23127), a branch of the Skiathos shop; it has modern ceramics and crafts—even a rainbow-hued hammock—as well as antiques. **Armoloi** (☎ 0424/22707), one of the neatest shops, displays an array of ceramics made by local potters, kilims, tapestries, embroideries, and bags crafted from fragments of old Oriental rugs and kilims. Also try **Ploumisti** (☎ 0424/22059) for kilims, bags, hand-painted T-shirts, and jewelry. **Kriezy's** (☎ 0424/23186) sells original jewelry and gifts. **Mesaio** has rag dolls, pottery, and watercolors. **Armonia** (☎ 0424/22392) has unusual ceramic, stone, and metal items. **Photo Gallerie** has a large collection of cards and photographs from all over the island.

Drachondoschisma

⑰ *Peninsula about 5 km (3 mi) south of Skopelos town.*

The road from Stafilos Beach runs southwest through the rounded Drachondoschisma peninsula, where Reginos dispatched the dragon.

Agnonda

⑱ *5 km (3 mi) south of Skopelos town.*

The tiny port of Agnonda is named after a local boy named Agnonas who returned here from Olympia in 546 BC wearing the victor's wreath.

Panormos Bay

⑲ *6 km (3¾ mi) west of Skopelos town, 4 km (2½ mi) northwest of Agnonda.*

Due northwest of Agnonda is Panormos Bay, the smallest of the ancient towns of Peparethos, founded in the 8th century BC by colonists from Chalkis. A few well-concealed walls are visible among the pine woods on the acropolis above the bay. With its long beach and its sheltered inner cove that's ideal for yachts, this is fast becoming a holiday village, although it retains its quiet charm.

Beaches

Just north of Panormos Bay is **Milia,** Skopelos's longest beach.

Lodging

$$–$$$ 🏨 **Adrina Beach.** Atop a picture-book cove, this terraced hotel boasts uninterrupted views of Panormos Bay from every level; multihued bougainvillea enchant the eye. The blue and white color scheme is carried throughout—from the balconies and stair railings to the slipcovers and cushions—and the warm terra-cotta floors complement it. Ornamental objects delight: plates adorn the walls, amphorae the corners. The large, comfy bedrooms have fans but no air-conditioning. The only fly in the ointment might be the stairs you must climb between the private beach, pool, taverna area, and your room, and the steep walk back from the little town. ⊠ *Adrina Beach 37003,* ☎ *0424/23373 through 23375,* 🖷 *0424/23372. Athens:* ☎ *01/682/6886. 45 rooms with bath, 10 duplex suites (each sleeps 4). Restaurant, bar, snack bar, minirefrigerators, pool, beach, jet skiing, sea parachuting, waterskiing, playground. AE, DC, MC, V. Closed Nov.–Apr.*

$$ 🏨 **Panormos Beach.** Guests come back to this hotel year after year. The
★ owner's attention to detail and perfection is found everywhere: in the beautifully tended flower garden; the immaculate, air-conditioned rooms with pine furniture and handwoven linens; the country dining room; and the entrance case displaying his grandmother's elaborate costume. Don't miss the delicious Skopelan mezedes prepared by his mother-in-law. This is a traditional, exceptionally quiet and peaceful hotel, and it's less than a 5-minute walk from the beach. ⊠ *Panormos Beach 37003,* ☎ *0424/22711,* 🖷 *0424/33005. 34 rooms with shower. Bar, snack bar, playground. No credit cards. Closed Nov.–Apr.*

Elios

 6 km (3¾ mi) west of Skopelos town, 4 km (2½ mi) north of Panormos Bay.

Elios is a development that houses residents of Klima who were dislodged in 1965 by the same earthquake that devastated Alonnisos. The origin of its name is more intriguing than the village: legend has it that when Reginos arrived to save the island from the dragon, which demanded human nourishment, he is supposed to have demanded, "Well, where in *eleos* (God's mercy) is the beast?"

Klima

 10 km (6¼ mi) northwest of Skopelos town, 3 km (1¾ mi) north of Elios.

Klima, clinging to the mountainside, is being slowly restored, but there are plenty of ruined houses still for sale. If you crave an island retreat, this could be your chance.

Loutraki

 11 km (7 mi) northwest of Skopelos town, 1 km (⅔ mi) northwest of Klima.

Loutraki is the tiny village where the ferries and hydrofoils stop. Three-hundred yards from Loutraki stand the remains of the **acropolis of Selinous,** the island's third ancient city. Unfortunately, everything lies buried except the walls.

Glossa

 19 km (11¾ mi) northwest of Skopelos town, 1 km (⅔ mi) north of Loutraki.

Glossa is the island's second-largest settlement, where picturesque red-roof houses are clustered on the steep hillside. The center is closed to traffic.

ALONNISOS

A visit to this island will show you what Greece was like 20 or 30 years ago. The little development that did occur happened late, and until very recently, most of its rugged coast was accessible only by boat. Barter was still the usual method of trade here until the late 1960s, when tourism catapulted Alonnisos into the 20th century. Alonnisos lacks pretension, chic beaches, and groovy nightclubs. For explorers, far better are the island's walks through forests, swimming at beaches where jet skis and parasailing are unknown, and boat trips to offshore islands. There are a few hotels, several rooms to rent, some nice tavernas, and a cheerful laid-back atmosphere. Restaurants and tavernas usually don't open until 6 PM. In August, it becomes an Italian colony.

Its 3,000 inhabitants (1,200 in winter) live in the port of Patitiri, hurriedly developed to house the 1965 earthquake victims, and in the adjacent cove of Votsi. Many fishing families live in Steni Vala, farther northeast. On a conical hill 183 meters (600 feet) above the port is Alonnisos town, or Chora, its houses lovingly restored by foreigners. It comes to life in summer, but in autumn it's almost deserted once more.

Though famous for its wine in ancient times, Alonnisos hardly gets more than a line or two in the history books, and because it has had many different names—Ikos and Liadromia—researchers find it difficult to trace. Peleus, Achilles' father, once lived on the island; Philip of Macedon coveted it; the Venetians erected a fortress here. Its waters cover dozens of fascinating shipwrecks, not to mention a ruined city or two, but little else is known otherwise. While Skiathos and Skopelos were sending merchant fleets to the Black Sea and Egypt in the 18th and early 19th centuries, sailors from Alonnisos were probably plundering them. When the Sporades and Greece gained independence, the pirates turned to fishing.

To explore beyond Patitiri and Old Alonnisos, you can either rent a motorbike or car or take a caïque; caïques also take you to the neighboring islands. The roads to the various beaches along the way are fairly decent dirt surfaces. The road from Patitiri to Steni Vala is now paved; north of Steni Vala are virtually no signs of habitation.

Patitiri

24 *7 km (4⅓ mi) southwest of Steni Vala.*

Everything is visible at a glance when you land at Patitiri, in a pretty cove flanked by white cliffs studded with pine trees. Along the waterfront are tavernas and cafés, a few hotels, the boat agency, and a gas station.

OFF THE
BEATEN PATH

The smaller islands closest to Alonnisos are reachable by caïque from Patitiri; day trips are organized for those interested in exploring them. Excursions can be arranged on Skiathos or Skopelos. **Peristera** (pigeon) is the island closest to Alonnisos. It has a tiny shepherd population and a few delightful beaches that the caïques buzz along. Take a caïque ride to **Skantzoura**, which has great beaches, a monastery with one monk in residence, and the submerged ruins of the ancient town of Skandyle. The biggest in the island group is **Kyra Panayia** (Pelagos), which has sometimes been identified as ancient Alonnisos. Here, too, there is a monastery (16th century) and traces of a neolithic settlement. Its two bays, Planitis and Ayios Petros, are often filled with flotillas—groups of yachts usually chartered by visitors. **Yioura** was once used as place of exile for undesirable politicos. A rare species of wild goat makes its home here, and the most impressive of its caves is said to be where Homer's Cyclops lived. **Psathoura,** the most northerly of the Sporades, is so low in the water it can hardly be seen until you're on top of it. Near its harbor are the ruins of yet another sunken city—perhaps ancient Ikos?

Dining and Lodging

$ ✕ **Flisvos.** By far the port's best restaurant, this is an excellent spot to while away the hours as you await the boat. Outdoor tables are across the road under a shady awning, right next to the water. The specialty is *tiropitta alonnisou* (a deep-fried cheese pie formed of swirls of pastry). Also served are freshly made pizza and pasta as well as all the usual taverna food. Don't miss the salad with locally produced olive oil—to die for. It's open at 7 AM for breakfast and lunch—a rarity here. ⊠ *Patitiri (on corner of main st. and seafront),* ☎ *0424/65307. No credit cards. Closed Oct. 16–Apr. 14.*

$$ 🏨 **Galaxy.** Gleaming among the pine trees on a cliff above town, this hotel's balcony views and friendly staff keep guests loyal, despite its drab public rooms, unadorned guest rooms, and boxy multilevel buildings. Beware of the challenging walk from the waterfront, although the hotel's minibus meets the boats as they arrive. ⊠ *Patitiri 37005,*

☎ 0424/65251, 0424/65254 or 0424/65363, ℻ 0424/65110. *Athens:* ✉ *13 Odhos Nikis,* ☎ *01/323–4869. 51 rooms with shower. Bar. AE, MC, V. Closed Oct.–Apr.*

$$ 🏨 **Liadromia.** Three quarters of the rooms in this three-story hotel overlook the port, but there's an even better view from the rooftop terrace bar and breakfast room. Rooms with dark wood, mustard and green striped bedspreads and curtains, and built-in beds lean toward the traditional; the halls portray family memorabilia and photos of Alonnisos before the quake. Some of the rooms have refrigerators, and some have double beds—ask if you want either of these. ✉ *Patitiri 37005,* ☎ *0424/65521,* ℻ *0424/65096. 20 rooms with shower. Bar. MC, V. Closed Nov.–Mar.*

$$ 🏨 **Paradise.** Although the rooms and balconies here are small and rudimentary, it's in a gorgeous setting: the hotel's flower garden is lovely, and just below, among the local pines and rocks, guests can have the pleasure of a swim at any time. Some hang out all day at the bar or shady terrace beside the pool, which doubles as a snack bar and breakfast area. ✉ *Patitiri 37005,* ☎ *0424/65160 or 0424/65213,* ℻ *0424/65161. 31 rooms with shower. 2 bars, pool. MC, V. Closed Nov.–Apr.*

Old Alonnisos

㉕ *1½ km (1 mi) west of Patitiri.*

If you can't hack the 45-minute hike up to Old Alonnisos, take the island's single bus to what must be the most spectacular village in the Sporades. At the top is a 360-degree view of the whole Aegean, several charming restaurants, and a couple of transient boutiques. The original town dates from the 10th century, when the population sought safety above the sea. Some walls from the Byzantine-Venetian fortress still crown the peak, and a few venerable churches stand out among the houses. The destruction caused by the 1965 earthquake is still being repaired, and only the houses at the top need renovation. You might decide to stay in rooms here rather than in the port below.

NEED A BREAK? **Kafereas** (✉ Near the top of the old village) serves up cool drinks or ice cream under shady awnings, with views of both coasts and the village below.

Dining

$$–$$$ ✗ **Astrofengia.** This restaurant, in a restored family house, has a stunning view and a delightful garden. From the varied, innovative menu choose one of the many salads, some Cypriot hummus, three-cheese pie, or tagliatelle with a choice of sauces, and tiramisu. It's just before the entrance to Old Alonnisos; take the path to the left as soon as you get off the bus. ✉ *Old Alonnisos,* ☎ *0424/65182. No credit cards. Closed Oct.–May. No lunch.*

$$ ✗ **Paraport.** At this little taverna, you will enjoy the setting as much as the food. The right table has views of the sea and nearby islands on both sides of Alonnisos. Tables spill out in both directions on the narrow, winding main street just underneath the picturesque ruins of the Kastro. Along with the usual taverna fare, try the potatoes au gratin. ✉ *Old Alonnisos,* ☎ *0424/65608. No credit cards. Closed Oct. 1– May 19. No lunch.*

Kokkinokastro

㉖ *4 km (2½ mi) northeast of Patitiri.*

At Kokkinokastro, where the cliff sides and pebbles radiate the red color of the stone, there are traces of an acropolis as well as a Ghisi fortress. Some experts think Kokkinokastro was also the site of the ancient city of Ikos.

The islet offshore, **Vrachos,** holds other secrets: stone tools found here, dating back between 30,000 and 100,000 years, show that it's one of the earliest inhabited sites in the Aegean.

Steni Vala

㉗ *3 km (1¾ mi) northeast of Kokkinokastro.*

Steni Vala, a fjordlike haven in any weather, has little to offer except that it's the headquarters of the International Centre for Research on the Mediterranean Monk Seal. The islands around Alonnisos are one of the last preserves of the endangered monk seal. Scientists are always on the lookout for orphans and they track mature animals, too. This is the gateway to the National Marine Park, which comprises all the islands in the vicinity, some of which are off-limits to visitors.

SKYROS

This southernmost and largest (209 sq km/81 sq mi) of the Northern Sporades, divided into two almost equal parts, has a split personality. The southern half of Skyros (meaning tough, stony) is forbidding, barren, and mountainous, its western coast outlined with coves and deep bays dotted with a series of offshore islets. The northern portion, attached by a narrow, flat isthmus, is virtually all farmland and forests and heavily populated. Their names reflect their characters—*Meri* or *Imero* (tame) for the north and *Vouno* (literally, mountain) for the south, with Mt. Kochilas its highest peak (792 meters/2,598 feet). Skyros lies in the middle of the Aegean, with nothing between it and Lesbos, off the coast of Turkey. Its nearest neighbor is the town of Kimi, on the east coast of Evia. Strangely enough, although the island is adrift in the Aegean, the Skyrians have never had a seafaring tradition, and they have always looked to the land for their living.

This isolation has brought about a unique set of island traditions, such as pre-Christian Carnival rituals. Found here is an almost extinct breed of pony, a town that has been occupied on and off for the last 3,300 years, and exceptional crafts—carpentry, pottery, embroidery—practiced by dedicated artisans. You will not find luxury accommodations or swank restaurants: This idiosyncratic island makes no provisions for mass tourism, but if you've a taste for the offbeat, you'll feel right at home.

From 1204, when Constantinople and the rest of the Greek world fell to the Crusaders, until the Ottoman Turks gained full control, Skyros seesawed between Venetian, Byzantine, and Turkish rule, and was on occasion ruthlessly pillaged by pirates. During all the early centuries—even from the Classical period through the Byzantine and medieval periods—until Greece won independence in 1831, all the island's population squeezed sardine-fashion into the area under the castle on the inland face of the rock. Not a single house was visible from the sea. Though the islanders could survey any movement in the Aegean for miles, they kept a low profile, living in dread of pirates based at Treis Boukes bay on Vouno.

There are a number of interweaving legends about Skyros in the Iliad: Before the Trojan War, Theseus, the hero-king of Athens, having been deposed from the throne, sought refuge in his ancestral estate on Skyros. Lykomedes, afraid of the power and prestige of Theseus, took him up to the acropolis one evening on the pretense of showing him the island, and pushed him over the edge of the cliff. Thus was Theseus' ignominious end. In historical times, however, Timon of Athens unearthed what he said were Theseus' bones and sword, and placed them in the Theseion in Athens (☞ Exploring Athens *in* Chapter 2), in what must be one of the earliest recorded archaeological investigations.

According to the island's other legend, the sea-nymph Thetis disguised her son Achilles as a girl, and hid him among the daughters of King Lykomedes, hoping to stop Odysseus from luring Achilles off to Troy, where she knew he would meet his doom. Odysseus delivered a number of presents to the palace, among which was a sword, and then pretended to attack; Achilles revealed himself by reaching for the sword to help in the defense. Having fallen into Odysseus' trap, he went to Troy where he could not avoid his fate.

Linaria

40 km (25 mi) northeast of Kimi on Evia.

All boats and hydrofoils dock at the tiny port of Linaria because the northeast coast is either straight, sandy beach or steep cliffs. There is no reason to explore this dusty, scruffy area, and very few people do: a bus to Skyros town meets arrivals.

Skyros Town

28 *10 km (6¼ mi) north of Linaria.*

Skyros town, often called *Horio, Hora, and Chora* (town), is where 90% of the island's 3,000 inhabitants live. The impression as you arrive is of crowded, squat buildings creeping up the hillside. The town is built among a tangle of labyrinthine lanes winding up, down, and around the dense patchwork of tiny houses and churches. Almost all activity takes place on Agora (Market) Street (familiarly known as Sisifos because of its steepness), or along its immediate side alleys. Found here are the town's two pharmacies, travel agencies, shops with wonderful Skyrian pottery, an extraordinary number of tiny bars, and tavernas. There are no boutiques and relatively little kitsch. Within one day, you will know where everything is.

As you stroll down from the Kastro, the highest part of the town, with various ruins and churches, or explore the alleyways off the main drag, try to take a discreet peek at the interiors of the houses. Walls and conical mantle pieces are richly decorated with European and Asian porcelain, copper cooking utensils, and embroideries. Wealthy upper-class families originally obtained much of the porcelain from the pirates in exchange for grain and food, and its possession was a measure of social standing. Then enterprising potters started making exact copies, along with the traditional local ware, leading to the unique Skyrian style of pottery. The furniture is equally beautiful, the most typical item being the miniature carved Skyrian chairs, which support adult posteriors, not just children's.

The tiny **Archaeological Museum** contains finds, mostly from graves, from prehistoric to Roman times. Weapons and jewelry are represented along with pottery. ⊠ *Eternal Poetry Sq. (at far end of Sisifos),* ☎ *0222/91327.* 💳 *500 dr.* ☉ *Tues.–Sun. 8:30–3.*

The **Faltaits Historical and Folklore Museum** has a rich collection of Skyrian decorative arts. This house, built after Independence, is far larger than the usual town dwelling, and it is almost overflowing with rare books, costumes, local embroideries, and other heirlooms of all kinds. The embroideries are noted for their flamboyant colors and vivacious renderings of mermaids, hoopoes (the Skyrians' favorite bird), and human figures whose clothes and limbs sprout flowers. ⊠ *Eternal Poetry Sq.*, ☎ *0222/91232.* ☎ *Free.* ⊙ *Daily 10–1, 5:30–8.*

You can't miss the **statue dedicated to Rupert Brooke** (⊠ Eternal Poetry Sq.) for the poet who was on his way to the Dardanelles in 1915 to fight in the first world war, but who died on the French ship *Duguay Trouin* just off Skyros on April 23, at the age of 28. He was buried the same night on Skyros, and his grave was immortalized in the words "that corner of a foreign field that is forever England." Brooke was a socialist, but he became something of a paragon for war leaders such as Churchill. The imposing statue, a classical nude bronze, provokes strong emotions (some of the islanders objected to the nudity). The Skyrians call this well-known landmark *To Brook,* and all streets seem to lead either to it or to the Kastro.

The best way to get an idea of the town and its history is to follow the sinuous cobbled lanes to the **Kastro** and the 10th-century fortified **Monastery of St. George,** which stand on the site of the ancient acropolis and Bronze Age settlement. There is little trace of the legendary fortress of King Lykomedes, portrayed in Skyros's two most colorful myths (☞ *above*), though lower down on the north and southwest face of the rock are the so-called Pelasgian bastions of immense rectangular fitted blocks, dated to the Classical period or later.

In the wall above the entrance to the monastery is a white marble lion, once thought to be left over from the Venetian occupation. It is now recognized as a Classical symbol, a reminder of when Skyros was under Athenian dominion and heavily populated with Athenian settlers to keep it that way. This part of the castle was built on ancient foundations (look right) during the early Byzantine era, and reinforced in the 14th century by the Venetians. The monastery itself was founded in 962 and radically rebuilt in 1600. Unfortunately, its once splendid frescoes are now mostly covered by layers of whitewash (look for the charming St. George and startled Dragon outside to the left of the church door), but its ornate iconostasis is considered a masterpiece. The icon of St. George on the right is said to have been borne by the waves from Constantinople to Skyros during the Iconoclast Controversy of the 9th century. He has a black face and is familiarly known as Ayios Georgis o Arapis (the Negro); the Skyrians view him as the patron saint of lovers as well as of their island.

The ruined church of **Episkopi** (⊠ Take the vaulted passageway from the monastery courtyard), the former seat of the bishop of Skyros, was erected in 895 on the ruins of a temple of Athena. This was the center of Skyros's religious life from 1453 to 1837; the remaining frescoes are being restored. Farther up, the summit is crowned with three tiny cubelike churches and the ruined Venetian cistern, once used as a dungeon. From here, you have a spectacular view of the town and surrounding hills. The roofs of the houses are flat, the older ones covered with a special dark gray shale that has splendid insulating properties. The house walls and roofs are interconnected; from above, the roofs look like a magnified form of cuneiform writing. Here and there, the shieldlike roof of a church stands out from the cubistlike composition of houses that fills the hillside with not an inch to spare.

Beaches

Around the northern tip of the island is a dirt road to **Theotokos** beach. The large Greek air base near the northern tip is off-limits.

Dining and Lodging

$$ ✕ Christina's Restaurant. This is where to go when you want a so-
★ phisticated, delicious meal in a romantic garden away from the crowds
on Sisifos. Australian by birth, Christina, the owner and chef, prepares
international and local cuisine with imagination and talent. The menu
changes regularly, but always includes the perennial favorites: hot herb
bread and a light, exquisite cheesecake—both rich but with a minimum
of fat or oil. Her barrel wine is excellent. To find the restaurant, look
for a sign a few minutes downhill from the taxi stand. ⊠ *Market St.,*
☎ *0222/91778. No credit cards. Closed Sun. June 1–Sept. 30 and week-
days Oct. 1–May 31.*

$$ ✕ Margetis Taverna. This vest-pocket taverna wedged in among the
others is known locally as the best place for meat and fish on the is-
land. It is very popular, so get there early (8–8:30). Though fish and
lobster are always pricey, they're cheapest here. Try the good barrel
wine. ⊠ *Market St.,* ☎ *0222/91311. No credit cards. Reservations not
accepted. No lunch.*

$$ ✕ Simposio. Opened in 1995, run by a husband and wife team, this
is the best choice for traditional taverna food. ⊠ *Market St.,* ☎
0222/92031. No credit cards. No lunch.

$ ✕ To Glaros. This small taverna is the place to get simple, good, pre-
cooked classics—stuffed tomatoes, moussaka, vegetable dishes—with
no frills. It might be your best choice for lunch, if you're not relaxing
on the beach.⊠ *Market St.,* ☎ *0222/92363. No credit cards.*

$$ ▥ Paliopirgos Hotel. This intimate, A-class hotel occupies the best island location: 5 minutes between both the beach at Magazia and the
main town center. Rooms are air-conditioned and decorated in a pristine, classic style; each has a small, well-equipped kitchen area, a single and a double bed, and a balcony with a sea view. The charming
Maria Makris is the perfect host. Breakfast is a relaxed affair in the
roof garden; in the evening, sip a cocktail in the same spot, and watch
the sun set and the moon rise. There are only nine rooms; be sure to
book in advance. The mopeds for rent are fun for tooling around the
island. ⊠ *Skyros town 37007,* ☎ *0222/91014 or 0222/92405,* ℻
*0222/92185. 9 rooms with shower. 2 bars. MC. Open winter with ad-
vance booking.*

Nightlife

BARS

Local bars with loud music are the extent of the nightlife on Skyros.
Calypso (⊠ Sisifos) is the oldest, opened in 1982. **Rodon** (⊠ Sisifos)
is popular and open late. **Renaissance** (⊠ Sisifos) is another hot spot
that goes on until the wee hours.

Shopping

FURNITURE

If you'd like to order some Skyrian furniture (it can be shipped anywhere), **Lefteris Avgoklouris** is a carpenter with flair; you may visit his
workshop (⊠ About 100 yards from square on right of rd. heading
down the hill, ☎ 0222/91106).

POTTERY

Although you will see Skyrian pottery all over town, the best places
to buy it are all on Market Street. First on the right near the square is
Emmanouil Andreou's (⊠ Market St., ☎ 0222/91631), which contains
both local and imported ceramics. Also on the right is **Stamatis Ftoulis's**
(⊠ Market St., ☎ 0222/91559 or 0222/91887), which has a very big
selection of plates, bowls, cups, and vases. You can watch him and his
assistants painting them at his workshop in Magazia. Perhaps the

most interesting for reproductions is **Kallio,** G. Nittis's tiny atelier (✉ On the left behind the pale blue kiosk, just before the turn for *To Brook,* ☏ 0222/92213). He is a mine of information and enjoys talking about his research over a glass of ouzo; he specializes in meticulously exact copies of historic pieces of Anatolian origin. You will not find pottery of this kind and quality outside Turkey.

Magazia and Molos

㉙ *1 km (⅔ mi) north of Skyros town.*

Magazia and **Molos** are coastal expansions of the town. This is where to go for a swim. Magazia, where the residents of Horio used to have their storehouses and wine presses, and Molos, where the small fishing fleet anchors, are growing fast. They can be reached in 5 minutes from the steps that lead down from Eternal Poetry Square past the archaeological museum.

Beaches
Just north of Molos, past low hills, fertile fields, and the odd farmhouse, is a dirt road to the beach at **Palamari.**

Nightlife
DANCE CLUB

For late-night dancing, the best club is **Skiropoulo** (✉ On the beach just before Magazia). Music is western and (later on) Greek, and its laser lighting system casts upon on the rocks of the acropolis after the sun has gone down. It can be reached from Eternal Poetry Square by descending the steps past the archaeological museum.

Atsitsa

㉚ *13 km (8 mi) west of Skyros town.*

Atsitsa, on the northwest coast, is home to the chapel of **Ayios Panteleimon** (✉ On dirt road south).

Skyros Centre, founded in 1978, was the first and remains the foremost center for holistic vacations. Participants come for a two-week session and can take part in activities as diverse as windsurfing, creative writing with well-known authors, art, tai chi, yoga, massage, dance, acting, and psychotherapy. Courses also take place in Skyros town, where participants live in rooms in villagers' houses. Skyros' courses are highly reputed and have been well reviewed, with even hardened journalists claiming that a holiday there changed their lives. For more information, contact the London office well in advance of leaving for Greece. ✉ *Skyros, 92 Prince of Wales Rd., London NW5 3NE, England,* ☏ *0171/267–4424 or 0171/284–3065,* 𝔽𝔸𝕏 *0171/284–3063.* ☏ *On Skyros: 0222/92279.*

Outdoor Activities and Sports
HIKING

Experienced hikers can take the 6-km (4-mi) walk around the headland from Atsitsa to Ayios Fokas, but the trek over the terrain takes skill to negotiate at times, and can be dangerous in bad weather.

Ayios Fokas

㉛ *12 km (7½ mi) west of Skyros town, 5 km (3 mi) south of Atsitsa.*

At Ayios Fokas, you will find three lovely beaches and the fabulous cooking of Kyria Kali, who serves her husband's fish with her own vegetables, cheese, and bread at her small taverna. If you're coming from

Atsitsa, the road south deteriorates into a rutted track, nerve-wracking even for experienced motorbike riders.

Beaches
The beaches at **Aherounes** and **Pefko** (✉ 7.5 km/5 mi southeast of Ayios Fokas, near Linaria) are most accessible from the Linaria–Horio main road. At Pefko, the dirt road south from Atsitsa becomes smooth and paved again.

Vouno

Access to southern territory starts at Ahilli, 4 km (2½ mi) south of Skyros town. Points south: Kalamitsa 4 km (2½ mi) south of Ahilli; Kolymbada 5 km (3 mi) south of Kalamitsa.

There is not much to see in Vouno, the southern half of Skyros, though a passable dirt road heads south at the eastern end of the isthmus, from ❸❷ **Aspous** to **Ahilli.** The little bay of Ahilli (whence Achilles is said to have set sail with Odysseus), is in the process of being made a yacht marina. There are some beautiful, practically untouched beaches and sea caves well worth the trip for hard-core explorers.

Thorny bushes warped into weird shapes, oleanders, and sharp rocks through which rivulets run are the predominant features here; only goats and Skyrian ponies can survive this desolate environment. Many scholars consider the beautifully proportioned diminutive horses to be the same breed as the horses sculpted on the Parthenon frieze. They are, alas, an endangered species; only 80 to 100 have survived.

❸❸ Pilgrims to **Rupert Brooke's grave** should continue along the wide dirt road through this wilderness down toward the shore. As you reach the valley with the olive grove, you'll catch sight of the grave under the trees on your left. Restored by the British Royal Navy in 1961, a stout wrought-iron and cement railing surrounds it. You can arrange for a visit to the grave by taxi or caïque in the town.

Beaches
The beach of **Kalamitsa** (✉ Western coast) is 4 km (2½ mi) along the road south from Ahilli. There are three tavernas there.

The inviting, deserted **Kolymbada** beach is found 5 km (3 mi) south of Kalamitsa.

For true explorers, the beaches at Vouno's impressive **Treis Boukes** natural harbor, Glyfada beach on Sarakino islet, and the dramatic sea caves around the southeast tip of the island await. Take a caïque to these spots; this can be arranged at Skyros Travel.

EVIA

In any other country, an island as large and beautiful as Evia would be a prime tourist attraction. In Greece, perhaps because it lies so close to the mainland, it is often ignored by foreigners. This was not the case in the past. In ancient times, Evia (then called Euboea) flourished early, and by the 7th century BC its four city-states—Chalkis (present-day Halkidha), Eretria, Kimi, and Histiaia—had colonies in Asia Minor and Italy, not to mention the Greek mainland. Their glory paled as Athens entered the ascendant, but Chalkis—which controlled the narrow Evripos Channel between mainland and island—was seen as a strategic prize by subsequent conquerors, from Philip of Macedon to the Romans, the Crusaders, and the Turks. A tour of the highlights of Evia could be done in a couple of days. This tour begins in Karystos, one of the ferry and hydrofoil ports, and ends in the north coast, characterized by fishing villages and miniresorts; you may also start where the boats also port (in Marmari, Eretria, Kimi, Aedipsos) or you can cross the bridge at Halkidha.

Karystos

90 km (56 mi) southeast of Halkidha.

At Karystos, in southeastern Evia, a 1-hour boat ride from the port of Rafina, the russet ruins of a Franco-Turkish castle overlook the neo-classical town and the fertile valley around it. To climb the 4,610-foot Mt. Ochi take the path from Myli in the lush slopes above the town to the bizarre half-hewn marble columns lying like felled logs among the rocks; near the summit is a structure called the Dragon's House, thought to be a temple of Hera. The mountain was a quarry site in the Roman era, and the Dragon's House, which is unlike anything Greek, may have been erected by workers from Asia Minor. On the coast below Karystos are some beaches; tucked among them is the lighthouse that marks the Cava d'Oro, the strait between Evia and Andros.

Marmari

80 km (49½ mi) southeast of Halkidha, 10 km (7 mi) northwest of Karystos.

The port of Marmari, rapidly growing with hotels and summer homes, is served by Rafina on the mainland. The road north goes inland along the middle of the island, flaunting glimpses of Frankish watchtowers and bisecting tiny villages. These villages are inhabited by Greeks of Albanian origin whose ancestors were brought by the Venetians during the 14th century and later the Turks to supplement the declining local population. Many still speak Albanian at home.

En Route On the drive from Marmari to Eretria you'll pass **Aliveri,** where smoke belches from a power plant, and then past fish tavernas and hotels patronized by package tourists.

Eretria

15 km (9 mi) southeast of Halkidha, 65 km (40 mi) northwest of Marmari.

Drab, dusty Eretria today is regarded as just a place where people board the 30-minute ferry to the mainland. Neither its interesting ruins nor its jewel of a museum is even signposted, but do persevere.

Eretria's **ancient theater** (⊠ North of the museum) has two vaulted passageways—one leading to the orchestra, the other under the orchestra—no doubt used for deus ex machina solutions and spectral apparitions.

The **museum** (⊠ Odhos Arheou Theatrou), set amid cypress trees, opened in 1991 in collaboration with the Swiss School of Archaeology, which is responsible for digging at Eretria. It has beautifully exhibited finds from the area—including magnificent black-figure vases, ex-votos galore, and children's toys and jewelry. ⊠ *Odos Archaio Theatrou,* ☎ *0229/62206.* ⊠ *500 dr.* ⊙ *Tues.–Sun. 8:30–3.*

Ask the guard to take you to the **House of the Mosaics,** 5 minutes away, to view the 4th-century BC treasures.

Kimi

50 km (31 mi) northeast of Halkidha, 40 km (29 mi) northeast of Eretria.

Kimi, the port for Skyros, has mulberry trees everywhere and spectacular beaches (follow the secondary roads). Probably the dried-fig capital of Greece, Kimi has a good deal of Victoriana and some diaphanous silk garments; it was known for its silk production in centuries past. It was also the birthplace of George Papanicolaou, who developed the Pap smear to detect uterine cancer.

In Kimi is a charming little **folk museum.** ⊠ *On rd. to the port,* ☎ *0222/22011.* 💴 *400 dr.* 🕙 *10–1 and 6–8:30.*

NEED A BREAK?	Stop to rest your feet at **To Balkoni** (⊠ Above the port) with its splendid view of the extravagant hillside vegetation and the sleepy, one-street port below.

Halkidha

90 km (56 mi) northeast of Athens.

Halkidha (Chalkis), Evia's largest town, has been linked by a bridge to the mainland since the 5th century BC. The current rushing through the 50-yard channel changes direction several times a day, confounding travel plans in past generations and perplexing scientists, including Aristotle, who is said to have thrown himself in the water in despair when he could not figure it out. Halkidha is still a major commercial center; cement factories blight its southern suburbs. Though the town may have more urban problems than blessings, you can dine royally in its fish tavernas for a pittance.

OFF THE BEATEN PATH	**STENI** – If you head 30 km (18½ mi) north from Halkidha's extended suburbs, you'll see signs for Steni, a pretty village halfway up Mt. Dirfis, Evia's highest mountain. At 1745 meters (5,725 feet), it's a challenge to hikers; a boon to botanists because of its many unique species; and to ordinary mortals a place of glorious views. You can drive a good way up it.

En Route On the coast going north from Halkidha to Prokopi, the road parallels a river shaded by enormous plane trees. One of them is so huge it takes 27 men to encircle its trunk.

Prokopi

40 km (25 mi) northwest of Halkidha.

Prokopi is a popular pilgrimage site, largely owing to the **shrine of Ayios Yannis o Rossos.**

Also in Prokopi is **Ahmet Aga,** the vast estate of the Noel-Baker family. The original Noel, a cousin of Lady Byron, bought the property from the Turks in 1830, and it has often been a source of violent resentment in this district inhabited by rather poor, often unemployed Greeks.

Limni

50 km (31 mi) northwest of Halkidha, 10 km (6¼ mi) west of Prokopi.

The west coast's Limni possesses a tranquil island atmosphere—and without the presence of tourists. Set alongside a stretch of water that is often as smooth as a lake (whence its name, which means lake) it has a couple of decent hotels, plenty of rooms, three ouzeris, and two good tavernas on the waterfront.

Sightseers can poke around the remains of the Roman baths, and the 15th-century convent of **Ayios Nikolaos,** built on the site of a temple of Apollo, where legend has it that Hera and Zeus got married.

En Route   On the way to Aedipsos you can stop at **Ayios David's monastery** at Rovies, 5 km (3 mi) north of Limni.

Aedipsos

80 km (50 mi) northwest of Halkidha, 30 km (18½ mi) northwest of Limni.

For a therapeutic spa, head to Aedipsos, where hot springs have been soothing aches and pains since antiquity, via the new corniche road full of spectacular views. Take a whiff of the sulfurous vapors, a look at the yellow rocks and, if you're stiff from all that driving, take a dip. The ferry here goes to Arkitsa, the National Road, and Athens.

THE NORTHERN SPORADES A TO Z

Arriving and Departing

By Bus and Ferry

For information, it is always best to first contact the EOT (☞ Visitor Information, *below*) where someone will be able to give you the information you need in English.

ALONNISOS, SKIATHOS, AND SKOPELOS

Leaving from Athens's terminal B, buses for Lamia stop in Ayios Konstandinos (usually just called Ayios), the main port for the Sporades; the trip takes about 2½ hours. The bus fare is 2650 dr. and the trip takes 2½ hours. There is at least one ferry per day during the summer, fewer in winter: check with the EOT's Athens office (☞ Visitor Information, *below*). Tickets are available from several travel agents on the dock. The trip costs 2,600 dr. to Skiathos and about 1,000 dr. extra to Skopelos or Alonnisos; the trip takes about 3½ hours to Skiathos, and about an hour between each island. Tickets for the islands can be bought at the **travel agencies** (☞ *below*).

SKYROS AND EVIA

A bus leaves Athens's Terminal B (✉ Behind Liossion 260, ☎ 01/831–7153) daily at 1:30 (Sun. 2:30) to catch the *Lykomedes* at Kimi on Evia. The bus fare is 2,600 dr. and the trip takes 3½ hours. You can buy boat tickets on the dock when you get off the bus. The boat trip from Kimi takes 2 hours and costs 1,700 dr. The return boat from Skyros leaves at 8 AM except Sun. (3 PM).

Buses: Athens–Ayios Konstandinos (☎ 01/831–7147); Athens–Skyros (☎ 01/831–7163).

Port Authorities: Alonnisos (☎ 0424/65595); Ayos Konstandinos (☎ 0235/31759); Skiathos (☎ 0427/22017); Skyros (☎ 0222/91475); Kimi (☎ 0222/22606); Skopelos (☎ 0424/22180).

By Car

SKIATHOS, SKOPELOS, AND ALONNISOS

You must drive to the port of Ayios Konstandinos (Ayios) and from there take the ferry. The drive to Ayios from Athens takes about 2 hours.

Visitors with cars might have to reserve a place on the car ferry a day ahead.

You must drive to the port of Kimi on Evia. From Athens, take the Athens–Lamia national road to Skala Oropou and make the 30-minute ferry crossing to Eretria on Evia (every half hour during daytime). No reservations are needed.

By Hydrofoil

The **Flying Dolphins** are about twice as fast as ferries and cost twice as much. They call at ports more frequently, and in summer with careful planning it is possible to use them to travel the entire distance from Evia to Skyros and the other Sporades, continuing on to either Volos or Ayios Konstandinos. Ask any travel agent for a timetable.

From Athens, a **Ceres Lines** bus (☎ Pireas: 01/428–0001 or 01/428–3555) leaves Syntagma (Constitution) Sq. to meet Flying Dolphins at Ayios Konstandinos. Ask for information when you book. Fares: bus from Athens to Ayios Konstandinos, 2,650 dr.; Ayios Konstandinos to Skiathos, Skopelos, and Alonnisos, at least three times per day, 4,000 dr.–5,500 dr.; Kimi to Skyros, the other Sporades and Volos, Tuesday only, 4,100 dr.–14,100 dr.

By Plane

Alonnisos, Skopelos, and Evia have no air service. Skiathos airport (✉ 5 minutes northeast of Skiathos town, ☎ 0427/22945) handles direct charter flights from many European cities and **Olympic Airways** (☎ Athens: 01/936–9111; ☎ Skiathos: 0427/22049) flights (at least daily, more in summer) from Athens's Ellinikon Airport West Terminal (☎ 01/969–9466). The trip takes 40 minutes; the fare is 12,200 dr. In summer there are daily **Olympic Airways** (☎ Skyros: 0222/91600) flights from Athens to Skyros airport (✉ 11 km/8 mi northwest of Skyros town, ☎ 0222/91625). The flight takes 50 minutes; the fare is 10,800 dr.

Getting Around

By Boat

Small motorboats can be rented at the **Marine Center** (✉ Near the airport runway, ☎ 0427/22888 or 0427/21178, FAX 0427/23262).

Boats can also be rented at the **Marine Center** (✉ Near the Elinoil gas station on the waterfront, ☎ 0424/65206).

By Bus

Buses on Skiathos leave Skiathos town to make the beach run as far as Koukounaries every 30 minutes from early morning till 11:30 PM.

Buses on Skopelos run six times a day from Skopelos Town to Glossa and Loutraki, stopping at the beaches.

Alonnisos has one bus that makes the trip from Patatiri to Alonnisos town (Chora) and back from 9 AM to 2 PM only.

Skyros buses carry ferry passengers between Linaria and Horio, stopping in Molos in summer.

All cities are serviced with frequent bus service. For information contact the KTEL bus station (☎ 0221/22026).

By Caïque
On all islands, caïques leave from the main port for the most popular beaches, and interisland excursions are made between Skiathos, Skopelos, and Alonnisos. You can also hire a caïque (and haggle over the price) to tour around the islands; they are generally the preferred way to get around by day. For popular routes, captains have signs posted showing their destinations and departure times. On Skyros, check with Skyros Travel (☞ Travel Agencies, *below*) for caïque tours. In Alonnisos, day trips are organized to the many smaller islands in the vicinity.

By Ferry or Hydrofoil
Journeys between islands are usually made by ferry or hydrofoil. There is at least one boat per day between Skiathos and Skopelos, and it usually serves Alonnisos as well. Hydrofoils usually ply between these islands at least three times per day. Between Skyros and the other Sporades there is no regular boat service; there is a hydrofoil on Tuesday, and sometimes on other days.

Because schedules are likely to change, keep an eye on the times listed outside travel agencies.

By Motorbike and Car
The road networks on all four islands are so rudimentary that cars are not really needed, but it's not a bad idea to rent one for a day to get a feel for the island, then use the bus or a motorbike thereafter. Jeeps and other cars can be rented everywhere. If you rent a motorbike, however, be extra cautious: many of those for hire are in poor condition. The locals are not used to the heavy summer traffic on their narrow roads, and accidents provide the island clinics with 80 percent of their summer business. Check with the travel agencies (☞ *below*) for information.

By Taxi
All the islands have taxis waiting at the ferry landings. Even Alonnisos has three. They are unmetered, so negotiate your fare in advance.

Contacts and Resources

Emergencies
SKIATHOS
Police (☎ 0427/21111). **Medical center** (☎ 0427/22222).

SKOPELOS
Police: Skopelos town (☎ 0424/22235); Glossa (☎ 0424/33333). **Medical center** (☎ 0424/22222).

ALONNISOS
Police (✉ Patitiri, ☎ 0424/65025). **Medical center** (☎ 0424/65208).

SKYROS
Police (☎ 0222/91274). **Medical center** (☎ 0222/92222).

EVIA
Police (✉ Karystos, ☎ 0224/22262; ✉ Marmari, ☎ 0224/31333; ✉ Eretria, ☎ 0229/61111; ✉ Kimi, ☎ 0222/22555; ✉ Halkidha, ☎ 0221/87000 and 0221/83333; ✉ Prokopi, ☎ 0227/41203; ✉ Limni, ☎ 0227/31209; ✉ Aedipsos, ☎ 0226/22456). **Medical center** (✉ Karystos, ☎ 0224/22207; ✉ Marmari, ☎ 0224/31300; ✉ Eretria, ☎ 0229/62222; ✉ Kimi, Oxylithos, ☎ 0222/96202; ✉ Halkidha, ☎

0221/21901; ✉ Prokopi, ☎ 0227/41212; ✉ Limni, ☎ 0227/32222; ✉ Aedipsos, ☎ 0226/22456).

Travel Agencies

SKIATHOS

Mare Nostrum Travel (✉ 21 Papadiamantis, 37002, ☎ 0427/21463 or 0427/21464, FAX 0427/21793), aside from handling all your inquiries and issuing boat and plane tickets, is the only American Express representative in the Sporades.

SKOPELOS

Madro Travel (✉ On the waterfront, ☎ 0424/22145, 0424/22300, 0424/22767, 0424/23060, or 0424/23061, FAX 0424/22941).

ALONNISOS

Ikos Travel (✉ On the waterfront, ☎ 0424/65320, 0424/65648, or 0424/65649, FAX 0424/65321).

SKYROS

Skyros Travel (✉ Market Street, Skyros Town 34007, ☎ 0222/91123, or 0222/91600, FAX 0222/92123) has a virtual monopoly on hydrofoil tickets, rooms, excursions, and car rentals.

Visitor Information

Greek National Tourist Organization (GNTO or EOT) office (✉ Karageorgi Servias 2, in the National Bank Building, Athens ☎ 01/322–2545). **Travel agents** can be helpful on Alonnisos and Skyros.

SKIATHOS

Tourist police (✉ At the inland end of Odhos Papadhiamndiou, ☎ 0427/23172).

SKOPELOS

Tourist offices and facilities (✉ On the waterfront under a row of mulberry trees or on the first street parallel to it). **Skopelos Municipality** (✉ Chora, ☎ 0424/22205).

5   Epirus and Thessaly

Ioannina, Metsovo, and the Meteora Monasteries

In remote Epirus—of spectacular mountain passes and hillside-perched enclaves—the inquisitive traveler will discover traditional shepherd villages with richly costumed women whispering the strange, secret Vlach vernacular. Epirus's capital Ioannina still bears the powerful influence of the Ottoman tyrant Ali Pasha. At Thessaly's Meteora, a spiritual center of Orthodox Greece, the quiet contemplation of generations of monks is preserved in wondrously frescoed monasteries hovering on rocky pedestals above the plain.

BORDERED BY ALBANIA AND THE IONIAN SEA, the province of Epirus is a land of stark mountains, lush forests, swift rivers, and remote villages with unique customs, language, and architecture. The tour described below begins in the Epirote capital of Ioannina, the city of the tyrant Ali Pasha, with its vestiges of the Ottoman occupation and a lovely islet. From Ioannina, it's easy to visit Dodona, the oldest oracle in Greece. The itinerary continues on to the thriving traditional village of Metsovo in the Pindos Mountains and over the Katara Pass on one of the most dramatic roads in Greece. It ends in the fertile province of Thessaly where, on the edge of the plain, the monasteries of Meteora seem to float in midair, built atop bizarrely shaped pinnacles that tower over the town of Kalambaka.

By Toula
Bogdanos

Updated by
Michael Boyd

Pleasures and Pastimes

Dining

The curious diner will muse at Epirus's local specialties. In Ioannina's lakeside restaurants you can sample unusual dishes like those using ingredients culled from lakes: frog's legs, eel, crayfish, and turtles. Those with a penchant for sweets will savor *bougatsa* (a local sweet custard pastry). For Greeks, Metsovo brings to mind the costly but delectable smoked Metsovone cheese and Katogi wine pressed from French Bordeaux grapes grown locally. Other Metsovo specialties include boiled goat, *trahanas* soup (made from cracked wheat boiled in milk and dried), and sausages stuffed with leeks. In all but the fanciest restaurants, check out what's cooking because the menus change seasonally. Informal dress is usually appropriate.

CATEGORY	COST*
$$$$	over 7,000 dr.
$$$	5,000 dr.–7,000 dr.
$$	2,500 dr.–5,000 dr.
$	under 2,500 dr.

per person for appetizer, main course, and fruit or dessert, including taxes and service charge, but no drinks.

Lodging

Except for the best hotels, rooms in the region are simply decorated. Though prices don't vary much within each government classification category, quality does. Ask to see the room first, and don't assume anything; if you have special requests, such as a mountain view; a *diplo krevati* (double bed) rather than a *diklino* (twin bed); a balcony; or a bathtub, speak up. Rooms are usually easy to find in Ioannina. Reservations might be necessary for Kalambaka, which is packed with tour groups in late spring and summer, and in Metsovo during ski season or the town's July 26 festival. In these two towns, private rooms are likely to be far cheaper than comparable hotel rooms—look for advertisements as you arrive. Off-season, prices drop drastically from those listed here, and you should always try to negotiate. Hotels in the $$$–$$$$ range are assumed to have air-conditioning and televisions; listings indicate them only when they are present in hotels in the $–$$ range.

CATEGORY	ALL AREAS*
$$$$	over 39,000 dr.
$$$	22,000 dr.–39,000 dr.
$$	13,000 dr.–22,000 dr.
$	under 13,000 dr.

for a standard double room in high season, including taxes but not breakfast, unless indicated.

Exploring Epirus and Thessaly

The region consists of two areas: the mountainous province of Epirus, with villages such as Metsovo and its capital, Ioannina, to the west; and the Thessalian plain, an agricultural heartland with Meteora at its edge.

Great Itineraries

The distance from Ioannina to Meteora is small, but the mountain road that connects the two cannot be negotiated swiftly; a tour of the region should take this into account. If you only have two or three days, visit the Meteora monasteries and head to Metsovo if you have time. Five days will allow you to cover, at a fair pace, all the sites described in this chapter or to concentrate in a smaller area. Eight days will allow a thorough exploration of the region, leaving the tourist trail to visit remote villages and sights.

IF YOU HAVE 2 DAYS

Numbers in the text correspond to numbers in the margin and on the Epirus and Thessaly map.

Base yourself in ⊞ **Kalambaka** ⑥ and spend as long as possible at the monasteries at **Meteora** ⑦. A full day should allow you to visit many of them.

IF YOU HAVE 5 DAYS

Start with ⊞ **Ioannina** ① and visit **Dodona** ③ in the morning to see the ancient oracle of Zeus. See the old town in the afternoon and the nearby island that night. The next morning head to ⊞ **Metsovo** ⑤, stopping at **Perama cave** ④ on the way; spend the day exploring **Metsovo,** and be sure to get a taste of the Metsovone cheese! On the following day move on to ⊞ **Kalambaka** ⑥ to make the trek along the monastery route of **Meteora** ⑦.

IF YOU HAVE 8 DAYS

With eight days you can explore the region at your leisure; if you prefer fast pace, you might find yourself with too much time on your hands. Start with ⊞ **Ioannina** ① and end with ⊞ **Kalambaka** ⑥ and the monasteries of **Meteora** ⑦. To get the most out of the experience, hire a car to visit the **Perama cave** ④ and to explore mountain villages surrounding ⊞ **Metsovo** ⑤.

When to Tour

As in all of Greece, places are more likely to be open in the mornings than the afternoons, and museums and sites are often closed on Monday. Although Metsovo might be delightful in high summer—the town festival is held July 26—the heat is oppressive elsewhere. The mountain roads to Metsovo are often blocked and impassable in winter; if you get there, however, the ski center will be open. The ancestral home of Baron Michalis Tositsa in Metsovo is closed on Thursday, so plan accordingly.

The Meteora monasteries are open Wednesday, Saturday, and Sunday year-round. They attract considerably fewer visitors in winter when you might find a sense of spirituality in their windy isolation.

EPIRUS

Ioannina, Dodona, and Metsovo

Ancient Epirus was once a huge country that stretched from modern-day Albania (an area the Greeks still call "Northern Epirus" and where Greek is still spoken) to the Gulf of Arta and modern Preveza. The region is bordered by the Mediterranean Sea to the west, the islands of Lefkadha to the south, and Corfu to the north. Inland it is defined by a tangle of mountain peaks and upland plains, and the climate is markedly Balkan.

Despite the region's natural physical barriers, it has been invaded many times. Its hinterland character has made it the perfect hideout for rebels and has led it to be inhabited by disparate peoples. In ancient times the province was ruled by a king, the last being the famous Pyrrhus (his victories were not worth the cost); the Macedonian, Roman, Byzantine, and Ottoman empires ruled the region in succession (but not always successfully). In modern times, the Italians failed and the Germans succeeded in passing through here.

Epirus became part of Greece in 1913, almost 100 years after Greece's liberation from the Turks, and the cultural influence from its Ottoman occupation is evident. Moreover it boasts a sizable non-Greek population, the Vlachs, said to be descendants of legionaries from garrisons on the Via Egnatia, one of the Roman Empire's main east–west routes. The Vlachs speak a Romance language (related to Italian and Romanian).

In this section we describe—in geographical succession—the capital of the province, Ioannina, with its rich Ottoman heritage; nearby Dodona, most ancient of Greek oracles; and the traditional Vlach mountain village of Metsovo to the west, perhaps the most accessible of these villages and a good base from which to explore.

Ioannina

❶ *305 km (189½ mi) northwest of Athens, 204 km (126¾ mi) west–southwest of Thessaloniki.*

On the rocky promontory of Lake Pamvotis lies Ioannina, its fortress punctuated by mosques and minarets whose reflections, along with those of the snowy peaks of the Pindos range, appear in the calm water. Although the city may seem noisy and undistinguished, its old quarter, encircled by the somber castle walls, and its peaceful islet, called Nissi or "island," where nightingales still sing and fishermen mend their nets, make it an ideal retreat from the bustle of Athens.

Founded by Emperor Justinian in AD 527, Ioannina suffered under many rulers: It was invaded by the Normans in 1082, made a dependence of the Serbian kingdom in 1345, and conquered by the Turks in 1431. Above all, this was Ali Pasha's city, where, from 1788 to 1821 the cunning despot carved a fiefdom from much of western Greece.

Born in the 1740s in Tepeline, Albania, Ali rose to power by unscrupulous means. He was made pasha of Trikala in 1787, and a year later seized Ioannina, the largest town in Greece. For the next 33 years, Ali pursued his lifelong ambition: to break from the Ottoman Empire and create his own kingdom. He paid only token tribute to the Sultan and allied himself according to his needs with the French, the British, and the Turks. In 1797 he collaborated with Napoléon; the next year he seized Preveza from the French; and by 1817 was wooing the British, who gave him Parga. His territory extended from the Ionian sea to the Pindos range and from Vaona in the north to Arta in the south.

While seeking British support against the French, who owned the Ionian islands, Ali invited prominent British visitors to meet him: Col. William Leake, sent to make a military survey of Greece; Queen Victoria's doctor Henry Holland, whom Ali consulted about his health; and C. R. Cockerell, the architect excavating Bassae and Aegina. In 1809, while on his first visit to Greece, Lord Byron met the pasha and was overwhelmed by the ruler's hospitality: "He received me standing, a wonderful compliment for a Mussulman, and made me sit down on his right hand." Ali, likewise, was taken with the poet's small ears, thought to be a mark of aristocratic breeding. In a letter to his mother, however, Byron revealed that "His highness is a remorseless tyrant, guilty of the most horrible cruelties, very brave, so good a general that they call him the Mahometan Buonaparte . . . but as barbarous as he is successful, roasting rebels, etc., etc."

The most notorious ruler of Epirus, Ali Pasha had a guard of assassins to carry out his plots of murder and brigandage. He combed the countryside looking for attractive concubines, and his harem numbered in the hundreds. He attacked the Turkish Porte (from "Sublime Porte" [or gate] of the Sultan's palace, where justice was administered; by extension, the Ottoman government), and he brutalized his Greek subjects. Perhaps Ali's most infamous crime was the drowning of the beautiful Kyra Frosini, his son's mistress, and 16 other women, by tying them in stone-laden bags and dumping them in the lake. Apparently, he was in love with Frosini, who rejected him, and, spurred on by his jealous daughter-in-law, Ali had Frosini killed for infidelity. He regretted his deed and ordered that 1,000 *kantaria* (100-kilogram weights) of sugar be thrown into the lake to sweeten the water Frosini would drink.

By 1820, the Porte had become fed up with Ali and sent 50,000 men to besiege Ioannina and execute the 80-year-old tyrant. He was killed while hiding in the guest house of an island monastery. His head was cut off and paraded around Epirus, then buried in Constantinople; his other remains are allegedly interred in the citadel in Ioannina.

The spacious, well-arranged **archaeological museum** is the best in the area, with finds from several sites. (Your children may prefer to stay in the nearby **playground**.) Of special interest are the artifacts from ancient Dodona, a 200,000-year-old Paleolithic stone tool found near Preveza, and two winsome bronze statuettes of children from the late 4th century BC. The bronze priapic warrior wearing nothing but a waist guard to protect his belly is of the Geometric period (first half of the 8th century BC). Best of all is the collection of inscribed lead tablets (6th–3rd centuries BC) found at the oracle. The questions for the gods are translated for your amusement: "Shall I take another wife?" "Has Pistos stolen the wool from the mattress?" "Will it be all right to buy the small lake by the sanctuary of Demeter?" Read the evolution of the temple of Zeus, especially if you plan to visit the site (☞ Dodona, *below*).

There's a delicately wrought funerary wreath of gold oak leaves (early 2nd century BC) from a grave near Arta; a silver-gilt pin and ring seal carved with images of Orestes and Clytemnestra from a grave near Preveza (late 5th century BC); an iron knife, coil bracelet, and other items from a Zagoria woman's grave (900–800 BC); and a dazzling collection of Roman coins and statues. ⊠ *Platia 25 Martiou,* ☎ *0651/33357, 0651/25490.* 🖭 *500 dr.* ◷ *Mon. 12:30–6, Tues.–Fri. 8–6, weekends 8:30–3.*

NEED A BREAK?	A number of pastry shops on Platia Dhimokrateia or Odhos Averoff offer *bougatsa* (sweet custard-cheese pie), for which the area is famous. Try **Select** (⊠ Platia Dhimokrateia) or **Bougatsopoleio** (⊠ Odhos Averoff). Alternatively, if it's morning, get a delicious hot and freshly baked cheese pie from **Artopeio** (⊠ Just outside entrance to fort).

Ioannina's other main attraction is the **citadel,** at the lakeside end of Odhos Averoff. The city's once-large Jewish population lived within the walls alongside Turks and Christians. The Jews were deported by the Nazis during World War II, never to return; there are only about 150 remaining today. Outside the citadel walls, near the lake, a mon-

Epirus and Thessaly

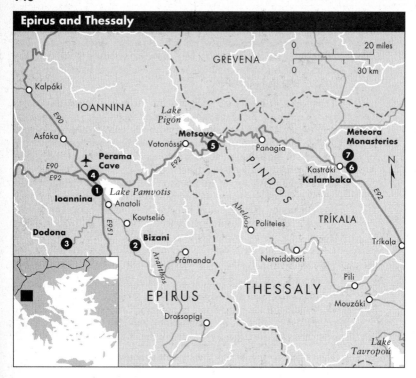

ument commemorates the slaughter. The citadel's massive stone walls, which once dropped into the lake on three sides, are more or less intact; Ali Pasha completely rebuilt them in 1815.

Tree-lined **Dionissiou Filosofou Street,** which circles the **castle** along the lake, is ideal for a late afternoon stroll. A moat, now filled, ran around the southwest landward side, and today the walls divide the old town—with rose-laden whitewashed houses, cobblestone streets, and birdsong—from the new. ⊠ *At lakeside end of Odhos Averoff.*

At the north end of the citadel is the remarkably well-preserved **Aslan Mosque,** now the municipal museum, whose collection recalls the three communities that lived together inside the fortress from 1400 to 1900. In revenge for a failed revolt against the Turks in 1611, Aslan Pasha destroyed the Church of Ioannis Prodromos and built this mosque in its place in 1618. Near the entrance are the ruins of the three-dome Turkish library. Make your way past the numerous stacked cannonballs and the many-arched *medresse,* with cells for Turkish imams, once part of the Koranic School of Ioannina. In front of the medresse and below the mosque there are other arches with fountains, where believers washed before entering to pray.

In Greece it is rare to glimpse the interior of a mosque. The vestibule has recesses for shoes and, inscribed over the doorway, is the name of Aslan Pasha and THERE IS ONLY ONE GOD, ALLAH, AND HIS PROPHET IS MAHOMET. The mosque retains its original decoration and *mehrab* (altar), which faces Mecca. Around the room are a walnut and mother-of-pearl table from Ali Pasha's period, clothes chests, and a water pipe. The *oulema* (priest) read the Koran from the seventh step of the pulpit. In the right corner, a small door leads to the minaret, up which the muezzin climbed five times a day to call the faithful to prayer. You can see Arabic graffiti on the columns. The mosque was active until most

Turks left in the disastrous 1922 population "exchange" after the war in Asia Minor.

The museum also displays Greek and Jewish objects donated by the communities, including silver jewelry handmade in Ioannina and costumes ranging from solemn, black Sarakatsani shepherd's outfits to the sumptuous purple and gold embroidered costume of an aristocrat. The Jewish section includes traditional clothing and gold-embroidered altar curtains from the 1790 synagogue, which still functions inside the citadel. ⊠ *North end of citadel,* ☎ *0651/26536.* 🎟 *500 dr.* ☉ *Weekdays 8–3, weekends 9–3.*

The **fortress,** called *Its Kale* by the Turks, is where Ali Pasha built his palace. Full-scale excavation and renovation are underway in this area, revealing remains from the Byzantine period; in 1995 the **Byzantine Museum** opened in the fortress. Its small collection of antiquities from all over Epirus is carefully arranged in the first half of the museum; there's much information in English on the walls. The second half of the museum houses an important collection of icons from the 16th and 17th centuries. Nearby is the *Fetiye* (Victory) **mosque,** which purports to contain Ali Pasha's tomb. ⊠ *Palace grounds, eastern corner of citadel,* ☎ *0651/25989.* 🎟 *500 dr.* ☉ *Tues.–Sun. 8:30–3; palace grounds daily 7 AM–10 PM.*

In the **old bazaar** (⊠ Clustered around the citadel's gates) some Turkish-era buildings and a smattering of the copper-, tin-, and silversmiths who fueled the city's economy for centuries still remain.

NEED A BREAK?	Stop for a drink in the **café** (⊠ Palace grounds) and enjoy a panoramic view of the lake.

The square **Platia Mavili** (⊠ On the waterfront) is lined with smart cafés, which are full of tourists having breakfast or waiting for the next boat to the nearby island; in the evening this is *the* place to hang out, where the youth of Ioannina while away the hours over frappés or long drinks. At sunset, catch the *volta* (ritual promenade) of showing off and gossiping.

NEED A BREAK?	One of the nicest café-bars on the square is **Makris** (⊠ Platia Mavili 9, ☎ 0651/79708), which serves creamy hot chocolate, drinks, and snacks. Even if you sit outside, take a peek at the brass ornamentation, marble-top tables, trompe l'oeil walls, murals, and the grand bar inside.

As you chug from the shore toward the tiny **island** or "Nissa," look back at the outline of the citadel and its mosques in a wash of green. The whitewashed lakeside island village, founded in the late 16th century by refugees from the Mani, seems centuries away from Ioannina. Ali Pasha once kept deer here for hunting. With its neat houses and flower-trimmed courtyards, pine-edged paths, runaway chickens, and reedy backwater, it's the perfect place to relax, have lunch, and visit some of the monasteries. Restaurants and tavernas abound here, even more than in Ioannina. The emphasis is strongly on fish and other creatures from the lake, although traditional taverna food can also be found.

Lake Pamvotis, now seriously polluted, is fed by streams from the northern Mt. Mitsikeli. Marshy to the north, it is about 12 meters (39 feet) deep to the south. In 1992 the city installed a sewage system and has recently brought in various fish from Hungary to nibble on the fast-growing reeds and keep them under control. Catch the boat below the citadel near Platia Mavili; it leaves every half hour from 8:30 AM to 10:30 PM; the ride takes 10 minutes and costs 200 dr.

The main attraction on Ioannina's island is the **Ali Pasha Museum.** It was in the monks' cells here on January 17, 1822 that Ali Pasha was killed, after holding out for almost two years. In the final battle, Ali ran into an upstairs cell, but the soldiers shot him through its floorboards from below. You'll hear more than one version of his last days, each more romantic than the last. Until recently you could see the original floorboards with the seven bullet holes, but the floor had to be replaced, and now newly drilled, circled holes indicate the position of the originals. The museum has a famous portrait of Ali Pasha sleeping on his wife Vasiliki's lap, the crypt where Vasiliki hid, prints and paintings of that era, an edict signed by Ali Pasha with his ring seal (he couldn't write), and his water pipe standing on the fireplace. ⊠ *On island, take left from boat landing and follow signs,* ☎ *0651/81791.* ☞ *100 dr.* ☉ *Open any time boats are running.*

Agios Nikolaos ton Filanthropinon has the best frescoes of the island's several monasteries. The monastery was built in the 13th century by an important Byzantine family, the Filanthropinos, and a fresco in the northern exonarthex depicts five of them kneeling before St. Nikolaos (1542); it's believed the oldest brother, Michael, is buried under this fresco. In the southern exonarthex, left of the door, are effigies of the seven ancient philosophers: Plato, Apollonios, Solon, Aristoteles, Plutarch, Thucydides, and Chilon. An inscription explains that though they didn't all live at the same time, they once met at an Athenian home and proclaimed the divine incarnation and presence of Christ. Many of the frescoes are by the Kontari brothers, who later decorated the mighty Varlaam in Meteora. You will note the similarities in the bold coloring, expressiveness, realism, and Italian influence—especially in the bloody scenes of martyrdom. The corner crypts were the meeting places of the secret Greek school during the Ottoman occupation. Instead of returning to the landing when you head back to the main road, follow signs for Filanthropini, which is on a grassy knoll at the other side of the village. Dress appropriately, pack a flashlight to see the frescoes better. The spry caretaker will let you in; if she doesn't see you immediately, hang around conspicuously for a few minutes. ⊠ *On island, follow signs.* ☞ *Leave 200 dr. donation.* ☉ *Daily 8–8.*

NEED A BREAK?	Stop for a lemonade in the shady square at the green-shuttered *kafenion* (traditional Greek coffeehouse) (⊠ On the island, center of village).

Only the 11th-century **Stratigopoulou monastery** (⊠ On the island, follow signs) can be visited—if the keeper is in—but the path goes through pine trees and wildflowers.

Dining and Lodging

$–$$ ✗ **Limnopoula.** If you arrive early enough you can take advantage of
★ the swimming pool or have a pre-dinner drink at the lakeside bar. The restaurant has tables inside and outside. The cook prepares standard taverna fare with plenty of traditional Epirote dishes, especially boiled meat, and the cook will prepare anything if you call in advance. A local specialty is *saganaki* cocktail (a mix of Roquefort, *kefalograviera,* feta, and Edam cheeses melted in a frying pan and served with pita bread). For dessert try the homemade *tis rinis* (halvah). The restaurant is in lush parkland a short drive from Limnopoula. Take a taxi from Platia Pirrou or from the entrance to the citadel; the ride is about 400 dr. ⊠ *Kanari 10, Limnopoula,* ☎ *0651/33288, 0651/39908. Reservations essential in August. AE, DC, MC, V.*

$ ✗ **Ivi.** Not much to look at, Ivi (written HBH in Greek) serves excellent *magirefta* (precooked dishes) in large portions for lunch; sometimes there's a line outside the door. Especially good are the vegetable dishes, such as leeks sautéed and baked with celery, green beans, or artichokes. Meat dishes include boiled goat, *tas* kebab (with bits of pork in red sauce), and beef with *kritharakia* (ricelike pasta). There's usually a fish entrée such as trout, cod with garlic sauce, or sea bream. Late at night, the cook serves pasta Ioannina style and a tripe soup with the cow's head and feet, said to be good for hangovers. Whatever is left over from lunch is served at dinner, and though it may not look as inviting, remember that magirefta taste just as good after sitting for hours. ⊠ *Platia Yoryiou 4,* ☎ *0651/27085. No credit cards. Closed Sun.*

$ ✗ **Propodhes.** Propodhes, near the museum, is said to be the best of the island's numerous eating places. When you ask to see the menu, however, don't be surprised if the owner produces various startled-looking frogs, turtles, fish, and birds from the cages and tanks in front of the restaurant—if you don't want to look your food in the eye, head elsewhere. Sweets include homemade *gliko* (preserves made from quince or cherries soaked in syrup). Try Zitsa, a dry white wine produced from the local Debina grape, with your meal. ⊠ *Island, outside entrance to Ali Pasha museum,* ☎ *0651/81214. No credit cards.*

$ ✗ **To Mandeio.** Opposite the entrance to the citadel, this spot is open all day and particularly popular for late meals. The menu has all the usual taverna favorites: order appetizers to share such as *koloukithakia* (fried zucchini), *gigantes* (baked giant beans), saganaki, and *piperato* (spicy cheese dip). The menu has entries in English and Greek; only the items with prices next to them are available, and they change with the seasons. ⊠ *Platia Yoryiou 15,* ☎ *0651/25452. No credit cards.*

$$$ ☲ **Xenia.** The nicest hotel in Ioannina, this was the site of a 1994 sum-
★ mit on Bosnia. Xenia is set back from a central street behind huge oak trees and a rose-studded gazebo. Its soothing lounge and eating areas, with mirrored columns and pastel upholstery, are pleasant retreats. The quiet guest rooms are done in the same gray-white-rose hues and have either mountain or garden views. The hotel has central heating, but no air-conditioning, which is rarely necessary. Buffet breakfast is included in the price. *Dhodhonis 33, 45221,* ☎ *0651/47301, 0651/47187, or 0651/47188,* FAX *0651/47189. 60 rooms with bath. Restaurant, refrigerators, bar, meeting rooms, parking. AE, DC, MC, V.*

$$ ☲ **Olympic.** Close to Platia Pirrou but relatively removed from the noise, the Olympic vies with the Palladion for comfortable, reasonably priced, downtown accommodations. Employees are helpful, and the pastel rooms have color televisions, tidy gray marble bathrooms, big closets, double-glazed windows to stifle noise. The best rooms are the newest eight on the fifth floor. ⊠ *Melanidhou 2, 45332,* ☎ *0651/25888, 0651/22233, or 0651/22403,* FAX *0651/22041. 54 rooms with bath. Restaurant, bar, air-conditioning, refrigerators, parking. No credit cards.*

$$ ☲ **Palladion.** Don't be put off by the plain exterior; inside, the lobby feels like a bar on a '30s cruise liner, from the polished wooden phone booths to the plush red sofas and neon clock. Upstairs there's a cozy lounge with a fireplace, and the hotel decor is eclectic (from African sculptures to abstract lithographs). The bathrooms are small, but about 40 rooms have great lake views. All have color TVs, though more adventurous visitors should pop into the outdoor summer cinema next door. Public rooms are air-conditioned in summer, and all rooms are heated in winter. ⊠ *Botsari 1, 45444,* ☎ *0651/25856 through 25859, 0651/34601, or 0651/34602,* FAX *0651/74034. 128 rooms, 120 with bath, 4 suites. Restaurant, bar, conference facilities, parking. AE, DC, MC, V.*

$ ☲ **Astoria.** It's the cheapest hotel in town, yet the Astoria is clean and centrally located near both the archaeological museum and the old citadel. ⊠ *Paraskevopoulou 2 (just off Odhos Averoff), 45444,* ☎ *0651/ 20755 or 0651/25438. 16 rooms, 8 with bath. Bar. No credit cards.*

$ 🏠 **Dioni.** Named after the goddess Dione worshiped at nearby Dodona, this well-managed hotel near the old town is good for those on a budget. The lounge, with its fireplace, bronze chandelier, and flagstone floor, belies the hotel's C-class rating. The rooms, although basic, all have color TVs, music, and balconies. It's conveniently located around the corner from the bus station. ✉ *Tsirigoti 10, 45444,* ☎ *0651/27864 or 0651/27032,* 🖷 *0651/29950. 44 rooms with bath. Bar, breakfast room. No credit cards.*

$ 🏠 **Pension Dellas.** What makes this place so special is the hospitality of the owners, Titika and Sotirios Dellas—freshly picked flowers, maybe a homemade *koulouraki* (cookie) made from their chicken's eggs, and hand-pressed linens. A delightful change from hotels in town, this lakeshore pension was originally built for the Dellas children. Rooms are immaculate, sunny, and quiet, with balconies or access to the courtyard, where neighbors often stop to chat. Most visitors come March through October since the pension has no central heating, but you'll get a portable heater and plenty of blankets in winter. Call beforehand and someone will meet you at the main dock, about 5 minutes away. ✉ *Island, 45444,* ☎ *0651/81494. 8 rooms, 1 with bath. No credit cards.*

Nightlife and the Arts

BARS

There are several excellent bars and clubs in Ioannina, including **Makris** (☞ *above*).

FESTIVAL

Ioannina hosts the **Epirotika festival** in July and August, with performances at the Frontzos theater. For information, contact the Ioannina Tourist Office (☞ Visitor Information *in* Epirus and Thessaly A to Z, *below*).

FILM

Several **cinemas** clustered around Platia Pirrhou feature an array of new releases and art-house movies.

Shopping

CRAFTS

On Odhos Averoff, near Platia Yoryiou, there are a number of junky-looking stores that sell locally produced beaten-copper artifacts. Avoid the shinier and brighter items in stores near the entrance to the citadel.

Bizani

❷ *293 km (182 mi) northwest of Athens, 12 km (7½ mi) south of Ioannina.*

Pavlos Vrellis wax museum, in the village of Bizani, is where you'll see a collection of historical Epirote figures, among them a tableau of Ali Pasha's murder sculpted by a local man. ✉ *Mouseio Pavlos Vrellis, Bizani,* ☎ *0651/92128.* 🎫 *1,000 dr.* ☉ *Daily 9:30–5.*

Dodona

❸ *308 km (191½ mi) northwest of Athens, 22 km (13½ mi) southwest of Ioannina.*

Said to be the oldest in Greece, the **oracle At Dodona** flourished from at least the 8th century BC until the 4th century AD, when Christianity succeeded the cult of Zeus. Homer, in the *Iliad,* mentions "wintry Dodona," where Zeus's pronouncements, made known through the wind-rustled leaves of a sacred oak, were interpreted by priests "whose feet are unwashed and who sleep on the ground." The oak tree was central to the cult, and its image appears on the region's ancient coins. It was here that Odysseus sought forgiveness for slaughtering his wife's suitors, and it was from this oak that the Argonauts took the sacred branch to mount on their ship's prow. According to one story, Apollo ordered the oracle moved here from Thessaly; Herodotus writes that it was locally believed a dove from Thebes in Egypt landed in the oak and announced, in a human voice, that the oracle of Zeus should be built.

As you enter the archaeological site of Dodona you pass the **stadium** on your right, built for the Naïa games and completely overshadowed by the **theater** on your left. One of the largest and best preserved on the Greek mainland, the theater once seated 17,000, and it has been restored for the annual summer festival. Its building in the early 3rd century BC was overseen by King Pyrrhus of Epirus, from whose name comes the phrase "Pyrrhic victory": His armies habitually won battles with great losses. His theater was destroyed, rebuilt under Philip V of Macedon in the late third century, and then converted by the Romans into an arena for gladiatorial games. Its retaining wall, reinforced by bastions, is still standing.

The remains of the **acropolis** behind the theater include house foundations and a cistern that supplied water in times of siege.

East of the theater are the foundations of the **bouleuterion** (headquarters and council house) of the Epirote League, built by King Pyrrhus, and a small rectangular temple dedicated to Aphrodite.

The remains of the **sanctuary to Zeus Naios** included the Sacred Oak and temples to Zeus, Dione, and Herakles; until the 4th century BC there was no temple. The Sacred Oak was surrounded by abutting cauldrons on bronze tripods. When struck, they reverberated for a long time, and the sound was interpreted by soothsayers. Fragments from as early as the 8th century have been recovered. In the 4th century BC, a small temple was built near the oak, and a century later the temple and oak were enclosed by a stone wall. By King Pyrrhus's time, the wall had acquired Ionic colonnades. After a 219 BC Aetolian attack, a larger Ionic temple was built, and the surrounding wall was enhanced by a monumental entrance. The oak tree currently on the site was planted by archaeologists; the original was probably cut down by Christians in the 4th century AD.

Near the sanctuary are traces of a 6th-century AD **Christian basilica** constructed on the sanctuary of Herakles to weaken the pagan influence. As with so many classical sites, local cults were assimilated into the Christian pantheon. In the Byzantine period, Dodona was the seat of a bishop.

Two buses leave daily from Ioannina's Vyzantinou station. For about 5,000 dr., you can hire a taxi, which will wait an hour at the site. Negotiate with one of the drivers near Ioannina's bell tower or call a radio taxi (☎ 0651/46777, 0651/45777, or 0651/25452). ✉ *Archaeological site,* ☎ *0651/82287.* 🎫 *500 dr.* ☉ *Weekdays 8–7, weekends 8:30–3.*

The Arts

For information about the **ancient Greek drama at Dodona** contact the Ioannina Tourist Office (☞ Visitor Information *in* Epirus and Thessaly A to Z, *below*).

Perama Cave

❹ *312 km (194 mi) northwest of Athens, 4 km (2½ mi) northwest of Ioannina.*

Perama cave's passageways, discovered in the early 1940s by locals hiding from the Nazis, extend for more than 1 km (⅔ mi) under the hills. The high caverns and many-hued limestone stalagmites and stalactites have names like Statue of Liberty and Sphinx, which you'll learn during the 45-minute guided tour that begins every 10 minutes; one of the guides will speak English. You can catch Bus 8 from Ioannina's clock tower. ⊠ *Along E 92 east from Ioannina,* ☎ *0651/81440.* ⌫ *1,000 dr.* ☉ *Summer 8:30–8, winter until sunset.*

Metsovo

❺ *293 km (182 mi) northwest of Athens, 58 km (36 mi) east of Ioannina.*

The traditional village of Metsovo cascades down the mountain below the 1,850-meter (6,069-foot) Katara Pass, which is the highest in Greece and which marks the border between Epirus and Thessaly. Early evening is a wonderful time to arrive. As you descend through the mist, dazzling lights twinkle in the ravine. Stone houses with slate roofs and sharply projecting wooden balconies line steep, serpentine alleys. In the square, especially after the Sunday service, old men—dressed in black flat caps and dark baggy pants, and wooden shoes with pom-poms—sit on the bench like crows on a tree branch. Should you arrive on a religious feast day, many villagers will be decked out in traditional costume.

Although most villages are fading, Metsovo, designated a traditional settlement by the Greek National Tourist Organization (GNTO or EOT), has become a prosperous community with a growing population. In winter it draws skiers headed for Mt. Karakoli, and in summer it is a favorite destination for tourist groups. Despite the souvenir shops that offer "traditional handicrafts" and may sell you imported weaving, the slate roofs that have been replaced with easier-to-maintain tile, and the kitsch that occasionally mars the scene, for the most part Metsovo has preserved its character.

The natives are descendants of nomadic Vlach shepherds, once believed to have migrated from Romania but now thought to be Greeks trained by Romans to guard the Egnatia Highway connecting Constantinople and the Adriatic. The Vlach language is so influenced by Latin that it was used during World War II to communicate with occupying Italian forces, and villagers still speak it among themselves. During winter, shepherds move their flocks from the mountains to the lowlands around Trikala, while their wives, nicknamed the white widows, tend the hearth as the village lies buried in snow. The shepherds numbers are dwindling, however (they herd about 15,000 sheep today), as many turn to tourism for their livelihoods.

In the early days of the Turkish occupation, Metsovo had a measure of political and economic autonomy. Villagers of Flokas were granted many privileges—reduced taxes, permission to herd large flocks, land rights, and the right to Orthodox worship and education—for guarding Katara Pass, the only viable route across the Pindos range and for once providing refuge for a Turk who had fallen from the Sultan's favor. A self-supporting Greek school was built in 1700, staffed by the foremost scholars of the time. These Flokan liberties are acknowledged today by the red ribbons worn by young women at weddings.

Metsovo became an important center of finance, commerce, handicrafts, and sheepherding. As the town grew, the Vlachs began trading farther afield—in Constantinople, Vienna, and Venice. Ali Pasha abolished the privileges in 1795, and in 1854 the town was invaded by Ottoman troops led by Abdi Pasha. In 1912 Metsovo was freed by the Greek army. Many important families lived here, including the Averoffs and Tositsas, who made their fortunes growing cotton in Egypt. They contributed to the new Greek state's development and bequeathed large sums to restore Metsovo and finance small industries.

After World War II, Baron Michalis Tositsa lived in Switzerland, had lost contact with his family, didn't speak Greek, and had never been to Greece. The statesman Evangelos Averoff, another Metsovite, wrote to Tositsa about plans to develop Metsovo. The aging, childless baron lent Averoff his name and left his fortune to set up the Foundation Baron Michalis Tositsa in 1950 (☞ *below*).

To get a sense of how Metsovites lived (and endured the arduous winters in style), visit the late Ottoman, restored, stone-and-timber **ancestral home of Baron Michalis Tositsa.** Now a museum of popular art, it is devoted to local Epirote crafts. Built in 1661 and renovated in 1954, this typical Metsovo mansion has carved woodwork, sumptuous textiles in rich colors, and Vlach handcrafted furniture.

In the stable you'll see the gold-embroidered saddle used for holidays and, unique to this area, a fanlight in the fireplace, ensuring that the hearth would always be illuminated. The goatskin bag on the wall was used to store cheese. The first floor also has an exhibit of Metsovite weapons. Next door is the women's working area, with dowry chests, looms, and traditional costumes. The last room is a large kitchen displaying everyday utensils.

Several pieces are exhibited in the second-floor salon, where the family carried out its official duties such as receiving foreign guests and local merchants. The *basi* (raised sleeping platforms) here are elaborately decorated; also of note are 16th-century icons, a silver foot warmer, and a hand mirror, which had to be turned to the wall at sunset to ward off bad luck. ⊠ *Up stone stairs to right off Tositsa (main rd.) as you descend to main sq.,* ☎ *0656/41024, 0656/41814.* ⊠ *300 dr.* ☉ *Fri.–Wed. 8:30–1, 4–6 (3–5 in winter). Guided tours every ½ hr; wait for the guard to open the door.*

NEED A BREAK?

Metsovo is famous throughout Greece for its expensive smoked cheeses. Sample one or two at the **cheese shop** in the main square. The owner is happy to let you taste before you buy.

The 18th-century church of **Agia Paraskevi** (⊠ Main sq.) has a flamboyant altar screen that's worth a peek.

At **Averoff Gallery** you may view Evangelos Averoff's personal collection: revolutionary scenes, local landscapes, and modern art by contemporary Greek artists. One painting known to all Greeks is Nikiforos Litras's *The Burning of the Turkish Flagship by Kanaris,* a scene from a historic battle in Chios. Look on the second staircase for Paris Prekas's *The Mosque of Aslan Pasha in Ioannina* to see what Ioannina looked like in the Turkish period. ⊠ *Main sq.,* ☎ *0656/41210.* ⊠ *300 dr.* ☉ *Wed.–Mon. 9–1:30 and 5–7:30 (winter 4–6).*

You may have noticed the **Foundation Baron Michalis Tositsa** (⊠ In the sq., ☎ 0656/41205), which helped the local weaving industry get a start (one year its stock was used in Yves St. Laurent's Paris collection) and supported the woodworking industry, which produces beehives and cheese barrels for all of Greece. It also financed a sawmill, a children's library, and the nearby ski resort (⊠ Just outside the village, ☎ 0656/41206), which has one chairlift, nestled in the slopes of Mt. Karakoli.

You can visit the **cooperative** (⊠ Metsovo village, ☎ 0656/41235) to see how cheeses are made; it's open daily 6:30–1:30. The **winery** (⊠ Outside the village, in the Upper Aoos Valley, ☎ 0656/41010) also welcomes visitors.

If you're staying in Metsovo a few days, visit **Politses** (✉ 4 km/2½ mi northwest of Metsovo, in the valley), a picturesque spot with several springs in a forest of beech, fir, and pine trees.

The **nearby mountain villages** of Votonosi, 5 km (3 mi) west of Metsovo, **Anthohori**, 5 km (3 mi) southwest, and **Chrysovitsa**, 9 km (5½ mi) west, are less tourist-trodden communities with plenty of local color.

OFF THE
BEATEN PATH

AYIOS NIKOLAOS MONASTERY – Not to be missed, unless you are pressed for time, is a visit to the restored 14th-century Ayios Nikolaos monastery, about 30 minutes into the valley, and an hour back up. The *katholikon* (main church) is topped by a barrel vault, and what may have once been the narthex was converted to a *ginaikonitis* (a woman's gallery). Two images of the Pantocrator, one in each dome—perhaps duplicated to give the segregated women a better view—stare down on the congregation. You can also see the monks' cells, with insulating walls of mud and straw; the abbot's quarters; and the school where Greek children were taught during the Turkish occupation. The porch still has the chains used for lunatics housed in the monastery. They were kept outside on a winter's night, and if they survived, they were deemed cured. The monastic community shut down in 1925. It seems the abbot sent the last two monks to work in the fields one day and made off with the altar furnishings. Years of neglect followed, with locals herding their sheep in the buildings and lighting fires in the chapel. In 1960, while on a summer stroll, Averoff scraped the blackened walls out of curiosity and discovered brilliant colors. With the help of the foundation, the 16th-century frescoes—depicting scenes from the life of Christ and various martyrdoms—were cleaned and illuminated. The church is still used on religious feast days. The keepers will give you a closely guided tour and explanation of the frescoes. ✉ *Down into valley via footpath (follow signs near National Bank of Greece; turn left where paving ends).* 🕭 *Leave a donation of 200 dr. in the box.* ⊙ *Usually until 7 PM (winter 1 PM).*

Dining and Lodging

$$ ✕ **Casa la Mounte Tirotaverna.** The owner has based his entire menu
★ around Metsovo's delightful, expensive smoked cheese. Strongly recommended is *hilopites* (oven-baked pasta with a little sauce and lots of cheese). Also try the freshly made pizza topped with Metsovo, and for true aficionados, cheese soup—it's truly different. ✉ *Tositsa, just up from sq.,* ☎ *0656/42600. No credit cards.*

$$ ✕ **Taverna Metsovitiko Saloni.** The dining room comforts customers with a large fireplace, Metsovo costumes on the walls, old photos, and carved wooden furniture. Try the various vegetable pies made from corn flour, unusual in Greece, and especially the saganaki with Metsovo cheese. Savor the large wine selection and a healthy choice of desserts, including Metsovitiko baklava, local thick sheep yogurt with pastry, honey, and walnuts, and gliko. ✉ *Tositsa 10, above post office,* ☎ *0656/42142. No credit cards.*

$ ✕ **Koutouki.** Koutouki (little box), aptly named for its interior, proves to be one of the best—it's popular among locals and is a good value. All the taverna favorites are here, but order something with the local cheese. Don't miss the strong barrel wine, because, as owner Kostas Todis jokingly points out, high altitudes go hand in hand with *zali* (giddiness). It's open late, until 3 AM. ✉ *Under post office,* ☎ *0656/41732. No credit cards.*

$$ 🏨 **Apollon.** The Apollon has a traditional lobby with a carved pine ceiling,
★ a fireplace, chandeliers, red and green woven upholstery, hammered-copper plates, and a pet bird, whose cheery song reminds guests of spring,

no matter what the season. Built in 1986 in typical Metsovo style with stone and wood, the hotel has cozy, carpeted rooms with pine furniture, televisions, and balconies overlooking the gorge. The best are those in the *sofrita* (attic); several have hot tubs. ⊠ *Near main sq., behind Tositsa Foundation, 44200,* ☎ *0656/41844, 0656/42442, or 0656/41833,* FAX *0656/42110. 42 rooms with bath, 4 suites. Restaurant, bar, breakfast room, refrigerators, parking. AE, DC, MC, V.*

$ ▥ **Athine Hotel.** For budget food and lodging, this hotel, the first built in the area, should be the first choice. The hospitality is superb: The owners, who sleep upstairs, have given up their quarters to guests. The rooms have no views, but they're comfortable enough, with carpeting and central heating. At the taverna, the mother prepares traditional fare and her own specialties—pies, soups, and meats—and there's usually a roaring fire in winter. The famous Katogi wine, made from French Bordeaux grapes, is available; almost as good is the restaurant's barrel red. Another local wine to savor is Balthazar, a dry white. Younger members of the family speak English. ⊠ *S. Klidi 2 (below National bank off main sq.), 42200,* ☎ *0656/41332, 0656/41725. 8 rooms with bath. No credit cards.*

$ ▥ **Bitounis.** Owned by the good-natured Bitounis couple, who might teach you a few words of Vlach, this hotel has a lounge with a fireplace, wooden ceiling, flagstone floors, and bright hand weavings. Rooms are plain, with televisions, radios, and phones; most have fantastic views of the valley, and, as Mr. Bitounis proudly proclaims, "You will find not a scratch." A sign in the breakfast area reads NO PLAYING AFTER MIDNIGHT to ward off late-night backgammon fanatics. Have the breakfast at least once—local yogurt and butter, jam, hot bread, eggs, juice, coffee, fruit, and a slab of delicious smoked Metsovo. The hotel is equipped for travelers with disabilities. ⊠ *Tositsa 48, 44200,* ☎ *0656/41217 or 0656/41700,* FAX *0656/41545. 39 rooms with bath, 6 suites. Bar, breakfast room, parking. V.*

$ ▥ **Filoxenia.** This pension at the edge of the gorge and near the Averoff gallery is a good budget choice. It fills quickly in high season; the owners also own the Athine and might offer you a room there if the Filoxenia is full. Downstairs you'll find a traditional lounge. Upstairs the clean, quiet rooms have views and are furnished simply; ask for one with a balcony. ⊠ *Behind main sq., 44200,* ☎ *0656/41021, 093/286334, or 0656/41725 (Athine). 16 rooms with bath. No credit cards.*

$ ▥ **Kassaros Hotel.** Quiet and reasonably priced, this hotel has its own travel agency, which books flights and arranges group trips to nearby sights. The lounge has brightly colored hand weavings and a U-shaped couch that runs along three walls. Rooms on the first floor have ubiquitous striped woolen curtains, as well as a television and balconies with either views of the Pindos or the garden. The newer rooms on the upper floor have better furnishings but no balconies. From July to September and during holidays the Continental breakfast is mandatory. ⊠ *Tsoumaka 6, 44200 (2-min walk form main sq.),* ☎ *0656/41800, 0656/41346, 0656/41662, 094/383131, or 093/407494,* FAX *0656/41262. 31 rooms with bath. Bar, breakfast room, parking. AE, DC, MC, V.*

THESSALY
Kalambaka and the Meteora Monasteries

Thessaly, a huge plain in central Greece, is almost entirely surrounded by mountains: Pindos to the west, Pelion to the east, Othrys to the south, and the Kamvounian range to the north. It is one of the country's most fertile areas and has sizable population centers in Lamia, Larissa, Trikkala, and Volos. Thessaly was not ceded to Greece until 1878, after five centuries of Ottoman rule; vestiges of this period remain. Archaeology enthusiasts will be intrigued by its neolithic sites to the east, Dhimini and Sesklo near Volos. Kalambaka and Meteora are in the northwest corner of the plain, just before the Pindos Mountains.

Kalambaka

❻ *154 km (95½ mi) southwest of Thessaloniki, 71 km (44 mi) east of Metsovo.*

Kalambaka, a drab modern town, seems to promise little as you approach it. Yet it is one of the most popular tourist destinations in Greece because of the Meteora monastery complex just north of town (☞ *below*). Spend a day at Meteora to get acquainted with the history and architecture of the Greek Orthodox Church and to experience living, vibrant traditions.

Burned by the Germans during World War II, Kalambaka has only one building of interest, the cathedral church of the **Dormition of the Virgin.** Patriarchal documents in the outer narthex indicate that it was built in the first half of the 12th century by Emperor Manuel Comnenos, but some believe it was founded in the 7th century on the site of a temple of Apollo (various classical drums and other fragments are incorporated into the walls, and you can glimpse mosaics under the present floor). The latter theory explains the church's paleo-Christian features, including its center-aisle *ambo* (great marble pulpit), which is usually to the right of the sanctuary; its rare *synthronon* (four semi-circular steps where the priest sat when not officiating) east of the altar; and its Roman basilica style, originally adapted to Christian use and unusual for the 12th century.

The church has vivid 16th-century frescoes, work of the Cretan monk Neophytos, son of the famous hagiographer Theophanes. A large underground crypt housed church vessels. The marble baldachin in the sanctuary, decorated with crosses and stylized grapes, probably predates the 11th century. ⊠ *North end of town, follow signs from Platia Riga Fereou or from central sq.,* ☎ *0432/24297.* ☑ *300 dr.* ☉ *Daily 7 AM–10 AM and 3:30–7.*

Dining and Lodging

$$ ✕ **Gertzos-Meteora.** A local favorite since 1925, Gertzos serves food
★ prepared by the family matriarch, Ketty. Expect lots of meaty main courses and some specialties from Asia Minor. For a light lunch, try the salads and a tasty local wine. ⊠ *Ekonomou 4, main sq.,* ☎ *0432/22316. No credit cards.*

$$ ✕ **Kipos.** This taverna's eclectic 140-dish menu—traditional Greek with Mexican and even children's dishes—might make the journey outside town worthwhile. The owners opened Kipos in December 1993, aiming to bring flawless service and quality at reasonable prices to Kalambaka; they have succeeded. You'll enjoy the garden setting, complete with waterfalls, and the antiques proudly pointed out by the owner. During winter weekends, there is live Greek music. It's open until 1 AM. ⊠ *Trikalon Rd., before entrance to Kalambaka,* ☎ *0432/23218. No credit cards.*

$–$$ ✕ **Vachos.** In the nondescript Riga Fereou Square, you could easily pass this taverna without a second glance. The secret is the flower-filled garden in the back, where you can enjoy the spectacular view of the Meteora rocks, which are floodlit at night (get a seat at the front). There's a large selection of the usual taverna *orektika* (starters) and meat and fish main dishes. Try the homemade desserts and barrel wine. ⊠ *Platia Riga Fereou,* ☎ *0432/24678. No credit cards. Closed Nov.–Feb.*

$$$ 🏨 **Amalia.** Built in 1991, Amalia's low-lying complex has spacious, handsome public rooms that somehow avoided the generic stamp. Relax in the sitting room, with a fireplace and floral murals, or enjoy the poolside bar, with glistening blue tiles and rustic rafters. Rooms are done in soothing colors with large beds and prints; some have televisions and balconies. Buffet breakfast is included in the price. ✉ *Trikalon 14, Theopetra, Kalambaka 42200,* ☎ *0432/81216,* FAX *0432/81457. 171 rooms with bath, 2 suites. Restaurant, 2 bars, cafeteria, pool, shops, meeting rooms. AE, DC, MC, V.*

$$$ 🏨 **Motel Divani.** This A-class hotel has optimal views of the Meteora
★   rocks from the room's balconies (an advantage over the Amalia). Its large open spaces, quiet corners, and private garden encourage relaxation. The exterior is plain, as are the rooms, but they're shielded from outside noise. The professional reception staff will arrange and negotiate a price for a leisurely taxi ride to the monasteries. It's on the edge of town, a few minutes from the center. An "American" breakfast is included. ✉ *Trikalon 1, 42200,* ☎ *0432/23330,* FAX *0432/23638. 165 rooms with bath. Restaurant, 2 bars, pool, shop, meeting rooms, parking. AE, DC, MC, V.*

$–$$ 🏨 **Hotel Edelweiss.** Bright and clean, this hotel sparkles. Comfortable rooms with televisions and air-conditioning look out over the pool and the towering Meteora rocks beyond. The bar has a lively, local crowd, and the hotel runs a Western and Greek popular music club right next door. ✉ *E. Venizelou 3, 42200,* ☎ *0432/23966, 0432/23884, or 0432/24918,* FAX *0432/24733. 60 rooms with bath. Restaurant, 2 bars, pool, dance club, parking. MC, V.*

$–$$ 🏨 **Hotel Famissi.** Should the Edelweiss be full and you need a low-priced hotel, try the slightly more expensive Famissi. Rooms are typical—white walls, wooden paneling, marble floors—with the added touch of icons over the beds; all have balconies and air-conditioning and those at the back have garden views. ✉ *Trikalon 103, 42200,* ☎ *0432/25090 through 25092 and 0432/24117,* FAX *0432/24615. 46 rooms with bath. Restaurant, bar, parking. MC, V.*

Nightlife

BARS

Kalambaka doesn't have much nightlife, but one or two **bars** stay open late in the central square and along the Trikala Road.

NIGHTCLUB

For dancing try the **Hotel Edelweiss club,** right next to the hotel (☞ *above).*

En Route   On the road to the Meteora monasteries, which begins just outside of Kalambaka in Kastraki, you'll pass the 12th-century **Chapel of the Virgin** (✉ At Doupani), where the monks first gathered. About 5 mi outside Kastraki you will spot what looks like a clothesline with brightly colored rags hanging high up in a crevice. According to legend, a woodcutter who lost his leg promised to give St. George all his wife's clothes if he was healed—he was. On St. George's day, women offer scarves or other items of clothing and young men scale the rocks to hang them up for the saint.

Meteora Monasteries

❼   *178 km (110½ mi) southwest of Thessaloniki, 3 km (1¾ mi) north of Kalambaka.*

The name Meteora comes from the Greek word *meteorizome* (to hang in midair) and the monasteries, perched on a handful of strangely shaped pinnacles that rise 300 meters (984 feet) above the Peneus Valley, seem to do just that. Their lofty aeries imbue them with an other-worldly quality; the azure heavens seem close enough to touch and the valley of worldly distractions is far below.

Looming between the Pindos range and the Thessalian plain, the rocks remain an enigma. Some geologists say a lake that covered the area 30 million years ago swept away the soil and softer stone as it forced its way to the sea. Others believe the Peneus River slowly carved out the towering pillars, now eroded by wind and rain.

By the 9th century ascetic hermits were living in the rocks' crevices. On Sunday and holidays they gathered at Stagi (present-day Kalambaka) and Doupiani, and they eventually formed religious communities. With Byzantine power on the wane and an increase in religious persecution from invading foreigners, the monks retreated to the inaccessible rocks. In 1336 they were joined by two monks from Mt. Athos, Abbot Gregorios of Magoula and his companion St. Athanasios. The abbot returned to Athos, but he commanded St. Athanasios to build a monastery here. Notwithstanding the legend that says that the saint flew up to the rocks on the back of an eagle, St. Athanasios began the backbreaking task of building the Megalo Meteoro (1356–1372) using pulleys and ropes to haul construction material. The monks themselves had to endure a harrowing ride in a swinging net to reach the top.

Despite St. Athanasios's strict rule, the monastery attracted many devotees, including, in 1371, John Urosh of Serbia, who turned down the throne to become the monk Ioasaph. His royal presence brought contributions to the monasteries, and their numbers grew quickly. By the 16th century, there were at least 20 smaller settlements and 13 monasteries, which were embellished with frescoes and icons by such great artists as Theophanis Strelitzas, a monk from Crete. The bigger monasteries prospered on revenues from estates in Thessaly and eastern Europe. During the late Byzantine period, they stood as a bastion of Christianity against Turkish domination.

The monastic communities disappeared for several reasons. Some of the wealthy monasteries were plagued by bitter power struggles that were their eventual undoing. Monasticism as a vocation gradually lost its appeal, causing even grand communities to dwindle. Smaller, poorer monasteries could not afford to maintain the old buildings; many monasteries were neglected or abandoned. Today only six monasteries at Meteora are open to the public. After the Greco-Turkish war of 1919–1922, the already diminished monastic lands and revenues were appropriated by the state for refugees from Asia Minor, another blow to the few remaining monasteries.

Visitors should dress decorously: men must tuck up long hair and wear long pants, women should wear a skirt to the knee, and both sexes should cover their shoulders. Some monasteries provide coverings at the entrance. Opening hours vary depending on the season, but information is readily available in Kalambaka from your hotel receptionist. All monasteries can be visited in one journey from Kalambaka—a 21-km (13-mi) round-trip by car. A bus leaves Kalambaka for Megalo Meteoro five times daily (once daily in winter). Megalo Meteoro and Varlaam are the two most rewarding to visit. You can hike along the footpaths between monasteries, but you must be in good shape because there are many steps up to most monasteries. Once on the monastery circuit, you'll find just a few overpriced concession stands; if you plan to make a day of it, stock up in town for a picnic.

The monastery of **Ayios Nikolaos Anapafsas** seems impossibly crammed atop a narrow rock. The katholikon was built in 1388 and was later expanded; the monastery itself dates from the end of the 15th century. Because of the rock's peculiar shape, the katholikon faces north rather than the usual east. Its superb 16th-century frescoes are the work of Theophanis Strelitzas. Though conservative, his frescoes are lively and expressive: mountains are stylized, plants and animals are portrayed geometrically. Especially striking are the Temptation, the scourging of Christ, and a scene of Adam naming the animals. The serpent has the form of the legendary basilisk, which could kill with a mere look or a breath. The rock's small area precluded a cloister, so the monks studied in the larger-than-usual narthex. Visitors are admitted in small groups. ⊠ *Along monastery route, about 3 km (2 mi) outside Kalambaka,* ☎ *0432/22375.* ☔ *400 dr.* ☼ *Daily 9–6.*

The inaccessible **Ayia Moni** monastery has been deserted since an 1858 earthquake. Locals believe the area is haunted owing to its ominous presence. ⊠ *Along monastery route, across from Agios Nikolaos monastery.*

Because of its breathtaking location, the compact **Ayia Barbara,** also called Roussanou, is probably the most photographed monastery. Abandoned in the early 1900s, it stood empty until nuns moved in and began its restoration some years ago. Its founding in 1288 by the monks Nicodemus and Benedict has yet to be confirmed, but it is known that 156 years later the monastery was restored for the first time. The main church, dedicated to the Transfiguration, has well-preserved frescoes from the mid-16th century. Most are gory, depicting scenes of martyrdom, but one shows lions licking Daniel's feet during his imprisonment. A smaller church houses the skull of St. Barbara. ⊠ *Along monastery route, across vertiginous bridges from Ayia Moni,* ☎ *0432/22649.* ☔ *400 dr.* ☼ *Daily 9–6.*

The highest and most powerful monastery is **Megalo Meteoro,** or the Church of the Metamorphosis (Transfiguration). Founded by St. Athanasios, the monk from Athos, it was built of massive stones on the highest rock, 415 meters (1,361 feet) above the valley. As you walk to the entrance, you will see the chapel with the cell where St. Athanasios once lived. The monastery had extensive privileges and held jurisdiction over the others for centuries; an 18th-century engraving in its museum depicts it towering above the rest.

The present church's sanctuary was the chapel built by St. Athanasios and then added to by St. Ioasaph. The rest of the church was erected in 1552 with an unusual transept built on a cross-in-square plan with lateral apses topped with lofty domes, like the Mt. Athos monasteries. To the right of the narthex are the tombs of Ioasaph and Athanasios; a fresco shows the austere saints holding a monastery in their hands. Also of interest are the gilded iconostasis, with plant and animal motifs of exceptionally fine workmanship; the bishop's throne (1617) inlaid with mother-of-pearl and ivory; and the 15th-century icons in the sanctuary. Their expressiveness and attention to color and detail have led art historians to conclude they may also be the work of Theophanis Strelitzas. In the narthex are frescoes of the Martyrdom of the Saints, gruesome scenes of persecution under the Romans. A chamber stacked with skulls and bones of monks is opposite.

The refectory now houses the treasury, with fine miniatures, golden bulls, historic documents, and elaborately carved crucifixes, including one that took the monk Daniel 10 years to carve. The front shows 10 scenes with several figures each and representations of 24 single figures. Portable icons include the Virgin by Tzanes, another well-known artist. The adjacent kitchen is blackened by centuries of cooking. ⊠

Along monastery route, 300 meters west of Megalo Meteoro, past the intersection for Varlaam monastery, ☎ *0432/22278.* 🖃 *400 dr.* ☉ *Wed.–Mon. 9–1 and 3:20–6 (winter hrs vary).*

The monks from **Varlaam,** which is atop a ravine and reached by 195 steps, were famous for their charity. Originally here were the Church of Three Hierarchs (14th century) and the cells of a hermitage started by St. Varlaam, who arrived shortly after St. Athanasios. Two brothers from the wealthy Aparas family of Ioannina rebuilt the church in 1518, incorporating it into a larger katholikon called Agii Pandes (All Saints). A church document relates how it was built in 20 days, after the materials had been collected atop the rock for 22 years. Its main attraction is the 16th-century frescoes—mostly of ascetic subjects, including the Life of John the Baptist and a disturbing Apocalypse with a yawning hell's mouth—which completely cover the walls, beams, and pillars. The frescoes' realism, the sharp contrasts of light and dark, and the many-figured scenes show an Italian influence, though in the portrayal of single saints they follow the Orthodox tradition (the West had no models to offer). Note the Pantocrator peering down from the dome. These are the work of Frangos Katellanos of Thebes, one of the most important 16th-century hagiographers.

Other buildings include the infirmary, a chapel to Sts. Cosmas and Damien, and the refectory, now a sacristy, which displays the manuscript Gospel Book of the Byzantine emperor Constantine Porphyrogennetus with his signature. There are storerooms with the monks' 12,000-liter (2,640-gallon) barrel and an ascent tower with a net and a winch. Until the 1920s the only way to reach most of the monasteries was by retractable ladder or net. A much-quoted story relates how an abbot, when asked how often the ropes were changed, replied "when they break." A bishop of Trikala decreed that steps be cut to all the monasteries, and today the ropes are used only for hauling up supplies. 🖃 *Along monastery route, 100 meters (328 feet) southwest of intersection,* ☎ *0432/22277.* 🖃 *400 dr.* ☉ *Sat.–Thurs. 9–1 and 3:20–6 (winter 3–5).*

The less-visited site, along the eastern route, is **Ayios Stephanos,** the oldest monastery. According to an inscription that was once on the lintel, the rock was inhabited before AD 1200 and was the hermitage of Jeremiah. By the beginning of the 14th century, the monks lived a common life (cenobitic). The Byzantine emperor Andronicus Paleologos stayed here in 1333 on his way to conquer Thessaly and made generous gifts to the monks, enabling the building of a church in 1350. About a half century later, the Lord of Hungro-Wallachia donated a piece of the True Cross, relics of John the Baptist, and property in Romania; his nephew gave the monastery the head of St. Haralambos, now housed in the katholikon (1798) that is named after that saint. A permanent bridge has replaced the movable one that once connected the monastery with the hill opposite.

Today Ayios Stephanos is an airy convent, where the nuns spend their time painting Byzantine icons, writing, or studying music; some are involved in the community as doctors and professors. The katholikon has no murals but boasts a fine carved wooden baldachin and an iconostasis depicting the Last Supper. A two-headed eagle, the symbol of the Byzantine Empire, embellishes the floor. You can also visit the **old church of Ayios Stephanos,** with late 15th-century frescoes, as well as a **small museum,** with icons by Tzanes, 17th-century illuminated manuscripts, and an exquisite Epitaphios cloth—used to cover the bier on Good Friday—embroidered with thread and sequins. 🖃 *Along eastern monastery route (from main rd. at intersection for*

Kalambaka, bear right at fork), ☎ *0432/22279.* 📧 *400 dr.* ☉ *Tues.–Sun. 9–1, 3:20–6 (winter 3–5).*

NEED A BREAK?	Although you may stop anywhere on the circuit, the stretch approaching Ayia Triada from Ayios Stephanos has the best views for a midday **picnic.** Just hike a few meters off the road to a spot overlooking the valley and unpack.

James Bond fans will recognize **Ayia Triada** from the movie, *For Your Eyes Only.* Of all the monasteries, it feels the most primitive and remote. (If you're pressed for time, skip this one.) According to local legend, the Monk Dometius was the first to arrive in 1438; the main church, dedicated to the Holy Trinity, was built in 1476, and the narthex and frescoes were added more than 200 years later. Look for the fresco with St. Sisois gazing upon the skeleton of Alexander the Great, meant to remind the viewer that power is fleeting. In the early 1980s thieves stole precious antique icons, which have never been recovered. The iconostasis has one icon (1662) that depicts Christ in local costume; another scene, of three angels, symbolizes the Holy Trinity. The apse's pseudo-trefoil window and the sawtooth decoration around it and beneath other windows lend grace to the structure. There are also a chapel dedicated to St. John the Baptist, a small folk museum, the monks' cells, a kitchen, a refectory, and cisterns. Ayia Triada is best known for its view, with Ayios Stephanos and Kalambaka in the south, and Varlaam and Megalo Meteoro to the west. A footpath near the entrance (red arrows) descends to Kalambaka, about 3 km (2 mi). ✉ *Along eastern monastery route, 200 meters (656 feet) north of Ayios Stefanos,* ☎ *0432/22220.* 📧 *400 dr.* ☉ *Fri.–Wed. 9–12:30, 3–5.*

EPIRUS AND THESSALY A TO Z

Arriving and Departing

By Bus

The **KTEL bus** system is preferable to the train. Eight or nine buses daily go from Athens's Terminal A (✉ Kifissou 100, ☎ 01/512–5954) to Ioannina station (✉ Between Sina and Zosimadou, ☎ 0651/27422); the trip takes about 7 hours. Some buses take the longer route east through Kalambaka and Trikala rather than the usual southern route to the Rion–Antirion ferry and the Peloponnese. The 110-dr. ferry ride is not included in the bus ticket.

From Athens's dismal Terminal B (✉ Near Liossion 260, ☎ 01/831–7153) seven buses leave daily for Trikala (6 hrs), where you then make the 25-minute connection to Kalambaka. On Sunday there is a reduced schedule for all towns.

For information in English on bus schedules, telephone the EOT in Athens (✉ Syntagma [Constitution] Sq., ☎ 01/322–2545).

By Car

Driving to Kalambaka or Ioannina from Athens takes most of a day. To reach Ioannina, take the National Road west past Corinth in the Peloponnese, to the Rion–Antirion ferry (9 km/5½ mi before Patras), then continue north past Mesolonghi, Agrinion, Amfiloxia, and Arta (447 km/277 mi). For Kalambaka, take the National Road north past Thebes and Lamia to N. Monastirio (about 53 km, 33 mi) north of Lamia, where there is a turnoff for Trikala and Kalambaka, (a total of 330 km/204 mi). You may then drive on to Metsovo and Ioannina (another 126 km/78 mi).

By Plane

Olympic Airways has at least one, and usually two, flights daily from Athens to Ioannina, and one flight daily from Thessaloniki. In Athens (☏ 01/966–6666); Thessaloniki (☏ 031/473720); Ioannina (✉ Katsadima 1, Platia Pyrrou, ☏ 0651/28526); airport (✉ 5 km/3 mi outside town, ☏ 0651/28218, 0651/39131).

By Train

The cheapest way to get to Kalambaka is by train, but it's not recommended. From Athens you must change trains at Palaiofarsalo and the trip takes at least 8 hours (the IC express cuts the time by an hour but costs 2,000 dr. extra). For more information, contact the **Greek Railway Organization**: Athens (✉ Karolou 1, ☏ 01/524–0601); Kalambaka (☏ 0432/22451).

Getting Around

By Bus

Four buses (KTEL) daily leave Ioannina for Metsovo (1½ hrs) and two buses make the full journey to Kalambaka (3 hrs); frequencies are the same in the opposite direction. One bus daily leaves Ioannina for Dodona, returning in the afternoon. There is a bus to most villages once a day, but traveling around is much easier in a rented car.

By Car

A rented car is by far the best way to explore the region, and it is necessary to go beyond the main sites. The road from Ioannina–Metsovo–Kalambaka is one of the most scenic in northern Greece, but it traverses the famous Katara Pass, which is curvy and possibly dangerous, especially in winter (snow chains are necessary).

Contacts and Resources

Car Rentals

Ioannina: Budget (☏ 0651/43901, airport ☏ 0651/33382); European (☏ 0651/70086).

Emergencies

IOANNINA

Police (☏ 100, 0651/25673, 0651/26431). **Hospital** (☏ 0651/99111, 0651/99504).

METSOVO

Police (☏ 0656/41233). **Health center** (☏ 0656/41111).

KALAMBAKA

Police (☏ 0432/22109). **Hospital** (☏ 0432/22222).

Guided Tours

In Athens **CHAT Tours** (✉ Stadiou 4, ☏ 01/322–2886) and **Key Tours** (✉ Kallirois 4, ☏ 01/923–3166) offers guided trips to Meteora and northern Greece. A three-day tour to Delphi and Meteora with lodging and half-board costs 66,000 dr.–73,000 dr.

Contact the **Greek Alpine Club** (☏ 0651/22138) for walking-tour information; it's open from 7 PM to 9 PM.

Travel Agencies

In Metsovo, **Kassaros Travel** (✉ Tsourmaka 3, ☏ 0656/41800, 0656/41346, 0656/41662, 093/407494, 094/383131 or 094/397778, FAX 0656/41262) can issue plane tickets, arrange accommodations, and occasionally organize trips to the nearby lake or ski center.

Visitor Information

IOANNINA

Greek National Tourist Organization (GNTO or EOT) (✉ N. Zerva 2, Platia Pyrrou, 45332, ☎ 0651/25086, FAX 0651/72148) is open weekdays 7:30–2:30 and 4–8, weekends 9–2:30. **Ioannina Tourist Office** (☎ 0651/25086).

KALAMBAKA

Tourist Police (✉ Hatzipetrou 10–11, ☎ 0432/22109.

6 Northern Greece

Thessaloniki, Chalkidiki, and the Alexander the Great Sites

Northern Greece remains the country's best-kept travel secret, allowing the exploring traveler a more intimate experience of Greece and its gregarious people. At Mt. Olympus, you can peek at the daily discoveries at Greece's most active archaeological site, walk empty beaches, hike virgin trails through rampant wildflowers, and experience the magic of the throne of Zeus. Thessaloniki was once home to Alexander the Great and crossroads of the ancient world; today you can roam its street markets and share anecdotes of modern life over ouzo.

By Tom Stone

THE REGION WE CALL NORTHERN GREECE, comprising Macedonia in the west and Thrace in the east, covers the Balkan frontier from Albania to Bulgaria, and also touches Turkey. It is both a meeting point and a crossroads between Europe, the Mediterranean, and Asia, imbued with the sights, sounds, and colors of many different cultures that sometimes blend in fascinating harmony, and at others clash in violent discord.

Enhancing the landscape and emphasizing its contrasts are the monuments and other artifacts of the various civilizations that have fought and lived here: marble temples and fortifications built by Athens and Sparta, rough-hewn Macedonian tombs, the arches and rotundas of Imperial Rome, the domes of Byzantium, and the minarets and *hamams* (baths) of the Ottomans.

The area first figured in Greek history when it was colonized by Greek city-states during the 7th century BC. In 512 BC, both Macedonia and Thrace were conquered by Darius I, the Persian, and later his son Xerxes marched through on his ill-fated expedition to Greece.

Then came the Macedonians. Within a hundred years, Philip II and his son Alexander the Great had conquered all of Greece except Sparta, and all of Persia as well. After Alexander's death his brother-in-law Cassander established Thessaloniki as the capital (316 BC), naming it for his new bride, Alexander's half-sister, Thessaloniki. She was the daughter of the much-married Philip, who had named her after a famous *niki* (victory) of his in Thessaly, where her mother had been one of his prizes.

Profiting from squabbles among Alexander's successors, the Romans took over Macedonia, and by 146 BC, the rest of Greece had become a Roman province. In 42 BC, after the assassination of Julius Caesar, Marc Anthony defeated Brutus and Cassius at the double battles of Philippi in Macedonia. Under the Pax Romana that followed, St. Paul twice traveled through on his way to Corinth, paving the way for the second great flowering of Greek and Macedonian culture—that of the Byzantine Empire.

Byzantium held sway for 1,100 years, the center of Greek civilization shifted from Athens to Constantinople, and Thessaloniki became the second most important city in the empire. It remained that way under the Ottoman Turks, who sacked Constantinople in 1453 and whose dominance over Northern Greece lasted until the 1912–13 Balkan Wars. Macedonia was then united with the rest of Greece, and the 1923 Peace of Lausanne established the present-day borders of Thrace—but two of the bloodiest battles were yet to come. In 1941, Mussolini's troops invaded Northern Greece and were pushed back into Albania, causing the German army to intervene and fight their way through the country from the north. Then, at the end of World War II, the region became the principal arena for the Greek Civil War (1946–49) between the Communists and Royalists.

Today, Northern Greece is once more feeling threatened, as the collapse of Yugoslavia has brought to life age-old ethnic and religious animosities. Because the Serbians are Orthodox Christians, they are natural allies of Greece in any confrontations against non-Christians. It has been difficult, therefore, for the Greeks to understand why the rest of the Christian world seems to be against their fellow believers. Nor can the Greeks comprehend how the rest of the world can be so blind to the threat posed by Skopje's insistence on calling itself "Macedonia" with the ancient Greek Macedonian sun as a symbol. The air these days is rife with rumors of international plots to redraw the map of the Balkans. Since such things have happened before, the Greeks see no reason why they won't again.

In spite of continuing tensions, both Northern Greece and Thessaloniki are flourishing. New hotels are being built, the highway connecting Macedonia with more remote regions of Thrace is being widened and extended, and Thessaloniki has been named the 1997 Cultural Capital of Europe. The natural, cultural, and historical attractions, along with the genuine hospitality of the people, make this region truly Greece's "secret garden."

Pleasures and Pastimes

Dining

Long Byzantine and Ottoman influence in Northern Greece has led to a cuisine of distinct Levantine character, with a liberal use of such spices as cinnamon and allspice. The cooks adapt to the seasons: in winter look forward to rich game—boar and venison—and in summer seafood and salads. Meals are always complemented by generous portions of wine and ouzo. The ritual of eating out is essential to Greek life, involving the sharing of emotions, making new friends, and bringing family together. It is always an event to be savored.

Every neighborhood is scattered with all types of tavernas and casual bars. Even at the best restaurants dress is often casual, and although at the higher-priced establishments reservations are theoretically possible, nothing is guaranteed. Therefore, it is prudent to arrive before 9:30, earlier than most Greeks like to eat, but take note that many places do not open before 8:30 or 9.

CATEGORY	COST*
$$$$	over 7,000 dr.
$$$	4,500 dr.–7,000 dr.
$$	2,500 dr.–4,500 dr.
$	under 2,500 dr.

*for a 3-course meal, including tax and service, but excluding drinks.

Hiking and Walking

Northern Greece is marked with hundreds of paths originated by shepherds, villagers, and some believed to be remnants of underground passageways from World War II. The area has many mountains and beach trails, easy to hike and rich with opportunities to meet villagers and swim in a crystal mountain pond or a still cove. The best hiking area in Northern Greece is, of course, through the paths of the national park area of Mt. Olympus, alive in spring with literally hundreds of species of rare wildflowers.

Lodging

Thessaloniki's hotels are nothing much to write home about. With the exception of the city's only luxury hotel, the Macedonia Palace, and the Electra Palace, they've mostly been geared to the needs of transient businesspeople, with little emphasis on capturing the unique spirit of place so appealing to visitors. Selection of hotels elsewhere in Northern Greece varies from exclusive seaside resorts to modest family-managed hostel-like housing on the slopes of Mt. Olympus.

The peninsulas of Chalkidiki and the island of Thasos have the best hotels in Northern Greece—and some say in all of Greece. Outside these areas, the hotels are mainly small, somewhat spartan affairs whose charm comes mainly from their surroundings. Some establishments, particularly in Chalkidiki, close for the winter (we've noted otherwise); it's best to make arrangements ahead.

CATEGORY	COST*
$$$$	over 30,000 dr.
$$$	15,000 dr.–30,000 dr.
$$	10,000 dr.–15,000 dr.
$	under 10,000 dr.

All prices are for a standard double room, including tax, service, and break-fast unless noted otherwise.

Monasteries

The most beautiful locations throughout the Greek countryside have been settled by monastic orders throughout the history of Greece. There are several unique monastic areas to visit in Northern Greece, the most impressive of which are found near the Ayion Oros (Holy Mountain) of Mt. Athos.

Exploring Northern Greece

The region is a delightful geographic mix: In the mountains, from snow-covered Mt. Olympus to the mineral-rich eastern ranges, forests of pine, spruce, juniper, oak, and chestnut abound. There are ski resorts and climbing opportunities.

Cosmopolitan Thessaloniki lies in the strategic center of Macedonia, nestled gracefully in the wide but protective arms of the Thermaic Gulf and buttressed on its inland side by a low-lying mountain range around which the Axios River flows south to the Aegean.

In the lowlands of Chalkidiki, Thasos, and parts of Thrace, as on other Mediterranean coasts, fruit and olive trees flourish with vineyards and tobacco plantations. In summer the air is redolent of thyme and oregano. White-sand beaches along miles of inletted coastline are lapped by a turquoise sea.

Great Itineraries

Thessaloniki's central location in Macedonia makes it a perfect base. Most of the sights are within an hour of the city by car or bus.

IF YOU HAVE 2 DAYS

Numbers in the text correspond to numbers in the margin and on the Exploring Thessaloniki and Northern Greece maps.

Starting in **Thessaloniki** ①–⑲, explore both the old and the new city, not missing the **archaeological museum** ②, the Kastro, and the **White Tower** ①. Take a long promenade on the boardwalk to people-watch and join all the Thessalonians for coffee by the sea. Overnight in **Thessaloniki.** Spend your second day visiting the famous Alexander the Great sites: **Pella** ⑳, **Vergina** ㉑, and **Dion** ㉒.

IF YOU HAVE 4 DAYS

Using **Thessaloniki** ①–⑲ as your base, on the first day visit **Pella** ⑳ and **Vergina** ㉑, and head back to **Thessaloniki.** On the second day explore the Byzantine face of the city; venture outside the old walls for dinner. On the third day visit **Dion** ㉒ and **Mt. Olympus** ㉓. On the fourth day drive down the coast of **Chalkidiki,** stopping at the **Caves of Petralona** ㉔ for a leisurely swim in the azure waters.

IF YOU HAVE 6 DAYS

Begin in your home base, **Thessaloniki** ①–⑲, taking a day to explore the city. On the second day head northeast to **Kavala** ㉙ and **Philippi** ㉚; you may then explore the wonderful seaside, and head to the island of **Thasos** ㉛ if you seek refuge. On the third day take a jaunt to

Alexander the Great territory, including **Pella** ⑳ and **Vergina** ㉑; on the next day hike or take a Jeep through the terrain of ⛰ **Dion** ㉒ and **Mt. Olympus** ㉓. If you wish, overnight in the village of ⛰ **Litochoro.** On the fifth day venture off the beaten path northwest to **Lake Prespas** and **Kastoria,** returning for the night to **Thessaloniki** for some early-morning exploration of city-center galleries and shops before departing for Athens.

When to Tour

With Thessaloniki the 1997 Cultural Capital of Europe, travel in 1997 is especially exciting, with special events going on year-round. Travel to Chalkidiki is best done from May through October, when all establishments are open.

When visiting sites in Thessaloniki and throughout Northern Greece, get an early start because the days heat up and the siesta hours cut days short. You'd do well to do as the Greeks: indulge in a siesta into every afternoon so you can partake in the native nightlife and enjoy the late hours!

THESSALONIKI

It has seen the rise and fall of all manner of civilizations: Macedonian, Hellenic, Roman, Byzantine, Ottoman, and that of the Jews and of the modern Greeks. Each of its successive conquerors has, unfortunately, tended to plunder, raze, and bury much of what went before. Thus, little evidence remains of the Macedonian-Hellenistic civilization that built the city's fortifications. When the Romans came they took most of what was of portable value back to Italy and buried the rest. The Roman temples then became Byzantine churches, and many other structures were torn down to refortify the walls and build the towers, where both Hellenistic and Roman elements can still be seen. The Ottoman Turks, in turn, transformed the Byzantine churches into mosques and demolished many other buildings for their minarets, hamams, imarets (almshouses), fountains, and private mansions. When the Greeks regained the city, they had their churches reconsecrated and tore down most of the minarets. Then, in 1917, a great fire destroyed much of what was left of the colorful, teeming blend of cultures that the Ottoman reign had packed in: the bazaars, the elegant hotels and banks, the beautiful Turkish town houses, and the distinctive European Christian, Jewish, and Greek quarters.

The Thessaloniki that you see today is largely a result of the spacious, orderly vision of the French architect, Ernest Hébrard, who rebuilt the city after the fire. Some of its more distant past can still be seen and sensed, and a little walking will be well rewarded.

Thessaloniki is very centralized and easy to become a part of; in fact, its greatest charm lies in its warmth and accessibility. It is a very pedestrian city that lends itself to lazy strolls, the exploring of in-town archaeological sites, and café-style people-watching.

Exploring Thessaloniki

We can suggest two routes for exploring some of the highlights of the city. The best tour, however, is to wander through the streets responding to what you encounter. It is hard to get lost, since the entire city slopes downhill to the bay where you can always align yourself with the White Tower and the city skyline.

The White Tower, Sintrivaniou Square, and Southern City Environs

An exploration of the area from the White Tower west along the gulf to Aristotelous Square reveals important icons of the city's history: grand monuments of Emperor Galerius, artifacts from the Neolithic period through the Roman occupation housed in the archaeological museum, prominent churches, and the city's most important landmark, the tower itself. The lively shopping streets, bustling markets, and cafés reward with retail and gastronomic therapy.

A GOOD WALK

This walk begins at the **White Tower** ①; after viewing the Byzantine works, take in the city's expanse from the rooftop. From the White Tower walk east on the seaside promenade Nikis until you see the dramatic bronze **statue of Alexander and his horse, Bucephalus.** Meander for 5 minutes through the lovely park to the north, with its inviting cafés and children's playground, and across the wide promenade cutting through the park is the renowned **archaeological museum** ②, with finds dating from prehistoric Greece to Alexander's Macedonia. The **Byzantine Museum** ③ is just east of the museum, and farther east, at the intersection of Vasilis Olgas and 25 Martiou (25th of March St.), is the **Pinacothiki** (Municipal Gallery).

Head across the street toward the city center to the beginning of the city's fanciest shopping street, **Tsimiski.** In the middle of the city block, after the second streetlight, is the beautiful pedestrian **Dimitriou Gounari street.** D. Gounari, lined with delightful shops and cafés, crosses Tsimiski and leads you north directly to the **Arch of Galerius** ④.

After trying to talk your way into the **Rotunda** ⑤, try to explore the narrow streets surrounding the area, rich with cluttered junk and antiques shops; on Wednesday you'll see the eclectic Russian Market.

Cross Egnatia again to the south side of the street and continue west on Egnatia. On the first corner you will find the lovely 14th-century **Church of the Metamorphosis** ⑥.

Continuing west on Egnatia, turn right and walk a half block up Ayios Sofias to the oldest Byzantine church in the city, the 5th-century **Panagia Archiropiitas** ⑦. Next head south again on Ayios Sofias for a short downhill walk to reach the 8th-century church of **Ayia Sofia** ⑧.

To explore a more contemporary part of the city center, exit via Ayios Sofias's parklike entrance, cross the street, and walk due west on Ermou. Ermou will carry you directly into **Modiano market** ⑨, the heart of the central marketplace, complete with a myriad of foods and faces to check out. Take a look at the evocative **Memorial to Grigoris Lambrakis** ⑩ just west of the market. You can quit now or head south to Aristotelous Square, the *kafenia-* (traditional Greek coffeehouses) lined village square of the city center, for a drink and postcard-writing session before a well-deserved Greek siesta.

TIMING

This walk should take a good part of a day, depending upon your speed. Plan to spend at least an hour at the archaeological museum. The best time to explore churches is during mass, especially on Sunday. Otherwise, hours are not set in stone; try from about 8 AM to noon and 5:30 to 7:30 on any day, unless where noted.

SIGHTS TO SEE

❹ **Arch of Galerius.** The arch, or *ee kamára*, is one of a number of monuments built by Galerius during his reign as co-emperor of Diocletian's divided Roman empire (☞ Rotunda and Platia Navarino, *below*). Originally it had four pediments and a dome and was intended to span not only the Via Egnatia but also a passageway leading north to the Rotunda. ⊠ *Egnatia Odos, Sintrivaniou Sq.*

★ ❷ **Archaeological museum.** A true Thessaloniki highlight is this unpretentious single-story white structure, which gives no hint from the outside of the breathtaking treasures within. In addition to a superb collection of artifacts from Neolithic times through the Roman occupation, including a bust of the Emperor Galerius, it houses stunning finds from the Royal Tombs of Vergina (☞ Central Macedonia, *below*), now universally accepted as those of Philip of Macedon and his family. You'll find delicately wrought gold laurel wreaths; Philip's crown, armor, and shield; his *larnax* (gold funerary box) embossed with the 16-point Macedonian sun (often erroneously called a star). Of particular interest are those items that seem most certainly Philip's: a pair of greaves (shin guards), one shorter than the other (Philip was known to have a limp), and a skull with clear evidence of the terrible arrow wound in the right eye that Philip is also known to have suffered. ⌧ *Hanth Sq.,* ☎ *031/830538.* ⌧ *2,000 dr.* ☉ *Mon. 12:30–7, Tues.–Sun. 8–7.*

★ ❽ **Ayia Sofia.** Experts disagree on the founding date of "Holy Wisdom": from its architecture it is believed to be late 8th century; ecclesiastics think it was after the first Council of Nicea (325), when Christ was declared a manifestation of Divine Wisdom; and other church historians say it was contemporaneous with the magnificent church of Ayia Sofia in Constantinople. In any case, its rather drab interior contains two superb mosaics: one of the *Ascension,* and the other of the Virgin Mary holding Jesus in her arms. This latter mosaic is of particular interest as an example of the conflict in the Orthodox Church (726–843) between the Iconoclasts (icon smashers, which they often literally were) and the Iconodules (icon venerators or "slaves"). It is possible to see that, at one point in this doctrinal struggle, the Virgin Mary in the mosaic was replaced by a large cross (still partly visible), and that only later, after the victory of the Iconodules, was it again replaced with an image of Virgin Mary holding baby Jesus. ⌧ *Pavlou Mela.*

Ayios Panteleimon. A prime example of Macedonian church architecture, the facades of this church reveal the ornamental interplay of brick and stonework and a dome displaying typical strong upward motion. ⌧ *Egnatia Odos.*

❸ **Byzantine Museum.** Inaugurated in 1994, this museum is still sparsely exhibited. This beautiful structure will gradually become the repository of most of the country's finest Byzantine art: priceless icons, frescoes, sculpted reliefs, jewelry, glasswork, pottery, and coins. At press time (October, 1996) the museum was planning its 1997 pièce de résistance: a June–November exhibition in conjunction with the Cultural Capital of Europe celebration that will display the coveted Byzantine collection from Mt. Athos. ⌧ *2 Leoforos Stratou,* ☎ *031/868570.* ⌧ *Free (at press time).*

Cemeteries. In ancient times, cemeteries were just outside the city gates, and Thessaloniki was no exception. At the northern end of Ethnikis Aminis are the city's main Orthodox and non-Orthodox Christian cemeteries. The Jewish cemetery, south of them, was dug up and desecrated during World War II by the occupying Germans. After the war the remaining Jewish community chose to offer this land to the city on the condition that a university be built there. Today **Aristotelian University,** or University of Thessaloniki, is the largest university in Greece. However, gravestones with Hebrew inscriptions can occasionally be found lying on lawns outside the university buildings or incorporated into walkways in various parts of the city. ⌧ *At northern end of Ethnikis Aminis.*

❻ **Church of the Metamorphosis.** This sunken church is a fine example of Macedonian church architecture, with a decorative mix of brick and stonework and the strong upward thrust of the dome. ⌧ *Egnatia Odos.*

Egnatia Odos. It was during the Byzantine period that Thessaloniki came into its own as a commercial crossroads because the Via Egnatia, which already connected the city to Rome (with the help of a short boat trip across the Adriatic), was extended east to Constantinople. Today Egnatia Odos virtually begins along the same path; it is Thessaloniki's main commercial thoroughfare, although not as upscale as the parallel Tsimiski Street, two blocks to the south. ⊠ *City points southwest to northeast.*

⑩ Memorial to Grigoris Lambrakis. Those who have read the novel *Z* by Vassilis Vassilikos or seen the Costas-Gavras film of the leftist member of parliament (played by Yves Montand) whose murder by rightists in 1963 precipitated the events that resulted in the 1967 takeover of the colonels' junta will find this of interest. A dramatic bronze head and arm rising out of the earth marks the site of the murder. ⊠ *Just west of Modiano market, on corner of Ermou and Eleftherios Venezelou.*

★ ⑨ Modiano market. This covered market is worth a visit even if you have no intention of buying anything there, as is the generally cheaper **open-air market** (⊠ On the north side of Ermou). Both are in the grand tradition of European markets: rich not only with all manner of fish, meats, vegetables, fruits, breads, spices, wines, and household items, but with true characters as well: the whole spectrum of colorful hangers-on who congregate at markets the world over, even strolling gypsy musicians best watched while eating and drinking in the market's ouzeris and tavernas. ⊠ *Along city block on south side of Ermou.*

Municipal Gallery (Pinacothiki). Housed in the 1905 Villa Mordoh, the art gallery has a collection of over 800 pieces, ranging from Byzantine icons to modern Thessaloniki artists. At press time, an important exhibition detailing the works of late 15th-century Italian painter Caravaggio and his followers was planned for April, 1997. ⊠ *162 Vasilis Olgas,* ☎ *031/425531,* ℻ *031/411101.* ◷ *Tues.–Fri. 9–1 and 5–9, Sat. 5 PM–9 PM, Sun. 9 AM–1 PM.*

⑦ Panagia Archiropiitas. This 5th-century Byzantine church marvels the eye with arcades, monolithic columns topped by elaborate capitals, and exquisite period mosaics of birds and flowers. An engraved statement by Sultan Murat states that he had conquered Thessaloniki in the 11th century. ⊠ *Ayios Sofias.*

Platia Navarino. The remaining structures in Galerius's city-center complex include a racetrack (hence the name of Platia Hippodromiou, which covers it today), a palace, and an octagonal structure that may have been his throne room. Parts of these buildings have been excavated and can be seen in sunken areas around the square and the pedestrian street bordering it. This tree- and awning-shaded square proper, its fountain a marvelous bronze of a young boy peeing, is a favorite drinking, eating, and nightlife hub among students. ⊠ *Directly south of Rotunda and Triumphal Arch.*

★ ⑤ Rotunda. Also known as Ayios Giorgios, this self-aggrandizing monument is thought to have been intended as Galerius's mausoleum. However, when he died in Bulgaria, his successor refused to have the body brought back. The Byzantines converted the Rotunda into a church; the Ottomans made it a mosque (whose minaret still stands), and today it is being restored after the damage suffered in a 1978 earthquake, and it occasionally houses art exhibits and concerts. In its collection is a series of superb mosaics of early Christian saints, and it is soon to become a museum of Christian art. If you have time, explore the narrow **surrounding streets**; on Wednesday the streets are flooded with the **Russian Market**, a novel commercial enterprise featuring tchotchkes and the occasional interesting heirloom, antique, or folk art piece hawked by Eastern European refugees, a good many of Greek descent. ✉ *Just off Sintrivaniou Sq.,* ☎ *031/213627.* ☉ *Special events.*

★ ❶ **White Tower.** In 1866, with the threat of piracy diminishing and opening the port to European commerce increasingly imperative, the Ottoman Turks began demolishing the city's formidable sea walls and their intermittent towers. The tower, the only one along the seafront the Ottomans left standing, was an infamous prison and place of execution, known as the Bloody Tower. But the Turks whitewashed it, perhaps in deference to the foreign businessmen whom they hoped to attract, and it has become the city's most famous landmark. These days, it houses an interesting collection of Byzantine art and artifacts. But even empty, the White Tower is well worth a brief visit, if only for its architecture and its lovely site on the seafront. ✉ *Waterfront Promenade, Nikis and Pavlou Melas sts.,* ☎ *031/267832.* ✑ *1,000 dr.* ☉ *Mon. 12:30–7, Tues.–Fri. 8–7, weekends and holidays 8:30–3.*

Upper City, Panagia Chalkeon, and Aristotelous Square

Upper City (Ano Polis) is called Ta Kastra (the castles) because of the castle of Eptapyrghion and the many fortified towers that once bristled along the walls. Other than Byzantine churches, there are few specific places of historical interest, but it's an experience in itself to wander the tangled pedestrian streets past gossipy women, grandfathers in cafés, and children playing in courtyards.

Unfortunately, getting there can be a chore, as taxi drivers often try to avoid the cramped, congested streets and fear missing a fare back down. Have your hotel find a willing driver, or take a local bus. Buses 22 or 23 leave from the terminal at Platia Eleftherios (✉ 2 blocks west of Aristotelous Sq.) every 10 to 15 minutes and follow an interesting route through the narrow streets of the Upper City.

A GOOD TOUR

Start this excursion with the superb aerial city view from the **Tower of Trigoniou** ⑪ then walk west along the inside of the seaward wall (the wall should be to your right). Walk a few meters past the second *portara* (large open gateway) and to your left you will see the entrance to the grounds of **Moni Vlatádon** ⑫, and its tiny chapel to Saints Peter and Paul. The **castle of Eptapyrghion** ⑬ is north along Eptapyrghiou. Backtrack to the Tower of Trigoniou and continue west along Eptapyrghiou street to the first wide street on your left, Dimitriou Poliorkitou, and take the broad flight of stairs to the beginning of the **Old Turkish Quarter** toward the sea. Follow Dimitriou Poliorkitou west, bearing left, and take the winding descent to the left and then to the right until you come to the doors of the 5th-century **Osios David** ⑭.

Turn right and continue down the narrow cobblestone street to the first intersection. Below a strange tin "palace" of the self-proclaimed "King of the Greeks," follow Akropoleos to the small Platia Romfei; walk along Eolou to the small but exceptional 14th-century **Ayios Nikolaos Orfanos** ⑮.

Walk downhill on Apostolou Pavlou, the legendary path Apostle Paul took to the Upper City to address the Thessalonians, and cross busy Kassandrou. At Ataturk turn right onto Ayiou Dimitriou, which can be crowded, noisy, and not very attractive, so you may choose to walk along a smaller, more pleasant parallel street.

Continue west about six blocks until you reach **Ayios Dimitrios** ⑯ church, named for the Thessaloniki's patron saint and where he was

Exploring Thessaloniki

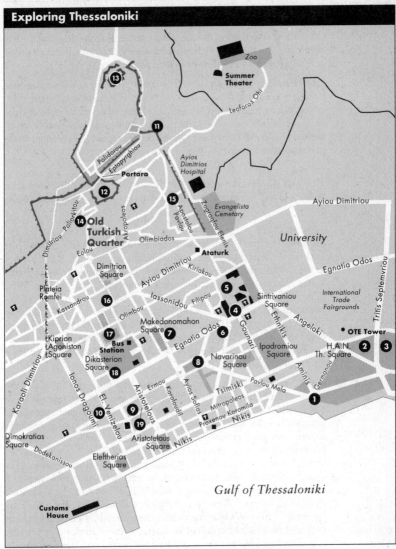

Arch of Galerius, **4**
Archaeological Museum, **2**
Ayia Sofia, **8**
Ayios Dimitrios, **16**
Ayios Nikolaos Orfanos, **15**
Byzantine Museum, **3**
Castle of Eptapyrghion, **13**

Church of the Metamorphosis, **6**
Jewish Community Memorial Museum, **19**
Memorial to Grigoris Lambrakas, **10**
Modiano Market, **9**
Moni Vlatádon, **12**
Osios David, **14**
Panagia Achiropiitas, **7**

Panagia Chalkeon, **18**
Roman Forum, **17**
Rotunda, **5**
Tower of Trigoniou, **11**
White Tower, **1**

martyred. Forge on downhill; one block south from the church to the very active excavation of the ancient **Roman Forum** ⑰. Walk west on Olimbou and turn left at the second corner onto short, diagonal Tositsa Street, and you'll will enter the **paliatzidiko** (flea market), the city's primo junk, antiques, and roaming-peddler promenade.

From **Panagia Chalkeon** ⑱, on the southwest corner of the immense Dikasterion Square, cross to the lower side of Egnatia Odos; a half block down, take a right on Aristotelous. Along Aristotelous, take a right on Vasiliou Irakleiou, the corner after Ermou, and walk half a block to the new **Jewish Community Memorial Museum** ⑲, a moving tribute to the persecution during World War II.

TIMING

This tour should take a few hours. You will want to spend some time at Ayios Dimitrios, especially to see a mass (☞ Timing *in* A Good Walk, *above*).

SIGHTS TO SEE

Ataturk. The birthplace of Mustafa Kemal, which also houses the Turkish consulate, should be visited by those interested in the history of the Turkish influence in Thessaloniki. In this modest, wood-frame house you can also explore a museum honoring his early life in Thessaloniki. The soldier and statesman who established the Turkish republic and became its president, Ataturk was born in Thessaloniki in 1881. He participated in the city's Young Turk movement, which eventually led to the collapse of the sultanate and the formation of the modern Turkish state. ⌧ *151 Ayiou Dimitriou,* ☎ *031/269964.* ⌧ *Free.* ☉ *Irregular hours.*

★ ⑯ **Ayios Dimitrios.** This magnificent church is a powerful tribute to the patron saint of Thessaloniki. It was rebuilt and restored from 1926 to 1949 with attention to preserving the details of the original; the marks left by a fire can still be seen throughout. In the time of the emperor Galerius, the young Dimitrios took to preaching Christianity in the coppersmith district, in contravention of a recent edict. He was arrested and jailed in a room in the old Roman baths, on the site of the present church. While he was incarcerated, he gave a Christian blessing to a gladiator friend named Nestor, who was about to fight Galerius's champion, Lyaios. When Nestor fought and killed Lyaios, after having made Dimitrios's blessing public, the enraged Galerius had Nestor executed on the spot and had Dimitrios speared to death in his cell. His Christian brethren were said to have buried him there. A church was built on the ruins of this bath in the 5th century AD but was then destroyed by an earthquake in the 7th century. The church was rebuilt in the 7th century and gradually the story of Demetrios and Nestor grew to be considered apocryphal until the great 1917 fire burned down most of the 7th-century church and brought to light its true past. The process of rebuilding uncovered rooms beneath the apse that appear to have been those very baths, and the discovery there of a reliquary containing a vial of bloodstained earth leaves little doubt that this is indeed the spot where Dimitrios was martyred. It can today be entered through a small doorway to the right of the altar. You may work your way through the catacombs or peruse the parish women's craft work cooperative. ⌧ *Ayiou Dimitriou and Ayios Nikolaos,* ☎ *031/270008.* ⌧ *Free.* ☉ *Tues.–Sun. 8:30–3.*

⑮ **Ayios Nikolaos Orfanos.** This small church is noted for its marvelous frescoes, intriguing mix of Byzantine architectural styles, and perhaps the most beautiful midnight Easter service in the city. ⌧ *Eolou and Apostolou Pavlou Sts., Upper City.*

⓭ Castle of Eptapyrghion. This 14th-century Byzantine bastion was used in modern times as a notoriously abysmal prison, closed in 1988. Plans for its future entail a cultural center. The walls and the area just inside the portara have been restored and made into a park, but that is about it. ✉ *Eptapyrghiou, Upper City.*

⓳ Jewish Community Memorial Museum. In that almost 95% of the once Jewish community was killed during World War II, its history is of great interest to those who want to really learn about this city. The small, but very active Jewish community recently opened a moving museum dedicated to its rich and impressive history in Thessaloniki. A **synagogue** is also at the site. ✉ *Vasiliou Irakleiou 24, 2nd floor,* ☎ *031/275701 or 031/277803.* ✆ *Free.*

⓬ Moni Vlatádon (Vlatades Monastery). Shaded with pine and cypress, this structure displays a mixture of architectural additions from Byzantine times to the present. The small central church just right of the apse has a tiny **chapel dedicated to Saints Peter and Paul,** though it is seldom open. It is believed to have been built on the spot where Paul first preached to the Thessalonians in AD 49. ✉ *Eptapyrghiou, Upper City.*

Old Turkish Quarter. During the Ottoman occupation, this area, probably the most picturesque in the city, was considered to be the best place to live in Thessaloniki. In addition to the superb views, in summer it catches whatever breeze there is. Until very recently the home of some of the poorest families in Thessaloniki, the area is rapidly gentrifying, thanks to EU development funds (which repaired the cobblestones), strict new zoning and building codes, and the zeal of young couples with the money to restore the old houses. ✉ *Upper City, south of Dimitriou Poliorkitou.*

★ ⓮ Osios David (Blessed David). This entrancing little church was built about 500, was later converted into a mosque, and somewhere along the line it lost its western side—the traditional place of entrance (in order to look east when facing the altar)—so you enter Osios David from the south. No matter; this entirely suits the rather battered magic of this tiny church, which has a kind of street-urchin feel to it. You can still see the radiantly beautiful mosaic in the dome of the apse, which shows a beardless, somewhat Orphic Christ, as he seems to have been described in the vision of Ezekiel.

The magic of this mosaic is fully complemented by the story of how it was forgotten for centuries and then found through a vision. To save it from destruction, it seems, the mosaic was hidden under a layer of calfskin during the Iconoclastic ravages of the eighth and ninth centuries. It was then plastered over by the Turks when the church was converted into a mosque and seems to have been forgotten until 1921 when an Orthodox monk in Egypt had a vision telling him to go to the church. On the day he arrived, which happened to be March 25 (the day of Greek Independence from the Turks), an earthquake shattered the plaster and revealed the mosaic to the monk—who promptly died. ✉ *Dimitriou Poliorkitou, Upper City.*

⓲ Panagia Chalkeon. The beautiful "Virgin of the Copper Workers" stands in what is still the traditional copper-working area of Thessaloniki. Completed in 1028, it is one of the oldest churches in the city displaying the domed cruciform style. You may encounter artisans and workers who frequently drop by during the day to light a candle to this patron of physical laborers. The area offers many shops featuring traditional copper crafts at low prices. ✉ *Southwest corner of Dikasterion Sq.*

⑰ Roman Forum. This large open area is undergoing vigorous excavation. Its small amphitheater is often the site of romantic concerts on balmy summer evenings. **Tositsa Street,** one block west, is the best junk, antiques, and roaming peddler street in the city, where good finds range from brass beds to antique jewelry. The area is flanked by coppersmith shops and the Church of the Panagia Chalkeon, the Virgin of the Coppersmiths, to the southeast. ⊠ *Between Olimbou and Filipou, just south of Ayios Dimitrios.*

⑪ Tower of Trigoniou. From here, you can see the city spread out below you in a graceful curve around the bay, from the suburbs in the east to the modern harbor in the west and, on a clear day, even Mt. Olympus, rising near the coastline at the southwest reaches of the bay. There is, however, little of historic interest to see within the walls. ⊠ *Upper City.*

Ano Polis (Upper City). The Upper City is also called Ta Kastra (The Castles) because of the castle of Eptapyrghion and the many fortified towers that once bristled along the walls. The area within and just outside the remains of the walls is like a village unto itself, a charming jumble of the rich, the poor, and the renovated. Rustic one-story peasant houses, many still occupied by the families that built them, sit side by side with houses newly built or restored by the wealthier class of Thessaloniki in something resembling the original style of the neighborhood. And, as the area continues to be upgraded, new tavernas, café-bars, and restaurants spring up to serve the visitors, both Greek and foreign, who flock there for a cool evening out. ⊠ *Elevated northern area of city.*

Dining

$$$$ ✕ **Aigli.** This is Thessaloniki's most authentically Greek restaurant, set
★ in a two-dome Turkish hamam with an old outdoor Greek cinema. Your palate will delight in delicately prepared and spiced dishes evocative of old Levantine Thessaloniki and Constantinople. In the evening, Aigli presents entertainment, from Greek and French singers to instrumentalists from Turkey. ⊠ *Corner of Kassandrou and Ayios Nikolaos, just behind Ayios Dimitrios church,* ☏ *031/270016. Reservations not accepted. No credit cards.*

$$$$ ✕ **B & B.** This restaurant pampers you with formal service among elegant appointments. The apartment it occupies is decorous but relaxed, with old-world European grandeur reminiscent of the home of an old wealthy friend. Dishes have a more European than Greek slant; the spinach crepe is marvelously delicate, and a treat to find in Greece. ⊠ *46 Tsimiski, 2nd floor,* ☏ *031/275731. Reservations essential. AE, MC, V.*

$$$$ ✕ **Krikelas.** The grandmother of the upscale restaurants, Krikelas is an old standby for the older Greek elite. It is famous for its wide variety of *mezedes* (appetizers) and venison, boar, and other specialty game dishes. Compared with most of the newer fancy restaurants, the decor is rather boring, but the food is great. Try the superb homemade cheese and the mixed grill. ⊠ *32 Ethnikis Antistasis, about 1 km east of the amusement park,* ☏ *031/411289. Reservations not accepted. DC.*

$$$$ ✕ **Porto Marina.** This is one of the best fish tavernas in Greece, with simple decor and friendly service. Come here for fresh, wonderfully cooked seafood, from grilled fish to lobsters, but be prepared for slightly elevated prices. You will find it in the noisy seafood restaurant strip in Krini, slightly out of the city center but worth the trek. ⊠ *79 Plastiras, Kalamaria,* ☏ *031/451333. Reservations essential weekends. AE, DC, MC, V.*

$$$$ ✕ **Syracuses.** While rubbing elbows with the beautiful people in this wood-beam villa, you will get a feel for the grand beauty of Thessaloniki gone by. From the glassed-in gazebo, you can survey the garden surrounding the house, or just have a long drink in the lovely front garden. Every dish is exceptional, and many claim their tiramisù to be the best in Greece. It's a 10- to 15-minute taxi drive from city center, and well worth the trip. ⊠ *Corner of Vasilis Olgas and Vulgari,* ☎ *031/414445. Reservations essential weekends after 10. AE, DC, MC, V.*

$$$ ✕ **Aristotelous Ouzerie.** Of all the ouzeris, this is the best—it is a great favorite among artists, scholars, and businesspeople, and it is consequently packed with glamorous and convivial patrons. Inevitably, you will have to wait, but once you're seated and have sampled the magnificent variety of mezedes, you'll understand why no one is in a hurry to leave. ⊠ *8 Aristotelous, in a hidden alleyway just off the rd.,* ☎ *031/230762. Reservations not accepted. No credit cards.*

$$$ ✕ **Buenos Serras/Totti's.** This Italian restaurant is clean, quiet, and always pleasurable. Most evenings feature a piano bar and a good view of people coming and going in the central square of Thessaloniki. You'll see the famous sign in the square. ⊠ *West side of Aristotelous Sq., just below Electra Palace,* ☎ *031/223216. Reservations not accepted. No credit cards.*

$$$ ✕ **Miami.** Reminiscent of a white and blue Cycladic beach house, this seafood taverna features mezedes and traditional seafood. Newly acquired by the owners of the institution Krikelas, the food is always good, and so is the atmosphere. ⊠ *18 Thetidos, Nea Krini, about 15 min from city center,* ☎ *031/447996. Reservations essential weekends after 9. AE, DC, MC, V.*

$$$ ✕ **Panselino** (Full Moon). This restaurant in a renovated neoclassical mansion has the charm of Syracuses and excellent food, but it will not break the piggy bank. The famous wine cava alone makes this restaurant worth visiting, as do the varietals of the many small lesser-known wineries in Northern Greece on the wine list. ⊠ *133 Vasilis Olgas,* ☎ *031/860978. Reservations essential weekends after 9:30. AE, DC.*

$$ ✕ **Gondola.** This beautiful family seaside taverna in the nearby village of Ayia Triada is a good-quality, low-cost option. The grilled octopus is to die for and their fried everything—from smelts to zucchini—is so light you can't get enough. Dress is very informal, and the seaside view is of the whole skyline of Thessaloniki. ⊠ *Ayia Triada, seafront restaurant strip, 40 min by bus or taxi from city center,* ☎ *0392/51311. Reservations not accepted. No credit cards.*

$$ ✕ **Gonia tis Soulis** (Souli's Corner). This unique secret is a family home converted into an intimate restaurant by Souli herself, which she decorated with all the family bric-a-brac. There is live music nightly but Souli provides the best entertainment, moving from table to table welcoming everyone to her "home" while they savor traditional mezedes. ⊠ *12 Raidestou, just below large church at top of hill at 40 Ekklesias, Upper City,* ☎ *031/201113. Reservations not accepted. No credit cards.*

$$ ✕ **Klimataria.** This grilled-meat taverna is frequented by young and old in Thessaloniki seeking a good meal in a simple atmosphere. The food is well cooked, served with care, and makes for one of the best deals in town. For a special after-dinner treat head across the street to the best chocolate shop in Greece, Hadjifotiou. ⊠ *34 Pavlou Mela, just behind Ayia Sofia church,* ☎ *031/277854. Reservations not accepted. No credit cards.*

$$ ✕ **Tiffany's.** A swank favorite among Thessalonians, one of the highlights at Tiffany's is the setup outside on a pedestrian walk, with the feel of Paris. Its grilled and ready-made foods are, in contrast, the essence of simplicity: tasty and traditional. There are no specialties to recommend—everything is good. ⊠ *3 Iktinou,* ☎ *031/274022. Reservations not accepted. No credit cards.*

Thessaloniki Dining and Lodging

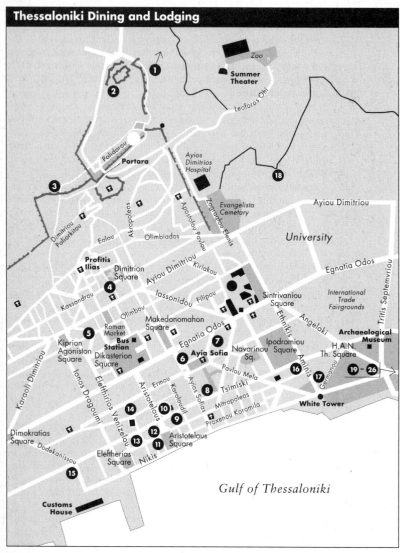

Dining
Aigli, **4**
Aristotelous
Ouzerie, **10**
B&B, **9**
Buenos Serras/
Totti's, **11**
Corner, **6, 17**
Gondola, **23**
Gonia tis Soulis, **18**
Klimataria, **7**
Krikelas, **20**
Miami, **21**
Panselino, **22**
Petros, **14**
Porto Marina, **24**
Syracuses, **25**
Tiffany's, **8**
To Makedoniko, **3**

To Yenti, **2**
Wolves, **19**
Zythos Dore, **16**

Lodging
Astoria , **15**
Electra Palace, **12**
Macedonia Palace, **26**
Olympia, **5**
Philippion, **1**
Tourist, **13**

$$ ✕ **To Yenti.** This charming taverna-ouzeri opened a few years ago in a wonderfully rustic area in the Upper City, with tables in the street, on the sidewalk, and under the trees. It serves delicious, well-prepared typical taverna food, grilled and ready-made, definitely the best in the old city. Try the *keftedes* (fried meatballs) and the excellent mezedes. It's now one of the in places to go in the evenings and on Saturday afternoons, so arrive before 9 PM. ✉ *7 Ioannis Papareka, outside gates of castle of Eptapyrghion,* ☎ *031/246495. Reservations not accepted. No credit cards. Closed Sun.*

$$ ✕ **Wolves.** The name comes from the original owner's allegiance to what was then England's number one soccer club. It's also called, in Greek, *Oi Lykoi,* and the name has nothing to do either with the menu or the attitude of the staff. It is renowned for classic Greek fare such as moussaka and *pastitsio* (a casserole of pasta, meat, and cheese with cinnamon). ✉ *6 Vasilis Olgas,* ☎ *031/812855. Reservations not accepted. No credit cards. No dinner Sun.*

$$ ✕ **Zythos Dore.** Named for the famous original Zythos, the Dore features beers from around the world and a casual menu. It's noisy and crowded, but lots of fun, and it has the best view of the White Tower. ✉ *7 Tsiroyiannis, across a little park near White Tower,* ☎ *031/279010. Reservations not accepted. No credit cards.*

$ ✕ **Corner.** This place makes the best pizzas in town, baked to perfection in a wood-burning oven. The ice cream and sweets are also tasty. It's a great favorite with the younger crowd. ✉ *42 Ayios Sofias, 1 block north of White Tower,* ☎ *031/426531. Reservations not accepted. No credit cards.*

$ ✕ **Petros.** It's small and packed with all kinds of characters from the market, including gypsy musicians. Petros and his son cook tasty mezedes, seafood casseroles, grilled meats, and batter-fried cod. ✉ *Inside western entrance of Modiano market. Reservations not accepted. No credit cards. Closed Sun.*

$ ✕ **To Makedoniko.** This extremely basic taverna is a favorite among university students and young professionals—hence crowded, but not touristy. Actually built into an arch on the western edge of the old walls of the Upper City, it remains rather unadorned. Favorites include mussels in broth and grilled meats. If you're feeling daring, order the local firewater called *tsipouro* (a variety of ouzo). ✉ *32 Giorgiou Papadopoulou,* ☎ *031/627438. Reservations not accepted. No credit cards. Closed Sun.*

Lodging

$$$$ 🏨 **Electra Palace.** The city's second-best, this functional, modern, well-
★ kept hotel is centrally located, with a view of the square and the sea. It's not immune, however, to noise from the streets and from the events—political and musical—that take place on the square. ✉ *9 Aristotelous Sq., 54624,* ☎ *031/232221 through 232229,* 🖷 *031/235947. 65 rooms with bath, 5 suites. 2 restaurants, bar, air-conditioning, refrigerators, limited convention center. AE, MC, V.*

$$$$ 🏨 **Macedonia Palace.** This especially delightful, historic luxury hotel
★ has reopened after a considerable face-lift. One of the only buildings rising on the coastline, this hotel offers stunning views of the city and bay from its rooftop bar. The adjacent boardwalk is great for early-morning or late-night runs, walks, and people-watching. The state-of-the-art convention center lures plenty of business travelers. ✉ *2 Alexander the Great Ave., 54640,* ☎ *031/861400,* 🖷 *031/832291. 272 rooms with bath, 16 suites. 3 restaurants, 2 bars, 3 pools, beauty salon, spa, shop, meeting rooms. AE, DC, MC, V.*

$$$ ⊞ **Astoria.** This newly renovated hotel is one of the city's best, although it's somewhat out of the way in an uninspiring, traffic-ridden commercial district. But the nearby picturesque area of Ladadika offers redemption—and it's clean, functional, and well kept, with TVs. ⊠ *7 Salaminos, at western end of Tsimiski, 54626,* ☎ *031/554902,* FAX *031/531564. 84 rooms with bath, 6 suites. Restaurant, bar, air-conditioning, minibars, meeting rooms, limited free parking. AE, MC, V.*

$$$ ⊞ **Olympia.** This clean, functional, modern hotel has the advantage of being near the flea market, copper market, Roman Forum, and Ayios Dimitrios. It is simple but very professionally managed. ⊠ *65 Olympou, 54631,* ☎ *031/235421,* FAX *031/276133. 115 rooms with bath. Restaurant, bar, cafeteria, air-conditioning, meeting rooms. AE, DC, MC, V.*

$$$ ⊞ **Philippion.** This is a perfect place for those who dislike staying in the city center, particularly in summer. Modern and well appointed, with color TVs and direct-dial phones, it sits in the middle of the forest of Sheih-Sou on a hilltop overlooking Thessaloniki. The city center is 5 km (3 mi) away, a 15-minute ride on the hotel shuttle bus, which leaves by prearranged schedule (available at the desk) mornings intermittently until 3 PM. The airport, too, is an easy 15-minute drive away, and the highway to Chalkidiki is readily accessible. ⊠ *Box 19002, 56610,* ☎ *031/203321,* FAX *031/218528. 84 rooms with bath, 4 suites. Restaurant, bar, coffee shop, grill, air-conditioning, minibars, 2 nightclubs, business services, meeting rooms, free parking. AE, DC, MC, V.*

$$ ⊞ **Tourist.** This extremely modest family-run hotel has none of the incipient sleaziness that hotels of its price range tend to adapt when they cater to students and businessmen. It's in a dignified high-ceiling building built around the turn of the century, and it has absolutely no frills: single rooms, for example, have bathrooms and toilets down the hall. But, for modest budgets, it is the best in the city. ⊠ *Mitropoleos 21, in city center, 1 block west of Aristotelous Sq., 54624,* ☎ *031/276335. 37 rooms, some with shared bath. No credit cards.*

Nightlife and the Arts

Nightlife

Thessaloniki's nightlife in winter is one of its true assets. The countless bars, pubs, breweries, discos, and clubs within the city center—particularly in the area east of Aristotelous Square—fill the streets with an endless barrage of young people in search of fun. In summer, most clubs close, as their clients flock to the beaches of Chalkidiki. There are several very classy discothèques on the road to the airport, but since they go in and out of fashion very quickly, it is best not to make recommendations among them. Ask at your hotel for the newest and best.

CASINO

A new and exciting addition to Thessaloniki nightlife is the **Hyatt Regency Casino** (⊠ Just outside of the airport, ☎ 031/491234, FAX 031/476129), said to be the largest and most elaborate in all of Europe. The entrance fee is 2,000 dr., which includes markers for slot machines; it's open daily 1 PM–8 AM.

CLUBS

One club that does stay open year-round is the extraordinary **Mylos** (⊠ 25 Andreadou Georgiou, on the southwest edge of the city just off October 28th St., ☎ 031/516945), a complex of clubs, bars, discothèques, bars and ouzeri-taverna, art galleries, and a concert stage that has become perhaps the best venue in all of Greece for jazz, folk, and pop groups, Greek and foreign. Visiting foreign and Greek pop, jazz, and folk artists occasionally appear at the **Palais de Sports** (⊠ International Trade Fairgrounds), and at Mylos.

To trumpet the cultural celebration, a 1997 **Jazz Week** was planned at press time for March 1–9, with seminars and concerts by jazz gurus at local clubs such as **Malt and Jazz, Indrogeios, The Mill,** and **Radio City.**

The Arts

As the Cultural Capital of Europe, in 1997 Thessaloniki will host a number of exhibitions, special performances, and excellent artists from all over Europe throughout the year. Check with your hotel or the Greek National Tourist Organization (GNTO or EOT) for current happenings.

FESTIVALS

No chapter on Northern Greece would be complete without mention of its famous *anastanarides* (fire dancers). Every year on May 21, the feast day of Saints Constantine and Eleni, groups of religious devotees in the villages of **Langadha** (⊠ 15 mi north of Thessaloniki) and **Ayia Eleni** (⊠ 50 mi northeast of Thessaloniki) take part in a three-day rite called the *pirovassia* (literally, "fire dancing") in which they dance barefoot unharmed over a bed of hot coals while holding the saints' icons. Although assumed to be of pre-Christian origin, the tradition adopted its Christian aspects about 1250 in the eastern Thracian village of Kosti. At this time the villagers are said to have rescued the original icons from a burning church, icons and rescuers unharmed by the blaze. For information, check with the EOT or American Educational Services (☞ Visitor Information *in* Northern Greece A to Z, *below*).

In mid-September the **International Trade festival** is celebrated at the Fairgrounds just north of the archaeological museum, marked by the modern, pinnacled tower of the Greek Telecommunications Organization (OTE), called the Pirgos Oté.

St. Dimitrios's feast is celebrated on October 26, but its secular adjunct has developed into a series of cultural events that brings an enormous amount of outside commerce. The October **Dimitria festival** exhibits works by artists and musicians from all over the country, including the Greek Film Festival (☞ *below*).

FILM

Most theaters in the city center close in summer, but there are a few outdoor cinemas in the city center and suburbs, which show movies in English with Greek subtitles. You'll be immersed in Greek community life; seeing friends meeting and greeting and neighbors watching from their balconies is part of the fun. Check the local papers and ask at your hotel. In October, there is an annual **Greek Film Festival,** but, as the title implies, movies are all in Greek.

MUSIC

A number of international orchestras will be performing throughout 1997. The **Municipal Orchestra of Thessaloniki** plays at its concert hall (⊠ In the university, just opposite the northern entrance of the International Trade Fairgrounds) from fall through spring.

THEATER

In winter, the State Theater of Northern Greece sponsors plays, ballets, and special performances of visiting artists at the **Kratiko Theatro** (State Theater) (⊠ Just opposite the White Tower (☎ 031/223785). In summer, performances are given at the **Theatro Kypou** (Garden Theater) (⊠ In Municipal Park off Germanou St. between State Theater and archaeological museum) and at **Theatro Dasous** (Forest Theater) (⊠ In the forest east of the Upper City, ☎ 031/218092). All performances are in Greek, although there are occasional visits by English-speaking groups.

Outdoor Activities and Sports

Beaches

Beaches in Thessaloniki and its suburbs are on water too polluted to be recommended, even though you may see locals swimming there.

The nearest safe beaches are in **Perea** and **Ayia Triada,** past the airport, about 15 and 25 km (10 and 15 mi, just over half an hour by bus) away, respectively, from the Thessaloniki city center. At **Ayia Triada,** on the headland of the bay, the EOT runs a bathing facility at
Akti Thermaikou (⊠ Ayia Triada, ☎ 0392/51352), with changing cabins, snack bars, tennis courts, and a children's playground.

Participant Sports

HORSEBACK RIDING

Contact **ALMA,** the eco-adventure tourism office, which can help you arrange daily riding or weeklong riding excursions in recommended areas (☞ Contacts and Resources *in* Northern Greece A to Z, *below).* The **Thessaloniki Riding Club** (⊠ Panorama, near Anatolia College, ☎ 031/270676) has riding outside of the city.

TENNIS

Courts can be rented at the **Poseidonion Athletic Center** (⊠ Nea Paralia and 25th of March St., at the eastern end of the seaside promenade, ☎ 031/428453). Outside the city try **Anatolia College** (⊠ On the road to Panorama after Pylea village, ☎ 031/323711) and **Akti Thermaikou** (⊠ Ayia Triada, ☎ 0392/51352).

Waterland, a water-activity amusement park (⊠ Off the highway to Chalkidiki, just past the airport exit), has six well-kept courts available at inexpensive prices. It's especially nice for families, as there is something for everyone—wave pools, water slides, children's pools, restaurants, and basketball courts.

Spectator Sports

BASKETBALL

Thessaloniki has three of the best basketball teams in the country: **Aris, Iraklis,** and **PAOK,** all three with one American and one or two Eastern Europeans on the roster. Aris and POAK play at the Palais de Sport, the domed athletic center within the International Trade Fairgrounds; Iraklis has its own large sports complex north of the university.

SOCCER

Two of the best teams in Greece—again **Aris** and **PAOK**—play their seasons in the spring and fall. The Aris stadium is in the suburb of Harilaou (⊠ Papanastasiou St., about a km north of the seafront amusement park, ☎ 031/305402). The PAOK stadium is several blocks northeast of the International Trade Fairgrounds (☎ 031/238560).

Shopping

Despite its cosmopolitan polish, Thessaloniki has nowhere near the choice or variety of goods for tourists' tastes as those found in Athens, although interesting items can be picked up in the shops of local craftspeople.

Complicated regulations control the opening and closing hours of shops. The afternoon siesta is still honored, which means that the shops are open from about 9 to 1:30 or 2, and most open again in the evenings, but only on Tuesday, Thursday, and Friday, and never in July.

The best shopping streets are Tsimiski, Mitropoleos, and Proxenou Koromila, which run east–west, between Pavlou Mela (the diagonal street connecting Ayios Sofias with the White Tower) and Eleftherios Venizelou.

Antiques

Several antiques shops on Mitropoleos Street between Ayios Sofias and the White Tower are perfect for leisurely browsing. One of the best is **Relics** (✉ 6 Giorgio Lassani, east of Mitropoleos cathedral), which has an interesting selection of non-Classical, exportable antiques; look for quality, not bargains. The best place to shop for antiques—besides prowling through the **street markets**—are in the narrow streets around the **Rotunda** and the **flea market** on Tositsa Street. The latter offers a marvelous jumble of fascinating, musty old shops, with the wares of itinerant junk collectors spread out on the sidewalks, intermingled with small upscale antiques shops.

Books

Newspapers and magazines are also sold at kiosks at the intersection of Tsimiski and Aristotelou streets and at another kiosk near the White Tower.

Both of the following two bookstores are rich with beautifully illustrated children's books on ancient Greek heroes and myths—a thoughtful gift to take home.

The oldest bookshop in the city is **Molchos** (✉ 10 Tsimiski, just west of Elefthirios Venizelou), which has a wide selection of newspapers and magazines in myriad languages, and specializes in English and French books. **Ianos** (✉ 7 Aristotelous St., just north of Electra Palace) is another well-stocked bookstore for foreign travelers.

Greek Souvenirs

The shop **ZM,** or Zeeta Mee (✉ 1 Proxeno Koromila), sells a high-class selection of various Greek crafts. In the entrance of **Ayios Dimitrios** you can find an interesting display of Greek handmade crochet and embroidery from the women of the parish, all proceeds of which go to various charities. **La Rose** (✉ 24 Tsimiski, at the lower end of Tottis Arcade) is an absolutely charming little shop featuring the popular Greek blown blue glass in every form imaginable. They also have an excellent selection of charms for protection from the Evil Eye.

Just south of Egnatia Odos, in the narrow streets between Aristotelous and Ayios Sofias, is a lovely area—chock-full of local color—in which many small craft shops have recently been opened by the craftspeople themselves. A most unusual one is named after **Haido,** the beautiful woman who creates works of art from tin and clay.

Jewelry

The jeweler at **Marina** (✉ 62 Mitropoleos) has worked for such famous houses as LALAoUNIS, and sells copies of their designs as well as her own. On the **Gold Strip** (✉ Area on Egnatia Odos between Aristotelous St. and Elefthirios Venezelou) you can window-shop the dozens of small, family-owned jewelry shops until the perfect bauble catches your eye.

Leather Goods

Elegant leather coats and accessories can be found in several shops on Tsimiski between Ayios Sofias and Aristotelous. In the southwest corner of the outdoor Modiano market, near the Grigoris Lambrakis memorial, a number of shops sell bags, sandals, and other leather items that are less expensive than they are elsewhere in Greece, but of good quality.

Perfumes

Aroma (✉ 62 Mitropoleos, next door to Marina) sells copies of famous scents and will mix your own cost-effective blend.

Sweets

It seems that every neighborhood in Thessaloniki can claim the city's best candy shop—and each has a delicious specialty. The truth is that as you walk through the city, you can usually find the best sweetshops by the seductive aroma. One of the best is **Agapitos** (⊠ North side of Tsimiski between Ayios Sofias and Karolou Dil), which aptly means "loved one," owned by the oldest son of a venerable Thessaloniki family.

Toys and Handicrafts

Very few toy stores here sell Greek toys, but a wonderful and inexpensive locally produced gift found in many of the city's toy stores is the playful **Kouvalias** pull toy. They are usually hidden away behind the more glamorous toys, but look for their bright paint and solid-wood construction.

One delightful store is **Skitso** (⊠ 11 Grigori Palama, a short diagonal street between Tsimiski and Platia Navarino), which sells a cornucopia of toys, ships, puppets, crosses, and other handmade objects. **Rotunda** (⊠ Just behind the Rotunda, off Sintrivaniou Sq.) offers some interesting Greek toys.

CENTRAL MACEDONIA

Pella, Vergina, Dion, Mt. Olympus

Pella, Vergina, and Dion are three major sites of Central Macedonia connected to Alexander the Great. You can explore all three on a day trip from Thessaloniki, or, after seeing the first two, spend the night near Dion or Mt. Olympus, and visit both of these the next day.

In the 7th century BC the Dorian Makednoi tribe moved out of the Pindos mountains (between Epirus and Macedonia), settled in the fertile plains below, and established a religious center at the sacred springs of Dion at the foot of Mt. Olympus. Perdiccas, the first king of the Macedonians, held court at a place called Aigai, now known to have been at Vergina, and in the 5th century BC, the king of that time, Archelaos (413–399), moved his capital from Aigai to Pella, which was then on a rise above a lagoon leading to the Thermaic Gulf.

In 359 BC, after a succession of kings and assassinations and near anarchy exacerbated by the raids of barbarian tribes from the north, the 23-year-old Philip II was elected regent. Philip II pulled the kingdom together through diplomacy and by his seven marriages, and then began expanding it, taking in the all-important gold mines of the Pangeon mountains, and founding Philippi there. In 356 BC, on the day that Alexander the Great was born, Philip II was said to have simultaneously taken the strategic port of Potidea in Chalkidiki, received news of his horse's triumph in the Olympic Games, and learned of a general's victory against the Illyrians. That was also the day the temple of Artemis at Ephesus was destroyed by fire, which later prompted people to say that the goddess was away on that day, tending to Alexander's birth. In 336 BC, Philip II was assassinated in Vergina at a wedding party for one of his daughters. It was assumed that his tomb there had been looted and lost, until it was discovered in 1977 by the Greek archaeologist Manolis Andronikos. Alexander, then 20, assumed power, and within two years he had gathered an army to be blessed at Dion, before setting off to conquer the Persians and most of the known world.

Pella

 40 km (25 mi) west of Thessaloniki.

Pella, Alexander's birthplace, is farthest from the sea of all sites. A sign on the right points to the modern-day village, but the archaeological site and its museum are both on the main road toward Edessa. It's best to visit the museum first to understand what you will see at the site.

The **museum** stands just northwest of the old lagoon; it contains artifacts of 7th-century BC Bronze and Iron Age settlers and from the first migrations of Neolithic era. There is a wonderful model of the 4th-century BC dwelling that stood across the road, as well as several beautiful mosaics from its floors. Note also the unique statuette of a horned Athena, apparently influenced by Minoan Crete, and the statue of Alexander sprouting the horns of Pan. ⊠ *Pella, Archaeological Site and Museum,* ☎ *0383/31160 or 0383/31278.* ☞ *800 dr.* ☉ *Weekdays 8–7, weekends and holidays 8:30–3.*

In 1914, two years after the departure of the Turks, the people who lived on the land were moved to a village north of here, and excavations of the **ancient site** began. Finds have since been made over an area covering about 5 sq mi, and in 1987, on a small rise to the north, the remains of the **palace** came to light, though at present they're of little interest to the general public. It's hoped that the **theater** where Euripides' *The Bacchae* was first performed may also be located (he is known to have written while in exile at the court).

Four important 4th-century BC **Macedonian tombs** with magnificent frescoes can be seen (⊠ Along the main road, before the turn off to Naoussa).

OFF THE
BEATEN PATH

KASTORIA AND LAKES OF PRESPA – Nestled in the Pindos mountains in Western Macedonia, 221 km (137 mi) west of Thessaloniki and 168 km (104 mi) west of Pella, is the beautiful town of Kastoria. It sits on a promontory projecting into a lake garlanded in poplar and willow trees and mirroring the mountains, while ducks, swans, and flat-bottom skiffs glide across the surface. In the Byzantine era, the town was famous for its Macedonian school of religious painting; its many fine Byzantine churches are richly decorated with frescoes and icons. Today, it is famous for its fur trade, and shops all over the city offer fur-tail key rings, slippers, vests, hats, and mink coats. Two hours by car northwest of Kastoria are the serenely lovely lakes of Prespa, along the border Greece shares with Albania and the former Yugoslavia. Officially designated bird sanctuaries, they are home to more than 250 species of birds—65 of which are internationally recognized as rare or endangered species.

Vergina

 135 km (84 mi) southwest of Thessaloniki.

After visiting the archaeological museum in Thessaloniki, you will be prepped for the archaeological site at Vergina. The **Royal Tombs** of Vergina were opened to the public only in 1993, 16 years after their sensational discovery. For years, both archaeologists and grave robbers had suspected that the large tumulus mound that stood on this site might contain something of value, but try as they might, neither of these professional groups were successful in penetrating its secret. In his fascinating book, *The Royal Tombs of Vergina,* Professor Andronikos theorizes that one of Alexander's successors, wanting to protect Philip's tomb from robbers, had covered it with broken debris and

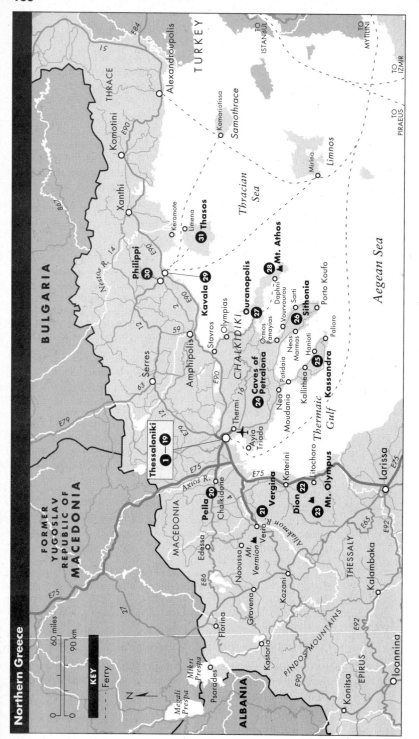

Northern Greece

tombstones to make it appear that the grave had already been plundered and then built the tumulus so that Philip's tomb would be near the edge rather than the center. But this was speculation after the fact: when Andronikos discovered it, on the last day of excavation in 1977 before closing the site for the winter, he had been trying one of the last approaches, with little hope of finding anything. Certainly not the tomb of Philip II, as pristine as the day it was closed.

This was the first intact Macedonian tomb ever found, and though its treasures were spirited off to Thessaloniki that very night (where they can be seen in the archaeological museum), the tombs themselves are very much worth visiting. You walk down a white sandstone ramp into the partially underground structure that contains the tombs. It is roofed over by a large earth-covered dome approximately the size of the original tumulus. In an open area on the left are two tombs and one altar that had been looted and destroyed in varying degrees by the time Andronikos discovered them. Macedonian Tomb III, on the right, found intact in 1978, is believed to be that of the young Prince Alexander IV, who was at first kept alive by his "protectors" after Alexander's death and then poisoned (along with his mother) when he was 14.

To the left of Tomb III is that of Philip II. He was assassinated a km or so away from here; his body was burned, his bones washed in wine, wrapped in royal purple, and put into the solid gold larnax with the 16-point sun that's now in the Thessaloniki museum. His wife, Cleopatra, was later buried with him. ⊠ *Archaeological site,* ☎ *031/830538.* 🎟 *1,200 dr.* ☉ *Tues.–Sun. 8:30–3.*

The winding road to the **site of Philip's assassination** goes through rolling countryside west of the village, much of it part of the vast royal **burial grounds of ancient Aigai.** On the way, you pass three more Macedonian tombs, rough-hewn stone structures in typical Macedonian style, of little interest. The palace itself is nothing more than a line of foundation stones that shows the outline of its walls. It was discovered by French archaeologists in 1861 but not thought to have any particular significance; ancient Aigai was then thought to be somewhere near Edessa. In the field just below are the remnants of the **theater,** located by Andronikos in 1982. It was on his way here for the wedding games that were to follow the marriage of his daughter to the king of Epirus that Philip was murdered.

Dion

22 *87 km (54 mi) southwest of Thessaloniki.*

At the foothills of Mt. Olympus lies ancient Dion. Even before Zeus and the Olympian gods, Mt. Olympus was home to the Muses and Orpheus, who entranced the men of the area with his mystical music. The story says that the life-giving force of Dion came from the waters in which the murderers of Orpheus (the women of Mt. Olympus, jealous for attention from their men) washed their hands on the slopes of the sacred mountain to remove the stain of their own sin. The waters entered the earth to cleanse itself, and rose again in the holy city of Dion. Today, underground streams from the sacred mountain emerge where ancient Dion was founded, consecrating the ground, as it were, with its bubbling, life-giving springs.

Although a lesser known ancient site to the non-Greek visitor, Dion is especially exciting because of daily discoveries throughout the year. The superb **museum** contains the best of a burgeoning number of finds from the area, which is still under intense excavation. It's best to visit the museum first and view the videotape (in English) prepared by the site's renowned archaeologist, Dimitris Pandermalis, which describes the excavations, the finds, and their significance. (His efforts to keep the artifacts in the place where they were found have won him the unqualified admiration of the villagers and established a new trend for decentralization of archaeological finds throughout Greece.) On the second floor, there is an excellent topographical relief of the area, and in the basement you'll see a wooden model of the ancient city and interactive learning centers set up for young people to better understand the daily life of ancient Greece.

Among the finds, which are grouped as they were found, are items from the oldest known sanctuary, that of Demeter, from the 5th century BC, and those of the early Christian and Byzantine eras. One of the most significant recent finds—particularly in light of Skopje's recent claims to the name of Macedonia—is of a stele from the mid-5th century BC inscribed in ancient Greek, which shows a strong Greek presence here many centuries before Tito gave the name Macedonia to the eastern province of his new confederation. The remains of the oldest known copper water-powered organ (2nd–1st century BC) were uncovered in 1992. ✉ *Next to archaeological site,* ☎ *0351/53206.* 🎫 *800 dr.* ⊙ *Mon. 12:30–7, Tues.–Sun. 8–7.*

The road from the museum divides the diggings at the **archaeological site** into two areas. On the left is the **ancient city** of Dion itself, with the juxtaposition of public toilets and several superb floor mosaics. On the right side is the **ancient theater** and, a bit farther on, the **Sanctuaries of Asklepios and Demeter** and the **Sanctuary of Isis.** In the latter, a vividly beautiful approximation of how it once looked, copies of the original statues, now in the museum, have been put in place.

Iron Age graves show a religious use of the area as early as the 7th century BC, but it was officially made a place of worship in the 5th century BC, when King Archelaos erected a sanctuary to Zeus, the theater, and a stadium. The northern Greek Olympics took place here at the same time as the southern Olympics. In the time of Philip and Alexander, Dion was used as a religious military center for giving thanks for victories and asking the gods for blessings, as Alexander did before setting off to conquer Asia. It is said, too, that at Dion, Alexander, age 12, received the gift of his famous horse, Bucephalus. The Romans, too, used Dion as a place of worship, as did the Christians, who established a bishopric there. A series of devastating earthquakes in the 4th–6th centuries AD caused the abandonment of the area. ✉ *Archaeological site,* ☎ *0351/53206.* 🎫 *800 dr.* ⊙ *Tues.–Sun. 8:30–3.*

Dining and Lodging

$$ ✕ **Dionysos.** This place looks like a combination tourist shop, café, and restaurant—which it is. In a setting of rather varnished modernity, it has excellent food and good, cheerful service. Try the specialty of the area, roast goat on a spit. Also recommended are the *loukaniko* (sausages), rolled, spiced, and spit-roasted meat, and the *saganaki* (fried feta or kefaloteri). ✉ *Village center, directly opposite museum,* ☎ *0351/53276. Open year-round. No credit cards.*

$ 🏨 **Dion Resort Hotel.** This resort's advantage is its proximity to the beach, Mt. Olympus, and the archaeological site. Every room has an excellent view, of either the sea or the peaks. Direct-dial phones are available. ✉ *Paralia Dion, 60100,* ☎ *0352/61222,* 🖷 *0352/61220. 200 rooms. Restaurant, bar, air-conditioning, minibars, snack bar, 2 pools, tennis court, limited water sports. AE, DC, MC, V.*

Mt. Olympus

㉓ *100 km (62 mi) southwest of Thessaloniki, 17 km (10½ mi) southwest of Dion.*

Driving from the sea to Mt. Olympus it appears as a conglomeration of thickly bunched summits and not as a majestic single peak. To understand how the mountain must have impressed the ancient Greeks and caused them to shift their allegiance from the earth-rooted deities of the Mycenaeans to those on the airy heights of Olympus, you need to see the mountain clearly from several different perspectives. From the south, if there is still snow on the range, it appears as a massive, flat-topped acropolis, much like the one in Athens, its vast snowy crest hovering in the air, seemingly capable of supporting as many gods and temples as the ancients could have imagined. On its northern side, the Olympus range catches all the clouds, gathering them in a turbulent, stormy bundle and letting fly about 12 times as many (surely Zeus-inspired) thunder-and-lightning storms as anywhere else in Greece. The third perspective comes from actually climbing the mountain, to the truly awe-inspiring summit at the throne of Zeus.

If you hike up Mt. Olympus (☞ *below*), when you descend from Prionia take time to visit the **monastery of Ayios Dionysus** (⊠ In the forest at the bottom of a turnoff to the right just below the refuge). During World War II, the monastery, rightly suspected of harboring resistance fighters, was blown up by the Nazis. It is now slowly being restored by the single monk who lives there, and in its unfinished state it has a stark and impressive beauty.

Lodging

$$ 🏨 **Aphrodite Hotel.** This one, on the village square, is of the same size and quality and has a decor similar to the Myrto's (☞ *below*), but lacks its character. ⊠ *Litochoro, 60200 Macedonia,* ☎ *0352/81415 and 0352/21868. 24 rooms, 10 with private baths, 14 with shared bath. No credit cards.*

$$ 🏨 **Hotel Myrto.** This is the best hotel in Litochoro village, bright and clean, and extremely well run. White walls and wooden decor give it a cheery Alpine flavor, and every room has a lovely view. ⊠ *Litochoro, a little off the main rd., 60200,* ☎ *0352/81498. 18 rooms with bath. No credit cards.*

Outdoor Activities and Sports

HIKING

Mt. Olympus also provides the traveler with some of the most beautiful nature trails in Europe. Mt. Olympus has hundreds of species of wildflowers and herbs in the spring, over 85 of which are found only on this mountain.

From **Litochoro** you can climb all the way on foot or take a car to the end of the road at Prionia and trek the rest of the way. The climb to Prionia takes about four hours; the ride, on a bumpy gravel road with no guardrails between you and breathtakingly precipitous drops, takes a little less than an hour, depending on your nerves. If you can manage to take your eyes off the road, the scenery is magnificent. There's a hiking refuge **Spilios Agapitos** (Refuge A) (⊠ Two-thirds of the way to the summit, ☎ 0352/81800) run by Kostas Zolotas, the venerable English-speaking guru of climbers. In the morning, it is just another two hours—some of it a bit hair-raising—to the Throne of Zeus and the summit, at 2,972 meters (9,751 feet). The trail is snow-free from about mid-May until late October. For further details, contact ALMA or the Hellenic Alpine Club (☞ Contacts and Resources *in* Northern Greece A to Z, *below*).

EASTERN MACEDONIA

Chalkidiki, Kavala, Philippi, Thasos

Eastern Macedonia, with its beautiful beaches and Mediterranean landscape, has had a considerably less violent history. It was colonized in the 5th century BC by settlers from Athens and Evia, and later in 1922 saw large numbers of Greek refugees resettled from Asia Minor in the exchange of populations.

Caves of Petralona

㉔ *50 km (31 mi) southeast of Thessaloniki.*

On the first peninsula of the three-fingered hand of Chalkidiki, you can stop at the dramatic Paleolithic caves of Petralona. A shepherd looking for a hole to hide in as German bombers flew over first stumbled on the caves in the early 1940s, but their significance was not understood until a villager looking for an underground stream in 1960 discovered the skull of a Paleolithic female, some 500,000 years old. These caves have now been made accessible; walkways take you through them, and dramatically lit grottoes contain life-size figures of cave dwellers squatting before their fires. ✉ *10 mi before turnoff for Nea Moudania,* ☎ *0396/31300.* 🎫 *800 dr.* ☉ *Daily 9–5.*

Kassandra

㉕ *69 km (43 mi) southeast of Thessaloniki, 19 km (11¾ mi) southeast of the Caves of Petralona.*

The peninsula of Kassandra was named after Cassander, the man who founded Thessaloniki. He also named a city on the peninsula after himself, presently called **Potidaia,** which once was important but gradually faded into insignificance as Thessaloniki became the major port. The small canal that leads to the town was cut across the isthmus in 1937.

Kassandra's marvelous beaches and its proximity to Thessaloniki have made it the most popular—and populous—resort area in Chalkidiki. Its variegated landscape and forested promontories isolate the resort areas from one another, so it never feels too crowded. Aside from a plethora of fast-food joints, discothèques, and shopping centers, it also has excellent hotels and resort complexes. For an interesting look at how the Greeks celebrate their vacations, take a dip into the energy being generated at the seaside villages of **Hanioti** and **Palioro** near the tip of the peninsula, particularly in the evenings.

Lodging

$$$$ ⚏ **Athos Palace.** Along with its sister hotel, the Pallini Beach, this is one of the best in the area. The modern building has well-landscaped grounds, excellent service, and a wonderful beach. But it also has a lot of guests. ✉ *Kallithea, 63077 Kassandra, Chalkidiki,* ☎ *0374/22100 through 22109,* 🖷 *0374/23605. 465 rooms with bath, 44 suites, 18 bungalows. 2 restaurants, 2 bars, air-conditioning, 2 pools, horseback riding, nightclub, meeting room. AE, DC, MC, V.*

$$$$ ⚏ **Pallini Beach.** Like the Athos Palace, next door, this is an excellent hotel, but it's crowded in summer. It shares the great beach with its next-door neighbor. All accommodations except bungalows are air-conditioned. ✉ *Kallithea, 63077 Kassandra, Chalkidiki,* ☎ *0374/22480 through 22489,* 🖷 *0374/22489. 345 rooms with bath, 98 bungalows. Restaurant, bar, cafeteria, pool, dance club, convention center. AE, DC, MC, V.*

Sithonia

 76 km (47½ mi) southeast of Thessaloniki, 26 km (16 mi) east of Kassandra.

The second peninsula, Sithonia, has perhaps the most beautiful scenery and coastline in all of Chalkidiki. A tour around the entire peninsula is highly recommended; with leisurely stops for lunch and a swim, the entire journey can be completed in 4 to 5 hours. Each small village is more inviting than the last, but keep in mind that most establishments on the peninsula are open only during the tourist season (May–late October).

The area of **Ormos Panayias** and its adjoining bay of **Vourvourou** provides the most idyllic setting in Northern Greece. Tiny pine-blanketed islands dot the shoreline and harbor, and passersby are instantly seized with an overwhelming desire to stay there forever.

On the drive south, excellent views of the holy peninsula of Mt. Athos rising in splendor across the bay fall short of epiphanic. **Sarti,** the next village down from Vourvourou, is the fishing port settled by refugees in the 1922 population exchange with Turkey. There is a favorable eclectic quality in the haphazard manner in which it was put together, with each family building its house according to its own dreams, resulting in a glorious lack of uniformity and, sometimes, taste. The beach is long and wide and it drifts right up to the little flower gardens in front of the houses. There are many rooming houses, and one hotel on the southern outskirts of the village.

The lovely secluded bay of **Porto Koufo,** on the western end of the tip of the peninsula, is almost completely encircled by rocky headlands. It has several tavernas, their setting warranting an eye-opening, relaxing drink. North of Porto Koufo are a succession of small, not-yet-overly-commercialized beach communities, of which nearby **Toroni,** with a few tavernas and cafés and an excellent beach, is probably the most picturesque.

In the fishing village of **Neos Marmaras,** north of Torini, caïques bob in the harbor and numerous cafés, tavernas, bars, and restaurants line the seafront. There are no hotels, however, just a number of rooming houses.

En Route If you are bypassing Kassandra and Sithonia peninsulas, the best route from Thessaloniki to Chalkidiki's easternmost peninsula is not, as it would seem, directly across the palm to Ouranopolis. The route from west to east involves much uphill driving, particularly frustrating if you get behind a bus or truck. Therefore, leave Thessaloniki at Platia Vardaris, take the E79 north toward Serres, then turn east onto the E90 toward Kavala. Continue past the long and beautiful lakes of **Koronia** and **Volvi** until you come to the forested turnoff for the coast, signposted to **Stavros** and **Olympias.** Between these charming little fishing villages (as yet relatively unravaged), you'll see some of the most spectacular landscape—rivaling Big Sur—as the road travels high above the coast through pine-scented forests. After Olympias comes the mining town of **Stratoni,** which appears irresistible from above, but is most depressing up close. You'll pass **Nea Roda,** near the site of Xerxes's Canal, dug by the Persian king in 480 BC in order to avoid the dangerous trip around Mt. Athos. Today the canal is barely visible in the grassy, marshy land.

Ouranopolis

110 km (68½ mi) east of Thessaloniki.

Ouranopolis is a charming cul-de-sac on the final point of land that separates the secular world from the sacred walled-off sanctuaries of

Mt. Athos. The village, noted for its rug and tapestry weaving, is particularly entrancing because of the bay.

Ouranopolis was settled by refugees from Asia Minor in 1922 and before that was occupied only by monks from Mt. Athos, who lived in the Byzantine **Tower of Proforion** (⊠ On the point), built in the 12th century by Emperor Andronicus II. When the villagers arrived, the monks fled, and the tower subsequently became the abode of Joice and Sydney Loch, a couple who worked with Thessaloniki's noted American Farm School to help the refugees develop their rug-weaving industry. The tower has now been fully restored and is occasionally open for various exhibitions by local artists.

Floating on its turquoise waters are the **tiny islands** and **atolls** of **Drenia** and **Amouliani,** which are reachable by a 15-minute caïque ride and by small outboard motorboats, which you can rent by the day. All have glorious white sand beaches and two—**Gaidoronisi** (part of the Drenia group) and **Amouliani**—have places to eat.

Dining and Lodging

$$ ✕ **Kritikos.** This family-run restaurant offers the village's best in freshness, prices, and seafood. The decor is provincial, but the food is divine. The family re-creates traditional village recipes—but never gives away the secrets. Try their lobster with pasta and delight in haute cuisine on paper tablecloths. The owner is a local fisherman, so everything is fresh catch of the day. ⊠ *Town center, just north of village sq. (You may have to ask the way). No credit cards.*

$$ ✕ **Skites Restaurant.** On a terrace overlooking the sea, in the hotel of
★   the same name, this restaurant serves some of the best food in the most interesting atmosphere. The home-cooked meals change from day to day, according to the season, but everything offered is bound to be good. ⊠ *Skites Hotel, southeast of Ouranopolis,* ☎ *0377/71140. No credit cards.*

$$ ✕ **Sugar.** Maybe this restaurant-bistro's newer status explains its affinity for light, good-quality fare. The pasta, drinks, and view of the marina and promenade leading to Mt. Athos are all worthy of a return trip. ⊠ *Port,* ☎ *0377/71319. No credit cards.*

$$$ ▦ **Xenia.** This hotel, tucked under tamarisk trees on the beach entering Ouranopolis, is definitely the best buy for the money. Its low-lying design makes it almost invisible from the village; likewise from within: the windows give way to only the blue of the sea. The wood exterior and clean, spartan rooms with functional furnishings make for a pleasantly unpretentious hotel. ⊠ *63075 Ouranopolis,* ☎ *0377/71202, 0377/71264, or 0377/71265. 22 rooms with bath, 20 bungalows. Restaurant, bar, air-conditioning. No credit cards.*

$$ ▦ **Skites.** Set on a bluff 1 km outside Ouranopolis, this is the peachiest hotel in the area. All its rooms are small, bungalow-style, with separate entrances, flower gardens, and privacy. You'll enjoy enlightening views from the restaurant's terrace and the earmarks of home: nostalgic cooking and an intimate and personal atmosphere. Note that there is no air-conditioning. ⊠ *63075 Ouranopolis,* ☎ *0377/71140. 17 bungalows with bath. Restaurant, bar. No credit cards.*

Mt. Athos

❷❽ *120 km (74½ mi) southeast of Thessaloniki.*

Visitors to Mt. Athos are very limited, and bookings, especially for the summer and Easter, must be made months in advance. Booking in hand, you must then go in person to the Directorate of Political Affairs in Thessaloniki to obtain your visa (☞ *Visitor Information in* Northern

Greece A to Z, *below*). Visas are issued only to adult males and boys if they are accompanied by an adult, who must make a formal declaration that the purpose of the visit is a religious one. Stays for non-Greeks are limited to four days.

The peninsula of Athos is called Ayion Oros (Holy Mountain) by the Greeks, although the peninsula does not become a mountain until its southernmost point, and there are no monasteries actually on its slopes. Nevertheless, the mountain is imposing and has a definite awe-inspiring grandeur. Its 2,033-meter (6,670-foot) height once prompted Alexander the Great's architect to suggest carving it into a replica of Alexander, a proposal that fortunately did not come to fruition.

It is said that the Virgin Mary, brought there by accident when a ship she was on from Ephesus was blown off course by a storm, also found the spot to be a holy one and asked that it be venerated as her own very special place. This story has since become the rationale for keeping it off-limits to all women but the Virgin herself.

In the 5th–6th centuries the peninsula was occupied by only a few cave-dwelling hermits, and in 885 the Byzantine emperor Basil I decreed the area to be exclusively the province of hermits and monks. It was not until the 11th century that another decree specifically prohibited "smooth-faced persons," i.e., women, young boys, children, and eunuchs, from entering. In 963, the first organized monastic community (*lavra*) was established at the foot of the mountain. Called Great Lavra, it is still functioning today. Nineteen other communities followed (including some Orthodox Russians), the last in the 14th century. Since then, a number of hermitages and the separate dependencies called *skites* have been built, some precariously clinging to the rocky slopes. In 1926, Athos was formally united with Greece, but it still remains theoretically autonomous in its administration. Hence the need for visas and a *diamonitirion* (official residence permit).

EXPLORING MT. ATHOS
A small boat leaves from the Ouranopolis dock daily at 9:45 AM. Before boarding, you go to the office near the dock with your visa to obtain the diamonitirion, which permits you to stay for the night. The boat then leaves you off at the tiny, somewhat disreputable-looking port of **Daphni,** a loading point for goods to and from the peninsula. From here, caïques take you to the monasteries along the western coast; otherwise, a rickety bus takes you up the steep side of the promontory to the administrative center at **Karyes,** and you are then on your own to walk or find a ride to the monastery of your choice. Be aware that most monasteries close for the night at sunset, about 9 PM in summer, and dinner is served at about 7.

An alternative excursion for those who cannot visit Mt. Athos would be one of the **daily cruises** around the spectacular coast of the peninsula. Book either in Thessaloniki (☞ Contacts and Resources *in* Northern Greece A to Z, *below*) or Ouranopolis at any of various agencies. You can see many superb monasteries that are built at the water's edge or clinging to rocky outcroppings.

Kavala

❷❾ *136 km (84½ mi) northeast of Thessaloniki.*

When Philip II founded Philippi to protect the eastern route to the mineral riches of the Pangeon mountains, he made Kavala (in those days Neapolis) its port. The imposing eastern promontory is dominated by a **Byzantine castle,** which looks down on a charming fishing harbor lined with seafaring caïques and a number of fine seafood tavernas. Visiting the castle is free, and can be done from Tuesday to Sunday from 8:30 to 3.

It was in the **archaeological museum** that the Apostle Paul disembarked on his first trip to Greece in AD 49 en route to Philippi. ⊠ *17 Erythrou Stavrou,* ☎ *051/222335.* ⊠ *800 dr.* ☉ *Tues.–Sun. 8:30–3.*

Dining and Lodging

$$ ✕ **The Beautiful Mytilini.** This extraordinary seafood taverna under the fortress promontory specializes in mussel pilaf and *fruits de mer.* ⊠ *Eastern end of harbor,* ☎ *051/223034 or 051/221777. MC, V.*

$$ 🏨 **Egnatia Hotel.** For the best hotel in the city, charming may not be the operative word, but the Egnatia is clean and well run. It's on the main road as you enter the city and is easily accessible—and there's a roof garden ⊠ *Evthono Meraxias 139, 65403, Kavala* ☎ *051/244891,* FAX *051/245396. 45 rooms with bath. Bar, dining room, meeting room, free street parking. MC, V.*

$$ 🏨 **Galaxia Hotel.** This classic international-modern style hotel has no charm, but it's clean and has the best location in the city. It's on the main drag on the port, which can be noisy at night, so get a back room. ⊠ *Elefthirios Venezelou 27, 65403,* ☎ *051/224811,* FAX *051/226754. 150 rooms with bath. Bar, dining room, roof garden, meeting rooms, free parking. MC, V.*

OFF THE
BEATEN PATH

EVROS – The ecological complex of Evros province is considered to be one of the most important areas in Europe for bird-watching. The delta of the Evros River (the largest river of southeastern Europe after the Danube) is a wetland of international importance for its biological richness protected under the Ramsar convention. More than 300 bird species—the likes of glossy ibises, black-winged stilts, and cormorants—use the 10,000 hectares of wetland for breeding, wintering, or as a migration stop. A few miles north is the forest of Dadia, one of the most important areas in Europe for birds of prey. A lovely 10-room guest house and information center has been built in the village of Dada, providing an ideal base for hikes in the forest through well-marked footpaths. For further information contact ALMA (☞ Contacts and Resources in Northern Greece A to Z, *below*).

Philippi

30 *150 km (93¼ mi) northeast of Thessaloniki, 14 km (8½ mi) west of Kavala.*

In AD 42 in Philippi, the armies of Antony and Octavian caught up with Caesar's assassins, Brutus and Cassius, and defeated them. The archaeological site of Philippi includes a **theater** where various performances are given in summer, the **cell** from which Paul was miraculously freed by an earthquake, and more noteworthy ruins. You can visit the place, just outside the west wall of Philippi on the banks of river Gangitis, where Apostle Paul baptized Lydia and her family, the first Christians baptized on European soil. *Archaeological site,* ☎ *051/516470.* ⊠ *800 dr.* ☉ *Tues.–Sun. 8:30–3. Museum,* ☎ *051/516251.* ⊠ *Free.* ☉ *Tues.–Sun. 8:30–3.*

Thasos

31 *About a 1-hour ferry ride from Kavala.*

The island of Thasos is one of the most beautiful, friendly islands in Greece. It is known as "the Green Island" because of its thickly forested mountain ranges and tracts of olive and fruit trees (which have suffered from fires in recent summers). Its coastline is wonderfully varied, etched out in coves and fine, white-sand beaches, not to mention 149 hotels at last count. Its main city of **Limenas** (also known as Thasos) has a small but excellent **museum** and some superb **Classical ruins,** including a **amphitheater** nestled in the forest above the town.

Dining and Lodging

$ ★ **✕ Sirtaki.** You'll like this restaurant's vantage point from under tamarisk trees on the edge of a tiny beach at the far end of the harbor. Try the fried squid or whatever fish happens to turn up on the menu—particularly the one called "sun-fried fish"—and any salad. All the vegetables are organically raised, and the care lavished on the preparation of the food is truly loving—which reflects the nature of the owners. ⊠ *East end of town, past the harbor,* ☎ *0593/22651. No credit cards.*

$$$$ ★ **☷ Makryammos Hotel.** This resort, in an absolutely superb setting, often seems more Caribbean than Greek. A series of private bungalows on the beautiful white-sand beach is surrounded by a lush game preserve with, for example, peacocks strolling through. The guest rooms, while adequate, are generic European in style. ⊠ *Limenas 64004,* ☎ *0593/ 22101 or 0593/22102,* 𝖥𝖠𝖷 *0593/22761. 196 bungalows with bath, 10 suites. Restaurant, bar, pool, 2 tennis courts. AE, MC, V.*

$$$ **☷ Hotel Amfipolis.** This converted mansion with a garden, one block inland from the harbor, is certainly the most elegant place to stay in Limenas. ⊠ *Limenas 64004,* ☎ *0593/23101 through 23104,* 𝖥𝖠𝖷 *0593/ 22110. 42 rooms with bath. Bar, dining room, outdoor café, air-conditioning. AE, MC, V.*

$$ **☷ Timoleon.** This is a modest, functional hotel. It's owned by the president of the Hotel Association of Thasos, and is, without a doubt, the most convenient place to stay on the island. ⊠ *Harbor, facing central bus stop and next to tourist police, Limenas 64004,* ☎ *0593/22177 through 22179;* 𝖥𝖠𝖷 *0593/23277. 30 rooms with bath. Dining room. AE, MC, V.*

NORTHERN GREECE A TO Z

Arriving and Departing

By Bus

The trip from Athens takes about 7 hours, with one rest stop. Buy tickets at least 1 day in advance (⊠ 100 Kifissou St., ☎ 01/514–8856); one-way fare is 6,800 dr.

By Car

Driving to Greece from Europe through the former Yugoslavia is possible but often time-consuming owing to many border problems. You may prefer to drive through Italy and take a car ferry from Bari, Ancona, or Brindisi to Igoumenitsa on the west coast of Greece. This more beautiful route takes 7–8 hours, either by the northern route via Ioannina and Kozani, or via Ioannina, Kalambaka (and the famous Meteora monasteries), and Larissa. Both drives are spectacular, but the one to the south, used by regional buses, is much less treacherous and marginally faster. The Athens–Thessaloniki part of the National Road (500 km/310 mi), the best in Greece, takes 5–7 hours.

By Plane

There are now direct flights to Thessaloniki from London, Amsterdam, Brussels, Paris, Frankfurt, Stuttgart, Munich, Zurich, and Vienna, with good connections from the United States. You can also take an

Olympic Airways flight to Thessaloniki from Athens. The airport is at Mikras (⊠ On the coast some 13 km/8 mi/20 minutes southeast of the city center). A municipal bus to the airport (30 mins; 200 dr. exact change) leaves at irregular intervals from the train station and makes a stop at Aristotelous Square opposite Electra Palace.

By Train

Three daily **express trains** connecting Athens and Thessaloniki take 5–6 hours; they are comfortable and air-conditioned. You can take an **overnight train** with sleeping accommodations. Make reservations a few days in advance at the station or, in Thessaloniki (⊠ 18 Leoforos Aristotelous, ☎ 031/517527 or 031/517517); express fare is 8,000 dr.; for other trains: first-class fare 5,580 dr., second class 3,750 dr.; sleeper surcharge ranges from 2,500 dr. to 7,500 dr. Tickets can also be purchased at Zorpidis Travel (⊠ Egnatia 76, corner of Egnatia and Aristotelous).

Getting Around

By Bus

Intercity **KTEL** buses connect Thessaloniki with locations throughout Greece. There are small ticket office terminals (*praktorio*) for each line, usually located on the side of the city toward their destination. Ticket offices for departure to Athens (⊠ 67 Monastiriou, opposite the Thessaloniki train station, ☎ 031/510834 or 031/516104); Chalkidiki (⊠ 68 Karakasi St., in the southeastern suburb of Harilaou, ☎ 031/924444); Kavala (⊠ 59 Langada St., on the northwest side of Thessaloniki, ☎ 031/525530). For information about other offices contact the EOT (☞ *below*) or check the listings in the daily newspaper of all buses, trains, and airlines.

By Car

The roads in general are good and well maintained. A good **4-lane highway** that begins in Athens (E90) goes to the border with Turkey (E84); beware, speeds may seem exceedingly fast. Mobil gas stations sell excellent **road maps.** You can get information from **The Greek Automobile Touring Club** (ELPA) (⊠ 228 Vasilis Olgas st., ☎ 031/426319 or 031/426320). You can reserve space for yourself and your car on **ships** and **car ferries** traveling between ports throughout Greece at the **Plaris Travel Agency** (⊠ 22 Pavlou Mela, ☎ 031/278613 or 031/232078, FAX 031/286825) and **Zorpidis Travel** (⊠ 76 Egnatius St., ☎ 031/286812 or 031/286825, FAX 031/285819). In summer you should reserve a month in advance.

By Plane

Domestic carriers connect Thessaloniki with a number of cities and Mykonos, Santorini, Crete, Rhodes, Corfu, Limnos, Chios, and Lesbos. There are usually at least five daily flights to and from Athens, which take 40–45 minutes.

By Ship

Nomicos Lines ships connect Thessaloniki to Chios, Heraklion (Crete), Lesbos, Limnos, Mykonos, Paros, Santorini, Skiathos, Skiros, and Tinos. Buy tickets at the **Karaharissis Agency** (⊠ N. Kountouriotous St., near Platia Eleftherios, ☎ 031/513005 or 031/524444).

By Train

The regional train service is not recommended; travel by bus is usually faster and always more dependable.

Contacts and Resources

Emergencies
Tourist Police (☎ 031/554871). **American Consulate** (☎ 031/242905). **Honorary British Consulate** (☎ 031/286696). **Honorary Canadian Consulate** (☎ 031/230456).

Guided Tours
Zorpidis Travel (☎ 031/244400). **Doucas Tours** (☎ 031/286696). **Athos City Tours**: Thessaloniki (✉ 5 Ayios Sofias, ☎ 031/264150); **Chalkidiki** (☎ 0377/71150, FAX 0377/71399).

Hiking and Climbing
ALMA eco-adventure tourism office (☎ 031/855629). **Hellenic Alpine Club** (✉ Thessaloniki, ☎ 031/278288 or 0352/81944). **Chalkidiki Hotel Association** (✉ 33 G. Papandreou, Thessaloniki, ☎ 031/429020, FAX 031/429021).

Pharmacies
Lists of late-night pharmacies are published in newspapers and posted in the windows of all pharmacies.

Visitor Information
The **Greek National Tourist Organization (GNTO or EOT)** regional office in Thessaloniki is open 8 AM–8 PM (✉ 8 Aristotelous Sq., ☎ 031/222935, FAX 031/265504); airport (☎ 031/471170, ext. 215); Kavala (✉ 5 Filellinon St., ☎ 051/228762 or 051/222425, FAX 051/223885).

American Educational Services (✉ 76 Egnatia, ☎ 031/264483).

MT. ATHOS
Applications for bookings and visas can be made by writing to or visiting the **Ministry of Foreign Affairs,** (✉ Department of Ecclesiastical Affairs, 3 Akadamias St., 6th Floor, Athens 10671, ☎ 01/3623144 or 01/3623264); Thessaloniki, write or go to the **Ministry of Macedonia and Thrace** (✉ Directorate of Political Affairs, Platia Dikasterion, Room 222, Ayiou Dimitriou St., Thessaloniki 54123, ☎ 031/270092 or 031/26106). You should have a note attesting to the religious nature of your proposed visit from your consulate in Greece.

A easier way of doing this, particularly from abroad, is to contact Christos Sigoulis, manager of **Athos City Tours** (☞ *above*). He can do all of the paperwork for your visa and bookings prior to your arrival.

7 Corfu

Temperate, multihued Corfu—of emerald mountains; turquoise waters lapping rocky coves; ocher and pink buildings; shimmering silver olive leaves; puffed red, yellow, and orange parasails; scarlet roses, bougainvillea, and lavender wisteria and jacaranda spread over cottages—could have inspired Impressionism. The island has a history equally as colorful, reflecting the commingling of Corinthians, Romans, Goths, Normans, Venetians, French, Russians, and British.

KERKYRA, OR CORFU, IS THE GREENEST, and many say the prettiest, of all Greek islands. Homer's "well-watered gardens," and "beautiful and rich land," was Odysseus' last stop on his journey home. Corfu is also said to be the inspiration for Prospero's island in Shakespeare's *The Tempest*. This northernmost of the seven major Ionian Islands has, through the centuries, inspired other artists, as well as conquerors, royalty, and of course, tourists. Today over a million visitors a year—most from England and many from Europe—enjoy, and in summer, crowd its evocative capital city, isolated beaches, stylish restaurants, and resorts.

By Daniel Gorney

Updated by Lea Lane

On the island of Corfu, Corcyra, a mistress of Poseidon, bore a son named Phaex, the first of the Phaeacians who inhabited the island. According to Homer, at the time of the Trojan War, when Odysseus, King of Ithaca, was shipwrecked on his long voyage home, he came ashore on Corfu and was befriended by the Princess Nausicaa (daughter of Alcinous, king of the Phaeacians), who was playing ball with her maidens near Ermones.

Corfu lies strategically in the northern Ionian Sea at the entrance to the Adriatic, off the western edge of Greece. The lush, mountainous landscape seems more classic European than Greek, and indeed, this flower-filled island is only 72 km (45 mi) from Italy, and ⅔ km (1 mi) or so from Albania; some geologists believe it is the top of a submerged mountain range that broke off from the mainland. Corfu is moderated by westerly winds, scored with fertile valleys, and punctuated by enormous, gnarled olive trees, planted over 400 years by the Venetians. Luscious figs, oranges, and grapes grow abundantly in the clear light and mild climate, and the sunny beaches, delightful towns, and cosmopolitan atmosphere complete its idyllic splendor.

The Ionian islands' proximity to Europe and their sheltered position on the East–West trade routes made them prosperous; both their wealth and strategic position assured them a lively history of conquest and counter-conquest. The Classical remains have suffered from this history and also from earthquakes; architecture from the centuries of Venetian, French, and British rule is most evident, leaving the towns with a pleasant combination of contrasting design elements.

In Classical times, Corinth colonized the northern islands, but Corfu, growing powerful, revolted and allied itself with Athens, a fateful move that triggered the Peloponnesian War. Subjection followed: to the tyrants of Syracuse, the kings of Epirus and of Macedonia, and in the 2nd century BC, to Rome.

After the Byzantine Empire shattered, the islands fended for themselves against sporadic Germanic and Saracen invasions, and from the 11th to the 14th century were ruled by Norman and Angevin kings. Then came the Venetians, who protected Corfu from Turkish occupation and provided a 411-year period of peace for commercial development and the flowering of arts and letters. Venice also made Italian the official language for a while, at least.

Napóleon Bonaparte took the islands, what he called "the key to the Adriatic," after the fall of Venice. "The greatest misfortune which could befall me is the loss of Corfu," he wrote to Talleyrand, his foreign minister. Unfortunately for Bonaparte, he lost it within two years to a Russo-Turkish fleet, though the island was never occupied by the Turks, so local culture continued to thrive here during the hated Turkish occupation of the rest of Greece. For a short time the French regained and fortified Corfu from the Russians, and their occupation especially influenced the island's educational system, architecture, and cuisine. A Greek-run republic—the first for modern Greece—whetted local appetites for the independence that arrived later in the 19th century.

In 1814 the islands came under British protection; roads, schools, and hospitals were constructed, and commercialism developed. Corfu was ruled by a series of eccentric Lord High Commissioners, beginning with the much-hated Sir Thomas Maitland, and then by Sir Frederick Adam, who married a Corfiot lady with a heavy mustache. Nationalism finally prevailed, and the islands were ceded to Greece in 1864.

Corfu is the most developed of the Ionians, with a population of about 100,000. The island's northeast section has been heavily built up, although stony, inland farming villages seem undisturbed by civilizations that have come and gone, or even by today's events. Although it was bombed when the Italians and Nazis occupied it during World War II, the town of Corfu remains one of the loveliest in all of Greece. The entire island has gracefully absorbed its many layers of history, and combines neoclassic villas and eco-sensitive resorts, horse-drawn carriages and Jaguars—simplicity and sophistication—in an alluring mix. But desirability comes at a price: Corfu is expensive. If price is a consideration, beware.

Pleasures and Pastimes

Boating

Calm waters in the coves and bays make boating a popular pastime. Sailors can moor boats at the new ports in Corfu town, at Gouvia Marina on the east coast, and at Paleokastritsa on the west coast. Motorboats and sailboats can be rented at the Old Port in Corfu town, in Paleokastritsa, Kondokali, and Kassiopi, and on the northeast coast. To charter a yacht or sailboat without a crew, you'll need a proficiency certificate from a certified yacht club. Corfu has customs and health authorities, passport control, supply facilities, and exchange services, and it is one of the few official entry-exit ports in Greece; from here you can sail throughout the islands.

Dining

The food and atmosphere at many restaurants in Corfu town is as European as it is Greek, although inexpensive tavernas and typical Greek cuisine predominate throughout Corfu. Restaurants cater to every taste, and prices vary depending upon season and location. As elsewhere in Greece, the demand for fresh fish often exceeds the supply. Be aware that lobster and seafood are often priced by the kilo, and injudicious ordering can easily produce an expensive meal in a moderate restaurant. To be sure, ask the price before ordering a dish, even if the waiter suggested it.

The Greeks have been successfully storing grape juice in barrels for thousands of years, producing wonderful wines. But it seems that the secret of bottling, a completely different process, has not been discovered in Corfu. There are certainly some great Greek whites—try Hadjimichalis or Strofilia—but consistency can be a problem, especially with Corfu's Theotoki wines and other labels. Unfortunately, *hima* (barrel wine) isn't readily available in Corfu, as there are too few vineyards and too many tourists. Occasionally, restaurants serve barrel house wine with meals, and sometimes sell it by the bottle to go; try it—you'll rarely be disappointed. Bottled water can be bought everywhere, and you'll want to order it because Corfu's tap water is *not* one of its many pleasures.

Corfiot specialties are served at most restaurants and tavernas. Those worth a try are *sofrito* (veal cooked in a sauce of vinegar, parsley, and plenty of garlic) served with rice or potatoes; *pastitsio* (beef cooked in a rich and spicy tomato sauce) served with spaghetti (always called "macaroni" in Greece); *bourdetto* (firm-fleshed fish stewed in tomato sauce with lots of hot red pepper); and *bianco* (whole fish stewed with potatoes, herbs, black pepper, and lemon juice).

If service has been satisfactory, it is customary to leave a tip of about 5% of the bill, since a service charge is included in the prices.

CATEGORY	COST*
$$$$	over 10,000 dr.
$$$	7,000 dr.–10,000 dr.
$$	3,000 dr.–7,000 dr.
$	under 3,000 dr.

for a three-course meal, including modest service charge and tax, but excluding drinks.

Golf

Corfu has one of the best golf courses on the Greek islands, near Ermones Bay in the Ropa Valley. The par-72, 18-hole course, with water hazards and well-kept fairways, is open to the public.

Lodging

Corfu has accommodations to satisfy every taste and budget, from in-town bed-and-breakfasts in renovated Venetian mansions to sleek resorts with children's camps and outdoor and indoor pools. If you're after peace and quiet, you can find it; but disco, drink, and crowds are readily available, too. Expect air-conditioning only in the $$$ or $$$$ category. Larger accommodations have historically catered to groups, but the explosion of tourism in recent years has led to prepaid, low-priced package tours; these masses can get rowdy and overwhelm otherwise pleasant surroundings. You'll recognize the haunts of these beer-guzzling revelers, mainly in towns along the southeast coast.

Bargain hunters should go to the Greek National Tourist Organization (GNTO or EOT), which has a list of basic accommodations that are usually clean, comfortable, and inexpensive (☞ Visitor Information *in* Corfu A to Z, *below*). Rates can be negotiable, but a double room should cost around 5,000 drachmas; Continental breakfast is often included, but you should ask. Telephones and radios are standard on the island, and hair dryers are not. Televisions are a rarity; it's noted below which places have them.

CATEGORY	COST*
$$$$	over 30,000 dr.
$$$	15,000 dr.–30,000 dr.
$$	10,000 dr.–15,000 dr.
$	under 10,000 dr.

All prices are for standard double rooms, usually including Continental breakfast and not including tax.

Tennis

Courts and lessons are available in Corfu town, at the oldest tennis club in Greece. It's played in Kefalomandouko, where you can also take lessons. Most large hotels also have courts.

Water Sports

Fishing is unrestricted in Corfu's clear coastal waters. For a special pleasure, join local fishermen, who often will take groups out if you negotiate a fair deal. Sand and pebble beaches and coves edge the island, but the west coast has the widest sand beaches for sunning and swimming. Snorkeling and diving are best in the many rocky inlets and grottos on the northwest coast, and Paleokastritsa, Ermones, and Ipsos have diving schools where you can take lessons and rent equipment. The winds on the west coast are best for windsurfing, although the water on the east coast is calmer. Sailboards are available, and pedal and rowboats can be rented at many beaches. Waterskiing, water polo, parasailing, jet skiing, and other water-related activities sponsored by resorts are easily available.

Exploring Corfu

Corfu, about 64½ km (40 mi) long and up to 29 km (18 mi) wide with 201 km (125 mi) of sparkling, indented coastline, is small enough to cover completely in a few days. Roads vary from gently winding to spiraling, but they're generally well marked. The focus is Corfu town, reminiscent of a stage set for a Verdi opera. Historic attractions are nearby, valley farming villages spread inland, and a series of coastal villages and towns are separated by mountains, coves, or beaches. Within a couple of turns the landscape can vary from flatland to rocky outcrop to mountain, but the green landscape and clear blue sea are constant.

Great Itineraries

Corfu must often be explored quickly by people off a cruise ship or ferry on a tour of the Greek islands. Two days allows enough time to visit Corfu Town's nearby environs and most famous sites. For those with four days, time can be spent exploring the island's other historic sites and natural attractions along both coasts. And those with six days will get a closer look at the museums, churches, and forts.

IF YOU HAVE 2 DAYS
Numbers in the text correspond to numbers in the margin and on the Corfu Town and Corfu maps.

On the morning of the first day meander along the narrow, cobbled lanes of ⊡ **Corfu town** ①–⑭, have a bite at one of the cafés along the Liston, and then take in view at the rooftop café of the Cavalieri hotel. Spend the afternoon just south of **Corfu town** at the acropolis at nearby **Analipsis** ⑯, the ruins of the **Temple of Artemis** ⑰, and **Kanoni** ⑱, where you can see the most famous vista on Corfu—**Pontikonisi** ⑲. On the second morning drive to **Gastouri** ⑳ and the Achilleion, the 19th-century palace built for Empress Elizabeth of Austria. Then follow the inland road north from **Corfu town** to reach the beautiful northwest-coast resort area of ⊡ **Paleokastritsa** ㉑. You can pedal-boat into the grottoes, snorkel, dive, or relax on the beach. If you choose, return to **Corfu town** area for an overnight stay.

IF YOU HAVE 4 DAYS
Because Corfu is small, if you're driving, you can return to the same accommodations each night. Spend the first day the same way as in the 2-day itinerary. On day two, start again at the Achilleion in **Gastouri** ⑳. In the afternoon, get to the beach resorts of **Ermones** ㉓ and/or ⊡ **Glyfada** ㉔. From ⊡ **Corfu town** ①–⑭, you hug the coast for a few miles with the mountains of Epirus a backdrop on your right; pass the bay at Gouvia, turn inland on Route 24, and explore the small farms in the fertile Ropa plain. On the third day go to ⊡ **Paleokastritsa** ㉑, and also see the ruins of Angelokastro in the mountains in **Lakones** ㉒. On the fourth day, take the coast road from **Corfu town** northeast around the bay, through a string of highly developed resort towns set among olive groves, beaches, hotels, and restaurants like ⊡ **Dassia, Ipsos, Pirgi,** and **Nissaki.** The pretty coastal road now leads north to the most moun-

tainous part of the island, to **Kouloura** ㉖, historic **Kassiopi** ㉗, and the northern beaches of **Roda** ㉘ and **Sidari** ㉙.

IF YOU HAVE 6 DAYS

Follow the four-day itinerary above. 🏛 **Corfu town** ①–⑭ is worth a second or third visit to shop, sightsee, and sit in the courtyards and absorb the pace of Corfian life. From **Kanoni** ⑱, you can take a boat trip to **Pontikonisi** ⑲. Those who don't mind tourist-filled towns can go farther south on the island, or head north to hike around **Mt. Pantokrator.** You might return to 🏛 **Glyfada** ㉔, where the beaches are the best on the island, or to 🏛 **Paleokastritsa** ㉑. Adventurers will take a day trip to Albania, only about a mile away from the northern part of the island. Or just spend the extra days relaxing in the Corfian sun.

When to Tour

The best time to enjoy Corfu is April through June, and September through October, when the weather is at its finest, crowds are smallest, and sites, dining, and lodging are up and running. Unlike most of the Greek Isles, winter months in Corfu can be rainy and cool, and although summers are not quite as hot as some of the more southern islands, overcrowding and humidity can make things uncomfortable.

Festivals are held throughout the year, especially around the Greek Orthodox holidays. Worth noting are Carnival, with a parade on the last Sunday before Lent; and Holy Week, including Easter Sunday, and the breaking of crockery on Holy Saturday. Bands accompany the processions carrying the remains of St. Spyridon, Corfu's patron saint, held four times a year: Palm Sunday, Holy Saturday, August 11, and the first Sunday in November. The Corfu Arts Festival is in September.

Visiting attractions and participating in activities early or late in the day will help you to avoid heat and long lines. Be sure to check on times and schedules before setting out, and watch out for the mid-afternoon closings. Greeks eat lunch and dinner quite late by American standards, so if you don't mind being unfashionable you can lunch at noon and dine at seven without having to battle for tables, saving precious time for sights or lazing around.

CORFU TOWN

16 km (10 mi) east of Glyfada, 26 km (16 mi) east of Paleokastritsa.

This capital and cultural, historical, and recreational center is just off the middle of the island's east coast. All ships and planes lead to Corfu town, on a narrow strip of land hugged by the Ionian Sea. Though beguilingly Greek, much of Corfu's old town displays the architectural styles of many of its conquerors—molto of Italy's Venice, a soupcon of France, and more than a tad of England.

❶ If you arrive from Igoumenitsa or Patras, on mainland Greece, your ferry will dock at the **Old Port** on the north side of town, west of the ❷ **New Fortress** (1577–1578) (⊠ On a promontory northwest of the old fortress and medieval town), built by the Venetians and added to by the French and the British to protect the town from a possible Turkish invasion. The fort was a Greek naval base until 1992, when it was opened to the public. You can now wander through the maze of tunnels, moats, and fortifications. A classic **British citadel** stands at its heart. The best time to come here is early morning or late afternoon, out of the noonday sun.

❸ The **Museum of Sea Shells** exhibits a great collection of shells, sponges, corals, sharks' jaws, snakes, and mysterious pickled creatures from

Corfu Town

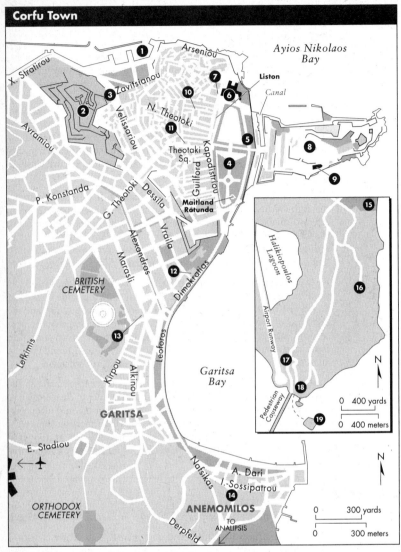

throughout the world. ⊠ *Old Port on Solomou St. just off New Fortress Sq.,* ☎ *0661/28568.* ⊠ *800 dr.* ⊗ *Daily 9–7.*

NEED A BREAK?	**Pizza Pete** (⊠ On the coast road), overlooking the bay near the New Fortress, is a popular, informal spot for drinks, snacks, and expansive views.

❹ The **Esplanade** (⊠ Between the Old Fortress and old town), the huge open parade ground on the land side of the canal, is central to the life of the town, and, many feel, the most beautiful *spianada* (esplanade) in Greece. It is bordered on the west by a street lined with seven- and eight-storied Venetian and English Georgian houses, and arcades, called the **Liston** (modeled on the Parisian Rue de Rivoli, by the French, under Napoleon). Cafés spill out onto the passing scene, and Corfiot celebrations, games, and trysts occur in the sun and shadows. Sunday cricket matches, a holdover from British rule, are played on the northern half of the Esplanade, and on the southern half are an ornate **Victorian bandstand,** a graffiti-covered **Ionic Rotunda,** in honor of Sir Thomas Maitland, and a **statue of Ioannis Kapodistrias,** a Corfu resident and the first president of Greece.

❺ On the walk east along the central path of the Esplanade is the **Statue of Count Schulenburg** (⊠ Esplanade), a monument to the hero of the siege of 1716, the Turks' last (and failed) attempt to conquer Corfu.

❻ The **Palace of St. Michael and St. George** is an elegant, colonnaded 19th-century Regency structure built as a residence for the Lord High Commissioner and headquarters for the order of St. Michael and St. George. The State Rooms were the setting for an EU summit meeting in June, 1994. It contains a notable collection of Asian porcelains and bronzes and Byzantine relics. ⊠ *At north end of Esplanade,* ☎ *0661/23124.* ⊠ *500 dr.* ⊗ *Tues.–Sat. 8:30–3, Sun. 9:30–2:30.*

❼ Just past the Palace of St. Michael and St. George is the oldest cultural institution in modern Greece, the **Corfu Reading Society,** with archives of the Ionian islands. One of the loveliest buildings in Corfu, it has an exterior staircase leading up to a loggia. ⊠ *Kapodistriou.* ⊗ *Daily 9–1, Thurs. and Fri. 5–8.*

❽ Originally, Corfu's population lived within the walls of the **Old Fortress** (⊠ On northeastern point of Corfu Town peninsula), or Citadel. Separated from the rest of the town by a moat once spanned by a movable wooden bridge, the fort is on the promontory mentioned by Thucydides. Its two heights, or *korypha*, gave the island its Western name. This striking landmark on the edge of the sea was built by the Venetians in 1546 on the site of a Byzantine castle. Most of the fortifications were blown up by the British when they left, but it's interesting to wander through the parts that remain.

❾ Visit the **Garrison Church of St. George** (1830), with its Doric portico. In summer there's folk dancing, and in August sound-and-light shows relate the fortress's history. The views from here, east to the Albanian coast and west over the town, are splendid. ⊠ *In middle of Old Fortress.* ⊠ *Free.* ⊗ *8–7.*

The narrow, winding streets and steep stairways that run west from the Esplanade take you into the large, traffic-free medieval **Campiello** (⊠ West of the Esplanade, between the two forts). Balconied Venetian buildings juxtapose multistory neoclassical 19th-century ones built by the British, and laundry often hangs between them. Small squares, some with wells, and high-belfried churches add to an utterly lovely urban space.

10 The **Church of St. Spyridon** (1596) (⊠ In the center of the old town) has a red-domed bell tower, the tallest on the island, and an especially large collection of silver. The patron saint's remains—brought here after the fall of Constantinople and contained in a silver reliquary—are carried in procession four times a year, along with his mummified body, which can be seen through a glass panel; his slippered feet are actually exposed so that the faithful can kiss them. The saint is said to have saved the island four times: once from famine, twice from the plague, and once from the hated Turks. Could this be why it seems half the males on Corfu are named Spiros?

Corfu's small, icon-filled **Orthodox Cathedral** (⊠ In the southwest of the medieval quarter, east of St. Spyridon), built in 1577, is dedicated to St. Theodora, the island's second saint, whose headless body lies in a silver coffin by the altar. Steps lead down to the harbor.

This twist of streets in the **Jewish Quarter** (⊠ South of the cathedral, next to the new fort) was the home to 5,000 Jews from the 1600s until 1940. The community was decimated, sent to Auschwitz by the occupying Nazis. A **synagogue** still stands at the southern edge of the ghetto, on Velissariou.

11 The ornate, marble, 17th-century **Town Hall** was built as a Venetian loggia and converted in 1720 into a theater, before becoming the town hall early in this century. ⊠ *Theotoki Sq.,* ☎ *0661/40401.* 🎟 *Free.* ☉ *9–1.*

12 The **Archaeological Museum** is where finds from the ongoing excavations are displayed. Note the Gorgon from the pediment of the 6th-century BC Temple of Artemis (☞ *below*), from the ancient capital—one of the best preserved pieces of archaic sculpture in Greece. It's inland just past the Corfu Palace Hotel. ⊠ *South of Esplanade along Leoforos Dimokratias,* ☎ *0661/30680.* 🎟 *800 dr.* ☉ *Daily 9–4:30.*

13 The walk south around Garitsa Bay is pleasant, with the gardens of the Garitsa neighborhood to the right. The **Tomb of Menekrates** (⊠ To the right of the obelisk dedicated to Sir Howard Douglas) is part of an ancient necropolis, items from which are in the Archaeological Museum (☞ *above*).

14 The suburb of Anemomilos (windmill) is crowned by the ruins of the Paleopolis church and the **Church of Ayios Iason and Ayios Sosipater** (⊠ At the south end of Garitsa Bay). Decorated with beautiful icons, it is a good example of 12th-century Byzantine churches, one of only two on the island (the other is in the northern coastal village of Ayios Markos).

Dining and Lodging

$$$$ ✕ **Albatros or Panorama Restaurant.** Both of these stylish restaurants, in the Corfu Palace Hotel, have Swiss chefs and fine service. The Albatros's terrace overlooks the pool, Garitsa Bay, and the gardens, and the Saturday night barbecue and buffet is a tradition; book well in advance. The Panorama is luxurious—replete with china flatware—but also comfortable. At both, the local specialties are particularly good, and the international cuisine is exceptional. They're expensive, but worth it. ⊠ *Leoforos Democratias 2, Corfu Palace Hotel,* ☎ *0661/39485. AE, DC, MC, V.*

$$$ ✕ **Aegli.** This 35-year-old restaurant on the Liston serves more than 100 different dishes, both local and international. The tables in front, with comfortable armchairs and spotless tablecloths, overlook the nonstop parade on the promenade. The swordfish with red-pepper sauce is a treat. For a more private meal, choose one of the 40 or so tables with white pine chairs inside, under the wood ceiling. ⊠ *Liston,* ☎ *0661/31949. AE, DC, MC, V. Closed Dec.–Feb.*

$$$ ✕ **Quattro Stagioni.** Although hard to find in the twisting, narrow streets of the old town, this place has a bright and airy old-world feeling. The snails with butter and garlic sauce or the baked feta are great for starters. Try the typical local specialties, or, for a light alternative, the salads and pastas. Dessert might be yogurt and honey, or Black Forest gâteau. ⊠ *Maniarisi and Arlioti 16, Kaduni Bisi,* ☎ *0661/43956. AE, DC, MC, V. Closed Dec.–Feb.*

$$$ ✕ **The Venetian Well.** On the most charming little square in the old town, built around a 17th century well, this romantic restaurant—its staff tiptoes around lingering lovers—seems too evocative and perfect to be true. The dining rooms in the handsome Venetian building are painted the classic Greek blue, one with a satirical fresco painted by the owner's ex-wife. Greek and international specialties are served to operatic music. Creative entrées might include duck with kumquats or wild boar. ⊠ *Across from Church of the Panayia; Kremasti Sq.,* ☎ *0661/44761. AE, DC, MC, V.*

$$ ✕ **Fish Taverna Roula.** This is the place for fresh fish: you can even come early in the morning—and do so during high season—to choose from the catch. When the fish runs out, Roula stops serving. Sit on the balcony under the enormous, ancient olive tree, and watch the boats on the bay. Follow the signs to the Kondokali Bay Hotel and continue on, keeping your eyes open for the sign to Roula's. ⊠ *Kondokali,* ☎ *0661/91832. Reservations essential in high season. No credit cards.*

$$ ✕ **The Rex Restaurant.** "We have air-conditioning," the waiter says, pointing up to a huge fan turning languidly, at this friendly, comfortable classic Greek taverna. Try the local specialties such as *stifado* (meat stewed with sweet onions, white wine, garlic, cinnamon, and spices) or the *lachano dolmades* (cabbage leaves stuffed with seasoned ground meat and rice). The *stamna* (lamb baked with potatoes, rice, beans, and cheese) is delicious. Outside tables are perfect for people-watching. ⊠ *Kapodistriou 66, just west of Liston,* ☎ *0661/39649. No credit cards. Closed 4:30 PM–8:30 PM and Sun.*

$ ✕ **O Yiannis.** One of the nicest in Corfu, this restaurant is unpretentious and full of locals. It's also cheap: you'll be hard-pressed to tally up 2,000 dr. on the great barrel wine and wonderful food. Try the stifado, the pork with Brussels sprouts, or the dolmades. For the bold, there's also *hordi* (intestines baked with a flavorful sauce). Order an ample supply of starters and hima, and eat in good company. Check out the ancient photos of Corfu's old-timers. ⊠ *Sophia Kremona and Iassonos-Sossipatrou 30, Anemomilos,* ☎ *0661/31066. Reservations not accepted. No credit cards.*

$$$$ 🏨 **Corfu Palace.** Overlooking the bay, 100 yards from the center of town, this elegant hotel is one of the most beautiful in all of Greece. Tasteful and comfortable best describe its Old World grandeur. The spacious rooms, furnished in various styles (Louis XIV and Empire) have TVs and wide balconies with splendid views. The bathrooms have hair dryers and telephones, and attention has been paid to every detail. Guests can play tennis at the nearby Corfu Tennis Club and may also use the facilities of the Corfu Yacht Club (☞ *below*). ⊠ *Leoforos Democratias 2, 49100,* ☎ *0661/39485,* 🅕🅐🅧 *0661/31749. 110 rooms with bath. 2 restaurants, 2 bars, minibars, room service, outdoor saltwater pool, indoor saltwater pool, health club, shops, baby-sitting, meeting rooms. AE, DC, MC, V.*

$$$$ 🏨 **Imperial Palace.** On a 14-acre peninsula jutting into Komeno Bay, 10 km (6 mi) north of town, this resort complex, formerly Astir Palace, has luxury rooms and bungalows that focus on comfort rather than elegance. Rooms have balconies with sea views. ⊠ *Komeno Bay, 49100,* ☎ *0661/91481,* FAX *0661/91881. 176 rooms and 124 bungalows with bath. Restaurant, 2 bars, pool, beauty salon, 2 tennis courts, beach, water sports, shops, dance club, laundry service. AE, DC, MC, V.*

$$$ 🏨 **Cavalieri Hotel.** In this venerable, eight-story building on the arcade of the Liston, get a room on the fourth and fifth floors with a number ending in 2, 3, or 4 for a breathtaking view of the Old Fort. The building is swank, yet graceful and chock-full of history. Have a drink at the usually empty but delightful English-style wood-paneled bar. Best of all is the roof garden, which offers light meals and the most remarkable view in town. ⊠ *4 Kapodistriou, 49100,* ☎ *0661/39041,* FAX *0661/ 39336. 50 rooms with bath. Restaurant, bar. AE, DC, MC, V.*

$$$ 🏨 **Kontokali Bay.** When you tire of exploring the streets and museums in town, this hotel about 6½ km (4 mi) north of town is just the place to relax. The pastel guest rooms, with modern wood appointments, are cheerful and sunlit, with balconies facing the sea, the mountains, or the lake. There's a buffet and grill restaurant that serves Greek and Italian cuisine. ⊠ *Kondokali Bay, 49100,* ☎ *0661/38736,* FAX *0661/91901. 234 rooms with bath. Restaurant, bar, room service, 2 tennis courts, beach, dock, water sports, dance club. AE, DC, MC, V.*

$$ 🏨 **Hotel Bella Venezia.** This two-story Venetian building in the center of town was operated as a hotel as early as the 1800s. Though in a lower classification—and price range—because it lacks views and a restaurant, its large lobby with a marble floor and wood-paneled ceiling and its huge garden make it quite pretty and grand. The rooms are small but tastefully furnished, and they have radios, telephones, and TVs. All in all, it's a good value for the money. It's just behind the Cavalieri Hotel. ⊠ *4 Zambelli, 49100,* ☎ *0661/46500. 32 rooms with bath. Lobby lounge, snack bar. AE, DC, MC, V.*

$ 🏨 **Hotel Cyprus.** Staying here will be an adventure, but the price is certainly right. The rooms at this hotel are clean, but the seemingly ancient building and the odds and ends of furniture—not to mention the masonry and walls—are in need of repair. Perhaps the Ministry of Culture is holding out on issuing a historic building special repair permit until the renovation of the neighboring church is completed. ⊠ *13 Ayios Pateron, 49100,* ☎ *0661/30032. 16 rooms with shared bath. No credit cards.*

$ 🏨 **Hotel Konstantinoupoulis.** A hotel for more than 200 years, this can be most ambitiously called traditional. But rooms are reasonably clean and acceptable if you're on a budget. Long-distance phone calls can be made in the lobby, a rarity in low-cost hotels. It's opposite the dock for car ferries to the islands, with a great view of the old port. ⊠ *Zavitsianou 11, Old Port, 49100,* ☎ *0661/39826. 44 rooms share bath. No credit cards.*

Nightlife and the Arts

BAR

Bill's Bar (⊠ On the main drag of the Commercial Center) has a quiet scene, with a definite trend toward music from the '60s, slower dancing, and even a taste of blues.

DISCOS AND NIGHTCLUBS

Just past the Commercial Center, 3 km (2 mi) west of town is a string of **discos** that really don't start swinging until after midnight. They have names like **Sax, Slik, Electron, bora bora, Slaze, Astral, Rondo, Mobile Club, Interview, Hippodrome,** and **LA Boom,** and they throb with all the latest international sounds and styles, from heavy metal to rap, techno, and fusion. Incredibly loud sound systems are just what the young T-shirted crowd needs to dance into the wee hours of the morning. A drink costs about 1,000 dr.

At **Ekati** (⊠ Opposite the main junction) crowds are more sophisticated and older, but the volume of the live music is nevertheless high for the *skiladiko* (roughly, dog party). Chichi is the theme here, with excessive baubles and Paris collections; buy a whisky bottle for your table, carnations to throw at your favorite performer, and a plate or two to break if you're in the mood. Drinks cost 1,500 to 2,000 dr. It's at the end of the disco strip.

FILM

Corfu town has an indoor cinema showing undubbed American flicks at the **Pallas** (⊠ North of Platia San Rocco). Go to the **outdoor theater** (⊠ Halfway down Marasli, seaside, on the right) on especially nice evenings.

MUSIC

Corfiots love music, from traditional bouzouki to classical. Corfu town has over a dozen **small orchestras,** a **choir,** and a **chamber-music group.** Sunday concerts are held at the bandstand on the esplanade throughout the summer, and brass bands can often be heard throughout the town. For entertainment information in English, tune into Radio Rama: 96.3 FM; Mon.–Sat. 3–5.

Outdoor Activities and Sports

SAILING

The **Corfu Yacht Club** (⊠ Corfu town, ☎ 0661/25759) offers sailing training courses.

TENNIS

The **Corfu Tennis Club** (⊠ Between I. Romanou and Kalosgourou streets, west of the Corfu Palace Hotel), founded in 1896, is the oldest in Greece. You may rent courts and take lessons.

OFF THE BEATEN PATH   **ALBANIA** – A day trip to nearby Albania on the European mainland was once practically impossible. But since the collapse of Communist rule in 1991, this mysterious country, just 1 nautical mile away, has opened its doors. Traveling from Corfu is the easiest and least expensive way to visit Albania, and it has become one of Corfu's most popular excursions. In Corfu town you clear customs and board a tour boat in the morning, which docks at the Albanian town of Saranda, a largely Greek-speaking settlement. The highlight of the day's itinerary is the Roman archeological site at Vouthrota. Much depends on the political situation, which remains volatile, so don't count on this trip, but if you're interested, check immediately upon arrival in Corfu where the boats leave the old port. The main tour operator to Albania is Petrakis Shipping Company (☞ Guided Tours *in* Corfu A to Z, *below*).

SOUTH OF CORFU TOWN

Just south of Corfu town, near the suburb of Kanoni, are ancient sites, the site of a former world summit, the lovely vista of Pontikonisi, famed throughout the world, and a controversial palace built by an Austrian empress. The villages farther south, such as Benitses, have become overrun with raucous package-tour groups, and have lost much of their original charm.

Mon Repos

4 km (2½ mi) mi south of Corfu town.

🅕 Along the road to Kanoni is the **palace of Mon Repos** (⊠ Near the public beach of Mon Repos), surrounded by gardens. It was built in 1831

Corfu

Avliotes

Sidari 29

Kavadades

Karoussades

Roda 28

Pelekito

Acharavi

Episkepsi

Mount Pantokrator ▲

Kassiopi 27

Ayios Stefanos

Makrades

22 **Lakones**

Ano Korakiana

Skripero

Barbati

26 **Kouloura**

Kalami

21

Paleokastritsa

Liapades

24

Pirgi

Ipsos

Nissaki

Sgombou

Dassia

Gianades

Gouvia

Kondokali

Ermónes 23

Vatos

Corfu Town 1 — 14

Ptihia

Myrtiotissa ■

Pelekas

25

Glyfada 24

Airport ✈ ★

15 **Mon Repos**

16 **Analipsis**

17 **Temple of Artemis**

Kinopiastes

Perama

18 **Kanoni**

19 **Pontikonisi**

Sinarades

Ayios Gordis beach

20 **Gastouri** ■ **Achilleion**

Pendati

Benitses

Strongili

Ayios Matheos

Moraitika

Mesonghi

Korissia

Hlomos

Boukari

Ayios Georgios beach

Argirades

Lefkimmi

Perivoli

TO IGOUMENITSA

Neohori

Paleohori

Dragotina

Kavos

TO PIRAEUS

N

KEY

----- Ferry

0 ——— 6 miles

0 ——— 9 km

by Sir Frederic Adam for his wife, and it was later the summer residence of the Lord High Commissioners. Prince Philip, Duke of Edinburgh, was born here. The house, which belongs to the former King Constantine of Greece, was expropriated by the Greek government in 1990; the king has appealed. Though the house is closed to the public, the extensive grounds are open.

NEED A BREAK?
Stop at the **café** (⊠ At the beach of Mon Repos), a pleasant spot in the shade of large plane trees, and have a drink.

Analipsis

⑯ *4 km (2½ mi) south of Corfu town, just south of Mon Repos.*

The village of Analipsis was built on the site of an acropolis, and a path leads to a spring where the Venetians watered their ships.

En Route Along the road to Kanoni, you'll pass through gardens and parks to
⑰ the ruins of the archaic **Temple of Artemis** and past the **lagoon of Halikiopoulou** down to the tip of the peninsula.

Kanoni

⑱ *5½ km (3½ mi) south of Corfu town. 1½ km (1 mi) south of Analipsis.*

At Kanoni, the site of the ancient capital, you may behold the most famous view on Corfu. A French cannon once stood in this hilly landscape, which is now built up and often noisy because of the nearby airport.

From Kanoni, against the backdrop of the green slopes of Mount Ayia Deka, is the serene view of two tiny islets: one, **Moni Viahernes,** is reached
⑲ by causeway. The other islet, **Pontikonisi,** called Mouse Island, has a **white convent** and, beyond, tall cypresses guarding the **13th-century chapel.** You can take a little launch or pedal boat to visit it—or even swim there.

NEED A BREAK?
The informal terrace bar and restaurant **To Balkoni** (⊠ On the hill overlooking Pontikonisi), where the tourist buses park, is a nice place to take in the view at your leisure.

Lodging

$$$$ ⊞ **Corfu Hilton International.** Though not quite as elegant or well located as the Corfu Palace, this hotel has extensive facilities. Modern wood-paneled rooms offer panoramic views. The less expensive "lake view" rooms in back look over the lagoon and the nearby airport. ⊠ *On beach at Kanoni, 49100,* ☎ *0661/36540,* FAX *0661/36551. 255 rooms with bath. 2 restaurants, bar, snack bar, room service, 2 seawater pools, sauna, 2 tennis courts, health club, beach, water sports, casino. AE, DC, MC, V.*

Gastouri

⑳ *19 km (11¾ mi) southwest of Corfu town, 23 km (14¼ mi) southwest of Kanoni*

The village of Gastouri, one of Corfu's loveliest and least spoiled, is the site of the palace **Achilleion,** in remarkable bad taste, but redeemed by lovely gardens stretching to the sea. This bizarre palace was built in the late 19th century by an Italian architect for the Empress Elizabeth of Austria. After Elizabeth was assassinated, Kaiser Wilhelm II

bought it. He lived here until the outbreak of World War I and throughout the war used it only as a summer residence. After the armistice the
Greek government received it as spoils of war.

The facade is fairly inoffensive, but the interior is a hodgepodge of a
pseudo-Byzantine chapel, a pseudo-Pompeian room, and a **pseudo-Re-
naissance dining hall,** culminating in a vulgar fresco called *Achilles in
His Chariot*. On the terrace, which commands a superb view over Kanoni
and the town, is an Ionic peristyle with a number of statues, in various degrees of undress. The best is *The Dying Achilles*, Elizabeth's favorite hero, for whom the palace was named. In 1962 the palace was
restored and leased as a gambling casino, which has since moved to
the Corfu Hilton International (☞ *above*). A **museum** on the ground
floor contains mementos and portraits, and rooms are available for meetings. ⊠ *Past resort area of Perama,* ☎ *0661/56210.* ▭ *700 dr.* ☉ *Season 9–4:30, off-season 9–2.*

Dining

$$$$ ✕ **Taverna Tripas.** It's best to experience this most famous restaurant
on Corfu, to which people ascend 13 km (8 mi) into the mountains southwest of Corfu town, in winter, when you're surrounded by dusty wine
bottles, hanging meats, and sundry stuffed birds and animals. It has now
become terribly tourist-ridden, though you might recognize important
politicians or ʾwell-known artists. You'll get an impressive array of
mezedakia (delicious tidbits) and do try the fine barrel retsina. Live music
and traditional Greek dances are performed. ⊠ *Kinopiastes,* ☎ *0661/
56333. Reservations essential in high season. AE, DC, MC, V.*

THE WEST COAST

The agricultural Ropa valley divides the sandy beaches of the lower
west coast from the dramatic mountains of the northwest. Hairpin bends
take you through orange and olive groves, over the mountainous spine
of the island to the rugged bays and promontories of the northwest
coast. Here the road descends to the sea, where two headlands, 39 meters (130 feet) high and covered with trees and boulders, form a pair
of natural harbors. This is an especially fine area for outdoor recreation.

Paleokastritsa

㉑   *25 km (15½ mi) northwest of Corfu town, 21 km (13 mi) northwest
of Kanoni.*

This area of grottoes and cliffs is identified by archaeologists as the
site of Homer's city of the Phaeacians; the big rock called Kolovri resembles the mythological ship that brought Ulysses home. The natural beauty and water sports of Paleo, as Corfiots call it, have brought
hotels, tavernas, bars, and shops to the hillsides above the bays, and
the beaches swarm with hordes of people on day trips from Corfu town.
But this spectacular spot of coves, rock formations, and turquoise waters is definitely worth a visit.

A **Byzantine monastery** is set among terraced gardens overlooking the
Ionian Sea. Its treasure is a 12th-century icon of the Virgin Mary, and
there's a small **museum** with some other early icons. Be sure to visit
the **inner courtyard** (go through the church), built on the edge of the
cliff, dappled white, green, and black by the sunlight on the stonework,
vine leaves, and habits of the hospitable monks. Under a roof of shading vines you look precipitously down to the placid green cove and the

torn coastline stretching south. ⊠ *On northern headland.* 🎫 *Free, but donation expected.* ⊘ *Daily 7–1 and 3–8.*

22 The village of **Lakones** (⊠ 5 km/3 mi northeast of Paleokastritsa) is on the steep mountain behind the monastery. Crested by the grim **ruins of Angelokastro,** it was built in the 13th century on an inaccessible pinnacle by a despot of Epirus, during his brief rule over Corfu. The road to this spot was reputedly built by British troops in part to reach Lady Adam's favorite picnic place, the **Bella Vista terrace.** Kaiser Wilhelm also came here to enjoy the magnificent view of Paleokastritsa's coves.

NEED A BREAK? Though it may be crowded, having a drink and savoring the view at the **Bella Vista Café** (⊠ On a bluff) is worth the wait.

Dining and Lodging

$$ ✗ **Chez George.** Sitting on the rock of the bay in Paleokastritsa, where Homer's wine dark sea touches forest green mountains, Chez George provides a sublime experience or a depressing tourist mistake. Whether you hit or miss, the pork chops are delicious and the *horiatiko* (village salad) is a tasty mix of carrot and onion with the hackneyed tomato, cucumber, feta, and olive combo. Do remember: order simply, don't buy the wine, and moderate prices seldom go with gorgeous views. ⊠ *The rock, Paleokastritsa,* ☎ *0663/41233. MC, V.*

$$ 🏨 **Fundana Villas.** On a hilltop in the mountains west of Corfu town, surrounded by gardens and olive and orange groves, this complex comprises 10 villas built in and around a 17th-century stone-and-mortar Venetian storehouse, with walls almost a yard thick. The common room–bar still contains the huge olive press and an old stone mill. You can really imagine life hundreds of years ago, and at the same time enjoy modern baths and kitchens. It's unique, and an ideal place for families interested in biking, exploring, and history. The villas are a short drive from the Paleokastritsa beaches; you will need your own transportation. ⊠ *Spyros Spathas, Box 167, 49100,* ☎ *0663/22532,* FAX *0663/22453. 10 villas with bath. Playground. No credit cards. Closed Nov.–Mar.*

Outdoor Activities and Sports

DIVING

The clear water is wonderful for underwater adventure. Diving lessons and equipment are available at the **Barracuda Club** (⊠ On the water in Paleokastritsa, ☎ 0663/41211).

Ermones

23 *16 km (10 mi) west of Corfu town, 6 km (3¾ mi) south of Paleokastritsa.*

South of Paleokastritsa, across the fertile Ropa Valley, is the resort of Ermones, with good, pebbly sand beaches, heavily wooded cliffs, water with plentiful fish, large hotels, and a backdrop of green mountains. The Ropa River flows into the Ionian Sea here.

Beach

The little sheltered **beach at Kondo Yialo** (⊠ Just south of Ermones) is especially beautiful.

Outdoor Activities and Sports

GOLF

The island's only golf course is here, at the **Corfu Golf Club** (⊠ Ermones, ☎ 066/94220), linked to the beach by an elevator. Look forward to a par-72, 18-hole course, with water hazards, well-kept fairways, rentals, lessons, a pro shop, and a clubhouse with a restaurant and bar. It's open to the public, and reservations can be booked through hotels.

Glyfada

㉔ *16 km (10 mi) west of Corfu town, 6 km (3¾ mi) south of Ermones.*

The large, sandy Glyfada beach is packed with busloads of bathers and sun worshipers on day trips from Corfu town. The area is filled with tavernas and discos.

In the village of Sinarades on the west coast, there's a **folk art museum** (✉ Sinarades, ☎ 0661/35673), exhibiting a private collection of local costumes, embroidery, furniture, and pottery. It's open Tuesday to Sunday 9:30 to 12:30.

Lodging

$$$ ⊞ **Louis Grand Hotel Glyfada.** Two patios with Japanese gardens redeem this otherwise overdone, quasi-Asian setting. The guest rooms are basic, and air-conditioning operates at the manager's whim. Buffets spotlight Greek specialties; the bar is done in a Viennese theme, a nod to the hotel's Germanic package tours. There's a children's program and a game room. The social staff keeps things jumping in summer, running courtesy cars to town and the golf course. The hotel is at the biggest, sunniest beach on the island. ✉ *46 Diadochou Pavlou, Glyfada 49100,* ☎ *0661/94201,* FAX *0661/7919. 242 rooms with bath. Restaurant, bar, saltwater pool, tennis courts, water sports, nightclub. AE, MC, V. Closed Nov.–Mar.*

Pelekas

㉕ *13 km (8 mi) west of Corfu town, 2 km (1¼ mi) north of Glyfada.*

Just inland from Glyfada is Pelekas, with a famous lookout point called the **Kaiser's Throne.** This rocky hilltop is known to Corfiots for its spectacular sunset views.

A monastery on the west coast is the hermitage of the **Myrtiotissa** (✉ Below Mt. Ayios Georgios), 3 km (2½ mi) or a 1-hour walk north of Pelekas, and a half-hour walk (2 km/1¼ mi) south of Vatos.

Beaches

The long, sandy **beach at Pelekas** is well-known and popular with nudists. The isolated **beach at Myrtiotissa,** between sheer cliffs, is noted for its beauty, excellent snorkeling, and nude sunbathing.

Dining

$$ ✕ **The Nornberg.** Everybody in the area knows this restaurant as Mihali's in Livadi Ropa, about a mountainous 13 km (8 mi) west of Corfu town. It's a *psistaria* (grill taverna), and it's one of the best. First savor fried eggplant, *tzatziki* (yogurt, chopped cucumber, and garlic), fresh salad, and feta. Mihali Moumouris bastes the best local meat—maybe *paidakia* (lamb chops) or pork chops—with lemon juice and local olive oil, sprinkles it with salt and fresh oregano, and grills it over charcoal. And don't forget to order some of his homemade retsina. ✉ *Livadi Ropa,* ☎ *0661/51473. No credit cards.*

NORTH OF CORFU TOWN

Mt. Pantokrator, at 905 meters (2,970 feet), forms the northeast lobe of the island. The northern coastal area is replete with pretty coves, and it has the longest sand beach in Corfu, curving around Roda to Archaravi.

Kouloura

26 *31 km (19¼ mi) northeast of Corfu town.*

This pretty harbor town is on a U-shape bay enclosed by cypress, eucalyptus, and palm trees and has a small, shingle beach with close views of the Albanian coastline. This is the part of Corfu immortalized by Gerald Durrell in *My Family and Other Animals* and by his brother Lawrence in *Prospero's Cell*; a taverna called the **White House** (⊠ In Kalami) was where the latter was written. Tavernas here still serve local wine.

Lodging

$$$ ⛶ **Corfu Chandris and Dassia Chandris Hotels.** This huge two-hotel complex is set in 25 acres of gardens, with private chalets and bungalows for groups. The public areas feature marble; the modern guest rooms are comfortable and basic, with large sea-view balconies, radios, and telephones. These two hotels are 11 km (7 mi) north of Corfu town, and about the same distance south of Kouloura. ⊠ *Dassia, 49100,* ☎ *0661/33871 through 33875,* 𝔽𝔸𝕏 *0661/93458; Athens:* ⊠ *Athens Chandris Hotel, 385 Syngrou, 17564 P. Faliron,* ☎ *01/941–4824 through 4826,* 𝔽𝔸𝕏 *01/942–5055. 526 rooms with bath. Restaurant, bar, lobby lounge, air-conditioning, room service, pool, beauty salon, 4 tennis courts, beach, water sports, shops, playground. AE, DC, MC, V. Closed Nov.–Mar.*

Outdoor Activities and Sports

HIKING

Drive inland from Pirgi, 10 km (6 mi) south of Kouloura. If you're in good shape, when the paved road ends, leave your vehicle and hike to the top of **Mt. Pantokrator.** You'll be rewarded with summit views of all of Corfu, the Albanian coast, and the Ionian islands of Paxos and Cephalonia. An unoccupied **17th-century monastery** is perched on the mountaintop.

Kassiopi

27 *36 km (22½ mi) northeast of Corfu town, 7 km (4⅓ mi) north of Kouloura.*

Kassiopi, north around the mountain, occupies a promontory between two bays. It was an important town during Roman times, with a shrine to Zeus that Nero and other emperors visited; Tiberius had a villa here. A **church** with a 17th-century icon and frescoes now occupies what was probably the site of Zeus's shrine.

During the Byzantine era this area rivaled Corfu town. When Kassiopi's fortress, built by the Angevins, was destroyed by the Venetians, the town declined. But now the fishing village has discovered the tourist trade and has become a busy resort.

Lodging

$$ ⛶ **Apraos Bay Hotel.** On the northern tip of the island sits this small, Venetian-style hotel. Rooms are fresh and airy with light-filled balconies. It's 40 yards from a private beach, with a fantastic view of the sea and the Albanian coast: a perfect place to relax in a friendly atmosphere, far from noise. Though it's almost completely isolated, just a mile away in the village of Kassiopi is all the action anyone could want; it's about 32 km (20 mi) from Corfu town. ⊠ *Loutses, 49100,* ☎ *0663/98331,*

FAX 0663/98336. *16 rooms with bath. Restaurant, piano bar, beach. AE, DC, MC, V. Closed Dec.–Feb.*

Roda

28 *37 km (23 mi) north of Corfu town, 8 km (5 mi) northwest of Kassiopi.*

On the north coast, Roda has good beaches and plenty of tourists, and though some spots farther west are less crowded, the roads to them are not as passable. Its narrow beach, which adjoins the beach at tiny Acharavi, has especially calm and shallow waters and a campsite, so it's popular with local families. The **remains of a 5th-century Doric temple** have been found here.

Sidari

29 *36 km (22½ mi) north of Corfu town, 4 km (2½ mi) west of Roda.*

At Sidari, unique striated cliffs are constantly being eroded into tunnels and caves, notably the "tunnel of love," which keeps changing its location. From here (or Kassiopi or Roda), you can hire a caïque for a daylong excursion to the sparsely populated fishing islands of Othanos, Erikoussa, and Mathraki, which form Greece's northwest border in the Ionian Sea.

CORFU A TO Z

Arriving and Departing

By Boat

Passenger ships stop at Corfu twice a week, April to October. **Minoan Lines** (⊠ Akti Poseidonos 28, Piraeus, ☎ 01/411–8211 through 8216, FAX 01/411–8631) runs the *Festos,* which connects Corfu with Ancona, Igoumenitsa, Heraklion, and Piraeus. The *Ariadne* connects Corfu with Kusadasi (Turkey), Samos, Paros, Kephallonia, and Ancona.

Ferries from Igoumenitsa on the mainland leave every hour in summer and every 2 hours off-season, landing in Corfu town (2 hours) and in Lefkimmi, at the southern tip of Corfu (45 minutes).

By Bus

KTEL Corfu buses (☎ 0661/39985 or 0661/37186) leave Athens (☎ 01/512–9443) three or four times a day. The trip, via Patras and the ferry from Igoumenitsa, takes about 9 hours. The fare is approximately 6,200 dr. each way.

By Car

The best route from Athens is the national road via Corinth to the Rion/Antirion ferry, then to Igoumenitsa (472 km/274 mi), where you take the ferry to Corfu. In winter, severe weather conditions often close the straits at Rion/Antirion, and the ferries from Igoumenitsa can also stop running. Call the **Touring Club of Greece** (☎ 104) for information.

By Plane

Olympic Airways (☎ 0661/30180) has three flights a day from Athens that land at Corfu's airport (⊠ Northwest of Kanoni, a few km/mi south of Corfu town). For a round-trip, the fare is 15,800 dr. each way; the one-way fare is 16,100 dr.

Getting Around

By Bus

Bus travel on Corfu is inexpensive, and the bus network covers the island. Buses tend to run fairly close to their schedules, and you can get timetables and information at the depots of the two bus companies and at many other places. Publications such as *Mythos Guide to Corfu, The Corfiot,* and *The Corfu Sun* all give good information.

The **Spilia** (✉ Avramiou St., ☎ 0661/30627) bus company's terminal is at the New Port. Buses also run from the **San Rocco** (✉ San Rocco Sq., ☎ 0661/31595) bus company's depot.

By Motorbike and Car

The gentle climate and rolling hills make Corfu ideal motorbike country, but you should drive very slowly until you feel comfortable. There is little or no system to Greek driving, and "depend on the other guy's brakes" best expounds the basic philosophy of many drivers. The road surfaces deteriorate as the tourist season progresses, and potholes abound. Helmets are rarely provided, and then only on request. Check the lights, brakes, and other mechanics before you accept a machine. Be warned and be careful.

By Taxi

Radio-controlled taxis (☎ 0661/33811) are available 24 hours a day, and rates, which are set by the government, are reasonable—when adhered to. Many drivers speak English and they know the island in a very special way. If you want to hire a cab and driver on an hourly or daily basis, you must negotiate the fee; ask for advice at your hotel's front desk. Always check the prices before you travel.

Contacts and Resources

Car and Motorbike Rental

A 50cc motorbike can be rented for about 3000 dr. a day (100cc for 6,000 dr.), but you can bargain, especially if you want it for two or more days. Rentals are available in even the most remote villages. In Corfu town, try **George's Bikes** (✉ El. Venizelou 38, ☎ 0661/32727).

Car rental can be considerably more expensive, starting at about 9,000 dr. a day for a Fiat 127 (100 km/62 mi minimum) plus insurance, delivery, and so forth. A four-wheel-drive Jeep, with the extras, can run to 25,000 dr. a day. In Corfu town you can try **Olympus Rent-a-Car** (✉ 29 National Stadium, ☎ 0661/36147). Also in Corfu, try **Suncars, Ginargirou Brothers Ltd.** (✉ 40 Alexandras, ☎ 0661/31565).

Emergencies

Police: (✉ Alexandras 19, ☎ 100).

Medical: hospital (✉ Polychroniou Kostanda, ☎ 0661/45811 through 45815). **Polyclinik** (✉ just outside town on the road to Paleokastritsa, ☎ 0661/22946).

Guided Tours

Many agencies run half-day tours of Old Corfu town, and tour buses go daily to all the sights on the island. Tickets and information are available at travel agencies all over town. **Vaba Travel** (✉ Ethnikis Antistaseos, New Port, ☎ 0661/44455, FAX 0661/22174) is reliable.

Most agencies offer an evening tour to **Danilia Village** (☎ 0661/91621, FAX 0661/91485), a fairly accurate reconstruction of an entire 17th-century Corfiot settlement in the countryside on the road to Afra, 16 km (10 mi) from Corfu town. This Corfu-style Williamsburg gives an interesting picture of how people lived at that time, and the tour includes live Greek and foreign music, dancing, food, and wine.

The main tour operator to Albania is **Petrakis Shipping Company** (✉ Eleftheriou Venizelou 9, next to the Old Port, ☎ 0661/31649). The cost is around 7,000 dr., plus $30 to cover port taxes and an entry permit to Albania.

Visitor Information

Greek National Tourist Organization (GNTO or EOT; ✉ Kapodistriou 1, ☎ 0661/37520, 0661/37638, or 0661/37639, FAX 0661/30298).

Tourist Police: ✉ Kapodistriou 1, ☎ 0661/30265.

8 Northern Peloponnese

Nauplion, Patras, and Olympia

The gods of ancient Greece blessed the Northern Peloponnese with natural beauty and the mysteries of forgotten civilizations. The ruined city of Mycenae, with giant tombs to the heroes of Homer's Iliad, *stands sentinel over the Argive plain, where warriors once assembled en route to Troy. In the rolling hills of Elis, Olympia plays host to the scattered remains of the ancient Olympic Games. And Nauplion, its ancient Greek, Venetian, and Turkish edifices jutting out into the Bay of Argos, is, to the Greeks, the embodiment of beauty.*

By Mark J. Rose and Toula Bogdanos

Updated by Terrence Moloney

NAMED FOR PELOPS, SON OF THE MYTHICAL Tantalos, this ancient land offers magnificent scenery; massive mountains covered with low evergreen oak and pines surround coastal valleys and loom above rocky shores and sandy beaches. Over the millennia this rugged terrain nourished kingdoms and empires and witnessed the birth of modern Greece. Traces of these lost realms—ruined Bronze Age citadels, Greek and Roman temples and theaters, and the fortresses, churches, and mosques of the Byzantines, Franks, Venetians, and Turks—attest to the richness of the land. The hand-shape Peloponnese is linked to the north by a narrow isthmus, from which the Gulf of Corinth leads west to the Adriatic, and from which the Saronic Gulf opens eastward into the Aegean. The Northern Peloponnese comprises the Argive peninsula, jutting into the Aegean, and runs westward past the isthmus and along the Gulf of Corinth to Patras and the Adriatic coast. The modern administrative districts, or nomes, are Argolida, Corinthia, Achaea, Elia, Lakonia, Arcadia, and Messinia.

The fertile Argive plain was the heart of Greece in the Late Bronze Age and the home of the heroes of Homer's *Iliad*. A walk through the lion gate to Mycenae, the citadel of Agamemnon, brings the Homeric epic to life, and the massive walls of nearby Tiryns glorify the age of might. The thriving market town of Argos, the successor to Mycenae and Tiryns, engaged in a long rivalry with Sparta, generally gets the short end of the stick. Corinth, the economic superpower of the 7th and 6th centuries BC, dominated trade and established colonies abroad. Although eclipsed by Athens, Corinth earned a reputation for wealth and easy living. Modern Corinth is a bustling, if unremarkable, regional center. Not far from Corinth is Epidauros, the sanctuary of Asklepios, god of healing, where in summer Greek dramas are re-created in the ancient theater. Far to the west lies Olympia, the sanctuary of Zeus and home of the ancient games.

After the armies of the Fourth Crusade (in part egged on by Venice) captured Constantinople in 1204, they conquered the Peloponnese, which became the Frankish principality of Achaea. The Franks settled in for the long haul, the Villehardouin family establishing the impressive Chlemoutsi Castle near Killini, but their dominion was brief, and Byzantine authority was restored under the Palaiologos dynasty at Mystras and Monemvassia in the Southern Peloponnese. Soon after Constantinople fell in 1453, the Turks, taking advantage of an internal rivalry, crushed the Palaiologoi and helped themselves to the Peloponnese. In the following centuries the struggle between the Venetians and the Ottoman Turks for control of the eastern Mediterranean was played out in Greece, and largely in the Northern Peloponnese. The two states alternately dominated the region until the Ottomans ultimately prevailed, as Venetian power declined in the early 1700s. The Turkish mosques and fountains and the Venetian fortifications of Nauplion recall this epic struggle. The Peloponnese played a key role in the Greek War of Independence, and from 1828 to 1834 Nauplion was the capital of Greece.

Today Patras is the chief city of the region and the third largest city in Greece. Agriculture and tourism are the economic bases of the Northern Peloponnese. Citrus, grapes (and wine), and currants are grown, as well as the ubiquitous olive. Modern resorts such as Porto Heli in the east and Killini in the west attract crowds seeking sun, sand, and sea.

Pleasures and Pastimes

Beaches
The beaches along the western coast of the Peloponnese are considered some of the best in Greece and are generally less crowded than other beaches. There are excellent beaches near Chlemoutsi castle. There are good beaches along the Gulf of Corinth, with spectacular views of the opposite shore, but some are of cobbles rather than sand. Xylokastro starts out cobbly but farther from town becomes sandy.

Dining
One of the best simple pleasures of Greece is a late dinner of traditional Greek food with good Greek wine, preferably from the barrel. In the small towns here, any restaurant that pretends to offer more than this should be viewed with suspicion. Dress is always casual and reservations unnecessary, although you might have to wait for a table if you're dining with the majority at 10 PM or later. Keep freshness and the season in mind; if you order fish, have a look at it before it's cooked—there's no reason to eat something frozen. Grape leaves are best early in the season, no later than early July, when they're young and tender. Ask to visit the kitchen; any chef worth his salt will tell you what's good and what's left over from lunch.

CATEGORY	COST*
$$$$	over 7,000 dr.
$$$	5,000 dr.–7,000 dr.
$$	2,500 dr.–5,000 dr.
$	under 2,500 dr.

for a 3-course meal, including tax, service, and usually beer or a small carafe of wine.

Hiking and Climbing
The mountainous terrain of the Northern Peloponnese is an ideal habitat for hikers and climbers. The **Greek Federation of Mountaineering Associations** in Athens operates several huts in the Peloponnese that are open to the public (☞ Contacts and Resources *in* Northern Peloponnese A to Z, *below*).

Lodging
Visitors accustomed to traveling in the United States and Europe should not expect to always find such amenities as color televisions, much less VCRs. Hotels in the $$$$ and $$$ categories have air-conditioning unless noted; it is mentioned when it exists in hotels of $$ and $ rank. Breakfast is not included in the price unless noted.

CATEGORY	COST*
$$$$	over 39,000 dr.
$$$	22,000 dr.–39,000 dr.
$$	13,000 dr.–22,000 dr.
$	under 13,000 dr.

for a standard double room in high season, including tax and service.

Nightlife
Bars and discos in the two liveliest spots, Nauplion and Patras, appear and disappear rapidly. What's "in" this season probably will be ignored the next. A recommendation today may be of little value to tomorrow's visitor.

Shopping
Olympia has many shops specializing in big-ticket gold jewelry—some very nice, some very gaudy. Patras is the best bet for fashion, especially downtown around Korinthos and Maizonos streets. If you are traveling by car, be on the lookout for roadside stands selling the wonder-

ful peaches and apricots—perfectly ripe and far superior to grocery-store fruit.

Greek vintners, faced with EU competition, are producing better wines than ever before. Look for red wines from the region around Nemea, between Corinth and Argos. Be sure to try Patras's sweet *mavro-daphne* (a heavy dessert wine, literally "black Daphne"), so called, because after the death of Daphne, Baron von Clauss's object of desire, he took his darkest grapes and made the sweet wine in her honor.

Tennis

Though you may not see Andre Agassi trotting around the courts of the Northern Peloponnese, tennis has a good following here. Some luxury hotels in Olympia and Porto Heli have courts, and the Patras Tennis Club is open to the public.

Water Sports

The popular beaches are well equipped: Paddle boats can be hired, and you can arrange windsurfing lessons at small "beach-bum" operations at many beaches, such as Tolo. In some resorts, like Porto Heli, waterskiing and jet skis are making an appearance.

Exploring the Northern Peloponnese

The Northern Peloponnese comprises several distinct geographical areas—on the eastern side is the Argolid plain and the Corinthiad, where we find Mycenae, Tiryns, Epidauros, and Nauplion, and on the western side the provinces of Achaea and Elis, home of ancient Olympia and the bustling port city of Patras. We describe each of these regions in its own section, below.

Great Itineraries

Visitors who spend less than a week in the Northern Peloponnese may spend much of their time asking themselves why they didn't allot more time to this fascinating area of Greece. The eastern and western portions of the Northern Peloponnese are easily divided into two separate three- to four-day itineraries; a thorough exploration of both requires about eight or nine days. Those with less time should consider investigating either the eastern or the western half; for travelers entering Greece from Italy, Patras and Olympia are a must, and for those entering Greece through Athens, Nauplion and the Argolid are only a short hop away.

IF YOU HAVE 2 OR 3 DAYS
Numbers in the text correspond to numbers in the margin and on the Northern Peloponnese, Nauplion, Tiryns, Mycenae, and Ancient Olympia maps.

The wealth of interesting sites on either side of the Northern Peloponnese will keep the intrepid occupied for at least three days, but if your schedule allows for only two days consider a day trip to 🔁 **Nauplion** ⑤–⑳ followed by a day spent exploring some of the highlights of the Argolid—**Mycenae** ㉜–㊷ and **Tiryns** ㉑–㉚, for example. A third day near **Nauplion** will allow a visit to the theater at **Epidauros** ② and perhaps the beaches at **Tolo** ④ or **Porto Heli** ③. For those entering Greece from Italy and with only a couple of days to spare, try spending a day in and around 🔁 **Patras** ㊾ followed by a day trip to 🔁 **Olympia** ㉛–㊻. An extra day on the western side of the Northern Peloponnese could be spent either enjoying a train ride along the picturesque **Vouraikos Gorge** ㊻ en route to **Kalavrita** ㊼ or clambering over the parapets of the Frankish **Chlemoutsi Castle** ㊿.

IF YOU HAVE 6 DAYS

Six days will allow you to see most of the major sites of the Northern Peloponnese. Spend two or three days in **Nauplion** ⑤–⑳ and use it as a base to explore the Argolid. You can get to **Nauplion** by boat, train, or car, and it is possible to rent transportation from there. After you have explored nearby **Mycenae** ㉜–㊷, **Tiryns** ㉑–㉚, **Epidauros** ②, and **Argos** ㉛, spend a day in **Patras** ㊾, visiting **ancient Corinth** ㊹ on the way, or forested **Kalavrita** ㊼ if you need a rest from antiquities! A fifth and sixth day can be divided between **Patras** and **Olympia** (51)–(68). Remember that this trip can be easily reversed if you are coming from Italy and arriving in **Patras.**

IF YOU HAVE 9 DAYS

Starting at the isthmus, journey south toward **Nauplion** ⑤–⑳, visiting **Isthmia** ①, **Kenchreai**, and **Epidauros** ② en route. Spend your second day in **Nauplion** ⑤–⑳, and perhaps visiting the beaches at nearby **Tolo** ④ or **Porto Heli** ③, both of which can be used as alternative bases for exploring the Argolid. The five major sites north of **Nauplion—Tiryns** ㉑–㉚, **Argos** ㉛, **Mycenae** ㉜–㊷, **ancient Nemea** ㊸, and **ancient Corinth** ㊹—could easily occupy two or even three days, using **Nauplion** as a base for daily excursions. **Olympia** (51)–(68) beckons the Peloponnesian traveler sooner or later, but don't rush! There's plenty to see en route from the Argolid, including the beaches of **Xylokastro** ㊺, and the alluring beauty of the **Vouraikos Gorge** ㊻ near **Kalavrita** ㊼, a sight best experienced from the train that winds its way up the **Vouraikos Gorge. Kalavrita** can be enjoyed as a side trip on the way to Patras, or as an overnight stay, followed by a quick hop to **Patras** ㊾, with fashionable shops, sophisticated cafés, and lots of energy. Stay in **Patras** for a couple of nights, exploring the city itself and the nearby sights, including the traditional village of **Halandritsa,** and the best preserved Frankish castle in the Peloponnese, **Chlemoutsi Castle** ㊿. Finally, take a languid trip through the verdant province of Elis to awesome ancient **Olympia,** where the Olympic Games were first held almost three millennia ago.

When to Tour

As in much of Greece late spring provides the optimum conditions for exploration—hotels, restaurants, and sites have begun to extend their hours of operation but the hordes of travelers have not yet arrived. In summer, mornings and early evenings are the best times on account of the heat, which can be a formidable obstacle. Remember that on Monday most state museums and sites are closed. On Sunday many are free off-season.

ARGOLID AND CORINTHIAD

Isthmus, Epidauros, Nauplion, Tolo, Porto Heli, Tiryns, Argos, Mycenae, Nemea, Corinth

Most of the sites in this area are in the Argolid—Tiryns and Mycenae gaze over the plain of Argos, which dominates the Argolid, and nearby Epidauros hosts audiences from around the world who come to see drama performed in its classical theater. Argos lies in the center of the plain of the same name; behind the mountains that surround the plain on all sides (except the south) is the Corinthiad, a hillier region, with ancient Corinth as its principal site.

Isthmus

75 km (46½ mi) southwest of Athens, 7 km (4⅓ mi) southeast of Corinth.

More of a pit stop than a town, the isthmus is where the Peloponnese begins. Were it not for this narrow neck of land less than 7 km (4 mi) across, the waters of the Gulf of Corinth and the Saronic Gulf would meet, making the Peloponnese an island; the name, in fact, means "Pelop's island." The tragic myths and legends surrounding Pelops and his family provided the grist for poets and playwrights from Homer to Aeschylus and enshroud many of the region's sites to this day.

For the ancient Greeks the isthmus was strategically important for both trade and defense; Corinth, with harbors on either side of the isthmus, grew wealthy on the lucrative east–west trade. Ships en route from Italy and the Adriatic to the Aegean had to go clear around the Peloponnese, so in the 7th century BC a paved roadway called the Diolkos was constructed across the isthmus on which ships were hauled using rollers. You can still see remnants near the bridge at the western end of the canal. Nero was the first to begin cutting a canal, supposedly striking the first blow with a golden pickax in AD 67. But the canal died with Nero the following year, and the roadway was used until the 13th century. The modern canal, built 1882–93, was cut through 87 meters (285 feet) of rock to sea level. The impressive sight is a fleeting one if you are traveling by bus, so keep a sharp lookout. The isthmus was not only a barrier to sea trade, but also a choke point on north–south land routes. As early as the Late Bronze Age (13th century BC) a wall was constructed across the isthmus, apparently to keep out invaders from the north, and throughout history other fortifications were erected, which generally failed when actually put to the test.

❶ **Isthmia,** an ancient sanctuary dedicated to Poseidon, scarcely a mile from the canal, isn't much to look at today, largely because its buildings were dismantled for stone to repair the Isthmian wall and to build a large fortress. Better preserved, not surprisingly, are the remains of the fortress, called the **Hexamilion,** and of the **wall** (east of the sanctuary is a stretch that rises more than 20 feet). Ancient Isthmia was an important place, the site, from 580 BC, of the Isthmian Games, biennial athletic and musical competitions on a par with those at Nemea, Delphi, and Olympia. The games, celebrated in the Odes of Pindar, may have originally honored the funeral of a hero. One tradition holds that during a famine, when a drowned boy, Melikertis, was taken ashore by a dolphin, the Delphic oracle declared the famine would stop only when the Corinthians honored the boy with a fitting burial and funeral games. ⊠ *1 km west of isthmus,* ☎ *0741/37244.* ▭ *500 dr.* ☉ *Tues.–Sun. 9–3.*

Dining

The line of **rest-stop restaurants** at the isthmus may be a more effective defense than the walls ever were. Be wary of these restaurants: It is better to enter the Peloponnese hungry than to eat the souvlaki here.

Outdoor Activities and Sports

BUNGEE JUMPING

Ev Zin (⊠ Syngrou 132, Athens, ☎ 01/921–6285 or 01/923–0263), an adventure travel agency that offers bungee jumping on Greek islands, is trying to get permission to organize jumps at the Isthmus Canal in Corinth. Given Greek bureaucracy, it's sure to take some time.

OFF THE   **KENCHREAI** – Much of ancient Corinth's port is underwater, including a
BEATEN PATH sanctuary of Isis, from which excavators retrieved the unique glass pan-

els depicting Nile scenes and Greek philosophers now on display at the Isthmia museum. It was from Kenchreai, 5 km south of Isthmia, that Paul sailed for Ephesus, having his hair cut before departure (Acts 18:18). Leaving Kenchreai, the road climbs into more rugged countryside, on the steep slopes overlooking small fjordlike inlets and the open waters of the Saronic Gulf. On the left you pass first the small post-Byzantine church of the Odigitria (Virgin Indicator of the Way) and second the 14th-century Monastery Agnounda.

Epidauros

② *41 km (25½ mi) east of Nauplion, 62 km (38½ mi) south of the isthmus. As you head south from the isthmus on Highway 70 you'll find the names confusing. You first pass a sign for Nea Epidauros; 6½ km (4 mi) later there's a turnoff marked for Palaio Epidauros (don't take this either). After this seaside village the road turns inland and gradually the tall pines give way to scrubby vegetation. Keep going—the Epidauros you want is about 8 km (5 mi) farther, about 3 km (1¾ mi) southeast of Ligourio.*

★ The **Sanctuary of Asklepios** at Epidauros is world renowned for one thing: its theater, whose extraordinary qualities were recognized even in the AD 2nd century. Pausanias of Lydia, an early traveler and geographer, writes, "The Epidaurians have a theater in their sanctuary that seems to me particularly worth a visit. The Roman theaters have gone far beyond all the others in the world . . . but who can begin to rival Polykleitos for the beauty and composition of his architecture?" Extolled for its acoustics, it is also the best-preserved Greek theater anywhere. Built in the 4th century BC with 14,000 seats, it was never remodeled in antiquity, and being rather remote, its stones were never quarried for building material. The summer drama festival staged in the theater is "worth a visit," as Pausanias might say. The quality of the theater, the setting, and the productions are outstanding, which cannot be said of any other festival in Greece. The rest of the site does not match the standard set by the theater. The **temple of Asklepios** is not well preserved; some copies of its sculptures are in the **site museum**, but the originals are in the National Museum in Athens. An exhibit of ancient medical implements is of interest, as are models of the sanctuary. The **reconstruction of the *tholos***, a circular building also possibly by Polykleitos, is noteworthy. ⊠ *Epidauros*, ☎ *0753/22009.* ☞ *1500 dr.* ☉ *Summer daily 8–7, winter 8–5, Mon. museum opens at 10 year-round.*

The Arts

FESTIVAL

The **Festival of Ancient Drama** (⊠ Stadiou 4 arcade, ☎ 0753/22006) in the theater at Epidauros takes place July to August, weekends only, at 9 PM. Many productions are in English and are produced by companies from around the world. Tickets can be bought at the theater before performances or in advance from the **Athens Festival box office** (⊠ 4 Stadiou, ☎ 01/322–1459).

Dining

$$ ✕ **Leonidas.** Rest your weary bones at this taverna, with liquid refreshment, excellent meals, and, in cold or wet weather, a blazing fire on the raised brick hearth. Actors from the theater hang out here, as the theatrical decorations attest. ⊠ *Epidauros Main rd.,* ☎ *0753/22115. No credit cards.*

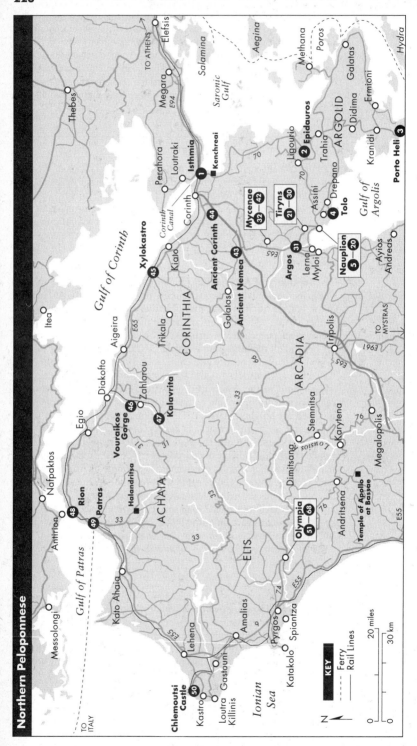

Northern Peloponnese

KEY
- - - - Ferry
───── Rail Lines

N

0 ——— 20 miles
0 ——— 30 km

TO ATHENS

Thebes

Elefsis

Megara
E94

Salamina

Saronic
Gulf

Aegina

Methana

Poros

Galatas

Hydra

Didima

Ermioni

Kranidi

3 Porto Heli

ARGOLID

Petrahora

Loutraki

Isthmia

1 Kenchreai

Corinth
Canal

Corinth

70

Ligourio

2 Epidauros

Trahia

Drepano

Assini

4 Tolo

Gulf of
Argolis

Mycenae **32**–**42**

Tiryns **21**–**30**

44 Ancient Corinth

43 Ancient Nemea

E65

31

Argos

Lerna
Myloi

Nauplion
5–**20**

Ayios
Andreas

Xylokastro

45

Kiato

Galatas

Gulf of Corinth

Itea

Aigeira

Diakofto

Trikala

CORINTHIA

Tripolis

TO
MYSTRAS

E65

1963

Egio

Zahlarou

46 Vouraikos
Gorge

47 Kalavrita

E65

31

31

ARCADIA

Stemnitsa

Loúsios

Karytena

76

Megalopolis

90

33

Nafpaktos

Rion

48

Patras **49**

Halandritsa

ACHAYA

33

33

33

Antirion

Gulf of Patras

Kato Ahaia

ELIS

Dimitsana

Andritsena

Temple of Apollo
at Bassae

E55

Olympia
51–**68**

76

Messolongi

**Chlemoutsi
Castle**
50

Kastro

Gastouni

Loutra
Killinis

Lehena

Amalias

9

Pyrgos

Spiantza

74

E55

Ionian
Sea

Katakolo

TO
ITALY

En Route From Epidauros, head south toward the resort town of Porto Heli. After 16½ km (10 mi), just beyond the village of Trahia, the road divides. Follow the left fork as it swings east to the coast, with a beautiful view across the Saronic Gulf to Aegina. After 30 km (18½ mi), a left turn takes you to the peninsula known as Methana, where a spa (⊠ In the small port) of the same name will treat you for rheumatism and skin disorders with hot sulfurous water. Continuing past Methana on the main road brings you to Galatas, overlooking the island of Poros. The road sweeps around the end of the peninsula and runs west along the coast to Ermioni, opposite Hydra, then to the beach at Kosta, opposite Spetses, and finally to Porto Heli.

Porto Heli

❸ *81 km (50⅓ mi) southeast of Nauplion, 54 km (33½ mi) south of Epidauros.*

A booming summer resort, Porto Heli is well supplied with tavernas, restaurants, souvenir shops, and discos. If you want traditional Greek culture, look elsewhere. On the south side of the bay are the **submerged ruins of the ancient city of Halieis.**

Beaches

The beach at **Kosta** (⊠ In the south of the Argolid, south of Porto Heli) is more pleasant and less crowded than those at Porto Heli.

Dining and Lodging

$$–$$$ ✕ **Papadias.** In a town of undistinguished dining options, this taverna near the church in the older part of Porto Heli stands out. Dishes include appetizers like shrimp or *midia saganaki* (mussels baked with cheese), rabbit *stifado* (a baked stew with meat, white wine, garlic, cinnamon, and spices) resplendent with onions, and grilled crayfish. The seafood is good, and in general fish is the high-water mark of Porto Heli cuisine. ⊠ *Beach Rd.,* ☎ *0754/52342. MC, V.*

$$$ 🏠 **Porto Heli.** This lodging of the former Kymata Club, like the other resorts around the sheltered bay, offers more than just a room for the night: the nearby beach has a range of water sports, and buffet breakfast is included in the price. The reasonably large white-stucco rooms have phones, stone floors, and, as wall decorations, colorful Byzantine-style plates. ⊠ *Beach Rd., 21300,* ☎ *0754/51490 through 51494. 210 rooms with bath, 8 suites. Restaurant, air-conditioning, pool, miniature golf, tennis courts, windsurfing, playground. MC, V. Closed Oct.–Apr.*

$$ 🏠 **La Cite.** The buildings climbing the hillside behind the beach here resemble gigantic white stucco Lego blocks. Inside, wood-frame furniture fills the rooms that, although clean and well kept, could be bigger. They do have balconies overlooking the beautiful bay, and each comes with a fan. There are rental bicycles and mopeds at the beach opposite, just 20 meters away. Continental breakfast is included in the price. ⊠ *Beach Rd., 21300,* ☎ *0754/51485,* 🖷 *0754/51265. 164 rooms with bath. 2 restaurants, bar, pool, miniature golf, 2 tennis courts, beach, water sports. AE, DC, MC, V. Closed Nov.–Mar.*

$ 🏠 **Rozos.** An alternative to the giant resorts, Rozos can be summed up in a few words: crafty on a budget. The rooms are clean and decorated with nautical photos. Some of the furniture in each room matches, and large ceiling fans, like salvaged propellers from B–29 bombers, ensure good air circulation. A saving grace for this establishment, if you deem one needed, is the front terrace, shaded by grapevines, lemon trees, and olive trees. ⊠ *Kosta 7, 21300,* ☎ *0754/51416,* 🖷 *0754/51415. 23 rooms with bath. Restaurant. MC, V.*

Nightlife

DISCOS

Disco Thea has enraptured multiseason visitors. **Disco Pop Rebel** has managed to stay in tourists' good graces for more than a summer.

Outdoor Activities and Sports

WATER SPORTS

Although its beach is not as good as others in the vicinity, Porto Heli's circular bay offers sheltered water for windsurfing, waterskiing, and other aquatic sports, and a safe harbor for sailboats. Waterskiing lessons are given at the **Porto Heli** hotel (⊠ Beach Rd., ☎ 0754/51546; ☞ *above*).

En Route The road north passes through Kranidi, a conservative town with plenty of good preconcrete slab architecture, and Didima, a small town in a large flat depression below the hulking mass of Mt. Didima. Perhaps because the sheer bulk of the mountain highlights its insignificance, Didima itself is depressing, and the long climb up the mountain, with many switchbacks and a steep grade, is like feeling the wind after being trapped in a closed room with stale air. At the top you can continue onward, through Trahia again and to Nauplion via Ligourio, or turn left and take the coast road to Nauplion, past the villages and beaches of Iria, Kandia, and Drepano along the Gulf of Argos.

Tolo

4 *11 km (7 mi) southeast of Nauplion, 77 km (47¾ mi) northwest of Porto Heli.*

Tolo is a resort center close to Nauplion, and it can be used as a base for exploring the northeastern Peloponnese. It has many fine beaches strung along the coast's crystalline waters, discothèques, and seafood tavernas supplied by the local fleet, but little in the way of traditional Greek culture. There is frequent bus service from Nauplion's KTEL station to Tolo.

Beaches

Just before Tolo, at the Bronze Age and Classical site of Asine, the road takes a sharp turn to a fine **beach** that's less crowded than Tolo's.

Dining and Lodging

$–$$ ✗ **Chryso Feggari (Golden Moon).** This seaside taverna, handed down from father George to son Dimitris, is one of Tolo's better restaurants, albeit that's no blue ribbon. Ask for *fagri* (sea bream), *barbounia* (red mullet), or a delicious local fish called *kotsomoura*. The taverna also serves Greek dishes such as *pastitsio* (a casserole of pasta, meat and cheese with seasonings and cinnamon), moussaka, *keftedes* (oniony meat balls), as well as pizzas and grilled meats. ⊠ *Aktis 52, about 100 meters from harbor,* ☎ *0752/59323. No credit cards. Closed Nov.–Feb.*

$ ✗ **Akroyiali.** Matriarch Anastasia Moutzouris is still cooking up good traditional Greek fare at this almost 40-year-old beach taverna. Appetizers include fried eggplant slices, tender broad beans, marinated octopus, and grilled squid. For a main course, there is fresh fish, as well as lamb and pork chops, souvlaki, and grilled chicken. The barrel wine (white and red) is light but potent; locals order it a kilo at a time. ⊠ *Aktis 10,* ☎ *0752/59789. No credit cards. Closed Dec.*

$$ 🏨 **King Minos.** One of the town's newest—it opened in 1992—this hotel offers amenities usually found in more expensive establishments. Almost all the rose and light-green rooms with bamboo touches have color TVs, hair dryers, air-conditioning, and balconies; many have sea views. Buffet breakfast is included in the price. ⊠ *Aktis 56, 21056,* ☎

0752/59902, FAX 0752/59968. *57 rooms with bath. Restaurant, 2 bars, air-conditioning, pool. MC, V. Closed Nov.–Feb.*

$$ ★ ▥ **Tolo and Tolo II.** These two hotels run by the Scalidis family are opposite each other on the town's main street. The rooms are straightforward in decor and well kept—nothing fancy. Tolo has the best views and immediate access to the nicest part of the beach. Buffet breakfast is included in the price. ✉ *Bouboulinas 15, 21056,* ☎ *0752/59248 or 0752/59464,* FAX *0752/59689. 59 rooms with bath. Restaurant, bar, air-conditioning. MC, V. Closed Nov.–Feb.*

$ ▥ **Aris.** The neat, clean rooms here have mahogany furniture, the ubiquitous blue and white fabric scheme, and balconies; be sure to ask for one with a sea view. Breakfast is included in the price. ✉ *Aktis 28, 21056,* ☎ *0752/59231,* FAX *0752/59510. 50 rooms with bath. Restaurant, bar, air-conditioning, recreation room. Closed Nov.–Feb.*

$ ▥ **Minoa.** This a pleasant hotel with relatively large, clean rooms done in the signature blue and white, all with radios and some with televisions. It is near the end of the town, and though there is a beach in front, it's a little walk to the wide sandy beach for which Tolo is known. Buffet breakfast is included in the price. ✉ *Aktis 56, 21056,* ☎ *0752/59207,* FAX *0752/59707. 44 rooms with bath. Bar, outdoor café, air-conditioning. AE, MC, V. Closed Nov.–Feb.*

Nauplion

★ *65 km (40½ mi) south of Corinth, 11 km (7 mi) northwest of Tolo.*

Oraia (beautiful) is the word Greeks use to describe Nauplion. They say the word with assurance and enthusiasm, wanting to convince you of Nauplion's beauty but knowing that it is self-evident and that you share their recognition of it. The town's old section, on a peninsula jutting into the Gulf of Argos, mixes Greek, Venetian, and Turkish architecture; narrow streets—often just broad flights of stone stairs—climb the slopes beneath the walls of Acronauplia; statues honoring heroes preside over tree-shaded plazas surrounded by neoclassical buildings, and the elegant Venetian fortress draped over the high cliff guards the town. The Greeks are right; Nauplion is beautiful. It deserves at least a leisurely day of your undivided attention.

Nauplion, known to the Venetians as Napoli di Romania, has an exquisite natural setting. On the north side of a rocky peninsula that juts into the Gulf of Argos is the oldest section of town, where the narrow streets are lined with the buildings of Greeks, Venetians, Turks, Franks, and Byzantines, and the stones are worn smooth by their feet. A central swath of flat land, given over to shady parks and plazas, lies below the sheer cliffs of a massive peak adorned with the Palamidi fortress, an elegant display of Venetian might from the early 1700s.

Though it's hard to imagine anyone not liking Nauplion, Henry Miller, in the late 1930s, whined about it at length in *The Colossus of Maroussi.* "Nauplia," he writes, "is dismal and deserted at night. It is a place which has lost caste. . . . There is a little military garrison, a fortress, a palace, a cathedral—and a few crazy monuments. There is also a mosque which has been converted into a cinema. By day it is all red tape, lawyers and judges everywhere, with all the despair and futility which follows in the train of these blood-sucking parasites. The fortress and the prison dominate the town. Warrior, jailer, priest—the eternal trinity which symbolizes our fear of life. I don't like Nauplia. I don't like provincial towns. I don't like jails, churches, fortresses, palaces, libraries, museums, or public statues to the dead."

232

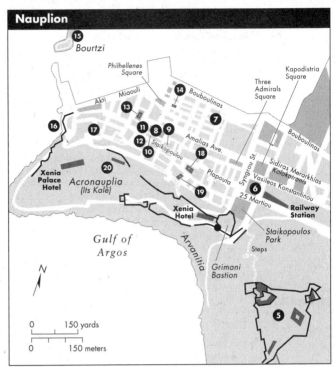

If you spend at least a day or two in Nauplion, your impression may be more positive. A full exploration could take an entire day; a quick tour, with some omissions, could be done in three hours.

Little is known about ancient Nauplion, although Paleolithic remains and Neolithic pottery have been found in the vicinity. It grew in importance in Byzantine times, and it was fought over by the Byzantines and the Frankish crusaders. It has been held by the Duke of Athens, the Venetians, and the Turks. In the War of Independence, the Greeks liberated the city, and it briefly became the capital. During World War II, German troops occupied Nauplion from April 1941 until September 1944. Today it is once again just a "provincial town," busy only in the tourist season and on weekends when Athenians arrive to get away from city pressures.

★ ⑤ Seen from the old part of Nauplion, the **Palamidi,** on its 700-foot peak, is elegant, with the red stone bastions and flights of steps that zigzag down the cliff face. A modern road lets you drive up the less precipitous eastern slope, but if you are in reasonable shape and it isn't too hot, try climbing the stairs. Most guidebooks will tell you there are 999 of them, but 892 is closer to the mark. From the top you can see the entire Argive plain and look across the gulf to Argos or down its length to the Aegean.

Built in 1711–1714, the Palamidi comprises three forts and a series of freestanding and connecting defensive walls. Sculpted in gray stone, the lion of St. Mark looks outward from the gates. The Palamidi fell to the Turks in 1715 after only eight days, and if you climbed those stairs, you'll be able to feel the desperation of the fleeing defenders racing down them with the Turks in hot pursuit. After the war, the fortress was used as a prison, its inmates including the revolutionary war hero Kolokotronis; a sign indicates his cell. On summer nights the Palamidi is illuminated with floodlights, a beautiful sight from below. ✉ *Above town*, ☎ *0752/28036.* ✉ *800 dr.* ☉ *Weekdays 8–6:30 (winter 8:30–1), weekends and holidays 8:30–2:30.*

<table>
<tr><td>NEED A BREAK?</td><td>For a respite, head to an area of flat ground occupied by a pleasant series of tree-shaded platias (✉ At foot of Palamidi). A playground, duck pond, and some small aviaries with songbirds offer entertainment for children. Benches here are perfect for sitting in the evening before dining.</td></tr>
</table>

In **Kolokotronis Park** (✉ On north side of pedestrian King Constantine St.), a bronze equestrian statue surrounded by four small Venetian cannons commemorates the revolutionary hero. South of the street is the **old train station** with a steam engine and vintage freight and passenger cars. In front of the station is a new **statue of Bouboulina,** the heroine of the revolution, shown with an alarming hair style the sculptor must have adapted from the *Bride of Frankenstein.* The **bust of Bouboulina** (✉ Bouboulina St.) is a much better, if more traditional, representation.

Just west of Kolokotronis Park is **Kapodistria Square** (✉ At Syngrou St. and Sidiras Merarkhias), with its marble statue of the Corfiote diplomat and father of modern Greece, standing statesmanlike, oblivious of the noise from the playground at his feet, from the tavernas across the street, and from the taxis and buses turning left onto Amalias Avenue.

Across Syngrou Street from the KTEL bus station is a **square** with yet another hero, Nikitaras the Turk-Killer, who directed the siege of Nauplion. Beyond this statue is the **Palace of Justice** (✉ Syngrou, 2 blocks down from Kapodistria Sq.). If Henry Miller loathed Nauplion for its lawyers and public buildings, you have to believe that he must have spent much of his time staring at the Palace of Justice, a building whose ugliness is magnified by its large size. This monumentality makes it useful as a landmark, however, since the telephone company (OTE) office and pay phones are in the next building.

<table>
<tr><td>NEED A BREAK?</td><td>South of the Palace of Justice, across Staikopoulos Street, is a small sun-drenched open area with a few benches, Staikopoulos Park (✉ At 25 Martiou and Syngrou). It is named for the conqueror of the Palamidi.</td></tr>
</table>

Three Admiral Square (✉ Syngrou and Amalias) is named for the English, French, and Russian admirals who sank Ibrahim Pasha's fleet in 1827.

A **miniature triangular park** (✉ Syngrou, North of Three Admiral Sq.) contains, inevitably, a monument to **admiral Konstantinos Kanaris,** a revolutionary hero; across from its far end is the **bust of Laskarina Bouboulina.** Twice widowed by wealthy shipowners, she built her own frigate, the *Agamemnon.* Commanding it herself, along with three small ships captained by her sons, Bouboulina blockaded the beleaguered Turks by sea, cutting off their supplies. **Bouboulina's pedestal** sits on the corner.

❼ The **Peloponnesian Folklore Foundation Museum** is an exemplary, small museum focusing on textiles. In 1981, it won the EC's Museum of the Year award for its displays. ✉ *Vas. Alexandrou 1, on block immediately north of Amalias, going up Sofroni,* ☎ *0752/28379.* ✉ *500 dr.* ☉ *Mar.–Jan., Wed.–Mon. 9–2:30.*

❽ Both Amalias and Vasileos Konstantinou streets lead to **Syntagma (Constitution) Square** (✉ Along Amalias and Vasileos Konstantinou Sts.), the center of the old town and one of Greece's prettiest platias. The latter street is more picturesque, with older buildings, and the more commercial Amalias is lined with butcher shops and grocery stores. In summer, the restaurants and patisseries along the west and south sides of Constitution Square—a focal point of Naupliote life—are boisterous with the shouts and laughter of children and filled with diners well into the evening.

9 Immediately to the left as you enter Constitution Square from Vasileos Konstantinou Street is an **old mosque** (✉ Constitution Sq.) that was once a movie theater—known for kung fu flicks—and a former school, court, and center for municipal offices.

NEED A BREAK?   Walking from the old mosque along the south side of Constitution Square, you pass a café and a store called **Odyssey** (✉ Constitution Sq.), the best place in Nauplion for newspapers and books in English; the owners are very helpful if you need advice or directions.

10 The **National Bank** (✉ Just south of Constitution Sq.) displays an amusing union of Mycenaean and modern Greek architectural elements with concrete. (The Mycenaeans covered their tholos tombs with mounds of dirt; the bank's ungainly appearance may explain why.)

Take a look at the **sculptures** (✉ On square next to National Bank) of a **winged lion of St. Mark** (which graced the main gate in the city's landward wall, long since demolished) and of Kalliope Papalexopoulou (a leader of the revolt against King Otho), whose house once stood in the vicinity.

11 The **archaeological museum,** in a red stone building on the west side of Constitution Square, was built in 1713 to serve as the storehouse for the Venetian fleet. To say that it is "well-constructed" is an understatement; its arches and windows are remarkably well proportioned. It has housed the museum since 1930, and artifacts from such sites as Mycenae, Tiryns, Asine, and Dendra are exhibited here. Of special interest are a Mycenaean suit of armor; jewelry from Mycenaean tombs in the area; and 7th-century gorgon masks from Tiryns. ✉ *West side of Constitution Sq.,* ☎ *0752/27502.* 🎫 *500 dr.* 🕙 *Tues.–Sun. 8:30–3.*

12 A **Turkish mosque** (✉ Next to archaeological museum and behind National Bank), ironically now the *Vouleftiko* (Parliament), was where the Greek National Assembly held its first meetings. The mosque is well built of carefully dressed gray stones. Legend has it that the lintel stone from the Treasury of Atreus was used in the construction of its large square-domed prayer hall. The mosque recently served as a music school, and occasionally the sound of a Rossini overture played on a piano could be heard. Today it is undergoing restoration and is not open to the public.

13 The **Church of the Virgin Mary's Birth** (✉ West of Constitution Sq.) is next to an **ancient olive tree,** where, according to tradition, Saint Anastasios, a Naupliote painter, was killed in 1655 by the Turks. Anastasios was supposedly engaged to a local girl, but he abandoned her because she was immoral. Becoming despondent as a result of spells cast over him by her relatives, he converted to Islam. Returning to his senses, he cried out, "I was a Christian, I am a Christian, and I shall die a Christian." A Turkish judge ordered that he be beheaded, but the mob, outraged by the insult to Islam, stabbed Anastasios to death. A local tradition holds that he was hanged on this olive tree, and it never again bore fruit. (Theologians debate whether such a miracle, minor at best and perhaps even dubious, is adequate recompense for Anastasios's unmerited martyrdom.) The church, a post-Byzantine three-aisle basilica, was the main Orthodox church during the Venetian occupation. It has an elaborate wooden reredos carved in 1870.

The quayside at the **Philhellenes Square** (⊠ North of Church of the Virgin Mary's Birth) is named for the memorial erected in 1903 to honor fighters in the revolution. The French, Germans, English, Swiss, and Americans who fought with the Greeks are called philhellenes, or "friends of Greece."

⑭ The church of **St. Nicholas** (⊠ Off Philhellenes Sq.) was built in 1713 for the use of sailors by Augustine Sagredo, the prefect of the Venetian fleet. The facade seen today and the belfry are recent additions. Inside, the church is furnished with a Venetian reredos and pulpit, and a chandelier from Odessa. From St. Nicholas westward along the quayside (called Akti Miaouli) is an unbroken chain of restaurants, most just average, and, farther along, more successful patisseries. It is pleasant in the afternoon for postcard writing, an iced coffee or ouzo, and conversation. Sparrows looking for handouts will flit around your feet; the air is warm and the sky blue; and Argos's high acropolis is clearly visible across the smooth sea.

⑮ If you like the view to distant Argos, the sight of the **Bourtzi** (⊠ In the harbor), Nauplion's pocket-size fortress, will captivate you. Built in 1471 by Antonio Gambello, one of those industrious Venetians, the Bourtzi (or Castelli) was at first a single tower, on a speck of land generously called St. Theodore's Island. Morosini is said to have massacred the Turkish garrison when he recaptured it for Venice in 1686. A tower and bastion were then added, giving it the shiplike appearance it has today. In 1822, after it was captured in the War of Independence, it was used to bombard the Turks defending the town. In the unsettled times after the revolution, the government retreated to the Bourtzi for a while; after 1865, it was the residence of the town executioners; and from 1930 until 1970 it was run as a hotel. During the day the Bourtzi is no longer menacing; a tree blooms bright red in its courtyard during spring. You can take a small boat out to it for spectacular views of the old part of Nauplion and the Palamidi. Illuminated by floodlights in summer, it is beautiful at dusk, but becomes grimmer as darkness falls. Extending from the extreme end of the quay is a large breakwater, the west mole, built by the Turks as the anchor point for a large chain that could be drawn up between it and the Bourtzi, blocking the harbor completely.

NEED A BREAK? A **small café** operates on the Bourtzi, where you can take in the view and refuel; it's open daily from 4 PM to 1 AM, May to September.

⑯ South of the Bourtzi is the bastion known as the **Five Brothers** (⊠ Near promontory of the peninsula), the only remaining part of the wall built around Nauplion in 1502. The name comes from the five guns placed here by the Venetians; there are five here today, all from around 1690 and all bearing the winged lion of St. Mark.

NEED A BREAK? A small taverna called the **Banieris** (⊠ Just south of Five Brothers) is a good place to sit with an ouzo and watch the sun set behind the mountains across the gulf. Keep an eye out for the arrival of the evening hydrofoil from Piraeus, as it comes up the gulf.

⑰ **Psaromachalas** (⊠ Along Kostouros St.), the fishermen's quarter, is a small district of narrow, alleylike streets running between cramped little houses that huddle beneath the walls of Acronauplia. The old houses, painted in brownish yellow, green, and salmon, have had all sorts of additions and overhangs added. The walk is enjoyable, but it is a poor neighborhood, and it's easy to feel like a voyeur scrutinizing the private lives of the locals.

The pretty miniature whitewashed chapel of **Ayios Apostoli** (⊠ Just off the parking lot of Psarmochalas) has six small springlets that trickle out of the side of Acronauplia.

The **promenade** around the peninsula, once a simple gravel pathway, is now paved with reddish flagstones and graced with an occasional ornate lamppost. Here and there a flight of steps goes down to the rocky shore below. (Be careful if you go swimming here, since the rocks are infested with sea urchins.) Just before you reach the very tip of the peninsula, marked by a ship's beacon, there is a little shrine at the foot of a path leading up toward the Acronauplia walls above. Little Virgin Mary or **Ayia Panagitsa** (⊠ At end of promenade) hugs the cliff on a small terrace and is decorated with an array of icons. During the Turkish occupation it hid one of Greece's secret schools. Two other terraces, like garden sanctuaries, have a few rose bushes and the shade of olive and cedar trees. They are very restful places to sit and not much frequented. Along the south side of the peninsula, the promenade runs midway along the cliff—it's 100 feet up to Acronauplia, 50 feet down to the sea. All along there are magnificent views of the cliff on which the Palamidi sits and the slope below, known as the Arvanitia.

On Plapouta Street is the **square dominated by Ayios Georgios** (⊠ 2 blocks west of Syngrou on Plapouta), a Byzantine church set at an angle, with five domes dating from the beginning of the 16th century and a Venetian arcade and campanile. Inside is the throne of King Otho. Around the square are several high-quality **neoclassical houses**—the one opposite the church is exceptional. Note the fine palmette centered above the door, the pilasters on the third floor with Corinthian capitals, the running Greek key entablature, and the end tiles along the roofline. This house is matched perhaps by the one at the intersection of Plapouta and Tertsetou streets, whose window treatments are especially ornate. Nauplion has many other fine neoclassical buildings; keep your eyes open and don't forget to look up once in a while.

⓲ Just west of Ayios Georgios is the square of **St. Spyridon** (⊠ Terzaki, St. Spirdonas Sq., Papanikolaou St.), a one-aisle basilica with a dome (1702). It has a special place in Greek history, for it was at its doorway that the statesman Ioannis Kapodistrias was assassinated in 1831 by the Mavromichalis brothers from the Mani, the outcome of a long-running vendetta. The mark of the bullet can be seen next to the Venetian portal. On the south side of the square, opposite St. Spyridon, are two of the four Turkish fountains preserved in Nauplion. A third is a short distance east (away from St. Spyridon) on Kapodistria Street, at the steps that constitute the upper reaches of Tertsetou Street.

⓳ King Otho returned the Venetian **Catholic Church of the Transfiguration** (⊠ 2 blocks south [uphill] from St. Spyridon) to Nauplion's Catholics. It is best known for the wooden arch erected inside the doorway in 1841, with the names carved on it of philhellenes who died during the War of Independence (Lord Byron is number 10). Note also the evidence of its use as a mosque by the Turks: the mihrab (Muslim prayer recess) behind the altar and the amputated stub of a minaret. The church boasts a small museum and an underground crypt in which can be found a recent sculptural work commemorating the defeat of the Turks at the hands of the Greeks and Philhellenes.

20 Potamianou Street, actually a flight of stone steps, ascends from St. Spyridon Square toward **Acronauplia.** The Turks called it Its Kalé. Until the Venetian occupation, it had two castles: a Frankish one on the eastern end and a Byzantine one on the west. The Venetians added the massive Castello del Torrione (or Toro for short) at the eastern end around 1480. If you have trouble locating the Toro, look under the Xenia Hotel (not the Xenia Palace), which was built on part of it. During the second Venetian occupation, the gates were strengthened and the huge Grimani bastion was added (1706) below the Toro. The Acronauplia is only accessible from the elevator on the west side, or by the road from the east side, near the Xenia Palace Hotel.

NEED A BREAK?

If you're headed back to Athens by bus and are waiting at the KTEL station (⊠ Syngrou 8), walk a few doors down to the *kafenion* (traditional Greek coffeehouse) and sweet shop for a plate of scrumptious, freshly made *loukoumades* (fritters doused in honey and sprinkled with walnuts).

OFF THE BEATEN PATH

AYIA MONI – Before or after exploring Nauplion, drive out the Epidauros road and turn right after 1 km (⅗ mi) to visit the fine Byzantine convent and church of Ayia Moni, a place of Christian devotion with a pagan twist. It was built in 1149 by Leo, the Bishop of Argos and Nauplion, and an inscription on the west gate records his efforts in building it and hopefully expresses the possibility that the Virgin will reward him by absolving him of his sins. In the monastery garden is a fountain said to be the spring Kanathos, where Hera annually renewed her virginity. On the way back to town, be sure to stop and see the Bavarian Lion, a beast of more than life size carved from a rock outcrop in the Pronoia section, Nauplion's modern suburb. The sleeping lion, a memorial to the Bavarian troops who died of typhus while serving King Otho, is a sad symbol of mortality compared to the invincible Venetian lions on Nauplion's fortresses.

Beaches

In Nauplion **Arvanitia Beach** (⊠ On south side of town nestled between Acronauplia and the Palomides) is rocky but nice for a plunge after a day of sightseeing, and it has convenient kiosks. If you want to make a day out of relaxing in the sun, you're better off heading for one of the beaches farther away from town. Close to Nauplion are **Kastraki** and **Plaka.** The closest is **Karathona,** favored by Greek families with children and picnic baskets and serviced by buses.

Dining and Lodging

With one or two exceptions you'll eat better for less at the restaurants on Constitution Square or just beyond on Staikopoulos Street than at the ones along the waterfront. After dining have a dessert at **Galaxia** (⊠ Constitution Sq.) or in one of the patisseries on the harbor.

$$ ✕ **Savouras.** Fresh seafood is served in this unpretentious taverna overlooking the bay; it is generally regarded as one of the best fish restaurants in the area. Specialties are red mullet, pandora, and dorado. Good side dishes are the eggplant dip and the fava with onions. ⊠ *Bouboulinas 79,* ☎ *0752/27704. No credit cards.*

$–$$ ✕ **O Arapakos.** Settle in on the waterfront for excellent Greek cooking, starting with grilled octopus and moving on to specialties like *yiouvetsi ton arapi* (beef with potatoes, tomatoes, carrots, and eggplants cooked in a ceramic dish) or *arnaki exohiko* (lamb stuffed with feta and potatoes). You can also have fresh fish, such as sea bream cooked over charcoal, or *bakaliaro skordalia* (dried cod, fried and served with a dollop of garlic sauce), all complimented by the light barrel retsina.

To further entice you, there's usually some pan dessert like *galakto-bouriko* (a sinful custard pastry) or baklava. ⊠ *Bouboulinas 81,* ☎ *0752/27675. V.*

$ ✗ **Hellas.** This reliable restaurant, probably the most inexpensive on Constitution Square, is also one of the most popular in Nauplion for classic Greek dishes just like *yiayia* (grandma) used to make. Ask to go back in the kitchen and see what's cooking, and if moussaka or pastit-sio has just finished baking, you're in luck—both are outstanding. The tomatoes stuffed with rice, the meatballs, and the grape leaves are also very good. ⊠ *Constitution Sq., opposite archaeological museum,* ☎ *0752/27278. V.*

$ ✗ **Karamanlis.** This simple taverna near the courthouse is crowded at lunch with civil servants who come for its tasty though limited num-ber of *magirefta* (precooked dishes). The light fish soup makes a good starter, followed by *yiouvarlakia* (meat-rice balls with avgolemono sauce), oven-baked potatoes, wild greens, and barrel retsina. Fresh fish is also available at very reasonable prices. ⊠ *Bouboulinas 1,* ☎ *0752/27668. No credit cards.*

$ ✗ **Ta Fanaria.** This is one of the finest restaurants in Nauplion. Fol-★ low this advice and enjoy: arrive late, sit at one of the tables in the nar-row alley beside the restaurant, and ask what's best that night. It's known for its *ladera* (vegetables cooked in olive oil), but the charcoal grilled lamb ribs, the *imam* (eggplant stuffed with onions), and the lamb baked with vegetables such as okra or green beans are equally deli-cious. ⊠ *Staikopoulos 13,* ☎ *0752/27141. V.*

$$$$ ▥ **Candia House.** Seventeen km (10½ mi) south of Nauplion on Kan-★ dia Beach, this beautifully decorated hotel is the creation of a Greek publisher, who has flawlessly matched good taste with comfort. Fresh flowers, antiques, paintings by Greek artists, hand-crafted mirrors, fire-places—all are just a taste of the embellishments of the suites. Each one is different in its decor, and their size ranges from palatial to truly enormous. All have balconies, sitting rooms, televisions, and refriger-ators, and buffet breakfast is included in the price. The hexagonal restau-rant with large windows looking onto the sea specializes in healthy meals, and the hotel offers hydromassage and botanotherapy treatments. ⊠ *Kandia-Irion, 21100,* ☎ *0752/94060 through 94063,* ℻ *0752/94480. 10 suites with bath. Restaurant, air-conditioning, pool, massage, ex-ercise room, recreation room. AE, DC, MC, V.*

$$$$ ▥ **Xenia Palace.** The view from the rooms in the Xenia Palace of the picturesque Bourtzi is exceptional; it appears in Greek National Tourist Organization (GNTO or EOT) television advertisements, and the view is possible only because the hotel was built on the ruins of the Frank-ish fortification atop Acronauplia. Modern art adorns the lobby, the relatively spacious rooms have exposed stonework, and the marble bath-rooms are, without qualification, among the best in Greece. Lighting in the rooms is dim, but some of the furniture needs reupholstering, and half board (included in the price) is mandatory. An elevator cut through the rock takes you to a tunnel leading straight into town, below. ⊠ *Acronauplia, 21100,* ☎ *0752/28981 through 28985,* ℻ *0752/28987. 48 rooms with bath, 3 suites. Restaurant, bar, air-conditioning, pool, dance club. AE, MC, V.*

$$$ ▥ **Amalia.** This attractive hotel occupies a fine neoclassical-style build-ing in large gardens 3 km (2 mi) outside Nauplion near ancient Tiryns. The public rooms are spacious and comfortable, the service attentive, and the buffet breakfast is included in the price. With an inviting swimming pool and a nearby beach, this makes for a relaxing stay. ⊠ *National rd. to Argos, 21100,* ☎ *0752/24401,* ℻ *0752/24400. 171*

rooms with bath. 3 restaurants, bar, cafeteria, air-conditioning, pool.
AE, DC, MC, V.

$$ ⊞ **Dioscuri.** This family-run hotel is nothing fancy but well looked after;
★ if you're not printing money but want a decent room, this could be it.
From the small balconies there is a good view of the harbor, and the
staff is especially helpful. Continental breakfast is included in the price.
⊠ Zigomala 6, 21100, ☎ 0752/28550 or 0752/28644, FAX 0752/21202.
51 rooms with bath. Restaurant, bar. V.

$$ ⊞ **Victoria.** Although it was built in the 1970s, the Victoria is well
maintained by its friendly managers, the Zoubelakis. It is spotless, and
the pink-and-green wallpaper is as new as the furnishings. So what if
the bathrooms are on the small side; the location in the heart of old
Nauplion is hard to beat, and from the balconies you can see either
the neoclassical houses or Acronauplia. ⊠ Spiliadou 3, 21100, ☎
0752/27420, FAX 0752/27517. 36 rooms with bath. Bar, air-conditioning.
V. Closed Nov.

$ ⊞ **Epidauros.** This hotel, a former merchant prince's home, is simple
★ but delightful. The two buildings feature an assortment of room styles,
all with pine decor. This was one of Nauplion's first three hotels. ⊠
Kokkinou 2, 21100, ☎ FAX 0752/27541. 35 rooms, 25 with bath.
Breakfast room, bar. No credit cards.

$ ⊞ **Leto.** There is a certain randomness about the Leto. No two rooms
are the same and not all rooms have baths, but they are all clean and
well kept. The neighborhood, just below the walls of Acronauplia, is
quiet and sees less tourist traffic than the town below. ⊠ Zigomala
28, ☎ 0752/28093. 11 rooms, 7 with bath. No credit cards. Closed
Nov.–Mar.

Nightlife

BARS AND DISCOS

Though Naupliotes drive to Tolo for their evening revels, Nauplion's
waterfront hot spots of the minute are **Disco Muses, Rainbow,** and **Disco
Gorilla.**

Shopping

Many stores in Nauplion and Olympia have the reproductions of
bronzes, frescoes, and vase paintings, the T-shirts, and the worry beads
for which your family, friends, and coworkers have been hankering.
Nauplion is better for antiques, especially toward the end of Staikopoulos Street in the old part of town.

GIFTS AND JEWELRY

It's fun to poke around at **Ithaki** (⊠ 9 Farmaleopoulou, ☎ 0752/22816
or 22091). For good-looking jewelry of fine quality, there's **Camara**
(⊠ Spiliadou 11 and ⊠ Konstantinou 10, ☎ FAX 0752/24093).

Tiryns

★ 5 km (3 mi) north of Nauplion.

Partly obscured by citrus trees are the well-preserved ruins of the
Mycenaean acropolis of Tiryns. Some tours skip the site in their mad
dash to cover everything in a single day, but if you see this citadel, with
its massive walls and its palace, before touring Mycenae, you can understand those rambling ruins more easily. Homer describes Tiryns as
"the wall-girt city," the only ancient literary reference to it, and Henry
Miller was repelled by the place, as he records in The Colossus of
Maroussi: "Tiryns is prehistoric in character. . . . Tiryns represents a
relapse. . . . Tiryns smells of cruelty, barbarism, suspicion, isolation."
Today the site seems harmless, home to a few lizards who timidly sun
themselves on the Bronze Age stones and run for cover if you approach.

Archaeological exploration of the site, which still continues, shows that the acropolis was occupied in Neolithic times.

Tiryns, called Tirintha in ancient times, was the birthplace of Herakles. Amphitryon, king of Tiryns, wed his virtuous and stunning cousin Alkmene, but before they could consummate the marriage he left to avenge the death of her brothers. Zeus, disguised as Amphitryon, took advantage of the king's absence to seduce Alkmene, and from her union with first a god and then a mortal, she bore two sons. One, Iphikles, who resembled her husband, was lacking in ability; the other, who took after Zeus, was the mighty Herakles. When still an infant of 18 months, he proved his demigod status by strangling the serpents that were sent to kill him by Hera, Zeus's jealous wife.

The citadel makes use of a long, low outcrop, on which was set the circuit wall of gigantic limestone blocks (of the type called "cyclopean" because the ancients thought they could have been handled only by the giant cyclops—the largest block is estimated at more than 15 tons).

㉑ Via the **cyclopean ramp** it was entered on the east side, through a gate leading to a narrow passage between the outer and inner walls. One could then turn right, toward the residential section in the **lower citadel** (now usually closed to the public) or to the left toward the **upper citadel**

㉒ ㉓ and **palace.** The heavy **main gate** and **second gate** blocked the passage to the palace and trapped attackers caught between the walls. After

㉔ the second gate, the passage opens onto a rectangular **courtyard,** whose

㉕ massive left-hand wall is pierced by a **gallery of small vaulted chambers,** or casemates, opening off a **long narrow corridor** roofed by a **corbeled arch.** (They were possibly once used to stable horses, and the walls have been worn smooth by the countless generations of sheep and goats who have sheltered there.) This is one of the famous galleries of Tiryns; another such gallery at the southernmost end of the acropolis also connects a series of five casemates with sloping roofs.

An elaborate entranceway leads west from the court to the upper citadel and palace, sited at the highest point of the acropolis. The

㉖ ㉗ complex included a colonnaded **court**; the *great **megaron*** (main hall) opened onto it and held the royal throne. Surviving fragments suggest that the floors and the walls were decorated, the walls with frescoes (now in the National Archaeological Museum of Athens) depicting a boar hunt, women riding in chariots, and a procession of women. Beyond the megaron, a large **court** overlooks the houses in the lower citadel;

㉘ ㉙ from here, a long **stairway** descends to a small **postern gate** in the west wall. At the excavated part of the lower acropolis a significant discovery

㉚ was made; two parallel **tunnels,** roofed in the same way as the galleries on the east and south sides, start within the acropolis and extend under the walls, leading to **subterranean cisterns** that ensured a continuous water supply.

From the palace you can see how Tiryns dominated the flat, fertile land at the head of the Gulf of Argos. The view would have been different in the Late Bronze Age: the ancient shoreline was nearer to the citadel, and outside the walls there was an extensive settlement. Profitis Ilias, the prominent hill to the east, was the site of the Tiryns cemetery. ✉ *On low hill just past suburbs of Nauplion,* ☎ *0752/22657.* 🎫 *500 dr.* ☉ *Weekdays 8–7 (winter 8–5), weekends and holidays 8–3.*

Argos

㉛ *12 km (7½ mi) northwest of Nauplion, 7 km (4⅓ mi) northwest of Tiryns.*

On the western edge of the Argive plain, amid citrus groves, is the city of Argos (population 21,000), the economic hub of the region. The fall

of Mycenae and Tiryns at the close of the Late Bronze Age proved favorable for Argos. Under King Pheidon, Argos reached its greatest power in the 7th century BC, becoming the chief city in the Peloponnese. In the mid-5th century, it consolidated its hold on the Argive plain by eradicating Mycenae and Tiryns. But like Corinth, Argos was never powerful enough to set its own course, following in later years the leadership of Sparta, Athens, and the Macedonian kings. Twice in its history, women are said to have defended Argos: once in 494 BC when Telesilla the poetess (who may be mere legend) armed old men, boys, and women to hold the walls against the Spartans; and again in 272 BC when Pyrrhus, king of Epiros, who was taking the city street by street, was felled from above by an old woman armed with a tile.

Remains of the Classical city are scattered throughout the modern one, and along Tripoleos Street you can see in a small area the extensive **ruins of the Roman bath, theater, odeon, and agora. The Kastro** is a Byzantine and Frankish structure incorporating remnants of classical walls, and it was later expanded by the Turks and Venetians. A small **archaeological museum** on the main platia, **Ayios Petros,** has well-displayed finds from Argos and nearby sites. ⊠ *Vasilissis Olgas,* ☎ *0751/28819.* 🎫 *500 dr.* 🕐 *Tues.–Sun. 8:30–3.*

Outdoor Activities and Sports

HIKING AND CLIMBING

A refuge for adventurers is at **Oropedia Ostrakinas** (⊠ On Mt. Menalo), which sleeps 26; contact the Tripoli Alpine Club (☎ 071/232243).

Shopping

MARKET

On Saturday morning, the platia is transformed into a huge open **household-merchandise and produce market** (dwarfing that at Nauplion). It's more fun than yet another tourist shop, and you can often find good souvenirs, such as wooden stamps used to impress designs on bread loaves, at prices that haven't been inflated. Argos is also well-known throughout Greece for its ouzo.

Mycenae

★ *21 km (13 mi) north of Nauplion, 9 km (5½ mi) north of Argos.*

The ancient citadel of Mycenae, which Homer describes as "rich in gold," stands on a low hill, wedged between sheer, lofty peaks but separated from them by two deep ravines. It commanded both the greater part of the plain stretching southward to the sea and the exit from the Dervenakia Pass; the Perseia Fountain, close to the entrance of the acropolis, ensured a continuous water supply; the fertile Argive plain provided food. The site's natural advantages thus enhanced its strategic position.

Mycenae was founded by Perseus, son of Zeus and Danae, and the Perseid dynasty provided many of its rulers. After the last of them, Eurystheus (famous for the labors he imposed on Herakles), the Mycenaeans chose Atreus, son of Pelops and Hippodamia, as their ruler. But Atreus hated his brother, Thyestes, so much that he offered Thyestes his own children to eat, thereby incurring the wrath of the gods. Thyestes pronounced a fearful curse on Atreus and his progeny; Atreus's heir, the renowned and energetic Agamemnon, was murdered on his return from the Trojan War by his wife, Clytemnestra, and her lover, Aegisthus (Thyestes's surviving son). Orestes and his sister Electra, the children of Agamemnon, took revenge for this murder, and Orestes became king of Mycenae. During the rule of his son, Tisamenus, the descendants of Herakles returned and claimed their birthright by force, thus satisfying the wrath of the gods and the curse of Atreus.

In the 17th century BC, Mycenae began an extraordinary growth in wealth and power that was to influence all of the eastern Mediterranean. The Mycenaean civilization, at first heavily influenced by that of Minoan Crete, spread throughout Greece, and by 1350 BC the Mycenaean culture was predominate not only on the mainland and the Aegean, but also on Crete. Clay tablets inscribed with Mycenaean Greek writing (called Linear B) have provided us with information about the society. At its height, it centered on palaces, from which kings or princes governed feudally, holding sway over various bakers, bronze workers, textile and perfumed oil manufacturers, masons, potters, and shepherds. And there were merchants, priests and priestesses, possibly a military leader, the nobility, and, perhaps, slaves. Some tablets record palace possessions (swords, textiles, furniture, and chariots) and commodities (grain, bronze, livestock, wool, and oil); other tablets record the elaborate system of tax collection for these various commodities. The dwellings of the elite were decorated with wall paintings depicting processions of ladies, hunting scenes, ox-hide shields, heraldic griffins, and such religious activities as priestesses bearing stalks of grain.

From the list of deities who received offerings, it seems that the Mycenaeans worshiped familiar classical deities, but the bizarre figurines found in a shrine at Mycenae (now in the Nauplion archaeological museum)—along with models of coiled snakes—are scarcely human, let alone godlike in the style of classical statuary. Mycenaeans usually buried their dead in chamber tombs cut into the sides of hills, but rulers and their families were interred more grandly, in shaft graves at first and later in immense tholos tombs—circular vaults, a hallmark of Mycenaean architecture, made by overlapping successive courses of stones, while reducing the diameter of the opening, until it was closed with a ·

single stone on top. The tholos was built into a hillside, like a chamber tomb, entered by a long passage or *dromos*, and covered with a mound of earth. Doors at the end of the dromos allowed the tomb to be opened and reused—not a bad feature, since the average life expectancy of a Mycenaean was about 36 years.

Massive fortification walls and gateways, also Mycenaean specialties, were necessary defenses in a culture whose economy of agriculture and trade was supplemented by occasional raiding and intercity warfare. The Mycenaeans had widespread trade contacts—their fine pottery has been found in Cyprus, southern Italy, Egypt, and the Levant. Wrecks of trading ships apparently headed toward Greece have yielded ox-hide-shape bronze ingots, aromatic resin, logs of ebony and ivory, and blue glass for jewelry. But the heyday of the Mycenaeans did not last. Drought, earthquake, invasion, and economic collapse have all been suggested individually and in combination for their fall. Around 1250 BC, arrangements were made to secretly secure the water supplies at Mycenae itself as well as at Tiryns and Athens. Coincidence? Some time around 1200 many sites, but not all, seem to have suffered some destruction. An uprising, invasion, or earthquake? Recovery and rebuilding took place, but it is likely that the palaces were no longer used, and it is certain that a major shift in political and economic administration was underway. By 1100 BC, when there may have been another round of destruction, Greece was heading into a Dark Age. Writing became a lost art, connections beyond the Aegean were nearly severed, and many sites were abandoned. Whatever the cause, or causes, the lights eventually went out.

In 1841, soon after the establishment of the Greek state, excavations of the **ancient citadel** by the Archaeological Society uncovered the parts of the Lion Gate that lay below the surface, and in 1874, Schliemann began to dig. Today you'll enter the citadel from the northwest

32 through the famous **Lion Gate.** The triangle above the lintel depicts in relief two lions, whose heads, probably of steatite, are now missing. They stand facing each other, their forepaws resting on a high pedestal representing an altar, above which stands a pillar ending in a uniquely shaped capital and abacus. Above the abacus are four sculptured discs, interpreted as representing the ends of beams that supported a roof. The **gate** was closed by a double wooden door sheathed in bronze. The two halves were secured by a wooden bar, which rested in cuttings in the jambs, still visible. The holes for the pivots on which it swung can still be seen in both sill and lintel.

33 Just inside on the right stands the **Granary,** so named for the many *pithoi* (clay storage vessels) that were found inside the building and held carbonized wheat grains. Between it and the Lion Gate a flight of steps used to lead to the top of the wall; today you see a broad ramp leading steeply

34 up to the palace; the staircase is modern. Beyond the granary is the **Grave Circle A,** which contains six **royal shaft graves,** encircled by a row of upright **stone slabs** interrupted on its northern side by the entrance. Above each grave stood a vertical stone stele. The "grave goods" buried with the dead were an array of personal belongings including gold face masks, gold cups and jewelry, bronze swords with ivory hilts, and daggers with gold inlay, now in the National Archaeological Museum of Athens. South

35 of the Grave Circle lie the remains of the **House of the Warrior Vase,** the

36 **37** **38** **Ramp House,** the **Cult center,** and others; farther south is the **House of Tsountas** of Mycenae.

The palace complex covers the summit of the hill and occupies a series of **terraces;** one entered through a monumental gateway in the north-

39 west side and, proceeding to the right, beyond it, came to the **Great Court-**

244

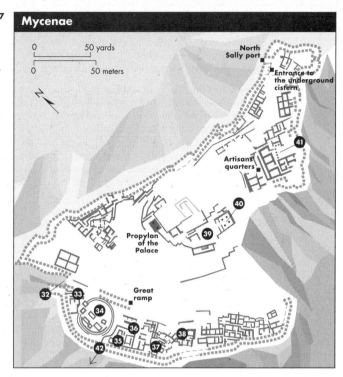

yard of the palace. The ground was originally covered by a plaster coating above which was a layer of painted and decorated stucco. East of the Great Courtyard is the **Megaron** with a **porch, vestibule,** and the **throne room** itself, which had four columns supporting the roof (the bases are still visible) and a circular hearth in the center. Remains of an **archaic temple** and a **Hellenistic temple** can be seen north of the palace, and to the east on the right, on a lower level, are the **workshops** of the artists and craftsmen employed by the king. On the same level, adjoining the workshops to the east, is the **House of the Columns,** with a row of columns surrounding its central court. The remaining section of the east wall consists of an addition made in around 1250 BC to ensure free communication from the citadel with the subterranean reservoir cut at the same time. ⊠ *Site,* ☎ *0751/76585.* ⊡ *1,500 dr.* ☉ *Weekdays 8–7 (winter 8–5), weekends and holidays 8–3.*

On the hill of Panagitsa, on the left along the road that runs to the citadel, lies another Mycenaean settlement, with, close by, the most imposing example of Mycenaean architecture, the **Treasury of Atreus.** Its construction is placed around 1250 BC, contemporary with the Lion Gate and after Grave Circle A was no longer used for burials. Like the other tholos tombs, it consists of a passageway built of huge squared stones, which leads into a domed chamber. The facade of the entrance had applied decoration, but only small fragments have been preserved. Traces of bronze nails suggest that similar decoration once existed inside. The tomb was found empty, already robbed in antiquity, but it must at one time have contained rich and valuable grave goods. Pausanias tells us that the ancients considered it the Tomb of Agamemnon, its other name. ⊠ *Across from ancient citadel.* ⊡ *Fee for citadel includes this site; hang on to your ticket.* ☉ *Weekdays 8–7 (winter 8–5), weekends and holidays 8–3.*

En Route Return to the main road north, which now climbs more sharply; 19 km (11¾ mi) from Argos it enters the narrow Dervenakia Pass, between the summits of Mt. Tretos. Near this pass, the revolutionary leader Theodoros Kolokotronis defeated the Turks in 1822. Four thousand Turks were slain in the battle and an additional 1,000 perished as they desperately tried to fight their way out of the Argolid. A statue of Kolokotronis (⊠ Near Nemea–Dervenakia train station) commemorates the victory.

Ancient Nemea

❋ *18 km (11 mi) north of Mycenae.*

Ancient Nemea was the site of a sanctuary of Zeus and the home of the biennial Nemean games, a Panhellenic competition like those at Isthmia, Delphi, and Olympia. *It was here that Herakles performed the first of the Twelve Labors set by the king of Argos in penance for killing his own children—he slew the ferocious Nemean lion living in a nearby cave.*

The main monuments at the site are the **temple of Zeus** (built about 330 BC to replace a 6th-century BC structure), the **stadium,** and an **early Christian basilica** of the 5th–6th century. Three columns of the temple still stand, and efforts have begun to re-erect two more. An extraordinary feature of the stadium, which dates to the last quarter of the 4th century BC, is its vaulted tunnel and entranceway. The evidence indicates that the use of the arch in building may have been brought back from India with Alexander, though arches were previously believed to be a Roman invention. A spacious **museum** displays finds from the site, including pieces of athletic gear, and coins of various city-states and rulers. Around Nemea, keep an eye out for roadside stands where local growers sell the famous red wine of this region. ⊠ *In upland valley,* ☎ *0746/22739.* 📷 *500 dr.* ☉ *Tues.–Sun. 8–3.*

En Route As the road emerges from the hills onto the flatter terrain around Corinth, the massive rock of Acrocorinth peaks nearly 1,900 feet on the left. The ancient city sat at the foot of this imposing peak, its long walls reaching north to the harbor of Lechaion on the Gulf of Corinth.

Ancient Corinth

★ ❌ *81 km (50½ mi) southwest of Athens, 35 km (21¾ mi) northeast of Nemea.*

West of the isthmus, the countryside opens up into a low-lying coastal plain around the head of the Gulf of Corinth. **Modern Corinth,** near the coast about 8 km (5 mi) north of the turnoff for the ancient town, is a regional center of some 23,000 inhabitants. Concrete pier-and-slab is the preferred architectural style, and the city seems to be under a seismic curse: periodic earthquakes knock the buildings down before they develop any character. It was founded in 1858 after one of these quakes leveled the old village at the ancient site; another flattened the new town in 1928; and a third in 1981 destroyed many of its buildings. Most tourists avoid the town altogether, visiting the ruins of ancient Corinth and moving on.

Ancient Corinth, at the base of the massive Acrocorinth peak (1,863 feet) was blessed: It governed the north–south land route over the isthmus and the east–west sea route. The fertile plain and hills around the city (where currants are grown, which are named for Corinth) are extensive, and the Acrocorinth afforded a virtually impregnable refuge. It had harbors at Lechaion on the Gulf of Corinth and at Kenchreai on the Saronic Gulf. Corinth was a wealthy city with a reputation for luxury and vice and a Temple of Aphrodite with more than 1,000 sacred prostitutes. These facts are emphasized too often today, and amid the titillation the real story of Corinth is lost.

The city came to prominence in the 8th century BC, becoming a center of commerce and founding the colonies of Syracuse in Sicily and Kerkyra on Corfu. The 5th century BC saw the rise of Athens as the preeminent economic power in Greece, and Athenian "meddling" in the Gulf of Corinth and in relations between Corinth and her colonies helped bring about the Peloponnesian War. After the war, Corinth made common cause with Athens, Argos, and Boeotia against Sparta, later remaining neutral as Thebes and then Macedonia rose to power.

In the second half of the 4th century, Corinth became active once more; in 344 BC the city sent an army to rescue Syracuse, which was threatened by local tyrants allied with the Carthaginians. Timoleon, the aristocrat who led the army, was in self-imposed exile after killing his own brother, who had plotted to become tyrant of Corinth. Corinthian opinion was divided as to whether Timoleon was the savior of the city or merely a fratricide, so no one objected to Timoleon's appointment to this dangerous mission (he wasn't present at the time). The Corinthian statesman Teleclides understood the challenge facing Timoleon perfectly, saying, "We shall decide that he slew a tyrant if he is successful; that he slew his brother if he fails." The tyrants were suppressed and Carthaginian armies expelled from Sicily; Timoleon, declared a hero, retired to a small farm outside Syracuse, where he died two years later.

Corinth was conquered by Philip II of Macedon in 338 BC, but it was named the meeting place of Philip's new Hellenic confederacy. After Philip was assassinated, Alexander immediately swooped down on Corinth to meet with the confederacy, to confirm his leadership, and to forestall any thoughts of rebellion. It's said that outside the gates Alexander encountered the philosopher Diogenes the Cynic, who espoused a creed of living as simply and cheaply as possible. When not carrying a lantern around in broad daylight on his quest for an honest man, he lived in a large storage jar, which is where Alexander found him. When Alexander the Great asked Diogenes if there was anything he could do for him, "Only step out of my sunlight," was the curt reply.

After the death of Alexander, the climate continued profitable for trade, and Corinth flourished. When the Roman general Flamininus defeated Macedonia in 198–196 BC, Corinth became the chief city of the Achaean confederacy, and in fact the chief city of Greece. Eventually the confederacy took up arms against Rome, attacking with more impetuosity than brains or training, and was crushed. The Romans under Lucius Mummius marched to Corinth and defeated a second Greek army, and Pausanias says: ". . . Two days after the battle he took possession in force and burnt Corinth. Most of the people who were left there were murdered by the Romans, and Mummius auctioned the women and children." Corinth was razed and its wealth sent back to Rome, and for nearly 100 years the site was abandoned. In 44 BC, Julius Caesar refounded the city, and under Pax Romana Corinth prospered as never before; its population (about 90,000 in 400 BC) was recorded as 300,000 plus 450,000 slaves.

The apostle Paul lived in Corinth for 18 months (AD 51–52), working as a tent maker or leather worker, making converts where he could. The city received imperial patronage from Hadrian, who constructed an aqueduct from Lake Stymfalia to the city, and Herodes Atticus made improvements to its civic buildings. Corinth survived invasions but was devastated by earthquakes and began a long decline with further invasions and plague. After 1204, when Constantinople fell to the Fourth Crusade, Corinth was a prize sought by all, but it eventually surrendered to Geoffrey de Villehardouin (the subsequent Prince of Achaea) and Otho de la Roche (soon to be Duke of Athens). Corinth was captured by the Turks in 1458, the Knights of Malta won it in 1612, the Venetians took a turn from 1687 until 1715, when the Turks returned, and it finally came into Greek hands in 1822.

The ancient city was huge. Excavations, which have gone on since 1896, have exposed ruins at several locations: on the height of Acrocorinth and on the slopes below, the center of the Roman city, and northward toward the coast. Most of the buildings that have been excavated are from the Roman era; only a few from before the sack of Corinth in 146 BC were rehabilitated when the city was refounded.

The **Glauke Fountain** is just past the parking lot on the left. According to Pausanias, "Jason's second wife, Glauke (also known as Creusa), threw herself into the water to obtain relief from a poisoned dress sent to her by Medea." Beyond the fountain is the **museum,** which displays examples of the pottery decorated with friezes of panthers, sphinxes, bulls, and such, for which Corinth was famous; some fine mosaics from the Roman period; and a variety of marble and terra-cotta sculptures. The remains of a temple (Temple E) adjoin the museum, and steps lead from there left toward the **Temple of Apollo.**

Seven of the original 38 columns of the Temple of Apollo are still standing, and it is by far the most striking of Corinth's ancient buildings, as well as being one of the oldest stone temples in Greece (mid-6th century BC). Beyond the temple are the remains of the **North Market,** a colonnaded square once surrounded by many small shops. South of the Temple of Apollo is the main Forum of ancient Corinth. A row of shops bounds the Forum at the far western end. East of the market is a series of small temples, and beyond is the Forum's main plaza. A long line of shops runs lengthwise through the Forum, dividing it into an **upper (southern)** and **lower (northern) terrace,** in the center of which is the bema (large podium), perhaps the very one where the Roman proconsul Gallio refused to act on accusations against St. Paul.

The southern boundary of the Forum was the **South Stoa,** a 4th-century building, perhaps erected by Philip II to house delegates to his Hellenic confederacy. There were originally 33 shops across the front, and the back was altered in Roman times to accommodate such civic offices as the council hall, or *bouleterion,* in the center. The road to Kenchreai began next to the bouleterion and headed south. Farther along the South Stoa were the entrance to the **South Basilica** and, at the far end, the **Southeast Building,** which probably was the city archive.

In the lower Forum, below the Southeast Building, was the **Julian Basilica,** a former law court; under the steps leading into it were found two starting lines (an earlier and a later one) for the course of a footrace from the Greek city. Continuing to the northeast corner of the Forum, we approach the facade of the **Fountain of Peirene.** Water from a spring was gathered into four reservoirs before flowing out through the arcade-like facade into a drawing basin in front. Frescoes of swimming fish from a 2nd-century refurbishment can still be seen. The Lechaion road heads out of the Forum to the north. A colonnaded courtyard, called the **Peribolos of Apollo,** is directly to the east of the Lechaion Road and beyond it lies a **public latrine,** with toilets in place, and the remains of a **Roman-era bath,** probably the Baths of Euryk-les described by Pausanias as Corinth's best-known.

Along the west side of the Lechaion road is a large basilica entered from the Forum through the **Captives' Facade,** named for its sculptures of captive barbarians. West of the Captives' Facade the row of **Northwest Shops** completes the circuit.

Northwest of the parking lot is the **Odeon,** cut into a natural slope, which was built during the AD 1st century, but it burned down around 175. Around 225 it was renovated and used as an arena for combats between gladiators and wild beasts. Just north of the Odeon is the **Theater** (5th century BC), one of the few Greek buildings reused by the Romans, who filled in the original seats and set in new ones at a steeper angle. By the 3rd century they had adapted it for gladiatorial contests and finally for mock naval battles.

North of the Theater, just inside the city wall, are the **Fountain of Lerna** and the **Asklepieion,** the sanctuary of the god of healing with a small temple (4th century BC) set in a colonnaded courtyard and a series of dining rooms in a second courtyard. Terra-cotta votive offerings representing afflicted body parts (hands, legs, breasts, genitals, etc.) were found in the excavation of the Asklepieion, and many of them are displayed at the museum; similar votives of body parts can be purchased and blessed at some Orthodox churches in Greece today. A stone box for offerings, complete with copper coins, was found at the entrance to the sanctuary. Off the lower courtyard are the drawing basins of the Fountain of Lerna. ⊠ *5 km west of Corinth,* ☎ *0741/31207.* ⊡ *1,200 dr.* ☉ *Daily 8:45–7, winter 8:45–3.*

On the slope of Acrocorinth is the **Sanctuary of Demeter,** a small stoa and a series of dining rooms with couches. The climb up to Acrocorinth is worth the effort for both the medieval fortifications and the view, one of the best in Greece. The entrance is on the west, guarded by a moat and outer gate, middle gate, and inner gate. Most of the fortifications are Byzantine, Frankish, Venetian, and Turkish—but the right-hand tower of the innermost of the three gates is apparently a 4th-century BC original. There is no access to the site; it can only be viewed. ⊠ *Below rd. to Acrocorinth and on its lower slopes.*

Xylokastro

🔞 *34 km (21 mi) west of Corinth.*

Xylokastro, a pleasant little town, is perfect if you want to soak your feet after trudging around Corinth. The road just west of town that climbs up Sithas Valley also climbs up to Ano Trikala, an alpine landscape where the peak (second-highest in the Peloponnese) stays covered with snow into June.

Beaches
A wide, paved promenade along the shore, with a beautiful view of the mountains across the gulf, leads to a good if somewhat pebbly **beach** (⊠ Beyond the east end of town).

ACHAEA AND ELIS
Vouraikos Gorge, Kalavrita, Rion, Patras, Chlemoutsi, Olympia

Achaea's wooded mountains guard the mountain steadfasts of Arcadia to the south, and mirror the forbidding mountains of central Greece on the other side of the Corinthian Gulf. Those who venture into Achaea will inevitably find their way to Patras, a teeming port city, with all the flavor, color, and vices of port cities. Elis, farther to the south, is bucolic and peaceful. It is a land of rolling hills green with forests and vegetation, and it is not surprising that the Greeks chose this region as the place in which to hold the Olympic Games.

Vouraikos Gorge

46 *Diakofto, the coastal access point: 47 km (29¼ mi) west of Xylokastro; Kalavrita: 25 km (15½ mi) south of Diakofto.*

The **Kalavrita Express**, a narrow-gauge train starting at Diakofto, heads up into the mountains through the Vouraikos Gorge, a fantastic landscape of towering pinnacles and precipitous rock walls. The diminutive train, a cabless diesel engine sandwiched between two small passenger cars, crawls upward, clinging to the rails in the steeper sections with a rack and pinion. The **Kalavrita Express** makes the round-trip from Diakofto six times daily; the first trip is at 6:48 AM, the last returns at 5:51 PM. ✉ *Fare: 1,000 dr. round-trip. Although the trip can be made from Athens (round-trip fare, Athens–Kalavrita: first-class 4,000 dr., second-class 2,800 dr.), it is best enjoyed between Corinth and Patras.*

A road goes directly from Diakofto to Kalavrita; the spectacular 25-km (15½ mi) drive negotiates the east side of the gorge. A cab from Diakofto to Kalavrita costs about 5500 dr.

Forty-five minutes into the trip the train pauses at Zakhlorou, where you can hike up a steep path through evergreen oak, cypress, and fir to the monastery of **Mega Spileo** (altitude 3,117 feet). This 45-minute trek offers superb views of the Vouraikos valley and distant villages on the opposite side. The occasional sound of bells carries on the wind from flocks of goats grazing on the steep slopes above. The monastery, founded in the 4th century, sits at the base of a huge curving cliff face and incorporates a large cavern (the monastery's name means "large cave"). You can tour the monastery to see an icon of the Virgin supposedly painted by St. Luke, vellum manuscripts of early gospels, and the heads of the founding monks. ✉ *Start hike on path in Zakhlorou.* ☉ *Daily 8–3.*

Beyond Zakhlorou, the gorge widens into a steep-sided green alpine valley for the last 11 km (7 mi) to Kalavrita (☞ *below*), a small town of about 2,000 nestled below snowcapped Mt. Helmos.

Kalavrita

47 *25 km (15½ mi) south of Diakofto.*

The ruins of a **Frankish castle, the Church of the Dormition,** and a **small museum** are worth seeing, but Greeks remember Kalavrita as the site of the Nazis' most heinous war crime. On December 13, 1943, the occupying forces rounded up and executed the town's entire male population over the age of 15, then locked women and children into the school and set it on fire. They escaped, but the Nazis later returned and burned the town to the ground. The clock on the church tower is stopped at 2:34 PM, marking the time of the execution.

Lodging

$$ 🏨 **Filoxenia.** This modern hotel caters largely to ski-season tours. All the rooms have balconies that look either to the Gorge or the mountains of the Peloponnese. The decor appears to be a holdover from the 70s, but the friendliness of the staff allows you to indulge such lapses in taste. ✉ *Kallimani, 25001,* ☎ *0692/22290 or 0692/22493,* FAX *0692/23009. 28 rooms with bath. Restaurant, bar. AE, DC, V, MC.*

Outdoor Activities and Sports
HIKING AND CLIMBING

Diaselo Avgou on Mt. Helmos has a refuge for hikers, with a capacity of 12 to 16. Contact the Kalavrita Alpine Club (✉ Top end of 25 Maritiou [25th of March St.], ☎ 0692/22611), open Monday through Friday from 7 to 3. The Athens travel agency **Trekking Hellas** runs a six-day "Mountains and Monasteries" hiking tour on Mts. Ziria and Helmos (☞ Contacts and Resources *in* Northern Peloponnese A to Z, *below*).

Rion

48 *5 km (3 mi) east of Patras, 49 km (30½ mi) west of Diakofto.*

Rion is distinguished by the **Castle of the Morea,** built by Sultan Bayazid II in 1499; it sits forlorn amid a field of oil-storage tanks. Here, the Turks made their last stand in 1828, holding out for three weeks against the Anglo-French forces. Along with the **Castle of Roumeli** on Antirion's shore opposite, it guarded the narrows leading into the Gulf of Corinth. A half-hourly car ferry connects Rion with Antirion, linking the Peloponnese with central and northwestern Greece. Of the titanic bridge proposed during the first Papandreou administration, there is no trace, although officially, the plan is still in the works.

Beaches
Try **Agios Vassilios** (✉ Near Rion), which received one of the highest cleanliness ratings from Perpa, Greece's ministry of the environment.

Patras

49 *135 km (84 mi) west of Corinth, 5 km (3 mi) west of Rion.*

Patras, the third-largest city in Greece, begins almost before Rion is passed. Like all respectable Greek cities, it has an ancient history. Off its harbor in 429 BC Corinthian and Athenian ships fought inconclusively, and in 279 BC the city helped defeat an invasion of Celtic Galatians. Its acropolis was fortified under Justinian in the 6th century, and Patras withstood an attack by Slavs and Saracens in 805. Silk production, begun in the 7th century, brought renewed prosperity, but control passed successively to the Franks, the Venetians, and the Turks, until the War of Independence.

Thomas Palaiologos, the last Byzantine to leave Patras before the Turks took over in 1458, carried an unusual prize with him—the skull of the apostle St. Andrew, which he gave to Pius II in exchange for an annuity. St. Andrew had been crucified in Patras and was the city's patron saint. In 1964 Pope Paul VI returned the head to Patras (apparently thinking that Pius II had gotten his money's worth, or that it had been a while since Thomas last collected his annuity). Today it graces St. Andrew's Cathedral, seat of the Bishop of Patras.

The major western port for freighters carrying the all-important currants, and for passenger and car ferries sailing to Italy, thoroughly modern Patras has the international, outward-looking feel common to port cities. The waterfront is pleasant enough, though not very interesting; you'll find lots of mediocre restaurants, a range of hotels, the bus and train stations, and numerous travel agents (caveat emptor). Back from the waterfront, the town gradually rises along arcaded streets, which provide welcome shade and rain protection but make some feel claustrophobic. Of the series of large platias, tree-shaded Queen Olga

Square is the nicest. A good walk is to take Ayios Nikolaos Street upward through the city until it comes to the long flight of steps leading to the ruined castle overlooking the harbor.

The **Archaeological Museum's** small rooms are choked with Mycenaean, Roman, and other ancient finds. It is a pleasant stop to see some antiquities in a city not known for them. ⊠ *Mezonos 42,* ☎ *061/275070.* 🎫 *Free.* ⊙ *Tues.–Sun. 8:30–3.*

Platia Olga (⊠ 2 blocks uptown from Othonos Amalias, off Kolokotroni) is one of Patras's many popular squares—locals sip their ouzo and observe their fellow townspeople and they eat, drink, shop, and play in this quintessentially Greek meeting place. Other popular squares include **Platia 25 Martiou (25th of March Square)**, and **Platia Ypsila Alonia.**

In the evening the **Kastro** (⊠ On hill uptown, southeast of train station) overlooking Patras draws many Greek couples seeking privacy and a spectacular view, and visitors are well advised to follow suit: the sight of the shimmering ships negotiating the harbor stirs even the most travel-weary. A word of advice: going without a date can make you feel really out of place!

A **Roman odeon** (⊠ Southwest of the Kastro, off 25th of March Sq.) remains in use in Patras, almost 2,000 years after it was first built. Today the productions of summer arts festivals are staged in the well-preserved theater, which was discovered in 1889 and heavily restored in 1960 (☞ *below*).

NEED A BREAK? Some wineries are now open for tours and tastings; among them is **Antonopoulos Winery** (⊠ Tripolis, 19 km/11¾ mi south of Patras, ☎ 061/277723), open daily 9–4, with shorter hours in summer. **Achaia Clauss** (⊠ 9 km/6 mi east of Patras, ☎ 061/325051) operates tours daily 9–7:30 and in winter 9–5. Call ahead for tours and tastings.

Beaches

The closest decent beach to Patras is **Kalogria** (⊠ About 32 km/20 mi west).

Dining and Lodging

Avoid the indifferent restaurants along much of Patras's waterfront. For lighter fare or after-dinner ice cream, coffee, and pastries, choose one of the cafés along upper Gerokostopoulou Street, which is closed to traffic.

$$ ✕ **Kalypso.** One of the city's better restaurants, Kalypso serves grilled meats and magirefta. Star dishes include fresh grilled red mullet and dorado, a lemony fish soup, its specialty, midia saganaki, and for dessert, a baked apple with whipped cream. Bacchus blesses the tables with several Patras vintages and barrel wine. ⊠ *Posidonios 21, 9 km/6 mi north of Patras,* ☎ *061/994739 or 061/994740. AE, DC, MC, V.*

$ ✕ **Faros.** By day the owner is out hauling in his catch, by night he is serving it up to locals. Ambience does not reign here: this bare-bones place—without tablecloths or even a menu—is often quite noisy, but it serves the freshest fish at the lowest prices. Nobody speaks English, but all you have to do is point to the fish you want (you're charged by weight), order an accompanying Greek salad, sit back, and enjoy yourself. ⊠ *Othonos-Amalias 101,* ☎ *061/336500. No credit cards. No lunch.*

$ ✕ **Trikoyia.** Down by the port, the Trikoyia family cooks delicious food in its traditional taverna, where a typical menu features *kalofaga* (beef baked with ham), fresh grilled fish, and octopus with macaroni and oregano. Enjoy the ocean view while you complete your meal with a piece of baklava. ⊠ *Othonos-Amalias 46,* ☎ *061/279421. AE, DC, MC, V.*

$$$ ⊞ **Astir.** Near the Patras waterfront, the genteel Astir is classy and con-
★   venient, with a well-trained staff. The decor may be nostalgic of the mid '60s, but what really sets this hotel apart is the rooftop patio view over the quayside to the mountains on the other side of the gulf; at night you can watch the brilliantly lighted ferries as they glide north-west toward Brindisi. The rooms are nice, some with TVs upon request, and there are plenty of public lounges. Continental breakfast is included in the price. ⊠ *Ayios Andreou 16, 26223,* ☎ *061/277502,* FAX *061/271644. 120 rooms with bath. Restaurant, bar, air-conditioning, pool, sauna, meeting rooms. AE, DC, V.*

$$ ⊞ **Galaxia.** The Galaxia is dependable. Its wallpapered rooms have TVs and clean, gray-tile bathrooms with tubs, and there is no hokey decor. Near, but not on, the waterfront, this hotel will allow you a good night's sleep without frills or annoyances, and Continental breakfast is included in the price. ⊠ *Ayios Nikolaos 9, 26221,* ☎ *061/275981 through 275983,* ☎ FAX *061/278815. 53 rooms with bath. Air-condi-tioning. AE, DC, MC, V.*

$ ⊞ **Adonis.** The Adonis has, for its class, very good, well-kept rooms,
★   and they all have TVs, a balcony, and views in those facing the gulf and the Adriatic. On the down side, the bathrooms are closetlike, with showers of the curb-and-curtain variety. Adonis adjoins the bus ter-minal, and some rooms may be noisy during the day. Buffet breakfast is included in the price. ⊠ *Zaimi and Kapsali 9,* ☎ *061/224235, 061/224213, or 061/224257;* FAX *061/226971. 56 rooms with bath. Bar, air-conditioning, AE, MC, V.*

$ ⊞ **Rannia.** This is an adequate hotel. Rooms could be larger, but they have pine furniture, and all have balconies; the view varies—some over-look Queen Olga Square, the nicest plaza in Patras. The location isn't bad either; it's a few blocks in from the waterfront, walkable from the train station and the bus station. Some rooms have TVs. ⊠ *Riga Fer-eou 53, 26221,* ☎ *061/220114. 30 rooms with bath. Bar. MC, V.*

Outdoor Activities and Sports

HIKING AND CLIMBING
There is a hiking and climbing refuge at **Psarthi** on Mt. Panahaiko (ca-pacity 50). Contact the **Patras Alpine Club** (⊠ Pantanassis 29, ☎ 061/273912) for information.

TENNIS
Patras Tennis Club (☎ 061/226028) is open to the public.

Nightlife and the Arts

BARS AND CAFÉS
For nightlife, in general it's best to ask around when you arrive. On the northern side of 25th of March Square are the steps at the head of **Gerokostopoulou Street,** below the odeon. Closed to traffic along its upper reaches, this street's myriad cafés and music bars make it a re-laxing place to spend an evening. It is the place to be for the young and hip of Patras.

FESTIVALS
Patras holds a lively **summer arts festival** (⊠ Office: 104 Ayios Geor-giou, ☎ 061/278206) with concerts and dance performances at the Roman odeon in the fortress. For more information, contact the Pa-tras tourist police or the Patras EOT (☞ *Northern Peloponnese A to Z, below*).

If you're lucky enough to be in Patras in February, you're in for a treat: the **Carnival** (✉ Office: 104 Agios Georgiou, ☎ 061/279008), which lasts for several weeks, is celebrated with masquerade balls, fireworks, and the Sunday Grand Parade competition for the best costume. Be warned, however: room rates can double or even triple during this time; tickets for seats (3,000 dr.) at the parade, which is held in front of the Múnicipal Theater at Platia Georgiou, are sold at the Carnival office.

NIGHTCLUBS

Worth a spin on the dance floor is the music club **Privé** (✉ Germanou 55, ☎ 061/274912). **Utopia Music Hall** (✉ Ayios Andreou 91, ☎ 061/222104) usually has a Greek bouzoukia variety program.

Shopping

Patras is a major city and thus it is possible to buy fashionable clothing, jewelry, and other products. However, unlike most other Greek cities, Patras also has shops that sell handmade and machine-made Greek icons, which make beautiful decorations. At night in the small narrow streets surrounding the Kastro one can find Greek craftsmen burning the midnight oil in their workshops and stores painting images of saints on wood and stone.

OFF THE
BEATEN PATH

HALANDRITSA – If you take an easy detour south from Patras on Highway 33 and turn left after 16 km (10 mi), you come to Halandritsa, seat of a prosperous Frankish barony, whose early stone churches and narrow streets make it a worthwhile stop. There are beautiful views across the coast to the open sea.

Chlemoutsi Castle

50   *56 km (34¼ mi) west of Patras.*

At the foot of Chlemoutsi Castle, the **Kastro** (✉ From Neokori 8 km/5 mi along the Loutra Killinis) is the best-preserved Frankish monument in the Peloponnese. Geoffrey I de Villehardouin, who built it from 1220 to 1223, named it Clairmont. The Venetians called it Castel Tornese, perhaps on account of the Frankish *tournoi* (coins) minted in nearby Glarentza, stamped with the facade of St. Martin's Church in Tours. The Byzantine despot Constantine Palaiologos captured it in 1427 and used it as a base from which to attack Patras, the last Frankish stronghold. The castle has a huge irregular hexagon keep, with vaulted galleries around an open court. After 1460 the Turks strengthened the gate and altered the galleries. It was captured by the Venetians in 1687, and shortly thereafter was ceded to the Turks. On the southwest side you can see a breach made by Ibrahim Pasha's cannon during the War of Independence.

Beaches

The coast south of Chlemoutsi Castle toward **Loutra Killinis** is a beach resort area, where its wide, sandy beach on the Adriatic is among the best in Greece. Farther south of the castle, near Gastouni and Pyrgos, are the fine beaches **Katakolo** and **Spiantza** (✉ Off Hwy. 9).

Olympia

★   *112 km (69½ mi) south of Patras, 65 km (40½ mi) southeast of Chlemoutsi Castle.*

Modern Olympia provides visitors to the ancient site with the services they need and has little else to offer. The village is a one-street town (Praxitelous Kondilis Street, to be exact), consisting largely of hotels and tourist shops with a smattering of tavernas. It's good for a stopover to soak up the pleasant hilly countryside, which is, for once in southern Greece, well watered and green.

Ancient Olympia, the ancient Sanctuary of Zeus, is one of the most popular sites in Greece. Two hours is the minimum necessary to see the ruins and the fine museum, and three or four hours would be even better. The ancient sanctuary occupies a compact, flat area at the base of the Kronion hill (on the north), where the Kladeos and Alpheios rivers join. It comprised the **sacred precinct,** or **Altis,** a large rectangular enclosure south of the Kronion, with **administrative buildings, baths, and workshops** on the west and south, and the **Stadium** and **Hippodrome** on the east. In 1829, a French expedition investigated the Temple of Zeus and brought a few metope fragments to the Louvre. The systematic excavation begun by the German Archaeological Institute in 1875 has continued intermittently to this day.

Although the first Olympiad is thought to have been in 776 BC, bronze votive figures of the Geometric period (10th–8th centuries) reveal that the sanctuary was in use before that date. The festival took place every four years over a five-day period in the late summer during a sacred truce, observed by all Greek cities. Initially only native speakers of Greek (excepting slaves) could compete, but Romans were later admitted. Foreigners could watch, but married women, Greek or not, were barred from the sanctuary during the festival on pain of death. One woman caught watching was spared, however, since not only all her sons but her husband and father had won Olympic victories. The events included the footrace, boxing, chariot and horse racing, the pentathlon (combining running, jumping, wrestling, and both javelin and discus throwing), and the *pankration* (a no-holds barred style of wrestling in which competitors could break their opponent's fingers and other body parts).

By and large the Olympic festival was peaceful, though not without problems. The Spartans were banned in 420 BC for breaking the sacred truce; in 364 BC there was fighting in the Altis between the Eleans and the Pisans and Arcadians in front of the crowd who had come to watch the games; the Roman dictator Sulla carried off the treasure to finance his army and five years later held the games in Rome. The 211th festival was delayed for two years so that Nero could compete, and despite a fall from his chariot, he was awarded the victory.

The long decline of Olympia began after the reign of Hadrian. In AD 267, under threat of an invasion, many buildings were dismantled to construct a defensive wall; Christian decrees forbade the functioning of pagan sanctuaries and caused the demolition of the Altis. Earthquakes settled its fate, and flooding of the Alpheios and the Kladeos, together with landslides off the Kronion hill, buried the abandoned sanctuary.

Olympia's ruins are fairly compact, so it's easy to get a quick overview in an hour and then investigate specific buildings or head to the museum. The site is very pleasant, with plenty of trees providing shade. **(51)** South of the entrance are the remains of a small **Roman bath** and the **(52) Gymnasion,** essentially a large open practice field surrounded by stoas (long, narrow porticoes). The large complex opposite the Gymnasion **(53)** was the **Prytaneion,** where the *prytaneis* (magistrates in charge of the games) feted the winners, and where the Olympic flame burned on a sacred hearth. Just south is the gateway to the Altis, marked by two **(54)** sets of four columns. Just beyond is the **Philippeion,** a circular shrine started by Philip II and completed after his death by Alexander the Great.

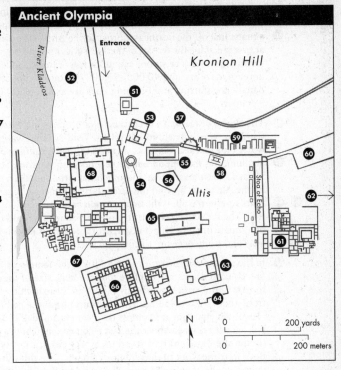

Ancient Olympia

55 Directly in front of the Philippeion is the large Doric temple of Hera, the **Heraion** (circa 600 BC). It is well preserved, especially considering that it is constructed from the local coarse, poros shell limestone. At first it had wooden columns, which were replaced as needed, so although they are all Doric, the capitals don't exactly match. Three of the columns have been set back up. A colossal head of a goddess, possibly from the statue of Hera, was found at the temple and is now in the site museum. Just south of the Heraion are the remains of a **sixth-century BC pentagonal wall** built to enclose the **Pelopeion** (Shrine of Pelops) at the time an altar in a sacred grove. According to Pausanias, the **Altar of Olympian Zeus** was southeast of the temple of Hera, but no trace of it has been found. Some rocks mark its supposed location, the most sacred spot in the Altis, where daily blood sacrifices are said to have been made.

56

57 There is no doubt about the location of the **Nymphaion,** or Exedra, which brought water to Olympia from a spring to the east. A colonnade around the semicircular reservoir had statues of the family of Herodes Atticus and his imperial patrons. The 4th-century **Metroon,** at the bottom of the Nymphaion terrace, was originally dedicated to Cybele, Mother of the Gods, and was taken over by the Roman imperial cult. Nearby, at the bottom of the steps leading to the Treasuries and outside the entrance of the Stadium, were **16 bronze statues of Zeus,** called the Zanes, bought with money from fines levied against those caught cheating at the games. Bribery seems to have been the most common offense, steroids not being available. Olympia also provides the earliest case of the sports-parent syndrome: In the 192nd Olympiad, Damonikos of Elis, whose son Polyktor was to wrestle Sosander of Smyrna, bribed the latter's father in an attempt to buy the victory for his son.

58

59 On the terrace itself are the city-state **Treasuries,** which look like small temples and were used to store valuables, such as equipment used in **60** rituals. Just off the northeast corner of the Altis is the **Stadium,** which at first ran along the terrace of the Treasuries and had no embankments for the spectators to sit on; embankments were added later, but were never given seats, and 40,000–50,000 spectators could be accommodated. The starting and finishing lines are still in place, 600 Olympic feet apart.

61 The **House of Nero,** a 1st-century villa off the southeastern corner of the Altis, was hurriedly built for his visit. Nearby was found a lead water pipe marked NER. AUG. Beyond this villa, running parallel to the **62** Stadium, was the **Hippodrome,** where horse and chariot races were held. It hasn't been excavated, and much has probably been eroded away by the Alpheios. Beyond the Altis's large southeastern gate, appended **63 64** to its southern wall, is the **Bouleuterion** and, just south of it, the **South Hall.** The Bouleuterion consisted of two rectangular halls on either side of a square building that housed the Altar of Zeus Horkios, where athletes and trainers swore to compete fairly.

65 In the southwestern corner of the Altis is the **Temple of Zeus.** Only a few column drums are in place, but the huge size of the temple platform is impressive. Designed by Libon, an Elean architect, it was built from about 470 to 456 BC. The **sculptures** from the pediments are on view in the museum at Olympia (☞ *below*). A gilded bronze statue of Nike (Victory) stood above the east pediment, matching a marble Nike (in the site museum) that stood on a pedestal in front of the temple. Both were the work of the sculptor Paionios. The cult statue inside the temple, made of gold and ivory, showed Zeus seated on a throne, holding a Nike in his open right hand and a scepter in his left. It was created in 430 BC by Pheidias, sculptor of the cult statue of Athena in the Parthenon, and was said to be seven times life size; it was one of the Seven Wonders of the Ancient World. It is said that Caligula wanted to move the statue to Rome and replace the head with one of his own, but the statue laughed out loud when his men approached it. It was removed to Constantinople, and destroyed by fire in AD 475. Pausanias relates that behind the statue there was "a woolen curtain . . . decorated by Assyrian weavers and dyed with Phoenician crimson, dedicated by Antiochos." It is possible this was the veil of the Temple at Jerusalem (Antiochos IV Epiphanes forcibly converted the Temple to the worship of Zeus Olympias).

Just outside the gate at the southwestern corner of the Altis stood the **66** **Leonidaion,** at first a guest house for important visitors and later a residence of the Roman governor of the province of Achaea. Immediately **67** north of the Leonidaion was the **Pheidias' workshop,** where the cult statue of Zeus was constructed in a large hall of the same size and orientation as the interior of the temple. Tools, clay molds, and Pheidias's own cup (in the museum) make the identification of this building certain. It was later used as a Byzantine church. North of the workshop **68** is the **Palaestra,** built in the 3rd century BC, for athletic training. The rooms around the square field were used for bathing and cleansing with oil, for teaching, and for socializing. ⊠ *½ km (⅓ mi) outside of Olympia,* ☎ *0624/22517.* 🎫 *1,200 dr.* ☽ *Weekdays 8–7, weekends 8:30–5.*

The **"new" museum at Olympia** (⊠ Across from ancient Olympia), officially opened in 1982, has in its collections the sculptures from the Temple of Zeus and the Hermes of Praxiteles, discovered in the Temple of Hera in the place noted by Pausanias. The Hermes was buried under the fallen clay of the temple's upper walls and is one of the best-preserved classical statues. Unfortunately the famous Nike of Paionios is in the old museum, which is closed, so it can't be seen by visitors. There's also a notable terra-cotta group of Zeus and Ganymede; the head of the cult statue of Hera; sculptures of the family and imperial patrons of Herodes Atticus; and bronzes found at the site, including votive figurines, cauldrons, and armor. Of great historic interest are a helmet dedicated by Miltiades, the Athenian general who defeated the Persians at Marathon, and a cup owned by the sculptor Pheidias. The central gallery of the museum holds the pedimental sculptures and metopes from the Temple of Zeus, depicting Herakles' Twelve Labors. ⊠ *Southern end of main rd.,* ☎ *0624/22529.* ⊡ *1,200 dr.* ⊙ *Weekdays 7:30–7, weekends 8:30–3.*

Dining and Lodging

$ ✕ **Ambrosia.** Don't let the tour groups deter you; there's a reason why they flock here. You, too, should try the tasty dishes, like rabbit or lamb *ladorigani* (with olive oil and dried crushed oregano), beef *yiouvetsi* (meat baked in a clay pot with orzo-like pasta), *briam* (a baked dish of potatoes, squash, and eggplant), fresh green beans, pastitsio, tart *dolmades* (stuffed vegetables, grape leaves, or fruit) in the traditional avgolemono sauce, and savory grilled meats. Save room for some homemade galaktobouriko for dessert. ⊠ *Near train station (no st. numbers outside the center),* ☎ *0624/23414,* ℻ *0624/22439. MC, V.*

$ ✕ **Taverna Praxitelous.** This taverna serves an array of mouthwatering appetizers; to sample them all, order the *pikilia* (variety) plate, which includes zucchini fritters, bourekakia, *tirolates* (ham and cheese fingers), *tzatziki* (yogurt-garlic dip), eggplant dip, and moussaka. Besides grilled meats, the typical magirefta like rabbit stifado and stuffed tomatoes go well with the barrel red or one of the local Achaea wines. In winter sit inside near the fireplace (the tables are always brightened with fresh flowers) and in summer sit out in the pedestrian zone. ⊠ *Spiliopoulou 7, near police station,* ☎ *0624/23570. V.*

$ ✕ **Thraka.** This family-run taverna has a large variety of Greek food, including *lahanokeftedes* (fried vegetable croquettes), *arnaki* (lamb) yiouvetsi, *kokkinisto* (beef in red sauce), and stifado made the old-fashioned way with vinegar and garlic. Desserts are from the family's nearby pastry shop. Off-season, the cook (and family matriarch) will prepare meals for you; just give her a call at home. ⊠ *Praxitelous Kondilis,* ☎ *0624/22575,* ☎ *Off-season 0624/22475. AE, DC, MC, V. Closed Dec.–Jan.*

$$$ ▥ **Antonios.** This first-class hotel, set on a hill at town's edge, has fairly
★ spacious rooms with TVs and balconies. There's a swimming pool and barbecue patio, and the hotel operates the adjacent Touris [sic] Club, which has a restaurant, bar, discothèque, folk dance performances, and a pool. Buffet breakfast is included in the price. ⊠ *Rd. to Krestena, 27065,* ☎ *0624/22348 or 0624/22349,* ℻ *0624/22112. 70 rooms with bath. Restaurant, bar, air-conditioning. V.*

$$ ▥ **Europa (Best Western).** Olympia's best, the Europa combines white stucco, pine, and red tiles in a traditional style but with high ceilings and large windows. The rooms have large beds, flokati rugs, marble bathrooms, and small terraces. Most face the pool. Rooms with TVs may be requested. Buffet breakfast is included in the price. ⊠ *Oikismou Drouba (off rd. to ancient Olympia), 27065,* ☎ *0624/22650 or 0624/22700,* ℻ *0624/23166. 42 rooms with bath. Restaurant, air-conditioning, pool, tennis court. AE, DC, MC, V.*

$ ▥ **Apollon.** Although the rooms at the Apollon are not exceptional, the wood furnishings and white walls do create a cheerful beach-bungalow atmosphere. The owner manages to keep things in good shape, renovating bit by bit every year. Apollon is in the center of the modern town, convenient to both bus and train stations; buffet breakfast is included in the price. ✉ *Douma 13, 27065,* ☎ *0624/22513 or 0624/22522,* ℻ *0624/23068. 96 rooms with bath. Restaurant, pool. AE, DC, MC, V. Closed Nov.–Feb.*

$ 🏨 **Kronion.** The rooms at the Kronion are uniform in many crucial respects: They're clean, and they have private baths, balconies, telephones, and high ceilings. The decor varies wildly, without apparent rhyme or reason; but the rationale for faux granite here or patterned wallpaper there is a matter for contemplation, not a drawback. The train station is close at hand. ✉ *Tsoureka 1, 27065,* ☎ *0624/22188,* ℻ *0624/22502. 32 rooms with bath. Restaurant. AE, DC, MC, V.*

$ 🏨 **Pelops.** This standard Greek hotel is pleasant and efficient. The rooms are more than adequate but not fancy: clean and well kept, with plain wood furnishings, orthopedic mattresses, and telephones. Shaggy throw rugs are scattered on the tile floors. It's away from the main street and fairly quiet, especially the vine-shaded terrace. ✉ *Varela 2, 27065,* ☎ *0624/22543,* ℻ *0624/22213. 25 rooms with bath. Breakfast room, bar. MC, V. Closed Nov.–Feb.*

NORTHERN PELOPONNESE A TO Z

Arriving and Departing

By Bus

The regional **bus associations** (KTEL) provide frequent service at reasonable prices to Patras, Pyrgos (for Olympia), Corinth, Argos, Epidauros, Kranidi, Nauplion (for Mycenae), Sparta (for Mystras and Monemvassia), and Xylokastro. Some sample prices: Corinth (every 30 minutes, 1½ hours, 1,150 dr.), Patras (every 45 minutes, 3 hours, 2,750 dr.), Nauplion (hourly, 2½ hours, 1,950 dr.), Olympia (four buses daily, 5½ hours, 4,300 dr.), Epidauros (two to three buses daily, 2½ hours, 1,850 dr.). Buses leave from Terminal A (✉ 100 Kifissou, ☎ 01/512–4910) on the outskirts of Athens (take Bus 51 at corner of Zinonos and Menandrou sts. near Omonia sq.). Pick up a bus schedule from the Athens EOT (☞ *below*) or call the following numbers for departure times or to reserve a seat: Corinth (☎ 01/512–9233); Sparta and Monemvassia, ☎ 01/512–4913; Patras (☎ 01/513–6185); Nauplion, Mycenae, and Epidauros, ☎ 01/513–4588.

By Car

Most people take the **toll highway** from Athens to the Isthmus of Corinth (84 km/52 mi, 1¼ hours) and on to Nauplion, Patras, and Olympia. Others take the **car ferry** between Patras and Italy (Ancona, Bari, or Brindisi). Car ferries for Brindisi or the Ionian islands leave from Patras's main terminal on the port; for Bari and Ancona, the pier is about 1 km (⅔ mi) west. An alternative route from Athens to Patras is via Delphi and the Rion–Antirion ferry.

By Ferry and Hydrofoil

Ceres (✉ Akti Miaouli 69, Piraeus, ☎ 01/459–1000) operates the Flying Dolphin hydrofoils (passengers only) from Zea Marina in Piraeus to ports on the east coast of the Peloponnese, sailing daily in summer to Porto Heli (1 hour 55 minutes, 3,375 dr.) and to Nauplion (3 hours, 4,040 dr.), and once or twice a day (3 hours 10 minutes, 5,541 dr.) to Monemvassia. In winter, there is a much-reduced schedule, especially because hydrofoils leave port only in the calmest weather. You may take your car only on the slower-moving ferry boats, which leave Athens a few times weekly for Monemvassia (car: 9,887 dr.–12,866 dr., passenger: 2,897 dr.) and Porto Heli (car: 8,986 dr.–10,397 dr., passenger: 1,995 dr.). Call the Piraeus port authority (☎ 01/422–6000) or the Athens EOT (☞ *below*) for a ferry schedule.

Nauplion port authority (☎ 0752/22974) and Patras port authority (☎ 061/341002) can advise you about entry and exit in their ports for yachts. Patras's EOT (☞ *below*) is at the port.

By Plane
There is no plane service to the Northern Peloponnese.

By Train
Traveling by train is convenient for the Northern Peloponnese and is relatively inexpensive. Trains from Athens depart from the Peloponnissos station (⌖ Sidirodromon); take Bus 057, which leaves every 10 minutes from Panepistimiou (fare 75 dr.). There are five departures daily to Nemea–Mykines–Argos–Nauplion (3 to 5 hours to Nauplion, 1,500 dr.); 13 trains daily to Corinth (2 hours, 780 dr.; on the IC, the Inter-City express, 1½ hours, 1,430 dr.); and eight daily to Patras (4½ hours, 1,580 dr.; IC 4 hours, 2,580 dr.). Going to Olympia by train isn't worth the trouble; the trip takes almost 8 hours, with a change at Pyrgos. For schedule information call (☎ 01/513–1601); some English is spoken.

Getting Around

By Bus
In addition to serving major centers, such as Nauplion, Argos, Corinth, and Patras, the coaches of the regional bus associations (KTEL) travel to virtually every village in the Northern Peloponnese. The bargain price and the extensive network makes bus travel a viable alternative to renting a car, although frequency decreases off the beaten track. Schedules are posted at local KTEL stations, usually on the main square or main street.

By Car
The roads are good in the Northern Peloponnese, and driving can be the most enjoyable (if not the most economical) way of seeing the region. **The Greek Automobile Touring Club (ELPA)** has an office in Patras (⌖ Patroon Athinon 18, ☎ 061/425411) and can assist with repairs and information. During the Epidauros Festival ELPA road-assistance vehicles patrol the roads around there.

By Train
Trains run from Athens to Corinth and then the route splits; you can go south to Argos and Nauplion or west along the coast to Patras and then south to Pyrgos and Kalamata. Alternatively you can go directly through the Peloponnese to Kalamata via Tripolis. On the western route the train stops at Kiato, Xylokastro, and Diakofto, where a wonderful narrow-gauge branch line heads inland to Kalavrita, and Aigion, before arriving in Patras. In high summer the trains between Patras and Athens can be crowded with young people arriving from or leaving for Italy on ferries from Patras. Branch lines leave the main line at Kavasila for Killini and at Pyrgos for Olympia. If you know you are returning by train, buy a round-trip ticket (good for a month); there is a substantial discount.

The *Kalavrita Express* train makes the round-trip from Diakofto–Kalavrita along the **Vouraikos Gorge** six times daily; the first trip is at 6:48 AM (leaving Diakofto), the last returns at 5:51 PM. The fare is 1,000 dr. round-trip. Although the trip can be made from Athens (round-trip fare, Athens–Kalavrita: first-class 4,000 dr., second-class 2,800 dr.), it is best enjoyed between Corinth and Patras.

Contacts and Resources

Emergencies
Tourist Police: Patras (⊠ Patreos 53, ☎ 061/220902 or 061/220903); **Corinth** (⊠ Ermou 51, ☎ 0741/23282); **Nauplion** (⊠ Fotamara 16, ☎ 0752/28131); **Olympia** (⊠ Spiliopoulou 15, ☎ 0624/22550).

Guided Tours
Many companies offer bus tours from Athens to the major archaeological sites in the Northern Peloponnese, including half-board accommodations, guide, and entrance fees. **Chat Tours** (⊠ Stadiou 4, ☎ 01/322–2886) and **Key Tours** (⊠ Kallirois 4, ☎ 01/923–3166) organize a 2-day tour to Corinth, Mycenae, and Epidauros (25,000 dr.) and a 6-day tour to all major sites in the Peloponnese, with accommodations at the best available hotels (120,000 dr.). Many local travel agents offer whirlwind day trips to sites, especially Epidauros (usually including the performance and stopping at some combination of Nauplion, Mycenae, and Corinth) and Olympia. These basic, no-frills tours are for those who don't expect a lot of hand-holding and have trouble planning in advance. They can be booked at travel agencies and at larger hotels.

Hiking and Climbing
For information on hiking and mountain climbing in the Northern Peloponnese, contact the **Greek Federation of Mountaineering Associations** in Athens (⊠ Milioni 8, Athens, ☎ 01/363–6617 or 01/364–5904), which operates several huts, open to the public; a detailed brochure is available at their offices.

Pharmacies
Pharmacies, clearly identified by red cross signs, take turns staying open late. A listing is published in the local newspaper; it is best to check at your hotel to find out not only which pharmacy is open, but how to get there.

Travel Agency
Trekking Hellas (⊠ Fillelinon 7, Athens 10557, ☎ 01/315–0853 and 01/325–0317).

Visitor Information
Greek National Tourist Organization (GNTO or EOT) Patras (⊠ Harbor, Terminal 6, Glyfada, ☎ 061/653358, ℻ 061/423866); Athens (⊠ Karageorgi Servias 2, ☎ 01/322–2545); Nauplion (⊠ 25th of March St., across from OTE, ☎ 0752/24444); and Olympia (⊠ Praxitelous Kondili 75, ☎ 0624/23100); **local tourist police** (☞ *above*).

9 Southern Peloponnese

Tripolis, Kalamata, Sparta, Mystras, and Monemvassia

From its ebullient ports to its ghostly Byzantine ruins, its sea of olive groves to its dizzying gorges and languorous beaches, the southern half of the Peloponnese is a land of extremes, its scenery unsubtle, almost theatrical. Cement-laden towns like Tripolis, Sparta, and Kalamata are sprawled across the region, their startling natural beauty juxtaposed with modern development. Despite the waves of invaders—the Franks, Venetians, and Turks—this land is considered the distillation of all that is Greek— indulged idiosyncrasy, intractable autonomy, appreciation of simple pleasures.

By Toula
Bogdanos

Updated by
Terrence
Moloney and
Susan Lupack

ANCIENT RUINS AND MEDIEVAL MONUMENTS pervade the landscape here more than in any other region in Greece. On a high plateau in the center of the Peloponnese ungainly Tripolis contrasts sharply with the forgotten stone towns of Arcadia: Stemnitsa, Dimitsana, and medieval Karitena shield themselves beneath the Taygettus's massive range. Those who penetrate the forbidding mountains discover not only crumbling towns but also the remote Temple of Apollo in Bassae. Farther south the sandy cape of Messinia offer refuge for those escaping from earthquake-ravaged Kalamata, while ancient Messene with its mammoth fortifications conjures up images of ancient civilizations. The Mycenaean ruins of Nestor's Palace are almost a millenium older than ancient Messene but only an hour away, as is Pylos, whose famous sea battle was immortalized in the *Guns of Navarone*. Across the Taygettus lies Laconia, where the ancient Spartans practiced their famously disciplined armies and where the final flourish of Byzantium has left us the astonishingly well-preserved Mystras. At the very tip of continental Europe dangles the Mani peninsula, from the charmingly dilapidated port of Gythion to the underground caves of Pirgos Dirou and to villages studded with tower houses, vestiges of the Mani's blood feuds and vendettas. Finally, on Laconia's southeast peninsula Monemvassia is perched, known as Greece's Mont-Saint-Michel, an inhabited medieval city.

Pleasures and Pastimes

Dining

You won't find many fancy restaurants in the southern Peloponnese, but the countless local tavernas and *estiatoria* (restaurants) serve memorable Greek home cooking and a great variety of fresh fish. Villages here in the south were the source of such international favorites as avgolemono soup and lamb fricassee. Don't go by looks; an underground hole-in-the-wall may serve the town's best meals, and what's available is what the butcher, fisherman, and grocer sold that day, despite what's printed on the menu. Local specialties to watch for: In the mountain villages near Tripolis, order *stifado* (beef with pearl onions), *arni souvla* (lamb on the spit), *kokoretsi* (entrails on the spit), and thick, creamy yogurt. In Sparta, look for *bardouniotiko* (a local dish of chicken stuffed with cheese, olives, and walnuts), and around Pylos, order fresh ocean fish (priced by the kilo). In the rest of Laconia, try *loukaniko xoriatiko* (village sausage), and in the Mani, ask for ham. As for wines, the light white from Mantinea is a favorite, and whenever possible, sample the *xima* (barrel wines), which range from light, dry whites to heavy, sleep-inducing reds. Except in some hotel dining rooms, casual dress is always acceptable, and unless noted, reservations are unnecessary or not accepted.

CATEGORY	COSTS*
$$$$	over 6,000 dr.
$$$	3,500 dr.–6,000 dr.
$$	2,000 dr.–3,500 dr.
$	under 2,000 dr.

for a three-course meal, including tax, service, and usually beer or a small carafe of wine.

Fishing

The bays of the Southern Peloponnese offer spear and boat fishermen a plentiful habitat of species. In Arcadia, the best place for spear and boat fishing is south of Leonidion, off the headlands of Capes Bournia and Tourkoviglas to Fokianou bay; in April every four years, Leonidion bay fills with schools of bonito. In Messinia, try offshore Kalamata for rock fish, and southeast at Kardamili and Stoupa for blackfish, red mullet, octopus, and sea bream. The Mani coast around Kotronas (in Laconia province) has plentiful octopus, grouper, and lobster. Also in Laconia you can catch blackfish, sea bream, and lobster in the waters near Monemvassia, and rockfish, lobster, and red mullet at Neapolis, down to Cape Malea. The waters of Aia Pelagia and Kapsali, though full of fish, are difficult to negotiate because of currents.

Greek Dancing

If local folk musicians play where you are staying, go to watch the dancing, which might include the popular *kalamatianos* (a circular dance from Kalamata), or the *tsakonikos* (in which the dancers wheel tightly around each other and then swing into bizarre spirals), which resembles the sacred dance of Delos, first performed by Theseus to mime how he escaped from the Labyrinth; the *tsamikos,* from Roumeli in central Greece, is an exclusively male dance for showing off agility and derring-do.

Hiking

Throughout the Peloponnese there are many small trails or *kalderimi* (mule paths) to hike, as well as the international E4 European Rambler Trail, which starts in the Pyrenees, winds through Yugoslavia, and traverses Greece to Gythion. The southern half, from Delphi to Gythion, is considered less difficult than the northern section and can be walked most of the year; the best time is mid-May to early October. Pick up the southern section at Menalon Refuge, and continue through Vresthena, Sparta, Taygettus Refuge and Panagia Yiatris monastery to Gythion. For more information, call the Tripolis Alpine Club, Sparta Alpine Club, or the Greek Federation of Mountaineering Associations; request a map from the Army's Geographical Service in Athens (☞ Contacts and Resources *in* Southern Peloponnese A to Z, *below*).

Lodging

Except for a few luxury complexes along the coast, most hotels are standard, with plain rooms and no air-conditioning, though the newer ones have more services and more of a decorative flair. Bathrooms usually have showers instead of tubs. it's important to reserve ahead if you plan to travel in the high season (July and August), especially in coastal hotels that cater to groups. It's often cheaper to book the larger hotels through a travel agent in the town or in Athens, and in most hotels you can negotiate a lower-than-official rate off-season. If the hotels are full, you can always find private rooms, though often without a private bath. Ask the tourist police or a local travel agency for assistance.

CATEGORY	COST*
$$$$	over 25,000 dr.
$$$	10,000 dr.–25,000 dr.
$$	6,000 dr.–10,000 dr.
$	under 6,000 dr.

for a standard double room in high season, including tax and service.

Nightlife

Beach towns always have their "in" bars, usually along the waterfront, and in more rural towns inland, you may observe a curious ritual called the *nymphopazaro* (bride bazaar), in which groups of young marriageable women walk arm-in-arm past the main square several times a night in view of the young men sitting at the *kafenion* (traditional Greek coffeehouse) A more sophisticated version of this is the *volta* (a sort of Saturday night stroll), in which young people of both sexes, along with black-garbed grandmothers and couples with baby carriages, amble back and forth all evening in a popular spot.

If you want something faster paced yet still traditionally Greek, try the ubiquitous *kentra* (the bouzoukia places that operate outdoors in summer). Be prepared for a lesson in decadence as dancers twirl in a frenzy, onlookers smash plates—though it's a no-no—and buy cases of champagne to toast the dancers, and singers wail away about forgotten love and remembered sins.

Water Sports

You can usually rent paddleboats and canoes on the beaches in front of major hotels; occasionally there are windsurfing and waterskiing instructors, though the rates are rather high. For example, waterskiing runs about 5,000 dr. for 15 minutes.

Sailing in Greece isn't restricted to the Aegean Islands. Many people prefer to sail to the islands near Methoni, with stops at Sapientsa, Skiza, and Venetiko. When you rent a sailboat or charter a yacht, the agency will usually indicate where to find water and fuel. The local port authority and the Naval Association can advise you on mooring information (☞ Contacts and Resources *in* Southern Peloponnese A to Z, *below*). You can moor at Gythion, which has water and fuel; in Kalamata repair service and moorings are usually available; for sailing around the Messinian cape, the port authority at Pylos can be of help.

Exploring the Southern Peloponnese

Politically, the Southern Peloponnese is divided into regions established by the ancients—Messinia in the southwest, Laconia in the southeast, and Arcadia to the north. Massive mountain ranges sweep down the fingers of the peninsula; the beaches are some of the finest and least developed in Greece. The area is considered somewhat isolated from the rest of Greece, especially politically, but its people are great respecters of *filoxenia* (hospitality). For the traveler, the regions are best divided into four: Arcadia, Messinia, Laconia, and a fourth, the Mani, part of which is administered by Messinia, and the other part by Laconia. We describe each of these regions in its own section, below.

Great Itineraries

Though it may be less accessible, this part of the Peloponnese holds forth for the visitor a less hectic pace, and fewer crowds. The best moments come to those who stray beyond the familiar, who take time to have a coffee in the square of a village on Mt. Taygettus, a picnic at the ruins of Bassae, or a sunset swim beneath the brooding towers of a Maniote fishing hamlet. A short visit forces the traveler to make some difficult choices: any of the four areas covered in this chapter can be explored in a few days, but not more than one. Arcadia is perhaps the most accessible from Athens. A longer stay will permit additions to the itinerary, and from Arcadia neither Messinia nor Laconia are far. The Mani at the tip of the Taygettus mountain range awaits those wise enough to plan an extended stay in this outpost of Greece and Europe.

IF YOU HAVE 3 DAYS
Numbers in the text correspond to numbers in the margin and on the Southern Peloponnese map.

Travelers who spend three days in the southern Peloponnese would best be served with a visit to ▣ **Tripolis** ①, from where you can visit the Arcadian mountain village of **Andritsena** ⑤ and the **Temple of Apollo at Bassae** ⑥. These can be explored in one or even two days at a leisurely pace. On the second day, either head south to 🏛 **Sparta** ⑳ and **Mys-tras** ㉑, or go southwest, over the forbidding Taygettus mountains to 🏛 **Kalamata** ⑦. In Kalamata enjoy a seaside meal, a stroll along the long promenade by the sea, or a visit to the nearby ruins of **ancient Messene** ⑧. On the third day simply cross the famous and exquisitely beautiful Langada Pass, going east to Sparta if you're coming from Kala-mata, or west to Kalamata if you're leaving Sparta.

IF YOU HAVE 6 DAYS

Begin by exploring Arcadia, basing yourself at 🏛 **Tripolis** ①, from which you can visit the surrounding mountain villages of **Stemnit-sa** ②, **Dimitsana** ③, **Karitena** ④, and **Andritsena** ⑤, and the Apollo **Temple at Bassae** ⑥. After two days make your way across the Tayget-tus to Messinia's major center 🏛 **Kalamata** ⑦. While in Messinia visit the ancient Mycenaean **Nestor's Palace** ⑩, and the port town of 🏛 **Py-los** ⑪, with an archaeological museum, castles, and a beautiful bay. Fi-nally, venture into the Mani and see **Kardamyli** ⑬; **Areopolis** ⑯, the sun-baked gateway to the Inner Mani; and the gloomy **Pirgos Dirou Caves** ⑰. If the Mani fills you with foreboding, or if you haven't seen your fill of fine Byzantine ruins, cross the Langada Pass from Kala-mata to 🏛 **Sparta** ⑳ where you can stomp about the Laconian Plain for a couple of days, seeing the last jewel in the Byzantine crown, **Mys-tras** ㉑, followed by a day's sojourn to the colorful crumbling Laco-nian port of **Gythion** ⑲.

IF YOU HAVE 10 DAYS

A trip of ten days will allow you to see most of the Peloponnese. Fol-low the 6-day itinerary above through 🏛 **Kalamata** ⑦. By the fifth or sixth day of your trip you should be starting down one of Greece's most spectacular highways, from **Kalamata** to 🏛 **Kardamyli** ⑬. The latter is a more remote, yet more sophisticated base for exploring the Mani than 🏛 **Areopolis** ⑯, which is farther south, but closer to the Inner Mani. Either will do, as you cruise up and down the last tip of the Taygettus range, stopping at **Itilo** ⑭, **Limeni** ⑮, the **Pirgos Dirou Caves** ⑰, and **Vathia** ⑱, soaking up the uniquely harsh but strangely inviting land-scape. If you manage to escape the alluring beauty, try the port **Gythion** ⑲, which is the Laconian gateway to the Mani. From there you can visit 🏛 **Sparta** ⑳ and **Mystras** ㉑, a site many consider the high-light of their trip. Finally, spend a day or two at 🏛 **Monemvassia** ㉓ on the eastern edge of the Peloponnese—the Gibraltar of Byzantium.

When to Tour

The Southern Peloponnese is not as popular a travel destination as the Northern Peloponnese, which means that those who choose to ven-ture here will find many unspoiled and uncrowded sites, but they will also discover that services and resources are proportionally limited: Be prepared to endure a reduced selection of hotels and restaurants. As with the rest of Greece, on Monday most state museums and sites are closed. On Sunday many have free admission.

ARCADIA

Tripolis, Stemnitsa, Dimitsana, Karitena, Andritsena, Bassae

Arcadia was named after Arcas, whom Zeus fathered with Callisto. Unfortunately, according to one version of the legend, Callisto's father chopped Arcas into bite-size pieces and served him to Zeus for dinner. Zeus managed to give his son new life as a bear, but in a fit of ingrat-itude, Arcas eventually had his wicked way with his mother. That's when

Zeus decided to turn both mother and son into the constellations Ursa Major and Minor, the Big and Little Dipper.

Arcadians are believed to be among the oldest inhabitants of the Peloponnese, a group of tribes that first united when they entered the Trojan War. They later founded the powerful Arcadian League, but after Corinth fell in 146 BC, the region slipped into decline. When the Goths invaded in AD 395, Arcadia was almost entirely deserted. Several centuries later the Franks conquered the area and built many castles; they were succeeded by the Byzantines and then the Turks, who ruled until the War of Independence.

No conqueror ever really dominated the Arcadians. Even when Tripolis was the Turks' administrative center, the mountain villagers lived much as they pleased, maintaining secret schools to preserve the rudiments of Greek language and religion, and harassing the Turks in roaming bands. In recent years, locals have abandoned their pastoral life to look for work in Athens; Arcadia now has no more people than Corinthia, a region half its size.

Tripolis

❶ *150 km (93¼ mi) southwest of Athens, 70 km (43½ mi) southwest of Corinth.*

Regardless of which direction you approach the southern half of the Peloponnese, history suggests you're sure to spend some time in Tripolis. In the days of the Ottoman Empire, this crossroads was the capital of the Turkish Pasha of the Peloponnese, and during the War of Independence, it was the first target of Greek revolutionaries. They captured it in 1821 after a six-month siege, but the town went back and forth between the warring sides until 1827, when Ibrahim Pasha's retreating troops burned it to the ground. Tripolis is a dreary town; one of its few redeeming features is Platia Areos, one of the largest and most beautiful *platias* (central squares) in Greece—definitely the place to while away the time if marooned in Tripolis. Tripolis is also the ideal jumping-off point for exploring the surrounding mountain villages in an area nicknamed the Switzerland of Greece.

Dining and Lodging

$$$ ✕ **Petit Trianon & Everyday Roma.** Locals no longer scowl at the gold
★   statues and mini obelisks: they've discovered the decent prices and great cooking. Special dishes include *argitiko* (beef with pearl onions slow-cooked in a ceramic dish) and bacon-wrapped filet mignon with mouthwatering potatoes. Beware: many appetizers and desserts are perilously heavenly. French and German wines are well matched. ⊠ *Platia Areos 2 & 4,* ☎ *071/237413,* FAX *071/241615. DC, MC, V.*

$$ ✕ **Café Kallisto.** Sit under the large white umbrellas of this café and order an exotic fruit tea; raisin crepes soaked in Grand Marnier; baklava; or the chef's special cake. Or savor drinks with a plate of *pikilia* (appetizers) such as meats, smoked trout, shrimp, olives, and cheese. The rosy pink interior with Hollywood prints is cozy, and a large evil-eye charm over the bar will protect you from jealous admirers. ⊠ *Platia Areos 5,* ☎ *071/237019. No credit cards.*

$$ ✕ **Sossoli.** Beyond the tacky plastic flowers is a real cosmic experience: a garden manicured into concentric circles. There are several unusual dishes on the menu, including moussaka made with artichokes, *sfirida spetsiota* (grouper simmered in fresh tomatoes), and *arni fricasse* (lamb cooked in lettuce leaves and red sauce). The waiters don't speak English, so you may have to point. ⊠ *Kennedy 40,* ☎ *071/222934. No credit cards.*

$$ ✕ **Touristiko Periptero.** Pine trees and birdsong surround this refuge, nestled in a park—replete with a peacock and pheasant aviary—just outside of town. Try the wild chicory salad, chicken *rollo* (stuffed with ham, bacon, and cheese), *sofrito* (beef with parsley and garlic), or just a coffee. In a small hut nearby, **To Xayiati**, drinks only are served. ✉ *Off Ethniki Antistasis in Agios Georgios township,* ☎ *071/238433 or 071/222971. No credit cards.*

$$ 🏨 **Arcadia.** Tripolis's hotels aren't as distinguished as its restaurants. This six-story green cement box with ordinary rooms is the town's most comfortable and convenient; saving graces are the high ceilings, heavy dark furniture, and the roof garden. It looks like thousands of others throughout Greece—at least you'll know you're not in Kansas. ✉ *Kolokotroni Sq. 1,* ☎ *071/225551 through 225553,* FAX *071/222464. 45 rooms with bath. Restaurant, bar. No credit cards.*

$ 🏨 **Artemis.** The tip-offs: black vinyl settees and '60s decor in the smoky bar—this is a typical modest Greek hotel. Several rooms overlook the garden next door or across to the main square. Ask for room 605, one of the nicest doubles. ✉ *Dimitrakopoulou 1,* ☎ *071/225221 through 225223,* FAX *071/233629. 69 rooms with shower, 3 with bath. Cafeteria, bar. No credit cards.*

$ 🏨 **Menelaon.** When it opened in 1939, the Menelaon was the grandest hotel in town. It served as a hospital after the war, and thus began its denouement, although in 1960 King Constantine and his queen spent the night. It's no longer plush, but it's a good choice; spacious, clean rooms have balconies overlooking the main square. Rooms vary quite a bit; ask to see a selection. ✉ *Platia Areos,* ☎ *071/222450, 071/224747, or 071/232740. 36 rooms with bath. Restaurant, air-conditioning. No credit cards.*

Outdoor Activities and Sports

HIKING AND CLIMBING

The **Ostrakina Refuge** (✉ On Mt. Menalon, ☎ 0796/22227), northwest of Tripolis, houses 26 hikers and climbers, with a kitchen, oil- and wood-burning stoves, tank water, and indoor toilets.

On Mt. Parnon at Arnomoussa, southeast of Tripolis, the **George Pierce Refuge** has accommodations for 40 people, a kitchen, oil stoves, spring water, a fireplace, and indoor toilets.

SKIING

Mt. Menalon ski center (☎ 071/22227) at Oropedio Ostrakina (4,310 feet) has five downhill runs and three tows; food and overnight accommodation are available. The center is 30 km (18½ mi) from Tripolis, with the last 2 mi a dirt road. For information, call the Tripolis Alpine Club (☞ Contacts and Resources *in* Southern Peloponnese A to Z, *below*).

SWIMMING AND TENNIS

There are municipal pools and public tennis courts at **Tripolis's Sports Center** (☎ 071/222761).

Stemnitsa

❷ *43 km (26¾ mi) northwest of Tripolis.*

The town, also called Ipsous, is wondrously perched 3,444 feet above sea level amid a forest of fir and chestnut trees. For centuries it was one of the Balkans' best-known metalworking centers, and today a minuscule school is still staffed by local artisans.

The unusual **folklore museum** devotes one floor to mock workshops for indigenous crafts such as candle making and bell casting; the other two floors house re-created traditional rooms and a haphazard collection of costumes, weapons, icons, and plates. ⊠ *Off main rd.*, ☎ *0795/81252.* ☞ *Free.* ☉ *Apr.–Sept. weekdays 4–6, weekends 11–1.*

<table>
<tr><td>OFF THE
BEATEN PATH</td><td>LOUSIOS GORGE – Stemnitsa is a good base for a serene 5-km (3-mi) long hike along the verdant Lousios Gorge to Ayios Andreas chapel; the ancient site of Gortys with acropolis walls, bath ruins, a temple to Asclepios, god of healing; and the 12th-century monastery Ayios Ioannis Prodromos (St. John the Baptist), wedged almost 1,000 feet above the Lousios. This tributary of the Alpheios is named from louzo (to wash), because it is said to be where Zeus bathed as a child. Cloistered away in the monastery are a tiny chapel with 14th- and 15th-century frescoes and relics of St. Athanasias, bishop of Christianoupolis. You may stay the night, but there are only a few beds, and these are often snatched up by far-flung pilgrims. Be prepared to camp or to perform the 2-hour ascent along well-graded switchback trails back to Stemnitsa. You can also reach the monastery by car; take a left on the road 2 km (1¼ mi) north of Stemnitsa. ⊠ Lousios Gorge. ☞ Free. ☉ Mornings and afternoons until 4 or 5. To be admitted into the church, women must wear skirts; men and women must wear long sleeves; no shorts.</td></tr>
</table>

Dimitsana

❸ *50 km (31 mi) northwest of Tripolis, 10 km (6¼ mi) north of Stemnitsa.*

Visit Dimitsana for a stunning view of the Arcadian mountains. Leave your car at the entrance of town and stroll the maze of narrow cobbled lanes. Archaeologists found ruins of a Cyclopean wall (irregular stones without mortar) and classical buildings near the town that belonged to the acropolis of Teuthis, the ancient city.

The **town library** displays manuscripts, rare books, and memorabilia from the Greek revolutionary period, when Dimitsana was a center for revolutionary activity against the Turks. Also explore the site of a **gunpowder mill** and the monk Hatzi Agapios's **School of Greek Letters,** which educated leaders such as Germanos, the bishop of Patras. ⊠ *Main sq.*, ☎ *0775/31219.* ☞ *Free.* ☉ *Weekdays 8–2. Closed Nov.–Mar.*

Karitena

❹ *54 km (33½ mi) west of Tripolis, 26 km (16 mi) south of Dimitsana.*

Karitena, a picturesque medieval village of stone houses topped by a Frankish castle, is depicted on the back of the 5,000 dr. bill. Now inhabited by fewer than 300 people, Karitena had a population of 20,000 during the Middle Ages. For a stunning view of the gorge and the town, walk over to the multiarched Frankish bridge that spans the Alpheios.

When the Franks took over from the Byzantines in 1209, they gave the town to Hugo de la Bruyeres, who built the **Frankish castle** in 1245, then bequeathed it to his son Geoffrey, the only well-liked Frankish overlord, who was praised in the *Chronicle of Morea* for his chivalry. The castle was known as the Toledo of Greece because of its strategic position at the mouth of the Alpheios Gorge. Later, during the Revolution, the hero Theodore Kolokotronis again made use of its location, repairing the fortifications and building a house and a church within the walls as his base, out of reach of Ibrahim Pasha.

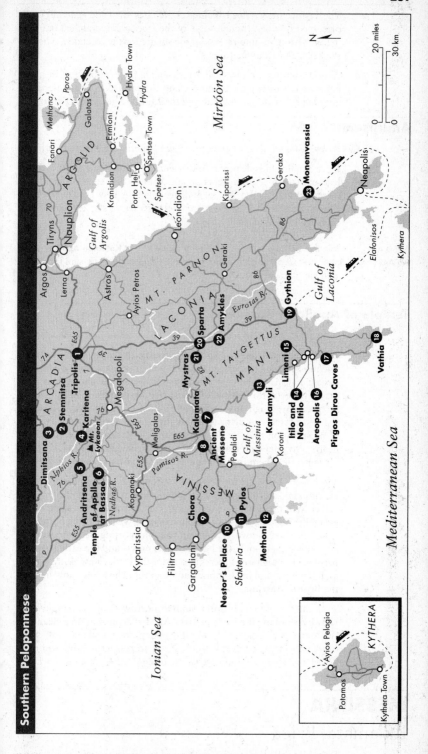

Southern Peloponnese

N

20 miles
30 km

Mirtóön Sea

Poros

Methana

Fanari

Galatas

Hydra Town

Ermioni

Hydra

Kranidion

Spetses Town

Porto Heli

Spetses

Kiparissi

Geraka

Monemvassia **23**

Neapolis

Leonidion

Elafonisos

Kythera

Nauplion

Tiryns 70

Gulf of Argolis

ARGOLID

Argos

Lerna

Astros

Ayios Petros

Geraki

Gulf of Laconia

MT. PARNON

LACONIA

Evrotas R.

Sparta **20**

Amykles

Gythion **19**

86

74

E65

Tripolis **1**

39

Stemnitsa **2**

ARCADIA

Karitena **4**

Mt. Lykaeon

76

Megalopoli

Mystras **21**

Kalamata **7**

MT. TAYGETTUS

MANI

Limeni **15**

Vathia **18**

Dimitsana **3**

1

Amykles **22**

39

Andritsena **5**

Temple of Apollo at Bassae **6**

Alphios R.

Nedhas R.

E65

E55

76

Meligalas

Ancient Messene **8**

Gulf of Messinia

Kardamyli **13**

Itilo and Neo Itilo **14**

Areopolis **16**

Pirgos Dirou Caves **17**

Pamisos R.

MESSINIA

Petalidi

Koroni

Kopanaki

Kyparissia

Filitra

Gargaliani

Chora **9**

Nestor's Palace **10**

Pylos **11**

Sfakteria

Methoni **12**

Ionian Sea

Mediterranean Sea

KYTHERA

Ayios Pelagia

Potamos

Kythera Town

The 11th-century **Ayios Nikolaos** church has vivid and generally well-preserved frescoes, though some of the faces were scratched out during the Ottoman Empire. Ask in the square for the caretaker, who has the keys. ✉ *Below the town sq.*

En Route   As you continue west toward Andritsena in the prefecture of Elis, you have views down into the gorge, and the road skirts narrow passes guarded by castles, known during the Middle Ages as the *Escorta.*

Andritsena

❺ *83 km (51½ mi) west of Tripolis, 29 km (18 mi) southwest of Karitena.*

Once a major hillside town, Andritsena's claim to fame today is a collection of 15th-century Venetian and Vatican first editions and documents relating to the War of Independence. A new library has been recently completed. ✉ *On main rd. 100 yds after the sq.,* ☎ *0626/22242.* ☞ *Free.* ⊘ *Weekdays 8:30–3.*

NEED A BREAK?	Join the old men relaxing under the plane tree at **Kafenion Apollon** (✉ In main sq). Order a cool Greek frappé, or iced coffee—be sure to have it with *me gala* (milk).

Temple of Apollo at Bassae

❻ *97 km (60¼ mi) southwest of Tripolis, 14 km (8½) south of Andritsena.*

The solitude of Temple of Apollo Epikourios at Bassae, with its craggy, uncompromising scenery, may catch you unprepared: the building is elegant and spare, and untouched by vandalism or commercialism. Pausanias believed this temple was designed by Iktinos, the Parthenon's architect. Although this theory has recently been disputed, it is one of the best-preserved Classical temples in Greece, superseded in its state of preservation only by the Hephaistion in Athens. The residents of nearby Phygalia built it atop an older temple in 420 BC to thank Apollo for delivering them from an epidemic; *epikourious* means "helper."

The Bassae temple, made of local limestone, has some unusual details: exceptional length compared to its width; a north-south orientation rather than the usual east-west (probably because of the slope of the ground); and Ionic half-columns linked to the walls by flying buttresses. It had the first known Corinthian column sporting the characteristic acanthus leaves—only the base remains now—and the earliest example of interior sculptured friezes illustrating the battles between the Greeks and Amazons and the Centaurs and Lapiths. The friezes now hang in the British Museum.

Take the time to climb to the **summit** northwest of the temple for a view overlooking the Nedhas River, Mt. Lykaeon, and on a clear day, the Ionian Sea. Despite its splendid setting, the temple has lost some of its impact, veiled as it is by a canopy to protect it from acid rain. ✉ *14 km south of Andritsena,* ☎ *0626/22254.* ☞ *Free.* ⊘ *Daily 8:30–3.*

MESSINIA
Kalamata, Pylos

Euripides called this region "a land of fair fruitage and watered by innumerable streams . . . neither very wintry in the blasts of winter, nor yet made too hot by the chariot of Hellos." Long, cool summers and

In case you want to see the world.

At American Express, we're here to make your journey a smooth one. So we have over 1,700 travel service locations in over 120 countries ready to help. What else would you expect from the world's largest travel agency?

do more ®

http://www.americanexpress.com/travel

Travel

In case you want to be welcomed there.

We're here to see that you're always welcomed at establishments everywhere. That's why millions of people carry the American Express® Card – for peace of mind, confidence, and security, around the world or just around the corner.

do more

Cards

In case you're running low.

We're here to help with more than 118,000 Express Cash locations around the world. In order to enroll, just call American Express before you start your vacation.

do more

Express Cash

And just in case.

We're here with American Express® Travelers Cheques and Cheques *for Two.*® They're the safest way to carry money on your vacation and the surest way to get a refund, practically anywhere, anytime.

Another way we help you...

do more ®

Travelers Cheques

mild winters may be Messinia's blessing, but nature was no ally in 1986 when an earthquake registering 6.2 on the Richter scale razed its capital, Kalamata. Though the port city started to rebuild immediately, jumbles of masonry and other reminders of the earthquake abound.

Kalamata

❼ *91 km (56½ mi) southwest of Tripolis.*

Though not Greece's finest city, Kalamata does have a pleasant mixture of sights, seaside restaurants, and beaches, and it makes an excellent base for exploring Messinia, one of Greece's most beautiful regions. Kalamata is built atop ancient Pharai, described by Homer as subject to the kingdom of Agamemnon. In the 8th century BC, Pharai was annexed as a province of Laconia, and like most towns in the area, was not independent again until the Battle of Leuctra ended Spartan domination, prompting the Theban general Epaminondas to erect the great fortifications of Messene.

The small, well-organized **Benakeion museum** exhibits local stone tools, proto-Geometric and Geometric pottery, and a 1st-century AD Roman mosaic floor depicting Dionysos with a panther and a satyr. ✉ *Benaki mansion, Benaki and Papazoglou Sts., near Platia 25 Martiou (25th of March Sq.),* ☎ *0721/26209.* ✆ *Free.* ☉ *Tues.–Sat. 8–2:30, Sun. and holidays 8:30–3.*

The earthquake felled the keep of the city's **Kastro** (✉ Hill overlooking town), but it's worth hiking the small hill for the view of the coast and the Messinian Plain. Only the theater area near the entrance is open.

In the early 13th century William de Champlitte divided the Peloponnese into 12 baronies, bestowing Kalamata on Geoffrey de Villehardouin, who built a winter **castle** (✉ At the end of Ipapandis). Through the centuries, the castle was bitterly fought over by Franks, Slavs, and Byzantines, and today it's difficult to tell what of the remains is original. From 25th of March Sq., walk up Ipapandis street past the church and take the first left at the castle gates, which are always open.

The oldest church in Kalamata is the 13th-century **Ayii Apostoli** (Holy Apostles), a small Byzantine church dedicated to the Virgin of Kalamata (of the good eye), from whom the town may get its name. Restored after its devastation in 1986, it is one of Greece's curious double churches with two naves—one for the Roman Catholics and one for the Orthodox—that resulted from 13th- and 14th-century ecumenical efforts. The Revolution was formally declared here on March 23, 1821, when Kolokotronis captured Kalamata from the Turks. Unfortunately the church is almost always closed; your best chance of finding it open is to visit in the late afternoon (5–7). ✉ *25th of March Sq.*

☾ Children will enjoy **Kalamata's train park,** which has seven steam engines, a Dietrich diesel engine, and several freight cars. There's a restored footbridge, a railway platform, and an old station, disguised as a café, where parents can relax while keeping an eye on their offspring. ✉ *South End of Aristomenous, near harbor.* ✆ *Free.* ☉ *Daily until dark.*

Beaches

☾ West of Kalamata at Petalidi is the beginning of a long chain of sandy beaches that are ideal for children because of the shallow water. Closer to town are **Verga** (✉ To the east) and the more crowded **Bouka** (✉ 7 km/4¼ mi to the west); both have showers and changing rooms.

Dining and Lodging

$$ ✗ **Selitsa.** Take in all of Kalamata and the Gulf of Messinia from the
★   tables at this hillside taverna. Wood, rock, and running water set the
stage for hearty meats such as *katsiki tou fournou* (roasted goat) and
roasted lamb. For a light snack, enjoy the special *paximadia* (rusks served
with oregano and oil) while quaffing a glass of barrel white. Next door
is a small castle, which in summer is a drinks-only bistro. ✉ *Take main
rd. out of Kalamata to Almiro; signs indicate where to turn for Selitsa
village,* ☎ *0721/41331 or 0721/41020. No credit cards.*

$ ✗ **Kaloutas.** At this waterfront restaurant, watch the men laying out
their nets to dry while you enjoy copious helpings of well-cooked
Greek food: tender beef *kokkinisto* (stew), and *arni lemonato* (lamb
cooked in a light lemon sauce). Mr. Kaloutas prides himself on his se-
lection and, if he's not too busy, he takes requests. He also prepares
large breakfasts with croissants, eggs, orange juice, and drip coffee in-
stead of the drearily ubiquitous *nes* (boiled Nescafé). ✉ *Navarinou 93,*
☎ *0721/29097. No credit cards.*

$ ✗ **Meltemi.** If you can't make it to this rustic taverna on the day they're
serving a whole roast pig, you can still be smitten with the fresh fish,
the *tsoutsoukakia* (rolls of spicy sausage), the *imam* (a Turkish version
of moussaka), or the *exohiko* (grilled lamb). Standbys are pizza, pork
chops, and the local retsina. Outdoor seating is on the harbor. ✉
Navarinou 25, ☎ *0721/21260. No credit cards.*

$$$ ▥ **Pharae Hotel.** This A-class hotel in downtown Kalamata is *the*
★   place to stay for those who can swing it. The lobby is handsome, with
tasteful green furniture and marble floors. The restaurant patio overlooks the sea, as will a rooftop patio that is being built. Rooms are
modern and immaculate, with all the amenities you would expect, such
as TVs. ✉ *Navarinou and Riga Fereou,* ☎ *0721/94421 through 94424,*
FAX *0721/93969. 76 rooms with bath. Restaurant, breakfast room, air-
conditioning, sauna, meeting room. MC, V.*

$$ ▥ **Haikos.** This modest beach hotel is a less-expensive alternative to
Kalamata's grand establishments, and it's meticulously run by the
Haikos brothers. The cool blue bedrooms have ocean views, showers,
and comfy sofas; a pebble-and-sand beach is just a few steps away. ✉
Navarinou 115, ☎ *0721/82886 and 0721/82888. 112 rooms with
shower. No credit cards.*

$ ⌂ **Elite.** Pitches here are set in an olive grove. Tennis courts at the Elite
Hotel are open to campers. ✉ *Verga beach, next to Elite Hotel,* ☎
*0721/25015. RV and tent sites. Bathrooms, hot showers, washing ma-
chine, water sports, children's playground. Closed Nov.–Mar.*

$ ⌂ **Maria's.** Also known as Sea and Sun, this site is almost as nice as
Grandma's garden, with a large mulberry tree, flowers, and a wooden
bar laced with vines. The restaurant at the entrance is built in the tra-
ditional local style; it's open year-round. ✉ *Verga beach, Near Agios
Sion chapel,* ☎ *0721/41314. RV and tent sites. Restaurant.*

Festivals

The annual **Independence Day celebration** is held March 23 (March
25 is the official date). Stick around for the festivities—dancing, local
bands, and a spirited parade. Contact the Greek National Tourist Or-
ganization (GNTO or EOT) for information (☞ Visitor Information
in Southern Peloponnese A to Z, *below*). In summer Kalamata holds
a **theater festival;** contact the **festival office** (☎ 0721/29909) for fur-
ther information.

Nightlife

Nightlife in Kalamata leaves a bit to be desired; to join the locals, head down to the waterfront to hang out.

Outdoor Activities and Sports

SWIMMING

Kalamata has public pools; call (☎ 0721/29717) for information.

Shopping

LOCAL SPECIALTIES

Kalamata is famous for its *pastelli* (sesame seed and honey candy), figs, fleshy black olives, olive oil, and the silk scarves handmade by nuns from the convent of the Virgin Ypapanti in the cathedral square.

Ancient Messene

8 *75 km (46½ mi) southwest of Tripolis, 31 km (19¼ mi) north of Kalamata.*

The ruins of ancient Messene near Mavromati are set on the slopes of majestic Mt. Ithomi (also known as Voulkanos). Epaminondas built Messene in 370–69 BC to provide a citadel, further undermining Sparta's authority. The Messenians had battled Sparta in two Messenian Wars (743–724 BC and 650–620 BC). Even after they were defeated and reduced to helots the Messenians seized the opportunity of a severe earthquake in 464 BC to wall themselves up in the stronghold of Ithome, so that Sparta had to beg Athens to help them recapture the acropolis.

Messene enjoyed prosperity under Theban protection, and after Thebes fell, allied itself with the Macedonians, later deserting them for the Achaean League. Even under the Romans, Messene managed to remain autonomous, only to be destroyed by the Goths in AD 395.

Its most striking ruin is the city's **circuit wall,** a feat of defensive architecture. Four gates remain; the best preserved is the north or **Arcadian Gate,** a double set of gates separated by a round courtyard. On the slabs of ancient paving stone below the arch, grooves worn by ancient chariot wheels are still visible. The heart of the walled city is now occupied by the village of **Mavromati,** but excavations have uncovered the most important public buildings, including a **theater,** whose seats have now been restored; the **Synedrion,** a **meeting hall** for representatives of independent Messene; the **Sebasteion,** dedicated to worship of a Roman emperor; the **sanctuary to the god Asklepios;** and a **temple to Artemis Orthia.** Outside the walls lie a **stadium** and a **cemetery.** The guard at the site usually has the key to the village's **small museum** if you want to examine the finds. ⊠ *From modern town of Messene, turn north at intersection of rd. to Mavromati; from village, you must walk the last 2 km (1¼ mi),* ☎ *0724/51257.* ☎ *Free.* ⊙ *Daily 8:30–1.*

Chora

9 *48 km (29¾ mi) west of Kalamata, 64 km (39¾ mi) west of ancient Messene.*

Stop in at Chora's **archaeological museum** to see the artifacts: golden cups and jewelry from the Mycenaean period, fragments of frescoes, including a warrior in a boar's-tusk helmet described by Homer, and plaster casts of the Linear B tablets—the originals are in the archaeological museum in Athens. ⊠ *Marinatou St. off town sq.,* ☎ *0763/31358.* ☎ *500 dr.* ⊙ *Tues.–Sun. 8:30–3.*

⑩ **Nestor's Palace** belonged to the king of Pylos, commander, according to Homer, of the fleet of "ninety black ships" in the Trojan War. Nestor founded the town around 1300 BC—only Mycenae was larger—but the palace was burned a century later. It was here, the *Iliad* tells us, that Telemachus came to ask for news of his father, Odysseus, from Nestor, who welcomed the young man to a feast at the palace.

Most of the palace rooms are clearly marked, but it's a good idea to buy the guidebook, available at the site, prepared by the University of Cincinnati, whose archaeologists excavated the site; the illustrations will help you imagine the palace in its original condition. Archaeologists believe the complex, excavated in 1952, was similar to those found in Crete and Mycenae, except that it was unfortified, an indication that surrounding towns had sworn strict allegiance to and depended economically on Pylos. In the **main building,** a simple **entrance gate** is flanked by a **guard chamber** and two **archives,** where 1,250 palm leaf–shape tablets were discovered on the first day of excavation. The tablets—records of taxes, armament expenses, and debts in Linear B script—were the first such unearthed on the Greek mainland, thus linking the Mycenaean and Minoan (Crete) civilizations, because the writing—like that in Knossos—was definitely Greek.

The entrance gate opens into a spacious **courtyard** with a balcony where spectators could watch the royal ceremonies. To the left are a **store-room** that yielded thousands of tall-stemmed vases and a **waiting room** with built-in benches. Beyond the courtyard a **porch of the royal apartments** and a **vestibule** open onto a richly decorated **throne room.** In the middle of the room is a ceremonial **hearth** surrounded by four wooden columns (only the stone bases remain) that probably supported a shaft. Now completely destroyed, the throne once stood in the center of the wall to the right. Each **frescoed wall** depicted a different subject, like a griffin (possibly the royal emblem) or a minstrel strumming his lyre. Even the columns and the wooden ceiling were painted. Along the southern edge of the throne room were seven **storerooms** for oil, which together with the one on the floor immediately above fueled the fire that destroyed the palace.

Off a corridor to the right of the entrance are a **bathroom,** where the oldest known bathtub stands, along with jars used for collecting bathwater. Next to it are the **Queen's apartments:** in the largest room a hearth is adorned with a painted flame, the walls with hunting scenes of lions and panthers. Other rooms in the complex include the **throne room** from an earlier palace, a **shrine, workshops,** and a **conduit** that brought water from a nearby spring. Several **beehive tombs** were also found outside the palace. ⊠ *On the hwy. 4 km/2½ mi south of Chora,* ☎ *0763/31437.* ⊠ *500 dr.* ☉ *Tues.–Sun. 8:30–3.*

Pylos

⑪ *52 km (32¼ mi) southwest of Kalamata, 22 km (13½ mi) south of Chora.*

Pylos, with its bougainvillea-swathed, pristine white houses fanning up Mt. Saint Nicholas, will remind you of an island. It was built according to a plan drawn by French engineers stationed here from 1828 to 1833 with General Maison's entourage. This port town was the site of a major naval battle in the War of Independence. Ibrahim Pasha had chosen Sfakteria, the islet that virtually blocks Pylos bay, to launch his attack on the mainland. For two years Greek forces flailed under Turkish firepower until in 1827, Britain, Russia, and France came in to support the Greek insurgents. They sent a fleet to persuade Turkey to sign a treaty, were accidentally fired upon, and found themselves retaliating. At the end of the battle, the allies had sunk 53 of 89 ships of the Turko-Egyptian fleet without a single loss of their 27 war vessels. The Sultan was forced to renegotiate, which paved the way for Greek independence. A column rising between a Turkish and a Venetian cannon in the town's main square, Platia Trion Navarchon (Three Admirals Square), commemorates the leaders of the fleets.

For a closer look of the bay, take an hour-long boat tour to the various monuments on **Sfakteria,** sunken Turkish ships, and the neighboring rock of **Tsichli-Baba,** which has a vast, much-photographed natural arch, nicknamed Tripito, a former pirate hideout with 144 steps. It's said that if a pregnant woman sails under this arch, she will have a boy. Boat rentals can cost up to 8,000 dr. (less expensive if you go with a group). They can also take you to the weed-infested 13th-century **Paleokastro,** one of the two fortresses guarding the channels on either side of Sfakteria, and make a stop also at **Nestor's cave.** Look for the many signs on the waterfront advertising captains' services. ⊠ *West of Pylos Port.*

For views of Pylos, the bay, and the Kamares Roman aqueduct, the **Neokastro,** the newer fortress that dominates the town, is unbeatable. It was built by the Turks in 1573 to control the southern—at that time, the only—entrance to the bay (an artificial embankment had drastically reduced the depth of the northern channel). Neokastro's well-preserved walls enclose a **church of the Transfiguration,** originally a mosque; cannons; and two anchors from the battle. The southwest wall, which could be attacked by sea, was especially strong. The highest point of the castle is guarded by a hexagonal fort flanked by towers. Until recently the fort was a prison, but unlike most Greek penitentiaries, which are fairly open, this was more secure, apparently to squelch feuds with the Mani prison, whose inmates were notoriously bellicose. ⊠ *Rd. to Methoni,* ☏ *0723/22897.* 🎟 *800 dr.* ☉ *Daily 8–3.*

The small **archaeological museum** of Pylos has a collection of Hellenistic pottery, Roman bronze statues, engravings, battle memorabilia, gold pots, jewelry, and other objects of the Mycenaean period. ⊠ *Methonis 8,* ☏ *0723/22448.* 🎟 *500 dr.* ☉ *Tues.–Sun. 8:30–3.*

Dining and Lodging

$$ ✕ **To Diethnes.** This rather nondescript restaurant serves solid Greek food. Especially good are the *briam* (a delicate mixture of potatoes and artichokes), *moschari psito* (roasted beef), and the squid. Look forward to an aromatic red barrel wine and a wide choice of Greek wines. Off-season, just the basics are served. ⊠ *Waterfront, next to police station,* ☏ *0723/22772. No credit cards.*

$ ✕ **Ta Pente Aderfia.** Blessed with perhaps the town's best sunset view, this unpretentious restaurant—a real treat—specializes in grilled meats, usual Greek *magirefta* (precooked dishes served at room temperature), and fresh seafood. Order the special dish called *navomaxia* (a seared fillet of beef) served in wine sauce, *psari macaronada* (an unusual combination of fish and pasta), which has to be ordered a day ahead, and the large mussels. After dinner, try the succulent local grapes or oranges. ⊠ *Waterfront,* ☏ *0723/22564. No credit cards.*

$$$ 🏨 **Karalis Beach.** This 60s minimalist Greek hotel has typical rooms in pale shades—the ones in the front, however, have beautiful sea views, balconies, and bathtubs; those in back overlook greenery. Relax in the roof garden. A large breakfast is served buffet style. The geographic advantages are its beach locale and its 4-minute walk to town center. ⊠ *Paralia,* ☏ *0723/23021 and 23022. 24 rooms with bath. Bar, air-conditioning. V. Closed Nov.–Mar.*

$$ ☒ **Miramare.** This hotel is perhaps best known for its plentiful English breakfast of ham, cheese, eggs, and—on request—bacon and sausage. Gentlemanly manager Nikos Houmas is always on the lookout for ways to improve his hotel. Windsurfers and canoes are now available for rent, and the sand and gravel beach is just steps away. All the rooms have ocean views. ☒ *Paralia,* ☎ *0723/22751,* ℻ *0723/22226. 16 rooms with bath. Restaurant (groups only), bar, water sports. AE, DC, MC, V. Closed Nov.–Feb.*

$ ⚓ **Ammos.** This site is on a fine sandy beach that offers boat rental, windsurfing, and waterskiing instruction. ☒ *Ammos; from Pylos head south for Ammos, 3 km (2 mi) before Finikoundas,* ☎ *0723/71262. RV and tent sites. Boating, waterskiing, windsurfing. Closed Nov.–Apr.*

Methoni

⓬ *98 km (61 mi) southwest of Kalamata, 14 km (8½ mi) south of Pylos.*

Methoni, a resort at a cape south of Pylos, is so delightful, so tempting, it was one of the seven towns Agamemnon offered Achilles to appease him after his beloved Briseis was carried off. According to Homer, Pedasos, as it was called, was "rich in vines," and tradition says that the town got its modern name because *onoi* (donkeys) carrying the town's wine became *methoun* (intoxicated) from the aroma.

Methoni's principal attraction is its **Kastro.** After the Second Messenian War, the victorious Spartans gave Methoni to the Nauplians, who had been exiled from their homeland for their Spartan alliance. The town remained autonomous under Roman rule and finally came into its own during the Middle Ages as an important stop on trade routes between Europe and the East. The Venetians, who had long had designs on its fine natural harbor, took control of Methoni in 1209, building the impressive Kastro along the shoreline. If you're feeling ambitious, cross the stone bridge over the dry moat to this imposing, well-kept citadel; various coats of arms mark the walls, including that of Genoa and Venice's Lion of St. Mark. A second bridge joins the fortified town with the **Bourtzi,** an octagonal tower built on an islet during the Turkish occupation (after 1500) and now a favorite lovers' haunt. ☒ *By the coast,* ☎ *0731/25363.* ▨ *Free.* ☉ *Daily, winter 8:30–3, summer 8:30–7.*

Dining and Lodging

$$ ✕ **Louis's (formerly Kali Kardia).** This newly named restaurant—the
★ owner's son Ilias (Louis) has taken the reins—still serves renowned food. In a neoclassical house, the restaurant's interior delights with checked tablecloths, lush plants, and family portraits. The swordfish, moschari psito flambée, and excellent desserts such as *ravani* (farina, almonds, and a heavy cognac-orange syrup) are all worthy of attention. Breakfast is also served. ☒ *Main rd. near castle,* ☎ *0723/31260. MC, V.*

$$ ✕ **Nikos's.** "The only time this kitchen closes is if I'm sick," says Nikos Vile, who insists on cooking everything from *mamboulas* (a moussaka made with tomatoes) to *maridakia* (lightly fried whitebait) each day. He also makes wonderful *fassolia* (beans) and *garides tsaganaki* (shrimp and cheese in a lemony red sauce). Or you may sip an aperitif at the bar or hide out in the secluded courtyard. ☒ *Miali Rd.,* ☎ *0723/31282. No credit cards.*

$ ✕ **Rex.** Right on the beach, surrounded by large shady pines, Rex serves delicious food: hearty dolmades, pungent *tzatziki* (garlic-yogurt-cucumber dip), fresh fish such as sea bream, and for dessert, local grapes, honeydew melons, and fragrant peaches. Throughout the summer, a nearby playground entertains kids. ✉ *On beach below fortress,* ☎ *0723/31239. No credit cards. Closed Nov.–Mar.*

$$$ 🏨 **Ulysses.** From the shady, well-manicured courtyard to the rooms' fresh-cut flowers, all feel welcomed at this hotel. A room bonus is individual cooling and heating units. The breakfast spread includes 22 items, such as fresh orange juice, omelets, and yogurt with honey. The hotel also charters yachts; for every week's hotel stay, guests receive a free day of yacht use. ✉ *Paralia,* ☎ *0723/31600. 12 rooms with bath. Restaurant, bar. MC.*

$$ 🏨 **Amalia.** Built in 1990, this modest hotel has basic rooms at very reasonable prices. All rooms have huge verandas that face the sea or town, both close. The lush garden is the pride of the Kalligas family. ✉ *Coastal rd. to Finikoundas,* ☎ *0723/31129 and 0723/31139,* FAX *0723/31195. 34 rooms with shower. Restaurant, bar. MC, V. Closed Nov.–Apr.*

Festival

On *Kathari Deftera* (Clean Monday), just before Lent, Methoni holds a mock Koutroulis village wedding at the town platia, a riotous annual performance, in which both the bride and groom are played by men.

MANI
Kardamyli, Itilo, Limeni, Areopolis, Vathia, Gythion

You now enter the Mani, which, on its western side, stretches from Kardamyli to Cape Tenaro, the mythical entrance to the underworld, and on its eastern side from Cape Tenaro up to Gythion. The western half is the Messinian Mani, while the eastern half is the Laconian Mani. Isolated and invincible, this was the land of bandits and blood feuds. The Dorians never reached this far south, Roman occupation was perfunctory, and Christianity was not established here until the 9th century. Neither the Venetians nor the Turks could quell the constant rebellions.

The Maniotes were thought to be descended from the ancient Spartans, and to have been expelled from northern Laconia by invading Slavs in the 7th century. An aristocracy arose—the Nyklians—whose clans began building defensive tower houses (the oldest dates to the 15th century) and fighting for precious land in this barren landscape. The object in battle was to annihilate the enemy's tower house, as well as its entire male population. Feuds could last for years, with the women—who were safe from attack—bringing in supplies. Mani women were famous throughout Greece for their singing of the *moirologhi* (laments), like the ancient choruses in a Greek tragedy.

A truce had to be called in long-lasting feuds during the harvest, but a feud only ended with the complete destruction of a family or its surrender, called *psychiko* (a thing of the soul) in which losers filed out of their tower house one by one, kissing the hand of the enemy clan's parents. The victor then decided under what conditions the humbled family could remain in the village. When King Otto tried to tame this incorrigible bunch in 1833, his soldiers were ambushed, stripped naked, and held for ransom.

Today, few people still live in the Mani. If you have the good luck to share a shot of fiery raki with a Maniote, you may notice a Cretan influence in his dress—older men still wear the baggy breeches, black headbands, and decorated jackets wrapped with heavy belts.

Kardamyli

⓭ *122 km (75¼ mi) southwest of Tripolis, 31 km (19¼ mi) southeast of Kalamata.*

Kardamyli is the gateway to the Mani on the Messinian side. It is considered part of the outer Mani, an area less bleak and stark than the inner Mani that begins at Areopolis. Here the foothills of Mt. Taygettus are still verdant and the sun is more forgiving. It has become a tourist destination for the more discerning traveler attracted to its remoteness and stark beauty, and it is particularly popular with the English. Kardamyli's most famous resident is Patrick Leigh-Fermor, an Anglo-Irish writer who has written extensively on Greece and on the Mani in particular.

Kardamyli is dotted with small clusters of **tower houses** that are being restored; some are occupied, but it is possible for the public to stroll through the paths that cut through the enclave. ⊠ *Northwest of modern town.*

Lodging

$$ 🏠 **Lela's Taverna & Pension.** Mrs. Lela is famous here for her cook-
★ ing; the secret is probably in the fragrant homemade olive oil and the exceedingly fresh tomatoes and herbs. Try the chicken with rosemary, the light moussaka, and the fish soup—even if you don't like fish. Good local barrel wine is usually available. There are also three rooms and two apartments behind the taverna in an oleander-, cyclamen-, and mulberry bush–covered building. Inside, therapeutic prints of indigenous flowers hang on the walls. The rooms face the sea and are very quiet; it is a respite from busy Kalamata. ⊠ *Seaside, above a rocky beach near old soap factory,* ☎ FAX *0721/73541. 3 rooms with bath, 2 apartments. No credit cards.*

$ 🏠 **Castle Pension.** This informal pension in a restored castle rents pleasant studio rooms and apartments with cooking facilities. There is a small balcony for everyone's use, and the public areas are filled with miscellaneous paintings and sculptures—thankfully not for sale. ⊠ *Main rd.,* ☎ *0721/73226 and 73396,* FAX *0721/73685. 10 rooms with bath, 5 apartments. Breakfast room. No credit cards.*

Itilo and Neo Itilo

⓮ *68 km (42¼ mi) southwest of Kalamata, 37 km (23 mi) south of Kardamyli.*

Itilo and Neo Itilo are the upper and lower parts of the same town. Neo Itilo is plunk on the curve of an enormous bay with a white pebble beach ideal for swimming; its uphill counterpart, Itilo, is nestled in a ravine amid slender cypresses. Formerly the capital of the Mani, verdant Itilo looks better from afar, with its red-tile roofs and bright blue window frames; up close, the houses are falling apart, neglected by a dwindling population. From the 16th to the 18th centuries, the harbor was infamous as a base for piracy and slave trading (Maniotes trading Turks to Venetians and vice versa, depending on who was in power).

Outraged by the piracy and hoping to control the pass to the north, the Turks built the nearby **Castle of Kelefa** (⊠ Across gorge from Itilo). You may walk or drive to Kelefa on a road that turns off to the right 4 km (2½ mi) before the Limeni junction.

Beach

Neo Itilo sits on a beautiful large bay with a **white pebble beach.** Enjoy a swim as you watch the fishermen fixing their nets, checking their ship hulls, and chattering amongst themselves amid the din of their portable radios.

Limeni

⓯ *70 km (43½ mi) southwest of Athens, 2 km (1¼ mi) south of Itilo and Neo Itilo.*

In Limeni the **restored tower** of Revolution hero Petrobey Mavromichaelis now guards little more than a string of cottages with their backs to the sea and a main street crammed with tiny shops. You may be mesmerized by the coastal scenery, but keep an eye out for donkeys, sheep, and flocks of goats that may suddenly trot into the road.

Areopolis

⓰ *74 km (46 mi) southwest of Kalamata, 4 km (2½ mi) south of Limeni.*

In Areopolis the typical Maniote tower houses began to appear in earnest, spooky sentinels in the harsh landscape. The town was renamed after the god of war Ares, because of its role in the Revolution: Mavromichaelis declared the local uprising against the Turks here (his statue stands in the square). Areopolis now enjoys protection as a historical monument by the government, but although the town seems medieval, most of the tower houses were built in the early 1800s; the Taxiarchis (Archangels) church, though it looks like it has 12th-century reliefs over the doors, was actually built in 1798. Still, it's easy to vicariously slip into a time warp as you meander down Kapetan Matapan Street through the fields to the sea or along the dark cobblestone lanes past the tower houses with their enclosed courtyards and low arched gateways.

Lodging

$$$ 🏨 **Londas Pension.** The diverse influences of Hans and Jacobis, Swiss
★ and Greek respectively, have created a unique "hotel." The restored tower house—with only four rooms and two terraces—is splashed with a white and blue island theme. Jacobis—whose cooking has been featured in newspapers as far away as Paris—cooks upon request in the small dining room. ✉ *Near Archangels church,* ☎ *0733/51360. 4 rooms, 2 with private bath. No credit cards.*

Pirgos Dirou Caves

⓱ *84 km (52¼ mi) southwest of Kalamata, 10 km (6¼ mi) south of Areopolis.*

Smack-dab in the middle of nowhere appears one of Greece's natural wonders, the Pirgos Dirou caves. Carved out of the limestone by the slow-moving underground river Vlychada on its way to the sea, the **Alepotripia** and **Glyfada** caves were places of worship in Paleolithic and Neolithic times and hiding places millennia later for Resistance fighters during World War II. Even earlier, Pirgos Dirou became known throughout Greece when Maniote women beat off Ibrahim Pasha's men with scythes when they tried to take the town. Cave paintings, stone implements, evidence of pottery making, and skeletons were found in Alepotripia. The skeletons were of unburied dead, leading to speculation that an earthquake early in the Bronze Age had blocked the cave, trapping the inhabitants.

Alepotripia is closed for excavation, but visitors can see Glyfada's fantastical grottoes, with luminous pink, white, yellow, and red stalagmites and stalactites. The cave is believed to be at least 70 km (43 mi) long, with more than 2,800 waterways, perhaps extending as far as Sparta. In the **Great Ocean room,** the flowing water is nearly 100 feet deep. Visitors can take a half-hour guided boat tour for 2 km (1¼ mi) through nine large **chambers** full of surreal "buildings" and mythical beasts, with names like Dragon's Lair, Cathedral, and Hanging Beds of the Water Sprites.

The close quarters in the passageways are not for the claustrophobic, and even in summer the caves are chilly. During the high season, you may wait up to two hours for a boat, so plan to arrive early. Next to the caves are a small bathing beach, snack bar, taverna, and changing room. ⊠ *Along southern coast,* ☎ *0733/52222 and 52223.* ☜ *3,500 dr.* ☉ *Daily 8–3 in winter, 8–5:30 in summer.*

En Route   En route to Vathia, farther south, you will pass the secluded cove of Mezapos, a road to the castle of Maina (locally called Tigani), built in 1247 by William Villehardouin, and the once-powerful village of Kitta where the last feudal war was suppressed in 1870 by a force of 400 federal soldiers.

Vathia

⑱   *107 km (66½ mi) southwest of Kalamata, 33 km (20 ½ mi) south of Areopolis.*

Vathia's two- and three-story stone towers, clustered around the hilltop, have small windows and tiny openings over the doors through which boiling oil was poured on the unwelcome. Vathia is worth a visit simply because of the density of the tower houses, and the pervasive feeling of emptiness. It is nearly a ghost town. Oddly enough, the **tower houses** are now guest houses, restored by the government to entice visitors to the village.

★

Lodging

$$$ ▣ **Traditional Settlements.** This is one of the government-restored tower houses, which loom over a square, a church, and abandoned domestic buildings. Rooms are simple, with regional handicrafts; the lobby, framed by heavy wooden beams and a stone floor, displays equipment from an olive press. ⊠ *Vathia,* ☎ *0733/54244. 50 rooms with bath. Restaurant. No credit cards.*

En Route   On the way to Areopolis, about 54 km (33½ mi), you'll pass the fine sandy beach of Mavrovouni and the castle of Passava. It's challenging to get to the top, albeit with no regular path, but the view takes in two bays. Originally constructed in 1254 by French baron Jean de Neuilly, the castle was rebuilt by the Turks in the 18th century, then abandoned.

Gythion

⑲   *46 km (28½ mi) south of Sparta, 79 km (49 mi) north of Vathia.*

Gythion, at the foot of the Mt. Taygettus range, is a welcome sight. Graceful 19th-century pastel houses march up the steep hillside, and along the harbor, fruit-laden donkeys sidestep the peanut vendors and gypsies hawking strings of garlic. Laconia's main port, the town is the Laconian gateway to the Mani peninsula. It claims Hercules and Apollo as its founders, and survives today by exporting olives, oil, rice, and citrus fruits.

Gythion has a few rather insignificant ruins, including a well-preserved **Roman theater** (✉ Archaio Theatrou St.) with stone seats intact. Some remains of the ancient town (Laryssion) are visible on **Mt. Koumaros** (✉ 2 km/1¼ mi along the road), a settlement that in Roman times exported the murex shell for dyeing imperial togas purple.

It is on the tiny islet of **Marathonissi** (✉ Just east of Gythion), once called Kranae, that Paris and Helen (wife of Menelaos) consummated their love affair after escaping Sparta, provoking the Trojan War described in the *Iliad*. A causeway now joins Marathonissi to Gythion. Recently, the EOT restored a castle-house on the islet as an ethnological museum. The **Pyrgos Tzannetaki Tower** occasionally displays interesting exhibits on the Mani such as traditional village settlements. ✉ *Marathonissi*, ☎ *0733/22676.* 🎫 *About 500 dr.* ⏰ *Daily 9–noon and 5–9.*

NEED A BREAK?

Take a late-afternoon break for grilled octopus and ouzo; Gythion is the octopus capital of Greece. The best place is **Nautilia** (✉ Southern end of waterfront, across from pier); look for the octopi dangling in the doorway.

Beaches
Near Gythion the best beaches (almost all are stony) are south on the coast between Mavrovouni and Skoutari; avoid the slightly littered public beach off the town waterfront.

Dining and Lodging

$$ ✗ **Poulikakos.** Word of mouth has made this small place a favorite for such traditional dishes as broiled stuffed peppers and *kotopoulo* (chicken) kokkinisto. Highlights are *soupies* (fresh cuttlefish) and octopus marinated in vinegar—excellent with ouzo. And sample the local barrel red if you're planning a beachside nap anyway. Heartwarming desserts, such as *rizogalo* (rice pudding with cinnamon), and a super breakfast are also served. ✉ *Platia Limani (harbor square),* ☎ *0733/22792. No credit cards.*

$ ✗ **Sinantisi.** Since its opening, this grill hasn't closed a day. The freshest seasonal local produce—artichokes in spring, squash and eggplant in summer, wild greens in winter—construct the *casserolas* (casserole)-style dishes. You may also order fresh fish, appetizers such as tzatziki and *taramosalata* (pink fish-roe dip), and homemade sweets like clove-scented baklava. ✉ *On sq. in Mavrovouni village, about 2 km (1¼ mi) outside town,* ☎ *0733/22256. MC, V. No lunch.*

$$$ 🏨 **Lakonis.** For romance, choose these white bungalows set like an am-
★ phitheater on a cliff 3 km (2 mi) out of town. Brilliant red and pink flowers dot the landscape, and the beach below is so popular, the hotel drained the Olympic-size pool. Nestle up to the bar and fireplace at the lofty circular restaurant, enjoying the vistas through the plate-glass windows; in summer, the informal beach restaurant is great for lunch. ✉ *Skalas 3,* ☎ *0733/22666 and 22667,* 🆎 *0733/23668. 100 rooms, most with bath. Restaurant, bar. No credit cards. Closed Nov.–Mar.*

$$ 🏨 **Aktaion.** This hotel is a pleasure. All rooms are squeaky clean and
★ modern, with subdued colors, seafaring balconies, and TVs. Lovely prints depict Maniote life. ✉ *39 Vassileos Pavlou,* ☎ *0733/23500 and 23501,* 🆎 *0733/22294. 22 rooms with bath. No credit cards. Breakfast room.*

$ 🏨 **Githion.** This good town-center hotel is booked a year in advance, so call ahead. All of the double or triple rooms are stark white with wood furniture and sea views. Request a room with two balconies and, if you're traveling with children, two housekeeping apartments for an economical alternative. ✉ *Vassileos Pavlou 33,* ☎ *0733/23777,*

*0733/23452, or 0733/23523. 7 rooms with bath. Dining room. No
credit cards.*

$ ⚛ **Gythion Beach.** A horseback-riding school, basketball and volley-
ball courts, and a sandy beach are the pleasures at this site, open year-
round. ✉ *Gythion beach,* ☏ *0733/22522 or 23441. RV and tent sites.
Bathrooms, hot showers, children's playground, common dining room,
satellite TV, pool. Closed Nov.–Mar.*

$ ⚛ **Meltemi.** This is one of the country's few A-class sites, set along a
sandy beach, encompassing thousands of trees. Campers can cook in
the dining room. ✉ *South of Gythion,* ☏ *0733/22833 or 23260. RV
and tent sites. Bathrooms, hot showers, children's playground, common dining room, satellite TV, pool. Closed Nov.–Mar.*

Outdoor Activities and Sports
SWIMMING

Gythion is best for daydreaming on the waterfront or swimming off
the rocks of Marathonissi.

LACONIA
Sparta, Mystras, Monemvassia

The Laconian Plain is surrounded on three sides by mountains, and
on one side by the sea. Perhaps it was the fear that enemies could descend those mountains at any time that drove the Spartans to make
Laconia their training ground, where they developed the finest fighting force in ancient Greece. A mighty power that controlled three-fifths
of the Peloponnese, Sparta contributed to the Greek victory in the second Persian War (5th century BC). Ultimately, its aggressiveness and
its jealousy of Athens brought about the Peloponnesian War, which
drained its resources, but left it victorious. The Greek world found Sparta
to be an even harsher master than Athens, and this fact may have led
to its losses in the Boetian and Corinthian wars, at the Battle of Leuctra, and in 222–221 BC at the hands of the Achaean League, who liberated all areas Sparta had conquered. A second period of prosperity
under the Romans ended with the barbarian invasions in the 3rd century, and Sparta declined rapidly.

Laconia can also claim two important medieval sites: Mystras and Monemvassia. Jewels in the Byzantine crown, the former is an intellectual
and political center, the latter a sea fortress meant to ward off invaders
from the east.

Sparta

⑳ *60 km (37¼ mi) south of Tripolis, 60 km (37¼ mi) east of Kalamata.*

For those who have read about ancient Sparta, the bellicose city-state
that once dominated the Greek world, the modern city is a disap-
pointment. Given the area's earthquakes and the Spartans' no-frills approach—living more like an army camp than a city-state—no elaborate
ruins remain, a fact that so disconcerted Otto, Greece's first king, that
in 1835 he ordered the modern city built on the ancient site.

The Spartans' relentless militarism set them apart from other Greeks.
They were expected to emerge victorious from a battle or not at all,
and for most of its existence Sparta was without a wall, because according to Lykourgos, its leader, who wrote Sparta's constitution,
"chests, not walls, make a city." From the 9th to the 4th centuries BC,
Spartans trained for a life of war. From the age of seven, boys in the

reigning warrior class submitted to a strict regimen, eating mostly herbs, roots, and the famous black broth. Rich foods were thought to stunt growth. Forbidden to work, they trained for combat and practiced stealing, an acceptable skill unless one was caught. One legend describes a Spartan youth who let a concealed fox chew off his arm rather than reveal his theft. Girls also trained rigorously in the belief they would bear healthier offspring; for the same reason, newlyweds were forbidden to make love frequently.

At the **Temple of Artemis Orthia** (⊠ Just outside of town on Tripolis Rd., down the path to the Evrotas River), the young Spartan men underwent *krypteia* (initiations) that entailed severe public floggings. The altar had to be splashed with blood before the goddess was satisfied. Traces of two such altars are among sparse vestiges of the 6th-century BC temple. The larger ruins are the remains of a grandstand built in the 3rd century AD by the Romans, who revived the flogging tradition as a public spectacle.

Ancient Sparta's **acropolis** (⊠ At north end of town) is now part archaeological site, and part park. Locals can be seen here strolling, along with many young couples stealing a romantic moment amid the fallen limestone and shady trees. The ruins include a **theater**, a **stadium**, and a **sanctuary to Athena**.

Stop a moment and contemplate the stern **Statue of Leonidas** (⊠ At end of Konstantinou St.). During the Second Persian War, with 30,000 Persians advancing on his army of 8,000, Leonidas, ordered to surrender his weapons, jeered, "Come and get them." For two days he held off the enemy, until a traitor named Efialtes (the word has since come to mean "nightmare" in Greek), showed the Persians a way to attack from the rear. Leonidas ordered all but 300 Spartans and 700 Thespians to withdraw, and when forced to retreat to a wooded knoll, he is said to have commented, "So much the better, we will fight in the shade," before his entire troop was slaughtered.

Enjoy an hour in the city's **archaeological museum,** tucked into a cool park. Its eclectic collection reflects Laconia's turbulent history: Neolithic pottery; jewels and tools excavated from the Alepotrypa cave; Mycenaean tomb finds; bright 4th- and 5th-century Roman mosaics; and objects from Sparta, including an expressive clay woman's head, a Parian marble statue of Leonidas (490 BC), prizes given to the Spartan youths, and ritual dance masks. Most characteristic of Spartan art are the bas-reliefs with deities and heroes; note the one depicting a seated couple bearing gifts and framed by a snake (540 BC). ⊠ *Ayios Nikonos between Dafnou and Evangelistria,* ☎ *0731/28575.* ⌑ *500 dr.* ☉ *Tues.–Sat. 8:30–3, Sun. and holidays 8:30–2:30.*

NEED A BREAK?	If you should find yourself waiting for a bus out of Sparta at dinnertime, cross the street to **Parthenon** (⊠ Vrasidou 106, ☎ 0731/23767) for the best gyro you may ever eat. The meat, which has a local reputation for being a cut above, is served in pita with just the right amount of chew and generous doses of onion, tomato, and tzatziki sauce.
OFF THE BEATEN PATH	**MENELAION** – The shrine of Menelaos and Helen is thought to date to the 5th century BC. (Earlier, during Mycenaean times, Sparta was still part of Menelaos's kingdom.) Excavations have unearthed cult objects, indicating that the hill, now known as Profitis Ilias, was a favorite place of worship. A bronze vase of the Archaic period (700–500 BC) is inscribed "to Helen of Menelaos" and a bronze tool is marked simply "to Helen." ⊠ *Beyond Evrotas River, off rd. to Geraki.*

Dining and Lodging

$$ ✕ **Diethnes.** Local vernacular claims this is one of Sparta's best restaurants. You'll be wowed by classic specialties that, here, translate into a special fish dish made with garlic, parsley, wine, oil, and rusks; bardouniotiko made with onions, *sfela* (a hard Kalamatan cheese), and red sauce; and occasionally delicacies such as sheep's heads cooked on a spit and *kokoretsi*. The summer courtyard rounds out a perfect meal. ⊠ *Paleologou 105, ☎ 0731/28636. No credit cards.*

$$ ✕ **Elysse.** A bit fancier than Diethnes, with wallpaper and flowers, Elysse serves essentially the same cuisine. Along with the smooth red barrel wine, you can get large portions of bardouniotiko, *perka* (a fish prepared in oil and lemon), moschari psito, excellent local sausage made with bits of orange, and Continental dishes. In summer you dine outdoors on the sidewalk. ⊠ *Paleologou 113, ☎ 0731/29896. No credit cards.*

$ ✕ **Semiramis.** This underground restaurant, with fluorescent lighting
★ and a linoleum floor, is no visual treat, but the simple Greek dishes are perfectly cooked. In spring, try the *anginares antidia* (wild artichokes with red sauce), and in summer the stuffed squash. The barrel wine is fragrant but deceivingly light. For dessert try the rich sheep yogurt with honey before you stagger outdoors. ⊠ *Paleologou 48, ☎ 0731/26640. No credit cards. No lunch alternate Sun.*

$$$ 🏨 **Lida.** This hotel is pricey for its category, but it provides flawless service. The owner's wife is an interior designer, as seen in the rooms and in the lobby with antique treadles, stones from flour mills and olive presses, and lithographs of Greek revolutionary heroes. Ask for a room above the third floor for views of Mt. Taygettus. ⊠ *Ananiou and Atreidon, ☎ 0731/23601 and 23602. 40 rooms with bath. Restaurant, bar. AE, MC, V. Closed mid-Nov.–Feb.*

$$ 🏨 **Hotel Maniatis.** It's hard to believe this hotel is so reasonably priced.
★ Though the color scheme is unfortunately reminiscent of Los Angeles in the '80s, it is unusually well run, with attention to detail. Ask for a room with a view, and, if you need a bathtub, a corner room. The hotel's new Dias restaurant is elegant, with specialities such as *arni araxobitiko* (lamb with onions, cheese, red sauce, and walnuts) and *bourekakia* pastries. ⊠ *Paleologou 72, ☎ 0731/22665, ℻ 0731/29994. 80 rooms with bath. Restaurant, bar, lobby lounge, air-conditioning. V.*

$$ 🏨 **Menelaion.** Sparta's dowager hotel presides over the main strip. To its old-fashioned high-ceiling lobby (check out the phone booths) and lounge with worn velvet chairs the town's old-timers come to play cards and chat over coffee. With their dark furniture, the guest rooms are just the place to retire with a dog-eared copy of *The Magus*. ⊠ *Paleologou 91, ☎ 0731/22161 through 22165. 48 rooms with bath. Restaurant, bar, air-conditioning, indoor pool. MC, V.*

Sports

SWIMMING

If you absolutely must have your daily swim, bring your goggles and fins to the public pool run by the Sparta Municipal Center (☎ 0731/24852).

Mystras

★ ㉑ *64 km (39¾ mi) southwest of Tripolis, 4 km (2½ mi) west of Sparta.*

Ethereal Mystras, with its abandoned gold and stone palaces, churches, and monasteries lining serpentine paths, is eerie. The scent of herbs and wildflowers permeates the air, goat bells tinker yonder, and the silvery olive trees glisten with the slightest breeze. An intellectual and cultural center where philosophers like Chrysoloras, "the sage of Byzantium," held forth on the good and the beautiful, it seems an appropriate place for the last hurrah of the Byzantine emperors in the 14th century.

In 1249 William de Villehardouin built the castle in Mystras in an attempt to control Laconia and establish Frankish supremacy over the Peloponnese. He held court here with his beautiful Greek wife, Anna Comnena, surrounded by knights of Champagne, Burgundy, and Flanders, but in 1259 he was defeated by the Byzantines. As the Byzantines built a palace and numerous churches (whose frescoes exemplified several periods of painting), the town gradually grew down the slope.

At first the seat of the Byzantine governor, Mystras later became the capital of the Despotate of Morea. It was the despots who made Mystras a cultural phenomenon, and it was the despots—specifically Emperor Constantine's brother Demetrios Palaiologos—who surrendered the city to the Turks in 1460, signaling the beginning of the end. For a while the town survived because of its silk industry, but after repeated pillaging and burning by bands of Albanians, by Russians, and by Ibrahim Pasha's Egyptian troops, the inhabitants gave up and moved to modern Sparta.

In spring Mystras is resplendent with wildflowers and butterflies like brimstones and swallowtails, but it can be oppressively hot in summer, so get an early start. Bring water and sturdy shoes for the slippery rocks and the occasional snake.

Among the most important buildings in the lower town (Kato Chora) is **Ayios Demetrios,** the *mitropolis* (cathedral) founded in 1291. Set in its floor is a stone with the two-headed Byzantine eagle marking the spot where Constantine XII, the last emperor of Byzantium, was consecrated. The cathedral's brilliant frescoes include a vivid depiction of the *Virgin and Child* on the central apse and a wall painting in the narthex of the *Second Coming,* its two red-and-turquoise winged angels sorrowful as they open the records of Good and Evil. One wing of the church houses a **museum** that holds fragments of Byzantine sculptures, including an eagle seizing its prey (11th century), later Byzantine icons, jewels, decorative metalwork, and coins. ✉ *Lower town.* 🎟 *1,200 dr. covers all Mystras sites.* ☉ *Daily winter 8:30–3, summer 8–7.*

In the **Vrontokion monastery** are Ayios Theodoros (AD 1295), the oldest church in Mystras, and the 14th-century **Church of Panagia Odegetria,** or **Afendiko,** which is decorated with remarkable murals. These include, in the narthex, scenes of the miracles of Christ: the *Healing of the Blind Man,* the *Samaritan at the Well,* and the *Marriage of Cana.* The fluidity of the brush strokes, its subtle but complicated coloring, and its resonant expressions suggest the work of extremely skilled hands. ✉ *Lower town, along path to the right.* 🎟 *1,200 dr. covers all Mystras sites.* ☉ *Daily winter 8:30–3, summer 8–7.*

The **Pantanassa monastery** is a visual feast of intricate tiling, rosette-festooned loops mimicking frosting on a wedding cake, and myriad arches. It is the only inhabited building in Mystras; the hospitable nuns still produce embroidery for sale. Step out onto the east portico for a view of the Evrotas river valley below. ✉ *Lower town.* 🎟 *1,200 dr. covers all Mystras sites.* ☉ *Daily winter 8:30–3, summer 8–7.*

Every inch of the tiny **Perivleptos monastery,** meaning "attracting attention from all sides," is covered with exceptional 14th-century illustrations from the New Testament, including the *Birth of the Virgin*—in a lush palette of reds, yellows, and oranges—the *Dormition of the Virgin* above the entrance (with Christ holding his mother's soul represented as a baby), and immediately to the left of the entrance, the famous fresco of the *Divine Liturgy.* ✉ *Lower town, in the southernmost corner.* 🎫 *1,200 dr. covers all Mystras sites.* ☉ *Daily winter 8:30–3, summer 8–7.*

In the upper town (Ano Chora) where most aristocrats lived, stands a rare Byzantine civic building, the **Palace of Despots,** home of the last emperor. The older, northeastern wing contains a guardroom, a kitchen, and the residence. The three-story northwest wing contains an immense reception hall on its top floor, lit by eight Gothic windows and heated by eight huge chimneys; the throne probably stood in the shallow alcove that's in the center of a wall.

In the palace's **Ayia Sofia chapel,** the Italian wives of emperors Constantine and Theodore Palaiologos are buried. Note the polychromatic marble floor and the frescoes that were preserved for years under whitewash, applied by the Turks when they transformed this into a mosque. Climb to the **castle** and look down into the gullies of Mt. Taygettus, where it's said the Spartans, who hated weakness, hurled their malformed babies. ✉ *Ano Chora,* ☎ *0731/93377.* 🎫 *1,200 dr. covers all Mystras sites.* ☉ *Daily winter 8:30–3, summer 8–7.*

Lodging

$ 🏕 **Mystera Camping.** Open year-round, this campsite has a pool, handy on hot summer days, as the sea is one mi away. Reed mats, orange and olive trees also lend shade; there is a shelter with a corrugated metal roof in case of rain. ✉ *Mystras,* ☎ *0731/22724. RV and tent sites.*

Outdoor Activities and Sports

HIKING AND CLIMBING

The Athens travel agency **Trekking Hellas** (☞ Contacts and Resources *in* Southern Peloponnese A to Z, *below*) arranges weekend hiking trips to Mystras and a six-day walk through the Taygettus foothills, with visits to the Mani and Mystras.

A mountain refuge, with a capacity of 24, is set up at **Varvara-Dereki** on Mt. Taygettus. It has a kitchen, an oil stove, a tank, spring water, and outdoor toilets. Contact the Sparta Alpine Club (☞ Contacts and Resources *in* Southern Peloponnese A to Z, *below*).

Shopping

EMBROIDERY

In Mystras the nuns at **Pantanassa** (✉ Lower town) monastery still make and sell their delicate embroidery.

Amykles

㉒ *67 km (41½ mi) south of Tripolis, 7 km (4¼ mi) south of Mystras.*

Achaean rulers made Amykles their capital, which was inhabited from the early Bronze Age on, and eventually one of Sparta's settlements.

The **Temple of Apollo** (✉ On the knoll) once housed a colossal statue of the god, which was engraved on coins of that period. Only a few traces of Amykles' **acropolis wall** (✉ On the knoll) remain, but the site is an excellent picnic spot. A *tholos* (Mycenaean beehive tomb; ✉ On a knoll at Vapheio) yielded important gold and silver artifacts, including two famous hammered gold cups depicting wild bulls savagely trampling a hunter, then peacefully grazing. The cups are now in Athens' archaeological museum.

Monemvassia

★ ❷ *96 km (59½ mi) southeast of Sparta, 89 km (55¼ mi) southeast of Amykles.*

The Byzantine town of Monemvassia clings to the side of the 350-meter (1,148-foot) rock that seems to blast out of the sea; in AD 375, it was separated from the mainland by an earthquake. Like Gibraltar, Monemvassia once controlled the sea lines from western Europe to the Levant. The name *moni emvasia* (single entrance) refers to the narrow passage to this walled community. If you come from Athens by ferry or hydrofoil, you'll get the most spectacular view; if you walk or take a taxi down the causeway from the adjoining town of Gefira, the rock looks uninhabited until you suddenly see castellated walls with an opening only wide enough for one.

The town was first inhabited in the 6th century AD, when Laconians sought refuge after Arab and Slav raids. During its golden age in the 1400s under the Byzantines, Monemvassia was home to families made wealthy by their inland estates and the export of malmsey wine, a sweet variety of Madeira praised by Shakespeare. When the area fell to the Turks, Monemvassia ended up under the Pope's control and then came under sway of the Venetians, who built the citadel and most of the fortifications.

Well-to-do Greeks once again live on the rock in houses they have restored as vacation homes. Summer weekends are crowded, but off-season, Monemvassia is nearly deserted. Empty houses are lined up along steep streets only wide enough for two people abreast, and remnants of another age—escutcheons, marble thrones, Byzantine icons—evoke the sense that time has stopped. It's worth a splurge to stay overnight here.

Christos Elkomenos (Christ in Chains; ✉ Platia Tzamiou, along the main st.) is reputed as the largest medieval church in southern Greece. The carved peacocks are symbolic of the Byzantine era; the detached bell tower—like those of Italian cathedrals—is a sign of Venetian rebuilding in the 17th century.

The 10th-century **Agios Pavlos** (✉ Across from Platia Tzamiou), though converted into a mosque, was allowed to function as a church under the Ottoman occupation, an unusual indulgence.

The **Panagia Hrissafitissa** (✉ Near southern ramparts), a third church, was restored by the Venetians (note the framed doorway with an oculus). A **tiny chapel** is built over the "sacred spring" (the only spring on the rock), believed locally to be effective in cases of sterility, especially when sons are desired.

For solitude and a dizzying view, pass through the upper town's wooden entrance gates, complete with the original iron reinforcement. Up the hill is a rare example of a domed octagonal church, **Agia Sofia** (✉ At top of the mountain), founded in the 13th century by Emperor Andronicus II and patterned after Dafni monastery in Athens. Follow the path to the highest point on the rock for a breathtaking view of the coast.

Dining and Lodging

$$ ✗ **Marianthi.** You'll feel like you're dropping in on someone at dinner here: family photos of stern mustachioed ancestors hang on the walls along with local memorabilia; someone's aunt is doing the cooking, and the service is just as homey. Order the wild mountain greens, any of the fish—especially the fresh red mullet—the addictive potato salad

(you may have to order two plates), and the marinated octopus sprinkled with oregano. ⊠ *Old town,* ☎ *0732/61371. No credit cards.*

$$ ✕ **To Kanoni.** After you roll out of bed, wander over to the Kanoni, which serves breakfast on a terrace overlooking the square's *kanoni* (cannon). Choose from omelets, ham and eggs, bacon, or thick, creamy yogurt and honey. Inside you'll find red-and-white checked tablecloths, 19th-century prints of Greece, and the same glorious sea view, accompanied by calming wave music. If you miss breakfast, you can always order a "toast" (grilled ham and cheese sandwich), a burger or beef *yiouvetsi* (meat baked in a clay pot with orzo-like pasta). ⊠ *Old town,* ☎ *0732/61387. No credit cards.*

$$ 🏠 **Byzantinon.** The Byzantinon is housed in an old building; the re-
★ quirement that owners get permission from the archaeological bureau before making any changes explains the rudimentary showers in some rooms. All the rooms are shaped differently, with beautiful decorations: a carved marble tile depicting a scale set in the floor; a Greek costume sketch adorning an alcove; sailor's lanterns for illumination. The best is Suite 1, a perfect hideout with an antique radio, marble bath, balcony, hidden kitchen, and large, cozy bed. ⊠ *Old town,* ☎ *0732/61351,* 🖷 *0732/61562. 25 rooms with showers. MC, V.*

$$ 🏠 **Malvasia.** A stay in this hotel is like living in a fairy tale; it is so en-
★ gaging you may prolong your stay. Rooms are tucked into nooks and crannies under cane-and-wood or vaulted brick ceilings. Each is decorated with bright patchwork rugs, embroidered tapestries, antique marble, and dark antique wood furniture. The hotel is in three buildings; the best is the one on the main street. Many rooms have sea views, some have fireplaces; suites are also available. ⊠ *Old town,* ☎ *0732/61323,* 🖷 *0732/61722. 66 beds with bath. Bar, breakfast room. AE, MC, V.*

$$ 🏠 **Ta Kellia.** Built in an old monastery (*kellia* means cells), this establishment is now run by the EOT. Though it's not glamorous like the competition, the rough-hewn rooms are a good alternative. Only a few rooms on the second floor have ocean views, and they can get quite hot in summer. ⊠ *Old town, on lower sq. opposite Church of Panagia Chrissafitissa,* ☎ *0732/61520. 11 rooms with showers. Breakfast room. No credit cards.*

$ 🏕 **Kapsis Paradise.** This simple site is arranged on terraces above a pebble beach, a paradise for beach lovers. It's open year-round. ⊠ *Above beach, 4 km (2½ mi) south of Monemvassia,* ☎ *0732/61123. RV and tent sites. Grocery, common kitchen.*

SOUTHERN PELOPONNESE A TO Z

Arriving and Departing

By Boat

In both winter and summer the costly **Flying Dolphin hydrofoils** (☎ 01/4280001) make the trip to Monemvassia several times a week. They leave from Piraeus's Marina Zea Harbor for Leonidion, Monemvassia, and Neapolis.

In the Peloponnese, call the local **port authority** for the latest information on boat travel: Gythion (☎ 0733/22262); Kalamata (☎ 0721/22218); Pylos (☎ 0721/23100); and Monemvassia (☎ 0732/61266).

By Bus

Buses leave Athens several times daily for Gythion, Kalamata, and Tripolis, and once a day for Andritsena, Monemvassia, or Pylos. For departure times, call the **KTEL station office** that handles your destination: Andritsena (☎ 01/5134574), Gythion (☎ 01/5124913), Kalamata (☎ 01/5134293), Monemvassia (☎ 01/5124913), Pylos (☎ 01/5134293), Sparta (☎ 01/5124913), and Tripolis (☎ 01/5134575).

To get to the station at **Kifissou 100** on the outskirts of Athens, take Bus 051 (24 hrs a day, every 10 mins) from the corner of Vilara and Menandrou off Omonia square.

In the Peloponnese, you may buy tickets at the **local station**: Andritsena (✉ Main sq., ☎ 0626/22239); Gythion (✉ Ebrikleous at north end of harbor, ☎ 0733/22228); Kalamata (✉ Artemidos 50, ☎ 0721/22851); Monemvassia ✉ Off main sq., ☎ 0732/61432); Pylos (✉ Platia Trion Navarchon, ☎ 0723/22230); Sparta (✉ Vrasidou and Paleologou, ☎ 0731/26441); Tripolis (✉ Platia Kolokotronis, ☎ 071/224314).

By Car

Even if **highways** have assigned numbers, no Greek knows them by any other than their informal names, usually linked to their destination. For those traveling on the E-92 from Athens to Tripolis, the new section of the highway (the Corinth–Tripolis road) now cuts travel time in half, to little more than two hours. From Olympia in the northwest Peloponnese, you may take a smaller local road (number 74, the Pirgos-Tripolis road). Both approaches have mountainous stretches that occasionally close in winter because of snow, but conditions are otherwise good. An accurate road map is essential: the Greek Motoring Association (ELPA) publishes one of the most detailed map books on Greece, available in most Athens bookstores (3,000 dr.).

By Plane

Olympic Airways offers daily 1-hour flights from Athens to Kalamata's airport, 10½ km (6½ mi) outside of town near Messinia. Call the Athens reservations line (☎ 01/9616161) or Olympic Airways's office in Kalamata (✉ Sidirodromikou Stathmou 17, ☎ 0721/22376). For the latest flight information in Kalamata, contact the airport (☎ 0721/69442).

By Train

Train travel into the area costs half the price but is slower and much more limited than journeying by bus. Buy tickets before you leave; prices shoot up 50% when purchased on board. If traveling during a national holiday, when many Athenians head to the Peloponnese for their villages, it's worth paying the extra fee for first class to ensure a seat, especially in no-smoking compartments. Train food is dismal, so stock up if you're taking a long trip.

Trains (lines 422, 424, 426, 428, and 436) run from Athens to Kalamata five times daily with stops in Corinth, Mycenae, and Tripolis, not to be confused with those traveling a second, longer route to Kalamata via Patras. Lines 421, 425, 427, 429, and 435 return from Kalamata to Athens. In Athens, the Greek National Railway (OSE) offices at (✉ Fillelinon 17, ☎ 01/3236747) or (✉ Sina 6, ☎ 01/3624402) are the most convenient for visitors staying near Platia Syntagma (Constitution Square); otherwise purchase your ticket before departure at the Peloponnese station (✉ Peloponnesou 3, ☎ 01/5131601). You can reach the station by catching Trolley 1 in front of Parliament above Syntagma Square (5 AM–midnight, every 10 mins).

In Kalamata depart from the station on (✉ Sidirodromikou Stathmou, ☎ 0721/23904) and in Tripolis from (✉ Grigoris Lambraki at Xeniou Dios, ☎ 071/222402).

Getting Around

By Boat

The *Martha* runs five times weekly in winter and daily in summer between Gythion, Neapolis, and Kythera. Call ticket offices in Gythion (☎ 0733/22996).

En route from Piraeus, **Flying Dolphin hydrofoils** stop once or twice a week in winter, depending on the weather, and almost daily in summer at Monemvassia (☎ 0732/61219 or 61419), and Neapolis (☎ 0734/22214). For departure information, you may also call the local port authority (☞ *above*).

By Bus

The network of bus routes lets you move easily about most of the towns mentioned, even to more remote sites such as the Pirgos Dirou caves, the Arcadian mountain villages, and Nestor's Palace museum in Chora. Keep in mind that there are fewer buses in winter and on weekends. For short distances, you may buy tickets on board; otherwise purchase them in advance at the station.

If you have trouble reaching a site—for example, there is no public transportation to ancient Messene—just take a taxi from a town's main square, which is always near the bus station. In rural areas, drivers may not switch on the meter if the destination has a fixed price, but make sure you agree on the cost before getting in—remember that it's the same price whether you're alone or in a company of four. It's the mileage that counts. When leaving town limits, the driver may switch his meter to the higher rate (Tarifa 2). Don't panic: this is perfectly legal, as is starting the meter at 200 dr. The price also goes up after midnight. If you think you've been had, don't hesitate to argue or threaten to report the driver to the police.

By Car

Especially off-season when buses don't run regularly, it's most rewarding to explore this region by car. In some areas—like the Mani peninsula—it's difficult to get around if you rely on public transportation. Rent a car in Athens or in any of the Peloponnese's bigger towns, like Kalamata, Tripolis, Gythion, and Sparta, thus leaving the harrowing prospect of exiting Athens up to someone else.

By Train

Within the region, train travel is limited to the lines that run from Kalamata to Tripolis.

Contacts and Resources

Camping

There are several camping sites throughout the southern Peloponnese; contact the **EOT** (☞ *below*) for a free camping guide.

Car and Moped Rental Agencies

Gythion: Motor Mani (✉ On waterfront near causeway to Marathonissi, ☎ 0733/22853); **Kalamata**: Maniatis (✉ Iatropoulou 1, ☎ 0721/25300 or 27694, and ✉ 202 Faron, ☎ 0721/26025); **Stavrianos**: (✉ Nedontos 89, ☎ 0721/23041 or 25370); **Pylos**: Venus Rent-A-Car (✉ Platia Trion Navarchon, ☎ 0723/22393); **Sparta**: Kottaras Rent-A-Car (✉ Menelaon 54, ☎ 0731/28966); **Tripolis**: Stephany's Tours (✉ Deligianni 23, ☎ 071/239577).

Emergencies

Police: Areopolis (☎ 0733/51209). Gythion (☎ 0733/22271 or 22316). Kalamata (☎ 0721/25444). Methoni (☎ 0723/31203). Monemvassia

(☎ 0732/61210). Pylos (☎ 0723/22316). Sparta (☎ 0731/28701 or 26229). Tripolis (☎ 071/222411 or 222519).

Medical assistance: Areopolis: first aid (☎ 0733/51259), hospital (☎ 0733/22315). Gythion: clinic (☎ 0733/22001/3). Kalamata: hospital (☎ 0721/23561), first aid (☎ 0721/25555). Methoni clinic (☎ 0723/31456). Pylos hospital (☎ 0723/22315). Sparta hospital (☎ 0731/28671 and 28672). Tripolis hospital (☎ 071/238542).

Guided Tours

Unlike in the northern Peloponnese, the choice of **English-language tours** in the south is limited. If an agency does venture into the region, it's usually a detour through Tripolis and Sparta for a cursory visit to Mystras, as part of a package to the Northern Peloponnese. Both **G.O. Tours** (✉ Voulis 31, Athens, ☎ 01/322–5951 and 322–5955) and **CHAT Tours** (✉ Stadiou 4, Athens, ☎ 01/323–0827 or 322–2886) offer a five-day combination called the Archaeological Tour for 81,000 dr., covering Corinth, Mycenae, Epidauros, Nauplion, Mystras, Olympia, and Delphi. CHAT also offers a more extensive six-day Grand Tour of the Peloponnese that adds Tiryns, a drive through Gythion to the Pirgos Dirou caves, Kalamata, Methoni, Nestor's Palace, and its museum at Chora, Bassae, and Patras for 150,000 dr. If you can't get to these tour companies, most travel agencies in Athens can book the tour as well.

Hiking and Climbing

Tripolis Alpine Club (☎ 071/232243). **Sparta Alpine Club** (☎ 0731/22574 or 0731/24135). **Army's Geographical Service,** Athens (✉ Evelpidou 4, ☎ 01/884–2811).

Greek Federation of Mountaineering Associations (✉ Milioni 8, Athens, ☎ 01/363–6617 or 01/364–5904).

Road Assistance

The Automobile and Touring Club of Greece (ELPA) provides assistance for light repairs around the clock (☎ 104 anywhere in the country). There are also ELPA main offices in Kalamata (✉ New Entrance, ☎ 0721/93366 or 9393376) and Tripolis (✉ Vassileos Pavlou 3, ☎ 071/224101).

Sailing

Naval Association (☎ 0721/23860). **Port authority** (☞ *above*).

Skiing

Mt. Menalon ski center (✉ Oropedio Ostrakina, ☎ 071/22227); call the Tripolis Alpine Club (☞ *above*).

Travel Agency

Trekking Hellas (✉ Fillelinon 7, Athens 10557, ☎ 01/315–0853 and 01/325–0317).

Visitor Information

Greek National Tourist Organization (GNTO or EOT): Kalamata (✉ Marina, ☎ 0721/22059); Sparta (✉ Platia Vassileos Georgios in the town hall, ☎ 0731/26517); Tripolis (✉ Ethnikis Antistaseos 43, ☎ 071/231844). **Tourist police** often speak English and help you find accommodations: Gythion (☎ 0733/22236); Kalamata (☎ 0721/23187); Sparta (☎ 0731/28701).

10 The Cyclades

Andros, Tinos, Mykonos, Delos, Naxos, Paros, and Santorini

The magical words "Greek island" conjure up images of fantasy. If you long for sun and sea, blazing bare rock and mountains, olive trees and vineyards, white peasant architecture and ancient ruins, fresh fish and fruity olive oil, the Cyclades are quintessential isles, the ultimate Mediterranean archipelago. "The islands with their drinkable blue volcanoes," wrote Greece's Nobel Prize poet Odysseus Elytis, musing of Santorini. That Homer—who loved the islands—is buried here is unverifiable, but spiritually true.

THE SIX MAJOR STARS IN THIS CONSTELLATION of is-
lands in the central Aegean Sea, Andros, Tinos,
Mykonos, Naxos, Paros, and Santorini, are the most
By Melissa
Dailey   famous and visited—the archetype of the islands of Greece. In a mag-
nificent fusion of sunlight, stone, and sparkling aqua sea, they offer
Updated by   both culture and hedonism: ancient sites, Byzantine castles and muse-
Jeffrey Carson   ums, lively nightlife, shopping, dining, and beaches plain and fancy.
On many of them the chief town, unofficially named Chora (meaning
"town"), is officially called by the name of the island.

These arid, mountainous islands are the peaks of a deep submerged
plateau, and their composition is rocky, with few trees. The prevailing wind is the northern *vorias*; called *meltemi* in summer, it keeps the
always sunny weather cool. Other popular Cycladic islands include Ios,
Siphnos, and Milos.

Well-to-do Andros, where shipowning families once lived, retains an
air of dignity, and its inhabitants go about their business largely indifferent to the visitors. It's a good place for adults in search of history, fine museums, and quiet evenings. Tinos has stayed authentically
Greek, since its heavy tourism is largely owing to its miracle-working
icon, and not to its beautiful villages. In the town of Mykonos, the whitewashed houses huddle together against the meltemi winds, and backpackers rub elbows with millionaires in the mazelike white-marble streets.
The island's sophistication level is high, the beaches fine, the shopping
varied and upscale, and it's the jumping-off place for a mandatory visit
to tiny, deserted Delos. That windswept dot, birthplace of Apollo, still
watched over by a row of marble lions, was once the religious and commercial center of the eastern Mediterranean.

Naxos, greenest of the Cyclades, makes cheese and wine, raises livestock, and grows potatoes, olives, and fruit. For centuries a Venetian
stronghold, it has a shrinking, aristocratic Roman Catholic population,
Venetian houses and fortifications, and Cycladic and Mycenaean sites.
Paros, a hub of the ferry system, has reasonable prices and is a good
base for trips to other islands. It's also good for lazing on long, white-
sand beaches and visiting fishing villages. Crescent-shape Santorini
(Thera), southernmost of the Cyclades, is the rim of an ancient drowned
volcano that exploded about 1500 BC. The sensational views across
its flooded caldera would be worth a visit even if it didn't have fascinating excavations and a dazzling white town where the shopping is
great and tourism highly developed.

Pleasures and Pastimes

Beaches and Water Sports
The best sport in the islands is swimming, and the islands gleam with
beaches, from long blond stretches of sand to tiny pebbly coves. Waterskiing, parasailing, jet skiing, scuba diving, and especially windsurfing
have become ever more popular, though venues change from season
to season. Anybody who invests in a mask, snorkel, and flippers has
entry to intense, serene beauty.

Classic Sites, Monasteries, and Churches
There are more of these than can be found on any map. The best reason to visit them may be the beauty of the walk, the impressiveness of
the location, and the hospitality you will likely find off the beaten track.
Many of the sites and buildings are often or permanently closed,
though the fencing around sites may have fallen, and monks and nuns

may let you in if you are polite and nicely dressed. And the gods are still out there.

Dining

Eating is a lively social activity in the Cyclades, and the friendliness of most taverna owners compensates for the lack of formal service. Unless you order intermittently, the food comes all at once. Reservations are not required unless otherwise noted, and casual dress is the rule.

Greek food, like English or indeed American, has a bad international reputation, and you can certainly find bad food in Greece easily. This is often a result of restaurants trying to adapt to the tastes and wallets of the throngs of tourists. For example: when a tourist asks for less of the islands' culinary gem—fruity, expensive olive oil—in a dish, the essence is lost. Greece produces top-quality tomatoes, lamp chops, melons, olive oil, and farmer's cheese. When Greeks go out to eat, they expect good, simple food culled from these elements, as should you. A few things to watch out for: "fresh fish" when the weather has been stormy; store-bought eggplant salad; frozen potatoes. Pay attention, and you will dine with much pleasure.

Dishes are often wonderfully redolent of garlic and olive oil; for an alternative, order grilled seafood and meat—grilled octopus with ouzo is a treat. A typical island lunch is fresh fried calamari with a salad of tomatoes, peppers, onions, feta, and olives. Lamb on a skewer and *keftedes* (spicy meatballs) are a couple of other favorites.

The volcanic soil of Santorini is hospitable to the grape, and Greeks love the Santorini wines. Greek wines have tripled in quality in the last decade. Santorini and Paros now proudly produce officially recognized "origin" wines, which are sought throughout Greece. Barrel or farmer's wine is common, and except in late summer when it starts to taste a bit off, it's often good. Try to be on Santorini on July 20 for the celebration of St. Elias's name-day, when a traditional pea and onion soup is served, followed by walnut and honey desserts and folk dancing.

Restaurant schedules on the Cyclades vary; some places close for lunch, most close for siesta, and all are open late.

CATEGORY	COST (ALL ISLANDS)*
$$$$	over 7,000 dr.
$$$	4,000 dr.–7,000 dr.
$$	3,000 dr.–4,000 dr.
$	under 3,000 dr.

per person for 3-course meal, including tax, service, and beer or barrel wine.

Hiking

The Cyclades are justly famous for their hiking. Ancient goat and donkey trails go everywhere—through fields, over mountains, along untrodden coasts. Rarely is the sea out of view, and almost never are you more than an hour's walk from a village. Since tourists tend to visit Greece for classical sites, for nightlife, and for the beach, walking is uncrowded even in July and August.

Lodging

Rooms in the islands have proliferated at a truly amazing rate. Although the charming simple room with oil lamp and grandmother's furniture is now hard to find, tasteful modern accommodations with all the amenities are everywhere. Managers—and quality—change year by year, but overall the already high quality is rising.

Island accommodations range from run-down pensions or an extra bedroom in a private house to first-class hotels. It is customary to leave your passport with the proprietor when you check in (for Greek tax records—and to ensure payment). Unless you're traveling at the very height of season (July 15–Aug. 30), you're unlikely to need advance reservations; often the easiest—and most recommended—way to find something on the spot is to head for a tourist office and describe your needs and price range. Rates, which are regulated by the Greek National Tourist Organization (GNTO or EOT), vary tremendously from month to month: In shoulder season you can pay 2,000 dr.–3,000 dr. less per room than you would in July or August. For budget travelers, room touts often meet the ferries with pictures advertising their properties: check the location. Alternatively, walk around town and ask where you can rent a cheap room, but take a good look first, and check the bathroom before you commit. If there are extra beds in the room, clarify in advance that the amount agreed on is for the entire room—owners occasionally try to put another person in the same room.

The best rooms and service (and noticeably higher prices) are on Mykonos and Santorini, where luxury out-of-town resort hotels are mushrooming—and our recommendations hardly represent the only choices. To experience the Cyclades properly, you should not go seeking technological amenities; make a room with a view your priority—preferably one with a balcony that overlooks the sea. Avoid hotels on main roads or near all-night discos. And an evening dip in a freshwater pool after swimming in the sea is a luxury.

Often only expensive hotels provide hot water 24 hours a day; in some hotels you must turn on a thermostat for a half hour to heat water for a shower (don't forget to turn it off). Signs tell you that water is in short supply in the Cyclades, reminding you to conserve it. Fresh water is often shipped from the mainland, and though faucet water is potable, you should not drink from fountains or springs. Most people drink bottled water, available everywhere.

Hotels close from November through March unless otherwise noted. Most do not serve breakfast, unless a restaurant or breakfast room is noted, and it usually costs extra.

CATEGORY	COST (ALL ISLANDS)*
$$$$	over 39,000 dr.
$$$	22,000 dr.–39,000 dr.
$$	13,000 dr.–22,000 dr.
$	under 13,000 dr.

All prices are for a standard double room in high season.

Nightlife
So many young backpackers and older holiday revelers pass through the islands in summer that lively all-night places have naturally cropped up. Greeks, too, like to stay out on balmy summer nights. All the major islands throb with bars, discos, and cafés. Young women especially will enjoy the opportunity to go partying unescorted in utter safety.

Shopping
Mykonos, with Santorini taking a close second, is the best island in the Cyclades for shopping. You can buy anything from Greek folk items to Italian designer clothes, cowboy boots, and leather jackets from the United States. Although island prices are better than in the expensive shopping districts of Athens, there are many tourist traps in the resort towns, with high-pressure sales tactics and inflated prices for inferior goods. The Greeks have a word for naive American shoppers—*Americanaki*. It's a good sign if the owner of a shop selling traditional crafts or art lives on the island and is not a hotshot Athenian over for the summer to make a buck.

Each island has a unique pottery style that reflects its individuality: in Santorini they are the bright shades of the setting sun, though the best pottery islands are Paros and especially Siphnos. Island specialties are hand-painted icons copying Byzantine originals; weavings and embroideries; local wines; and gold worked in ancient and Byzantine designs.

Don't be surprised when the stores close between 2 and 5:30 in the afternoon and reopen in the evenings; even on the chic islands everybody takes a siesta.

Traditional Festivals

Ano Approvato, a village south of Batsi on Andros, holds a *paneyiri* (festival) on August 15, for the Dormition of the Virgin Mary, with feasting and dancing along with the religious rites.

In Tinos town (Chora) on Tinos the icon is paraded with much pomp through town on poles on Annunciation Day, March 25, and especially Dormition Day, August 15. As it passes over the heads of the faithful, including thousands of bedecked gypsies who make Tinos seem a gigantic glittering encampment, cures are effected, and religious emotion runs high. On July 23, in honor of Saint Pelagia, the icon is paraded from Kechrovouni Nunnery and afterwards the festivities continue long into the night, with music and fireworks.

Naxos Town celebrates the Dionysia festival during the first week of August, with concerts, folk dancing in costumes, and free food and wine in the square. At other times, feast days are honored with a paneyiri. For example, during Carnival, preceding Lent, "bell wearers" take to the streets in Apeiranthos and Filoti, running from house to house, making as much noise as possible with strings of bells tied around their waists. They're a disconcerting sight in their hooded cloaks, with scarves concealing their faces, as they ritually escort a man dressed as a woman around the houses collecting eggs. In Apeiranthos, you can hear villagers square off in rhyming-verse contests: On the last Sunday of Lent, the *paliomoskari,* their faces blackened, challenge each other in improvising *kotsakia* (satirical couplets). At the May Day Festival in Koronis, wildflower garlands are made, and there's lively dancing. On July 14, Ayios Nikodemos Day is celebrated in Chora with a procession of the patron saint's icon through town, but the Dormition of the Virgin on August 15 is, after Easter and Christmas, the festival most widely celebrated, especially in Sangri, Filoti (August 4th), and Apeiranthos.

On Paros, each year on August 23 Naousa celebrates the heroic naval battle against the Turks, with children dressed in native costume, great feasts, and traditional dancing. The day ends with 100 boats illuminated by torches converging on the harbor.

Villages

Despite its depredations, the automobile has brought life back to the villages. Many closed-up houses are now being authentically restored, and much of the traditional architecture is still there. Oia on Santorini, Kardiani on Tinos, and Apeiranthos on Naxos are part of any deep experience of the islands.

Exploring the Cyclades

Great Itineraries

There is no bad itinerary for the Cyclades. The islands are remarkably different from one another, and all beautiful. It is possible to "see" any island in a day, for they are small and the "must-see" sights are few—

Delos, Santorini's caldera, the Minoan site at Akrotiri, and Paros's Church of a Hundred Doors. So planning a trip depends on your sense of inclusiveness, your restlessness, your energy, and your ability to adjust to changing boat schedules.

IF YOU HAVE 2 OR 3 DAYS

Numbers in the text correspond to numbers in the margin and on the Cyclades, Mykonos Town, Delos, Naxos, and Santorini maps.

For a 3-day trip that promises shopping, nightlife, a serious summer beach scene, classical Greece, and traditional Greece, go directly to **Mykonos** ①–⑩, the next morning visit **Delos** ⑪–㉛, and in the afternoon go to **Tinos** for its landscape, villages, and church.

IF YOU HAVE 5 DAYS

If you want to see the two most popular islands in 5 days you can visit **Mykonos** ①–⑩ (and **Delos** ⑪–㉛) and **Santorini** ㊻–(51), with its volcanic bay, ancient site, and Greece's most photographed village.

IF YOU HAVE 8 DAYS

If you want some hiking, Byzantine churches, and relaxation between Mykonos and Santorini, visit **Naxos** and **Paros** for an overfilled eight days. And if you have two weeks really to see the Cyclades, start the 4-day itinerary in elegant nontouristy **Andros,** then go to **Tinos,** **Mykonos** ①–⑩ (and **Delos** ⑪–㉛), then **Naxos** ㉜–㊺, **Paros,** and **Santorini** ㊻–(51), You may continue on to explore the other Cycladic islands—they are endless.

When to Tour

Most people come to Greece in the summer, when Zeus's sky is faultlessly azure, Poseidon's sea warm, and Dionysus's nightlife swinging. But in summer—especially August—Greece is crowded and less personal, and the penetrating sun has its way with hot afternoons.

Walkers, nature lovers, and devotees of classical and Byzantine Greece would do better to come in the spring and fall, both less temperate and tourist riddled. Spring's islands burst with thousands of varieties of wildflowers, and sprightly crimson poppies dapple stern marble blocks, but the sea is cold. Autumn's days are short but the sea remains alluringly swimmable. Zesty olives are gathered and bulging grapes are pressed.

ANDROS

The northernmost and second-largest of the Cycladic islands, Andros is about 32 km by 16 km (nearly 20 mi by 10 mi), and its rugged, mountainous geography is best seen by car. The highest peak, Mt. Kouvari, reaches 994 meters (3,260 feet). An array of springs gives birth to streams, which whirl down from the mountaintops, feeding lush valleys; unlike most of the Cyclades, Andros is green with pines, sycamores, mulberries, fig trees, and lemon trees. In ancient times it was called Hydroussa, or "Watery Isle." Not only do the springs and streams have a cooling effect, but the prevailing northern wind, or meltemi, which sweeps across Andros throughout the summer, ameliorates the scorching heat. Locals say that when the meltemi subsides, the gentler, *notias* winds arrive from the south, bringing hotter weather and bothersome jellyfish.

Tourism is in an early stage on Andros, and most of the islanders are indifferent to it. Perhaps the reason for this snobbishness toward tourists is that Andros is historically a wealthy island. The well-known Goulandris shipping family from Andros founded two museums of modern art and the archaeological museum in Andros town, arguably the best in the Aegean. Among Greeks, Andros is considered an island for the cultured elite. Prices are, surprisingly, still in line with the Greek economy, and restaurants and hotels are less expensive than they are in Mykonos or Santorini.

Across the entire landscape of Andros you will notice an interesting network of stone walls that mark boundaries between the fields of different owners. In a building style unique to Andros, the walls are interrupted at regular intervals, and each gap is filled with a large flat slab set on its edge longitudinally. Not only did this save stone and labor, but it also allowed herders to lay the large slab flat temporarily, to allow the passage of animals.

Another common feature of Andros (also seen on Mykonos and especially Tinos) is the dovecotes: square towers whose pigeonholes form decorative geometric designs. The Venetians introduced them in the 13th century. Eventually many of the dovecotes fell into disuse, but when hard times struck the islands in this century, local farmers started breeding the pigeons and preserving and selling them abroad as a delicacy. Today only a few of the dovecotes are inhabited and cared for.

Gavrion

75 km (46½ mi) east of Rafina Port, 35 km (21¾ mi) northeast of Andros town.

Gavrion, on the northwest coast, is Andros's dull, dusty little port town. Although there are some accommodations here, most people go south to Batsi, the island's only resort, or to Andros town, on the opposite side of the island. It's a good idea to buy a map of the island.

Few visitors are adventurous enough to take the small dusty roads **north of Gavrion.** In the remote mountain villages live the descendants of Orthodox Albanians who left their native Epirus in the 14th century and found a safe haven here. Many of them still speak an Albanian dialect.

Before leaving Gavrion you may want to take a short detour northeast on a side road shown on the island map, available at newsstands in each town, to see the round **watchtower of Ayios Petros** (✉ Far up in hills above rd. between Gavrion and Batsi). The hike from Gavrion takes about an hour. The tower is built of enormous brown blocks 2 meters (6½ feet) long, fitted without mortar. You have to bend down to get through the low entranceway and, once inside, you can attempt to climb the stone steps 20 meters (65 feet) to the top. It is thought to be one of a series of signal towers used during the Byzantine era to communicate across long distances, or perhaps to protect nearby mines from pirates.

Lodging

$ ⚠ **Camping Andros.** Settle in a grove of olive trees, just 328 yards from the port of Gavrion and 273 yards from the beach. ✉ *Near Gavrion port,* ☎ *0282/71444. Tent sites. Bathroom, hot showers, grocery, snack bar.*

Outdoor Activities and Sports

TENNIS

The **Andros Holiday Hotel** (✉ Gavrion, ☎ 0282/71443, ℻ 0282/71097) has tennis courts open to the public.

Batsi

27 km (16¾ mi) northwest of Andros town, 8 km (5 mi) southeast of Gavrion.

Originally a little fishing village, Batsi has developed only over the last 10 years, and as a new resort town, many of the businesses have a

The Cyclades

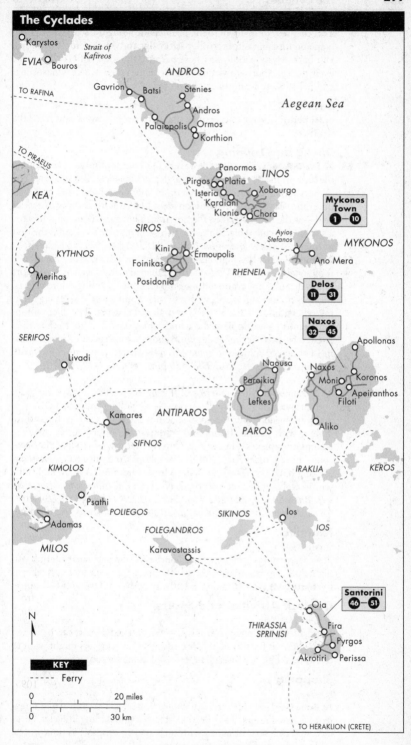

Karystos

EVIA Bouros

Strait of Kafireos

TO RAFINA

ANDROS

Gavrion Batsi Stenies

Palaiopolis Andros

Ormos

Korthion

Aegean Sea

TO PIRAEUS

KEA

Panormos *TINOS*

Pirgos Platia

Isteria Kardiani Xobourgo

Kionia Chora

Mykonos Town ① — ⑩

SIROS

Ayios Stefanos

MYKONOS

Ano Mera

KYTHNOS

Kini Ermoupolis

Foinikas

Posidonia

RHENEIA

Delos ⑪ — ㉛

Merihas

Naxos ㉜ — ㊺

SERIFOS

Apollonas

Livadi

Naousa

Naxos

Moni Koronos

Paroikia Apeiranthos

Lefkes Filoti

Kamares *ANTIPAROS*

PAROS

Aliko

SIFNOS

IRAKLIA

KEROS

KIMOLOS

Psathi

POLIEGOS

SIKINOS

Ios

IOS

Adamas

FOLEGANDROS

MILOS

Karavostassis

Santorini ㊻ — ㊼

Oia

THIRASSIA

Fira

SPRINISI

Pyrgos

Akrotiri Perissa

N

KEY

- - - - Ferry

0 _____ 20 miles

0 _____ 30 km

TO HERAKLION (CRETE)

friendly, nonhustling nature. On the hillside, a few lovely houses from a century ago look down to the promenade along the sea, where Athenian and foreign visitors stroll, patronizing the new restaurants, shops, and bars. Many people stay here because the social life is a bit more lively than in Andros town and because of the beach, where windsurfing, paddleboats, and canoes can be rented.

Beach

Batsi beach is sandy, accessible, and offers some protection from the winds.

Dining and Lodging

$$ ✕ **The Dolphins.** This popular taverna has outdoor tables overlooking the harbor; inside, a colorful mural depicts the local fishing scene. The owners Jannis Fotiou and his German wife Gesa both cook and wait on tables. Try their forte—onion stew loaded with chunks of tender veal—or the liver or grilled filet mignon. The seafood includes lobster, a special fish called blacktail, and fish soup that locals claim is the best in town. ⊠ *South end of harbor,* ☎ *0282/41635. No credit cards.*

$$ ✕ **Stamatis.** Pity this high-class taverna has no sea view, but the food—
★   traditional Greek since 1965—is better than at many. Outside, blue chairs and red tables are crammed into the narrow, gleaming white streets. Inside is homey and rustic, with a fireplace and a wall displaying hunting relics (dinner's harbinger?) and an old clarinet. The chef will invite you to have a look at the wonderful dishes. Try the fresh stuffed roasted chicken or the tender lamb chops with a special Andros stuffing. For dessert splurge on *galactoboureko* (here, scrumptious milk pie). ⊠ *On side st., to right of The Dolphins,* ☎ *0282/41283. MC, V.*

$$$–$$$$ ⊞ **Epaminondas.** The exterior of this quiet complex is stark and odd,
★   with brown stone and small windows—something between a dovecote and a monastery. But the cool, spacious interiors are tasteful and relaxing, with marble floors and traditionally embroidered curtains. Rooms or duplexes range in size, with room for two to six people. Some rooms have kitchenettes, and all have phones and huge balconies overlooking Batsi Bay. The hotel's deep freshwater pool is lit all night. It's within walking distance of town center. ⊠ *On rd. to lower Batsi, on left, Batsi 84500,* ☎ *0282/41682 and 0282/41683,* ℻ *0282/41681. 32 rooms with bath. Kitchenettes, freshwater pool. No credit cards.*

Nightlife

NIGHTCLUBS

Beware, evenings at the open-air **Sunrise** (⊠ On perimeter rd. of Batsi) nightclub can extend into the wee hours. More remote but livelier is the **Marabout** (⊠ On main rd. halfway between Batsi and Gavrion).

Outdoor Activities and Sports

WATER SPORTS

Windsurfing equipment, jet skis, canoes, and pedal boats can be rented by the hour at Batsi Beach. More adventurous travelers might want to try waterskiing or parasailing, tethered behind a motorboat.

Shopping

JEWELRY

At **Batsi Gold** (⊠ Harbor St., Batsi, ☎ 0282/41575) skillful and imaginative goldsmiths sell a collection of jewelry (including bracelet, necklace, and ring sets) designed with such ancient symbols as honey bees, bull's horns, and the Macedonian star.

Palaiopolis

18½ km (11½ mi) southwest of Andros town, 9 km (5½ mi) south of Batsi.

Unfortunately, most of Palaiopolis, the ancient capital of Andros, lies beneath the sea, destroyed either by an earthquake or a landslide during the 4th century. The town today is a quiet but gorgeous village that stretches down the slope of Mt. Kouvari to the shore.

The road cuts through the **upper town,** where you'll find a **café** and an excellent roadside **taverna.** From the taverna you can look up to the hill and see the site of an **ancient acropolis,** 300 meters (984 feet) above the sea, now occupied by a small **Orthodox chapel;** some **waterfalls** are a short climb up. In 1832 a farmer turned up the famous **statue of Hermes** in this area, which is now on display in the archaeological museum in Andros town (☞ *below*).

Opposite the café, 1,039 steps lead down through the **lower village,** in the shade of flowering vines and trees heavy with lemons and limes. Scattered about the **beach** are marble remnants of early buildings and statues. Though it has not been systematically excavated, archaeologists did enough digging around here in 1956 to conjecture that the bits and pieces are remains from the ancient agora.

Nightlife

BOUZOUKI CLUB

The **Panorama** (⊠ Main rd.) in Palaiopolis features live bouzouki shows.

NEED A BREAK?

Stop in Menites (⊠ ½ km/⅓ mi off main rd., halfway between the fork in the road and Andros town) to see the sacred springs and have a glass of local wine and a bite to eat at one of two **shaded tavernas,** which both serve nice whole rooster. Mineral spring water tumbles from a series of spouts along a stone wall, and hidden by greenery in the background is **Panayia tis Koumoulous,** an Orthodox church supposedly built on the site of a major temple to Dionysos. According to legend, these are the very springs whose water turned to wine each year on the god's feast day.

Andros Town

27 km (16¾ mi) south of Batsi.

Andros town (Chora) has been the capital of the island since the Venetian occupation in the 13th century. The city is built on a long, narrow peninsula.

On a **small island** at Andros town's tip are the remains of a **Venetian castle** built about 1220.

Overlooking the castle is the statue of *The Unknown Sailor,* by Michael Tombros, whose works are exhibited in the Museum of Sculpture (☞ *below*).

Take a leisurely stroll down the center's **marble promenade** (⊠ Main St.), past the impressive 13th-century **Palatiani Church** and the interesting **gift shops** that sell local Andros pottery. Handsome stone mansions of the 19th century line the streets, and over their doors are carved galleons, large three-masted sailing ships, indicating that the original owners were shipowners or sea captains. The town is deliberately kept traditional, and its tidy appearance and the distinction of its neoclassical houses bear witness to its long-standing prosperity.

The main street leads to **Kairis Square** (⊠ At tip of peninsula), where in the center stands a bust of **Theophilos Kairis,** a local hero. Born in Andros town in 1784, Kairis was educated in Paris and returned to Andros in 1821 to become one of the leaders in the War of Independence. A philosopher, scholar, and social reformer, he toured Europe to raise money for an orphanage and school, which he founded in 1835. The school became famous in Greece, and enrollment eventually rose to 600, but the Orthodox church closed it down and tried Kairis as a heretic for his individualistic religious beliefs. He died in a Siros prison in 1852.

The **Museum of Modern Art** is the first of the three museums on Andros funded by the Goulandris Foundation. It stages exhibitions of such notable international and Greek artists as the sculptor Alberto Giacometti. ⊠ *Andros town,* ☎ *0282/22650.* 🖾 *700 dr. (free Sun.).* ☉ *Sat.–Mon. 10–2.*

The **Museum of Sculpture** displays rotating exhibitions by Greece's best modern painters and a permanent collection of the works of sculptor Michael Tombros (1889–1974), whose parents were born on Andros. ⊠ *Andros town,* ☎ *0282/22444.* 🖾 *Free.* ☉ *Sat.–Mon. 10–2.*

The pride of Andros's **Archaeological Museum** is the statue of Hermes discovered in Palaiopolis, thought to be a copy of a Praxiteles original. The museum presents sculpture from the Archaic through the Roman periods on the lower floor. Upstairs is an extensive display on Zagora, the earliest known settlement in Andros, a town built during the Geometric Period on the southwest coast, on a promontory 161 meters (529 feet) above sea level, surrounded by jagged cliffs. It was the main settlement from 900 BC to 700 BC, before the rise of Palaiopolis. The Athens Archaeological Society and the University of Sydney are excavating Zagora. The site is not open, but the museum provides a model of the town and displays many of the archaeological finds. ⊠ *Kairis Sq.,* ☎ *0282/23664.* 🖾 *500 dr.* ☉ *Tues.–Sun. 8:30–3.*

OFF THE
BEATEN PATH

BAY OF KORTHION – The Bay of Korthion (⊠ 22 km/14 mi south of Andros town) is where a pretty village extends down to a beach on a deep indentation of the sea. High on a hill above the bay are the ruins of the Medieval Venetian fortress called Kastro tis Grias (the Castle of the Old Woman). A legend says that an old Greek woman tricked the guard into allowing her access to the castle gate, which she later opened to the waiting Ottoman Turks. After the soldiers slaughtered the Venetians, the old woman, filled with remorse, leapt to her death from a cliff now known as Tis Grias to Pidema, or Old Lady's Leap.

The Arts
Check the art museums for lectures, recitals, and opening nights.

Beaches
Adjacent to Andros town is a **beach** (⊠ North of Chora) that provides a view of the castle ruins, but the nearby road and development in the area are distractions. There's a nice sandy beach at **Nimborio Bay** (⊠ About 2 km/1¼ mi north of Andros town). South of Andros town is another **beach** (⊠ In bay below Korthion and Yialia, near village of Stenies) with a taverna and some cheap rooms.

Dining and Lodging
$ ✕ **Parea.** This shaded taverna perched high above a windswept beach is the perfect place to try *fourtalia* (the island's oven-baked omelets packed with potatoes, cheese, sausage or bacon, a handful of broad beans, and herbs). Other favorites are veal in lemon sauce, and long,

Your passport around the world.

- Worldwide access
- Operators who speak your language
- Monthly itemized billing

MCI Calling Card

415 555 1234 2244
J.D. SMITH

Use your MCI Card® and these access numbers for an easy way to call when traveling worldwide.

Austria (CC)♦†	022-903-012
Belarus	
From Gomel and Mogilev regions	8-10-800-103
From all other localities	8-800-103
Belgium (CC)♦†	0800-10012
Bulgaria	00800-0001
Croatia (CC)★	99-385-0112
Czech Republic (CC)♦	00-42-000112
Denmark (CC)♦†	8001-0022
Finland (CC)♦†	9800-102-80
France (CC)♦†	0800-99-0019
Germany (CC)†	0130-0012
Greece (CC)♦†	00-800-1211
Hungary (CC)♦	00▼800-01411
Iceland (CC)♦†	800-9002
Ireland (CC)†	1-800-55-1001
Italy (CC)♦†	172-1022
Kazakhstan (CC)	1-800-131-4321
Liechtenstein (CC)♦	155-0222
Luxembourg†	0800-0112
Monaco (CC)♦	800-90-19

Netherlands (CC)♦†	06-022-91-22
Norway (CC)♦†	800-19912
Poland (CC)✛†	00-800-111-21-22
Portugal (CC)✛†	05-017-1234
Romania (CC)✛	01-800-1800
Russia (CC)✛♦	747-3322
For a Russian-speaking operator	747-3320
San Marino (CC)♦	172-1022
Slovak Republic (CC)	00-42-000112
Slovenia	080-8808
Spain (CC)†	900-99-0014
Sweden (CC)♦†	020-795-922
Switzerland (CC)♦†	155-0222
Turkey (CC)♦†	00-8001-1177
Ukraine (CC)✛	8▼10-013
United Kingdom (CC)†	
To call to the U.S. using BT ■	0800-89-0222
To call to the U.S. using Mercury ■	0500-89-0222
Vatican City (CC)†	172-1022

To sign up for the MCI Card, dial the access number of the country you are in and ask to speak with a customer service representative.

MCI

http://www.mci.com

It helps to be pushy in airports.

Introducing the revolutionary new TransPorter™ from American Tourister® It's the first suitcase you can push around without a fight. TransPorter's™ exclusive four-wheel design lets you push it in front of you with almost no effort–the wheels take the weight. Or pull it on two wheels if you choose. You can even stack on other bags and use it like a luggage cart.

Stable 4-wheel design.

TransPorter™ is designed like a dresser, with built-in shelves to organize your belongings. Or collapse the shelves and pack it like a traditional suitcase. Inside, there's a suiter feature to help keep suits and dresses from wrinkling. When push comes to shove, you can't beat a TransPorter™. For more information on how you can be this pushy, call 1-800-542-1300.

Shelves collapse on command.

Making travel less primitive.®

round fresh *kannelonia* (cannelloni) stuffed with mincemeat. At the end of a meal Andriotes like their *dopio* (local feta) with fresh fruit. You will, too. ⊠ *Kairis Sq., Chora,* ☎ *0282/23721. V.*

$$$ 🏨 **Hotel Pighi Sarisa.** This white three-story hotel flies the EU, United States, British, and Greek flags. It's on a mountain road near the Sarisa mineral springs, and it is wonderful for a break from the heat. The air is cool, and you can hike along many mountain trails nearby. Rooms are clean and simple, with TVs. The restaurant has an international menu. This hotel is open all winter. ⊠ *Apikia Rd., 3 km (2 mi) north of Andros town, 84500,* ☎ *0282/23799,* 🖷 *0282/22476. 42 rooms with bath. Restaurant, minibars, freshwater pool, sauna, recreation room. DC, V.*

$$$ 🏨 **Paradise Hotel.** The best rooms in this white colonial-style hotel have white lacy curtains and canopy double beds; all have balconies from which you can view the sea or the mountains, but try to book one away from the main road. It's just outside of town center, within walking distance of the shops, museums, and the beach; you can also take the hotel van to better beaches. ⊠ *Main St., Andros town 84500,* ☎ *0282/22187 and 0282/22188,* 🖷 *0282/22340. 41 rooms with bath. Bar, cafeteria, minibars, tennis court. MC, V.*

Outdoor Activities and Sports

BOATING

The **Andros Naval Club** (⊠ Nimborio port, just north of Andros town) offers rowing and sailing.

HIKING

The mountainous geography and lush greenery make Andros a pleasant island for hiking, especially around Andros town and near Messaria (south), Apoikia (west), and Stenies (north). The 5-km (3-mi) hike from the little village of Lamira to Andros town is popular.

Shopping

GIFT SHOPS

A number of gift shops on the **main street** and **Paraporti** (⊠ Kairis Sq., ☎ 0282/23777) sell local pottery, embroidery, ship models, and other handmade objects. Notable are the ceramic bowls in bright colors with flowers molded in the centers.

TINOS

Perhaps the least visited of the major Cyclades, Tinos (or as archaeologists spell it, Tenos) is among the most beautiful, and most fascinating. The third-largest of the Cyclades after Naxos and Andros, with an area of 195 sq km (121 sq mi), it is home to nearly 10,000 people, many of whom still live the traditional life of farmers or craftsmen. Its long mountainous spine, rearing amid Andros, Mykonos, and Siros, makes it forbidding, and in a way it is. It is not popular among tourists for several reasons: The main village, Tinos town (Chora), lacks charm; the beaches are mediocre; there is no airport; and the prevailing north winds are the Aegean's fiercest, so much that passing mariners used to sacrifice a calf to Poseidon—ancient Tinos's chief deity—in hopes of avoiding shipwrecks. For Greeks, a visit to Tinos is essential: its great Church of the Evangelistria is the Greek Lourdes, a holy place of pilgrimage and miraculous cures; 799 other churches have also been erected. Encroaching development here is to accommodate those in search of their religious elixir, and not, as on the other islands, beach-and-bar tourist development.

Tinos is renowned for its 1,300 dovecotes which, unlike on Mykonos or Andros, are mostly not falling into disrepair; on the contrary, new ones are being built. Two stories high, with intricate stonework, carved-dove finials, and thin schist slabs arranged in intricate patterns resembling traditional stitchery, the dovecotes have been much written about—and are much visited by doves.

Tinos is dotted with possibly the loveliest villages in the Cyclades, which, for some welcome reason, are not being abandoned. The dark arcades of Arnados, the vine-shaded sea views of Isternia and Kardiani, the Venetian architecture of Loutra, the gleaming marble squares of Pirgos: these finally, are what make Tinos unique. A map, available at kiosks or rental agencies, will make touring these villages by car or bike somewhat less confusing—there are nearly 50 of them!

Tinos Town

55 km (34 mi) southeast of Andros's port, Gavrion.

Civilization on Tinos island is a millennium older than **Tinos town,** or Chora, founded in the 5th century BC. On weekends and during festivals, Chora is thronged with Greeks attending church, and with restaurants and hotels catering to them. As the well-known story goes: In 1822, a year after the War of Independence began (Tinos was first of the islands to join in), the Virgin sent the nun Pelagia a dream about a buried icon of the Annunciation. On January 30, 1823, it was unearthed amid the foundations of a Byzantine church, and it started to heal people immediately.

The Tiniots, hardly unaware of the potential of the icon's healing power, immediately built the splendid **Panayia Evangelistria,** or Annunciate Virgin, on the site using the most costly marble from Tinos, Paros, and (alas) Delos. The church's **marble courtyards** (note the green-veined Tiniot quarry stone) are paved with pebble mosaics and surrounded by **offices, chapels, a health station,** and **seven museums.**

Inside the **upper three-aisle church,** dozens of beeswax candles and precious votives—don't miss the golden orange tree near the door donated by a blind man granted sight—dazzle the eye. You must wait in line to see the little icon, which is encrusted with jewels as thanks for cures. To beseech the icon's aid, a sick person sends a young female relative and a mother brings her sick infant. As the pilgrim descends from the boat, she falls to her knees, with traffic indifferently whizzing about her, and crawls painfully up the main street—half a mile—to the church. In the church's courtyards, she and her family camp for several days, praying to the magical icon for a cure, which sometimes comes. This procedure is very similar to the ancient one in Tinos's temple of Poseidon.

The **lower church,** called the Evresis, celebrates the finding of the icon; in one room a baptismal font is filled with silver and gold votives. The chapel to the left commemorates the torpedoing, on Dormition Day, 1940, of the Greek ship *Helle* by the Italians; in the early stages of the war, the roused Greeks amazingly overpowered the Italians. ✉ *Chora, at end of Megalohari,* ☎ *0283/22256.* 🎟 *Free.* ⊙ *8:30–3.*

On the main street, near the church, is the small **Archaeological Museum;** its collection includes a sundial by Andronicus of Cyrrhus, who in the 1st century BC also designed Athens' Tower of the Winds. Here, too, are Tinos's famous huge red storage vases, from the 8th century BC. ✉ *Megalohari,* ☎ *0283/222670.* 🎟 *500 dr.* ⊙ *Tues.–Fri. 8–2.*

Beaches

There is a series of beaches between Chora and Kionia (and beyond for walkers). **Stavros** is the most romantic. **Ayios Yannis** (⌧ Near Porto) is long, sandy, and peaceful. **Pachia Ammos** (⌧ Past Porto, reached by a dirt road) is undeveloped and sparkling.

Dining and Lodging

$$$ ✕ **Xinari.** On a tiny square with a marble fountain, a curved gray mar-
★   ble staircase leads to the town's fanciest restaurant, with balconies and rooms with high ceilings, terra-cotta tile floors, rose tablecloths, and dark furniture. For starters try *bekri* (drunkard's) meze or pork in a piquant sauce. Exceptional entrées include eggplant stuffed with meat chunks and pork fillet with plums, white wine, and cream. For dessert, try the house specialty, *spitiko* (sweet bread in syrup with custard and whipped cream). Xinari bottles its own good wine, which is also served in its winter quarters in Athens. ⌧ *Evangelistria,* ☎ *0283/23337. Reservations essential in high season. MC, V.*

$$ ✕ **Alonia.** In a terraced hotel with magnificent views of fields and sea,
★   you can savor home-style meals prepared by the owners. To begin, try homemade onion focaccia (which they call bread), eggplant olive salad, or marinated raw saury fillets (recipe: debone sauries; salt well; drain 30 hours; rinse well; marinate in lemon juice 2 hours). Homespun entrées may be chicken breasts stuffed with bacon, cheese, and herbs, beef in cream sauce with mushrooms, and grilled treats—the menu changes. The wine is barrel or bottle. ⌧ *2 km (1½ mi) from Chora toward Porto (Ayios Ioannis), Alonia Hotel,* ☎ *0283/23541 through 23543,* ℻ *0283/ 23544. MC, V.*

$$ ✕ **Old Pallada.** Choose this popular old taverna, near the busy center of things, over its neighbors—locals do. The outdoor area, in a pedestrian's alley, is shaded over with grapevines. Trusty starters are roasted peppers with garlic and parsley, and stuffed squid. The stuffed zucchini blossoms, when in season, are a treat. Chef's favorites are roast lamb and his homemade wine. It's open all year. ⌧ *Kontogiorgi alley, facing the sq.,* ☎ *0283/23516. No credit cards.*

$$$ 🏨 **Porto Tango.** This ambitiously up-to-date, popular resort-hotel strives for the best in decor and service. Greece's late prime minister, Andreas Papandreou, stayed here during his last visit to Tinos (he had previously stayed at the Tinos Beach Hotel). Modular Cycladic architecture lends privacy; the lobby, where an art exhibition is usually in progress, has a wooden ceiling, marble floors, and Tiniot furnishings, modern and antique. Rooms are simple, white, and private, with wooden furniture and TVs. ⌧ *Cement rd. up hill, Porto 84200,* ☎ *0183/24410 through 24415,* ℻ *0283/24416. 62 rooms with bath. Restaurant, bar, air-conditioning, freshwater pool, sauna, exercise room. D, V.*

$$ 🏨 **Akti Aegeou.** The family that runs this little resort must know they are lucky to own such a valuable piece of property. Akti Aegeou, or "Aegean Coast," is in fact right on the fine, uncrowded beach at Porto. All airy rooms come with balconies, marble floors, traditional rag rugs, and personal service, including minibus service. The restaurant, specializing in fresh fish, is very good. It must take a lot of water to keep the lawns so green under the blazing Aegean summer sun. ⌧ *Beach of Ayios Ioannis, Porto 84200,* ☎ *0283/24248,* ℻ *0283/23523. 5 rooms with bath, 6 apartments. Restaurant, bar, kitchenettes, pool. No credit cards.*

$$ 🏨 **Alonia Hotel.** This hotel is not exciting, aesthetically interesting, in
★   town, or near the beach (1 km/⅔ mi away). It is, however, Tinos's best. Comfortable, family-run, and quietly efficient, it is the best bet if you dislike snazzy resorts and want to be out of hectic Chora. The fairly large rooms all have dazzling views (rooms overlooking the pool are

best), telephones, and bathrooms *with* bathtubs. Tinos's largest fresh-water pool is surrounded by lawns, trees, and gardens—not baking cement. And the restaurant is superb, often frequented by Tiniots. An hourly minibus makes the run to Chora; the hotel is open in winter for groups. ⊠ *2 km (1½ mi) from Chora toward Porto (Ayios Ioannis) 84200,* ☎ *0283/23541 through 23543,* FAX *0283/23544. 34 rooms with bath, 4 air-conditioned suites. Restaurant, bar, café, freshwater pool. MC, V.*

$$ 🏨 **Leandros.** If you want to be in Chora, but you also desire peace and quiet, this charming 11-room hotel, run by Jack and Anna Paravalos (he also runs the local tree farm), is the place. The lobby and breakfast room are of all wood, stone, and whitewash. Traditional Tiniot marble carvings are everywhere. A plant-filled outdoor stairway leads to the rooms, which have balconies. The whitewashed walls of the rooms are textured with traditional *sardeles* (sardines) stripes made with a trowel—Jack did much of the work himself. ⊠ *Behind new dock, Chora 84200,* ☎ *0283/23545,* FAX *0283/24390. 11 rooms with bath. Breakfast room. No credit cards.*

$$ 🏨 **Tinion.** This hotel dating to 1925 is the handsome old-timer of Tinos. It's old in the good sense: spacious, neoclassic, and authentic—but it has no elevator for its three stories. The lobby and rooms are all elaborately tiled, and some of the rooms (you should ask for these) have balconies and telephones. Traditional furniture, brass beds, and old-fashioned wardrobes add to the charm. It's conveniently located on the waterfront, though at one end it's angled to avoid the worst of the traffic and hubbub. ⊠ *Constantinou Alavanou, just off quay, Chora 84200,* ☎ *0283/22261,* FAX *028324754. 21 rooms with bath. Breakfast room. MC, V.*

$ 🏕 **Camping Tinos.** 200 meters east of Chora and 100 meters from Ayios Phocas beach, Tinos's only campsite is shady and pleasant. A songful aviary greets you at the reception. Simple rooms with bath can also be had. ⊠ *Ayios Phocas beach, Chora 84400,* ☎ *0283/22344. Tent sites and some rooms with bath. Bathrooms, hot shower, cafeteria, grocery, telephones.*

Nightlife

Tinos has fewer **bars** and **discos** than the other big islands, but there is plenty of late-night bar action just behind the waterfront on the way to the new dock.

BAR

The one **bar** in the village of Falatados (⊠ 12 km/7½ mi north of Tinos town) on occasion throbs with all-night Greek dancing.

Outdoor Activities and Sports

Of all the major islands, Tinos is the least developed for sport. The strong winds discourage water sports, and their concessions come and go.

Shopping

FARMERS AND FLEA MARKETS

Tinos is a rich farming island, and in season on every day but Sunday farmers fill the **square** (⊠ Between new and old docks) with vegetables, herbs, and flowers from all the far-flung villages. In the next square closer to town, the local pelican (a rival to Mykonos's) can often be found cadging snacks from the **fish market.**

Tinos produces a lot of milk. A short way up from the harbor, on the right, is the little store of the **Enosis,** or Farmer's Cooperative (⊠ Megalohari, up from harbor, ☎ 0283/23289), which sells milk, butter, and a variety of cheeses, including Mykonos's famous, very sharp *kopanisti*, perfect with ouzo.

Evangelistria, the street parallel to the church, is closed to traffic and is a kind of **religious flea market,** lined with shops hawking immense candles, chunks of incense, tacky souvenirs, tin votives, and sweets. There are several good jewelers' shops on the market street where, as always on Tinos, the religious note is supreme.

JEWELRY

The selection at **Ostria** (✉ Evangelistria, ☎ 0283/23893) is especially good; in addition to delicate silver jewelry, it sells silver icon covers, silver plate, and 22-karat gold. **Anna Maria** (✉ Chora waterfront, on patio of Avra hotel, ☎ 0283/23456) sells traditional Greek silver jewelry amid much culture.

WEAVINGS

The 100-year-old weaving school, or **Biotechniki Scholi** (✉ Evangelistria, ¾ way up), sells traditional weavings—aprons, towels, spreads—by its students, local girls. The biggest of its three high-ceiling, wooden-floored rooms is filled with looms and spindles.

OFF THE
BEATEN PATH

MARKOS VELALOPOULOS'S OUZERI – One and a half kilometers (1 mile) from Chora you'll see a copse of pines shading a small parking lot, whence a path leads down to Stavros (Holy Cross) chapel; right on the water is the unmarked Markos Velalopoulos's Ouzeri (✉ Under church, ☎ 0283/23276), which serves *strophia* (raki), ouzo, and traditional snacks like fried cheese or figs with sesame. This is Tinos's most romantic spot to watch the sunset. It is also good for swimming. The sunken mole along the coastal road in Stavros Harbor is ancient.

MOUNTAIN VILLAGES ABOVE CHORA – At night the lights of the villages above Chora, in the hills before Tinos's highest mountain, Mt. Tsiknias, 725 meters high and the ancient home of Boreas (the wind god), glitter like fireworks. By day they are worth visiting. Take the good road that runs through Dio Horia and Monastiri, which ascends and twists around switchbacks, passing fertile fields and a few of Tinos's most fanciful old dovecotes. After 9 km (5½ mi) you reach **Kechrovouni,** or just Monastiri, which is a veritable city of nuns, founded in the 10th century. One cell contains the head of Saint Pelagia in a wooden chest; another is a little icon museum. Though a nunnery, Kechrovouni is a lively place, since many of the church's pilgrims come here by bus. Out front, a nun sells huge garlic heads and braids to be used as charms against misfortune; because of the huge cloves, the Greeks call these "California garlic." One kilometer (½ mile) farther on, Tinos's telecommunications towers spike the sky, marking the entrance to **Arnados,** a strange village 488 meters (1,600 feet) up, overlooking Chora. Most of the streets here are vaulted, and thus cool and shady, if a bit claustrophobic; no medieval pirate ever penetrated this warren. In one alley is the **Ecclesiastical Museum,** which displays icons from local churches. Another 1½ km (1 mi) farther on are the **Dio Horia** (Two Villages), with a marble fountain house, which is peculiar in Tinos. The spreading plane tree in front of it, according to the marble plaque, was planted in 1885. Now the road starts winding down again, to reach **Triandaros,** which has a good restaurant; many of the pretty houses in this misty place are owned by Germans. Yannis Kyparinis, who made the three-story bell tower in Dio Horia, has his workshop and showroom here.

Kionia

2½ km (1½ mi) northwest of Tinos town.

The large, untended **Sanctuary of Poseidon** (✉ Northwest of Tinos town) is also dedicated to the bearded sea god's lovely consort, Amphitrite.

The present remains are from the fourth century BC and later, though the sanctuary is a lot older. The sanctuary was a kind of hospital, where the ailing came to camp and solicit the god's help. The marble dolphins from the museum were discovered here. According to the Roman historian Pliny, Tinos was once infested with serpents (goddess symbols) and named Serpenttown (Ophiousa), until super-masculine Poseidon sent storks to clean them out. The sanctuary functioned well into Roman times.

Beaches

The Kiona road ends at a long sheltered **beach**, unfortunately being worn away by cars heading for the two pretty **coves** beyond, including the **Gastrion cave**, whose entrance shows Byzantine inscriptions.

Dining and Lodging

$$ ✕ **Tsambia.** Abutting the sanctuary of Poseidon, this multilevel taverna prepares homemade traditional fare. For starters try a mélange of indigenous specialties: *louza* (smoked peppered pork roll coated and preserved in wax), local Tiniot cheeses, and local vegetables. Fresh fish is available, weather depending. Tried-and-true are *stifado* (rabbit stew), the strictly local meat, and the outstanding codfish croquettes in garlic sauce. Just before the Sanctuary of Poseidon follow signs for TRA-DITIONAL GREEK RESTAURANT. ⊠ *Cement rd., Kionia 84200,* ☎ *0283/23142. No credit cards.*

$$$ 🏨 **Tinos Beach.** Part of the government's all-too-successful sponsorship to promote tourism in the '70s, this is Tinos's most varied resort. In the large, cool lobby, with lots of wood and tiles, pianists sometimes play at night. Though the carpeted rooms show some signs of age, many rooms have a splendid sea view, and there are suites and bungalows that sleep four, with marble floors. ⊠ *Tinos beach, at end (3 km/1¼ mi) of Kiona Rd., just past sanctuary to Poseidon, Kionia 84200,* ☎ *0283/22626 and 0283/22627,* FAX *0283/23153. 80 rooms with bath, suites and bungalows. Restaurant, bar, café, taverna, 2 pools, tennis courts, gift shops. MC, V.*

Outdoor Activities and Sports

HIKING

Ktikados village is a beautiful hour-long walk up into the panoramic mountains; 9th-century BC graves have been found in the settlement.

RACQUET SPORTS

Tennis and Ping-Pong are usually going on at **Tinos Beach Hotel** (⊠ Kionia, ☎ 0283/22626).

VOLLEYBALL

You can usually join—or organize—a pick-up game of volleyball at **Tinos Beach Hotel** (⊠ Kionia, ☎ 0283/22626).

Kardiani

21 km (13 mi) northwest of Tinos town.

The mountainside village of Kardiani is 4,000 years old; views here are spectacular and its elegant peasant architecture preserved.

Isternia

24 km (15 mi) northwest of Tinos town, 3 km (1¼ mi) north of Kardiani.

The village of Isternia (Cisterns) is verdant with lush gardens. Many marble plaques seen here over doorways—a specialty of Tinos—often indicate the owner's profession, e.g., a sailing ship for a fisherman or captain. A long, paved road winds down from here to a little **port,** with a **beach** and two **fish tavernas;** a small boat ferries people from here to Chora in good weather.

Pirgos

32 km (20 mi) northwest of Tinos town, 8 km (5 mi) north of Isteria.

The village of Pirgos, second in importance to Chora, overlooks the little harbor of **Panormos.** Pirgos, a prosperous town, is famous for its sculpture school (the town's highest building) and marble workshops, where craftsmen make fanlights, fountains, tomb monuments, small objects for tourists, or whatever you order. The cemetery here is, appropriately, a showplace of marble sculpture. The marble-working tradition survives from the last century, and is going strong.

The **Kardamites Museum** features the work of Pirgos' renowned sculptor, Iannoulis Chalepas. ⊠ *1 block from bus stop.* ⊡ *300 dr.* ⊙ *Daily 10–2.*

Tinos is famous for marble carving; Pirgos is the traditional center for this art and craft. The village's **main square** is aptly crafted of all marble. In fact, the quarries for the green-veined marble are just north of here, reachable by car; when it's raining, they shine emerald green.

NEED A BREAK?   Rest your feet at the **Platonos café** (⊠ Main sq.) under a century-old *platonos* (plane) tree.

Beaches

The beaches next to Panormos are popular in summer.

Shopping

CARVINGS

A number of marble carvers are, properly, found in Pirgos. You may visit the shop of probably the best master carver, **Lambros Diamantopoulos** (⊠ Near main sq., ☎ 0283/31365), who accepts commissions for work all over Greece. He makes and sells all the traditional designs to other carvers and to visitors who may bring a portable slab home to copy.

Panormos

35 km (21¾ mi) northwest of Tinos town, 3 km (1¾ mi) north of Pirgos.

Panormos, an unpretentious port, has several seafood restaurants and a good beach with a collapsed sea cave. More coves with secluded swimming are beyond, as is the islet of Panormos.

Xobourgo

12 km (7½ mi) north of Tinos town.

Tinos is dominated by the sharp, ominously cloudy peak of Xobourgo, 640 meters (2,100 feet) high. Battered by winds, haunted by crows, Xobourgo was Tinos's chief town before 500 BC, though the only obvious remains are stones from a temple to Demeter. When the Venetians conquered the island after the traitorous fourth crusade (1204), they made their castle in this unconquerable spot; its ruins are strewn about. Tinos was the last island to pass from Venetian to Ottoman rule, in 1714. It did not revive from this calamity until the miraculous icon made it a lucrative pilgrimage center.

OFF THE
BEATEN PATH

VOLAX, XYNARA, AND LOUTRA – Volax is strewn with boulders as if in a moonscape. It used to export 1,500 baskets a week to Smyrna for packing figs; you can observe several families here making—and selling—their wares. The town's excellent taverna is famous for its galactoboureko. Xynara, south of Volax, houses, in a splendid building, the Catholic archives of Tinos. Loutra, another Catholic town, has a weaving school in the Ursuline Convent, and a Jesuit church from 1661.

MYKONOS AND DELOS

The dry, rugged island of Mykonos is one of the smallest of the Cycladic group: It's only 16 km (10 mi) long, 11 km (7 mi) wide, and its two highest peaks, both named Profitis Ilias, are less than 365 meters (1,197 feet) above sea level. An ancient myth tells us that the rocks strewn across its barren landscape are the solidified remains of the giants slain by Hercules. Despite its deserted appearance, Mykonos has become one of the most popular (and expensive) of the Aegean islands. Tourists from all over the world are drawn to its many stretches of sandy beach and the upscale bars and restaurants crowded into the port town, Mykonos. The town's whitewashed streets, its cubical houses and churches with their dashes of sky-blue doors and domes, are the best example of classic Cycladic architecture.

The islanders seem to have been able to fit the tourists gracefully into their way of life. You may see, for example, an old island woman leading a donkey laden with vegetables through the narrow streets of the town, greeting the suntanned vacationers walking by. But Mykoniots regard a good tourist season as a fisherman looks at a good day's catch. For many, the money made in July and August is the money they will live on for the rest of the year. Not long ago Mykoniots had to rely on what they could scratch out of the island's arid land for sustenance, and some remember the time of starvation under Axis occupation during World War II. In the 1950s a few tourists began trickling into Mykonos on their way to see the ancient marvels on the nearby islet of Delos. There are no restaurants or hotels on Delos, and so they came to know Mykonos and to appreciate its appeal.

For almost 1,000 years Delos was the religious and political center of the Aegean, host every four years to the Delian games, the region's greatest festival. The population of Delos actually reached 20,000 at the peak of its commercial period, and throughout antiquity Mykonos, eclipsed by its holy neighbor, depended on this proximity for income, as it partly does today. Visitors interested in antiquity should plan to spend a morning on Delos. Most travel offices in Mykonos town run guided tours that cost 7,500 dr. and up, including boat transportation and entry fee. Alternatively, take one of the small ferries that visit Delos daily from the port: The round-trip costs about 2,000 dr., and entry to the site (with no guide) 1,500 dr.

Mykonos Town

16 km (10 mi) southeast of Tinos town.

❶ The **archaeological museum** affords insight into the intriguing history of the shrine. The museum houses Delian funerary sculptures discovered on the neighboring islet of Rhenea, many with scenes of mourning. The most significant work from Mykonos is a 7th-century BC *pithos* (storage jar), showing the Greeks emerging from the Trojan horse. ⊠ *Ayios Stefanos Rd., between boat dock and town,* ☎ *0289/22325.* ☒ *500 dr.* ☉ *Tues.–Sun. 8:30–3.*

A bust of Mando Mavroyennis, the island heroine, stands on a pedestal in the **main square.** In the War of Independence the Mykoniots, known for their naval and seafaring skills, volunteered an armada of 24 ships, and in 1822, when the Ottomans later landed a force on the island, Mavroyennis and her soldiers forced them back to their ships. After independence, a scandalous love affair caused her exile to Paros, where she died.

The best time to visit the **central harbor** is in the cool of the evening, when the islanders promenade down the **esplanade** to meet friends and go to the numerous cafés. Along the waterfront where the boats dock, the town mascot, Petros the Pelican, can be seen preening himself. In the 1950s a group of migrating pelicans passed over Mykonos, leaving behind one exhausted bird. Vassilis the fisherman nursed it back to health, and locals say that the pelican in the harbor is the original Petros, though there are several, enjoying the spotlight and carrying on tradition.

The main shopping street, **Matoyanni** (⊠ Perpendicular to harbor) is lined with jewelry stores, clothing boutiques, chic cafés, and candy shops. The **Public Art Gallery** (⊠ Matoyanni, ☎ 0289/27190) is also here, with exhibitions changing weekly.

NEED A BREAK?	For homemade ice cream, stop at **Snowstorm** (⊠ In middle of shopping area, ☎ 0289/24995), which has been making its creamy product, in 40 flavors, for 17 years.

Any visitor who has the pleasure of getting lost in the narrow, whitewashed streets of Mykonos town will appreciate the fact that its confusing layout was designed to foil attacking pirates. After Mykonos fell under Turkish rule in 1537, the Ottomans allowed the islanders to arm their vessels against pirates, which had a contradictory effect: Many of them found that raiding other islands was more profitable than tilling arid land. At the height of Aegean piracy, Mykonos was the principal headquarters of the corsair fleets—the place where pirates met their fellows, found willing women, and filled out their crews. Eventually the illicit activity evolved into a legitimate and thriving trade network.

Housed by the charming **Aegean Maritime Museum** is a collection of model ships, navigational instruments, old maps, prints, coins, and nautical memorabilia. The backyard garden displays some old anchors and ship wheels and a reconstructed lighthouse from 1890, once lit by oil. ⊠ *Enoplon Dynameon,* ☎ *0289/22700.* ⊡ *200 dr.* ☉ *Tues.–Sat. 8:30–3.*

Take a peek into **Lena's House,** an accurate restoration of a middle class Mykonos house of the last century. ⊠ *Enoplon Dynameon.* ⊡ *Free.* ☉ *Tues.–Sat. 8:30–2 and 6:30–8.*

Many of the early ship captains built distinguished houses directly on the sea here, with wooden balconies over the water. Today, this neighborhood, at the southwest end of the port, is called **Little Venice** (⊠ Mitropoleos Georgouli). A few of the old houses have been turned into stylish bars, which are quite romantic at twilight. In the distance across the water, lined up like toy soldiers on the high hill, are the famous **Mykonos windmills,** echoes of a time when wind power was used to grind the island's grain.

The **Mykonos Agricultural Museum** displays a 16th-century windmill, traditional outdoor oven, waterwheel, dovecote, and more. ⊠ *Petassos, at top of Mykonos town.* ⊡ *Free.* ☉ *Tues.–Sat. 8:30–2 and 6:30–8.*

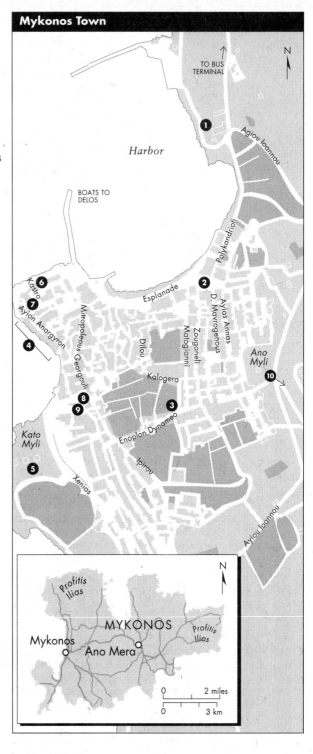

6 The **folk museum,** housed in an 18th-century house, exhibits a bed-room furnished and decorated in the fashion of that period. On display are looms and lace-making devices, Cycladic costumes, old photographs, and Mykoniot musical instruments that are still played at festivals. ⊠ *South of boat dock,* ☎ *0289/22591 or 0289/22748.* 🎫 *Free.* ⊙ *Mon.–Sat. 5:30–8:30, Sun. 6:30–8:30.*

Mykoniots claim that exactly 365 churches and chapels dot their landscape, one for each day of the year. The most famous of these is the **7** **Church of Paraportiani** (Postern Gate) (⊠ Ayion Anargyron, near folk museum). The sloping, whitewashed conglomeration of four chapels, mixing Byzantine and vernacular idioms, has been described as "a confectioner's dream gone mad," and its position on a promontory fac-**8** ing the sea sets off the unique architecture. The **Greek Orthodox Cathedral of Mykonos** (⊠ On sq. that meets both Ayion Anargyron and Odos Mitropolis) has a number of old icons of the post-Byzan-**9** tine period. Next to the Greek Orthodox Cathedral is the **Roman Catholic Cathedral** (⊠ On sq. that meets both Ayion Anargyron and Odos Mitropolis), from the Venetian period. The name and coat of arms of the Ghisi family, who took over Mykonos in 1207, are inscribed in the entrance hall.

Beaches

There is a beach for every taste in Mykonos. **Beaches near Mykonos town,** within walking distance, are **Tourlos** and **Ayios Ioannis. Ayios Stefanos,** about a 45-minute walk from Mykonos town, has a mini-golf course, water sports, restaurants, and umbrellas and lounge chairs for rent. The **south coast**'s **Psarou,** protected from wind by hills and surrounded by restaurants, offers a wide selection of water sports and is often called the finest beach. Nearby **Plati Yialos,** popular among families, is also lined with restaurants and dotted with umbrellas for rent. From here you can take a caïque to **Paranga, Paradise, Super Paradise,** and **Elia,** on all of which nudity is common. All have tavernas on the beach. At the easternmost end of the south shores is **Kalafatis,** known for package tours, and between Elia and Kalafatis there's a remote beach at **Kato Livadhi,** which can be reached by taxi. The great indentation on the **north coast** of the island, called **Panormos Bay,** has unprotected sandy beaches, which can get windy.

Dining and Lodging

$$$–$$$$ ✕ **Edem.** Prompt service and excellent food is well received at the cool
★ white garden of Edem; some tables are also on a platform over the lighted pool. The extensive menu offers five lamb dishes; lamb wrapped in vine leaves with a wine sauce is especially good. Fresh fish and lobster are specialties. For appetizers, choose from dolmades, baked potatoes stuffed with spiced meat and cheese, and Edem shrimp cooked in a garlic, olive oil, and tomato sauce. ⊠ *At an alley end off Matogianni (follow signs) behind the Panachra church,* ☎ *0289/22855 or 0289/23355. AE, DC, MC, V.*

$$$ ✕ **Chez Cat'rine.** This restaurant is hidden, but the Greek and French
★ cuisine and formal hospitality are worth the search. The splendid interior mixes Cycladic arches and whitewash with the feeling of a French château, plus a faded 16th-century mural from Constantinople. Candles and classical music set the tone for baby squid stuffed with rice and Greek mountain spices, or soufflé, puffed to perfection and loaded with cheese, mussels, and prawns. For entrées, try grilled swordfish, leg of lamb, and tournedos langoustine (a beef fillet with lobster sauce, flamed with cognac). After dinner try the strawberry pie or kopanisti served with fresh fruit. ⊠ *Ayios Gerasimos, Mykonos town,* ☎ *0289/22169. Reservations essential on weekends. AE, DC, MC, V.*

$$ ✕ **Phillipi.** This old, lovely restaurant features authentic Greek dishes in a beautiful garden. Fish-roe salad, eggplant salad, fried calamari, and many other traditional dishes have stayed old-fashioned here. ⊠ *Just off Kaloyera,* ☎ *0289/22295,* ℻ *0289/23382. No credit cards.*

$ ✕ **Kounelas.** This is the long-established fresh-fish taverna where many fishermen themselves eat, for no frills and solid food. The menu depends on the weather—low winds: lots of fish. ⊠ *Just off the port near Delos boats. No credit cards.*

$$$$ 🏨 **Cavo Tagoo.** This hotel seems to emerge from its cliff-side backdrop
★ and reach out to the sea 45 meters (150 feet) below. Recognized for its unique architecture in a national competition sponsored by the EOT, this medley of cream cubical suites features roof sunset terraces and an alluring saltwater pool. The reception area, restaurant, and guest rooms all have marble floors, dark beamed ceilings, and wooden furniture. It's a 10-minute walk to the harbor. Another hotel lurks nearby with the exact same name but lower standards. ⊠ *Follow Polykandrioti, north of the port, Mykonos town 84600,* ☎ *0289/23692, 0289/23693, or 0289/23694,* ℻ *0289/24923. 72 rooms with bath. Restaurant, bar, snack bar, saltwater pool. AE, MC, V.*

$$$$ 🏨 **Kivotos Clubhotel.** Spyros Michopoulos's deluxe hotel is architec-
★ turally ambitious, in a richly decorative island style, with statues in niches and stone-mosaic work, and unexpected little courtyards with bright flowers. The rooms, most with sea views, display local crafts. A hotel minibus runs into town, about 2 mi away, and to the airport. ⊠ *Ornos Bay, a mile from Mykonos town, 84600,* ☎ *0289/25795 or 0289/25796,* ℻ *0289/22844. 30 rooms with bath, 4 suites. 2 restaurants, bar, air-conditioning, freshwater pool, hot tub, sauna, exercise room, racquetball, beach. AE, MC, V.*

$$$–$$$$ 🏨 **Petinos.** This casual resort community of four hotels on Plati Yialos beach is comfortable, convenient, and friendly, a favorite among extended vacationers and families. The wind-protected crowded beach, dotted with umbrellas and lounge chairs, is noisy with water sports, snack bars, and restaurants; a boat goes to five other beaches. In the seaside taverna, which comes to life two nights a week with Greek music and dancing, pink tablecloths and flower arrangements brighten the painted wooden tables. Fresh fish is good, or try the salad bar for 1,000 dr. Make reservations on weekends. Frequent port and airport buses (4 km/2½ mi) stop by the hotel. **Petinos Beach,** the most popular, is yards away from the beach and has a saltwater pool. **Petinos Hotel,** a short walk up the street, has less-expensive, smaller rooms, with showers instead of bathtubs, and studios with kitchenettes upstairs. The elegant and pricier new **Palladium,** 500 yards up the road and so quiet, is all cool colors and green marble. Farther up, the cheaper **Nissaki** completes the complex. Top-floor rooms with a balcony are best. All the hotels have the standard wooden beds with multicolor spreads, desks, and chairs. ⊠ *Plati Yialos Beach, a mile from Mykonos town, 84600,* ☎ *0289/22913, 0289/23903, or 0289/23680. 130 rooms with bath. Restaurant, bar, snack bar taverna, 2 pools, hot tub, exercise room, laundry service. AE, MC, V.*

$$$ 🏨 **Ilio Maris.** At this high-quality hotel, a 5-minute walk from the main shopping streets, enjoy extras such as stereos and phones in the white, cubic rooms, and suites with TVs. The stone-paved lobby has traditional furniture with striped fabric, wooden beams, and lots of whitewash. Here you'll find easy parking, and it's open all year (with central heating). ⊠ *Despotika area, 1 block out of town, 84600,* ☎ *0289/23755,* ℻ *0289/24309. 22 rooms with bath. Bar, breakfast room, air-conditioning, pool. AE, V.*

$$ ⚄ **Myconian Inn.** One of the inexpensive, unpretentious, and practical hotels right in town is the Myconian Inn. The small rooms are tastefully furnished in island style, on several uneven levels, with TVs and balconies overlooking the port. Breakfast is included. The owner, George Ghikas, also runs Sunspots Travel. ⊠ *Petassos, edge of town, 84600,* ☎ *0289/22663 or 0289/23420,* ℻ *0289/27269. 13 rooms with bath. Air-conditioning, refrigerators. No credit cards.*

$ ⚠ **Mykonos Camping.** This site, under the trees of Paraga Beach, is a 10-minute walk from Plati Yialos. ⊠ *Paraga Beach, 84600,* ☎ *0289/24578. Tent sites. Bathrooms, restaurant, bar-café, grocery, and cooking and laundry facilities.*

$ ⚠ **Paradise Beach Camping.** Near one of the best beaches, this is popular among young backpackers. ⊠ *Paradise beach, 84600,* ☎ *0289/22852. Tent sites and bungalows. Bathrooms, hot showers, restaurant, bar, grocery.*

Nightlife and the Arts

BARS

Little Venice is a good place to begin an evening, and the **Caprice Bar** (⊠ Little Venice), with whitewashed low ceilings, blown-glass chandeliers, a piano, and elegance, is full of the romance of the neighborhood. **Montparnasse** (⊠ Little Venice, ☎ 0289/23719) has Toulouse-Lautrec posters and a superb sunset view, with live music; cabaret and musicals are featured. Leave your habit and robes behind when you go to **Thalami** (⊠ Near Paraportiani Church, ☎ 0289/23291), a small underground bar with Greek dancing in a cozy nightclub setting. As the night goes on you feel the heightened energy level, which continues to build as dawn approaches. **Diva** (⊠ Little Venice, near the Caprice, ☎ 0289/27271), also in Little Venice, is a popular cocktail bar with a view. And at the famous gay **Pierro's** (⊠ Matoyanni), you can find late-night wild dancing to American and European rock. In summer, Greeks dance all night at **Cava Muses** (⊠ Ayios Stefanos), which is off the beaten path, but worth it.

PERFORMING ARTS

The **Anemo Theatre** (⊠ Steno Roharis, ☎ 0289/23944) is a nonprofit open-air center for the performing arts set in a unique olive garden in the center of town, where, between July and September, distinguished international artists present an eclectic array of concerts, performances, and seminars.

Outdoor Activities and Sports

DIVING

For exciting diving and certification, try **Lucky Scuba Divers** (⊠ Mykonos town, ☎ 0289/22813). or **Psarou Diving Center** (⊠ Mykonos town, ☎ 0289/24808).

HORSEBACK RIDING

Equestrians will find a horseback-riding program—for the novice or expert—at the huge and luxurious **Aphrodite Beach Hotel** (⊠ Kalafati Beach, ☎ 0289/71367), where you have beach access.

TENNIS

The Kochyli Hotels (⊠ On hill above Mykonos town, ☎ 0289/22929 or 0289/22107) has courts. **Aphrodite Beach Hotel** (⊠ Kalafati Beach, ☎ 0289/71367) also has courts.

WATER SPORTS

Aphrodite Beach Hotel (⊠ Kalafati Beach, ☎ 0289/71367, ℻ 0289/71525) has water sports. The windy **northern beaches on Ornos Bay** are best for water sports; you can rent surfboards and take lessons.

There's windsurfing and waterskiing at **Ayios Stefanos**, **Plati Yialos**, and **Ornos**. The program at **Surfing Club Anna** (⊠ Agia Anna, ☎ 028971205) is well organized.

You can work out at the **Body Work Gym** (⊠ From taxi sq. go to Alexis Snack Bar and turn right), run by a Dutch couple.

Shopping

FASHION

Yiannis **Galatis** (⊠ Platia Manto, opposite LALAoUNIS, ☎ 0289/22255) has outfitted such famous women as Elizabeth Taylor, Ingrid Bergman, and Jackie Onassis. He will probably greet you personally and show you some of his coats and costumes, hostess gowns, and long dresses. He also has men's clothes. **Pan Boutiques** (⊠ 29 Matoyanni, ☎ 0289/24114) has designer clothes for men and women, especially from Calvin Klein and Armani. **Armonia** (⊠ Laka Sq., ☎ 0289/23930) carries a more risqué, racier selection of men's and women's fashions by such designers as Gottex, Plus Zero, Daniel Hechter, and Options.

FINE AND DECORATIVE ART

The **Mono Ena** Gallery of Contemporary Art (⊠ Megali Panagia in Little Venice, ☎ 0289/26869) is run by the dynamic Marina Petri, a Mykoniot artist who studied in London. Besides changing exhibitions of contemporary Greek artists, the gallery sells an interesting range of local artwork, ceramics, folk art with a contemporary twist, handmade cards, posters, and prints. In **Nikoletta** (⊠ Little Venice, ☎ 0289/27503), Mykonos's last traditional weaving shop, Nikoletta Xidakis sells her skirts, shawls, and spreads made from local wool. The **Mykonos Antiques Centre** (⊠ In garden of the Edem restaurant off Matoyanni, ☎ 0289/27597) offers traditional antiques and other objets d'art in a gallery-like setting.

JEWELRY

Ilias LALAoUNIS (⊠ 14 Polykandrioti, near taxi sq., ☎ 0289/22444, FAX 0289/24409) is known internationally for jewelry based on classic ancient designs, especially Greek. Silver bowls, candlesticks, and decorative objects—some with semiprecious stones—make perfect gifts. **The Gold Store** (⊠ On waterfront) is Mykonos's oldest jewelry shop.

SWEETS

Since 1921, Nikolaos Skaropoulos and family have been making traditional almond biscuits and almond milk at **Skaropoulos** (⊠ Pano Matoyanni, ☎ 0289/24983); now a number of confection shops carry them. Nikolaos's grandson claims that their cookies were a favorite of Winston Churchill. You can also visit the **factory** and **shop** (⊠ A short way up past Ano Mera turnoff on left).

Ano Mera

8 km (5 mi) east of Mykonos town.

Monastery buffs should head to Ano Mera, a village in the central part of the island, where the **Monastery of the Panayia Tourliani,** founded in 1580 and dedicated to the protectress of Mykonos, stands in the central square. Its massive baroque iconostasis (altar screen), made in 1775 by Florentine artists, has small icons carefully placed amid the wooden structure's painted green, red, and gold-leaf flowers. At the top are carved figures of the apostles and large icons of New Testament scenes. The hanging incense holders with silver molded dragons holding red eggs in their mouths show an eastern influence. In the hall of the monastery, an interesting **museum** displays embroideries, liturgical vestments, and wood carvings. ⊠ *On central sq.,* ☎ *0289/71249.* ☉ *By appointment only, call in advance.*

Delos

20- to 25-minute caïque ride from Mykonos.

The obvious question that arises regarding Delos is how such a small islet, with virtually no natural resources, could have become the religious and political center of the Aegean. The answer is that Delos, shielded on three sides by other islands, provided the safest anchorage for vessels sailing between the mainland and the shores of Asia.

The great Zeus fell in love with gentle Leto, the Titaness, and she became pregnant. When Hera discovered this infidelity, she forbade Mother Earth to give Leto refuge and ordered the serpent Python to pursue her. Poor Leto wandered the earth, and finally Poseidon, taking pity on her, anchored the floating island of Delos with four diamond columns to give her a place to rest. She gave birth first to Artemis, goddess of the hunt and virginity, and nine days later, to Apollo, god of truth and light, while Zeus looked down from nearby Mt. Kynthos.

By 1,000 BC the Ionians, who inhabited the Cyclades, had made Delos their religious capital, introducing the cult of Apollo. A Homeric hymn mentions this cult in the 7th century BC. A difficult period began for the Delians when Athens rose to power and developed aspirations to Ionian leadership, seeking to conquer the political and religious center. In 543 BC an oracle at Delphi conveniently decreed that the Athenians must purify the island by removing all the graves to Rhenea, a dictate designed to alienate the Delians from their past.

After the defeat of the Persians in 478 BC, the Athenians organized the Delian alliance, with its treasury and headquarters at Delos (in 454 BC the funds were transferred to the Acropolis in Athens). The Delians paid a yearly tax and supplied ships to the Athenian fleet in exchange for protection. A second "purification" was ordered in 426 BC, and in 422 Athens forced the entire population of Delos to move to Asia Minor. Delos had its second and perhaps greatest period in the late Hellenistic and Roman times, when an international merchant community grew up. It was declared a free port and quickly became the financial center of the Mediterranean, the focal point of trade, and a slave market, where 10,000 people were said to be sold every day. Foreigners from as far as Rome, Syria, and Egypt lived in this cosmopolitan port, in complete tolerance of one another's religious beliefs, and each group built its various shrines.

In 88 BC Mithridates, the king of Pontus, in a revolt against Roman rule, ordered an attack on the unfortified island. The entire population of 20,000—natives and foreigners—was killed or sold into slavery. Delos never fully recovered, and later Roman attempts to revive the island failed because of pirate raids. After 70 BC the island was gradually abandoned.

In 1872, the French School of Archaeology began excavating on Delos—a massive project, considering that much of the island's 4 sq km (1½ sq mi) is covered in ruins. Their work continues today.

⓫ On the left from the harbor is the **Agora of the Competialists** (circa 150 BC), members of Roman guilds, mostly freedmen and slaves from Sicily, who worked for Italian traders. They worshiped the *Lares Competales,* the Roman "crossroads" gods; in Greek they were known as Hermaistai, after the god Hermes, protector of merchants and the crossroads. The **Sacred Way,** east of the Agora, was the route, during the holy Delian festival, of the procession to the sanctuary of Apollo.

Delos

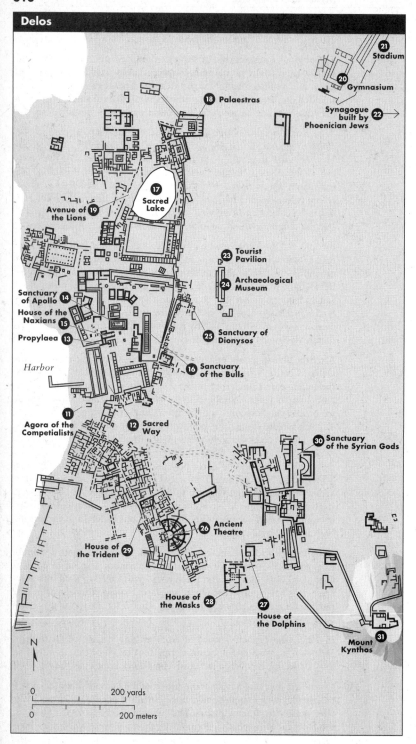

21 Stadium

20 Gymnasium

22 Synagogue built by Phoenician Jews →

18 Palaestras

17 Sacred Lake

19 Avenue of the Lions

23 Tourist Pavilion

24 Archaeological Museum

14 Sanctuary of Apollo

15 House of the Naxians

13 Propylaea

25 Sanctuary of Dionysos

16 Sanctuary of the Bulls

Harbor

11 Agora of the Competialists

12 Sacred Way

30 Sanctuary of the Syrian Gods

26 Ancient Theatre

29 House of the Trident

28 House of the Masks

27 House of the Dolphins

31 Mount Kynthos

N

0 — 200 yards

0 — 200 meters

⑬ The **Propylaea,** at the end of the Sacred Way, was once a monumental white marble gateway with three portals framed by four Doric
⑭ columns. Beyond the Propylaea is the **Sanctuary of Apollo;** though little remains today, when the Propylaea were built in the mid-2nd century BC, the sanctuary was crowded with altars, statues, and
temples—three of them to Apollo. Just inside the sanctuary and to the
⑮ right is the **House of the Naxians,** a 7th- to 6th-century BC structure
with a central colonnade. Items dedicated to Apollo were stored in this
shrine. Outside the north wall is a massive rectangular **pedestal,** once
supporting a colossal statue of Apollo (one of the hands is in Delos's
archaeological museum, and a piece of a foot is in the British Museum).
Near the pedestal a bronze palm tree was erected in 417 BC by the Athenians to commemorate the palm tree under which Leto gave birth. According to Plutarch, the palm tree toppled in a storm and brought the
statue of Apollo down with it.

⑯ Southeast of the Sanctuary of Apollo are the ruins of the **Sanctuary of
the Bulls,** an extremely long and narrow structure built, it is thought,
to display a trireme, an ancient boat with three banks of oars, dedicated to Apollo by a Hellenistic leader thankful for a naval victory. Maritime symbols were found in the decorative relief of the main halls, and
the head and shoulders of a pair of bulls were part of the design of an
interior entranceway. A short distance north of the Sanctuary of the
⑰ Bulls is an oval indentation in the earth where the **Sacred Lake** once
sparkled. It is surrounded by a stone **wall** that shows the original pe-
riphery. According to islanders, the lake was fed by the River Inopos
from its source high on Mt. Kynthos until 1925, when the water
stopped flowing and the lake dried up. Along the shores are two an-
⑱ cient **palaestras,** buildings for exercise and debate.

⑲ One of most evocative sights of Delos is the 164-foot-long **Avenue of
the Lions.** The five Naxian marble beasts crouch on their haunches, their
forelegs stiffly upright, vigilant guardians of the Sacred Lake. They are
the survivors of a line of at least nine lions, erected in the second half
of the 7th century BC by the Naxians. One was removed in the 17th
century and now stands before the Arsenal of Venice. Northeast of the
palaestras is a large square courtyard, nearly 40 meters (131 feet) long
⑳ on each side, which once was the **gymnasium.** The long, narrow struc-
㉑ ture farther northeast is the **stadium,** the site of the athletic events of
the Delian Games. East of the stadium site, by the seashore, are the re-
㉒ mains of a **Synagogue built by Phoenician Jews** in the 2nd century BC.

㉓ A road south from the gymnasium leads to the **tourist pavilion,** which
㉔ has a restaurant and bar. The **Archaeological Museum** is also on the
road south of the gymnasium; it contains most of the antiquities found
in excavations on the island: monumental statues of young men and
women, steles, reliefs, masks, and ancient jewelry. The museum keeps
the same hours as the site.

㉕ Immediately to the right of the museum is a small **Sanctuary of
Dionysos,** erected about 300 BC; outside it are several monuments dedicated to Apollo by the winners of the choral competitions of the Delian
festivals. Each is decorated with a huge phallus, emblematic of the
orgiastic rites that took place during the Dionysian festivals. Around
the base of one of them is carved a lighthearted representation of a
bride being carried to her new husband's home. A marble phallic bird,
symbol of the body's immortality, also adorns this corner of the
sanctuary.

㉖ Beyond the path that leads to the southern part of the island is the **ancient theater,** built in the early 3rd century BC in the elegant residential quarter inhabited by Roman bankers and Egyptian and Phoenician merchants. Their one- and two-story **houses** were typically built around a central courtyard, sometimes with columns on all sides, and they were floored with decorative mosaics, which channeled rainwater into cisterns below. The colorful mosaics show fantastical natural themes: panthers, birds, and dolphins; the best preserved can be seen in the **House ㉗ ㉘ ㉙ of the Dolphins,** the **House of the Masks,** and the **House of the Trident.** A dirt path leads east to the base of Mt. Kynthos, where there are re-㉚ mains from many **Middle Eastern shrines,** including the **Sanctuary of the Syrian Gods,** built in 100 BC. A flight of steps goes up (112 m/368 ㉛ ft) to the summit of **Mt. Kynthos** (after which all Cynthias are named), on whose slope Apollo was born. ⊠ *Delos island and historic site, take a caïque from Mykonos town,* ☎ *0289/22259.* ◺ *1,500 dr.* ☉ *Apr.–Oct., Tues.–Sun. 8:30–3.*

NAXOS

"Great sweetness and tranquillity" is how Nikos Kazantzakis, premier writer of Greece, described Naxos, and indeed a tour of the island leaves you with an impression of abundance, prosperity, and serenity. The greenest, most fertile of the Cyclades, Naxos, with its many potato fields, its livestock and its thriving cheese industry, and its fruit and olive groves framed by the pyramid of Mt. Zas (3,295 ft., the Cyclades' highest), is practically self-sufficient. Inhabited for 5,000 years, the island offers today's visitor memorable landscapes—abrupt ravines, hidden valleys, long sandy beaches—and towns that vary from a Cretan mountain stronghold to the seaside capital, strongly evoking its Venetian past.

Naxos Town

㉜ *7 hours by ferry from Piraeus; no service from Mykonos; 35 km (21¼ mi) east of Paros town.*

As your ferry chugs into the harbor, you see before you the white houses of Naxos town (Chora), the capital, on a hill crowned by the one remaining tower of the Venetian castle. The tiny church of **Our Lady of Myrtle** (⊠ Perched on a rock beside the waterfront) watches over the local sailors, who built it for divine protection.

Naxos's most famous landmark is the **Portara** (⊠ At harbor's far edge), a massive doorway that leads to nowhere. The Portara stands on the islet of **Palatia,** which was once a hill (since antiquity the Mediterranean has risen quite a bit) and in the 3rd millennium BC was the acropolis for a nearby Cycladic settlement. The Portara, an entrance to an unfinished Temple of Apollo that faces exactly toward Delos, Apollo's birthplace, was begun about 530 BC by the tyrant Lygdamis, who said he would make Naxos's buildings the highest and most glorious in Greece. He was overthrown in 506 BC and the temple was never completed; by the 5th and 6th centuries AD it had been converted into a church; and under Venetian and Turkish rule it was slowly dismembered, so the marble could be used to build the castle. The gate, built with four blocks of marble, each 5 meters (16 feet) long and weighing 20 tons, was so large it couldn't be demolished, so it remains today, along with the temple floor. Palatia itself has come to be associated with the tragic myth of Ariadne, princess of Crete.

Ariadne, daughter of Crete's King Minos, helped Theseus thread the labyrinth of Knossos and slay the monstrous Minotaur. In exchange, he promised to marry her. Sailing for Athens, the couple stopped in

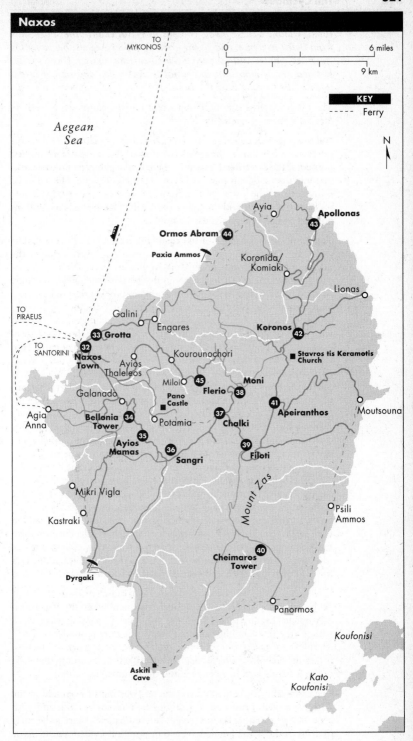

Naxos

TO MYKONOS

0   6 miles

0   9 km

KEY

------- Ferry

N

Aegean Sea

Ayia

Apollonas 43

Ormos Abram 44

Koronida/ Komiaki

Paxia Ammos

Lionas

TO PIRAEUS

Galini

Engares

Koronos 42

33 **Grotta**

32 **Naxos Town**

Ayios Thaleleos

Kourounochori

Stavros tis Keramotis Church

Miloi

45 **Flerio**

Moni

Galanado

38

Pano Castle

37

Apeiranthos 41

Moutsouna

Agia Anna

Bellonia Tower 34

Potamia

Chalki

Ayios Mamas 35

36 **Sangri**

39 **Filoti**

Mikri Vigla

Mount Zas

Psili Ammos

Kastraki

Cheimaros Tower 40

Dyrgaki

Panormos

Koufonisi

Askiti Cave

Kato Koufonisi

TO SANTORINI

Naxos, where Theseus, sailing away while she slept, abandoned her. Jilted Ariadne's curse made Theseus forget to change the ship's sails from black to white, and so his grieving father Aegeus, believing his son dead, plunged into the sea. Seeing her tears, smitten Dionysos descended in a leopard-drawn chariot to marry her, and set her bridal wreath, the Corona Borealis, in the sky, in eternal token of his love.

The myth inspired one of Titian's best-known paintings, as well as Strauss's opera, *Ariadne auf Naxos.*

Old town (✉ Along causeway to Naxos town, on left at first big sq.) possesses a bewildering maze of twisting cobblestone streets, arched porticoes, and towering doorways, where you're plunged into cool darkness and then suddenly into pockets of dazzling sunshine. The old town is divided into the lower section, **Bourgos**, where the Greeks lived during Venetian times, and the upper part, called **Kastro** (castle), still inhabited by the Venetian Catholic nobility.

You won't miss the gates of the **castle** (✉ Kastro). The south gate is called the **Paraporti,** but it's more interesting to enter through the northern gate, or **Trani** (strong), via Apollonos Street. Note the vertical incision in the gate's marble column—it is the Venetian yard against which drapers measured the bolts of cloth they brought the noblewomen. Step through the Trani into the citadel and enter another age, where around silent courtyards still stand sedate Venetian houses, emblazoned with their coats of arms and bedecked with flowers, the only sign of present-day occupants the drying clothes fluttering occasionally from a balcony. The citadel was built in 1207 by Marco Sanudo, a Venetian who, three years after the fall of Byzantium, landed on Naxos as part of the Fourth Crusade. For two months he laid siege to the Byzantine castle at t'Apilarou, and upon its downfall made Naxos the headquarters of his duchy. He divided the island into estates, distributing them to his officers, who built the *pirgi* (tower houses) that still dot the countryside. When in 1210 Venice refused to grant him independent status, Sanudo switched allegiance to the Latin Emperor in Constantinople, becoming Duke of the Archipelago. Under the Byzantines, "archipelago" had meant "chief sea," but after Sanudo and his successors, it came to mean "group of islands," i.e. the Cyclades. For three centuries Naxos was held by Venetian families, who resisted pirate attacks, introduced Roman Catholicism, and later rebuilt the castle in its present form. In 1564 Naxos came under Turkish rule, but even then, the Venetians still ran the island, while the Turks only collected taxes. The rust-colored **Glezos tower** was home to the last dukes; it displays the coat of arms: a pen and sword crossed under a crown.

Few Turks settled on Naxos, and those who did were in constant fear of the pirates, who preyed exclusively on them; when the War of Independence began in the 1820s, the only Turk remaining was a clerk who, at the first rumblings, sailed away. The only reminder of Turkish rule is a ruined fountain on the road from Naxos town to Engares; it was the lack of schools under Turkish rule that led to the founding of the Kastro's Ursuline convent and the commercial school.

The **cathedral** (✉ At the Kastro's center) was built by Sanudo in the 13th century and restored by Catholic families in the 16th and 17th centuries. The marble floor is paved with tombstones bearing the coats of arms of the noble families. Venetian wealth is evident in the many gold and silver icon frames. The icons reflect a mix of Byzantine and Western influences: The one of the Virgin Mary is unusual because it shows a Byzantine Virgin and Child in the presence of a bishop, a cathedral benefactor. Another 17th-century icon shows the Virgin of the

Rosary surrounded by members of the Sommaripa family, whose house is nearby.

The **convent and school of the Ursulines** (⊠ A few steps beyond cathedral) was begun in 1739. In a 1713 document, a General of the Jesuits, Francis Tarillon, mentions that the proposed girls school should be simple; grandeur would expose it to the Turks' covetousness. Over the years, extensions were added, and the Greek state has now bought the building for cultural purposes.

The **French School of Commerce** is marked by an escutcheon bearing a fleur-de-lis surrounded by the collar of the Order of the Holy Spirit. The school was run in turn by Jesuits, Lazarists, and Salesians. Under the latter it enjoyed its most distinguished period (1891–1927); the Cretan writer Nikos Kazantzakis attended the school for two years. Its library, archives, and opulent furnishings were destroyed during the German–Italian occupation, but it's easy to imagine rows of schoolboys running to class as you enter its vast, cool halls.

Today the Convent and school of the Ursulines (☞ *above*) houses the **archaeological museum,** best known for its Cycladic and Mycenaean finds. During the Early Cycladic period (3200 BC–2000 BC), there were settlements along Naxos's east coast and just outside Naxos town at Grotta. The finds are from these settlements and graveyards scattered around the island. Many of the vessels exhibited are from the Early Cycladic I period, made of coarse-grained clay, sometimes decorated with a herringbone pattern. Gradually, the variety of shapes and decoration increased—new forms appeared, such as candlesticks, wine pourers, and sauce boats with spiral patterns, fish, or the typical many-oared boat. One common shape is known as the "frying pan," though archaeologists are uncertain of its use. Some believe it held water and served as a mirror; others think that skins were stretched across the pan to make a drum for funeral processions.

Though the museum has too many items in its glass cases for a short visit, you should try not to miss the white marble Cycladic statuettes, which range from the early "violin" shapes to the more detailed female forms with their tilted flat heads, folded arms, and legs slightly bent at the knees. The male forms are slightly more complex and often appear sitting. Again, some archaeologists have suggested these correspond to heroes and nymphs; others believe they represent such divinities as gods of fertility and were meant to protect the dead on their journey to the underworld.

A period of notable prosperity in Naxos was the Late Mycenaean period (1400 BC–1100 BC), and much of the museum's collection comes from a Mycenaean settlement near Grotta. The finds include seal rings, false-necked amphoras, water pitchers with sculpted snakes, and many vessels with the octopus motif, the spaces between the tentacles filled with designs of plants and animals. In the museum's courtyard there is a mosaic pavement from a 3rd-century AD house depicting a Nereid astride a bull rising from the sea. ⊠ *Kastro,* ☎ *0285/22725.* ⌑ *500 dr., free Sun.* ☉ *Tues.–Sun. 8:30–3.*

The **Greek Orthodox cathedral** (⊠ Bourgos) was built in 1789 on the site of a church called Zoodochos Pigis (Life-giving Source). The cathedral was built from the materials of ancient temples: The solid granite pillars are said to be from the ruins of Delos. Amid the gold and the carved wood, there is a vividly colored iconostasis painted by a well-known iconographer of the Cretan school, Dimitrios Valvis, and the Gospel Book is believed to be a gift from Catherine the Great of Russia.

Excavations of the ruins of the **agora,** the center of the ancient city, have revealed a 167-foot-by-156-foot square closed on three sides by Doric stoas, so that it looked like the letter "π". A shorter fourth stoa bordered the east side, leaving room at each end for an entrance. The *heroon* (shrine for a hero) and bases for statues stood in front of the stoas; the inscriptions recovered indicate Artemis was worshiped here.

Beaches

Venture past Chora's beach, **Ayios Georgios,** to the long, mostly sandy stretches farther south. **Ayios Prokopios** has a small leeward harbor. Ayios Prokopios gives way to the small cape of **Ayia Anna. Plaka,** ringed by sand dunes and bamboo groves, is about 8 km (5 mi) south of town. **Mikri Vigla** is sandy and edged by cedar trees. **Kastraki,** with its creamy white marble sand, is due south of Mikri Vigla.The next south is **Pyrgaki,** with idyllic crystalline water.

Dining and Lodging

$$$ ✕ **The Old Inn.** Dieter Ranizewski, a trained chef and instructor of chefs from Berlin, has built his "dream place," maybe the best in the Cyclades. In a courtyard under a chinaberry tree, with rough whitewashed walls and bits of ancient marble, two of the old church's interior sides open into the wine cellar and gallery; on the fourth side, with beams and wood paneling, is a fireplace, handy for the winter months. The menu is extensive; for starters you might try smoked ham, jellied pork, or liver paté—all homemade. For entrées, Berlin liver with apples and onions, and the fresh trout with almonds and parsleyed potatoes, are especially good. For dessert the homemade red forest–berry jelly with vanilla cream beckons voluptuously. Kids love both the small playground with miniature merry-go-round and the children's menu. ✉ *Naxos town, up car rd. around the town, 2 alleys in on right from waterfront,* ☎ *0285/26093,* ⅁ *028923325. No credit cards.*

$$ ✕ **I Apothiki tou Ballidras/Kraemerladen.** Though the service may be slow, this taverna is worth the wait, for the traditional and local specialties you don't usually find. After the fried zucchini appetizer, for instance, sample the *boxa* (lamb, mountain greens, and a lemon sauce cooked slowly in a ceramic pot) or the *kouneli krasato* (rabbit in red wine). Most dishes come with the island's delicious potatoes, lightly covered with olive oil and dill. I Apothiki also serves fresh fish, some non-Greek dishes, and several of the well-known local cheeses like the salty *kefalograviera* and a creamy, almost sweet, *mizithra*—perfect after your meal. ✉ *Naxos town waterfront,* ☎ *0285/24242. MC, V.*

$$ ✕ **Nikos.** Don't be fazed by the 30-pound fish hanging in the glass case, along with eels, sharks, and other edible marine denizens. Step inside this fine Greek restaurant, with prompt service and enthusiastic clientele. Start your meal with *kakavia* (a delicate fish soup made from small catch); for an entrée, you might try the *bitock* (beefsteak with an egg on top) or hearty macaroni with bite-size octopus chunks. *Fasolia mavromatika* (black-eyed peas) cooked in fragrant olive oil, and fava dip are good side dishes. The wine list is long and varied, with Cycladic and Italian selections. Finish off your meal with a piece of Greek apple pie. ✉ *Chora waterfront above Commercial Bank,* ☎ *0285/23153 or 0285/23381,* ⅁ *0285/23379. V.*

$$ ✕ **O Kontos.** If you're staying at Orkos Village or visiting the Plaka, stop here for a bite. Proprietor Maria Salteri-Antoniou runs the spacious kitchen like home. The main dish might be an irresistible plate of *ambelo-fasolia* (green beans cooked in oil), *kokkinisto* (beef in red sauce), or grilled fish basted in lemon and oil: red mullet, *sargos* (bream), and *lithrinia* (pandora). The good barrel retsina usually runs out by summer, but ask anyway. She also serves breakfast. ✉ *Central*

Rd. between Orkos and Mikri Vigla beaches, south of Chora, ☎ *0285/75278. No credit cards.*

$ ✕ **Meltemi.** Mihalis Mathiassos's restaurant is typically Greek, with fluorescent lighting and plastic-wrap tablecloths, but it is by the sea and set among vines. It's known locally as the place to go for inexpensive Greek staples like souvlaki, lamb *exohiko* (cooked in paper with vegetables), barbecued fillets of Mihalis's daily catch, and pans and pans of *gigantes* (giant white beans in olive oil) and *tsoutsoukakia* (meat patties made from spicy sausage). *Kaloyero* (eggplant with ham and béchamel) is a bit more unusual. The crème caramel is heavenly. The gentlemanly, ever-so-jaded waiters are fast and efficient, even when the place is packed. ✉ *Chora waterfront, at other end of dock,* ☎ *0285/ 22654. No credit cards.*

$ ✕ **Panorama.** This seaside taverna is ideal for those frequenting the popular Ayia Anna beach, just south of town. The easygoing crowd ranges from German couples with dreadlocks to local patriarchs twirling their worry beads. In the large shaded terrace with blue-and-white checked tablecloths, you can get a hefty lamb chop sprinkled with oregano, crisp roast chicken, or fresh fish barbecued over charcoal, all well cooked and low priced. The messy but delicious crab, served in a mustard-lemon-olive oil sauce, is an especially good deal, and another great appetizer is the garlicky *tzatziki* (a yogurt dip). A breakfast of omelets, yogurt with honey, toast, and coffee is also served. ✉ *Beach Rd. south into Ayia Anna from Chora. No credit cards.*

$$$ 🏨 **Chateau Zevgoli.** Each room in this fairy-tale pension, in a comfortable
★ Venetian house, is different. The living room is filled with dark antique furniture, gilded mirrors, old family photographs, and locally woven curtains and tablecloths. One of the nicest bedrooms has a private bougainvillea-covered courtyard and pillows handmade by Despina's great-grandmother; the honeymoon suite has a canopy bed, a spacious balcony, and a view of the Portara. Rooms can sometimes be had off-season for half price. The owner, Despina Kitini, also owns several charming studios in Chora old town; you can get details at her EOT in the harbor (☞ Visitor Information *in* The Cyclades A to Z, *below*). ✉ *Chora old town (follow signs stenciled on walls), 84300,* ☎ *0285/22993 or 0285/24358,* 🖷 *0285/25200;* ☎ *Athens: 01/651–5885. 10 rooms with showers. Breakfast room. No credit cards.*

$$$ 🏨 **Galaxy.** As you approach this hotel, it seems to shimmer in the distance, all whitewash and marble. Its three buildings rather resemble grand pueblos, except that they have wide stone arches; wooden doors in shades of green, purple, and turquoise; and balconies with grillwork depicting swans. Archways also span the large rooms, which have beamed ceilings and trim orange accessories, plants, kitchenettes, dining areas, telephones, and cable TV. Most rooms have ocean views (the beach is about 10 minutes away); all have balconies. Though mostly shadeless, the carefully tended grounds are a pleasure, with yellow roses and a fountain. ✉ *Ayios Georgios Beach, 84300,* ☎ *0285/22422 or 0285/22423,* 🖷 *0285/22889. 54 rooms with bath. Snack bar, air-conditioning, pool, playground. V.*

$$$ 🏨 **Lianos Village.** Yannis Lianos, a Naxian, has just built an attractive resort that imitates the Cycladic village style he grew up with. A 10-minute walk from Ayios Prokopios beach, it has island furnishings, very private rooms with magnificent sea views across the straits to Paros, immaculate and unobtrusive service, and heavenly quiet. A restaurant is nearby. The bus stops here twice a day. ✉ *Ayios Prokopios beach, 84300,* ☎ *0285/26366, 0285/23865, and 0285/26361,* 🖷 *0285/26362. 30 rooms with bath. Bar, café pool. V.*

$$$ ⊞ **Orkos Village.** When Norwegian doctor Kaare Oftedal first saw Orkos beach years ago, he fell in love with the almost isolated strand ringed by sand dunes and cedars. Today he returns from Norway every spring to open his small, popular hotel, whose guests seem perfectly content never to leave their idyllic surroundings to go to town. The hotel's white cubist bungalows that stagger down the hillside to the sea's edge are simply furnished and decorated (dried flowers and blue wooden shutters just about covers it). They all have sea views and verandas; a few have an additional sitting area. Guests love to hang around the friendly stone bar, where the doctor's wife Katerina leads Greek dances and serves up classic Greek meals, and to ramble downhill to the beach. The hotel shuttle bus is infrequent. ⊠ *Orkos beach between Plaka and Mikri Vigla, 84300,* ☎ *0285/75321,* FAX *0285/75320 (Nov.–Mar.* ☎ *Norway: 033/28888,* FAX *033/10954). 26 rooms with bath. Restaurant, bar, kitchenettes. No credit cards.*

$$ ⊞ **Iria Beach.** Maria Refene's hotel is right on the beach, and echoes
★ Chora's old town, with its stucco arches, peaceful nooks and crannies, sunlit courtyard, and bright red and blue shutters. The reception area is quite luxurious, with its huge glass doors, cool marble floor, and brass details. The owners have eschewed the usual Greek hotel furniture for unlacquered wood with a gray wash and an interior color scheme of light blue, gray, and white for the spacious one- and two-room apartments. Guests always enjoy hanging out in the shady beach bar and restaurant. ⊠ *Ayia Anna, 84300,* ☎ *0285/24178, 0285/24022, and 0285/24023,* FAX *0285/23419 and 0285/24656. 21 rooms with bath, 4 apartments . Restaurant, bar, kitchenettes. MC.*

$ ⚇ **Camping Apollon.** This site sits near windsurfers' hangouts about 3 km (2 mi) outside Naxos town. It has a friendly staff, and many of the sites have excellent views of the Kastro. The camp arranges transfers from town in its buses. ⊠ *Between Ayios Georgios and Ayios Prokopios, 84300,* ☎ *0285/24117, 0285/24117, 0285/22372, and 0285/23330,* FAX *0285/23419. Tent sites. Bathrooms, showers, cafeteria.*

$ ⚇ **Maragas.** Opt for this site if a better beach means more to you than proximity to town. ⊠ *Ayia Anna, 84300,* ☎ *0285/24552. Tent sites.*

Nightlife

BARS

Nightlife in Naxos is quieter than it is on Santorini or Mykonos, but there are several popular bars at the south end of Chora. **Veggera** (⊠ Chora waterfront near Ayios Georgios Beach, ☎ 0285/23567) has a garden that's a respite from the rap and rock music inside. Next door to Veggera, in a small white house, **Ecstasis** (⊠ Chora waterfront near Ayios Georgios Beach) has a spacious bar, happy hours, strong drinks, all kinds of music from surf to blues, and a terrace overlooking the sea. For Greek music try the **Greek Bar** (⊠ On Chora waterfront, ☎ 0285/24675).

Outdoor Activities and Sports

SAILING

To rent a sailboat, contact the **Rental and Travel Center** (⊠ Chora, ☎ 0285/23395 or 0285/23396); call the port authority (☎ 0289/22300) for information about where to go in Chora for gas, water, and repairs.

TENNIS

The **Mathiassos Village Hotel** (⊠ Just outside new section of Chora, ☎ 0285/22200) has a court open to the public.

WATER SPORTS

At **Ayios Prokopios** and **Ayia Anna** beaches the wind and water conditions are ideal for inexperienced windsurfers, and there are also waterskiing equipment rentals, and instruction for both sports. Jet skis can also be rented at **Ayios Prokopios.** The Mikri Vigla hotel complex has a **windsurfing center** (⊠ South of Chora, ☎ 0285/75241 or 0285/75242), but experienced windsurfers prefer **Kastraki, Pyrgaki, Moutsouna,** and **Agiassos beaches,** where wind speeds can reach 7 on the Beaufort scale.

Shopping

BOOKS

At Eleftherios Primikirios' **Zoom** (⊠ Chora waterfront, ☎ 0285/23675 or 0285/23676) there's an excellent selection of English-language history and picture books about Naxos. Zoom also has another shop (⊠ On cemetery sq., ☎ 0285/24357).

FOOD, WINE, AND LIQUEUR

A large selection of the famous *kitro* (citron liqueur) and preserves, as well as Naxos wines and thyme honey, packed in attractive gift baskets, can be found at **Promponas Wines and Liquors** (⊠ Chora waterfront, ☎ 0285/22258), which has been around since 1915. Free glasses of kitro are always offered.

TRADITIONAL KNITS, JEWELS, AND LINENS

The embroidery and knitted items made by women in the mountain villages are known throughout Greece; they can occasionally be bought in a Chora tourist shop like **Old Market Naxos** (⊠ Old Town, ☎ 0285/24767) or from villagers hawking their wares in front of tourist sites. For a wide selection of old designs for jewelry, linens, household items, and so forth, try **Techni,** which has three shops (⊠ Near entrance to Chora's old town, ☎ 0285/24767 or 0285/25673).

JEWELRY

For a large selection of beautiful jewelry, try **Midas** (⊠ Old Town, up the main st. behind Pampronas on the Chora waterfront, ☎ 0285/24852); Midas also has a smaller store (⊠ On waterfront, ☎ 0285/26291). The owner, Fotis Margaritis, creates talismans in different settings that feature a "Naxos eye," which is the operculum, or door, of a seashell the fishermen bring him, with a spiral design. The workshop-gallery of **Angelos V** (⊠ Exarchopolou, Old Town, ☎ 0285/23187) sells one-of-a-kind pieces distinguished by their fluid shape and bold design.

MARBLE

Since ancient times the island has been lauded for its marble. For an unusual gift, pick up some tiles, art items, or designs for a marble fireplace at **Naxos Marble** (⊠ Chora new town).

En Route On your way to Bellonia, on the main road from Naxos town, you'll go southeast past Galanado, and drive through the reeds, cacti, and plains of the Livadi Valley.

Grotta

❸❸ *Just a few steps east of Naxos town.*

Grotta flourished from the 7th to the 6th centuries BC, and for a time, Naxiots were the administrators of the Delos sanctuary. Wealthy Naxos was an early leader in marble sculpture: The famous Delos lions and several large kouroi were done here. Gifts from Naxian donors were found in many sanctuaries of that period, such as the temple of Apollo at Delphi and the temple of Athena on the acropolis at Athens.

That was the time of the oligarchs, known as the *pacheis* (fat ones), after which one-man rule was established by Lygdamis during the latter 6th century BC. When he was overthrown, the Persians destroyed the island in 490 BC and sold off the inhabitants as slaves. Naxos came under Athenian rule in 471, and never recovered its former splendor. The island passed successively from Macedonian to Egyptian to Rhodian rule, and in 41 BC became a Roman province. When the Romans were succeeded by the Byzantines in the 5th century, Naxos regained some importance as the seat of the provincial governor who controlled one-third of the Aegean. Then, after the fall of Constantinople in 1204, the Byzantines lost the island to the Venetians, as mentioned above.

In Grotta you can sometimes see **underwater remains of Cycladic buildings** strewn along an area of about 39 meters (130 feet), a series of large worked stones, perhaps the remains of the mole, and a few steps that locals say go to a tunnel leading to the islet of Palatia.

Bellonia Tower

❸❹ *5 km (3 mi) south of Naxos town.*

The graceful **Bellonia tower** (Pirgos Bellonia) belonged to the area's ruling Venetian family, and like other fortified houses, it was built as a refuge from pirates and as part of the island's alarm system. The towers were located strategically throughout the island; if there was an attack, a large fire would be lit on the nearest tower's roof, setting off a chain reaction from tower to tower and alerting the islanders. Bellonia's thick stone walls, its lion of St. Mark emblem, and flat roofs with zigzag chimneys are typical of these pirgi. The unusual 13th-century **"double church" of St. John** (⊠ In front of Bellonia tower) exemplifies Venetian tolerance. On the left side is the **Catholic chapel,** on the right, the **Orthodox church,** separated only by a double arch. A family lives in the tower and the church is often open. From here, take a moment to gaze across the peaceful fields to Chora and imagine what the islanders must have felt when they saw pirate ships on the horizon.

Ayios Mamas

❸❺ *8 km (5 mi) south of Naxos town, 3 km (1¾ mi) south of Bellonia Tower.*

A half mile past a valley with unsurpassed views is one of the island's oldest churches (9th-century), Ayios Mamas. St. Mamas is the protector of shepherds and is regarded as a patron saint in Naxos, Cyprus, and Asia Minor. Built in the 8th century, the stone church was the island's cathedral under the Byzantines. Though it was converted into a Catholic church in 1207, it was neglected under the Venetians and is now falling apart. You can also get to it from the Potamia villages.

Sangri

❸❻ *11 km (7 mi) south of Naxos town, 3 km (1¾ mi) south of Ayios Mamas.*

Sangri is the center of an area with so many monuments and ruins spanning the Archaic to the Venetian periods, it is sometimes called "little Mystras." The name Sangri is a corruption of Sainte Croix, which is what the French called the town's 16th-century monastery of **Timios Stavros** (Holy Cross). The town is actually three small villages spread across a plateau. During the Turkish occupation, the monastery served as an illegal school, where children met secretly to learn the Greek language and culture. Above the town, you can make out the **ruins of t'Apilarou** (⊠ On Mt. Profitis Ilias), the castle Sanudo first attacked.

Chalki

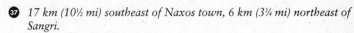 *17 km (10½ mi) southeast of Naxos town, 6 km (3¾ mi) northeast of Sangri.*

You are now entering the heart of the lush Tragaia Valley, where in spring the air is heavily scented with honeysuckle, roses, and lemon blossoms, and many tiny Byzantine churches hide in the dense olive groves.

Chalki is home to one of the most important of these Byzantine churches: the white, red-roof **Panayia Protothrone** (First Enthroned Virgin). Restoration work has uncovered frescoes ranging from the 6th through the 13th centuries, and the church has remained alive and functioning for 14 centuries. The oldest layers, in the apse, depict the Apostles. ✉ *On main rd.* ☉ *Mornings.*

Chalki itself is a pretty town, known for its neoclassical houses in shades of pink, yellow, and gray, which are oddly juxtaposed with the plain but stately 17th-century Venetian **Frangopoulos tower.** ✉ *Main rd., next to Panayia Protothrone.* ☉ *Sometimes in the morning.*

Moni

23 km (14¼ mi) east of Naxos town, 6 km (3¾ mi) north of Chalki.

At Moni is one of the Balkans' most important churches, **Panayia Drosiani,** which has rare Byzantine frescoes from the 6th and 7th centuries. Its name means Our Lady of Refreshment, because once during a severe drought, when all the churches took their icons down to the sea to pray for rain, only this church's icon got results. The frescoes are visible in layers: To the right when you enter are the oldest—one shows St. George the dragon slayer astride his horse, along with a small boy, an image one usually sees only in Cyprus and Crete. According to legend, the saint saved the child, who had fallen into a well, and there met and slew the giant dragon that had terrorized the town. Opposite him is St. Dimitrios, shown killing barbarians. The church is made up of three chapels—the middle one has a space for the faithful to worship at the altar rather than in the nave, as was common in later centuries. Next to that is a very small opening that housed a secret school during the revolution. Walk to the back of the church for a view of its odd configuration; the undulating curves are reminiscent of a Gaudi building. If the church is closed when you arrive, ring the bell loudly, and a local woman who is usually in the fields or in town will come to open it; it's usually open mornings and again after siesta.

Filoti

20 km (12½ mi) southeast of Naxos town, 6½ km (4 mi) south of Moni.

Filoti, a peaceful village on the lower slopes of Mt. Zas, is the interior's largest. Nothing much seems to happen here, but if you're lucky, you may see a festive bridal procession. According to custom, the groom, accompanied by musicians, goes to the bride's house to collect her and her family, and then the party strolls through the village picking up well-wishers. A three-day festival celebrating the Dormition starts on August 4. In the center of town is another Venetian tower that belonged to the Barozzi, and the main church with its fine marble iconostasis and carved bell tower.

Hiking

Filoti is better known as the starting place for several walks in the countryside, for example, the climb up to **Zas Cave,** where obsidian tools and pottery fragments have been found; beware, there's lots of bats inside! Mt. Zas, or Zeus, is one of the god's birthplaces; on the path to the summit lies a block of unworked marble that reads *Oros Dios Milosiou,* or "boundary of the temple of Zeus Melosios." (Melosios, it's thought, is a word that has to do with sheep.) The islanders say that under the Turks the cave was used as a chapel, and two stalagmites are called the Priest and the Priest's wife, who are said to have been petrified by God to save them from arrest. It's best to ask directions for the start of the path (⊠ Southeast of town off a small dirt track).

40 For less determined walkers and hikers, there is a flatter 3½-hour walk with excellent views of the island, which culminates at the **Cheimarros Pirgos** (Tower of the Torrent), a cylindrical Hellenistic tower preserved up to 13 meters (45 feet), with marble blocks perfectly aligned. The tower, which also served as a lookout post for pirates, is often celebrated in the island's poetry: "O, my heart is like a bower/And Cheimarros's lofty tower!" The bad dirt road, drivable by Jeep, begins from the main road to Apeiranthos, just outside Filoti.

NEED A BREAK?	Take a frappé, the Greek version of iced coffee, break under the plane tree at **Gratzias** *kafenion* (traditional Greek coffeehouse) (⊠ Filoti's Sq.), where the owner's name and the date of its founding (1926) are inscribed over the doorway, so you don't confuse it with the other two competing kafenia.

Apeiranthos

41 *32 km (20 mi) southeast of Naxos town, 12 km (7½ mi) northeast of Filoti.*

Apeiranthos is very picturesque, with fine views and marble-paved streets running between the Venetian Bardani and Zevgoli towers. As you walk through the arcades and alleys, notice the unusual chimneys—no two are alike. The elders sit in their doorsteps chatting, while packs of children shout "Hello, hello" at any passerby who looks foreign.

A very small archaeological **museum,** established by a local mathematician, Michael Bardanis, displays Cycladic finds from the east coast. The most important of the artifacts are unique gray marble plaques from the 3rd millennium BC, with roughly hammered scenes of daily life: hunters and farmers and sailors going about their business. If it's closed, ask in the square for the guard. ⊠ *Off main sq.* ☎ *Free.* ☉ *8:30–3.*

The villagers of Apeiranthos have always been considered somewhat a breed apart because they are of Cretan origin. Indeed, travel literature of the late 1800s mentions that other islanders hesitated to travel in the north, fearing the thievery of Apeiranthiotes! Today the local dialect still resembles Cretan, and the people preserve many Cretan traditions, like the singing of *kotsakia* (rhyming eight-syllable couplets that praise virtue and condemn infidelity, desertion, and the like):

Oh, you have made me lose my mind
And babble in the street;
My love is such that I dissolve
Whene'er we chance to meet.

During festivals, the singing often develops into a poetic contest between boisterous bards. Apeiranthos also has a strong weaving tradition; most families have their own loom, and until recently the women made clothing for their families, along with decorative tablecloths and curtains. Although these last are usually not for sale, more and more often you may find women spreading out their wares for tourists near the local sights.

Moutsouna

39 km (24¼ mi) southeast of Naxos town, 7 km (4½ mi) east of Apeiranthos.

A steep paved road from Apeiranthos cuts down to the coast at Moutsouna, a small bay with a few houses and a beachside taverna.

Beaches

The road south of Moutsouna follows the coast and leads to a number of small, deserted coves perfect for swimming. **Psili Ammos** ("fine sand"), with white dunes and sandy beaches, is the best, but it's 7 km (nearly 5 mi) south of Moutsouna, and the unpaved road requires a Jeep.

Koronos

㊷ *36 km (23½ mi) east of Naxos town, 4 km (2½ mi) north of Apeiranthos.*

The paved road from Apeiranthos, winding and narrow in places, passes through the lovely village of Koronos, which tumbles spectacularly down the green mountainside. On the right you come to the **Stavros tis Keramotis church,** the only point from which you can see both the east and west coasts of Naxos.

Apollonas

㊸ *54 km (33½ mi) northeast of Naxos town, 12 km (7½ mi) north of Koronos via road from Komaki.*

Apollonas is a small resort town on Naxos's northeast corner. Look for the steps leading to the unfinished 35-foot **kouros** of Apollonas, which lies in an ancient quarry. It's thought to represent Dionysos. Initially, the Greeks represented gods with small idols, but after the Homeric epics, the gods were seen as anthropomorphic, though much larger than a tall man, and were depicted by these giant, highly stylized statues. This early 6th-century kouros was probably abandoned because cracks developed in the marble while the work was in progress. It lies on its back, eroded by the winds, but still, somewhat eerily, in the shape of a bearded man. ⊠ *On main rd. past Apollonas, on the left.* ☏ *Free.*

Beaches

In the far northeast, **Apollonas** is a spread-out beach with small white marble pebbles. Much more rewarding are the **bays** of Abram, Ayias Mamas, Xilia Brisi, and **Paxia Ammos,** small sand beaches to the west that are seldom crowded. Most of these can be reached by bus.

Dining and Lodging

$$$ ✕ **Apollon.** In Apollonas the pickings are slim, and this is the best of the tavernas encircling the harbor. Between frying potatoes and garnishing Greek salads, the sweet-faced grandmother-chef can often be found sitting down to chat (or gesture) with customers or joining a table of local women stringing garlic in the corner. Her food is basic—fresh fish such as red mullet, *paidakia* (bite-size lamb chops) with oregano and dolmades. ⊠ *Apollonas waterfront,* ☏ *0285/81324. No credit cards.*

$–$$ ⌸ **Flora's.** The apartments and rooms at Flora's, the best bet in Apollonas, overlook the owner's fields and the tiny bay below. To get to the hotel, you must cross the potato patch, fording irrigation rivulets, which can be a bit annoying. But the spacious apartments all have marble floors, comfortable beds, and pine furniture. Most have a bedroom and a sitting area, and are large enough for a family of four, but no maid service is provided. ⊠ *Above waterfront, Apollonas 84300,* ☎ *0285/81270. 9 rooms with bath. Kitchenettes, coin laundry. No credit cards.*

Ayia

2½ km (1½ mi) west of Apollonas.

The partially unpaved coast road from Apollonas to Naxos town passes, in a lush valley, the **Ayia tower,** once a lookout post for northwestern Naxos. At the nearby church, during the feast of the Dormition (August 15), women who had taken a vow to the Virgin used to attend the service after walking barefoot from Apollonas along the rough paths.

Beaches
The road from Apollonas to Chora runs along steep cliffs, traversing
❹❹ inlets and secluded beaches; the most accessible is **Ormos Abram,** 5 km or 3 mi from Apollonas, which is pleasant when the north winds aren't blowing, and has a pension and taverna.

Flerio

❹❺ *12 km (7½ mi) east of Naxos town.*

The island's second famous **kouros** is at Flerio, in the Melanes valley, which, although smaller (8 meters/26 feet), is more detailed and lies in a beautiful private orchard; it has become one of Naxos's more popular sights. The silent kouros, like Ozymandias, is a reminder of a once-glorious age. Archaeologists think the 6th-century statue was abandoned either because the artist made a mistake or because the client who commissioned it died. Also, when the tyrant Lygdamis came to power, he confiscated all the orders of the rich that were still in the quarries. When he couldn't find a way to dispose of some of the kouroi, he tried to sell them back to former owners. ⊠ *On right just before small white shack; through small gate.* ☎ *Free.* ☉ *May–Oct., daily 8–sunset.*

NEED A
BREAK?
> After seeing the kouros, relax in the **garden** (⊠ On right before small white shack), among bougainvillea and lilac, and order the local family's homemade kitro preserves or a shot of citron liqueur.

PAROS

Paros lacks the chic of Mykonos and has fewer top-class hotels, but at the height of the season it often gets Mykonos's overflow, and people are delighted by the island's lower prices, golden sandy beaches, and charming fishing villages. It is large enough to accommodate the traveler in search of peace and quiet, yet the port towns of Paros town (also called Parikia) and Naousa also have an active nightlife. Paros town is a focal point of the ferry network, and many people stay here for a night or two while waiting for a connection. It's particularly good for bars and discos, though Naousa has a more authentic island atmosphere.

Paros Town

35 km (21¾ mi) west of Naxos town, 10 km (6¼ mi) southwest of Naousa.

One of your first impressions of Paros town will be the many travel agencies dispensing information on the waterfront and a multitude of car and motorbike rental agencies nearby. If you walk east on the harbor road you will see a lineup of bars, fast-food restaurants, and cof-

fee shops—some owned by Athenians who come to Paros to capital-
ize on tourism during the summer. Past them are the bus stop, fishing-
boat dock, ancient graveyard, and post office; then the beaches start.
The better restaurants and the shopping district are in the interior of
the town, where it is easy to get lost in the maze of narrow, stone-paved
streets that intersect with the streets of the quiet residential areas.
Though the tourist culture has not blended in as smoothly as it has on
Mykonos, and Paros has looked neglected in the past, much restoration work, especially in the area around the great church, has recently
been undertaken.

The splendid square above the port, to the northwest, was built in 1996
to celebrate the church's 1,700th anniversary. From there you will see
a white gate, the front of the former monastic quarters that surround
★ the magnificent **Panayia Ekatontapyliani** (Hundred Doors) church, the
earliest remaining Byzantine church in Greece. According to legend,
99 doors have been found in the church and the 100th will be discovered
only after Constantinople is Greek again. Inside, the subdued light mixes
with the dun, reddish, and green tufa. The columns are classical and
their capitals Byzantine. At the corners of the dome are two fading Byzantine frescoes depicting six-winged seraphim. The 6th-century iconostasis (with ornate later additions) is divided into five frames by marble
columns. One panel contains the just-restored 14th-century icon of the
Virgin, with a silver covering from 1777. The Virgin is carried in procession on the church's crowded feast day, August 15, the Dormition.
The adjacent **Baptistery** has a marble font, and bits of mosaic floor.

In 326, Saint Helen, the mother of the emperor Constantine the Great,
took ship for the Holy Land to find the True Cross. Stopping on Paros,
she had a vision of success, and vowed to build a church. She found
it, and died. Her son built the church in 328 as a wooden-roof basilica. Two centuries later Justinian the Great, who ruled the Byzantine
Empire in 527–565, had it splendidly rebuilt with a dome. He appointed
Isidorus, one of the two architects of Constantinople's famed Ayia Sophia,
to design it; Isidorus sent an apprentice, Ignatius, to Paros. Upon its
completion Isidorus arrived in Paros for an inspection and found such
a magnificent church that, consumed by jealousy, he pushed the young
apprentice off the top of the dome. Ignatius grasped his master's foot
as he fell, and the two tumbled to their death together. Two folk sculptures by the toilets at sanctuary's Baroque left portal portray them as
two fat men, one pulling his beard with remorse and the other holding his cracked head. The church **museum**, at right, contains fine post-
Byzantine icons. ✉ *250 meters east of the dock,* ☎ *0284/21243.* 🖻
Free. ☉ *Daily 8–1 and 4–9.*

The **Archaeological Museum** is another must-see site on Paros. It contains a fragment of the famed Parian chronicle, which recorded cultural events in Greece from about 1500 BC until 260 BC (a larger
section is in the Ashmolean Museum in Oxford). What has interested
scholars is the fact that the historian inscribed valuable information
about only the lives of artists, poets, and playwrights, completely ig-
noring wars and shifts in government. Some primitive pieces from the
Aegean's oldest settlement, Saliagos (an islet between Paros and Antiparos), are exhibited in the same room, to the left.

In the large room to the right rests a marble slab depicting the poet
Archilochus in a banquet scene, lying on a couch, his weapons nearby.
The ancients ranked Archilochus, who invented iambic meter and wrote
the first signed love lyric, second only to Homer. When he died in bat-
tle against the Naxians, his conqueror was cursed by the oracle of
Apollo for putting to rest one of the faithful servants of the muse. Also

there are a monumental Nike, and three superb just-found pieces: a waist-down kouros, a gorgon, and a dancing-girl relief. ⊠ *Behind Church of a Hundred Doors,* ☎ *0284/21231.* ⊡ *500 dr.* ☉ *Tues.–Sun. 8:30–2:30.*

Beaches

Pounda Beach is packed with young sun worshipers. Sometimes the beaches on the waterfront in Paros town get murky owing to their proximity to the port. From Paros town boats leave throughout the day for beaches across the bay: to sandy **Krios** or the quieter **Kaminia.**

Dining and Lodging

$$$ ✕ **Kalakonas Restaurant.** This restaurant is a bit hard to find, and—despite good food and a romance atmosphere—it is rarely crowded. Greek specialties predominate the extensive menu. To begin, the Parian country sausages are tasty, as is the marinated crayfish, mussels, and clams dish. Sure bets for entrées are chicken livers in white wine and oregano, pork in wine sauce, pasta, and fresh fish. For dessert treat yourself to an ice cream sundae in a cantaloupe half. If you go for lunch, take your bathing suit for a dip in the bay. ⊠ *Across Paros Bay, between Livadia and Krios,* ☎ *0284/22751. MC, V.*

$$$ ✕ **Porphyra.** For the most civilized dining on Paros, Porphyra is unique
★ in the islands because the owner farms his own shellfish in Paros's pellucid waters (his two tall sons are both divers and waiters); the fresh oysters, shell of Venus, clams, and cockles are Aegean-sweet. His wife Roula cooks; her mussels Provençal are a great favorite. Fresh fish, fish salads, and local seasonal vegetables round out the menu. And where else can you taste sea-urchin salad or marinated ray? The inside, popular in winter, is simple and authentic. ⊠ *Paros town (along waterfront toward post office),* ☎ *0284/22693. AE, MC, V.*

$$$–$$$$ ▨ **Xenia Hotel.** If you want a good night's sleep away from the pulse of Paros town, but you don't want to give up shopping, nightlife, restaurants, and cafés, the Xenia is the best choice. Built on a hill with a splendid view overlooking Paros Bay, the hotel's lobby looks like an enormous living room, with low, cushioned seats around circular wooden tables, a stone fireplace with antique key chains, and a cozy bar. The veranda off the lobby is perfect for sunset watching. The rooms are sparsely decorated; half have balconies. ⊠ *East of Paros town, up hill at Ayia Anna church, 21009,* ☎ *0284/21394,* ☎ *Athens: 01/360–5611,* ℻ *0284/23501. 24 rooms with bath or shower. Bar, breakfast room. AE, MC, V.*

$ ⚠ **Camping Koula.** Though you're near a beach, expect large crowds here. ⊠ *About 1 km (½mi) northwest of Paros town's harbor, 84400,* ☎ *0284/22082. Tent sites. Bathrooms, hot showers, snack bar.*

$ ⚠ **Parasporos.** This site is newer and larger than Camping Koula. ⊠ *One mi south of Paros town, 84400,* ☎ *0284/21100. Tent sites. Bathrooms, hot showers.*

Nightlife and the Arts

MUSIC AND BARS

Turn right along the waterfront from the port in Paros town to find Paros's famous bars; then follow your ears. But **Evinos** and **Pebbles** (⊠ On the Kastro hill) play classical and overlook the sunset. **Pirate** (⊠ Market St.) is partial to jazz and blues.

At the far end of the Paralia is the laser-light-and-disco section of town, which you may want to avoid. In the younger bars, cheap alcohol, as everywhere in tourist Greece, is often added to the more colorful drinks. **Delfini** (⊠ A 15-min walk south from Paros town and on the beach) often presents passing or local bands, and Japanese food in the afternoon.

The **Aegean Center for the Fine Arts** (⊠ At end of Market St., Paros town, ☎ ⨍⨍ 0284/23287) periodically stages readings and exhibitions of students' work. It is run by John Pack, an American photographer who lives on the island with his family, and since 1966 the center has offered courses in writing, painting, and photography, among other disciplines; it even takes a group to Tuscany.

The **Archilochos Cultural Society** (⊠ Near bus stop, behind Splash disco, ☎ 0284/23595) runs a film club in winter, stages art exhibitions during the summer, and offers a program of concerts and lectures throughout the year. Watch for posters.

Outdoor Activities and Sports

GYM

To stay in shape, Fotis Skiadas's well-appointed **Gymnasium** (⊠ Hotel Zanet, near Livadia beach, ☎ 0284/22233), for aerobics and body-building, is air-conditioned and has a sauna.

HORSEBACK RIDING

For riding along the coast **Time Riding Center** (⊠ Livadi, Paros town, ☎ 0284/23408) has fine animals; it costs 5,000 dr. for 1½ hours.

MOUNTAIN BIKING

For organized mountain-bike tours (one includes Naxos) and rental, there's **Hellas Bike Travel** (☎ 0284/52010, ⨍⨍ 0284/51720).

WATER SPORTS

Many of the Paros beaches have various water sports, especially wind-surfing. Every summer the **F2 Windsurfing Center** (⊠ New Golden Beach, at Philoxenia Hotel, near Marpissa, ☎ 0284/41878) hosts the **International Windsurfing World Cup.**

Shopping

JEWELRY

Vangelis Skaramangas and Yannis Xenos have been making their own delicate, precious jewelry at **Jewelry Workshop** (⊠ Paros town, at the far end of Market St., ☎ 0284/21008) for 15 years.

TEAS, HERBS, AND SPICES

Teapot (⊠ On an alley off middle of Market St., ☎ 0282/21177) sells locally gleaned spices, teas, and herbs—perfect lightweight gifts.

En Route Halfway from Paros town to Naousa, on the right, the 17th-century **Monastery of Longovarda** shines on its mountainside; these days only seven monks reside there. The monastic community farms the local land, and makes honey, wine, and olive oil. Only men, dressed in conservative clothing, are allowed inside, where there are post-Byzantine icons, 17th-century frescoes depicting the Twelve Feasts in the Life of Christ, and a library of rare books; it's usually closed.

OFF THE BEATEN PATH

ANTIPAROS – On the small island of Antiparos, southwest of Paros, an enormous cave descends 70 meters (230 feet) into the earth. Even in August, travelers will feel damp and chilly as they descend the 400 cement steps into the cave. Famous visitors have carved their names on the walls, including Lord Byron and King Otho, the King of Greece in 1840. On three occasions the French ambassador, Count M. de Nouantelle, celebrated midnight mass here, using an enormous truncated stalagmite as an altar. At its base is this inscription: HIC IPSE CHRISTUS / EJUS NATALIE DIE MEDIA CELEBRATO / MDCLXXIII (Here midnight mass was celebrated on Christmas, 1673). Islanders claim an older inscription that has been lost was written by runaways who had been wrongfully accused of attempting to assassinate Alexander the Great and were hiding in fear of retribution. Boats from Paros town take passengers directly to the landing stage on the shore below the cave, and drivers wait there with donkeys for those who want a ride up the hill of St. John to the cave's entrance. Or go to Pounda and take the car ferry across—a 5-minute ride.

Naousa

10 km (6¼ mi) northeast of Paros town.

Naousa, impossibly pretty, long ago discovered the benefits of tourism. Its outskirts are mushrooming with villas and hotels that exploit it further. Along the harbor, red and navy-blue boats knock gently against one another as fishermen repair their nets and foreigners relax in the ouzeries—Barbarossa being the traditional favorite—by the water's edge. Navies of the ancient Persians, flotillas from medieval Venice, and the imperial Russian fleet have anchored in this harbor. The half-submerged ruins of the Venetian fortifications still remain, and they are even more intriguing in the evening when they are lit.

Beaches

There are a number of spots from which to swim along the bay east of Naousa. Boats go to **Lageri Bay** (⊠ North of Naousa), a long sandy beach with dunes. Boats stop at **Santa Maria** (⊠ Northeastern shore of Paros), the windsurfers' beach. Boats also buzz to **Kolimbithres** (⊠ In Lageri Bay west of Naousa), famous for its rock formations, with water sports, a choice of tavernas, and several luxury hotels. Take a boat to **Ayios Ioannis** (⊠ On small western peninsula of Lageri Bay), though only if you want a nudist beach.

Dining and Lodging

$$$ ✕ **Lalula.** The delicious Mediterranean cooking and fine service here
★ induce repeat dining. You'll be soothed by the mood music, small garden, calming aqua walls, and subdued lighting. The menu changes, but the chicken liver paté with pink peppercorns and onion confiture hors d'oeuvre and the butterfly shrimp fried in sesame sauce are unforgettable. Vegetarians are also spoken for here. The daily fixed-price menu is a good deal at 3,000 dr. ⊠ *Naousa, opposite Minoa Hotel* ☎ *0284/51547. Reservations essential in August. No credit cards.*

$$$ ✕ **Taverna Christos.** Christos has been improving yearly for 20 years—
★ no wonder it's so good! In a spacious garden in the heart of Naousa, Christos is bright and fresh, with graceful service and good Mediterranean cuisine. Excellent first courses include *haloumi* (fried Cypriot cheese with fresh tomato and basil) and sautéed baby squids in a delicate wine sauce. The sole with almonds and butter entrée is also exceptional. The pasta dishes are cheaper and yummy. For dessert, a specialty is prunes stuffed with walnuts and topped with cream. ⊠ *Naousa, up hill from central sq.,* ☎ *0284/51442. AE, V. Closed Nov.–mid-May.*

$$$$ 🏨 **Astir of Paros.** Across the bay from Naousa twinkle the lights of this luxurious resort hotel, along with the Porto Paros (☞ *below*). This is more elegant and expensive, with greener lawns, palm trees, gardens, an art gallery. Rooms are prettier and more spacious—perfect for romantic couples—with antiques, artwork, and views of the sparkling Naousa Bay. Its Greek restaurant is excellent. ⊠ *Take Kolymbithres Rd. from Naousa, 84400,* ☎ *0284/51976 or 0284/51984,* FAX *0284/51985. 57 rooms with bath (suites and doubles). Restaurant, bar, air-conditioning, refrigerators, freshwater pool, sauna, miniature golf, tennis court, exercise room, windsurfing, waterskiing, baby-sitting, laundry service. AE, DC, MC, V.*

$$$$ ☷ **Porto Paros.** This resort, 1 km (⅔ mi) from the Astir of Paros, has a better beach, out of the north wind; and more organization, and it is perfect for families. Exposed stone echoes the spectacular rock formations of the area. Rooms are simply furnished, with marble bathrooms, balconies, and phones, and most have sea views; challenge yourself with the excellent sports facilities. It is served by an hourly boat from Naousa. ⊠ *Kolymbithres Rd. going from Naousa to Parikia, 84400,* ☎ *0284/52010 or 0284/52017,* FAX *0284/51720. 191 rooms (suites and doubles). Restaurant, bar, air-conditioning, refrigerators, freshwater pool, beauty salon, 5 tennis courts (2 floodlit), surfing, jet skiing, waterskiing, laundry service. AE, MC, V.*

$$$ ☷ **Sovronos Bungalows.** These bungalow apartments always seem to be full. The owner and his daughter tend the garden, and the comfortable rooms and Cycladic whitewashed courtyards are decorated with antiques and objects from his extensive travels. This is convenient and quiet, with easy access to Naousa's lively shopping and nightlife. Breakfast is included. ⊠ *Behind big church, 1 block in from Santa Maria Rd., Naousa 84400,* ☎ *0284/51211 or 0284/51409,* FAX *0284/52281. 20 apartments with bath. Bar. No credit cards.*

$ ⚠ **Santa Maria Campgrounds.** This site is a ½-hour walk from Naousa, with lots of great accommodations. ⊠ *Santa Maria beach, Naousa 84400,* ☎ *0284/51013 or 0284/52420* FAX *0284/51937. Tent sites. Bathrooms, hot shower, taverna, pool, grocery, volleyball, windsurfing, jet skiing, pool, laundry room, public phone.*

Nightlife and the Arts

BARS

The bar, **Leonardo's** (⊠ Fishing harbor), is lively and is open into the wee hours. **Agosta** (⊠ Fishing harbor) is a pretty spot.

DANCE

The group **N.E.L.E.** (☎ 0284/51082 or 0284/51480), formed in 1988 to preserve the traditional dances and music of Paros, performs all summer long in Naousa in the costumes of the 16th century and has participated in dance competitions and festivals throughout Europe. Keep an eye open for posters, or ask travel agents about times and locations of performances.

Outdoor Activities and Sports

WATER SPORTS

Also popular is the **Santa Maria Surf Club** (⊠ Santa Maria beach, about 4 km/2½ mi north of Naousa), with windsurfing, jet skis, waterskiing, and diving.

Shopping

LOCAL JEWELRY AND ART

Metaxas gallery (⊠ On second st. from harbor toward main church, Naousa, ☎ 0284/52667) shows painting, photography, sculpture, and especially jewelry, all done by Paros residents. One of the jewelers, Gregory Altamirano, makes his elegant designs in his workshop (⊠ Near Monastery of Saint Andreas), with a splendid view overlooking Naousa Bay.

Marathi

10 km (6¼ mi) east of Paros town.

During the Classical period the island of Paros had an estimated 150,000 residents, many of them slaves who worked the ancient marble quarries in Marathi. The island grew rich from the export of this white, granular marble known among ancient architects and sculptors for its ability to absorb light. They called it *lychnites* ("won by lamplight").

Marked by a sign, **three caverns** (⊠ A short walk from the main rd.) are bored into the hillside, the largest of them 91 meters (300 feet) deep. The most recent quarrying done in these mines was in 1844, when a French company cut marble here for Napoleon's tomb.

Shopping
LOCAL CRAFTS
At Stelios and Monique Ghikas' **Yria Studios** (⊠ 3 km/1¾ mi east of Marathi, in mountains above Kostos village, ☎ 0284/29007) potters and other craftsmen can be seen at work; also done there are book design, house decoration, industrial design, flower arrangements, paintings—it is a true Renaissance workshop. Both the ceramic tableware and the works of art make use of Byzantine and Cycladic motifs in their designs, and some pieces incorporate Parian marble. Many organized tours stop here, or you can take a bus or taxi, or drive.

Lefkes

10 km (6¼ mi) southeast of Paros town, 6 km (3¾ mi) south of Marathi.

Rampant piracy in the 17th century forced thousands of people from the coastal regions to move inland; thus for many years the scenic village of Lefkes, built on a hillside in the protective mountains, was the island's capital. It remains the largest village in the interior and has preserved a peaceful, old European feeling, with narrow streets fragrant of jasmine and honeysuckle. Farming is a major source of income, as you can tell from the maintained stone walls and olive groves.

Two **17th-century churches** of interest are **Ayia Varvara** (St. Barbara) and **Ayios Sotiris** (the Savior). The big 1830 neo-Renaissance **Ayia Triada** (Holy Trinity) is the village's pride.

Beaches
Piso Livadi (⊠ On rd. past Lefkes) was the ancient port for the marble quarries and today is a small resort town at the center of Paros's main beach colony.

Lodging
$$$ ⌂ **Lefkes Village.** All island-style rooms in this elegant new hotel have
★ magnificent views down the olive-tree valley and over the sea to Naxos. The lobby is tasteful and comfortably simple. The restaurant is noted for its traditional Greek food; the small folk museum makes for an interesting exploration. ⊠ *Just east of Lefkes on the main rd., 84400,* ☎ *0284/41827 through 24158,* FAX *0284/41827. 20 rooms with bath. Restaurant, bar, air-conditioning, refrigerators, pool. AE, DC, MC, V.*

Shopping
On the way to the little main square, near the café with olive-wood tables, are several **weaving shops.**

WEAVING
In the little weaving shop named for her, **Anna Kritikou** (⊠ In Lefkes, on the main st.) has her loom set up and makes everything she sells: elegant bedspreads, rag rugs, and donkey saddlebags, the first two most practical for gift ideas.

Petaloudes Park

4 km (2½ mi) south of Paros town.

A species of moth returns year after year to mate in Petaloudes (the Valley of the Butterflies), a lush oasis of greenery in the middle of this dry, barren island. In May, June, and perhaps July, you can watch them as they lie dormant during the day, their chocolate-brown wings with yellow stripes still against the ivy leaves. In the evening they flutter upward to the cooler air, flashing the coral-red undersides of their wings as they rise. A notice at the entrance asks visitors not to disturb them by taking photographs or shaking the leaves. ⊠ *Petaloudes.* 🎫 *300 dr.* ⊙ *9–8. Closed Oct.–mid-May.*

NEED A
BREAK?

Even when the "butterflies" are not there, it is pleasant to have coffee in the small **kafenion** (⊠ Inside entrance to park) and enjoy the shade of the cypress, olive, chestnut, mulberry, and lemon trees.

On the summit of a hill just beyond the garden reigns a lopped **Venetian tower.** Its founder's name, Iakovos Alisafis, and the date 1626, are inscribed on it. It's said that during the Ottoman period, when the Turks ruled Paros from Istanbul, appearing once a year to collect taxes, the lack of a continuous military presence allowed piracy to spread, and Algerian corsairs raided south Paros. The 12 Alisafis brothers barricaded themselves in their castle with a large supply of food and access to a secret spring outside the tower, but when the pirates discovered the spring, the brothers knew they were doomed. They killed their sister rather than let her be taken and waged a valorous battle before they were killed.

En Route A 15-minute walk back toward Paros town from the Valley of the Butterflies leads to the convent known as **Christos sto Dasos** (Christ of the Wood), where there's a marvelous view of the Aegean. The convent contains the tomb of Ayios Arsenios (1800–1877), who was a schoolteacher, an abbot, and a prophet; the Parians say he was also a rainmaker and that his prayers ended a long drought and saved Paros from starvation. The nuns are a bit leery of tourists. If you want to go in, be sure to wear long pants and a shirt that covers your shoulders, or the sisters will offer you makeshift black-and-white striped skirts that look like prison uniforms.

Alyki

12 km (7½ mi) south of Paros town, 8 km (5 mi) south of Petaloudes.

Southern Paros is more sparsely inhabited. South of the airport, in the less touristy seaside village of Alyki, fishermen can be seen at sunrise in the distant sea, hauling in the day's catch.

Beaches

The **town's beach** is popular among the locals. Some think the nearby beach of **Farangas** is the prettiest on the island.

The island's longest beach is **Chrysi Akti** (Golden Beach) (⊠ 3 km/1¾ mi east of Dryos), with fine sand and sparkling, clear waters.

Outdoor Activities and Sports

TENNIS

You can rent courts at the **Holiday Sun Hotel** (⊠ Pounda, ☎ 0284/91284 and 91285, 🕿 0284/91288), which also has an exercise room and sauna.

SANTORINI

Santorini is undoubtedly the most extraordinary island in the Aegean, and thus it's dreadfully crowded in summer. Arriving by boat you are met by one of the world's truly breathtaking sights, the **caldera**: a crescent of cliffs, striated in black, pink, brown, white, and pale green, rising 335 meters (1,100 feet), with the white clusters of the towns of Fira and Oia perched along the top. The encircling cliffs are the ancient rim of a still-active volcano, and you are sailing east across its flooded caldera.

Santorini and its four neighboring islets are the fragmentary remains of a larger landmass that exploded in about 1625 BC: The core of the island volcano blew up, and the sea rushed into the abyss to create the great bay, which measures 10 km by 7 km (6 mi by 4 mi) and is 394 meters (1,292 feet) deep. The other island pieces of the rim, which broke off in later eruptions, are Thirassia, home to a few hundred people, and deserted, little Aspronissi ("The White One"). In the center of the bay, black and uninhabited, are two still-smoldering cones, the "Burnt Isles" of Palea Kameni and Nea Kameni, which appeared between 1573 and 1925. The ancients called Santorini's island group Strongyle ("Round One") and Kalliste ("Most Beautiful"); the island was named Thera, and it still officially is. Its medieval name of Santorini (a corruption of Santa Irene) is more common.

There has been a great deal of speculation about the possible identification of Santorini with the mythical Atlantis, mentioned in Egyptian papyri and discussed by Plato (who says it's in the Atlantic), but myths are hard to pin down. This is not true of arguments about whether or not tidal waves from Santorini's cataclysmic explosion destroyed the Minoan civilization on Crete. The latest carbon-dating evidence clearly indicates that the Minoans outlasted the eruption by a couple of hundred years.

Since antiquity, Santorini has depended on rain collected in cisterns for drinking and irrigation—the well water is mostly brackish—and the serious shortage is alleviated by the importation of water from elsewhere. The fertile volcanic soil produces small, intense tomatoes with tough skins used for tomato paste; the famous Santorini fava beans, which have a light, fresh taste; barley; wheat; pistachio nuts; and white-skinned eggplants. The locals say that in Santorini there is more wine than water, and it may be true; wine is the island's largest export. The volcanic soil, high daytime temperatures, and humidity at night produce 36 varieties of grape, and these unique growing conditions are ideal for the production of a strong red wine that is gaining international recognition. Farmers twist the vines into a basketlike shape, in which the grapes grow, protected from the wind.

Fira

46 *10 km (6¼ mi) west of the airport, 14 km (8½ mi) southeast of Oia.*

Tourism, the island's major industry, adds more than 1 million visitors per year to its population of 7,000. As a result, Fira, the capital, midway along the west coast of the east rim, is no longer just a picturesque town but a major tourist center, overflowing with discos, shops, and restaurants. Many of its employees don't speak a word of Greek; they are young travelers extending their summer vacations.

The modern Greek Orthodox cathedral of **Panayia Hypapantis** (✉ Southern part of town) is a major landmark; the local priests, with somber faces, long beards, and black robes, look strangely out of place in summertime Fira. Along **Eikostis Pemptis Martiou** (25th of March St.) (✉

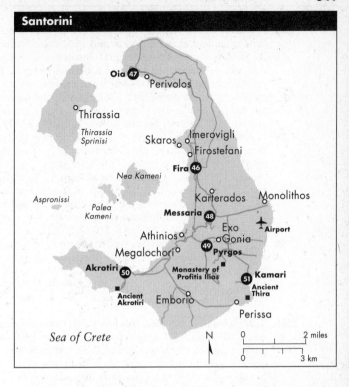

East of Panayia Hypapantis) is where you'll find inexpensive restaurants and accommodations. The blocked-off Hypapantis Street (⊠ West of Panayia Hypapantis) leads to **Kato Fira** (Lower Fira), built into the cliff side overlooking the caldera, where prices are higher and the vista wonderful. For centuries the people of the island have been digging themselves rooms with a view right in the cliff face—many bars and hotel rooms have actually been made out of caves—which lowers building costs and provides constant temperatures.

The **Ghyzis Palace,** Fira's cultural museum, is housed in a restored 17th-century mansion once owned by the Catholic church. The collection includes old maps, engravings, photographs, and paintings by 20th-century Greek artists. ⊠ *Stavrou and Ioannis Sts.,* ☎ *0286/22244 or 0286/22721.* ☑ *500 dr.* ☉ *Tues.–Sun. 8:30–3.*

The **Archaeological Museum** displays an interesting collection of pottery, statues, and grave artifacts found at excavations on the island (mostly from Ancient Thira), which represent the Archaic, Classical, Hellenistic, Roman, and Byzantine periods. ⊠ *Stavrou and Nomikos Sts.,* ☎ *0286/22217.* ☑ *800 dr.* ☉ *Tues.–Sun. 8:30–3.*

OFF THE BEATEN PATH

NEA KAMENI – If you'd like to peer down into a live, smoldering volcano, join one of the popular excursions to Nea Kameni, the larger of the two Burnt Isles. After disembarking, you hike 131 meters (430 feet) to the top and walk around the edge of the crater, wondering if the volcano is ready for its fifth eruption in this century—after all, it has been quite some time since the last, in 1956. Tours are scheduled regularly (☞ Contacts and Resources *in* The Cyclades A to Z, *below*).

Dining and Lodging

$$$ ✕ **Kastro.** There's very little here that's authentically Greek, but the expansive outdoor dining area is usually packed and festive throughout the evening. European dishes reign: Danish or Russian caviar and prosciutto with melon can even be paired with Dom Perignon. You can have your filet mignon prepared in seven ways, and five different scrumptious soufflés have been dreamed up. Grilled shrimp, lobster, and swordfish are sold by the kilo. The upstairs cafeteria serves American breakfasts and fast food. ✉ *Ayios Ioannis Walkway,* ☎ *0286/22503. AE, MC, V.*

$$ ✕ **Archipelago.** The food at this restaurant is delicious, the inside dreary. But if you arrive early, there may be room on the small balcony overlooking the caldera. Try "the Archipelago" of shredded chicken, ham, corn, cheese, and a special dressing. "Something like ratatouille" is a traditional dish called *briam* (eggplants, tomatoes, and olive oil). Another good entrée is the *yiartou* (meatballs and yogurt served in a warmed pita). ✉ *Entrance on Hypapantis Walkway, (take staircase down),* ☎ *0286/23673. AE, DC, MC, V.*

$$ ✕ **Nicholas.** This is Santorini's oldest taverna, where you'll find locals in winter. Island dishes are prepared well and served in a simple, attractive room. Try the yellow lentils and, for a delicious entrée, the lamb fricassee with an avgolemono sauce. ✉ *2 sts. in from cliff side on Erythrou Stavrou, Fira. No credit cards.*

$$$$ 🏨 **Aiglialos Houses/Villas.** This new hotel (1995) mixes tradition with
★   modern comfort and luxury perfectly. Ocher neoclassic cubes are juxtaposed with classic white Cycladic ones, with neoclassic details. The one-, two-, or three-bedroom "villas," with cooking facilities, marble bathrooms, and balconies, also have terraces overlooking the incredible caldera. There's satellite TV and maid service twice daily. ✉ *South end of Hypapantis Walkway (left from Hotel Atlantis), Fira 84700,* ☎ *0286/25191 through 25195,* ℻ *0286/22856. 16 villas with bath. Bar, air-conditioning, kitchenettes, refrigerators, pool, spa. AE, MC, V.*

$$$$ 🏨 **Hotel Aressana.** The only drawback to the Aressana is that it's behind another major hotel and has no view of the volcano. Its advantages are its freshwater pool (with classical music piped in) and its location, a short walk from Fira's business district. If you want a spanking-new room with white tile floors, a balcony, and a spotless bathroom, this is a good bet. ✉ *South end of Hypapantis Walkway, Fira 84700,* ☎ *0286/23900 or 0286/23901,* ℻ *0286/23902. 50 rooms with bath. Bar, freshwater pool. AE, DC, MC, V.*

$$$$ 🏨 **Hotel Atlantis.** One of the oldest, most distinguished, and most expensive hotels in Santorini, the Atlantis is perched on Fira's volcanic rim, and most of the rooms have balconies. The floors and staircases are white marble; the curtains and walls depict lush bamboo shoots and cheerful flowers. Unfortunately, beer for Fira's bars is delivered outside the hotel in the wee hours of the morning. ✉ *South end of Hypapantis Walkway, Fira 84700,* ☎ *0286/22232 or 0286/22111,* ℻ *0286/22821. 25 rooms with bath. Bar, cafeteria. AE, MC, V.*

$$$ 🏨 **Panorama Hotel.** From the cliff side of Fira, this lofty, white hotel provides a breathtaking view of the caldera from every room, all with balconies. There's a great roof garden. A travel desk in the reception area can book tours, rent cars, and exchange money. ✉ *Hypapantis Walkway, Fira 84700,* ☎ *0286/22481,* ℻ *0286/23179. 23 rooms with bath. Café, air-conditioning, travel services. AE, MC, V.*

$$ 🏨 **Delphini II.** Owner-manager Vassilis Rousseas says he has "prices for everyone." Delphini II has spacious apartments, all different in architecture and decor, which once were village homes. (Ask to see the one with the old stove.) ✉ *Down hill in front of Atlantis Hotel, Fira*

84700, ☎ 0286/22780. *7 studios and apartments with bath. Kitchenettes or refrigerators. No credit cards.*

$–$$ ⊡ **Delphini I.** Vassilis's other property, Delphini I (☞ *above*), is less expensive and has no views. ⊠ *Near hospital, Fira 84700,* ☎ *0286/22780. 10 rooms with bath. Refrigerators. No credit cards.*

Nightlife and the Arts

DISCO

Bar 33 (⊠ Fira, ☎ 0286/23065) has bouzouki music and a celebratory atmosphere. And the **Koo Club** (⊠ Fira, ☎ 0286/22025) is Fira's most popular outdoor disco by far.

MUSIC

As the sun sets on the caldera, **Palia Kameni** (⊠ Fira, ☎ 0286/22430) is the relaxing place to go for well-selected jazz, classical, and passionate Greek music. Try a strawberry margarita or one of the other reasonably priced drinks. **Franco's Bar** (⊠ Fira) plays calm, classical music.

FESTIVAL

The **International Santorini Music Festival** (⊠ Estis Hall, ☎ 0286/22220) takes place in late August–early September. The performance schedule, including internationally known musicians, is announced during the summer and posted about town.

Outdoor Activities and Sports

SAILING

The **Santorini Sailing Center** (⊠ Merovigli, ☎ 0286/23058, ☎FAX 0286/23059) arranges charters and runs weekly 2- to 3-day sailing trips around the Cyclades for groups up to 10.

TENNIS

The **Santorini Tennis Club** (⊠ Santorini Tennis Club Hotel, Kartaradoes, ☎ 0286/22122) has two concrete courts where two can play in high season for the equivalent of $6.50 per hour; it's open Apr.–Oct.

The **Santorini Image Hotel** (⊠ Messaria, middle of island, ☎ 0286/31874 or 0286/31875) also has a court.

Shopping

LOCAL LIQUEURS

Kava Liquor Store (⊠ Aghiou Ioannou) carries 10 kinds of ouzo, including the sweet Canava from Santorini and a local brand in a hand-painted bottle, and 12 kinds of Metaxa (another Greek liqueur)—not to mention the numerous Santorini wines.

JEWELRY

Kostas Antoniou Jewelry (⊠ Ayios Ioannou, ☎ 0286/22633). *Vogue* and *Marie Claire* have taken photographs of the pieces displayed in this shop, which is a favorite among cruise-ship passengers. Imagine the magnificence of solid gold necklaces named Earth's Engravings, Ritual, and Motionless Yielding! Antoniou also carries a selection of Van Cleef & Arpels watches from Paris. Thankfully, they take plastic (AE, MC, V).

Oia

★ ㊼ *80 km (50 mi) southeast of Paros town (with a ferry connection on Ios), 14 km (8½ mi) northwest of Fira.*

At the tip of the northern horn of the island sits Oia (pronounced and sometimes spelled Ía), Santorini's second-largest town and surely the most beautiful settlement in the Aegean. Marked by a cultural taste that Fira lacks, Oia's cubical white houses stand out against the green, brown, and rust-color layers of rock, earth, and solid volcanic ash that rise from the sea. Every summer evening, travelers from all over the world congregate at the caldera's rim—sitting on whitewashed fences, staircases, and beneath the town's windmill—each looking out to sea in anticipation of the performance: the Oia sunset. The two-hour rim-edge walk from Oia to Fira at this hour is unforgettable.

In the middle of the quiet caldera, the volcano smolders eerily away, adding an air of suspense to an already awe-inspiring scene. Its most recent eruption, in 1956, caused tremendous earthquakes (7.8 on the Richter scale) that left 48 people dead and hundreds injured, and top-pled 2,000 houses. The island's west side—especially Oia, until then the largest town—was hard hit, and many residents emigrated to Athens, Australia, and America. And although Fira, also damaged, rebuilt rapidly, the people from Oia proceeded slowly, sticking to the traditional architectural style. The perfect example of that style is the restaurant 1800, a renovated ship-captain's villa (☞ Dining and Lodging, *below*).

Beaches

There are no beautiful beaches close to Oia, but if you hike down Oia's cliff side, you can catch a bus to the small sand beach of **Baxedes** (⊠ Port of Armoudhi).

Dining and Lodging

$$$ ✕ **1800.** The goal here is to revive the special homelike atmosphere
★ of a captain's house. Indeed this historic Venetian-style building, with tall windows and a cathedral ceiling, was owned by a sea captain. It was abandoned after the 1956 earthquake until its purchase (with an-tique furniture intact) and restoration a few years ago. Try the zucchini pie with onions, eggs, and cheese, or the veal cooked in tomato sauce and served with smashed eggplant. There's occasional live music, with flute and oboe duets. ⊠ *Main St., central Oia,* ☎ *0286/71485. AE, DC, MC, V.*

$$$ ✕ **Kyklos.** This restaurant invites you to explore its intersecting cav-erns, with arched ceilings, black slate floors, and no windows. Try the appetizer plate of varied dips made from local yellow lentils, eggplant, and garlic with yogurt. The *graviera* cheese dipped in beer, floured, and fried crisp is worth the calories, and the Santorini lamb with rosemary is delicious. ⊠ *Follow signs,* ☎ *0286/71145. V.*

$$$–$$$$ 🏨 **Atlantis Villas.** Each "villa" is actually built inside a cave in Oia's
★ cliff face, making this one of the most unusual and dramatic places to stay in the world. The caves, linked into a small complex by steep walk-ways, are quiet, always cool, and furnished with traditional woven rugs and curtains. They all have private balconies fitted with umbrellas, and a glorious view, 183 meters (600 feet) up, across the caldera. As you watch the sunset, you'll agree it's hard to beat this hotel anywhere in the Cyclades. ⊠ *Oia cliff face, just before main town,* ☎ *0286/71214 or 0286/71236,* ℻ *0286/71312. 20 apartments with bath. Kitch-enettes, refrigerators, saltwater pool, laundry service. AE, MC, V.*

$$$–$$$$ 🏨 **Eagle's Nest, Artemis, Apollo, and Athena.** These four traditional villas, originally part of a Traditional Settlement of the EOT, have been renovated by Cycladic Environments, an American architectural-preser-vation firm. The villas have arched ceilings and balconies and can sleep from two to six people; one has a pool. They have been done in a charm-ing vernacular style, with handicrafts and stippled walls, prints, and colored handwoven rugs. ⊠ *On the cliff side. Reservations: Box 352622, Cambridge, MA 02238–2622,* ☎ *800/719–5260,* ℻ *617/492–5881. 6 double rooms with bath. Kitchenettes.*

$$$–$$$$ 🏨 **Oia's Sunset.** This modern hotel looks like a castle made from miniature Cycladic chapels. The rooms, decorated in traditional style, all have balconies. ⊠ *Near main sq., Oia 84700,* ☎ *0268/71420 or 0268/71490,* FAX *0286/71421. 8 rooms with bath, 7 two-bedroom apartments. Pool. AE, MC, V.*

Nightlife

BARS

In Oia, sophistication and architectural splendor are the selling points of the **1800** bar and restaurant (☞ *above*). Those in search of a happy-hour beer go to **Zorba's** (⊠ On the cliff side).

Shopping

This is the best town for finding locally crafted items. The inhabitants are sophisticated, and here you will find the best art galleries, antiques shops, crafts shops, and stores that sell reproductions of Byzantine icons.

ART

Art Gallery (⊠ Main shopping st., ☎ 0286/71448) sells large three-dimensional representations of Santorini architecture by Bella Ko-keenatou and Stavros Galanopoulos. Their lifelike depth invites the viewer to walk through a door or up a flight of stairs. **Art Gallery Oia** (⊠ Main shopping st., ☎ 0286/71463) is the place to find a water-color to take home; painter Manolis Sivridakis captures the special light of Santorini with remarkable agility.

CLOTHING

Meteor (⊠ Main shopping st.), a white store with purple trim, has the best hats in the Cyclades: in many colors and shapes, with various rib-bons and dangling decorations—whatever the heart desires. Check out the handmade silk and cotton shawls and the funky dresses from the l950s. Meteor now also sells unusual antiques, such as jewelry, and traditional artwork. **Gemini** (⊠ Hypapantis Walkway, Fira, ☎ 0286/23242) carries Italian Diesel jeans, American Levis, and clothes with the Replay and Union Trade labels.

SOUVENIRS

Yordani (⊠ Near main sq., ☎ 0286/71117) is the perfect shop for in-expensive handmade souvenirs, such as shiny ceramic apples, hand-painted tiles, and gold jewelry, all made in Greece. The delicate blown-glass chandeliers are spectacular but are not so easy to take home in your suitcase.

Messaria

48 *3 km (1¾ mi) south of Fira, 9 km (5½ mi) south of Oia.*

Messaria's **Archontiko Argyrou Museum,** a splendid neoclassical house with painted walls and traditional furniture of the 19th century, is well worth a stop on the way to the Monastery of Profitis Ilias. ⊠ *Messaria,* ☎ *0286/31669,* FAX *0286/33064.* ▨ *1,000 dr.* ☉ *Hourly guided tours 11–7.*

Nightlife

MUSIC AND DANCING

You can see the best traditional Greek music and dancing at **Canava Roussos Winery** (⊠ Mesagonia, ☎ Reservations: 0286/31276), the old-est on the island, founded in 1838, where professional and local dancers in costume perform nightly 8–midnight.

Pyrgos

 5½ km (3½ mi) south of Fira, 2½ km (1½ mi) south of Messaria.

Stop in Pyrgos to see its medieval houses, stacked on top of one another and back to back for protection against pirates. And you can also see the crumbling walls of the old Venetian castle here.

The **Monastery of Profitis Ilias** is at the highest point on Santorini, which spans to 565 meters (1,856 feet) at the summit. From here you can see the surrounding islands and, on a clear day, the mountains of Crete, more than 100 km (66 mi) away. You may also be able to spot Ancient Thira on the peak below Profitis Ilias (☞ *Kamari, below*). Unfortunately, radio towers and a NATO radar installation provide an ugly backdrop for the monastery's wonderful bell tower.

Founded in 1711 by two monks from Pyrgos, Profitis Ilias is cherished by islanders because here, in a secret school, the Greek language and culture were taught during the dark centuries of the Turkish occupation. A **museum** in the monastery contains a model of the secret school in a monk's cell, another model of a traditional carpentry and blacksmith shop, and a display of ecclesiastical items. The monastery's future is in doubt because there are so few monks left. ⊠ *Pyrgos, at highest point on Santorini.* ⊙ *No visiting hours; try to find a caretaker early in morning.*

NEED A
BREAK?

If you are heading south to Akrotiri, stop at Boutari (⊠ Megalochori, ☎ 0286/81011), Santorini's largest winery, and take a tour of the modern facility. An oenologist leads a wine tasting, and a slide show describes local wine production.

Akrotiri

 13 km (8 mi) south of Fira, 7 km (4⅓ mi) west of Pyrgos.

★ If you visit only one archaeological site during your stay on Santorini, make sure it is **ancient Akrotiri,** near the tip of the southern horn of the island.

In the 1860s, in the course of quarrying tephra (volcanic ash) for use in making water-resistant cement for the Suez Canal, workmen discovered the remains of an ancient town. The town was frozen in time by layers of pumice that buried it at the time of the eruption 3,600 years ago, long before Pompeii's disaster. In 1967 Spyridon Marinatos of the University of Athens began excavations, which occasionally continue. It is thought that the 40 buildings that have been uncovered are only one-thirtieth of the huge site and that excavating the rest will probably take a century. You enter from the south, pass the ticket booth, and walk 100 yards or so up a stone-paved street to a vast metal shed that protects 2 acres of the site from wind and sun. A path punctuated by explanatory signs in English leads through the ancient town.

Marinatos and his team discovered great numbers of extremely fine and well-preserved frescoes depicting all aspects of Akrotiri life, now displayed in the Archaeological Museum in Athens; Santorini is trying to get them back. Meanwhile, postcard-size pictures of them are posted outside the houses where they were found. The antelopes, monkeys, and wildcats they portray suggest trade with Africa. One notable example, apparently representing a festival, shows two ports: the left village has ordinary people in skins and tunics, and a symbolic lion runs overhead; and the other, probably Akrotiri, which has more aristocratic folks, has in its center a fleet of sailing ships at sea, with playful dolphins swimming alongside. Another fresco shows that Akrotirian ladies wore makeup and jewelry and ornate two-piece garments that, as was the fashion in Crete, bared their breasts.

There is general agreement that Akrotiri was culturally an outpost of Minoan Crete. Although it was settled as early as 3,000 BC, it was not until about 2,000 BC that the civilization reached its height and developed its trade and agriculture and settled the town being uncovered today. The inhabitants cultivated olive trees and grain, and their advanced architecture—four-story frescoed houses faced with fine masonry (some show evidence of balconies) and public buildings of sophisticated construction—is evidence of an elaborate lifestyle. A sanitary system emptied into drains beneath the streets; ceramic storage jars in 50 shapes were made (many have been left in situ); and many of the houses had wood posts inserted in their stonework to make the walls more flexible in case of earthquakes (the mortar that held the beams in place was decorated with seashells and pebbles). Unlike at Pompeii, no human remains, gold, silver, or weapons were found here. It appears that the earthquakes preceding the eruption gave enough warning to enable the inhabitants to pack their belongings and flee. After the explosion Santorini was uninhabited for about two centuries while the land cooled and plant and animal life regenerated. The site is accessible by public bus or with a guided tour. ⊠ *South of modern Akrotiri, near tip of southern horn,* ☎ *0286/81366.* 🎟 *1200 dr.* ⊗ *Tues.–Sun. 8:30–3.*

Beaches

There's a quiet **beach** (⊠ On southwest shore just below Akrotiri) that's known for its red sand near here.

Kamari

51 *6 km (3¾ mi) south of Fira, 6½ km (4 mi) east of Akrotiri.*

Die-hard archaeology buffs may want to visit the site of **Ancient Thira.** There are relics of a Dorian city, with 9th-century BC tombs, Hellenistic houses and public buildings, and traces of Byzantine fortifications and churches. At the sanctuary of Apollo, graffiti dating to the 8th century BC record the names of some of the boys who danced naked at the god's festival (Satie's popular Gymnopédies reimagine these). To get there, hike up from Perissa or take a taxi up **Mesa Vouna,** a mountain in the southeast corner of the island, which overlooks the black beaches of Perissa and Kamari. On the summit are the scattered ruins, excavated by a German archaeology school around the turn of the century. ⊠ *On a switchback up the mountain, 643 meters (2,110 feet) high,* ☎ *0286/31366.* 🎟 *1,200 dr.* ⊗ *Tues.–Sun. 8:30–3.*

Beaches

If you're a beach bum, it's better to stay at the long **black beaches** in **Kamari** or **Perissa** (Perissa's is volcanic sand, not rock). The black beaches are a natural treasure of Santorini, but some stretches are becoming polluted with cigarette butts and garbage left by tourists. Deck chairs and umbrellas can be rented at both beaches, and tavernas and *cantines* (drink stands) abound.

Dining and Lodging

$$$–$$$$ ✕ **Camille Stéfani.** This fine restaurant, on the black beach of Kamari,
★ serves superb international cuisine with the local stamp of approval. For appetizer, you can't do better than the *poikilia* ("variety" of calamari, octopus, fried tomato balls, deep-fried eggplant, and zucchini). For an entrée, Aris especially recommends beef fillet with green peppercorns and Madeira. A variety of fresh fish is also usually available. For dessert, chocolate crepes with whipped cream are sure to satisfy. It's open all year. ⊠ *At end of coast rd.,* ☎ *0286/31716. AE, MC, V.*

$-$$ ⊞ **Hotel Astro.** This hotel is a short walk to the black sandy beach and minutes away from the local nightlife. Rooms have phones, and those on the lower level have verandas; those on the second floor have balconies facing the mountains or the Aegean. After spending the day at the sea, it's great to take a dip in the pool in the evening. And it's not far from Camille Stéfani restaurant, Kamari's best. ⊠ *Central Kamari 84700,* ☎ *0286/31366. 36 rooms with bath. Coffee shop, pool. No credit cards.*

$ ⚠ **Camping Perissa Beach.** This is the most popular site, which even has a disco. ⊠ *Next to Perissa beach, 84700,* ☎ *0286/81343. Tent sites. Bathrooms, hot showers, restaurant, grocery, disco.*

$ ⚠ **Kamari Camping.** Here, you can be lulled by the waves, just 875 yards away. ⊠ *Off the main rd. to Kamari, near beach, 84700,* ☎ *0286/ 31451 or 0286/31453. Tent sites. Bathrooms, hot showers, restaurant, cafeteria, grocery, coin laundry.*

Nightlife

DISCO

In Kamari the younger set heads for the **Yellow Donkey** disco (⊠ Promenade, ☎ 0286/31462) and the other bars along the beach promenade.

Outdoor Activities and Sports

WATER SPORTS

Perissa beach has windsurfing and waterskiing. **Kamari** offers parasailing, windsurfing, and waterskiing.

THE CYCLADES A TO Z

Arriving and Departing

By Plane

There are no airports on **Andros** or **Tinos.**

MYKONOS

Some European countries now have charter flights to Mykonos. **Olympic Airways** (⊠ Athens, ☎ 01/966–6666) is the only domestic carrier. It has seven flights daily to Mykonos (10 daily during peak tourist season); reservations are always a good idea. There are also flights between Mykonos and Santorini, Heraklion (on Crete), and Rhodes. The Olympic Airways offices in Mykonos are at the port (☎ 0289/22490 or 0289/22495) and at the airport (4 km/1½ mi southwest of Mykonos town, ☎ 0289/22327).

NAXOS

Olympic Airways has two flights daily between Athens and Naxos airport (⊠ A few km outside Naxos town, ☎ 0285/23292).

PAROS

Olympic Airways (⊠ Paros town, ☎ 0284/21900) has five daily flights to the Paros airport (⊠ Near Alyki village, 9 km/6 mi south of Parikia, ☎ 0284/91257) from Athens and up to nine a day in high season.

SANTORINI

Olympic Airways (⊠ Ayia Athanassiou, Fira, ☎ 0286/22493 or 0286/22793) flies six times daily to Santorini airport (⊠ Monolithos, on east coast, 8 km/5 mi from Fira, ☎ 0286/31525) from Athens in peak season. From Santorini, flights go to Mykonos, Heraklion (Crete), and Rhodes about three times per week.

By Boat

Most visitors use the island's extensive ferry network, which has been much improved in recent years. Watching the islands, the sparkling Aegean, and occasional dolphins from the deck will let you know where you are. Ferries sail from Piraeus (Port Authority, ☎ 01/451–1311 or 01/415–1321) and from Rafina, 35 km (22 mi) northeast of Athens (Port Authority, ☎ 0294/22300). Leaving from Rafina cuts traveling time by an hour; buses make the one-hour trip from Rafina to Athens every 20 minutes 6 AM–10 PM. Traveling time from Piraeus to Mykonos is six hours; to Santorini, 8–11 hours. Interisland catamarans and hydrofoils are faster, less pleasant, and more dependent on weather.

Third-class boat tickets cost roughly one-quarter the airfare, and passengers are restricted to seats in the deck areas and often-crowded indoor seating areas. A first-class ticket, which sometimes buys a private cabin and better lounge, costs about half an airplane ticket. For information on interisland connections, contact the port authorities on the various islands (☞ *below*). The tourist season is April through October; boats are less frequent in the off season. Very advance schedules must be checked, as they change with the season, for big holidays, and for weather.

ANDROS

For Andros, you must take a ferry from Rafina (not Piraeus); they leave at least three times a day in summer, and the trip takes about two hours. From Andros (✉ Port Authority, Gavrion, ☎ 0282/22250) boats leave twice daily for Tinos and Mykonos. Boats leave once weekly for Paros, Naxos, Ios, and Crete; they leave once a week for Skiathos and Salonica also. An excursion boat goes daily to Mykonos and Delos, returning in the late afternoon.

TINOS

Tinos is served in summer by two boats a day from Piraeus and one from Rafina. There are daily connections with Andros and Mykonos, several boats a week for Paros, Naxos, and Santorini, and a weekly boat to Skiathos and Salonica. An excursion boat goes daily to nearby Delos, returning in the afternoon. The Port authority in Chora gives information, but it's not more reliable than that given at the agencies clustered near the old harbor (☎ 0283/22348).

MYKONOS

In summer, there are two to three ferries daily to Mykonos from Piraeus and Rafina. From Mykonos (Port Authority: ✉ Harbor, above National Bank, ☎ 0294/22218) there are daily departures to Paros, Tinos, and Andros and five to seven departures per week for Santorini, Naxos, Ios, and Crete.

NAXOS

In summer, ferries leave Piraeus for **Naxos** at least four times a day (The trip takes about seven hours). A boat goes daily from Naxos (Port Authority, ☎ 0285/22300) to Mykonos, Ios, and Santorini. There are daily connections with Paros, Ios, and Santorini, and weekly trips to Skiathos and Salonica. Boats from Naxos serve the Little Cyclades, Iraklia, Schinousa, Koufonis, and Donousa.

PAROS

About four ferries leave Piraeus for **Paros** every day in summer. Paros (Port Authority, ☎ 0284/21240) has daily ferry service to Santorini, Ios, and Naxos. There are also boats to Tinos, Andros, Crete, Rhodes, Kos, Siphnos, Anaphe, Samos, Skiathos, and Salonica. Cruise boats leave daily from Paros town and Naousa for excursions to Delos and Mykonos.

SANTORINI

Santorini is served at least twice daily from Piraeus; from Santorini ferries make frequent connections to the other islands—daily to Paros, Naxos, and Ios, and regularly to Mykonos, Anaphe, Crete, Tinos, and Andros. Almost all ferries dock at Athinios port, where taxis and buses take passengers to Fira, Kamari, and Perissa Beach. Travelers bound for Oia take a bus to Fira and change there, though sometimes the boats stop first below Oia, and small caïques transport passengers to waiting donkeys at the bottom of the cliff below the village. The port below Fira is used only by small ferries and cruise ships. Passengers disembarking here face a 45-minute hike, or they can ride up on the traditional donkeys or take the cable car. The port police (☎ 0286/22239) can give information on ferry schedules.

Getting Around

By Bus

ANDROS

About six buses a day from Andros town (⊠ To right of marble walkway, ☎ 0282/22316) go to Gavrion and back, in conjunction with the ferry schedule; all buses stop in Batsi. Daily buses also go to and return from Stenies, Apoikia, Strapouries, Pitrofos, and Korthion.

TINOS

Buses run several times daily from the quay of Chora to nearly all the many villages in Tinos (☎ 0283/22440), and in summer buses are added for beaches.

MYKONOS

In Mykonos town the Ayios Loukas station near the Olympic Airways office is for buses to Ornos, Ayios Ioannis, Plati Yialos, Psarou, the airport, and Kalamopodi. Another station near the archaeological museum is for connections to Ayios Stefanos, Tourlos, Ano Mera, Elia, Kalafatis, and Kalo Livadi. For bus information, dial ☎ 0289/23360.

NAXOS

The bus system is reliable and fairly extensive. Daily buses go from Chora (⊠ Waterfront, ☎ 0285/22440) to Engares, Melanes, Sangri, Filoti, Apeiranthos, Koronida, and Apollonas. In summer there is added daily service to the beaches, including Ayia Anna, Pyrgaki, Ayiassos, Pachy Ammos, Ayios Mamas, and Abram. The bus office is near the dock.

PAROS

From the Paros town bus station (⊠ 3 min east of the dock, ☎ 0284/21133) there is service every hour to Naousa, and less frequent service to Alyki, Pounda, and to the beaches at Piso Livadhi, Chrissi Akti, and Drios. Schedules are posted.

SANTORINI

Buses leave from the main station in central Fira (⊠ Deorgala) for Perissa and Kamari beaches, Oia, Pyrgos, and other villages.

By Caïque

On all islands, caïques leave from the main port for the most popular beaches and interisland trips. You can also hire a caïque (and haggle over the price, of course) for your tour of choice. For popular routes, captains have their signs posted showing their destinations and departure times.

By Car, Motorbike and Bicycle

To take cars on ferries you must make reservations in advance. All the major islands have car- and bike-rental agencies at the ports and in the business districts. Car rental starts at about 10,000 dr. per day, with unlimited milage and third-party liability insurance. Full insurance costs about 2,000 dr. a day more. Motorbikes and scooters start at 2,500 dr. a day, including third-party liability coverage. Jeeps and dune buggies are also available in Santorini, Mykonos, Paros, Tinos, and Naxos. Choose a dealer that offers 24-hour service and a change of vehicle in case of a breakdown. Beware: Too many travelers end up in Athenian hospitals owing to poor roads, slipshod maintenance, and partying.

ANDROS

Though there is bus service on this large and mountainous island, it is much more convenient to travel by car. Cars can be rented at **Rent a Car Tasos** (⊠ Gavrion, near the ferry boat quay, ☎ 0282/71391 or 0282/71040) or from **Hermes Rent-a-Car** (⊠ Batsi, below The Dolphins taverna, ☎ 0282/41371).

TINOS

Vidalis Rent-a-Car (⊠ Zanaki Alavanou, ☎FAX 028323400) and **Dimitris Rental** (⊠ Zanaki Alavanou, ☎ 0283/23585, FAX 0283/22744), almost next door to each other, are reliable.

MYKONOS

There are several agencies near the windmill bus stop; no cars are permitted in town.

NAXOS

The roads don't go everywhere and are sometimes poor. Often it's easier just to take the bus, especially to places like Apollonas, where the road is steep and twisting. Still, if you drive carefully, you shouldn't have any problem. Car-rental outfits are concentrated in the Chora new town: try **The Jeep Rent-A-Car** (⊠ Chora new town, ☎ 0285/23396) or **Tourent A Car** (⊠ Chora new town, ☎ 0285/23330 or 0285/23331).

PAROS

It is a good idea to rent a vehicle here, because the island is large, there are many beaches to choose from, and taxis are in demand. Among the many agencies near the port, **Vintsi Travel** (⊠ A little past the bus stop, ☎ 0284/21830, FAX 0284/23666) is reliable.

SANTORINI

Extreme caution is advised on Santorini, the car- and bike-accident capital of the Cyclades; the narrow roads are extremely crowded with inexperienced (and often drunk) drivers. Cars can be rented at **Avis** (⊠ Fira, ☎ 0286/23742) or at **Hertz** (⊠ Fira, ☎ 0286/22221).

By Taxi

ANDROS

Taxi stands (⊠ Off main st., near bus station in Andros town; in Batsi at the small quayside sq. beneath The Dolphins restaurant, ☎ 0282/22171).

TINOS

Taxis wait on the quay (⊠ Near central boat dock, ☎ 0283/22470).

MYKONOS

Taxi stand (⊠ Harbor near Mando Mavroyennis statue, ☎ 0289/22400 or 0289/23700). Meters are not used; standard fares for each destination are posted on a notice bulletin board.

NAXOS

Taxi stand (⊠ Near the harbor, ☎ 0285/22444).

Taxi stand (⊠ Across from windmill on the harbor, ☎ 0284/21500); in high season taxis are often busy.

SANTORINI
Taxi station (⊠ Near Fira's central sq. on 25th of March St., ☎ 0286/22555).

Contacts and Resources

Emergencies

ANDROS
Police: (⊠ Gavrion ☎ 0282/71220; ⊠ Batsi, ☎ 0282/41204; and in ⊠ Andros town, ☎ 0282/22300). **Medical assistance**: If you cannot find a doctor, contact Batsi medical assistance (⊠ Batsi, ☎ 0282/41326; ⊠ Gavrion, ☎ 0282/71210). **Health center** (⊠ Andros town, ☎ 0282/22222).

TINOS
Police (⊠ Chora, ☎ 028322255; ⊠ Pirgos, ☎ 0283/31371). **Medical assistance**: Health Center (⊠ East end of town, ☎ 0283/22210; ⊠ Isternia, ☎ 0283/31206).

MYKONOS
Police (☎ 0289/22235). **Medical assistance**: hospital (⊠ Mykonos town, ☎ 0289/23994) has 24-hour emergency service with pathologists, surgeons, pediatricians, dentists, and X-ray technicians; first aid (⊠ Ano Mera, ☎ 0289/71395).

NAXOS
Police (⊠ Chora, ☎ 0285/22100 or 0285/23280; ⊠ Filoti, ☎ 0285/31244). **Medical assistance**: health center (⊠ Just outside Chora, ☎ 0285/23333 or 0285/23676) is open 24 hours a day; Medical Center of Naxos (☎ 0285/23234, ℻ 0285/23576).

PAROS
Police (⊠ Paros town, ☎ 0284/23333; ⊠ Naousa, ☎ 0284/51202). **Medical Center**: Paros town health clinic (⊠ Paros town, ☎ 0284/22500); (⊠ Naousa, ☎ 0284/51216); (⊠ Antiparos, ☎ 0284/61219).

SANTORINI
Police (⊠ Fira, ☎ 0286/22649). **Medical assistance**: first aid (⊠ Fira, ☎ 0286/22237; ⊠ Oia, ☎ 0286/71227).

Guided Tours

ANDROS
Greek Sun Holidays (⊠ Batsi, ☎ 0282/84503) arranges island tours, and tours to Tinos.

TINOS
Windmills Travel (⊠ Above new dock behind playground, ☎ ℻ 0283/23398) runs daily guided coach tours of the island for 2,000 dr., a variety of specialty tours by Jeep, and unguided Delos–Mykonos trips (4,000 dr.).

MYKONOS
Sunspots Travel (⊠ Near airport bus stop, into town, on left, second floor, ☎ 0289/24196, ℻ 0289/23790) takes a group every morning for a day tour of Delos (7,500 dr.). It has half-day guided tours of the Mykonos beach towns, with a stop in Ano Mera for the Panagia Tourliani Monastery. **Delos Tours** (⊠ Fabrica Sq., ☎ 0289/26442) runs all-day excursions (about 7,500 dr.) to nearby Tinos to visit the marble studios, monasteries, and a Venetian ruin.

NAXOS

The **Tourist Information Center** (✉ Waterfront, ☎ 0285/22993), run by Despina Kitini of the Chateau Zevgoli (☞ Naxos *in* Exploring, *above*) offers round-the-island tours, and a weekly boat trip, Mykonos by Night, for 5,000 dr. **Zas Travel** (✉ Chora, ☎ 0285/23330 or 0285/23331, FAX 0285/23419; ✉ Ayios Prokopios, ☎ 0285/24780) runs two good one-day tours of the island sights with different itineraries, each costing about 4,000 dr., and one-day trips to Delos and Mykonos (7,500 dr.), and Santorini (8,000 dr.).

PAROS

A variety of trips by land and sea, such as around Antiparos, are arranged by Kostas Akalestos's **Paroikia Tours** (☎ 0284/22470 or 0284/22471, FAX 0284/22450). **Simitzi Tours** (✉ Naousa, ☎ 0284/51113, FAX 0284/51761) are good. Most agencies handle Delos–Mykonos trips for about 4,000 dr.

SANTORINI

Bellonias Tours (✉ Fira, ☎ 0286/22469 or 0286/23604; ✉ Kamari, ☎ 0286/31721) runs coach tours to Akrotiri, Ancient Thera, and Oia, and daily boat trips to the volcano and Thirassia; they also arrange private tours. **X-Ray Kilo** (☎ 0286/22624 or 0286/23243) has tours to the same sights, and to the island's wineries and the Monastery of Profitis Elias.

Visitor Information

ANDROS

The Greek National Tourist Organization (GNTO or EOT) is housed in a converted dovecote (✉ At port of Gavrion, near Batsi Rd., ☎ 0282/71785). **Police station** (✉ Gavrion, across from ferry dock, ☎ 0282/71220) lists available accommodations. To locate a room, call **Dolphin Hellas** (☎ 0282/41185, FAX 0282/41719), **Greek Sun Holidays** (✉ Batsi, ☎ 0282/41198, FAX 0282/41239), or **Achivada Travel** (✉ Gavrion, ☎ FAX 0282/71571).

TINOS

From June to October, the Town Hall (✉ Evangelistria) runs a **Greek National Tourist Organization (GNTO or EOT)** (☎ 0283/22255). For all tourist services (schedules, room bookings, tours, happenings), see friendly Sharon Turner, manager of **Windmills Travel** (✉ Above new dock behind playground, ☎ FAX 0283/23398); she's a mine of information—there's nothing she doesn't know about her adopted island.

MYKONOS

Tourist police (✉ Harbor, near departure point for Delos, ☎ 0289/22716). George Ghikas' **Sunspots Travel** (✉ Near airport bus stop, into town, on left, second floor, ☎ 0289/24196, FAX 0289/23790) is super-efficient, with a multitude of services.

NAXOS

The well-organized **Greek National Tourist Organization (GNTO or EOT)** (✉ Waterfront, ☎ 0285/24525, 0285/24358, or 0285/22993) has free booking service, bus and ferry schedules, international dialing, luggage storage, and foreign exchange at bank rates.

PAROS

The **Greek National Tourist Organization (GNTO or EOT)** (✉ Paros town, in café across from dock, ☎ 0284/22079) is sometimes open. For efficient and friendly service—tickets, villa rentals for families, apartments, and quality hotel reservations—try Kostas Akalestos's **Paroikia Tours** (☎ 0284/22470 or 0284/22471, FAX 0284/22450). Kostas, both efficient and full of the Greek spirit, has many returning customers. **Simitzi Tours** (⊠ Naousa, on main sq., ☎ 0284/51113, FAX 0284/51761) is helpful.

SANTORINI

There's no EOT on Santorini, but at **X-Ray Kilo** (⊠ Eikostis Pemptis Martiou, Fira, ☎ 0286/22624 or 0286/23083), English-speaking agents book ferries, sell plane tickets, and represent American Express. Another reputable office is **Nomikos Travel** (☎ 0286/23660 or 0286/22660), which has offices in Fira and Perissa.

11 Crete

To Greeks, Crete is the Megalonissi
(Great Island), a hub of sophisticated
ancient art and architecture, where
rebellion was endemic for centuries—
against Arab invaders, Venetian
colonists, Ottoman pashas, and
German occupiers in World War II.
Mountains, split with deep gorges and
honeycombed with caves, rise in sheer
walls from the sea. Snowcapped peaks
loom against sandy beaches, vineyards,
and olive groves. Hospitality is still
important; in the more remote areas
you may be offered plentiful tsikouthia
(the local firewater) and be sent on
your way with grapes or oranges.

By Kerin Hope

Updated by
Stephen
Brewer

CRETE HOLDS A SPECIAL PLACE IN HISTORY as the cradle of European civilization: The Minoans, prehistoric Cretans, founded Europe's first urban culture as far back as the third millennium BC, and the island's rich legacy of art and architecture strongly influenced both mainland Greece and the Aegean islands in the Bronze Age. From around 1900 BC the Minoan palaces at Knossos (near present-day Heraklion), Mallia, Phaistos, and elsewhere were centers of political power, religious authority, and economic activity—all concentrated in one sprawling complex of buildings. Their administration seems to have had much in common with contemporary cultures in Egypt and Mesopotamia. What set the Minoans apart from the rest of the Bronze Age world was their art. It was lively and naturalistic, and they excelled in miniature techniques. From the scenes illustrated on their frescoes, stone vases, seal stones, and signet rings, it is possible to build a picture of a productive, well-regulated society. Yet new research suggests that prehistoric Crete was not a peaceful place; there may have been years of warfare before Knossos became the island's dominant power, in around 1600 BC. It is now thought that political upheaval, rather than the devastating volcanic eruption on the island of Santorini, triggered the violent downfall of the palace civilization around 1450 BC.

Vestiges of the Minoan civilization abound at Knossos, Phaistos, and many other archeological sites around the island. In addition to enjoying miles of beaches, evocative ruins, and fascinating towns and cities, immersing oneself in the island's lifestyle can be an immense pleasure. Even in the large cities Cretans remain family oriented, rooted in tradition and openly inviting to their visitors who want to experience the real Greece.

Pleasures and Pastimes

Bicycling

Crete is rewarding biking country. Though the rugged White Mountains of the west are for hardened addicts, there is plenty of pleasant riding in the gentler landscapes of eastern Crete. Bicycle rentals are available in most Cretan towns. Mountain bikes for cycling in the uplands are now easier to find.

Bird-Watching

Bird-watchers have access to a huge variety of bird life, though most species are not indigenous. A bird sanctuary is being set up east of Heraklion at the Gouves estuary, which is a stopover for a large range of migratory birds. Mt. Iuktas, south of Heraklion, is the place to spot vultures.

Dining

Crete cannot claim to be a center of gastronomy, but ingredients are always fresh, and the family-run tavernas take pride in their cooking. The island produces top-quality fruit and vegetables—cherries from the Amari valley in June, oranges from the groves around Hania in winter, tomatoes and cucumbers all year round, and, increasingly, avocados and bananas. The Cretans enjoy grilled meat, generally lamb and pork, but there is also plenty of fresh fish. Cretan *graviera* cheese is prized, along with *mizythra* (a creamy white variety). Cretan olive oil is famous throughout Greece, though it's heavier than other varieties. The island's wines are improving fast: look for Boutari Kritikos, a crisp white, and Minos Palace, a smooth red. Wine from the barrel is best in eastern Crete, where local growers produce full-bodied reds. Retsina is not part of the Cretan tradition, but it can be found in town restaurants.

In restaurants, *magirefta* (precooked dishes served at room temperature) are prepared in the morning and are best eaten at lunch. Never feel shy about looking them over in the kitchen. In a fish taverna, you will be expected to select your own fish from the ice tray: to check its freshness, make sure the eyes gleam brightly and lift the gills to see if they are a healthy pink. As a rule, it is hard to go hungry in Crete; in a village *kafenion* (traditional Greek coffeehouse), you can almost always order salad and an omelet or eggs fried with graviera cheese. Make sure you try the tsikouthia (also known as raki), the Cretan firewater, which is drunk at any hour, often accompanied by a dish of raisins, or walnuts drenched in honey.

You will almost certainly eat better in a taverna or restaurant than at a hotel, where, unless you are staying at a first-class resort, the menu is usually of the bland "international" variety. Hotel desk clerks willingly recommend a choice of tavernas. Dress is invariably casual, though shorts are not worn in the evening, and reservations are unnecessary unless noted. Credit cards are usually accepted only in more expensive restaurants.

CATEGORY	COST*
$$$$	over 8,000 dr.
$$$	5,000 dr.–8,000 dr.
$$	3,000 dr.–5,000 dr.
$	under 3,000 dr.

per person for a 3-course meal, including tax and service, but excluding drinks.

Hiking

Crete provides both the casual walker and the experienced hiker with challenging opportunities. There are no island-wide trails yet, but the Greek Federation of Mountaineering Associations operates refuges in the White Mountains and on Mt. Ida and has marked numerous paths, especially in the south of the island.

Lodging

Crete has luxury resort hotels with sports and entertainment facilities that compare with anywhere in the Mediterranean. For a more authentic way to experience Crete, opt for the simple whitewashed, cement-floor rooms in mountain and seaside villages. Unfortunately, Crete also has many undistinguished, concrete-block hotels, mostly along the north coast, that defile the landscape and have little character. Some of Greece's finest hotels line the shores of Elounda peninsula, just outside the town of Ayios Nikolaos. In the west especially, old houses, Venetian mansions, and 19th-century consulates are being sensitively restored as small hotels. Hania has several such hotels, and they are excellent.

Unless the months of closing are noted, a hotel is open year-round. Prices rise sharply in June and come down again in mid-September, but even in high season you can often negotiate a discount at medium-price hotels if you are staying more than a night or two. Resort hotels sometimes require half board (MAP); many will give substantial discounts at the beginning and end of the season. If you are staying in Hania or Heraklion in July or August, you may want to pay a little more for a room with air-conditioning. Travel agencies, the local Greek National Tourist Organization (GNTO or EOT) offices, and the tourist police all will help you find accommodation at short notice. In villages, ask at the kafenion about rooms for rent. Standards of cleanliness are high in Crete and service is almost always friendly.

CATEGORY	COST*
$$$$	over 25,000 dr.
$$$	14,000 dr.–25,000 dr.
$$	9,000 dr.–14,000 dr.
$	under 9,000 dr.

All prices are for a standard double room including breakfast, service, and tax.

Nightlife and the Arts

An evening out in Crete is generally spent in a *kentron* (a taverna that features traditional Cretan music and dancing). The star performer is the *lyra* player, who can extract a surprisingly subtle sound from the small pear-shape instrument, held upright on the thigh and played with a bow. Cretan dances range from monotonous circling to astonishing displays of athletic agility, but much depends on the *kefi* (enthusiasm) of the participants. In winter, the kentron moves indoors and becomes a more typical bouzouki joint. Ask at your hotel where the best-known lyra players are performing. Throughout the warmer months, almost every town and village celebrates the feast of its patron saint with a *panayiria* (celebration), with food, drink, and traditional music and dancing usually lasting until dawn. If you are lucky, you may be invited to a *glendi* (local party), or even a traditional Cretan wedding, where the celebrations can last 24 hours.

There are discos in every resort hotel and almost every seaside village. Heraklion and Hania have a wide variety of bars: check with your hotel to find out which are the hot spots. Most resort hotels organize weekly displays of Cretan dancing; many also offer lessons, so guests can join in.

Crete has few serious arts activities and events. Though the island attracts painters from all over Europe, they rarely exhibit locally. In Heraklion, Rethymnon, and, occasionally, Hania, however, local authorities sometimes organize concerts, theater, and folk dancing events during the summer. Athenian and even some foreign musical groups stage open-air performances in the Koules fort at Heraklion and the Fortessa at Rethymnon. Ask at the EOT offices for up-to-date booking information (☞ Visitor Information *in* Crete A to Z, *below*). In winter, both local and visiting choirs and chamber-music groups perform occasionally. The town hall will have information on times and bookings.

Shopping

Crete is a serendipitous place for the shopper. Little serious attempt has been made to adapt the island's traditional crafts to the demands of foreign customers, but by poking around the backstreets of Heraklion, Rethymnon, and Hania, you can find things both useful and exotic— and sometimes even beautiful. Crete was famous even in Minoan times for its weaving. You still occasionally come across the heavy scarlet-embroidered blankets and bedspreads that formed the basis of a traditional dowry chest. Woven wool rugs in plain geometric designs from the village of Axos on the slopes of Mt. Ida are attractive, as are heavy sweaters in natural oily wool. All of the villages on the Lashiti plateau have shops selling embroidered linens, made in front of the stove during the long winter months when snow blocks roads in and out of the area. All over the island, local craftsmen produce attractive copies of Minoan jewelry in gold and silver, as well as some with original modern designs. A shepherd's kit, a striped woven haversack, and a staff are useful for the hiker. Boot-makers in Heraklion and Hania will make you a pair of heavy Cretan leather knee boots to order. A Cretan knife, whether plain steel or with a decorated blade and handle, makes a handy kitchen or camping implement. In the village of Thrapsano, 20 km (12½ mi) southeast of Heraklion, at one of the potteries you can choose a new *pithos* (the tall Ali Baba–style jar used by the Minoans for storing wine and oil and still popular today, often as a flowerpot); have it air-freighted home. Also, some Cretan produce travels well: perhaps a can of olive oil, or of Cretan olives; a packet of dittany, a tangy herb used for making tea; a supply of crunchy barley rusks; and, in cool weather, a small graviera cheese.

Water Sports

Water-sports enthusiasts will find windsurfers available for rent on any beach frequented by tourists. Scuba diving, snorkeling, dinghy sailing, and yacht rentals are available at large resort hotels or can be arranged through local travel agencies.

Exploring Crete

From the glossy beach resorts along the north coast—with the faint echoes of Minoan hedonism in their stunning settings—to the backpackers' haunts in the south, there are destinations to suit every tourist's taste. English is spoken everywhere. Local travel agents offer an increasingly imaginative range of tours, to frescoed Byzantine churches deep in the countryside, beaches reachable only by boat, or offshore islets inhabited mostly by birds and sheep.

Crete is a long narrow island, and therefore as a matter of convenience most visitors tend to approach it in halves. Western Crete is especially rugged, with inland mountains and the equally craggy southern shoreline; some of the best beaches on the island are on the western coast, surrounding the town of Falasarna. Hania and Rethymnon, both lovely, mysterious old cities that trace their roots to the Arab and Venetian worlds, are here in the west. In both the east and the west of Crete, you'll find the most development on the north shore, while for the most part the southern coast remains blessedly unspoiled.

Great Itineraries

Although Crete is a large island, in the north, at least, it is crossed by a good highway and serviced by a good bus system. Even on a one-day stopover you can see the greatest of the island's Minoan sights, though beware: you will be tempted to stay longer. A three-day tour allows you to taste the pleasures of Heraklion and the cities of western Crete, and seven days will allow time to see most of the major towns and sights on a circular tour of the island.

IF YOU HAVE 1 DAY

Numbers in the text correspond to numbers in the margin and on the Eastern Crete, Heraklion, Palace of Knossos, Palace of Mallia, Western Crete, and Palace of Phaistos maps.

Many visitors stop off in Crete for only a day, often en route from Santorini to Rhodes. This stopover doesn't allow much time, but you can begin in ⊞ **Heraklion** ①–⑬ with a visit to the **archaeological museum** ⑬, with its stunning displays of Minoan culture, then move onto ★ the island's largest and most well-preserved Minoan sight, the **Palace** ★ **of Knossos** ⑭–㉔. In the afternoon, make the hour-long trip to the **Palace of Phaistos** ㊌–㊲, another great Minoan site overlooking the south coast, and before returning to **Heraklion** enjoy a drink or a meal in the pretty nearby resort of **Matala** ㉑.

IF YOU HAVE 3 DAYS

⊞ **Heraklion** ①–⑬ is the best starting point for a visit to the island. Spend one day visiting that city, its **archaeological museum** ⑬ and the ★ **Palace of Knossos** ⑭–㉔. From there, follow the north coast west to the city of 🔲 **Rethymnon** ⑦, with its Venetian and Arab heritage, and later in the afternoon travel on to 🔲 **Hania** ⑧, one of the most beautiful cities in Greece and, with its gorgeous harbor and fascinating old town, a delightful place to spend an evening. En route back to **Heraklion,** drive south from **Rethymnon** to the Minoan **Palace of Phaistos** ㊌–㊍, returning for the night to **Heraklion** or staying in seaside 🔲 **Matala** ㊆ or, for a taste of rural Cretan life, one of the other nearby villages.

IF YOU HAVE 7 DAYS

A week allows time to see all of Crete, if not exactly at leisure, at least at an enjoyable pace. The place to begin is 🔲 **Heraklion** ①–⑬, where a stay of a day and a night allows enough time to the see city, the **archaeological museum** ⑬, and the **Palace of Knossos** ⑭–㉔. From there you can explore the island on a more or less circular tour. However, since there is no road directly across the south shore, you will return to the north shore frequently as you travel. Heading east from **Heraklion,** your first stop is the **Lasithi Plateau** ㉕, where you'll get a taste of one of the most scenic corners of rural Crete. After lunch there, you'll want to return to the north shore and, after a stop (via the 20-year-old north coast road still labeled NEW ROAD) at the Minoan ruins at the **Palace of Mallia** ㉗–㊱, continue on to **Ayios Nikolaos** ㊲. The nearby peninsula, 🔲 **Elounda** ㊳, with its fine hotels and wonderful views of the Gulf of Mirabello, is an excellent place to stay. The next day head south to the Minoan city of **Gournia** ㊹, and continue on to **Ierapetra** ㊺. After lunch and maybe a swim, it's back up to the north coast to 🔲 **Siteia** ㊽. The next morning you'll want an early start to the beautiful beach at **Vai** ㊿. The afternoon is devoted to driving, all the way to 🔲 **Rethymnon** ⑦ on the western side of the island—however, the distance is only a little more than 200 km (120 mi) and the highway along the north coast is wide and well paved. After an evening in **Rethymnon,** preferably staying in the charming old town, make the short trip on to 🔲 **Hania** ⑧. You may want to spend two nights here, allowing time to see the city and to explore the area. You might, for instance, want to take a day trip to the **Samaria Gorge,** to the beaches in the far west, or to the rugged southern coast around **Paleochora** or **Hora Sfakion** ㊸. From **Hania,** take the long route back to **Heraklion,** making a loop south at **Rethymnon** to visit the Minoan **Palace at Phaistos** ㊌–㊍ then turning back to the north coast.

When to Tour

The best times for visiting Crete are April and May, when every outcrop of rock is ablaze with brilliant wildflowers, or October, when the sea is still warm and the light golden but piercingly clear. In July and August the main Minoan sites and the coastal towns come close to overflowing. Places like Mallia and Limin Hersonissos, hideously developed towns where bars and pizzerias fill up with heavy-drinking northern Europeans, should be avoided especially in summer and in any other season as well. Driving can be especially hazardous in July and August amid the profusion of buses, Jeeps, and motorbikes, not to mention the impatient Cretan drivers.

EASTERN CRETE

Eastern Crete includes the towns and cities of Heraklion, Ayios Nikolaos, Siteia, and Ierapetra, as well as the archaeological sites of Knossos and Gournia. Of course, many natural wonders lie between these man-made places, including the palm-fringed beach at Vai and the stunning Elounda Peninsula.

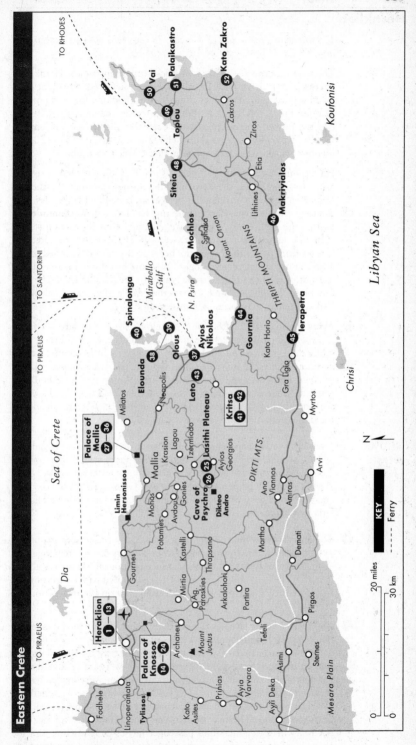

Eastern Crete

TO RHODES

TO SANTORINI

TO PIRAEUS

TO PIRAEUS

Sea of Crete

Dia

Libyan Sea

Koufonisi

Chrisi

Mirabello Gulf

Spinalonga

Mesara Plain

THRIPTI MOUNTAINS

DIKTI MTS.

50 Vai

51 Palaikastro

52 Kato Zakro

49 Toplou

48 Siteia

Zakros

Ziros

Etia

Lithines

46 Makriyialos

47 Mochlos

Sphaka

Mount Ornon

N. Psira

44 Gournia

Kato Horio

45 Ierapetra

Gra Ligia

Myrtos

Arvi

Amiras

Demati

Pirgos

Sternes

Ayii Deka

Asimi

Ayia Varvara

Tefeli

Partira

Arkalohori

Ano Viannos

Martha

38 Elounda

39 Olous

40

37 Ayios Nikolaos

43 Lato

41 **42** Kritsa

Neapolis

Milatos

Ayios Georgios

Lasithi Plateau

25 **26** Cave of Psychro

Dikteo Andro

Ayios Georgios

Tzermiado

Lagou

Krasion

27–36 Palace of Mallia

Mallia

Mohos

Avdou

Gonies

Potamies

Limin Hersonissos

Gournes

Kastelli

Mirtia

Thrapsano

Ag. Paraskies

Archanes

Mount Jouctus

14–24 Palace of Knossos

1–13 Heraklion

Fodhele

Linoperamata

Tylissos

Kato Asites

Prinias

Ayia Varvara

N

KEY

----- Ferry

20 miles

30 km

0
0

Heraklion

175 km (108¾ mi) south of Piraeus, 78 km (48½ mi) east of Rethymnon, 69 km (43 mi) west of Ayios Nikolaos.

The narrow, crowded alleys and thick stone ramparts of Heraklion, Crete's largest city and the fourth largest city in Greece, recall the days when soldiers and merchants clung to the safety of a fortified port. In Minoan times, this was a harbor for Knossos, the largest palace and effective power center of prehistoric Crete. But the Bronze Age remains were built over long ago, and now Heraklion, with more than 120,000 inhabitants, stretches far beyond even the Venetian walls.

Heraklion's town center is typical of many of Greece's larger towns: a few traffic-jammed streets around the open-air market. Eleftheriou Venizelou Square is a triangular pedestrian zone filled with cafés, and

1 a stately marble Renaissance fountain, The Lions or **Ta Leontaria** (⊠ Eleftheriou Venizelou). The square is named after the Cretan statesman who united the island with Greece in 1913. But for hundreds of years before then it had been the heart of the colony founded in the 13th century, when Venice bought Crete, and Heraklion became an important port of call on the trade routes to the Middle East. The city, and often the whole island, known then as Candia, was ruled by the Duke of Crete, a Venetian administrator.

2 **Ayios Markos** (⊠ Eleftheriou Venizelou), the 13th-century church (now an exhibition center), is named for Venice's patron saint, but, with its modern portico and narrow interior, it bears little resemblance to

3 its grand namesake in Venice. The **Loggia** (⊠ 25th Avgoustou [25th of August St.]) was built in the early 17th century by Francesco Basilicata, an Italian architect, as a gathering place for the island's Venetian nobility. Recently restored to its original Palladian elegance, it adjoins the old Venetian Armory, now the City Hall.

NEED A
BREAK?

There are two **bougatsa shops** (⊠ Eleftheriou Venizelou), side by side, where you can stop for this envelope of flaky pastry stuffed with a sweet creamy filling dusted with cinnamon and sugar, or with soft white cheese. A double portion served warm with Greek coffee is a nice change from a hotel breakfast, especially if you've just arrived off the ferry from Piraeus.

---

4 The church **Ayios Titos** (⊠ Set back from 25th of August St.) you pass as you head north toward the harbor is named for Crete's patron saint. A **chapel** to the left of the entrance contains the saint's skull, set in a silver-and-gilt reliquary. Ayios Titos is credited with converting the islanders to Christianity in the 1st century AD on the instructions of St. Paul.

5 The Turkish-named **Koules,** a miniature fortress, dominates Heraklion's **inner harbor.** Fishing boats land their catch and yachts are now moored at what was once the city's Venetian port. To the right rise the tall vaulted tunnels of the arsenal; here, Venetian galleys were repaired and refitted and timber, cheeses, and sweet malmsey wine were loaded for the three-week voyage to Venice. The Koules was built by the Venetians, and three stone lions of St. Mark, symbol of Venetian imperialism, decorate the exterior. The view from its battlements takes in both the outer harbor, where freighters and passenger ferries drop anchor, and the sprawling labyrinth of concrete apartment blocks that is modern Heraklion. To the south rises Mt. Iuktas and to the west, the pointed peak of Mt. Stromboli. ⊠ *Inner harbor, end of 25th of August St.* 🕿 *800 dr.* ☉ *Tues.–Sun. 8:30–3.*

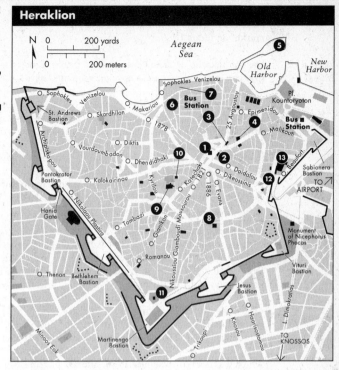

Heraklion

The **Marina Café** (⊠ Old harbor) is a favorite gathering place for young Herakliots. It serves cakes, ice cream, coffee, and cold drinks. Even in high summer there is usually a breeze, and you can watch the comings and goings of the fishermen.

6 A shell now remains of **St. Peter's church** (⊠ West of harbor along the seashore rd.), the medieval church heavily damaged during World War **7** II in the bombing before the German invasion in 1941. The **Historical and Ethnological Museum,** housed in an imposing mansion, contains a varied collection of early Christian and Byzantine sculptures in the basement and several rooms filled with Venetian and Ottoman stonework. Look out for a splendid **lion of St. Mark,** with an inscription that says in Latin I PROTECT THE KINGDOM OF CRETE, and some striking tombstones of Ottoman officials, topped with stone turbans. Left of the entrance is a room stuffed with memorabilia from Crete's bloody revolutionary past: weapons, portraits of mustachioed warrior chieftains, and the flag of the short-lived independent Cretan state set up in 1898. The 19th-century banner in front of the staircase sums up the spirit of Cretan rebellion against the Turks: ELEFTHERIA I THANATOS (Freedom or Death). Upstairs, look in on a room arranged as the study of Crete's most famous writer, Nikos Kazantzakis, the author of *Zorba the Greek* and an epic poem, *The Odyssey, a Modern Sequel.* The top floor contains a stunning collection of **Cretan textiles,** including the brilliant scarlet weavings typical of the island's traditional handwork, and another room arranged as a comfortable domestic interior of the early 1900s. ⊠ *Sophocleous Venizelou, opposite St. Peter's church,* ☎ *081/226092.* ⊞ *800 dr.* ☉ *Tues.–Sun. 8–3.*

8 The square, **Platia Cornarou** (⊠ At top of Odos 1866, south of Ta Leontaria and across Kalokairinous), is graced with a Venetian fountain and an elegant Turkish stone kiosk. Fruit and vegetable stalls alternate with butchers' displays of whole lambs and pigs' feet at the lively **open-air market** on Odos 1866.

NEED A
BREAK?   You can stock up at **Platia Cornarou** for a picnic: Grocers sell cheese (you can taste a sliver before buying), wine, and olives.

9 **10** Lofty **Ayios Minas** (✉ Kyrillou Loukareos, main rd. west from Platia Cornarou) is a huge but unprepossessing 19th-century cathedral. **Ayia Aikaterina** of Sinai, nestled in the cathedral's shadow, is one of Crete's most attractive small churches. Built in 1555, it is now a **museum of icons** by Cretan artists, who traveled to Venice to study with Italian Renaissance painters. Look for six icons (Nos. 2, 5, 8, 9, 12, and 15) by Michael Damaskinos, who worked in both Byzantine and Renaissance styles in the 16th century. ✉ *Kyrillou Loukareos.* 🎫 *500 dr.* ☉ *9:30–1; closed Tues. and Sun.*

Martinengo Bastion (✉ South of Kyrillou Loukareos on N. G. Mousourou) is the largest of six bastions shaped like arrowheads jutting out from the well-preserved Venetian walls. Designed by Micheli Sanmicheli, the bastions were built in the 16th century to keep out Barbary pirates and Turkish invaders. When the Turks finally overran Crete in 1648, the garrison at Heraklion held out for another 21 years in one of the longest sieges in European history. General Francesco Morosini finally surrendered the city to the Turkish Grand Vizier in September 1669. He was allowed to sail home to Venice with the city's archives and such precious relics as the skull of Ayios Titos—which was not returned until 1966. Literary pilgrims come to the Martinengo to visit the **burial place of Kazantzakis.** The grave is a plain stone slab marked by a weathered wooden cross. The inscription, from his writings, says: I FEAR NOTHING, I HOPE FOR NOTHING, I AM FREE.

12 The city's biggest square is **Platia Eleftherias,** or Treis Kamares (✉ At end of Daidalou St., 1 st. east of Ta Leontaria, just south of Ayios Markos). Daidalou, which follows the line of an early fortification wall, is now a pedestrian walkway lined with tavernas, boutiques, jewelers, and souvenir shops.

★ **13** The **archaeological museum** is best visited early in the morning before tourist buses start disgorging their passengers. Installation of air-conditioning has been recently completed, and all galleries are open. The Minoan collection compares to that in any of the great museums of western Europe. Even before the great palaces were built, around 1900 BC, the prehistoric Cretans excelled at metalworking and in carving stone vases, seen in the box in Gallery I with a lid whose handle is in the shape of a lazing dog. They were also skilled at producing fine pottery, such as the eggshell-thin Kamares ware decorated in delicate abstract designs (in Gallery III), and miniature work like the superbly crafted jewelry (in Galleries VI and VII) and the colored seal-stones (in Gallery III) that are carved with lively scenes of people and animals.

Though naturalism and an air of informality distinguish much Minoan art from that of contemporary Bronze Age cultures elsewhere in the eastern Mediterranean, you will also see a number of heavy, rococo set pieces, such as the fruit stand with a toothed rim and the punch bowl with appliquéd flowers (both in Gallery III). The Linear B script, inscribed on clay tablets (Gallery V), is now recognized as an early form of Greek, but the earlier Linear A script (Gallery V) and that of the Phaistos Disk (Gallery III) have yet to be deciphered.

The Minoans' talents at modeling in stone, ivory, and a kind of glass paste known to archaeologists as faience, peaked in the later palace period (1700 BC–1450 BC). A famous rhyton (vase for pouring libations) carved from dark serpentine in the shape of a bull's head has eyes made of red jasper and clear rock crystal with horns of gilded wood (Gallery IV). An ivory acrobat—perhaps a bull-leaper—and two bare-breasted faience goddesses in flounced skirts holding wriggling snakes (both Gallery IV) were among a group of treasures hidden beneath the floor of a storeroom at Knossos. Bull-leaping, whether religious rite or a favorite sport, inspired some memorable Minoan art. Three vases of serpentine (probably covered originally in gold leaf) from Ayia Triada (Gallery VII) are carved with scenes of Minoan life thought to be by artists from Knossos: boxing matches, a harvest-home ceremony, and a Minoan official taking delivery of a consignment of hides. The most stunning rhyton of all, from Zakro, is made of rock crystal (Gallery VIII). Commodities were stored in the palaces: An elephant tusk and bronze ingots (Gallery VIII) were found at Zakro and Ayia Triada. Make sure to save some time and energy for the fresco galleries upstairs. Dating from the later palace period, they show both the Minoans' preoccupation with religious ritual and enjoyment of their island's natural beauties. ⊠ *Platia Eleftherias,* ☎ *081/226092.* ⊠ *1,000 dr.* ☉ *Mon. 12:30–5, Tues.–Fri. 8–7, weekends 8:30–3:30.*

Dining and Lodging

$$ ✕ **Kyriakos.** With its pink tablecloths and green chairs, this is no ordinary taverna. Just a short walk from the Galaxy Hotel, Kyriakos offers a wide range of well-prepared salads, grills, and fish dishes. Watch for seasonal Cretan specialties, such as snail stew in summer and *volvi* (baked iris bulbs in olive oil and vinegar) in spring. There is a good wine list, with Cretan and mainland wines. ⊠ *Leoforos Dimokratias 43,* ☎ *081/224649. AE, DC, V.*

$ ✕ **Ionia.** Frequented by villagers doing business in town, this old-fashioned restaurant near the open-air market offers a variety of magirefta, such as lamb fricassee and lamb *yiouvetsi* (baked with orzo), Greek lunchtime staples that are hard to find in the tourist resorts. ⊠ *Odos Evans,* ☎ *081/283213. MC, V.*

$ ✕ **Terzakis.** This unassuming establishment is one of Heraklion's most popular *mezedopolio* (a meze joint) in which you choose half a dozen or more dishes from a long list of fish, dips, and salads. Traditionally mezes are accompanied by ouzo, but beer or wine are equally acceptable. ⊠ *Loh. Marineli 17, behind Ayios Dimitrios church,* ☎ *081/221444. No credit cards. No dinner Sun.*

$ ✕ **Yacoumis.** This hole-in-the-wall is reputed to be the best of the small restaurants in the covered Meat Alley: follow the aroma of roasting meat and clouds of steam wafting out between the stalls. Sizzling chunks of spit-roasted lamb and pork are sold by weight, accompanied by salads of roughly sliced tomatoes and onions, drenched in thick Cretan olive oil. ⊠ *Meat alley, leading off market. No credit cards. Closed Sun.*

$$$ ⊡ **Galaxy.** This modern hotel on the road to Knossos is efficiently run and popular with Greek businessmen, but its decoration and furnishings are on the drab side. However, there are two good reasons for making it your base—the swimming pool and the coffee shop, which offers the best patisserie in town. To avoid traffic noise, make sure you ask for an inside room on an upper floor. ⊠ *Leoforos Dimokratias 67, 71306,* ☎ *081/232157 or 081/238812,* 𝐅𝐀𝐗 *081/211211. 120 rooms with bath. Restaurant, coffee shop, air-conditioning, pool, sauna. DC, MC, V.*

$$ 🏨 **Astoria Capsis.** Conveniently located opposite the archaeological museum in the liveliest area of the city, this recently refurbished hotel has delightful, modern-style rooms decorated in cool shades and furnished with sleek blonde wood; it has a rooftop swimming pool, as well as a delightful poolside bar, and it is fully air-conditioned. ⊠ *Platia Eleftherias, 71201,* ☎ *081/229002,* FAX *081/229078. 120 rooms with bath. Restaurant, bar, coffee shop, air-conditioning, pool. AE, DC, MC, V.*

$ 🏨 **Atrion.** This well-run hotel tucked away on a quiet street behind the
★   archaeological museum is rather drab and dark, but it has its advantages: a generous breakfast buffet and drinks are served in the evening in a tiny patio-garden. ⊠ *Palaiologou 9, 71202,* ☎ *081/229225 or 081/242830,* FAX *081/223292. 50 rooms with bath or shower. Restaurant, air-conditioning, free parking. DC, MC, V.*

$ 🏨 **Daedalos.** On a pedestrian street in the city center, this small hotel is shabby but extremely friendly. The owner, Takis Stoumbidis, used to run an art gallery, and the rooms and corridors are lined with Cretan landscapes. The ground-floor bar is a local gathering place, where you may run into a distinguished archaeologist or folklorist downing a glass of tsikouthia. ⊠ *Daidalou 15, 71202,* ☎ *081/224391 through 224395. 60 rooms with shower. DC, MC, V.*

Outdoor Activities and Sports
BICYCLING
Bicycle rentals are available in all Cretan towns. Mountain bikes for cycling in the uplands are now easier to find. To rent a bike in Heraklion, ask at the **Creta Tours** (⊠ Epimenidou 20–22, ☎ 081/227002).

BIRD-WATCHING
For details regarding the bird sanctuary now being set up east of Heraklion at the Gouves estuary contact the Grecotel group, which runs the **Creta Sun Hotel** (☎ 0831/71602).

Shopping
BOOKSTORES
In Heraklion, you can find **English-language books** at Kouvidis-Manouras (Daidalou 6, ☎ 081/220135) or Astrakianakis (⊠ Eleftheriou Venizelou, ☎ 081/284248). **Newspapers and magazines** are available in Platia Venizelou.

Palace of Knossos

180 km (111¾ mi) south of Piraeus, 5 km (3 mi) south of Heraklion.

The palace of Knossos belonged to King Minos, who kept the Minotaur, a hybrid monster of man and bull, in an underground labyrinth.

★   A low hill at the site of the Minoan Palace of Knossos was occupied from Neolithic times, and the population spread to the land around. Around 1900 BC, the hilltop was leveled and the first palace constructed; around 1700 BC, after an earthquake destroyed it, the later palace was built, surrounded by houses and other buildings. Around 1450 BC, another widespread disaster occurred, perhaps an invasion: palaces and country villas were razed by fire and abandoned, and though Knossos remained inhabited, the palace suffered some damage. But around 1380 BC the palace and its outlying buildings were destroyed by fire, and, at the end of the Bronze Age, the site was abandoned. Still later, Knossos became a Greek city-state. Fine houses with mosaic floors and statuary have been excavated. Evidence of the Minoan civilization was unearthed in the early 1900s, when Crete had just achieved independence after centuries of foreign rule by Venice and then by the Ottoman Turks.

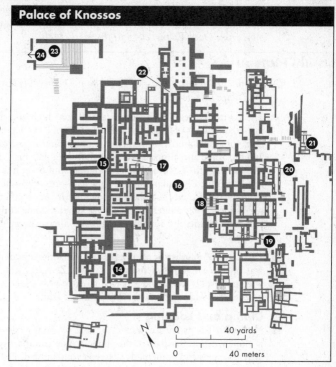

Palace of Knossos

You enter the palace from the west, passing a **bust of Sir Arthur Evans,** the British archaeologist who excavated at Knossos on and off for more than 20 years after 1900. Opinions vary about his concrete restorations and copies of the **frescoes.** But without them, it would be impossible to experience, even at second hand, the ambience of a Minoan palace, with its long pillared halls, narrow corridors, deep stairways and light wells, and curious reverse-tapering columns. But the restorations themselves are in need of renovation; some areas of the palace are now closed off. **(14)** A path leads you around to the monumental **south gateway;** the **(15)** **west wing** encases lines of long narrow storerooms where the true wealth of Knossos was kept in tall clay jars: oil, wine, grains, and honey. The **(16)** **central court,** about 50 meters (164 feet) by 25 meters (82 feet), lies **(17)** before the cool, dark **throne room complex,** with its griffin fresco and tall, wavy-back gypsum throne.

(18) The most spectacular piece of palace architecture is the **Grand Staircase,** on the east side of the court, leading to the domestic apartments. Four flights of shallow gypsum stairs survive, lit by a deep light well. Here you get a sense of how noble Minoans lived; rooms were divided by sets of double doors, giving privacy and warmth when closed, coolness **(19)** and communication when open. The **Queen's Megaron** (apartment) is decorated with copies of the colorful Dolphin fresco and furnished with stone benches. Beside it is a bathroom, complete with a clay tub, and next door a toilet, whose drainage system permitted flushing into a channel flowing into the Kairatos stream far below. The **(20)** east side of the palace also contained **workshops.** Beside the staircase **(21)** leading down to the **east bastion** is a stone water channel made up of parabolic curves and settling basins: a Minoan storm drain. Northwest **(22)** of the east bastion is the **north entrance,** guarded by a relief fresco of **(23)** a charging bull. Beyond is the **theatrical area,** shaded by pines and overlooking a shallow flight of steps, which lead down to the **Royal Road.**

This was perhaps the ceremonial entrance to the palace. ⊠ *Site.* ☎ *1,250 dr.* ⊙ *Weekdays 8–5, weekends 8:30–3. Bus 2 leaves every 15 mins from Odos Evans, close to the market.*

Lasithi Plateau

㉕ *52 km (32¼ mi) southeast of Heraklion, 47 km (29¼ mi) southeast of the Palace of Knossos.*

The Lasithi Plateau, 853 meters (2,800 feet) high and the biggest of the upland plains of Crete, lies behind a wall of barren mountains. Covered with mechanical windmills pumping water for fields of potatoes and the apple and almond orchards that are a pale haze of blossom in early spring, the Lasithi plateau is remote and breathtakingly beautiful. It is ringed by small villages that in winter are sometimes cut off from the outside world by heavy snowfalls. It appears that the villagers spend these long winter months weaving and doing embroidery, and their handicrafts are for sale at shops in almost every village on the plateau.

㉖ The **Cave of Psychro** is an impressive, stalactite-studded cavern that was once a Minoan sanctuary. It's where Zeus, the king of the gods, was supposedly born, and it is well worth a visit. ⊠ *Descend slippery path near village of Psychro.* ☎ *800 dr.* ⊙ *Daily 8–5.*

Dining and Lodging

$ ✗ **Kronio.** The promise of a meal in this cozy, family-run establishment is alone worth the trip up to the plateau. A delicious array of meat and vegetable pies and homemade casseroles and lamb dishes emerge from the kitchen, and the charming young proprietors, Vassilis and Christine, will encourage you to linger over your wine and raki. ⊠ *Lasithi Plateau,* ☎ *0844/22375. No credit cards. Closed Nov.–Mar.*

$ 🏨 **Kouritas.** The large, tile-floored rooms are simple but extremely pleasant, and all have modern baths. Each room opens to a balcony that overlooks surrounding fields and windmills, and a terrace downstairs is a nice place to contemplate the cool evenings over a beer. The hotel provides bikes free of charge for a spin around the plateau. ⊠ *Tzermiado,* ☎ *0844/22194. 20 rooms with bath. Restaurant, bicycles. MC, V.*

Shopping

HANDICRAFTS
Katepiva (⊠ In village of Tzermiado) has an especially fine selection of weavings and embroidery.

Mallia

37 km (23 mi) east of Heraklion.

In its effort to serve mass tourism, Mallia has also submerged whatever character it might once have had. Its sandy beach, overlooked by the brooding Lasithi mountains, is backed by a solid line of hotels and vacation apartments.

Mallia itself may not be worth a visit, but the Minoan Palace of Mallia on its outskirts definitely is. Like Knossos and Phaistos, it was built around 1900 BC, but it was less sophisticated both in architecture and decoration. The layout, however, is similar. Across the west court,

㉗ along one of the paved raised walkways, is a double row of **round granaries** sunk into the ground, which were almost certainly roofed.

㉘ East of the granaries is the **south doorway,** from which to see the

㉙ large, circular limestone table, or **kernos** (on which were placed

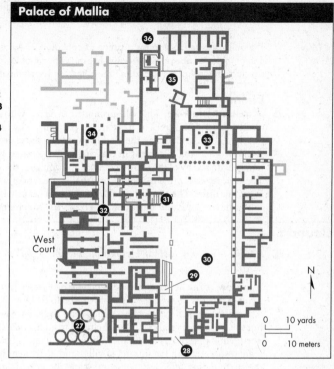

Palace of Mallia

offerings to a Minoan deity), with a large hollow at its center and 34 smaller ones around the edge. The **central court** has a shallow pit at its center, perhaps the location of an altar. To the west of the central court are the remains of an imposing **staircase** leading up to a second floor, and a terrace, most likely used for religious ceremonies; behind is a long corridor with **storerooms** to the side. In the north wing is a large **pillared hall,** part of a set of public rooms. The **domestic apartments** appear to have been in the northwest corner of the palace, entered through a narrow dogleg passage. They are connected by a smaller **northern court,** through which you can leave the palace by the **north entrance,** passing two giant *pithoi* (storage jars). Much excavation has been done nearby, but only a few of the sites are open. ⊠ *3 km (2 mi) northeast of Mallia,* ☎ *0841/22462.* ✉ *800 dr.* ⏱ *Tues.–Sun. 8:30–3.*

Ayios Nikolaos

★ ③⑦   *69 km (43 mi) east of Heraklion, 32 km (20 mi) southeast of Mallia.*

Ayios Nikolaos, built just over a century ago by Cretans from the southwest of the island, is clustered around the **Gulf of Mirabello,** a dramatic composition of bare mountains, islets, and deep blue sea. Behind the crowded harbor lies a natural curiosity, tiny Lake Voulismeni, linked to the sea by a narrow channel. The **museum** at Ayios Nikolaos displays some unique finds, such as the *Goddess of Myrtos,* an Early Minoan rhyton from a site on the southeast coast. The goddess is an appealing figure cradling a large jug in her spindly arms. There are also fine examples of Late Minoan pottery in the naturalistic marine style, with lively octopus and shell designs. The Triton stone vase found at Mallia is carved with an unusual scene of a Minoan religious ritual. A Roman cemetery on the edge of the town yielded a rare find: a skull adorned with a gold wreath, perhaps an athlete who died young. ⊠ *Odos Palaiologou,* ☎ *0841/22462.* 🖃 *800 dr.* ☉ *Tues.–Sun. 8:30–3.*

NEED A BREAK?	The quietest place to stop for a coffee or cool drink in Ayios Nikolaos is one of the **cafés above the Kitomilia beach** (⊠ South of town). There's a spectacular view of the island of Pseira and the Thripti mountains.

Dining

$ ✕ **Itanos Restaurant.** This old-fashioned taverna, with a formal arrangement of palm trees at its center, is patronized by locals, as it offers much better value than the establishments on the seafront. The wine comes from a row of barrels in the kitchen. In summer you dine on a terrace with a view of the town's comings and goings in the square below. The *soutzoukakia* (oven-cooked meatballs) are tender and spicy, and vegetable dishes like braised artichokes or green beans with tomato are full of flavor. ⊠ *Platia Iroon,* ☎ *0841/25340. No credit cards.*

Elounda

③⑧   *80 km (49¼ mi) east of Heraklion, 11 km (7 mi) north of Ayios Nikolaos.*

A narrow corniche road with spectacular sea views runs north from Ayios Nikolaos around the Gulf of Mirabello to Elounda. This is not an area renowned for beaches, which tend to be narrow and pebbly, but the water is crystal clear and sheltered from the *meltemi* (the fierce north wind that blows in summer). Elounda village is becoming a full-scale resort, serving the dozens of villas and apartment hotels dotting the surrounding hillsides. You can escape the crowds in Elounda by

③⑨   following signs for **Olous,** 3 km (2 mi) east of Elounda, an ancient city whose sunken remains are still visible beneath the sea as you cross a causeway to Spinalonga.

Dining and Lodging

$$ ✕ **Marilena.** If the scenery alone doesn't lure you out to the village of Elounda, this delightful family-run restaurant might. In good weather, meals are served in the large rear garden, although you can also choose a table on a sidewalk terrace overlooking the harbor. The Gaitanos brothers serve an excellent selection of fresh grilled fish and a rich fish soup, and any meal should begin with a platter of assorted appetizers. ⊠ *Elounda Village,* ☎ 🖷 *0841/41322. MC, V.*

$$$$ 🏨 **Elounda Beach.** This is one of Greece's most renowned resort hotels, set in 40 acres of gardens looking across the Mirabello Gulf. It ★ has inspired imitations on a half dozen other Aegean islands. The architecture reflects Cretan tradition: whitewashed walls, shady porches, and cool flagstone floors. You can have a room in the central block or a bungalow at the edge of the sea. The hotel has two sandy beaches and a wide range of beach and water sports, including scuba diving. ⊠ *Elounda, 72053,* ☎ *0841/41412 or 0841/41413,* 🖷 *0841/41373. 150 rooms with bath, 150 bungalows. Air-conditioning, sauna, Turkish bath, miniature golf, tennis courts, windsurfing, boating, parasailing, waterskiing. AE, DC, MC, V. Closed Nov.–Mar.*

$$$$ 🏨 **Elounda Mare.** If you plan to stay in one luxurious hotel in Crete, ★ make it this extraordinary Relais & Chateau property on the Mirabello Gulf, one of the finest hotels in Greece, if not the world. More than half of the rooms, all bathed in cool marble and stunningly decorated in traditional but luxurious Greek furnishings, are in villas set in their own gardens with private pools. The service is what you would expect from the best European hotel, yet the atmosphere is relaxed and wel-

coming. Verdant gardens line the shore above a sandy beach and terraced waterside lounging areas, a stone's throw from the large pool. Menus in three restaurants, all with outdoor dining, range from Greek to Continental cuisine, with an excellent selection of fresh seafood and extensive wine lists. Scuba diving is also offered. ⊠ *Box 31, 72100, Ayios Nikolaos,* ☎ *0841/41102 or 0841/41103,* FAX *0841/41307. 95 rooms and bungalows with bath. 3 restaurants, air-conditioning, sauna, Turkish bath, tennis courts, windsurfing, boating, waterskiing, scuba diving. AE, DC, MC, V. Closed Nov.–Mar.*

$ ⊞ **Akti Olous.** This friendly, unassuming hotel on the edge of the Mirabello Gulf is just a step away from a strip of sandy beach and a short swim from the sunken city of Olous—its remains are easy to spot while snorkeling. The rooftop bar, next to the swimming pool, has a stunning view across the gulf, especially at sunset, and there is a waterside taverna and beach. The rooms, decorated in a handsome modern neoclassical style, all have balconies overlooking the sea. ⊠ *Elounda, 72053,* ☎ *0841/41270,* FAX *0841/41425. 75 rooms with shower. No credit cards. Closed Nov.–Mar.*

Outdoor Activities and Sports

SWIMMING

There is good swimming off the rocks of **Olous** (☞ *above*).

Spinalonga

40 *82 km (51 mi) east of Heraklion, 2 km (1¼ mi) east of Elounda.*

Spinalonga, a small, narrow island in the center of the Mirabello Gulf, is a fascinating if somewhat macabre place to visit. The Venetians built a huge, forbidding fortress here in the 17th century, and in the early 1900s the island became a leper colony. To reach it you must take an excursion boat from Ayios Nikolaos. Ask at the harbor; there are two or three trips every day in summer, some including a midday beach barbecue and a swim on a deserted islet. As you cruise past the islet of Ayioi Pantes, look for the *agrimi* (the Cretan wild goat), with its impressive curling horns. The islet is a reserve for about 200 of this protected species.

Kritsa

41 *80 km (50 mi) east of Heraklion, 20 km (12½ mi) south of Elounda.*

The village of Kritsa, 9 km (6 mi) west of Ayios Nikolaos, is renowned for its weaving tradition. If you visit only one Byzantine church in Crete,
42 it should be the whitewashed **Panayia Kera.** It has an unusual shape, with three naves supported by heavy triangular buttresses. Built in the early years of Venetian occupation, it contains some of the liveliest and best-preserved medieval frescoes on the island, painted in the 13th century. ⊠ *On main rd. just before town, Kritsa.* ▦ *200 dr.* ☉ *Sat.–Thurs. 9–3.*

43 One of the best views in Crete can be had at **Lato** (⊠ *1 km/½ mi beyond Kritsa's church of Panayia Kera; follow the dirt track*), an ancient city built in a dip between two rocky peaks. Make your way over the ancient masonry to the far end of the site: On a clear day, you can see the island of Santorini, about 135 km (84 mi) across the Cretan Sea.

Shopping

WEAVING

Among the tourist items in Kritsa, you can usually find a rug or bag in natural wool—usually in colors of off-white, gray, or brown.

Gournia

44 *98½ km (61 mi) southeast of Heraklion, 18½ km (11½ mi) east of Kritsa.*

The Minoan site of Gournia was excavated in 1904 by Harriet Boyd Hawes, the first woman archaeologist to work here, along with her team of Cretan workmen and a chaperon. Most of what you see dates from the later Palace period, though Gournia had only a small mansion set among dozens of small houses. Finds indicated that it was a fishing and weaving community, destroyed around 1400 BC and never resettled. ✉ *To right of main hwy., on low hillside.* 🎟 *Free.* ⊙ *Mon.–Sat. 8:30–3, Sun. 9:30–2:30.*

Ierapetra

45 *113½ (70¼ mi) southeast of Heraklion, about 15 km (9 mi) south of Gournia.*

From Gournia, a road branches to the right and crosses the narrowest part of the island to Ierapetra. The only major town on the south coast, Ierapetra is a flourishing agricultural center, its prosperity based on the plastic-covered greenhouses where early tomatoes and cucumbers are grown and exported all over Europe. The climate in this part of Crete is north African; you are nearer to Libya than to mainland Greece.

Beaches

46 Tourism is fast developing to the east of Ierapetra, where there are some fine sandy beaches. At the village of **Makriyialos,** 28 km (17 mi) east of Ierapetra, you can take your pick; even in high summer you might have most of a cove to yourself.

Lodging

$$ 🏨 **Astron.** Opened in 1992, all rooms at this comfortable hotel have a terrific vantage point, with balconies, of a quiet stretch of waterfront at the edge of town. The beach is just a minute away. The coffee shop looks onto a pleasant interior courtyard with a fountain. ✉ *Mihail Kothri 56, 72200,* ☎ *0842/25114 through 25117,* 𝔽𝔸𝕏 *0842/25917. 70 rooms with bath. Restaurant, coffee shop, snack bar, air-conditioning, minibars. V. Closed Nov.–Apr.*

Mochlos

47 *50 km (31 mi) east of Ayios Nikolaos, 35 km (21¾ mi) northeast of Ierapetra.*

If you feel like a swim, or a leisurely taverna meal, wind along the north coast road between the base of the mountains and the sea to the island of Mochlos, separated from shore by a swimmable channel. On the island is a Minoan cemetery excavated early in this century, now being re-excavated by a team of American archaeologists. Mochlos is a good place for lazing in the hottest part of the day; there are several pleasant tavernas on the shore and, if you want to stay longer, rooms to rent.

Siteia

48 *73 km (45 mi) east of Ayios Nikolaos, 23 km (14¼ mi) east of Ierapetra.*

Like Ierapetra, Siteia is an unpretentious town where agriculture is at least as important as tourism: raisins and, increasingly, bananas are the main crops. Siteia's waterfront, lined with cafés and tavernas, is lively in summer. From Siteia you can take a plane or ferry to Rhodes via the small islands of Kassos and Karpathos.

A Venetian fort, the **Kazarma** (⊠ Follow rd. up from waterfront) overlooks Siteia from a height on the west: it offers a spectacular view across the bay. Siteia's archaeological museum contains a unique find:

★ a **Minoan ivory and gold statuette of a young man,** found at Palaikastro on the east coast. The figure dates from around 1500 BC and, though incomplete, is a masterpiece of Minoan carving. ⊠ *Outskirts of town.* 🕭 *800 dr.* ☉ *Tues.–Sun. 9–3.*

49 The fortified monastery of **Toplou** (12½ km/8 mi east of Siteia on the road for Palaikastro and Zakro) is set among barren hills where the sparse trees are twisted into strange shapes by the fierce north winds that sweep this region. Only a few monks live here now, though the monastery is slowly being renovated. Inside the tall loggia gate, built in the 16th century, the cells are arranged around a cobbled courtyard with a 14th-century church at its center. It contains a famous icon, composed of 61 scenes, each inspired by a phrase from the Orthodox liturgy.

Beaches
A long sandy beach stretches to the east of the waterfront.

Lodging
$ 🏨 **Hotel El Greco.** This friendly establishment on a narrow street several blocks above the waterfront is perfectly comfortable and not without charm. Many of the simple rooms have balconies overlooking the old town and the sea, and the manager, Jankov Marjan, goes out of his way to help guests. ⊠ *G. Arkadiou, 72300,* ☎ 𝔽𝔸𝕏 *0843/23133. 20 rooms with shower. MC, V. Closed Dec.–Apr.*

Vai, Palaikastro, and Kato Zakro Beaches

Vai is 170 km (105½ mi) east of Heraklion, 27 km (16¾ mi) east of Siteia.

★ **50** The palm grove of the renowned beach at **Vai** (⊠ 7½ km/4½ mi northeast of Toplou) existed in classical Greek times; it is unique in Europe. The sandy beach with offshore islets set in clear turquoise water is one of the most attractive in Crete, but in summer it is very crowded.

51 Follow a dirt track through olive groves to the sandy beach at **Palaikastro** (⊠ 9 km/6 mi south of Vai, follow sign for Marina Village). It is rarely crowded, and service is friendly at the waterside tavernas. The sprawling Minoan town, currently being excavated by British and American archaeologists, lies off to the right.

At **Ano Zakro,** 20 km (12 mi) south of Palaikastro village, a path leads down through a deep ravine past caves used for early Minoan burials

★ **52** to the Minoan palace site at **Kato Zakro** (⊠ Ask at one of the cafés for directions to the start of the path). The walk down takes about one hour. You can also drive 9 km (6 mi) down to the site by a circuitous but spectacular route. The village of Kato Zakro, on a fine beach, is a cluster of tavernas with a few rooms to rent. Kato Zakro's **Minoan palace,** smaller than those of Knossos, Phaistos, and Mallia, is surrounded by a terraced town with narrow cobbled streets, like Gournia. A roofed area to the right of the entrance covers a bathroom, suggesting that visitors to the palace may first have undergone a ritual cleansing. The splendid rock-crystal rhyton and other treasures now in the Heraklion Museum were found in a treasury in the west wing. The kitchen area was in the north section of the west wing, and the east wing contained a large cistern. The site is badly in need of conservation but, by climbing up to the town above, you can get a clear idea of its ground plan. ⊠ *Ascend paved Minoan Rd. from harbor,* *through once-covered gateway, reaching northeast court down stepped ramp,* ☎ *0841/22462.* 💶 *500 dr.* ☺ *Tues.–Sun. 8–3.*

WESTERN CRETE

Western Crete, with soaring mountains, deep gorges, and rolling green lowlands planted with olives and oranges, is much less affected by the growth of mass tourism than is the rest of the island. There are a wealth of interesting byways to be explored. This region is rich in Minoan sites, Byzantine churches, Venetian monasteries, and friendly upland villages. There are some outstanding beaches on the west and south coasts. South and west of Heraklion lies the traditional agricultural heartland of Crete: long, narrow valleys where olive groves alternate with vineyards growing sultana grapes for export.

Mesara Plain and Gortyna

Gortyna is 45 km (28 mi) south of Heraklion.

After climbing through a vine- and olive-clad valley, the narrow road south from Heraklion to Gortyna swings toward the Mesara plain. The plain, filled with silver-gray olives interspersed with plastic greenhouses for growing early tomatoes and cucumbers, rises again to the craggy **Asterousia Mountains;** beyond them is the Libyan Sea. In summer especially, the temperature rises sharply as you descend. The village of **Ayia Varvara,** with the whitewashed church of Profitis Ilias built high on a rock, said to mark the center of Crete, lies some 32½ km (20½ mi) south of Heraklion.

54 The village of **Ayii Deka** (14 km/8 mi south of Ayia Varvara) is home to the church of **Ayios Titos** (✉ Follow signs from rd.), an early 6th-century Christian basilica, reputedly the saint's burial place.

55 Ayios Titos is at the entrance to the Greco-Roman city of **Gortyna,** a huge expanse of scattered ruins sliced through by the main road. At Gortyna, which was made a capital by the Romans in AD 67, sights include the **Odeion,** a small amphitheater where musical recitals were staged in the 1st century AD. In the brick building behind it the **Gortyna Law Code** is displayed. Inscribed on a set of stone blocks, this is Europe's earliest code, dating from the first half of the 5th century BC. In 600 lines it details the laws concerning marriage, divorce, inheritance, adoption, assault and rape, and the status of slaves. From the ruins of Gortyna, a path climbs a few hundred feet uphill to the **acropolis of Gortyna** (✉ Above Gortyna), which has a fine view across the plain. Italian archaeologists, who have dug here since the 1880s, recently completed a detailed topographical survey. A plan is posted at several points around the site, enabling you to find your way through the olives to **several temples, a small theater,** and the **public baths.** Although it was destroyed by Arab raiders in the 7th century and never rebuilt, Gortyna did provide most of the building material for the town of Ayii Deka. Fragments of ancient sculpture and inscriptions can still be seen in the 13th-century village **church.**

Phaistos

★ *50 km (31 mi) south of Heraklion, 18 km (11 mi) west of Gortyna.*

Mires, a flourishing market town, lies some 5 km (3 mi) west of Gortyna. From here, a road crosses the Geropotamos river and climbs a hill to the superbly situated Minoan **palace of Phaistos.** Like Knossos and Mallia, it was built around 1900 BC and rebuilt after a disastrous earthquake around 1650 BC. It was burned and abandoned in

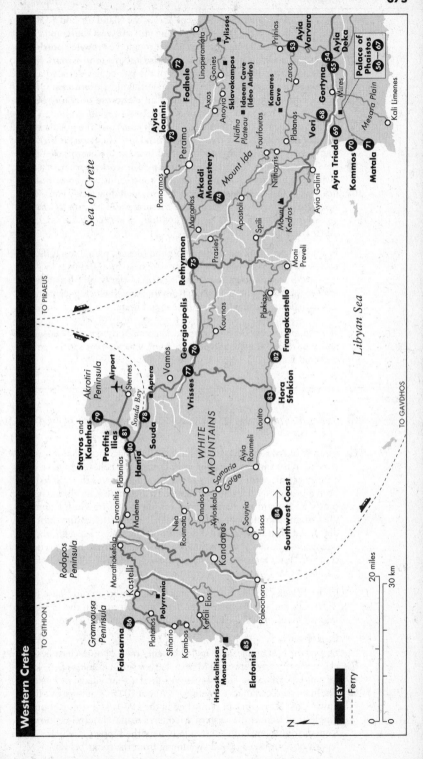

Western Crete

Sea of Crete

Libyan Sea

TO PIRAEUS

TO GITHION

TO GAVDHOS

KEY

Ferry

0   20 miles
0   30 km

Tylissos
Ayia
Varvara
Prinias
53
Ayia
Deka
54
55
**Palace of
Phaistos** 56—67
Gortyna
Linoperamáta
Gonies
68 Vori
Sklavokampos
**Idaean Cave
(Ideo Andro)**
**Kamares
Cave**
Zaros
Mires
Mesara Plain
Kali Limenes
72
Fodhele
Axos
Anoyia
Nidha Plateau
Fourfouras
Platanós
69 Ayia Triada
70
71 Matala
Kommos
**Ayios
Ioannis**
73
Perama
**Arkadi
Monastery**
74
Mount Ida
Niflaynis
Ayia Galini
Mount
Kedros
Panormos
Margoos
Prasies
Apostoli
Spili
Moni
Preveli
75
Rethymnon
Kournas
Plakias
Georgioupolis
76
82 **Frangokastello**
Vamos
Akrotiri
Peninsula
Airport
Sternes
Aptera
77 **Vrisses**
83 **Hora
Stakion**
Souda Bay
79
Stavros and
Kalathas
81 **Profitis
Ilias**
80 **Hania**
78 Souda
Platanias
Tavronitis
Loutro
Ayia
Roumeli
Rodopos
Peninsula
Maleme
Nea
Roumata
Omalos
Xyloskala
Samaria
Gorge
Souyia
84
Southwest Coast
Lissos
Marathokefala
Kastelli
Kandanos
Gramvousa
Peninsula
Polyrrenia
86
Falasarna
Platanós
Sfinario
Kambos
Kefali Elos
Paleochora
**Hrisoskalitissas
Monastery**
85
Elafonisi

**WHITE
MOUNTAINS**

Libyan Sea

N

the wave of destruction that swept across the island around 1450 BC.
(56) You enter down a flight of steps leading into the **west court,** and climb
(57)(58) a **grand staircase.** From here you pass through the **Propylon porch** into
(59)(60) a light well and descend a **narrow staircase** into the **central court.** Much
of the southern and eastern sections of the palace have eroded away.
(61) But there are large pithoi still in place in the old **storerooms.** On the
(62) north side of the court the recesses of an **elaborate doorway** bear a
rare survival: red paint in a diamond pattern on a white ground. A pas-
(63)(64) sage from the doorway leads to the **north court** and the northern **do-**
(65) **mestic apartments,** now roofed and fenced off. The **Phaistos Disk** was
found in 1903 in a chest made of mud brick at the northeast edge of
(66) the site. East of the central court are the **palace workshops,** with a metalworking furnace fenced off in the east court. South of the workshops
(67) lies a set of southern **domestic apartments,** including a clay bath. They
have a memorable view across the Mesara plain. ⊠ *From Gortyna,*
cross Geropotamos River and ascend hill, ☎ *0892/22615.* 🎫 *1,200*
dr. ☉ *Daily 8–7.*

From Phaistos, looking north across the Mesara plain, you'll be able
to see twin-peaked **Mt. Ida,** Crete's highest mountain (2,457 me-
ters/8,058 feet), known locally as Psiloritis. A gray blur beneath Mt.
Ida's right-hand peak marks the **Kamares Cave,** which gave its name
to the delicate Minoan pottery first found there.

NEED A   You can enjoy as good a view as the Minoans had from the **Phaistos**
BREAK?   **tourist pavilion** (⊠ Near site parking area), which serves snacks, coffee,
            and cold drinks.

Vori

(68) *65 km (40½ mi) southwest of Heraklion, 5 km (3 mi) north of the palace*
of Phaistos.

(69) The site of **Ayia Triada** dates from the later palace period and was destroyed at the same time as Phaistos. It was once believed to have been
a summer palace for the rulers of Phaistos, but now is thought to have
been a group of villas and warehouse areas. There's another magnificent view toward the Paximadia islets in the Mesara Gulf. Rooms in
the L-shape complex of buildings were paneled with gypsum slabs and
decorated with frescoes: Two now in the Heraklion Museum show a
woman in a garden and a cat hunting a pheasant. A road from the upper
courtyard leads to the sea. ⊠ *Follow signs from main rd.,* ☎ *0892/91360.*
🎫 *500 dr.* ☉ *Daily 8–5.*

In the village of Vori, a well-arranged museum in an old house illustrates Cretan farm life before mechanization started in the 1950s. ⊠
Just off main sq., ☎ *0892/91394.* 🎫 *500 dr.* ☉ *Daily 10–6.*

Beaches

One of the best and least crowded beaches on the south coast lies just
(70) below the recently excavated Minoan harbor site of **Kommos** (⊠ 3 km/2
mi south of main rd. from Mires to Matala, near village of Pitsidia).
(71) The main road continues to **Matala** (⊠ About 10 km/6 mi west of Mires),
now a popular resort but renowned in the 1960s as a stopover on the
hippie trail across the eastern Mediterranean. The 2nd-century-AD
Roman tombs cut in the cliff side (where the hippies lived) are now
fenced off, but there's good swimming from the rocks below.

En Route   The **north coast highway,** as it heads west from Heraklion toward
            Rethymnon and Hania, climbs away from Heraklion bay and then hugs

Palace of Phaistos

West
Court

N

| 0 | | 20 yards |
| 0 | | 20 meters |

the coastline. There are plenty of places to turn off the broad corniche road and go for a swim.

Tylissos

24 km (15 mi) southwest of Heraklion, 65 km (40½ mi) from Phaistos.

The road to the Minoan site at Tylissos, via the Heraklion–Rethymnon road turning at the town of Gazi, just west of Heraklion, winds uphill through vineyards. The pine-shaded complex reveals three later Palace-period buildings: workshops, living quarters, and storerooms. ⊠ *To left of rd. at the 14-km (9-mi) mark.* ⊡ *500 dr.* ☼ *Tues.–Sun. 8:30–3.*

The road west from Tylissos cuts through another Minoan building of the same period, the villa of **Sklavokampos** (⊠ 5 km/3 mi west of Tylissos). **Anoyia** (⊠ 11 km/7 mi west of Sklavokampos), in the foothills of Mt. Ida, is a sprawling mountain village with a tradition of weavings done in bright colors. Its buildings are modern because Anoyia was razed during World War II in reprisal for the capture of the commander of the German occupying force.

The **Nidha Plateau** spans south from Anoyia 1,402 meters (4,600 feet) above sea level, where the scenery is magnificently wild and dotted with shepherds' stone huts. There is a newly discovered Minoan villa at **Zominthos** (⊠ 15 km/9 mi south of Anoyia), which is now being excavated by Greek archaeologists.

Ideo Andro or **Idaean cave** (⊠ West of Zominthos) was a place of pilgrimage for thousands of years, from Minoan through Roman times.

When Zeus was a baby he was hidden in the Idaean cave to protect him from his jealous father, Kronos.

After you park outside the café at the base of the slope, a 15-minute walk takes you up to the cave. It is now fenced off to protect the antiquities inside, but the air is invigorating and the view superb.

Fodhele

72 *12 km (7½ mi) west of Heraklion, 10 km (6¼ mi) northwest of Tylissos.*

The straggling village of Fodhele is said to be the birthplace of Domenico Theotocopoulos, the 16th-century Cretan painter known as El Greco.

NEED A   Take a respite from driving in **Fodhele,** and refuel with a coffee beneath
BREAK?   a spreading plane tree.

73 The monastery of **Ayios Ioannis** (✉ 23 km/14 mi west of Fodhele) is dedicated to John the Baptist. It is just above the highway, with a spectacular view from its terrace across the Cretan Sea.

Arkadi Monastery

★ **74** *30 km (18½ mi) west of Heraklion, 18 km (11½ mi) from Fodhele.*

Running parallel to the coast highway, the old Heraklion–Hania road follows a gorge inland before emerging into the flat pastureland that is part of the holdings of the Arkadi Monastery. The monastery is a place of pilgrimage for Cretans and one of the most stunning pieces of Renaissance architecture on the island. Built in the 16th century, of honey-color local stone, it has an ornate facade decorated with Corinthian columns and an elegant belfry above. In 1866, the monastery was besieged during a major rebellion against the Turks, and Abbot Gabriel and several hundred rebels, together with their wives and children, refused to surrender. When the Turkish forces broke through the gate, the defenders set the gunpowder store afire, killing themselves together with hundreds of Turks. ✉ *Just south of town of Perama.* ☎ *Free.* ☉ *Daily 8–5.*

Rethymnon

75 *78 km (48½ mi) west of Heraklion, 54 km (33½ mi) west of Arkadi Monastery.*

Rethymnon is Crete's third-largest town, after Heraklion and Hania. As the population (about 30,000) steadily increases, villagers move into new houses on the outskirts of town; the old Venetian quarter is being restored; and the port has been expanded, allowing Rethymnon to have its own ferry service to and from Piraeus. Unfortunately, a long strip of beach to the east of the old town has been tastelessly developed with large hotels and other resort facilities catering to tourists on package vacations, diminishing much of the charm that Rethymnon once had.

Thankfully, some of Rethymnon's remaining charm perseveres in the **old section** (✉ Town center). Wandering through the narrow alleyways you come across handsome carved-stone Renaissance doorways belonging to vanished mansions, fountains, archways, and wooden Turkish houses. One of the few surviving minarets in Greece is in the **Neratzes mosque** (✉ Old town), now a concert hall, and you can climb its 120 steps for a panoramic view. Don't miss the carefully restored **Venetian loggia** (✉ Near center of town on Arkadiou St.), the clubhouse of the local Rethymnon nobility. Rethymnon's small **Venetian harbor,** with its restored 13th-century lighthouse, comes to life in summer, with restaurant tables cluttering the quayside.

Rethymnon is dominated by the huge Venetian castle known as the **Fortessa.** High, well-preserved walls enclose a large empty space occupied by a few scattered buildings and filled with wildflowers in spring. Forced labor from the town and surrounding villages built the fortress from 1573 to 1583, but it never fulfilled its purpose of keeping out the Turks: Rethymnon surrendered after a three-week siege. ⊠ *At village's western end.* ☉ *Daily 8–8.*

The **archaeological museum** is in what used to be Rethymnon's Turkish prison. Look for the collection of beautifully made bone tools from a Neolithic site at Yerani, west of Rethymnon. An unfinished statue of Aphrodite, the goddess of love, is interesting: the ancient chisel marks show clearly. ⊠ *Western end, next to entrance of Fortessa,* ☎ *0831/29975.* ⊠ *800 dr.* ☉ *Tues.–Sun. 8:30–3.*

Dining and Lodging

$$$ ✕ **Cavo D'Oro.** This is the most stylish of the handful of fish restau-
★ rants around the tiny Venetian harbor, and one of the finest restaurants in Crete. Lobster and a wide range of innovative fresh fish dishes are always served. The high, wood-paneled dining room was once a medieval storeroom, and diners also sit on the old cobbled waterfront. ⊠ *Nearchou 42–43,* ☎ *0831/24446. DC, MC, V.*

$ ✕ **Castelvecchio George.** Just down from the Venetian Fortessa, this pleasant taverna just above the narrow streets of the old town catches a refreshing evening breeze in summer. George's specialties, among the traditional Greek and international dishes, are pepper steak and *stifado* (a rich stew made with lamb and sometimes with hare). George has also recently added four simple guest rooms to his establishment. ⊠ *Heimaras 29,* ☎ *0831/55163. No credit cards.*

$$$ 🏨 **Hotel Fortessa.** This newer hotel has many of the advantages of the
★ larger hotels that have sprung up farther out of town on Rethymnon's charmless beach strip, yet it is only steps from the Fortessa, the old town, and the beach. The tile-floored rooms, with handsome traditional furnishings, are built around a marble atrium and sunny courtyard; many have balconies. The nicest rooms face the street, which is closed to vehicular traffic during tourist season, and the fortress. ⊠ *Melisinou 16,* ☎ *0831/23828 or 0831/55552,* ℻ *0831/54073. 54 rooms with bath. Restaurant, snack bar, air-conditioning, pool, free parking. AE, DC, MC, V.*

$$$ 🏨 **Palazzo Rimondi.** This all-suite hotel was formed from combining
★ several 15th-century houses in the heart of the old quarter. All of the tasteful, stylish rooms have sitting and sleeping areas and kitchenettes; many retain such architectural details as vaulted or paneled ceilings, fireplaces, and latticed Venetian windows. A courtyard with a tiny swimming pool offers a nice retreat from the tourist clamor. ⊠ *Xanthoudidou 21, 74100,* ☎ *0831/51289,* ℻ *0831/26757. 21 rooms with bath. Bar, air-conditioning, pool. AE, DC, MC, V.*

$ 🏨 **Liberty.** This quiet, friendly, family-owned hotel opposite a park has a roof garden with an attractive view up to the hills overlooking the town. The rooms are small but comfortable. ⊠ *Themis Moatsou 8, 74100,* ☎ *0831/55851, 0831/55852, or 0831/55853,* ℻ *0831/55850. 24 rooms with shower. DC, MC, V.*

Outdoor Activities and Sports

BICYCLING

For bicycle rentals in Rethymnon, ask at the **Grecotel Rithymna Beach** hotel (⊠ Rethymnon, 74100, ☎ 0831/71002 or 0831/29491).

Shopping

BOOKS AND NEWSPAPERS

One or two souvenir stores on the waterfront sell English-language books and newspapers.

Georgioupolis

76 *99½ km (61½ mi) west of Heraklion, 21½ km (13½ mi) west of Rethymnon.*

Georgioupolis was named for Prince George of Greece, the high commissioner of Crete from 1898 to 1906. Here, at the mouth of the Vrysanos river, where migrating birds gather, he built a shooting lodge, which is closed to the public. There are several good fish tavernas and many rooms to rent.

Vrisses

77 *30 km (18½ mi) west of Rethymnon, 5 km (3 mi) west of Georgioupolis.*

Vrisses is famous throughout Crete for its thick, creamy yogurt. Served in the cafés beneath the plane trees as you come into the village, it's best eaten with a large spoonful of honey on top.

Souda Bay and the Akrotiri Peninsula

71½ km (45 mi) west of Rethymnon, 20 km (12½ mi) northwest of Vrisses.

The road from Vrisses to Hania climbs across the Vamos peninsula, and approaches Souda Bay. This deep inlet, considered the best harbor in the eastern Mediterranean, can shelter the entire U.S. Sixth Fleet. Looking north across the bay to the Akrotiri peninsula, you can spot a small islet topped with a **Venetian fort,** guarding the harbor's inner reaches, which is now part of a large Greek naval base with installations all around the harbor. Taking photos is forbidden around Souda Bay, a regulation to be taken seriously: if you are caught doing so you **78** may be charged with spying. At the top of Souda bay is **Souda** port, where passenger ferries arrive from Piraeus dock.

Beaches

79 There are good beaches at **Stavros** and **Kalathas** on the Akrotiri peninsula.

Hania

80 *78 km (48½ mi) west of Rethymnon, 6½ km (4 mi) west of Souda.*

As you approach Hania—one of the most attractive towns in Greece—a long avenue lined with eucalyptus trees takes you to the outskirts, where signs lead you around the one-way system to the large cross-shape covered market in the town center. Highlights include its well-★ preserved **Venetian quarter** and harbor. It was here that the Greek flag was raised in 1913 to mark unification with Greece, and until 1971 Hania was the island's capital.

On Sunday, Hania's time-honored flag-raising ceremony is repeated at the **Firka,** the old Turkish prison, now the naval museum. ⊠ *Waterfront, at far west end of port.* ☉ *Tues.–Sun. 10–2 and 10–4. Closed Nov.–Apr.*

From Hania's market, work your way through a maze of narrow streets to the **waterfront,** which is a pedestrian zone in summer. Walk around Hania's **inner harbor,** where the fishing boats moor, and east past the **Venetian arsenals.** If you head around to the **old lighthouse,** you'll get a magnificent view of the town with the imposing White Mountains looming beyond.

The **Janissaries mosque** (⊠ East side of harbor), now an information center, was built when the Turks captured the town in 1645 after a two-month siege. The **Kastelli hill** (⊠ Above harbor), where the Venetians first settled, remained the quarter of the local nobility, but it had been occupied much earlier; parts of what may be a Minoan palace have been excavated at its base.

Both **Theotocopoulou and Zambeliou streets** (⊠ Behind outer harbor) lead you into the narrow alleyways with predominantly **Venetian and Turkish houses.** Look for an old **synagogue** (⊠ In Parodos Kondylaki, behind outer harbor), formerly the Venetian church of St. Catherine and now a warehouse.

The **archaeological museum** occupies the Venetian church of St. Francis. Finds on display come from all over western Crete: the painted Minoan clay coffins and elegant Late Minoan pottery indicate that the region was as wealthy as the center of the island in the Bronze Age, though no palace has yet been located. ⊠ *Venetian Church of St. Francis, Chalidron St.,* ☎ *0821/20334.* ⊐ *800 dr.* ☉ *Tues.–Fri. 8:30–3.*

⑧¹ **Profitis Ilias** (⊠ 4½ km/3 mi east of Hania in the Halepa suburb), the burial place of Eleftheriou Venizelou, Crete's great statesman, is lined with fine neoclassical mansions dating to the turn of the century, when Britain, France, Russia, and Italy were active in Cretan politics. A panoramic view from here takes in Hania and its surrounding villages, along with much of the northwest coast.

OFF THE
BEATEN PATH

XYLOSKALA AND SAMARIA GORGE – At Xyloskala (wooden staircase) (⊠ 44 km/27½ mi south of Hania), the 17-km-long (10½-mile-long) Samaria Gorge, the longest in Europe, descends in a steep curve to the Libyan Sea. The hike down takes six hours and is one of the most memorable experiences you can have on Crete. You should start early in the morning, descending the precipitous staircase from the high Omalos plain. The going is stony in places: Wear tough shoes, and take a water bottle and a swimsuit—the reward at the end is a dip in the sea. From Ayia Roumeli, where the gorge debouches on to the coast, you take a boat to Hora Sfakion (☞ *below*) and make the return trip to Hania by bus. Unless you are prepared to wrestle with local bus timetables, it is best to go with an organized tour. Late June and October are the ideal times; do avoid making the trek on Sunday in summer, when the gorge is crowded.

Dining and Lodging

An almost unbroken row of **tavernas** lines Hania's old harbor in summer. Their menus are nearly identical and almost all offer grills and fresh fish at reasonable prices. Among those frequented by Haniots are **Apostolis** (⊠ Inner harbor) and **Karnagio** (⊠ Outer harbor), with tasty Cretan specialties.

$$ ✕ **The Well of the Turk.** Part of the adventure is finding this restaurant on a narrow alley near the minaret in the old Arab quarter, just behind the Venetian warehouses on the harbor; you will have to ask your way, but just about everyone in the neighborhood knows this place. The food ranges from simple Greek fare—a prerequisite is the wonderful appetizer platter, a meal in itself—to some Continental dishes, such as sautéed chicken in a wine sauce. ⊠ *Kalinikou Sarpaki 1–3 Splantiza,* ☎ *0821/545487. No credit cards.*

$$$$ ⊞ **Casa Delfino.** This small hotel in the heart of the old town was once
★   part of a Venetian Renaissance palace, and it now belongs to two descendants of Pedro Delfino, an Italian merchant who lived in the house in the 1880s. The cool pastel rooms are set behind graceful stone archways surrounding a courtyard paved in pebble mosaic; most have stylish modern furniture and are on two levels. The view takes in the medieval harbor and the old town, but you are protected by thick stone walls from the noise of nearby bars and tavernas. ⊠ *Theofanous 9, Palio Limani, 73100,* ☎ *0821/93098 or 0821/87400,* FAX *0821/96500. 12 rooms with bath. Air-conditioning, minibars. AE, DC, MC, V.*

$$$$ ⊞ **Doma.** This converted 19th-century mansion facing the sea, on the outskirts of town, accomplishes the feel of a private house, and was once the Austrian consulate and later the British vice-consulate. Traditional Cretan-style furnishings grace the salons and guest rooms. The best bedrooms overlook the garden, best seen from the rooftop terrace in one of the suites. The Doma is one of the best places in town to dine; one of the owners prepares a traditional dinner each evening, which nonguests also enjoy. Breakfast features breads to be slathered with homemade jams, and yogurt comes with a Turkish topping: a delicious mix of spices, quince preserves, and honey. ⊠ *124 Eleftheriou Venizelou St., 73100,* ☎ *0821/51772 or 0821/51773,* FAX *0821/41578. 22 rooms with shower, 3 suites. DC, MC, V. Closed Nov.–Mar.*

$$$$ ⊞ **Villa Andromeda.** This elegant neoclassical mansion, with gleaming marble floors and painted ceilings, on the eastern outskirts, was formerly the German consulate. The service is friendly, and all suites are luxuriously furnished in a modern, neoclassic style. Next to the swimming pool in the large, luxuriant garden is a curious historic remnant: a much smaller pool built for General Rommel in World War II. ⊠ *150 Eleftheriou Venizelou, 73133,* ☎ *0821/28300 or 0821/28301,* FAX *0821/28303. 8 suites with bath. Poolside bar, air-conditioning, kitchenettes. AE, DC, MC, V. Closed late Nov.–Dec.*

$$$ ⊞ **Porto Veneziano.** From this hotel's modern waterfront block you may gaze at the Mediterranean, its medieval harbor filled with fishing boats and guarded by a Venetian lighthouse. Breakfast is served in a shady garden on a landing stage, where you can watch the fishermen hanging out freshly caught octopus to soften in the sun. The hotel belongs to the Platsidakis family, who are congenial and knowledgeable about the local scene. The rooms are tastefully decorated in cool pastel shades, and the air-conditioning is a welcome relief from the Cretan heat. ⊠ *Palio Limani, 73100,* ☎ *0821/27100,* FAX *0821/27105. 53 rooms with bath or shower, 6 suites. Bar, café, air-conditioning. AE, DC, MC, V.*

$ ⊞ **Porto del Colombo.** Occupying a renovated Venetian house, this pleasant hotel is full of architectural surprises: wooden ceilings, small deepset windows, two-floor rooms with loft areas. Furnishings are traditional and comfortable. Weather permitting, breakfast is served on the narrow street out front. ⊠ *Old town, Theofanous and Moshon Sts., 73100,* ☎ FAX *0821/70945. 10 rooms with shower. MC, V.*

Outdoor Activities and Sports

BICYCLING

You may arrange bike rentals through the **G & A Travel Agency** (⊠ Halidon 25, ☎ 0821/28817).

HIKING

The **Greek Federation of Mountaineering Associations** operates refuges in the White Mountains (☎ 0821/24647) and on Mt. Ida (☎ 081/267110). For details on trekking from Hania; ask at the EOT office (☞ Visitor Information *in* Crete A to Z, *below*).

Shopping

ANTIQUE BLANKETS AND RUGS
Exceptional finds may be had at **Top Hanas** (⊠ Odos Anghelou, #3), which sells a fine selection of antique blankets and rugs, most of them made for dowries from homespun wool and natural dyes.

BOOKS AND NEWSPAPERS
One or two souvenir stores on the waterfront sell English-language books and newspapers.

GOURMET GOODS
Take a stroll through Hania's **covered market** (⊠ Town center), where local merchants sell rounds of Cretan cheese, jars of golden honey, lengths of salami, salt fish, lentils, and other pulse from sacks.

JEWELERS AND CRAFTS
The silver jewelry and ceramics are especially striking at **Carmela** (⊠ Odos Anghelou, #7), which represents contemporary jewelers and other craftspeople from Crete and throughout Greece.

En Route To venture to the southern coast of Crete, backtrack east to Vrisses to the turnoff for a spectacular drive traversing the Askyphou plain, watched over by an Ottoman fort perched on a knob-shape hill, and then descending to the Libyan Sea along the **Nimbros gorge.**

Hora Sfakion

62 km (38½ mi) southwest of Rethymnon, 36 km (22½ mi) south of Vrisses.

82 83 **Frangokastello,** 10 km (6 mi) east of Hora Skafion, is a medieval Venetian fort (with rooms to rent), overlooking a fine sandy beach. **Hora Sfakion** is the landing point for the boat trip from the mouth of the Samaria Gorge, farther west. The gorge gets crowded with buses and walkers in the early evening, but is otherwise a tranquil place where you can find a taverna.

84 In summer, a boat service operates along the **southwest coast** from Hora Sfakion to Loutro, Ayia Roumeli, Souyia, Lissos, and Paleochora, the main resort on the southwest coast. You can easily rent a room for the night in these towns.

85 At the far southwestern corner of Crete is the islet of **Elafonisi,** with white-sand beaches, black rocks, and a turquoise sea (to get there, you wade across a narrow channel).

Beaches
A good road that now traverses the west coast north of Elafonisi has opened up access to uncrowded beaches, even in summer. One of these **86** is the fine beach at **Falasarna** (⊠ North of Elafonisi), near Crete's northwest tip.

OFF THE BEATEN PATH

GAVDHOS – The southernmost point of Europe, Gavdhos is a two-hour boat journey from Paleochora at the western end of the south coast.

Legend has it that on Gavdhos, covered with juniper bushes, the beautiful sorceress Calypso seduced Odysseus, who was on his way home from Troy, and kept him prisoner for seven years.

More prosaically, Gavdhos was a prison island in the 1920s and 1930s for political exiles, who built some of the rough stone houses scattered across the island. Now there are just 60 residents, who rely on an experimental solar power station for electricity—enough is generated to keep drinks cool at the two fish tavernas where you can also find rooms

to rent. There are superb sandy beaches at Korfos, Sarakiniki, and Potamos. For the boat timetable, check with the Paleochora Harbor Authority
(☎ 0823/41214) or Sfakia Harbor Authority (☎ 0825/91292).

CRETE A TO Z

Arriving and Departing

By Boat

Heraklion and Souda Bay (5 km/3 mi east of Hania) are the island's
main ports. Two **Cretan shipping companies,** Anek (⊠ 25th of August
St. 33, Heraklion, ☎ 081/222481) and **Minoan Lines** (⊠ 25th of August St. 78, Heraklion, ☎ 081/229646) have daily ferry service to both
ports from Piraeus year-round. **Rethymniaki Lines** (⊠ Arkadiou 250,
Rethymnon, ☎ 0831/21518) has service from Piraeus to Rethymnon
three or four times a week. The overnight crossing takes 10–12 hours.
You can book a berth in a first-, second-, or tourist-class cabin or an
aircraft-style seat. Make reservations for summer crossings through a
travel agent several days in advance. At other times of the year, you
can buy a ticket from a dockside agency in Piraeus an hour before the
ship sails. Before buying, make sure your cabin is air-conditioned.
There are cafeterias in second and tourist classes and a dining room
in first class. All ferries take cars: a discount may be available if you
buy a round-trip ticket for the car. In summer, you should make your
return-trip reservation several days in advance at the shipping company: both Anek and Minoan Lines have offices in all the main towns
on the island. A one-way first-class fare costs about 11,000 dr., second-class about 8,000 dr., and tourist class 6,000 dr., with little or no
discount for round-trips. Car fares are 16,000 dr. to 20,500 dr., one-
way, depending on size. Other **ferry services** change from year to year,
but there are weekly trips in summer from Piraeus to Siteia and to Kastelli
Kissamou. A small ferry links Siteia with the Dodecanese islands of Kassos, Karpathos, and Rhodes, and both ferries and catamarans operate
in summer between Santorini and Heraklion. There is also a weekly
sail from Heraklion to Limassol in Cyprus, and to Haifa, Israel. Ferries sometimes sail to Kusadasi, Turkey, and Alexandria, Egypt. Travel
agents can advise you on schedules.

By Plane

The principal arrival point on Crete is **Heraklion airport** (⊠ Center of
island, 5 km/3 mi east of city, ☎ 081/228402) where up to six flights
daily arrive from Athens and two flights arrive weekly from Rhodes.
Heraklion is also serviced directly by flights, many of them charters,
from other European cities. There are several daily flights from Athens
to **Hania airport** (⊠ In the west, 15 km/10 mi east of town, ☎
0821/63224). There are flights two or three times weekly to **Siteia airport** (⊠ Eastern Crete, 2 km/1¼ mi west of the town, ☎ 0843/24424).
Twice-weekly flights from Rhodes via Karpathos also land in Siteia.

A municipal **bus** outside Heraklion airport will take you to Platia
Eleftherias (⊠ Town center), known locally as Treis Kamares. Tickets
are sold from a kiosk next to the bus stop; the fare is 200 dr. From
Hania and Siteia airports, Olympic Airways buses take you to the airline office in the town center. The fare is 400 dr. from Hania airport
and 150 dr. from Siteia airport. **Cabs** are lined up outside Heraklion
and Hania airports; the fare into town is 1,000 dr. from Heraklion and
1,800 dr. from Hania. Taxis usually turn up to meet flights into Siteia
airport, but if there are none to be seen, ask the information desk to
call one from town. The fare will be approximately 800 dr.

Getting Around

By Boat

To reach the island of **Spinalonga,** you must take an excursion boat from Ayios Nikolaos. Ask at the harbor; there are two or three trips every day in summer, some including a midday beach barbecue and a swim on a deserted islet.

In summer, a boat service around the **Samaria Gorge** operates along the southwest coast from Hora Sfakion to Loutro, Ayia Roumeli, Souyia, Lissos, and Paleochora, the main resort on the southwest coast.

For the boat timetable from **Paleochora to Ghavdos,** check with the **Paleochora Harbor Authority** (☎ 0823/41214) or **Sfakia Harbor Authority** (☎ 0825/91292).

By Bus

The **public bus companies (KTEL)** have regular, inexpensive service among the main towns. You can book seats in advance at whichever bus station is the terminus for the district of the island you're going to. The efficient village bus network operates similarly, from the bus station in each *komopolis,* or market town. In **Heraklion,** the bus station for western Crete (☎ 081/221765) is opposite the Historical Museum; the station for the south (☎ 081/283287) is just outside the Hania Gate to the right; and for the east (☎ 081/282637), the station is just east of the traffic circle at the end of Leoforos D. Bofor, close to the old harbor.

By Car

Roads on Crete are not congested but, apart from the north coast highway, tend to be winding and narrow. Most are now asphalt, but dirt tracks between villages are still found in mountainous regions. Most road signs are in Greek and English. Gas stations are not plentiful outside the big towns, and road maps are not always reliable, especially in the south. Driving in the main towns can be nerve-racking, especially during the lunchtime rush hour. Drive defensively wherever you are, as Cretan drivers are aggressive and liable to ignore the rules of the road. In summer, tourists on motor scooters can be a hazard. Sheep and goats frequently stray onto the roads, with or without their shepherd or sheepdog. Night driving is not advisable.

With Children

There is practically no provision made on Crete for the specific amusement of children, but people take them everywhere, and Cretans will welcome yours. Just remember that there is a limit to most children's tolerance for ruins, which can be greatly extended by frequent administrations of ice cream and cold drinks, and many dunks in the sea, a pleasure in itself.

Contacts and Resources

Bicycling

Hania: G & A Travel Agency (✉ Halidon 25, ☎ 0821/28817). **Heraklion:** Creta Tours (✉ Epimenidou 20–22, ☎ 081/227002). **Rethymnon:** Grecotel Rithymna Beach hotel (✉ Rethymnon, 74100, ☎ 0831/71002 or 0831/29491).

Bird-Watching

For Gouves estuary, contact the Grecotel group, which runs the **Creta Sun Hotel** (☎ 0831/71602).

Car Rentals

You can rent cars, Jeeps, and motorbikes in all the island's towns, or you can arrange beforehand with a major agency in the United States or in Athens to pick up a car on arrival in Crete. **Hertz** (☎ 081/229702) and **Avis** (☎ 081/225421) have offices at Heraklion airport as well as in the city, but other reliable companies, like **Hellascars** (☎ 081/223240) and many local agencies, have cheaper rates. A medium-size, 4-door car costs about 15,000 dr.–30,000 dr. a day with 100 km (63 mi) of free mileage (extra mileage costs about 50 dr. per km) including insurance and taxes. Weekly prices are negotiable, but with unlimited mileage they start at about 60,000 dr.

Emergencies
Police, fire, and **ambulance services** (☎ 100). Your hotel will call an **English-speaking doctor. Pharmacies** stay open late by turns, and a list of those open late is displayed in their windows.

Tourist police: Heraklion (☎ 081/283190). Hania (☎ 0821/45871). Rethymnon (☎ 0831/28156). Ayios Nikolaos (☎ 0841/26900). Ierapetra (☎ 0842/24200). Siteia (☎ 0843/24200).

Guided Tours
Resort hotels and large travel agents organize guided tours by air-conditioned bus to the main Minoan sites; excursions to spectacular beaches like Vai in the northeast and Elafonisi in the southwest; and trips to Santorini and to some offshore islands like Gaidouronisi, south of Ierapetra, and Spinalonga, a former leper colony off Ayios Nikolaos.

Heraklion: Creta Travel (✉ Epimenidou 20–22, ☎ 081/227002); Adamis Tours (✉ 25th of August St. 23, ☎ 081/246202). **Hania:** G.A. Travel (✉ Halidon 25, ☎ 0821/24965); Canea Travel (✉ Tzanakaki 28, ☎ 0821/28817); El Greco Tours (✉ Theotocopoulou 63, ☎ 0821/21829) organize hikes through the Samaria Gorge and other local excursions. For example: a tour of the Heraklion Museum and Knossos costs 4,500 dr.; a tour of Phaistos and Gortyna plus a swim at Matala costs 6,000 dr.; a trip to Omalos and the Samaria Gorge, returning to Sfakia by boat, about 9,000 dr. Travel agents can arrange for personal guides, whose fees are negotiable.

Hiking
The **Greek Federation of Mountaineering Associations** operates refuges in the White Mountains (☎ 0821/24647) and on Mt. Ida (☎ 081/267110). For details on trekking from Hania, ask at the EOT.

Hospitals
Heraklion: Venizeleion Hospital (✉ Knossos, ☎ 081/237502), Apolloneion General Hospital (✉ Albert and M. Moussourou, ☎ 081/229713). **Hania** General Hospital (☎ 0821/27231). **Rethymnon** town hospital (☎ 0831/27814). **Ayios Nikolaos** town hospital (☎ 0841/25221). **Ierapetra** town hospital (☎ 0842/22488). **Siteia** town hospital (☎ 0843/24311).

Post Offices and Telephones
Post offices are open weekdays 8–8. You can sometimes buy stamps at a kiosk. **Heraklion** (✉ Platia Daskaloyianni). **Hania** (✉ Tzanakaki 3). **Rethymnon** post office and OTE (✉ Koundourioti).

You can often make metered calls overseas from kiosks and kafenions (coffee shops), even in small villages. To avoid heavy surcharges imposed by hotels on long-distance calls, you can make them from offices of the Greek phone company, known as **OTE**. OTE office **Heraklion** (✉ El Greco Park). **Hania** (✉ Tzanakaki 5). **Rethymnon** post office and OTE (✉ Koundourioti).

Visitor Information

The **Greek National Tourist Organization (GNTO or EOT)**: Heraklion (⊠ Xanthoudidou 1, ☎ 081/228203) and Hania (Odos Kriari 40, ☎ 0821/92943) are open 8 AM–2 and 3–8:30.

Community-run information offices: Rethymnon (⊠ Venizelou 20, ☎ 0831/21143), Ayios Nikolaos (⊠ Akti Koundourou 20, ☎ 0841/22357), Ierapetra (⊠ Town Hall, ☎ 0842/28658), and Siteia (⊠ Iroon Polytechneiou Sq., ☎ 0843/24955).

Water Sports

Local **travel agencies, large resort hotels,** municipal information offices, or the **Greek National Tourist Organization (GNTO or EOT)** (☞ *above*) can help with information and arrangements for renting windsurfers, dinghies, yachts, and the equipment for scuba diving and snorkeling.

12 Rhodes and the Dodecanese

Kos, Patmos, and Symi

The Dodecanese (Twelve Islands) are the easternmost holdings of Greece, wrapped enticingly around the shores of Turkey and Asia Minor. Romans, Crusaders, Turks, and Venetians have left their mark here in a remarkable array of temples, castles, fortresses, and exotic towns of shady lanes and tall houses. But what is most likely to capture the visitor is the landscape— from the rugged mountains of Patmos to the verdant fields of Kos and lush hillsides of Rhodes—and a way of life that, despite invasions of armies and sunseekers, remains essentially and delightfully Greek.

By Catherine
Vanderpool

Updated by
Stephen
Brewer

AT THE EASTERN EDGE OF THE AEGEAN SEA, bordering the west coast of Asia Minor, lie the southernmost group of Greek Islands, the Dodecanese, sometimes known as the Southern Sporades. Of them, the largest by far is Rhodes, for many years one of the most popular vacation spots in the Mediterranean; best known of the others are Kos, Patmos, and Symi. The dozen islands, plus additional tiny members of the archipelago, have long shared a common history and fate. The landscapes, however, are sharply contrasting. Patmos, Karpathos, Symi, and Kassos, for example, resemble in some ways the Cycladic islands: rugged hills and mountains almost devoid of vegetation, with villages and towns clinging in picturesque disarray to craggy landscapes. Rhodes and Kos unfold in fertile splendor, creased with streams and dotted with large stretches of green; their major towns lie on almost flat land next to the sea, embracing exceptionally large and well-protected harbors facing the mainland of Asia Minor. Leros, perhaps the greenest, is seldom visited by foreigners; its splendid harbor is adorned with monumental examples of Italian fascist architecture constructed in the 1930s in expectation of a glory that never came. Kalymnos, home to what was once one of the major sponge-diving fleets of the Mediterranean, still shows traces of its former prosperity, and its native sons have done well by their island and their town, whose colorfully painted houses ornament the amphitheatrical harborside. At the very edge of the archipelago, connected only administratively, is Kastellorizo, a lonely outpost that has lost much of its population to emigration.

Pleasures and Pastimes

Beaches
On both the south and north coast of Kos there are highly developed little resort towns with sandy beaches, showers, and umbrellas and sun beds for rent. Paradise Beach is broad, sandy, and scenically magnificent, curving around an enchanting bay. In the morning, caïques make regular runs from Skala to the beaches of Patmos. Most of Patmos's beaches are coarse shingle, but there are sand-and-pebble strips with cafés and tavernas nearby. In 1993, 27 of the beaches in Rhodes were awarded EU Blue Flags for cleanliness and infrastructure; another 15 received the *Golden Starfish* for outstanding natural beauty and limited number of bathers. Rhodes town and the more sheltered east coast have exquisite stretches of fine-sand beaches, while the west side, which is subject to prevailing on-shore winds, can be choppy.

Bicycling
Kos's north coast is especially good for bicycling: in a word, flat. You can rent bicycles just about anywhere in the Dodecanese, in towns and at the more popular resorts.

Dining
Although Dodecanese cooking doesn't differ greatly from that of the mainland, there are some restaurants with unique locations and imaginative preparation. Rhodes produces most of its own foodstuffs, so you can count on fresh fruit and vegetables and, of course, an array of fish (as everywhere, very expensive). Kos, too, is a garden island with lush fields, and fresh vegetables are easy for chefs to come by and even simple salads can be delicious. Eating well is not quite so easy on Patmos and Symi, neither of which have much homegrown produce; the lack seems to have dulled the senses of the cooks, so the fare in tavernas tends toward the mediocre. Always check the food on display in

the kitchen, and ask about the specialty of the day. Dress on all the islands is casual and reservations are not necessary unless mentioned.

CATEGORY	COST*
$$$$	over 9,000 dr.
$$$	6,000 dr.–9,000 dr.
$$	3,000 dr.–6,000 dr.
$	under 3,000 dr.

per person for an appetizer, main course, and dessert, including service and tax, but not drinks.

Diving
Rhodes offers the most opportunities for divers. At Thermes Kallitheas, on the island of Rhodes, a company with customized boats provides 30-minute theory lessons to beginning divers. After practicing in shallow water, you'll descend to a moderate depth to explore the underwater world.

Fishing
No license is required for trolling or line fishing on most of the islands. The best fishing is reputed to be on Rhodes, off Kameiros Skala, Kallithea, Lindos, and Gennadi. Sometimes the commercial fishing boats that moor opposite St. Catherine's Gate in Rhodes town will take visiting anglers out on their trips.

Golf
There is an 18-hole golf course at the village of Afandou, a few mi outside Rhodes town. The Rhodos Open takes place here in October.

Lodging
Except for Athens, Rhodes probably has more hotels per capita than anywhere else in Greece. Almost all of them are resort or tourist hotels; a few of the most luxurious cater to conference and incentive business as well. Some of the most elaborate, at the edge of town, have sea views and easy access to the beaches, which are extremely crowded in high season.

You may have difficulty finding a room in Rhodes; it is best to book through an agent in high season. The hotels in Kos tend to be more modest in size and facilities. For a cozy few days for two, a favorite pastime is staying in a small bed-and-breakfast on Symi or Patmos. Both islands offer a greater number of small hotels with charm, since neither island has encouraged the development of mammoth caravansaries. Many hotels in Rhodes and throughout the Dodecanese are closed from November through April. Hotels in only the first two categories are air-conditioned unless noted otherwise.

CATEGORY	COST*
$$$$	over 39,000 dr.
$$$	22,000 dr.–39,000 dr.
$$	13,000 dr.–22,000 dr.
$	under 13,000 dr.

All prices are for a standard double room in high season, without breakfast unless indicated.

Shopping
Although Rhodes is no longer a duty-free port, some people still consider shopping to be one its major attractions. Upscale shops sell furs and jewelry as well as more affordable trinkets. The styling of the jewelry can be extremely attractive, but the prices are no better than in Athens and are often even higher. In both Rhodes town and in Lindos, you can buy good copies of Lindos ware, a fine pottery with green and red floral designs. Patmos, an upscale tourist island, has some elegant

boutiques selling jewelry and crafts, including antiques mainly from the island. In Chora, you'll find a wide selection of traditional ceramics, icons, and silver jewelry.

Tennis

Several first-class and luxury hotels, mostly on Rhodes, have courts, where equipment can be rented and where nonguests can usually play.

Water Sports

The larger resort hotels in Rhodes offer windsurfing, waterskiing, and in some cases, jet skiing and parasailing. Windsurfing is best near Ixia and Ialyssos; waterskiing, on the sheltered east coast. It's also possible to rent dinghies for sailing and sculling.

Exploring Rhodes and the Dodecanese

Of the Dodecanese, we highlight four: strategically located Rhodes has played by far the most important role in history; Kos comes in second, particularly in its vestiges of antiquity, when its famous Sanctuary of Asklepeios, a center of healing, drew people from all over the ancient world. Both islands are worth visiting for several days each. Symi, easily accessible from Rhodes, is a virtual museum of 19th-century neo-classical architecture, and Patmos, where St. John wrote his Revelations, became a renowned monastic center during the Byzantine period and continues as a significant focal point of the Greek Orthodox faith.

Great Itineraries

If you have a few weeks, exploring the Dodecanese by boat makes for a marvelous, and unusual, holiday, but boats to the less-visited islands are infrequent, especially in winter, and no boats sail if the weather is bad—so you have to allow time for getting stranded.

Most travelers, though, don't have the luxury of waiting for the next boat to carry them off to one more remote island, but they can still get a satisfying taste of the Dodecanese on a shorter visit. With its own towns and fine beaches, Rhodes alone is a fine place to spend a few days or a week, and from there you can make a day trip or an overnight excursion to Symi, with its neoclassic architecture and strikingly arid landscape. If you have time to visit just another island a little farther afield, you might consider Patmos, with its stunning beaches and hilly landscape that is as mystical as its famous monastery.

IF YOU HAVE 3 DAYS
Numbers in the text correspond to numbers in the margin and on the Rhodes and the Dodecanese map.

Confine your visit to ☷ **Rhodes** ①–⑧, where you can spend a day walking through the fascinating old town and visiting the Grand Palace of the Masters and other sights. You will definitely want to make a day trip to the old city of **Lindos** ②, where you can also enjoy a fine beach, and stop in **Petaloudes** ⑦, the Valley of the Butterflies, en route back to Rhodes town. Another day trip takes you by boat to Symi, close to Rhodes but quiet and unspoiled.

IF YOU HAVE 5 DAYS
☷ **Rhodes** ①–⑧ is the best place to begin a longer tour of the Dodecanese. You will want to spend several days there, following your own version of the itinerary above, then on the fourth day take the hydrofoil or slower ferry to ☷ **Patmos.** Of course you'll want to visit the famous monastery and the chora, and leave a day to relax on your own stretch of beach.

IF YOU HAVE 7 DAYS

Again after exploring ⊞ **Rhodes** ①–⑧ and ⊞ **Symi,** you will want to take a hydrofoil or ferry to ⊞ **Kos,** and spend a couple of days exploring this island with its Greek and Roman excavations, Venetian and Turkish architecture, and beautiful flat landscape—perfect biking terrain. After touring the mosque and narrow streets of ⊞ **Kos town,** which is also a good place to stay, make the trip just out of town to the archeological site of Asklepieion, then venture farther afield to other archeological sites and the island's excellent beaches. From ⊞ **Kos,** you can travel on to ⊞ **Patmos** by ferry or hydrofoil.

When to Tour

The best time to tour Rhodes and the Dodecanese is during high season, from about March or April to November, when all establishments are open and the weather is most agreeable.

RHODES

The island of Rhodes (1,400 sq km/540 sq mi) is, after Crete, Evia, and Lesbos, the largest Greek island and, along with Sicily and Cyprus, one of the great islands of the Mediterranean. Rhodes is a country unto itself, and in the years before tourism, it was easily self-sufficient. It lies almost exactly halfway between Piraeus and Cyprus, 18 km (11 mi) off the coast of Asia Minor, and it was long considered a bridge between Europe and the East. Geologically similar to the Turkish mainland, it was probably once a part of it, separated by one of the frequent volcanic upheavals this volatile region has experienced. A central mountain range thickly forested with pine and cypress stretches roughly northeast–southwest along its westernmost half. Most of the rainfall occurs in the northwestern flank of the range; yet the runoff makes the island's eastern side also extremely fertile. Rhodes has almost twice as much rainfall as Athens and Attica, and the climate is extremely mild.

Rhodes saw successive waves of settlement, culminating with the arrival of the Dorian Greeks from Argos and Laconia sometime early in the first millennium BC. They settled in Ialyssos, Lindos, and Kameiros, and together with Dorians from Kos, and from Knidos and Halicarnassos in Asia Minor, formed a kind of loose confederation, later known as the Hexapolis (Six Cities). From the 8th to the 6th centuries BC the three Rhodian cities established settlements in Italy, France, Spain, and Egypt, and actively traded with mainland Greece, exporting pottery, oil, wine, and figs.

By the end of the 6th century BC, the flourishing independence, creativity, and expansion came to an abrupt halt when the Persians took over the island, later forcing Rhodians to provide ships and men for King Xerxes's attack on the mainland in 480 BC. The Persian failure resulted in their final expulsion from the mainland and the creation of a league of city-states under Athenian leadership. In 408 BC the inhabitants of the three cities established the united city of Rhodes, on the site of the modern town; much of the populace moved there, and the earlier towns eventually became mainly religious centers.

The new city grew and flourished, and its political organization was the model for the city of Alexandria in Egypt. At the end of the 4th century BC the Rhodians commissioned the sculptor Chares, from Lindos, to create the famous Colossus, a huge bronze statue of the sun god, Helios, one of the Seven Wonders of the Ancient World. The next two centuries were prosperous for Rhodes's economy, thanks to its superb location on trade routes. In 227 BC, when an earthquake razed the city, help poured in from all quarters of the eastern Mediterranean, attesting to the city's importance. After the calamity the Delphic oracle advised the Rhodians to let the great Colossus lie where it had been toppled in the quake. So it lay, for some eight centuries, until AD 654, when it was sold as scrap metal and carted off to Syria allegedly by a caravan of 900 camels. After that, we know nothing of its fate.

In 42 BC, Rhodes came under the hegemony of Rome, and through the years of the empire, it was fabled as one of the most beautiful of cities, with parks and gardens and the straight streets that had been laid out in the 4th century BC. The roads were lined with porticoes, houses, and gardens, and according to Pliny, who described the city in the 1st century AD, it possessed some 2,000 statues, at least 100 of them colossal.

The sculptural school flourished through the Hellenistic period, and one of its most famous exemplars—probably executed in the 1st century BC—was the *Laocöon*, showing the Trojan priest who warned the Trojans to beware of Greeks bearing gifts, and his sons, in their death struggles with a giant serpent, a work that Pliny reports having seen in Rome in the 1st century AD. Excavations in Rome in 1506 uncovered the statue, which stands in the Vatican today. The intellectual life of Rhodes was also dazzling, attracting students and visitors from around the Mediterranean; its schools of rhetoric and philosophy found great favor among young Romans.

There is almost nothing left of the ancient glory of Rhodes. The city was ravaged by Arab invaders in AD 654 and again in 807, and only with the expulsion of the Arabs, and the reconquest of Crete by the Byzantine emperors, did the city begin to revive. Rhodes was a crucial stop on the road to the Holy Land during the Crusades. It came briefly under Venetian influence, then Byzantine, then Genoese, but in 1309, when the Knights of St. John took the city from its Genoese masters, its most glorious modern era began.

The Knights of St. John, an order of Hospitalers organized in Jerusalem to protect and care for Christian pilgrims, were grouped into "tongues" by country of origin. Each tongue's inn, its place of assembly, was under the orders of a bailiff; the bailiffs were ruled by an elected Grand Master. By the beginning of the 12th century the order had become military in nature, and after the fall of Acre in 1291, the Knights fled from Palestine, withdrawing first to Cyprus, and then to Rhodes. In 1312, the Knights inherited the immense wealth of the Templars (another religious military order, which had just been outlawed by the Pope), and used it to fortify the city.

But for all their power and the strength of their walls, the Knights could not hold back the Turks. By the 16th century they manned the last bastions against the Turks in the eastern Mediterranean, as one by one the towns and cities of Byzantium fell. In preparation for the attack they knew would come, the Knights continually enlarged the moats and reinforced the sea walls, building new towers, fortifying gates, and installing artillery of all sizes. In 1522, the Ottoman Turks, with 300 ships and 100,000 men under Süleyman the Magnificent, began what was to be the final siege, taking the city after six months. During the Turkish occupation, Rhodes became a possession of the Grand Admiral, who collected taxes but left the Rhodians to pursue a generally peaceful and prosperous existence. They continued to build ships and to trade with Greece, Constantinople (later Istanbul), Syria, and Egypt. The Greek mainland was liberated by the War of 1821, but Rhodes and the Dodecanese remained part of the Ottoman Empire until 1912, when the Italians took over. After World War II, the Dodecanese were formally united with Greece in 1947.

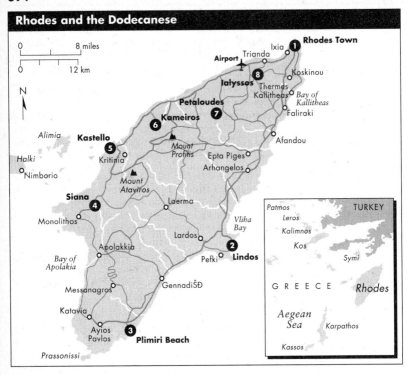

Rhodes and the Dodecanese

[Map showing Rhodes Town, Ixia, Trianda, Airport, Koskinou, Ialyssos, Thermes, Kallitheas, Bay of Kallitheas, Faliraki, Petaloudes, Kameiros, Kastello, Kritinia, Mount Profitis, Epta Piges, Arhangelos, Afandou, Alimia, Halki, Nimborio, Mount Ataviros, Siana, Laerma, Monolithos, Vliha Bay, Lardos, Apolakkia, Pefki, Lindos, Bay of Apolakia, Messanagros, GennadiSÐ, Katavia, Ayios Pavlos, Plimiri Beach, Prassonissi. Inset map showing Patmos, Leros, Kalimnos, Kos, Symi, GREECE, TURKEY, Rhodes, Aegean Sea, Karpathos, Kassos. Scale: 0–8 miles, 0–12 km.]

Rhodes Town

★ ❶ *250 km (155 mi) east of Piraeus.*

Early travelers described Rhodes as a town of two parts: a castle or high town (Collachium) and a lower city. Today Rhodes town is still a city of two parts, but now the divisions are the **old town,** which incorporates the high town and lower city, and the **new town,** the modern metropolis that spreads away from the walls that encircle the old town. Old town contains numerous Orthodox and Catholic churches (many of which have disappeared), Turkish structures, and fine houses, some of which follow the ancient orthogonal plan. All the public buildings are similar in style, creating a harmonious whole, which has been enhanced in recent years by careful reconstruction. Staircases are on the outside, either on the facade or in the court; the facades are elegantly constructed of well-cut limestone from Lindos. Windows and doors are often outlined with strongly profiled moldings and surmounted by arched casements.

In the castle area, a city within a city, the Knights built most of their monuments. The Palace of the Grand Masters, at the highest spot of the medieval city, is the best place to begin a tour of Rhodes; here you can get oriented before wandering through the labyrinthine old town. Also a great help is the permanent exhibition on the downstairs level, with extensive displays on the building, and maps and plans of the city. A large rectangular building with a broad central courtyard, the palace was so solidly built that it withstood unscathed the Turkish siege, but in 1856, an explosion of ammunition stored nearby in the cellars of the Church of St. John devastated the palace; the present buildings are Italian reconstructions. Note the Hellenistic and Roman mosaic floors throughout, which came from the Italian excavations in Kos. ⊠ *Cas-*

tle, old town, ☎ *0241/23359.* ✍ *800 dr.* ☺ *Tues.–Fri. 8:30–7 (winter till 3), weekends 8:30–3.*

The Knights of St. John were buried in the church that once stood at the site of the **Loggia of St. John** (✉ Old town, in front of court of Palace of the Grand Masters), which was also almost totally rebuilt by the Italians. From the Loggia, the **Street of the Knights** descends toward the **Commercial Port,** bordered on both sides by the **Inns of the Tongues,** where members ate and held their meetings.

The **Inn of France** (✉ About halfway down St. of the Knights from Loggia) was largest of the Knights' gathering spots. The ground floor of this typically Rhodian building is occupied by vaulted utility areas opening onto the road; the first floor is reached by a stairway rising from the central courtyard. The facade is carved with flowers and heraldic patterns, and bears an inscription that dates the building between 1492 and 1509.

The **Hospital** (✉ At end of St. of the Knights) was the largest of the Knights' public buildings. The imposing facade of this building, completed in 1489, opens into a courtyard, where cannonballs remain from the siege of 1522.

The main floor of the **Archaeological Museum,** which contains a collection of ancient pottery and sculpture, including two well-known representations of Aphrodite, the *Aphrodite of Rhodes,* who, while bathing, pushes aside her hair as if she's listening; and a standing figure, known as *Aphrodite Thalassia,* or "of the sea," as she was found in the water off the northern city beach. Other important works include the 6th-century kouroi found in Kameiros and the beautiful 5th-century BC funerary stele of Timarista bidding farewell to her mother Crito. ✉ *Platia Mouseou (Museum Sq.), reached by wide staircase from Hospital,* ☎ *0241/27657.* ✍ *800 dr.* ☺ *Tues.—Fri. 8:30–7 (winter until 3), weekends 8:30–3.*

The impressive **Palace of Castellania** (✉ Hippokratous Sq., just inside Arsenal Gate) is an early 16th-century building that was the courthouse of the Knights.

The southernmost side of the old city was once the **Jewish Quarter** (✉ Follow Aristotelous, from south side of Hippokratous Sq.). A **synagogue** still stands here, but it is usually kept closed. Rhodes's Jewish population, once numbering 2,000, was decimated in World War II. At this end of the city Süleyman and his forces were able to breach the walls and end two centuries of the Knights' rule.

The soaring vaults of **Our Lady of the Bourg** (✉ In ruins just inside remains of wall), the magnificent Gothic cathedral, are a startling reminder of Rhodes's Frankish past. The **Commercial Harbor** (✉ Just past St. Catherine's Gate) is Rhodes's largest, close to the cathedral.

The **Mosque of Süleyman** (✉ At top of Sokratous) was built soon after 1522 and rebuilt in 1808. The **Turkish Library** (✉ Sokratous, opposite mosque) dates to the late 18th century. Striking reminders of the Ottoman presence, the library and the mosque are still used by those members of Rhodes's Turkish community who stayed behind after the population exchange of 1922.

The **walls** of Rhodes in themselves are one of the great medieval monuments in the Mediterranean. Wonderfully preserved (even before the extensive Italian reconstruction), they illustrate the engineering capabilities as well as the financial and human resources available to the Knights. Each stretch of the wall was called a "curtain" and its defense was the responsibility of a tongue. For 200 years the Knights strengthened the walls by thickening them, up to 12 meters (40 feet) in places, and curving them to deflect cannonballs. The moat between the inner and outer walls never contained water; it was a device to prevent invaders from constructing siege towers. Part of the road that runs along the top for the entire 4 km (2½ mi) is accessible through municipal guided tours. ⊠ *Old town,* ☎ *0241/21954.* ⊡ *800 dr.* ⊙ *Tours Tues. and Sat. 2:45 (arrive at least 15 minutes early); departure from palace entrance.*

The medieval city of Rhodes is now completely surrounded by the **new city** (⊠ North of medieval walls, bordering small Mandraki Harbor); many of the city's official buildings are found here, their style heavily influenced by the Grand Masters' Palace and other medieval monuments, and making abundant use of Lindos stone, crenelation, and Gothic architectural detail.

Rhodes's harbor is dominated by the **cathedral** (⊠ Harbor), modeled after the destroyed Church of St. John in the Collachium. The **Governor's Palace** (⊠ Harbor, next to cathedral) is constructed in an arcaded Venetian Gothic style. Other buildings in the vicinity include the **port authority** and **customs offices,** the **municipal buildings,** and a huge **open-air bazaar** now faced by fancy confection shops. The **main shopping areas** of new Rhodes are just behind these buildings.

To the west of Rhodes town rises **Mt. Smith,** its slopes still dotted with villas and gardens that in the early part of this century made Rhodes look like a miniature Italian Riviera. Many of them, unfortunately, have been torn down to make way for modern apartment buildings.

The **acropolis** contains the remains of many ancient buildings, including a heavily restored **theater,** a **stadium,** the three restored columns of the **Temple of Apollo Pythios,** and scrappy remains of the **Temple of Athena Polias.** For a dramatic view, walk to the westernmost edge of Mt. Smith, which drops in a sharp and almost inaccessible cliff to the shore below, now lined with enormous hotels. ⊠ *At top of Mt. Smith,* ☎ *0241/21954.* ⊡ *Free.*

Beaches

Elli beach (⊠ Modern town) has fine sand, an easy slope, chairs and umbrellas for rent, showers, pedal boats, and Windsurfers. Much of the coast around Rhodes town is developed, so you can reach some of the best beaches only through the hotels that occupy them.

Dining and Lodging

$$$ ✕ **Alexis.** Carrying on the tradition begun by his father in 1957, Yiannis Katsimprakis spares nothing to bring his loyal clientele the very best
★ seafood, speaking passionately of eating fish as though it were a lost art. Don't bother with the menu; just look at the day's offerings, and if you're a neophyte, ask for suggestions. Whether its beluga caviar, mussels in wine sauce and garlic, smoked eel, oysters, or sea urchins, you'll savor every bite. He even serves *porphyra* (murex), the mollusk yielding the famous purple dye for the Byzantine emperors. A side dish might be sautéed squash with local greens like *vlita* (notchweed) and *glistrida* (purslane). Yiannis also offers bountiful menus for two, which include champagne. Eat your meal on the quiet, shady terrace, perhaps with the new local dry white, Rodos 2400 (in honor of the city's 2,400th anniversary), and don't miss the house salad and the dessert called *hilli* (baklava with ice cream). ⊠ *Sokratous 18, old town,* ☎ *0241/29347 or 0241/26717. AE, V. Closed Nov. No lunch Sun. in summer.*

$$$ ✕ **Ta Kioupia.** Just outside Rhodes town in a group of humble farm
★ buildings, Ta Kioupia is anything but modest. The white-stucco rooms with exposed ceiling beams are elegant: antique farm tools are displayed,

and there are linen tablecloths and napkins, fine china, and crystal. Regular customers get their own engraved plate and glass. Food arrives on large platters and you select what you fancy: pine-nut salad, *tiropita* (four-cheese pie), an eggplant dip that customers joke can't be beat, *bourekakia* (phyllo pastry stuffed with cheese and nuts), *korkorosouvlaki* (rooster kebab) . . . the list goes on—and the food is extraordinary in its variety and quality. ⊠ *Tris, about 7 km (4¼ mi) west of Rhodes,* ☎ *0241/91824. AE, V. Closed Sun. Oct.–May. No lunch.*

$$ ✕ **Dinoris.** In a great hall built in 1530 as a stable for the Knights, Dinoris has long specialized in fish. The food and service lure appreciative and demanding clients, from the mayor to hotel owners and visiting VIPs. Rusticity prevails, with embroidered tablecloths, brightly painted pottery, and thick, seemingly handwoven draperies on the windows. For mezes, try the variety platter, which includes *psarokeftedakia* (fish balls made from a secret recipe) as well as mussels, shrimp, and lobster. Other special dishes are coquilles St. Jacques, grilled prawns, and the sea urchin salad. ⊠ *Museum Sq. 14a, old town,* ☎ *0241/25824 or 0241/35530. Reservations essential for the garden and for weekends in high season. AE, MC, V.*

$$ ✕ **Palia Istoria.** Never mind that this *mezedopolio* (meze joint) is a bit out of the way. Gregarious former actor Haris Kerasiotis has created a visual treat in the space ensconced in an old house with high ceilings, beautiful floors, and genteel murals. Begin your meal with the garlic bread, thin slices topped with *kefalotiri* (a hard cheese) and roquefort; scallops with mushrooms and artichokes baked in béchamel; and plump mussels either sautéed or with piquant *tsouska* peppers. Deciding among the entrées can be tantalizing—*ameletes piperaki* (testicles in pepper sauce), shrimp ouzo with orange juice, pork tenderloin in garlic and wine sauce. The flambéed banana dessert wrapped in phyllo, followed by the portlike Komantaria liqueur from Cyprus and an espresso will complete this serendipitous meal. The extensive wine list accents small Greek producers and a prize-winning Hatzimichali 1992 merlot. ⊠ *Mitropoleos 108 and Dendrinou, Ammos Marasia, south of old town (about 800 dr. by taxi),* ☎ *0241/32421. Reservations essential. MC, V. No lunch.*

$ ✕ **Kavo d'Oro.** This simple taverna is one of the few places in the old town where you can get a good, inexpensive roast chicken, veal, and lamb and grilled meat dishes. Especially good are the *papoutsakia* (eggplant "shoes" stuffed with mincemeat). The decor is taverna style: plain whitewashed walls, with the typical rush-seat, straight-back chairs, and a vine-shaded courtyard at the back for warm-weather dining. The same management runs a second taverna by the same name at Orfeous 40–42. ⊠ *Parodos Sokratous 41 (st. behind Sokratous), old town,* ☎ *0241/36181. Reservations not accepted. No credit cards. Closed Nov.–Mar.*

$ ✕ **Taverna Kostas.** Though slightly more expensive than Kavo d'Oro, this, too, is a good alternative in an area with overpriced, rather mediocre food. Enjoy the plentiful fried squid, and the tender, perfectly grilled chicken souvlakia. Other dishes include pork chops, swordfish, crab, and a mixed seafood plate, which is more than enough for two. ⊠ *Pythagora 62, old town,* ☎ *0241/26217. No credit cards. Closed Nov.–Mar.*

$$$ ▥ **Grand Hotel Summer Palace.** A cut above other resort hotels in the area, the Grand is actually in Rhodes, near the beach, the old town, and the new town's nightlife scene. Though not exceptional from the outside, once you enter the name makes sense: the atrium lobby is spacious, with giant plants and views onto the porticoed pool and garden. The best rooms are in the newer wing, with pink marble floors and pretty paintings of nymphs and goddesses. They feature subdued blue and rose

furnishings, trompe l'oeil touches, alcoved bathtubs, and key cards that automatically turn on the lights. Breakfast is included. ⊠ *Akti Miaouli 1, new town, 85100,* ☎ *0241/26284,* FAX *0241/35589;* ☎ *Athens: 01/291–7027. 362 rooms, 18 suites. Restaurant, bar, 1 indoor pool, 2 outdoor pools, wading pool, sauna, exercise room, tennis court, shops, casino, nightclub, conference rooms. AE, DC, MC, V.*

$$$ 🏨 **Rhodos Imperial.** Resortlike stacked red, blue, and yellow cement boxes zigzag down the hill and end in a swirl of waterfalls and pools. The spacious public rooms are sleek; the pièce de résistance is a glass-ceiling lobby cut from local marble and decorated with huge banners. The crisp, modern rooms are warm peach and gray or blue and sea green, with nice touches like ceramic lamps in ancient style. All rooms have balconies (about half with sea views) and color satellite TV, and all come with buffet breakfast. For diversion, evening shows, Greek-language and dancing lessons, and volleyball and table-tennis competitions are organized. There are supervised children's activities, and free baby cots, high chairs, and children's menus at this parent-friendly hotel. ⊠ *Ialyssou Ave, Ixia, 85100, 4 km (2½ mi) from Rhodes town,* ☎ *0241/ 37489,* FAX *0241/25390;* ☎ *Athens: 01/725–3219,* FAX *01/721–7739. 356 rooms, 48 suites. 2 restaurants, refrigerators, 1 indoor pool, 2 outdoor pools, sauna, steam room, 4 tennis courts, exercise room, squash, boating, waterskiing, recreation room, meeting rooms. AE, DC, MC, V. Closed mid-Nov.–mid-Mar.*

$$$ 🏨 **Rodos Palace.** At this giant resort nestled in gardens just outside town,
★   the guest rooms—some done in shades of ocher, orange, and brown, others in blue and green—are bungalows and in a 20-story tower. All have satellite color TV, balconies, and direct-dial phones; many have sea views. Rooms in the deluxe executive wing have walnut desks and leather sofas, individually controlled air-conditioning, phones for international dialing and voice mail, TVs that permit teleconferencing, and credit-card checkout. ⊠ *Trianton, Ixia, 85100,* ☎ *0241/25222 and 0241/26222,* FAX *0241/25350. 785 rooms with bath, and suites, apartments, and bungalows. 5 restaurants, 4 bars, coffee shop, no-smoking rooms, 3 pools, massage, sauna, 3 tennis courts, exercise room, boating, waterskiing, shops, dance club, recreation room, business services, meeting rooms. AE, DC, MC, V. Closed Dec.–Feb.*

$$ 🏨 **Ibiscus Hotel.** Superbly set on Elli beach, the Ibiscus is good for families who want to be close to the beach and also have the convenience of being close to monuments and museums. Many of the plain, beige and white rooms have wonderful views from their balconies. Continental breakfast is included in the price. In August, half board is mandatory, boosting the price about 6,000 dr. for a double. ⊠ *Nissirou 17, new town, 85100,* ☎ *0241/24421, 0241/24422, or 0241/24423,* FAX *0241/24421. 206 rooms with bath. Restaurant, bar. AE, DC, MC, V. Closed Nov.–Mar.*

$$ 🏨 **S. Nikolis Hotel.** One of the finest accommodations in the old town—and one of the most charming in Rhodes—occupies a restored house. The small but tidy rooms are enlivened by arches and other architectural details, and many have balconies overlooking a lovely garden. Breakfast is served on the roof terrace. Excellent service, including laundry, is caringly administered by Sotiris and Marianne Nikolis. ⊠ *Odos Ippodamou 61, old town, 85100,* ☎ *0241/32034. 10 rooms with bath, 4 apartments. Breakfast room. AE, MC, V.*

$ 🏨 **Pension Sofia.** The old town is full of rooms to rent, but budget-priced Sofia's, run by the same people that own Kavo d'Oro, is bright, pleasant, and framed by trailing jasmine; each room has a little bath. ⊠ *Aristofanous 27, old town, 85100,* ☎ *0241/36181. 10 rooms with bath. No credit cards. Closed Dec.–Mar.*

$ ⚏ Spartalis Hotel. The hotel lives up to its name: it is Spartan, plain, and simple, but it is just off Mandraki Harbor, a few minutes from the gates of the old city. Insist on a room with a harbor orientation; the rooms on the street are noisy. ⊠ *Plastira 2, 85100,* ☎ *0241/24371 or 0241/24372,* ℻ *0241/20406. 79 rooms with bath. Bar, breakfast room. AE, DC, MC, V. Closed Nov.–Mar.*

Nightlife and the Arts

BARS AND DISCOS

It's claimed that Rhodes has more bars and discos per person than New York, Berlin, and Paris—most are in the new town and resort areas like Faliraki. They come and go, so it's best to check with your concierge or the free *Rodos News,* available at the Greek National Tourist Organization (GNTO or EOT) office (☞ Visitor Information *in* Rhodes and the Dodecanese A to Z, *below*).

CASINO

Rhodes's casino (⊠ Next to Grand Hotel Summer Palace, new town, ☎ 0241/28109) is open all year; you must show your passport to get in. The entry fee is 1,500 dr., and it is open from 8 PM to 2 AM.

GREEK DANCE

Performing since 1971, the **Nelly Dimoglou Folk Dance Theatre** (⊠ Andronikou 7, behind Turkish baths, old town, ☎ 0241/20157) keeps alive the tradition of Greek dance, with strict adherence to authentic detail in costume and performance. From May until September, they can be seen weekdays at 9:20 PM for 2,500 dr. They also give dance lessons.

SOUND AND LIGHT SHOW

From April through October the **Sound-and-Light Show** (⊠ Grounds of the Palace of the Grand Masters, ☎ 0241/21922) tells the story of the Turkish siege. English-language performances are Monday and Tuesday 8:15 PM; Wednesday, Friday, and Saturday 9:15 PM; and Thursday 10:15 PM. From mid-May to July performances start one hour later; the cost is 900 dr.

Outdoor Activities and Sports

DIVING

The **Dive Med Center** (⊠ Dragoumi 5, new town, ☎ 0241/33654 or 0241/23783) offers a "resort dive" (11,000 dr.) for first-time divers and for those who don't have a certificate. Customized boats will take you to Thermes Kallitheas, the only place where you can dive on the island. After a 30-minute theory lesson and practice in shallow water, you'll descend to a moderate depth to explore the underwater world. The center also offers courses leading to PADI or NAUI certification. Keep in mind that even if you are certified, it is illegal to dive on your own in Greece. The center is open from May to October.

FISHING

No license is required for trolling or line fishing in Rhodes. The best fishing is reputed to be off Kameiros Skala, Kallithea, Lindos, and Gennadi. Sometimes the commercial fishing boats that moor opposite St. Catherine's Gate will take visiting anglers out on trips.

GOLF

There is an 18-hole golf course in the village of **Afandou** (⊠ About 20 km/12 mi outside Rhodes town, ☎ 0241/51451). The course is open daily 8 to 8; a round costs 4,000 dr. and a weekly pass worth seven rounds costs 22,000 dr. Prices are lower off-season. The Rhodos Open takes place here in October.

HORSEBACK RIDING

Mike's Riding Horses (✉ On rd. between Ialyssos and Filerimos, follow signs for 3 km/2 mi from Hotel Anoixi, ☎ 0241/21387) offers hour-long rides with a guide for 4,000 dr; it's open from 8 to 1:30 and 4 to 8.

SAILING

Information can be obtained on dinghy sailing and sculling from the **Nautical Club of Rhodes** (NOR) (✉ Platia Kountouriotou 9, Rhodes new town, ☎ 0241/23287). To rent yachts, call the **Yacht Agency Rhodes Ltd.** (✉ Amerikis 95, ☎ 0241/22927, 0241/30504, or 0241/30505).

TENNIS

Several first-class and luxury hotels have courts, where equipment can be rented and where nonguests can usually play. The **Rhodes Town Tennis Club** (☎ 0241/25705) is open to nonmembers. Prices are 1,600 dr. per hour for two people, 3,200 dr. for four.

WATER SPORTS

The larger resort hotels offer windsurfing, waterskiing, and in some cases, jet skiing and parasailing. Windsurfing is best near Ixia and Ialyssos; waterskiing, on the sheltered east coast.

Shopping

BOUTIQUES

The **old city's shopping center** (✉ Intersection at Sokratous) is lined with boutiques selling furs, jewelry, and other high-ticket items.

POTTERY

In Rhodes town you can also buy good copies of **Lindos ware,** a fine pottery decorated with green and red floral motifs.

AROUND THE ISLAND

The island's east coast, particularly the stretch between Rhodes town and Lindos, is blessed with white sandy beaches and dotted with copses of trees, interspersed with fertile valleys full of figs and olives. Unfortunately, its beauty has meant that long stretches of this country are now given over to vast resort hotels and holiday villages. Even so, there are still some wonderfully untrammeled sections of beach to be found all around the island, and the town of Lindos alone warrants an excursion from Rhodes town.

Faliraki

16 km (10 mi) south of Rhodes town.

As you leave Rhodes town and travel south along the East Coast, you approach a strange sight: **Thermes Kallitheas** (✉ About 10 km/6 mi south of Rhodes town; 6 km/3½ mi north of Faliraki), a group of buildings that look as if they've been transplanted from Morocco. In fact, this is a spa built in 1929 by the Italians, now much neglected. The great physician Hippocrates of Kos extolled these mineral springs in the early 2nd century BC for alleviating liver, kidney, and rheumatic ailments.

Beaches

Faliraki Beach (✉ 6 km/3½ mi south of Thermes Kallitheas) is a splendid strip of sandy beach now ringed by hotels. At **Afandou Beach** (✉ About 7 km/4⅓ mi past Faliraki), you'll see on the right small tavernas spread out under grape arbors in the brilliant sun. Before or after your meal, you can run across the road to the beach for a dip.

Dining

$$ ✕ **Epta Piges.** If you've had enough of Afandou beach, take an easy, uphill walk through a pleasant ravine to a deeply shaded glen surrounding Epta Piges, or Seven Springs. Here an enterprising local shepherd began serving simple fare to visitors about 40 years ago, and his sideline turned into the busy taverna of today. He imported peacocks and turned them loose in the woods, where they pierce the silence with their scratchy shrieks and flaunt their bright plumage high up in the trees. If you arrive before mealtime, you can have a glass of freshly squeezed orange juice. ✉ *About 2 km (1¼ mi) from Afandou Beach via the footpath. No credit cards. Closed Oct.–Mar.*

Lindos

➋ *60 km (37 mi) southeast of Rhodes town, 30 km (18 mi) southwest of Faliraki.*

Lindos, cradled between two harbors, had a particular importance in antiquity. Before the existence of Rhodes, it was the island's principal maritime center. Perhaps the poverty of Lindos's land, which could barely support a few fig trees and vines, in combination with the fine harbor, forced the Lindians to turn outward for survival and led to their maritime success. Lindos possessed a revered sanctuary, consecrated to Athena, whose cult probably succeeded that of a pre-Hellenic divinity named Lindia, and the sanctuary was dedicated to Athena Lindia. By the 6th century BC, an impressive temple dominated the settlement, and after the foundation of Rhodes, the Lindians set up a *propylaia* (monumental entrance gate) on the model of Athens's. In the mid-4th century BC, the temple was destroyed by fire and almost immediately rebuilt, with a new wood statue of the goddess, covered by gold leaf and with arms, head, and legs of marble or ivory. In the Hellenistic period, the Acropolis was further adorned with a great portico at the foot of the steps to the propylaia. Lindos prospered into Roman times, during the Middle Ages, and under the Knights of St. John. Only at the beginning of the 19th century did the age-old shipping activity cease. The population decreased radically, reviving only with the 20th-century influx of foreigners.

For 500 dr., donkeys can be hired for the 15-minute climb from the modern town to the **Acropolis.** The winding path leads past a gauntlet of Lindian women who spread out their lace and embroidery over the rocks like fresh laundry. The final approach ascends a steep flight of stairs, past a marvelous 5th-century BC **relief** of the prow of a Lindian ship, carved into the rock; and through the main gate of the **Crusader castle.**

The **entrance** to the Acropolis, almost all of it undergoing restoration, takes you through the **medieval castle,** with the Byzantine **chapel of St. John** on the next level above. On the **upper terraces** are the remains of the elaborate **porticoes** and **stoas,** initially restored by the Italians. As is the case with Sounion (☞ Chapter 3), the site and temple command an immense sweep of sea, making a powerful statement on behalf of the deity and city to which they belonged; the lofty white columns on the summit must have presented a magnificent picture. The main portico had 42 Doric columns, at the center of which an opening led to the staircase up to the **propylaia.** The temple at the very top is surprisingly modest, given the drama of the approach. There is no encircling colonnade; instead, as was common in the 4th century BC, both the front and the rear are flanked by four Doric columns, like the Nike Temple on the Acropolis of Athens. Numerous inscribed statue bases were found all over the summit, attesting in many cases to the work of Lindian sculptors, who were clearly second to none.

From the southwest side of the Acropolis you have a good view over the small harbor—where St. Paul supposedly landed bringing his message to Lindos. At the foot of the slope you can see the remains of the ancient theater and, slightly to its right, the ancient agora. ⊠ *Acropolis of Lindos*, ☎ *0244/31258.* ⊠ *800 dr.* ☉ *Tues.–Sun. 8:30–2:45.*

Lindos town (⊠ On land side of Acropolis) is remarkably well preserved, and many 15th-century houses are still in use. Everywhere are examples of the Crusader architecture you saw in Rhodes town: substantial houses of finely cut grayish Lindos limestone with inner courtyards containing stairs to the upper level. The facades are pierced by doors and windows crowned with stone arches, often elaborately carved in the characteristic rope patterns. Many floors are paved with the typical Rhodian black and white pebble mosaics. Intermixed with these Crusader buildings are other houses of almost Cycladic appearance: white geometric shapes pierced by plain square windows framed with blue shutters are nestled in gardens filled with bougainvillea and hibiscus.

Like Rhodes town, Lindos town is enchanting off-season and almost unbearably crowded otherwise, since pilgrims make the trek from Rhodes daily. The main street is lined with shops selling clothes and trinkets of all types; the streets are medieval in their narrowness and twisting course, so the passage slows to a snail's pace. Lindos town can be reached only on foot from the parking lot.

The **Church of the Panayia** (⊠ Just off main platia) is a graceful building with a fine bell tower, now in perilous condition. The body of the church probably antedates the Knights, although the bell tower bears their arms with the dates 1484–1490. The interior has frescoes painted in 1779 by Gregory of Symi.

Gennadi and the South Coast

80 km (50 mi) south of Rhodes town, 20 km (12½ mi) south of Lindos.

The area south of Lindos is less traveled than the rest of the island. The land is not as attractive as in the north, the sandy beaches are fewer, and the soil is less fertile, so there is much less development. The village of Gennadi offers some inexpensive pensions and rooms for rent, as well as tavernas.

Beach

❸ There's a detour to **Plimiri Beach** (10 km/6 mi south of Gennadi), a good place for a swim to break the long drive. The ancient city Kyrbe is believed to have stood in the hills behind the town until it was destroyed by a *plimiri* (flood); hence the name of the village.

NEED A   The **Plimiri Beach taverna** (⊠ Take turnoff along the narrow country
BREAK?   road, ☎ 0244/43250), on a deserted beach, serves very simple
             food—though expensive if you have fish—but the location is hard to
             beat. It closes from November to mid-April.

En Route   From Gennadi, turn inland on a road that leads west across the island, through a river valley dotted with curious hillocks, to the town of Apolakkia, where you bear right at the crossroads to begin your return trip north. The road to Siana climbs through spectacularly wooded hills.

Siana

❹ *60 km (37¼ mi) southwest of Rhodes town, 20 km (12 mi) northwest of Gennadi.*

The town of Siana perches above a vast, fertile valley and sits in the shadow of a rock outcropping crowned with the ruin of a castle.

Shopping

LOCAL SPECIALTIES

Siana is known for *souma* (a local liqueur distilled from grapes, resembling unflavored schnapps). Its renowned honey and walnuts can be obtained at **Tasia's Kafenion** (✉ Just past town church on the main road) or any of the other **cafés** at which hordes of tourist buses occasionally stop.

En Route   Beyond Siana, the road continues on a high ridge through thick pine forests, which carpet the precipitous slopes dropping toward the sea. To the right looms the bare stony massif of **Mt. Ataviros,** Rhodes's highest peak 1,215 meters (3,986 feet).

Kritinia

35 km (21¼ mi) southwest of Rhodes town, 12 km (7½ mi) from Siana.

❺ The **Kastello** (✉ South of Kritinia), a fortress built by the Knights in the late 15th century, is an impressive ruin, situated high above the sea with fine views in every direction.

Kameiros

❻ *25 km (15½ mi) south of Rhodes town, 17 km (10½ mi) northeast of Kritinia.*

The site of ancient Kameiros is one of the three ancient cities of Rhodes. The apparently unfortified ruins, excavated by the Italians in 1929, lie on a slope above the sea. Most of what is visible today dates to the Classical period and later, including impressive remains of the early Hellenistic period. ✉ *Kameiros archaeological site,* ☎ *0241/41435.* 🎟 *400 dr.* ⏱ *Tues.–Fri. 8:30–4:45 (winter to 2:45), weekends 8:30–2:45.*

Petaloudes

❼ *22 km (13½ mi) from Kameiros, 20 km (12½ mi) from Rhodes town.*

Petaloudes, the Valley of the Butterflies, lives up to its name, especially in July and August. In summer the *kalimorpha quadripunctaria,* actually a moth species, cluster by the thousands around the low bushes of the pungent storax plant, which grows all over the area. Don't agitate the butterflies. Over the years, unfortunately, their number has diminished, partly owing to busloads of tourists clapping hands to see them fly up in dense clouds, startled by the slightest sound. ✉ *Petaloudes.* 🎟 *300 dr.* ⏱ *Butterfly season, May–Sept.*

❽ Mt. Filerimos is capped by the site of **Ialyssos,** the third of the ancient Rhodian communities. There are some remains of an early Hellenistic Temple of Athena, as well as those of a Byzantine church. Because of its strategic position, Filerimos also was used by the Knights for a fortress, which stands above a monastery of Our Lady of Filerimos. ✉ *Acropolis of Ialyssos; take turnoff, going on the coast road west from Petaloudes, at Trianda and head south for 5 km (3 mi),* ☎ *0241/92202.* 🎟 *400 dr.* ⏱ *Tues.–Fri. 8:30–5 (winter to 3), Sat.–Mon. 8:30–3.*

SYMI

The island of **Symi,** a wonderful 11 km/7 mi day trip north of Rhodes, is an enchanting place, with a 19th-century town that was built up in just a generation or two, and then virtually abandoned almost as quickly. Fortunately, the island has no beaches—in fact almost no flat land—so it is not attractive to developers. Nireus, the ancient king of Symi, who sailed with three vessels to assist the Greeks at Troy, is mentioned in Homer. Symi was later part of the Dorian Hexapolis dominated by Rhodes, and it remained under Rhodian dominance throughout the Roman and Byzantine periods.

The island has good natural harbors, and the nearby coast of Asia Minor had plentiful timber. The Symiotes were fine shipbuilders, fearless seafarers and sponge divers, and finally, rich and successful merchants. Under the Ottomans their harbor was proclaimed a free port and attracted the trade of the entire region. Witness to their prosperity are the fine neoclassical mansions that were fashionable elsewhere in Greece at the same time. The Symiotes' continuous travel and trade and their frequent contact with Europe led them to incorporate foreign elements in their furnishings, clothes, and cultural life. At first they lived in Chorio, high on the hillside above the port, and in the second half of the 19th century spread down to the seaside at Yialos. There were some 20,000 inhabitants at its acme, but under the Italian occupation at the end of the Italo-Turkish war in 1912, the island declined; the Symiotes lost their holdings in Asia Minor and were unable to convert their fleets to steam. Many emigrated to work elsewhere, and now there are just a few thousand inhabitants in Chorio and Yialos.

Yialos

11 km (7 mi) north of Rhodes, 452 km (281 mi) east of Piraeus.

The boat from Rhodes to Symi usually stops first at the inlet of Pedhi, a small village. If you prefer, you can stay aboard and visit Yialos first. Rounding the last of many rocky barren spurs, the boat suddenly comes in view of the town, at the back of a deep, narrow harbor. The shoreside is lined with shops and houses; the esplanade at the head of the harbor, once the site of shipyards, is now full of cafés. The Church of Ayhios Ioannis (⊠ Near center of Yialos village), built in 1838, incorporates in its walls fragments of ancient blocks from a temple that apparently stood on this site.

Chorio

1 km (⅔ mi) east of Yialos.

It's a 10-minute walk from the main harbor of Yialos up to Chorio, up a road that's actually a staircase of some 500 steps, known as **Kali Strata.** It is flanked by many elegant pastel stucco houses of neoclassical design, with fine, often classical stonework, lavish use of pediments, and intricate wrought-iron balconies. Just before the top of the stairs, to the left, a line of windmills crowns the hill of **Noulia.**

In Chorio, alleys branch out in every direction from Kali Strata, winding through neighborhoods in various states of repair. Many of the houses, older than the neoclassical mansions, are built in typical Aegean style, occasionally modernized by a bit of neoclassical ornament.

The collection at the archaeological museum displays Hellenistic and Roman sculptures and inscriptions; and more recent carvings, icons, costumes, and handicrafts. ⊠ *Laikos Milos Sq., Chorio,* ☎ *0241/71114.* ☑ *Free.* ☉ *Tues.–Sun. 8:30–2.*

Most of Chorio's many churches date to the 18th and 19th centuries, and many are ornamented with richly decorated iconostases and ornate bell towers. The **Kastro** (⊠ At top of town on Chorio's ancient Acropolis) incorporates fragments of Symi's history in its walls. The view from here takes in the village of Pedhi as well as both Chorio and Yialos.

Outdoor Activities and Sports

HIKING

A 5-hour hike south following the island's only road will bring you to the **Monastery of Taxiarchis Michael Panormitis** (☞ *below*); along the way you will enjoy the scenery and the smell of the fennel, thyme, rosemary, and basil growing in great profusion.

Southern Area

Monastery is 7 km (4⅓ mi) south of Chorio.

The main reason to venture to the atypically green, pine-covered hills surrounding the little gulf of Panormitis is to visit the **Monastery of Taxiarchis Michael Panormitis,** Symi's patron saint, and also the protector of sailors. The entrance to the site is surmounted by an elaborate **bell tower,** of the multilevel wedding-cake variety already seen in Yialos and Chorio. In the **courtyard,** which is surrounded by a vaulted stoa, the floor is adorned with a black-and-white pebble mosaic. The **interior** of the church, entirely frescoed in the 18th century, contains a marvelously ornate wooden iconostasis, flanked by a heroic-size 18th-century representation of Michael, completely covered with silver. Note also the collection of votives, including ship models, gifts brought from all over, and a number of bottles with money in them, which, according to local lore, traveled to Symi on their own after having been thrown into the sea. Some rooms are available for lodging. ⊠ *Symi's south side, at harbor,* ☎ *0241/71581.* 🖪 *Free.* ☉ *Daily.*

Dining and Lodging

$ ✕ **Trawlers.** Expect to eat simply in Symi; Trawlers does simple cooking better than most places on the island, and it is reasonably priced. ⊠ *Yialos. No credit cards.*

$$ 🏨 **Aliki Hotel.** Right on the water at the edge of Yialos, the Aliki has been converted from a traditional 19th-century structure into a comfortable, modern facility. The rooms are simply furnished in island-rustic style, as are the public areas; for those who love sea views, the Aliki's can't be beat. ⊠ *Symi, 85600,* ☎ *0241/71665,* 🖷 *0241/71655. 15 rooms with bath. Bar, breakfast room. No credit cards. Closed Nov.–Mar.*

$$ 🏨 **Dorian Hotel Apartments.** You can cook your own meals in these
★ small efficiency apartments in Yialos, each with a miniature living and dining room and a cozy loft-style bedroom, both with dark wood furniture. ⊠ *Symi, 85600,* ☎ *0241/71181, 0241/71811, or 0241/71307. 2 rooms with bath, 7 apartments. No credit cards. Closed Nov.–Mar.*

$ 🏨 **Village Hotel.** Spotlessly restored in 1992, the Village Hotel is set
★ in a traditional neoclassical mansion that has been enlarged. In Chora, it has good views in all directions . . . and a steep climb home after you've had a morning coffee in the port. All the rooms open onto a balcony or terrace. ⊠ *Symi, 85600,* ☎ *0241/71800. 17 rooms with bath. Breakfast room. No credit cards. Closed Nov.–Mar.*

KOS

The island of Kos, the third-largest in the Dodecanese, is certainly one of the most beautiful, with verdant fields and tree-clad mountains, surrounded by miles of sandy beach. Its highest peak, part of a small mountain range in the northeast, is less than 1,000 meters (3,280 feet). All this beauty has not gone unnoticed, of course, and Kos undeniably suffers from the effects of mass tourism: Its beaches are often crowded, and the main town is noisy and busy between June and September.

In Mycenaean times and during the Archaic period, the island prospered. In the 6th century BC it was conquered by the Persians, but later joined the Delian League, supporting Athens against Sparta in the Peloponnesian War. Kos was invaded and destroyed by the Spartan fleet, ruled by Alexander and various of his successors, and has twice been devastated by earthquakes. Nevertheless the city and the economy flourished, as did the arts and sciences. The painter Apelles, the Michelangelo of his time, came from Kos, as did Hippocrates, father of modern medicine. Under the Roman Empire, the island's Asklepieion and its renowned healing center drew emperors and ordinary citizens alike. The Knights of St. John arrived in 1315 and ruled for the next two centuries, until they were replaced by the Ottomans. In 1912, the Italians took over, and in 1947, the island was united with Greece.

Kos Town

370 km (230 mi) east of Piraeus, 92 km (57 mi) north of Rhodes.

The modern town lies on a flat plain surrounding a spacious, round harbor called Mandraki. The fortress, which crowns its west side, where Hippocrates is supposed to have taught in the shade of a large plane tree, is a good place to begin your exploration of Kos town.

On one side of Platia Platanou, the little square named after the tree, stands the graceful Loggia (⊠ Platia Platanou), actually a mosque, built in 1786.

The **Castle of the Knights,** built mostly in the 15th century and full of ancient blocks from its Greek and Roman predecessors, is a repository of fragments of ancient inscriptions, funerary monuments, and other sculptural material. A walk around the walls affords fine views over the town, whose flat skyline is pierced by a few remaining minarets and many palm trees. ⊠ *Over bridge from Platia Platanou,* ☎ *0242/ 28326.* 🎫 *400 dr.* ☉ *Tues.–Sun. 8:30–3.*

Excavations have uncovered the **Roman agora and harbor** (⊠ Over bridge from Platia Platanou, just behind Castle of the Knights), as well as portions of 4th-century BC and Hellenistic buildings. The **ruins,** which are not fenced, blend charmingly into the fabric of the modern city; it's a shortcut for people on their way to work, a place to sit and chat, an outdoor playroom for children. The ruins are now overgrown, and in spring they're covered with brightly colored flowers, which nicely frame the ancient gray and white marble blocks tumbled in every direction.

★ Kos town's **archaeological museum** contains extremely important examples of Hellenistic and Roman sculpture by Koan artists. Among the treasures is a group of sculptures from various Roman phases, all found in the House of the Europa Mosaic, and a Hellenistic series of Hellenistic draped female statues mainly from the Sanctuary of Demeter at Kyparissi and the Odeion. ⊠ *Platia Eleftherias, west of agora through gate leading to main sq.,* ☎ *0242/28326.* 🎫 *400 dr.* ☉ *Tues.–Sun. 8:30–3.*

The **West Excavations** (⊠ Just below ancient Acropolis) have uncovered a portion of one of the main Roman streets with many houses, including the **House of the Europa Mosaic.** Part of the **Roman baths** (⊠ Near main Roman st.), it has been converted into a basilica. The **gymnasium,** distinguished by its partly reconstructed colonnade, and the so-called **Nymphaion,** a lavish public latrine that has been restored, are also of interest.

Beaches

Kardamena (⊠ On south coast of Kos), and **Tingaki** (⊠ On north coast of Kos), are both highly developed little resort towns with sandy beaches, showers, and umbrellas and sun beds for rent. At **Mastichari** (⊠ On north coast, farther from Kos town), another resort, there's a wide sand beach, tavernas, rooms for rent, and a pier where boats sail on day trips to the uncrowded islet of Pserimos. **Paradise Beach** (⊠ On southeast coast) has plenty of parking, and thus crowds, but the broad, sandy beach is magnificent, curving around an enchanting bay. If you must get wet but can't leave **Kos town,** try the **narrow pebbly strip** (⊠ Just south of main harbor).

Asklepieion

4 km (2½ mi) west of Kos town.

One of the great **healing centers** of antiquity is framed by a thick grove of cypress trees and laid out on several **broad terraces** connected by a monumental staircase. The lower terrace probably held the Asklepieian Festivals. On the middle terrace is an **Ionic temple,** once decorated with paintings by Apelles, including the renowned depiction of Aphrodite often written about in antiquity and eventually removed to Rome by the emperor Augustus. On the uppermost terrace is the **Doric Temple of Asklepeios,** once surrounded by colonnaded porticoes. ⊠ *Asklepieion,* ☎ *0242/28763.* ⊠ *600 dr.* ☉ *Tues.–Fri. 8–7, weekends 8:30–3.*

Antimacheia

25 km (15½ mi) southwest of Kos Town, 6 km (3¾ mi) southwest of Asklepieion.

Built by the Knights, the lonely complex of the **Castle of Antimacheia** was once a large town that, because of its isolation, was not quarried for stone. Most of its buildings lie where they have fallen, in heaps of rubble picturesquely shrouded in thick vegetation. Two small **churches** still stand at the center of the site, one dating to 1494, according to an inscription over its door; the other, a **Latin-type basilica** with a single nave and no transept is now dedicated to Ayia Paraskevi and is still in use.

Bay of Kamares

35 km (21¾ mi) southwest of Kos Town, 10 km (6 mi) south of the Castle of Antimacheia.

Close to shore here is a little rock formation holding a **chapel to St. Nicholas,** and opposite are the ruins of a magnificent 5th-century **Christian basilica** (⊠ On mainland, edge of public beach).

Beach

A good chunk of the public beach (⊠ Mainland) is now occupied by a Club Méditerranée.

<table>
<tr><td>OFF THE
BEATEN PATH</td><td>**NISIROS AND MANDRAKI** – From the resort town of Kardamena, on Kos's south coast, excursion boats make a 1-hour trip daily to Nisiros, a nontouristy island with an active volcano in the middle. Buses transport you up over the mountain rim and into the crater, where fumaroles give off hot sulphurous steam. You can also visit the picturesque, unspoiled main town of Mandraki and its 15th-century monastery.</td></tr>
</table>

Dining and Lodging

$$ ✕ **Panorama.** You will need a car to get here, but the evening will be
★ well spent in the large paneled dining room with exposed beams and
fireplace, or on the terrace nestled among vistas. You'll enjoy the del-
icately fried *kolokithakia tiganita* (summer squash), octopus with oil
and vinegar, fluffy *tiropitakia* (little cheese pies), and the marvelous sal-
ads. Even if you don't like retsina, try the local Theokritos; it may con-
vert you. ⊠ *Bagiati-Asfendiou,* ☎ *0242/29367. Reservations essential
Fri. and Sat. in high season. No credit cards. Closed Nov.–Dec.*

$ ✕ **Aklipios.** A memorable meal in Kos can be had at a little restaurant
★ near the Asklepieion, in the village of Platani. Sit in the shade of an
ancient laurel tree and try the exquisite selection of mezedes: home-
prepared *dolmadakia* (stuffed vine leaves), bourekakia, *imam bayaldi*
(baked eggplant). Even the boiled cauliflower is perfect. ⊠ *Platani,* ☎
0242/25264. No credit cards.

$$$ ⊞ **Astron Hotel.** Most of the rooms in this quasi-waterfront hotel are
a sparse white with touches of brown, and have balconies and a view
over the town's main harbor. Although the location is picturesque, scooters and late-night revelers make the area noisy in season; rooms on the
third floor are quietest. ⊠ *Akti Kountouriotou,* ☎ *0242/22814 or
0242/23704 through 23707. 58 rooms with bath. Bar, cafeteria, pool.
AE, MC, V.*

$$$ ⊞ **Ramira Beach.** This is one of the better resort hotels for family hol-
idays, just outside Kos town. Most of the white and blue rooms have
sea views. ⊠ *Psalidi Beach,* ☎ *0242/22891 through 22894. 268
rooms. Restaurant, bar, pool, 2 tennis courts. AE, DC, MC, V. Closed
Nov.–Mar.*

$$ ⊞ **Titania Hotel.** This in-town hotel, right on the sea, delivers good quality at a good price. Modern outside and in, its rooms are plain but com-
fortable. Because it's on the main road, the rooms may be noisy in high
season, but offsetting this, you are within walking distance to town,
and there's a little strip of beach right across the street. ⊠ *6b Vasileos
Georgiou,* ☎ *0242/22556. 58 rooms with bath. Bar, lobby lounge. No
credit cards. Closed Nov.–Apr.*

Outdoor Activities and Sports

BICYCLING

The flat island of Kos, particularly the area around the town, is good
for bicycle riding. Ride to the **Asklepieion** for a picnic, or visit the **Castle of Antimacheia.** Note: Be aware of such danger points as cistern
openings; very few have fences around them. You can rent bicycles everywhere—in Kos town and at the more popular resorts. Try the many
shops along Eleftheriou Venizelou Street in town. Renting a bike costs
about 600 dr. per day; scooter rentals begin at about 2,000 dr.

PATMOS

Rocky and barren, the small island of Patmos, northwest of Kos, is
the site of the famed Monastery of St. John the Theologian. Most of
the island's approximately 2,500 people live in three villages: Skala,
medieval Chora, and the small rural settlement of Kambos.

The early history of Patmos remains shadowy: classical references are
few and the area has not been the object of extensive excavation.
There is scattered evidence of Mycenaean presence, and walls of the
Classical period indicate the existence of a town near Skala. In AD 95,
during the emperor Domitian's persecution of Christians, St. John
was banished to Patmos, where he lived until his reprieve two years
later. He writes that it was on Patmos that he "heard . . . a great voice,

as of a trumpet," commanding him to write a book and "send it unto the seven churches."

Patmos was virtually abandoned after the 6th century, and reemerges in history at the end of the 11th century with the founding of the Monastery of St. John the Theologian by Hosios Christodoulos, a man of education, energy, devotion, and vision. Born in Bythynia in Asia Minor, he had spent some years as a hermit, then built the Theotokos Monastery in Kos, and came to Patmos in 1088. He wrote, "My ardent desire was to possess this island at the edge of the world, for there were no people, all was tranquillity, no boats dropped anchor here." So he traveled to Constantinople for permission to set up a monastery, receiving Patmos in exchange for his holdings on Kos.

Skala

302 km (187½ mi) east of Piraeus, 161 km (100 mi) north of Kos.

Skala, the island's main port, is its commercial center and the location now of almost all the hotels and restaurants. It's also a popular port of call for cruise ships, and in summer, huge liners often loom over town for several hours every day. There is not much to see in the town, but strict building codes have been enforced and even new buildings have traditional architectural detail.

Beaches
In the morning, caïques make regular runs from Skala to the beaches, and prices vary with the number of people making the trip (or with the boat). Ask for several "bids" to find out the going rate and the time of return, and remember to negotiate. Most of Patmos's beaches are coarse shingle. Melloi Beach (⊠ A 20-min walk north of Skala, or a quick caïque ride) is a sand and pebble strip with cafés and tavernas nearby. The beach at **Kambos Bay** (⊠ 15–20 min caïque ride), mostly fine pebble and sand, is the most popular on the island, with nearby tavernas, windsurfing, waterskiing, and pedal boats. Both **Psiliamo** and **Little Psiliamo** (⊠ On south shore) have fine sand, but they're hard to get to: a 45-minute caïque ride or a 2-hour walk from Skala.

Dining and Lodging
$ ✕ **Grigoris.** This old favorite near the ferry landing is a good place to wait for the night boat to Athens. You can have grilled fish and meat, or a selection from the *magirefta* (pre-cooked dishes). The interior is carefully decorated in rustic taverna style and the tables under the spreading laurel tree are an especially pleasant place to take in the passing (and noisy) scene. ⊠ *Skala,* ☎ *0247/31515. No credit cards. Closed Nov.–Mar.*

$ ✕ **O Kipos.** This tiny hole-in-the-wall really comes to life in warm weather, when tables are pulled out into the street, next to a large *kipos* (garden). Try the *kolokithopita* (squash pancakes), the delicious boiled octopus in vinegar, or *koukia* (flat beans), among other well-prepared traditional dishes. The restaurant is distinguished by the small boat and nets the owner has hung in the tree just outside, a memento of his previous pursuits. ⊠ *Skala,* ☎ *0247/31884. No credit cards.*

$ ✕ **Pandelis Restaurant.** Just a few steps back from the port, Pandelis offers good taverna-style cooking, with a good selection of the chef's choice of traditional Greek dishes. Sit outside at one of the tables in the little sunny alley in front of the restaurant, or move inside, but not too close to the noisy TV. ⊠ *Emmanuel Xenou, Skala,* ☎ *0247/31230. No credit cards.*

$$ 🏠 **Captain's House.** One of the very special places to stay in Patmos, ★ largely because the owners are so pleasant, the Captain's House faces

the sea at the edge of Skala. The feel of old Patmos has been re-created with stone arches accenting the white-painted rooms and simple wood furniture. ⊠ *Skala,* ☎ *0247/31793,* ⅛ *0247/32277. 14 rooms with bath. Breakfast room. AE, DC, MC, V. Closed mid-Oct.–Mar.*

$ ⌂ **Blue Bay Hotel.** An enterprising Greek-Australian family has returned
★ to open this hotel just outside Skala, but within a 10-minute walk of everything. Its location, with a view over the open sea (shared by all but two of the rooms), is one of its great charms, as are the neatly decorated, immaculate rooms. ⊠ *Skala,* ☎ *0247/31165. 22 rooms with bath. Breakfast room. No credit cards. Closed Nov.–Mar.*

$ ⌂ **Delfini.** The bright and cheerful interior of this hotel reflects the taste of the owner's Swiss wife. Half the rooms look out to the sea, the other half toward the monastery and the hotel's lovely inner garden and patio. ⊠ *Skala,* ☎ *0247/32060,* ⅛ *0247/32061. 12 rooms, some with bath. Breakfast room. No credit cards. Closed Dec.–Mar.*

Chora

2½ km (1½ mi) south, and above, Skala.

The village of Chora, clustered around the walls of the Monastery of St. John the Theologian, has become a preserve of international wealth; many of the houses, now exquisitely restored, are owned by Athenians and foreigners, who discovered the settlement some years ago.

According to tradition, St. John wrote the text of Revelations in the little cave, the Sacred Grotto, now built into the **Monastery of the Apocalypse** (⊠ 2 km/1¼ mi along the cobbled road from Skala heading to Chora, ☎ 0241/31234). It is decorated with wall paintings of the 12th century and icons of the 16th. The monastery, constructed in the 17th century from architectural fragments of earlier buildings, and further embellished in later years, also contains chapels to St. Artemios and St. Nicholas.

★ The **Monastery of St. John the Theologian,** high above Skala, is one of the finest extant examples of a fortified medieval monastic complex. From its inception, it attracted monks of education and social standing, who made sure that it was ornamented with the best sculpture, carvings, and paintings. It was an intellectual center, with a rich library and a tradition of teaching, and by the end of the 12th century, it owned land on Leros, Limnos, Crete, and Asia Minor, as well as ships, which carried on trade exempt from taxes. A broad staircase leads to the entrance, which was fortified by towers and buttresses. The complex consists of buildings from a number of periods: in front of the entrance is the 17th-century **Chapel of the Holy Apostles;** the **main church** dates from the time of Christodoulos; the **chapel of the Virgin, refectory, kitchen,** and some of the **cells** are 12th century.

The monastery contains three of the most important cultural treasures of the Orthodox Church. The **library,** with a wonderful series of illuminated manuscripts, approximately 1,000 codices, and more than 3,000 printed volumes, was first catalogued in 1200; of the 267 works of that time, the library still has 111. Later catalogues make it possible to reconstruct the library's history and the monastery's intellectual life. The oldest codices, dating to the early 6th and the 8th centuries, contain parts of the Gospel of St. Mark and the Book of Job.

The documents in the **archives** (not open to the public) preserve a near-continuous record, down to the present, of the history of the monastery as well as the political and economic history of the region. The **treasury** contains a wide range of relics, icons, silver, and vestments, most dating from 1600 to 1800. Many of the objects are votives dedicated by the clerics, nobles, and wealthy individuals: one of the most beautiful is an 11th-century icon of St. Nicholas, executed in the finest of mosaics, in an exquisitely chased silver frame. The more than 600 vestments are of luxurious fabrics, elaborately embroidered with gold, silver, and multicolored silks. ⊠ *Along cobbled rd. from Skala to Chora,* ☎ *0241/21954.* ▨ *800 dr., free on Sun.* ☉ *Tues.–Sun. 8:30–3.*

Shopping

Patmos has some elegant boutiques selling jewelry and crafts, including antiques mainly from the island. **Katoi** (⊠ Chora, on the main rd. to monastery, ☎ 0247/31487 or 0247/32107) has a wide selection of ceramics, icons, and silver jewelry of traditional design.

RHODES AND THE DODECANESE A TO Z

Arriving and Departing

By Boat

Of the several ferry lines serving the Dodecanese, the **Dane Sea Line** (⊠ Piraeus: Akti Miaouli 33, ☎ 01/429–3240; ⊠ Rhodes: Amerikis 95, ☎ 0241/77070) has the largest boats and the most frequent service, sailing daily out of Piraeus. The Athens–Dodecanese ferry schedule changes seasonally, so call the **Piraeus port authority** (☎ 01/422–6000), any Athens EOT (☎ 01/322–2545), or a travel agency, before booking.

Those traveling by ferry to **Rhodes** should try to get one of the few ferries that goes direct (like the *Rhodos*); most stop first at Patmos, Leros, Kalymnos, and Kos, often arriving, inconveniently, between midnight and 6 AM. Fares from Athens to Rhodes are about 6,500 dr.–10,000 dr., cars 13,241 dr.–17,441 dr., not including taxes. Strintzis Line's *Ionian Sea* (represented by Skevos Travel, ⊠ Amerikis 111, ☎ 0241/22461 or 241/75655) leaves Rhodes for Piraeus every Sunday at 3:30 PM, hitting seven islands, including Tilos, Nissiros, Kos, and Kalymnos, along the way. Ferry fares from Athens to **Patmos** are 3,405 dr.–5,828 dr., cars 13,160 dr.–17,441 dr.

By Car

If you drive to Greece, you may take your car to the Dodecanese on one of the large ferries that sail daily from Piraeus to Rhodes and less frequently to the smaller islands.

By Plane

At least four flights per day fly to Rhodes from Athens, and extra flights are added during high season. The flight, via **Olympic Airways** (☎ Athens: 01/966–6666, ℻ 01/921–9933; ⊠ Rhodes: Ierou Lochou 9, ☎ 0241/24571 through 0241/24575, reservations ☎ 0241/24555), takes less than an hour and costs 22,800 dr. one way. You can also fly to Rhodes from Heraklion four to five times a week (45 minutes; 18,800 dr.) and from Thessaloniki usually twice weekly (75 minutes; 26,800 dr.). It is possible to fly directly to Rhodes from a number of European capitals, especially on charters.

Rhodes airport (☎ 0241/92839) is about 20 minutes from Rhodes town, and it's best to take a taxi (about 1,600 dr.). Though private vehicles must have permits to enter the old town, a taxi may enter if carrying luggage, no matter what a reluctant driver tells you. In Kos, the Olympic Airways office is in Kos town (⊠ 22 Vasileos Pavlou, ☎ 0242/28331 or 0242/28332) and a bus runs between the office and the **Kos airport** (☎ 0242/51229), about 45 minutes away, to meet the twice-daily flights from Athens. The smaller islands of **Leros, Karpathos, Kassos,** and **Kastellorizo** also have airports with less frequent service.

Getting Around

By Boat

There are frequent local boats, and in summer, hydrofoils connect the Dodecanese with one another. For information, contact the **Rhodes Port Authority** (☎ 0241/22220) or the Rhodes hydrofoil office (☎ 0241/24000 or 0241/20272).

By Bus

There is a good bus network on all the islands. Buses from Rhodes town leave from the bus stop (✉ Alexander Papagou, near Platia Rimini, ☎ 0241/27706) for points on the east side of the island, and from Averoff Street (✉ Beside new market, ☎ 0241/26300) for the west side.

By Car and Bicycle

On **Rhodes,** the roads are good, there are not many of them, and good maps are available. It is possible to tour the island in one day if you rent a car. Traffic is likely to be heavy only from Rhodes town to Lindos, and again as you near Kameiros. You can rent bicycles, including mountain bikes, in Rhodes town from **Mike's Motor Club** (✉ Kazouli 23, ☎ 0241/37420). In **Kos,** a car is advisable only if you are very pressed for time; most of what you want to see in Kos can by reached by bicycle or public transportation. Bicycle shops are plentiful. In **Patmos,** there is no point in renting a car unless you want to explore the outer edges of the island, since both monasteries are easily reached by bus, on foot, or even by taxi. There are no roads suitable for cars on **Symi,** and exploration is done on foot or by boat. The other Dodecanese islands are also best visited by public transportation.

By Plane

Olympic Airways (☞ *above*) runs five flights a week from Rhodes to Kos (30 minutes, 9,000 dr.) and other flights to the less-visited islands of Karpathos (8,800 dr.), Kassos (8,800 dr.), and Kastellorizo (7,000 dr.); the latter two are not served directly from Athens. You can also hook up with the Cycladic islands by flying to Mykonos (weekly flight, 15,000 dr.) or Santorini (three times weekly, 15,000 dr.). Schedules are reduced in winter.

By Taxi

Taxis are available throughout the island of **Rhodes,** with ranks in most resorts—cars can be flagged down anywhere. The central rank is in Rhodes town (✉ Off Platia Rimini, ☎ 0241/27666). If you call a radio taxi (☎ 0241/64712, 0241/64734, 0241/64778, or 0241/64790), the pick-up charge is an extra 200 dr. Typical fares from Rhodes town are: to Ixia, 600 dr.; to Ialyssos/Trianda, 900 dr.; to Faliraki, 1,600 dr.; and to Lindos, 5,000 dr. Fares almost double between midnight and 6 AM.

Contacts and Resources

Car Rental

RHODES

Hertz (✉ Griva 16, ☎ 0241/21819 and 0241/25888; ✉ Rhodes airport ☎ 0241/92902; ✉ Lindos, ☎ 0244/31347). **Interrent-EuropCar** (✉ 28th of October St. 18, ☎ 0241/21958; ✉ Airport, ☎ 0241/93105; ✉ Lindos, ☎ 0244/31132). **Just Rent a Car** (✉ Orfanidou 45, ☎ 0241/31811, 0241/75421, or 0241/33842).

KOS

Interrent-EuropCar (✉ Eleftheriou Venezelou 28, ☎ 0242/24070 or 0242/24071, FAX 0242/25180).

Emergencies

As elsewhere in Greece, **pharmacies** in the Dodecanese post in their windows a list showing which stores are open 24 hours, on which days.

RHODES

Hospital (☎ 166 or 0241/22222). **Police** (✉ Ethelondon Dodekanissou 45, new town, ☎ 100). **Tourist police** (✉ On Museum Sq., old town, ☎ 0241/27423).

KOS

Police (☎ 0242/22222). **Tourist police** (☎ 0242/22444).

PATMOS

Hospital (☎ 0247/31211). **Police** (☎ 0247/31303).

Guided Tours

A wide variety of local boat and land tours offered in Rhodes, Kos, Patmos, and Symi will take you to the usual sites (which you can probably reach by yourself anyway), and will give you a day picnicking on a remote beach, or even visiting the shores of Turkey.

RHODES

From April to October **Triton Holidays** (✉ Plastira 9, ☎ 0241/21778, 0241/21690, or 0241/21691; ℻ 0241/31625), for example, organizes a visit to Lindos by boat; a caïque leaves Mandraki Harbor in Rhodes in the morning, deposits you in Lindos for a day of sightseeing and beachgoing, and returns you to Rhodes in the evening (3,500 dr.–4,500 dr.). Triton also offers day cruises down the east coast of Rhodes (3,500 dr.), to Symi (3,500 dr.), Kos (10,000 dr.), and Marmaris, Turkey (17,000 dr.), as well as a half-day inland hike (5,000 dr.); a half-day tour of Kameiros, Filerimos, and Petaloudes (5,000 dr.); and a scuba diving trip (9,000 dr.).

KOS

Aeolos Travel (✉ 8 Annetas Laoumzi, ☎ 0242/26203 through 0242/26205, ℻ 0242/25948) organizes one-day cruises to other islands.

SYMI

Symi Tours (✉ Symi Harbor, ☎ 0241/71307, ℻ 0241/72292) will take you on a boat trip to the magical islet of Seklia (with a barbecue) for about 5,000 dr., or on a round-the-island trip for 5,000 dr.

PATMOS

Apollon Travel (✉ Skala Harbor, ☎ 0247/31324, 0247/31356, or 0247/31724; ℻ 0247/31819). **Astoria Travel** (✉ Skala Harbor, ☎ 0247/31205 or 0247/31208; ℻ 0247/31975).

Visitor Information

RHODES

The **Greek National Tourist Organization** (GNTO or EOT; ✉ Archbishop Makarios and Papagou, in the new city, close to the medieval walls, ☎ 0241/23655, 0241/23255, or 0241/27466) has brochures and bus schedules.

The centrally located **Rhodes Municipal Tourism Office** on the east side of Platia Rimini near the bus station (☎ 0241/35945; ☉ May–Oct., weekdays 8–7, Sat. 8–6) is helpful with information and can exchange money for a 2% commission.

KOS

EOT (✉ Koundouriotis, ☎ 0242/28724 or 0242/24460).

PATMOS

EOT (✉ Skala, ☎ 0247/31666 or 0247/31158).

13 The Northern Islands

Chios, Lesbos,
Limnos, and Samos

Each of these far-flung Aegean islands is distinct: Though ravaged by fire, Chios is extraordinary for its bazaar, mansions, Byzantine monasteries, and stenciled-wall houses; Lesbos, Greece's third-largest island and birthplace of legendary artists and writers, is dappled with mineral springs and a quirky petrified forest; Limnos is imprinted with mournful volcanic outcroppings, sand dunes, and ancient ruins; and lush, mountainous Samos, land of wine and honey, whispers of the classic wonders of antiquity.

CLOSER TO TURKEY'S COAST THAN TO Greece's mainland—and quite separate from one another—the northeastern Aegean islands of Limnos, Lesbos, Chios, and Samos—dotted in a zigzag pattern from north to south, respectively—form a startling and rather arbitrary archipelago. Even less traveled are the three sister islands—Ikaria, Samothraki, and Thasos—and four islets: Fourni, southeast of Ikaria; Psara and Inousses, flanking Chios to the west and east; and Agios Efstratios, south of Limnos. Despite the Northern Islands' proximity to Asia Minor, they are the essence of Greece, the result of 4,000 years of Hellenic influence that lasted until 1923.

By Toula
Bogdanos

Updated by
Lea Lane

Although Limnos, Lesbos, Chios, and Samos fell into obscurity in later centuries, especially under the Ottoman Empire, in the ancient world they prospered gloriously as important commercial and religious centers. They also were cultural hothouses, producing geniuses like Pythagoras, Sappho, and probably Homer.

Whether or not they once again become centers of art and culture, these islands are on the verge of becoming popular travel destinations, despite their military presence (most visible in Limnos), and the occasional acid remark about the neighbors to the east. After Turkey's invasion of Cyprus in 1974, tension was aggravated by subsequent squabbles over oil deposits. Despite the rhetoric—mostly instigated by the two governments—islanders don't hesitate to shuttle people back and forth to Turkey. And why not, when tourism has at last arrived?

Mountainous, with uncrowded beaches, natural attractions, noteworthy architecture, and historic sites, these are the Greek islands to one-up your well-traveled friends with; they probably haven't even heard of most of them. Much as the Cyclades may have been 50 years ago, they are not "party" islands that come alive only in summer, but towns and villages operating on a year-round schedule. People here go about their business as they have for centuries, with a gratifying Greek temperament of open-mindedness and optimism.

Pleasures and Pastimes

Beaches

All of these islands have good beaches, ranging from golden sand to black and red pebbles. The relative lack of tourism often results in deserted stretches, rare in the more popular Greek islands. Many beaches allow topless sunbathing, unless they're part of the town's waterfront, but there is always a designated non-nude stretch where families congregate. Nude bathers should use discretion; in general, if you choose your spot carefully, you should have no problem with local people or the law.

Dining

Although waterfront restaurants in the touristed areas are generally mediocre, you can still find delightful meals, especially in the villages. Unless noted, reservations are unnecessary, and casual dress is always acceptable. Be adventurous: go to the kitchen and point to what you want. The thing to order is fish, which, except for smaller catch, is rather expensive. Remember how to translate what restaurants often call "lobster," *astakos* (actually a sort of salt-water crayfish; its smaller cousin is called *karavides*). Shrimp is usually frozen, but most fish is fresh, except for the dried cod used in *bakaliaro* (fried cod with garlic sauce). If you can find it, try *kakavia* (a fishermen's soup with small catch, stewed with onions and tomatoes).

In Limnos, specialties include halvah, often served hot with lemon squeezed over it to cut the sweetness. Limnos is also the place for octopus grilled over embers and sweet *trahanas* (wheat kernels boiled in milk and dried). Besides its mastic products, Chios is known for tangerines, eaten fresh or preserved in *gliko koutaliou* (a thick sugar syrup).

In Lesbos, try the *keskek* (a special meat mixed with wheat served most often at festivals), and Kalloni bay sardines, the fleshiest in the Mediterranean; eat them with lemon and oil. Octopus simmered in wine, another island dish, goes perfectly with the famous island ouzo, most of which is made in Plomari. Fresh figs, almonds, and raisins are delicious; a local dessert is *baleze* (almond pudding). Samos is known for its thyme-scented honey; its wines, both pale dry white and Samian *moskhato* (sweet dessert wine); *yiorti* (the local version of keskek); and *revithokeftedes* (garbanzo patties).

CATEGORY	COST*
$$$$	over 10,000 dr.
$$$	7,000 dr.–10,000 dr.
$$	3,000 dr.–7,000 dr.
$	under 3,000 dr.

per person, for a 3-course meal, of appetizer, entrée, and dessert (usually fruit), service and tax, but no drinks.

Fishing

Fish thrive in these clear Aegean waters. In Chios, locals usually fish the bays of Komi, Kardamila, and Limnia. In Lesbos you can catch sea bream, horse mackerel, dorado, and blackfish everywhere. Most fishing in Limnos is in Plateos Bay and off Cape Moudros. In Samos, sea bream, dorado, red mullet, and blackfish are plentiful in Marathokambos and Kerveli bays.

Hiking

Mountains and deep valleys, deserted towns, and craggy coasts provide for great walking or hiking. Be it along flat coastal areas or trekking to summits, hikers can indulge in a variety of terrains.

Lodging

With the exception of summer you'll have little trouble finding accommodations. Most hotel rooms are basic, with simple pine furniture and sparse furnishings often created by local craftspeople. These islands are still less costly than most, but prices are starting to go up and deluxe resorts are expensive.

Reserve early for better-category hotels, especially in Pythagorio on Samos and Molyvos on Lesbos. Off-season you can usually bargain over the official prices and avoid paying for a compulsory breakfast. Hotels are not air-conditioned unless noted, and, even in those that are, you must sometimes insist that it be turned on. Islanders are extremely friendly hosts, and although they may get a little irritable when the hordes descend in August, they still consider you a guest rather than a billfold. Unless noted otherwise, all hotels are open year-round.

CATEGORY	COST*
$$$$	over 30,000 dr.
$$$	15,000 dr.–30,000 dr.
$$	10,000 dr.–15,000 dr.
$	under 10,000 dr.

Prices are official rate for a standard double room with bath in high season, including tax and service and excluding breakfast. For those hotels in which half board is compulsory, meals (one is breakfast) for two are included in price.

Monasteries

Some of Greece's best-preserved Byzantine monasteries are scattered throughout these islands, especially on Chios, Lesbos, and Samos. Sometimes they are in marvelous villages that are also filled with Byzantine treasures; often they are set high in the hills, so you can hike and enjoy the scenery and views as well.

Nightlife and the Arts

Outdoor movie theaters are popular summer entertainment for islanders and tourists alike. They can be found in Mytilini, Molyvos, Eressos, Limnos, Kokkari, and Karlovassi. Check the billboards in the town square for showings. Every summer brings a new wave of trendy bars and discos, usually clustered on the beach. They come and go, so ask what's new when you arrive.

Island municipalities often organize cultural events that range from philosophy conferences to evenings of folk music. Chios usually is host to the summer conference of the International Society of Homeric Studies. In summer on Limnos, the Kehayiades folklore association presents island festivities. The best-known celebration is the Molyvos Theater Festival (tickets, ☎ 0253/71323; tourist office, ☎ 0253/71347) held July–August in Lesbos.

Sailing

Boat rentals are available on all the islands; repair services, fuel, and water are available at many of the larger ports on the islands, and moors are available at some. The ragged coastlines, calm, uncrowded waters, strong and refreshing winds, and deserted beaches make sailing a particular pleasure. Your charter agency can usually give basic details about where to find fuel and water.

Shopping

Products found here are hard to find in Athens—and on other Greek islands—and they make interesting and original gifts. Snatch up the Samian wine, honey, and ceramics. On Lesbos, olive oil, chestnuts, local liquors, and local fabrics and pottery are popular. On Chios look for the unique mastic products, ceramics, handwoven fabrics, and ouzo. Limnos is known for its honey, pistachios, ouzo, white wine, and dried figs and blue-black plums.

Tennis

Only a few of the better-class hotels have courts. If you're not a guest you might still persuade the management to let you play, but it's unlikely during high season.

Traditional Festivals

Festivals offer the visitor a wonderful view into age-old traditions—and lots of fun.

Samos sometimes hosts a wine festival in early fall with Panhellenic dances. Swimming races in Pythagorio commemorate the battle of Cavo Fonias on August 6, a day of celebration for the entire island. On Samos, on September 7 and 8 at Vourliotes village and the nearby Vrondiani monastery, there's dancing in the square and a distribution to the faithful of yiorti to celebrate the birthday of the Virgin. On September 14, the Timiou Stavrou monastery on Samos celebrates its feast day with a service followed by a *paniyiri* (feast), with music, firecrackers, booths of coconut candy, plastic toys, and *loukoumades* (honey-soaked dumplings). In October, Platanos, on Samos, throws a big bash when the new batch of wine and raki is ready. The firewater flows freely, served with *mezedes* (appetizers) and fruit macerated in alcohol.

One of Limnos's biggest festivals takes place September 7 at Ayios Sozon monastery, at the southern tip of the island, with island dances and songs.

On Lesbos on the archangel's feast day, usually the third weekend after Easter, you will see an ancient, probably pagan, custom. A bull and several sheep decorated with flowers are sacrificed in the monastery's courtyard. The faithful dip handkerchiefs in the blood, marking their foreheads to protect themselves from sickness. The next day everyone feasts on keskek. Bull roasts and horse races also take place. The same occurs at Ayia Paraskevi where horse races are held after the distribution of the meat. On August 15 the islanders of Lesbos flock to Agiassos to celebrate the Feast of the Assumption of the Virgin with dancing, drinking, and eating. On Clean Monday at the end of Carnival in February, costumed islanders take part in a custom known as *vallia* (an improvised exchange of satirical verse).

On Chios, festivities are held the last Sunday in Lent in Mostra Thymianon. In Thimiana, on Chios, on the last Sunday of Carnival (late February), islanders reenact the expulsion of the pirates in the Festival of Mostras; youths wave swords and dance the vigorous *talimi*. On Chios in Pirgi on August 15 and August 23 villagers perform local dances to commemorate the passing of the Virgin, the second most important religious holiday of the Greek Orthodox Church. On Chios on Easter Saturday night the effigy of Judas is burned in Mesta. Olympoi, southeast of Mesta, is host to festivities on the first Monday of Lent.

Turkish Jaunts

All within a few kilometers of the Turkish coast, the islands are good springboards for day trips (and longer) to ports such as Bodrum, İzmir, and Kuşadasi in Turkey. Ferry schedules can be checked at individual ports on the islands, and at travel agencies. Day-trippers must carry passports.

Water Sports

Snorkeling is not really popular here, but if you bring your own equipment you can find calm coves on all the islands. Most resort hotels provide water sports on their beaches. Scuba is prohibited in most areas because of underwater antiquities.

Exploring the Northern Islands

Visitors to Limnos, Lesbos, Chios, and Samos tend to be Greeks or Europeans who have previously traveled to other Greek islands. Charters are just beginning, and English is not spoken as frequently as it is in more touristed areas. These islands do not offer much trendy nightlife. Instead, you may revel in quiet charms, and a feeling of discovery. Each island is worth a visit, although in some cases, it may have to be a quick one.

Great Itineraries

Seeing all four islands without having to rush—or hang around terminals—will take some preparation, as interisland transportation may not be as frequent as it is on the more touristed islands. Check ahead for transportation schedules. Whenever possible, take hydrofoils rather than ferries; they are more costly, but they can cut time in half. Lesbos has daily air service from Athens and Salonica and daily ferry service from Piraeus; it makes a good base from which to start exploring.

The packed four-day itinerary will give you a brief overview of each island; more relaxed travelers can pick and choose among the islands. The 7- and 10-day itineraries will allow you to explore each island more in depth, pursuing what strikes your fancy. In general, it is best to arrive on Lesbos and head north to Limnos; the two are connected by ferry, hydrofoil, and daily air service. Then head back to tour Lesbos. Ferry or hydrofoil to nearby Chios and then to Samos, the most southerly island of the four. You can go on from Samos to other Greek islands, the Turkish coast, or back to Athens or Piraeus, as connections are good by sea, and sometimes by air.

IF YOU HAVE 4 DAYS

Numbers in the text correspond to numbers in the margin and on the Limnos and Lesbos and Chios and Samos maps.

This is a real challenge, but you can manage an overview of each island. You will need to rent vehicles to get around, and you must make sure that the ferry from ⊠ **Lesbos** ⑨–㉕ to ⊠ **Limnos** ①–⑧ is running on the day you start out. Day one starts with a quick tour of **Limnos,** encompassing **Myrina** ① port and the **Cabiri** and prehistoric **Poliochni** sites (only for archaeological diehards). Return to **Myrina,** where you can catch the ferry or fly to **Lesbos.** On day two move from the capital, **Mytilini** ⑨, to northern villages like **Petra** ⑰ and dreamy Molyvos ⑯, to Sappho's birthplace in **Eressos,** to Agiassos hill village and **Plomari,** a fishing hamlet that's also a resort. Day three begins on ⊠ **Chios** ㉖–㊲ in the Ottoman quarter of **Chios town** ㉖. It continues to **Nea Moni monastery** ㉛, with its fine mosaics and tragic history. From hilltop Avgonima, head west down to the coast road, then travel via **Lithi** and **Vessa,** to the southern mastic villages of stenciled **Pirgi** ㉝ and labyrinthine **Mesta** ㉟. Day four circles ⊠ **Samos** ㊳–㊿, including **Pythagorio** ㊳ and the **Temple of Heraion** ㊴, one of the Seven Wonders of the Ancient World. Then travel through mountain villages such as **Pirgos** ㊶ to the tiny harbor of **Ormos Marathokambou** ㊸, and the fishing village of **Kokkari** ㊼, ending at **Samos town** ㊽, the capital.

IF YOU HAVE 7 DAYS

Enhance the four-day schedule, exploring your interests in greater depth. Depending how you add the time, for the three extra nights you could remain in one favorite place to cut down on travel. You might add another day on ⊠ **Chios** ㉖–㊲, traveling north from the capital to **Daskalopetra** ㉗ (Teacher's Rock), where Homer is said to have taught, visiting the Byzantine village there, and the isolated beaches of the north. You could spend more time in **Pirgi** ㉝ and **Mesta** ㉟, with time for shopping, and relaxing at the volcanic beach at **Emborio** ㉞, near the mastic villages. On ⊠ **Lesbos** ⑨–㉕, you could visit the hot springs around **Eftelo,** east of Mithymna. Or on ⊠ **Samos** ㊳–㊿, meander on the trails around the picturesque hill villages between **Kokkari** ㊼ and **Kondakeika.**

IF YOU HAVE 10 DAYS

Stick to the seven-day schedule, adding three extra days wherever they fit best, on the islands of your choice, for relaxing and recreation— hiking, enjoying water sports, shopping, or just lazing on an Aegean beach. You might bird-watch on ⊠ **Samos** ㊳–㊿, study ancient ruins on ⊠ **Lesbos** ⑨–㉕, or just veg out in one of the new deluxe beach resorts on ⊠ **Limnos** ①–⑧. You could visit the other nearby north-Aegean islands and islets, or take a ferry to ⊠ **Turkey** from Chios or Samos.

When to Tour

May through June and September through October is when the weather is ideal, the wildflowers and shrubs are in bloom, and the crowds have thinned. Since these four islands are not yet overrun with tourists even in summer, you will find isolated nooks where you can enjoy the therapeutic sounds of the wind, the birds, and the lapping water.

When booking, keep in mind the enlightening cultural events and religious festivals, called **paniyiri,** which usually take place on a saint's day or patriotic holiday. On Lesbos a cultural week of drama, dance, and music exhibitions occurs each May. On Chios, festivities take place during Lent and summer.

LIMNOS

Low and gently rolling on the Aegean, near the Dardenelle straits and Turkey, Limnos is essentially an agricultural and garrison island guarding the entrance to the Black Sea. On the route less traveled, for years the island attracted few visitors except for Greek families who came for the beaches; German windsurfers; and British subjects on cruise ships who wanted to see Moudros Bay, an important site of the Gallipoli campaign. But today, resort development is slowly turning Limnos into a sun and fun hideaway.

The island is divided into west and east by deeply indented Moudros Bay on the south and Pournias Bay on the north. Tiny villages of stone houses punctuate a checkerboard of hay and grain fields decorated with gaudy scarecrows; calm plains give way to dark volcanic rocks and remote sandy beaches. Once well wooded, the island's interior is now so barren that, when giving directions, villagers might tell you to turn at "the tree." Green enough in spring, the island becomes crackling brown in summer, and villages often shut off water in the evenings to conserve. Dirt roads cover much of the island and the southern part is filled with sand dunes, unusual for Greece, and dubbed rather grandly "The Sahara of Limnos."

The ancient civilizations here had contact with the Trojans across the straits. Limnos sided with Athens during the Peloponnesian wars, and in AD 395, with the Roman Empire split, it became a part of Byzantium. The Genoese ruled Lesbos starting in 1462, and the Turks conquered it in 1478 and ruled until 1912.

The god Hephaistos (Vulcan in Roman mythology) landed on Limnos when Zeus, his father, furiously hurled him from Mt. Olympus for daring to defend Hera, his unruly mother. At his foundry on Limnos, Hephaistos made a race of cast-gold maidens, who stoked the furnace, causing the disturbances that ruptured the island. When his wife Aphrodite left him for Ares, the strapping god of war, Limnian women flung her statue into the sea. The miffed Aphrodite retaliated by giving the women body odor, which drove their men into the arms of captive Thracian women. The frustrated wives then poisoned their husbands' wine, slit their throats, and threw them into the sea. They then lived alone until the arrival of Jason and the Argonauts, who helped them repopulate the island.

Today, Limnos's volcanic origins are reaped from its hot springs and the once-famous Limnian earth. From antiquity, this special soil, high in sulfur, was exported in limited amounts to heal festering wounds and snakebites. Once a year, on August 6, the precious earth is still dug up under the surveillance of a priest, who allows only one wagon load to be carted off. Islanders use it, and you can buy it from pharmacies in Myrina or Moudros.

Myrina

❶ *25 km (15½ mi) west of Moudros.*

Myrina, the capital on the west end, was a flourishing town during antiquity; today, new deluxe resorts are making the area prosperous again.

A 13th-century **Genoese-Turkish fortress** melds with the rust-brown rock formations cleaving the bay in two. The castle was begun by Byzantium then fell to the Venetians, the Genoese, and finally in 1479 to the Turks. It's a short hike to the top, and although not much is there except some cisterns, at sunset on a clear day distant Mt. Athos seems to rise, shimmering out of the western sea. ⊠ *Above town.* ☏ *Free.* ☉ *Daily.*

Backing up to the castle are white, wind-hammered houses with wood balconies, many of them mariners' homes, interspersed with the occasional Ottoman stone mansion. **The Romeikos Yalos** (⊠ On waterfront below fortress) is the best place to stroll, especially in the fading purple twilight.

The recently overhauled provincial **archaeological museum** chronicles the island's history with finds from Poliochni, Hephaestia, the Cabiri sanctuary (☞ *below*), and ancient Myrina. Gold jewelry and bronze cheese graters share space in a room of metal objects. Presentation is chronological, and better than at many larger museums. In fact, in 1996 it was named by the European Council of Culture as the fifth-best small museum in Europe. ⊠ *Romaikos Gialos beach,* ☎ *0254/22990.* ☏ *500 dr.* ☉ *Tues.–Sun. 9–3.*

The Arts

The **Kehayiades folklore association** presents island dances in costume, accompanied by the local version of a Cretan lyre; contact the Myrina tourist office (☞ Visitor Information *in* The Northern Islands A to Z, *below*).

Beaches

The closest beach to town is **Avlonas,** past Akti Myrina. Just southeast of Myrina are two lovely, quiet beaches. The beach at **Plati** village, down the road about 2 km (1¼ mi), is long and sandy, with sheep grazing below. The beach near **Thanos** village, 4 km (2¼ mi) south of Myrina and easily reached by car or moped, is huge and set between volcanic crags—reputed to be the best on Limnos. **Ayios Pavlos** is a nearly 1-km-long (⅔-mi-long) stretch of beach near Kondias.

Dining and Lodging

$$ ✕ **Zimbabwe.** The food at this café-ouzeri, with seating under a huge jujube tree, belies its humble appearance and is quite popular among locals. Grills such as octopus, sausage, or chops, or mezedes like *melitsanosalata,* or beets—are tasty and carefully prepared, but not inexpensive. The friendly English-speaking chef and his wife spent 30 years in Africa, as the name suggests. Go early to be sure of a table. ⊠ *Plati village, off main sq.,* ☎ *0254/24954. No credit cards.*

$ ✕ **Avra.** Although the service may be slow (who's in a rush?), this excellent taverna serves substantial portions of *magirefta* (here, casseroles) and grilled items in the evenings. Try the spit-roasted chicken basted with lemon-oregano sauce, moussaka, and the *tzoutzoukakia* (sausage meatballs). ⊠ *Next to Myrina port authority, on harbor sq.,* ☎ *0254/22523. No credit cards.*

$ ✕ **O Platanos.** This family-style taverna sits in a charming square among old houses and two huge plane trees planted a century ago. The owner has a limited menu of traditional dishes: *kokkinisto* (stewed meat) with okra, spinach, or peas; *makaronada* (pasta); *stifado; horiatiki* (large Greek salads); and *lakhano* dolmades (grape leaves stuffed with cabbage and rice). The barrel wine is a hefty red from the village of Ayia Sofia. ⊠ *Odos Kyda, main bazaar st., Myrina,* ☎ *0254/22070. No credit cards.*

$$$$ ⊞ **Akti Myrina Bungalows.** This special, luxurious, yet rustic complex
★ dominates the scene and is seemingly part of a fortified hill overlooking the water. The wood-and-stone chalets are spacious, with large baths and local artwork and furnishings. Bungalow 312's sunset view is one of the best, and you must book far in advance, because many guests return. ✉ *Myrina 81400,* ☎ *0254/22681 through 22685 (*☎ *Athens: 01/413–7907),* FAX *0254/22352. 125 rooms with bath. 4 restaurants, air-conditioning, 2 pools, 3 tennis courts, health club, beach, windsurfing, jet skiing, parasailing, waterskiing, recreation room. AE, DC, MC, V. Closed Nov.–Apr.*

$$$$ ⊞ **Kaviria Palace.** This plush resort on the water is tasteful, with guest rooms and bungalows designed of local materials and craftsmanship. Indoor-outdoor restaurants, social programs, gardens streaming with bougainvillea, and much more are in the details. The clientele is mostly northern European—tanning by day, partying by night. ✉ *Tigani Bay, Kontopouli Myrina 81400,* ☎ *0254/41600,* FAX *0254/41609. 242 rooms with bath, 40 bungalows. 2 Restaurants, 2 bars, air-conditioning, in-room safes, minibars, 3 pools, 2 tennis courts, health club, shops, meeting room. AE, MC, V. Closed Mar.–Nov.*

$$$$ ⊞ **Portomyrina Palace.** Opened in 1995 with angled architecture and red roofs, this resort is just as upscale as the competition, but smaller. White umbrellas crisply line a shimmering Olympic-size pool with mosaic tiles the color of the sea beyond, a fine place for sun worshippers. Rooms are set up for people with disabilities; this practice is uncommon at Greek hotels. ✉ *Myrina 81400,* ☎ *0254/24805 and 24806,* FAX *0254/24858. 150 rooms and bungalows with bath. 2 restaurants, 3 bars, in-room safes, 1 indoor and 1 outdoor pool, 3 tennis courts, shops, conference room. AE, MC, V. Closed Apr.–Nov.*

$$$ ⊞ **Astron.** Several notches below Akti Myrina, this hotel is good for families and for lengthy stays, which afford a discount. Although none of the rooms has a water view, the beach is close by. Astron's larger housekeeping apartments can accommodate six. In early spring the rates are significantly lower. ✉ *Garofalidi 3, Myrina 81400,* ☎ *0254/24392 or 0254/24393,* FAX *0254/24396. 12 apartments with bath. Café, laundry service. V.*

$$$ ⊞ **Villa Afroditi.** Panayiotis Papasotiriou, Afroditi, his wife, and son George provide energetic multilingual service at this hotel and the Afroditi Apartments in Myrina. The garden hotel has careful landscaping, generous buffet breakfasts, and an enduringly popular pool flanked by a bar and restaurant. Giant *kioupia* (ceramic urns) salvaged from an old olive-oil mill dot the lawn, and live guitar music is a bonus after dinner in summer. ✉ *150 yards inland from Plati beach, 81400,* ☎ *0254/24795,* FAX *0254/24504. 20 rooms with bath, 2 family suites. Restaurant, air-conditioning, bar. No credit cards.*

$$ ⊞ **Afroditi Apartments.** The owners run this hilltop hotel with cheerful efficiency, and it could easily belong to a higher category. Just a few yards from Romaïkos, this complex is surrounded by geraniums, roses, petunias, and fruit trees. Besides the housekeeping apartments, five rooms are on the roof. The spic-and-span rooms are sprightly, with cane-and-bamboo furniture and orthopedic mattresses. Guests can go for a spin on the speedboat or rent the hotel caïque—prices are negotiable. ✉ *Riha Nera area, across from Ayios Pandelimon, Myrina 81400,* ☎ *0254/23489,* FAX *0254/24504;* ☎ *Athens: 01/964–1910. 5 rooms with bath, 16 apartments. Minibars, kitchenettes. AE, DC, MC, V. Closed Nov.–Mar.*

Outdoor Activities and Sports

SAILING

Ports at both Myrina and Moudros (☞ *below*) have fuel, water, and repair services.

WATER SPORTS

You can usually rent paddleboats and canoes on **Romaikos Gialos beach** (⊠ East of Kastro) in Limnos.

En Route The east side of the island, with streams and fruit groves, is more agricultural than the barren west, and it contains most of the ancient sites. On your way to Moudros you first take the road to Repanidi, 26 km ❹ (16 mi) east of Myrina, where you can turn off for **Kotsinas** village and its view of Pournias Bay.

Moudros

❺ *25 km (15½) mi east of Myrina.*

Moudros is the island's second-biggest town. In 1915, the Allies launched an attack on the Dardanelles from this large, protected harbor. Here in 1918 the Turks surrendered to the British a few days before the Germans sued for peace. A thousand or so Allied war graves are in the **East Moudros Military Cemetery** (⊠ One km out of town on Roussopoli Rd.), a hint of this town's former importance.

Outdoor Activities and Sports

SAILING

The port at Moudros has fuel, water, and repair services.

Poliochni

❻ *32 km (20 mi) east of Myrina, 20 km (12½ mi) south of Cabirion.*

At Poliochni, on a bluff overlooking a rocky beach, Italian archaeologists, sometimes working on site, may offer their expertise. They have uncovered four layers of settlements, the oldest predating the Minoan kingdoms in Crete. The only architectural remnants—an extremely thick wall and house foundations—come from the second-oldest level, the 2000 BC city where the oldest baths in the Aegean were found. The third dates to the Late Bronze Age, and the last settlement is a contemporary of Mycenae, a close contact of Poliochni in ancient times (1500 BC–1100 BC). ⊠ *On bluff overlooking rocky beach.* 🎫 *Free.* 🕐 *Daily 9:30–5:30.*

Kondopouli

❼ *26 km (16 mi) northeast of Myrina, 9 km (5½ mi) northeast of Moudros.*

Archaeology buffs should watch for signs to the ruins of ancient **Hephaestia** (sometimes called Paliopoli), inhabited since prehistory. During classical times, it was the principle city on Limnos. Excavations have so far uncovered traces of houses, a 6th-century BC sanctuary, a cemetery, and a Roman theater. This and Cabirion (☞ *below*) are informal sites—they will be disappointing for those expecting grand ruins. ⊠ *On dirt rd. on rocky promontory.* 🎫 *Free.* 🕐 *Daily 9:30–3:30.*

Chloe

30 km (18½ mi) northeast of Myrina, 3 km (1¾ mi) northeast of Kondopouli.

❽ Near the village of Chloe, **Cabirion** is the ruins of one of the oldest sanctuaries of the Cabiri cult, which worshiped the underworld gods. Archaeologists found a large stoa with 11 columns and many inscriptions giving clues to early Limnian life. According to legend, Cabirion is also the site of the famous cave of Philoctetes, the hero of the Trojan War who supposedly hid here with a gangrenous leg, and whose story is detailed in Sophocles' play. ⊠ *Across silted-up bay from Hephaestia, reached via a separate rd. toward Plaka.* 🎫 *Free.* 🕐 *Daily 9:30–3:30.*

Limnos and Lesbos

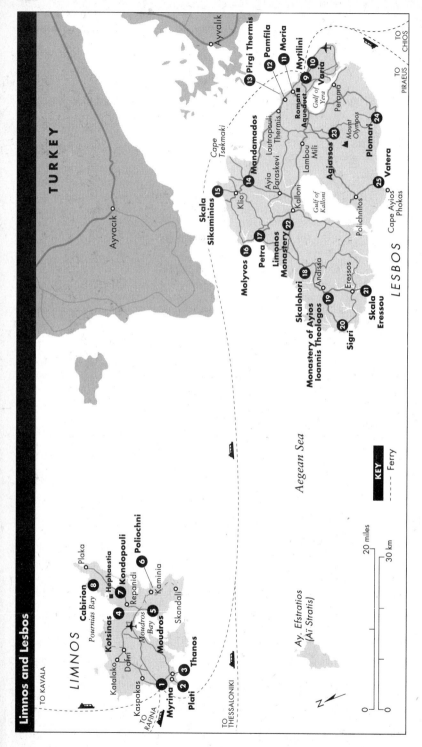

LESBOS

When you first land, Lesbos may not strike you as particularly enchanting, but its treasures are not geographical. Greece's third-largest island, Lesbos was once a major cultural center, known for its Philosophical Academy, where Epicurus and Aristotle taught; it was the birthplace of the philosopher Theophrastus, who presided over the Academy in Athens; of the great lyric poet Sappho; of Terpander, the "father of Greek music"; and of Arion, who influenced the later playwrights Sophocles and Alcaeus, inventors of the dithyramb (a short poem with an erratic strain).

Even in modernity, artists emerged from Lesbos: Theophilos, a poor villager who earned his ouzo by painting some of the finest naive art modern Greece has produced; novelists Stratis Myrivilis and Argyris Eftaliotis; and more recently, the latest Greek Nobel prizewinner, poet Odysseus Elytis.

The island's history stretches back to the 6th century BC, when the two mightiest cities, Mytilini and Mithymna, settled their squabbles under the tyrant, Pittahos, considered one of Greece's Seven Sages. Thus began the creative era, but later times brought forth the same pillaging and conquest that overturned other Greek islands. In 527 BC the Persians conquered Lesbos, and the Athenians, Romans, Byzantines, Venetians, Genoese, and Turks took their turns adding their influences.

Lesbos has more inhabitants than either Corfu or Rhodes, with only a fraction of the tourists. It looks like a giant jigsaw-puzzle piece, carved by two large sandy bays, the gulfs of Yera and Kalloni. The Turks called Lesbos the "garden of the empire" for its fertility: Olive trees abound on the undulating hills, reputedly producing Greek's finest oil. Wildflowers and grain cover the valleys, while the higher peaks wear wreaths of dark green pines.

Mytilini

🍷 *42 km (26 mi) northeast of Plomari.*

The main town and port, Mytilini was the scene of one of the most dramatic moments in Greek history. Early in the Peloponnesian War, it revolted against Athens but surrendered in 428 BC. The Athens assembly decided to kill all men in Lesbos and enslave all women and children as punishment, and a boat was dispatched to carry out the order. The next day a less vengeful mood prevailed and the assembly repealed its decision and sent a second ship after the first. Its crew worked in shifts, eating and drinking as they rowed. Picture the second ship, pulling into the harbor just as the first commander finished reading the death sentence. Mytilini was saved.

Set on the ruins of an ancient city, Mytilini sprawls across two bays like an amphitheater. The intervening pine-covered headland—a nice spot for a picnic—supports a **stone fortress,** its walls intact, seemingly to protect the town even today. Built by the Byzantines on a 600 BC temple of Apollo, it was repaired with available material (note the ancient pillars crammed between the stones) by Francesco Gateluzzi of the famous Genoese family. Look above the gates for the two-headed eagle of the Palaiologos emperors, the horseshoe arms of the Gateluzzi family, and inscriptions made by Turks, who enlarged it; today it is a **military bastion.** Inside the castle there's only a crumbling **prison** and a **Roman cistern,** but you should make the visit for the fine view. ✉ *On pine-covered hill,* ☎ *0251/27297.* 🎫 *400 dr.* ☯ *Daily sunrise–sunset.*

The only vestige of ancient Mytilini is a **Hellenistic theater** (⊠ In pine forest northeast of town), one of the largest in ancient Greece. Pompey admired it so much that he copied it for his theater in Rome; it is currently under excavation.

The bustling waterfront just south of the headland is where most of the town's sights are clustered. Stroll the main bazaar street, **Ermou,** past the fish market, where men haul in their sardines, mullet, and octopi. Narrow lanes are filled with antiques shops and grand old mansions. The enormous post-Baroque church of **St. Therapon,** built in the 19th century, is reminiscent of some styles in Italy. It has an ornate interior, a frescoed dome and, in its courtyard, a **Byzantine museum** filled with icons. ⊠ *Southern waterfront,* ☎ *0251/28916.* 🗃 *200 dr.* ☉ *Mon–Sat. 10–1.*

In front of the cathedral of **Ayios Athanasios,** there is a **traditional Lesbos house,** restored and furnished in 19th-century style. Call owner Marika Vlachou to arrange a visit. ⊠ *Mitropoleos 6,* ☎ *0251/28550.* 🗃 *Free.* ☉ *By appointment only.*

The **archaeological museum,** in a neoclassic mansion, will help you imagine Lesbos's past. Among its treasures are finds from prehistoric Thermi, mosaics from Hellenistic houses, and reliefs of comic scenes from the 3rd-century Roman House of Menander. ⊠ *Argiri Eftaliotis 7, behind the ferry dock,* ☎ *0251/28032.* 🗃 *500 dr.* ☉ *Tues.–Sun. 8:30–3.*

Dining and Lodging

$$ ✕ **Dimitrakis.** As many as 10 types of decidedly fresh fish are available at this restaurant, which locals call the "little boat grill" because of its nautical decor. Start your meal with *bourekakia* (ham and *kasseri*-cheese pie); favorites are the simple grilled fish or the bakaliaro. This restaurant is hopping, but you can enjoy dinner outside, lulled by the sounds of rocking boats. ⊠ *Hristouyennon 1944 Rd., Fanari quay of Mytilini,* ☎ *0251/23818. No credit cards.*

$ ✕ **Asteria.** This Mytilini institution offers seven or eight magirefta nightly and a complete grill selection, including thick, juicy beef patties and *exohiko* (meat baked in a pot with vegetables). Among the specialties are eggplant with artichokes and *yiouvetsaki politiko* (beef cooked in a clay pot with aromatic sweet spices). In summer, you sit at tables facing the harbor. ⊠ *Koundourioti 56, Mytilini,* ☎ *0251/22689. No credit cards.*

$$$ 🏨 **Mytilana Village.** Several buildings circling a pool make up this hotel on a predominantly pebbled beach in the Gulf of Yera. The rooms have blond pine furniture and balconies. The half-board option, which includes two meals, is convenient, since most restaurants are a taxi drive away. A local bus makes the round-trip into town once a day. ⊠ *Ethniki Odos, 6 km (4 mi) outside Mytilini toward Kalloni, 81107,* ☎ *0251/20653, 0251/20654, or 0251/29655;* 🆎 *0251/26572. 50 rooms with bath. Restaurant, bar, minibars, pool. AE, DC, V. Closed Nov.–Mar.*

$$ 🏨 **Rex.** This peaceful hotel, in one of the town's well-heeled neighborhoods, is covered with such glorious bougainvillea that tourists often stop to photograph the entrance; but the facade may be its best feature. Mirrors and high ceilings in the rooms create a spacious feeling despite the dark carved furniture. ⊠ *Katsakouli 3, behind archaeological museum, Mytilini, 81100,* ☎ *0251/28523. 16 rooms, some with bath. No credit cards.*

$$ 🏨 **Villa 1900.** This renovated neoclassical house, in a fairly quiet lo-★ cation near the stadium, is a real treat, with stonework, a lush garden, and old-fashioned details such as iron beds, family photographs, and, in a few rooms, ceilings painted with women and flowers. The best rooms are the three in the converted garret. Guests sit in the garden

for breakfast, which includes fresh juice from the hotel's fruit trees. ✉ *Vostani 24, Mytilini 81100,* ☎ *0251/23448 or 0251/43437;* ☎ *Athens: 01/806–5770 or 01/228–9379,* ℻ *01/201–4190. 11 rooms with bath. Breakfast room. No credit cards. Closed Nov.–Mar.*

$$ 🏨 **Zaira.** Set in a former olive mill dating to 1909, this hotel displays the mill's original stonework, its smokestack, and the large red olive press, as spied in the lounge. The rooms line a courtyard; there are four suites with fireplaces. Just a few steps away is a small harbor, where a boat stops daily to take guests to the cove of Ayios Ermoyenis. ✉ *Loutra, about 7 km (5 mi) outside Mytilini 81100,* ☎ *0251/91004, 0251/91100 through 91102. 21 rooms with bath, 4 suites. Restaurant, air-conditioning, meeting room. No credit cards.*

Nightlife

BARS

The newest bar—packed on summer nights—is **To Musio** (The Museum) (✉ Vournazi 21, Mytilini, ☎ 0251/42140), so called because it's ensconced in a neoclassical house with traditional furnishings.

A popular music bar for a youngish crowd is **The Music Cafe** (✉ Corner of Mitropoleos and Vernardaki) with jazz, blues, and classical tapes and live jazz. It opens at 7:30 PM and stragglers can stay until 2.

Outdoor Activities and Sports

WATER SPORTS

You can moor at most large coastal villages in Lesbos, including Mytilini, Molyvos, Skala Sikaminias, Sigri, Plomari, and Skala Eressou, for fuel and water.

Paddleboats, canoes, and sailboarding equipment are available on Lesbos at Sigri, Molyvos, Petra, Vatera, and Skala Eressou.

En Route Lesbos is one of the few Greek islands in which the Turks settled into the countryside, away from the protection of the larger towns. Throughout your explorations keep your eyes open for the crumbling traces of the Ottoman legacy, such as a minaret or arching bridge, popping up in a field of flowers or a turn in the road.

Varia

⑩ *4 km (2½ mi) southeast of Mytilini.*

This suburb is a cultural center, the home village of early 20th-century painter Theophilos. Displayed in the **Theophilos museum** are 80 of his whimsical works—great washes of color detailing the everyday life and fantasies of another age—and the works of other evocative, primitive local painters. Theophilos lived in poverty, but painted airplanes and exotic cities—which he'd never seen. ✉ *Near the sea,* ☎ *0251/28179.* 🎫 *500 dr.* ☉ *Tues.–Sun. 10–1 and 4:30–8.*

The **Museum of Modern Art,** home of Stratis Eleftheriadis, better known by his French name, Thériade. This artist and critic helped publicize Theophilos and rose to fame as the foremost publisher of graphic art in Paris. The museum exhibit includes his publications—*Minotaure* and *Verved* magazines—and his collection of works (mostly lithographs) by Picasso, Matisse, Chagall, and Miró. ✉ *Next to Teriade Library,* ☎ *0251/23372.* 🎫 *600 dr.* ☉ *Tues.–Sun. 9–2 and 3–5.*

Moria

⑪ *6 km (3¾ mi) northwest of Mytilini, 7 km (4⅓ mi) northwest of Varia.*

Moria's **Roman aqueduct** dates back to the 2nd century. It was in Lesbos that Julius Caesar first made his mark. Sent to Bythinia to drum up a fleet, he hung around so long at King Nicodemus's court that he was rumored to be having an affair with the king, but he finally distinguished himself by saving a soldier's life.

Pamfila

⑫ *8 km (5 mi) north of Mytilini, 4 km (2½ mi) north of Moria.*

In the 19th century, Pamfila's traditional tower mansions were used by wealthy families as summer homes. The views across the straits to Turkey are wonderful here.

Pirgi Thermis

⑬ *8 km (5 mi) northwest of Mytilini, 2 km (1¼ mi) east of Pamfila.*

Pirgi Thermis is known for its tower mansions and for its 12th-century church, **Panayia Tourloti** (✉ Near the outskirts).

The village of **Loutropouli Thermis,** about 3 km (1¾ mi) northwest of Pirgi Thermis, is aptly named for its *loutra* (hot springs). These sulphur baths are dramatically enclosed with vaulted arches. A settlement existed here from before 3000 BC until Mycenaean times, centered on the spa's curative properties. In all, remnants of five cities have been excavated at this site.

Mandamados

⑭ *36 km (22½ mi) northwest of Mytilini, 7 km (4¼ mi) northwest of Pirgi Thermis.*

Mandamados is a pretty village of stone houses, wood carvings, and the ruins of a medieval castle. It is famous for its pottery, *koumari* urns (that keep water cool even in scorching heat), and for its black icon of Archangel Michael in the 18th-century monastery, **Taxiarchis Michail** (✉ Just north of village). Visitors used to make a wish and press a coin to the archangel's forehead; if it stuck, the wish would be granted. Owing to wear and tear on the icon, the practice is now forbidden.

Skala Sikaminias

⑮ *35 km (21¾ mi) northwest of Mytilini, 5 km (3 mi) north of Mandamados.*

At the northernmost point of Lesbos, past Pelopi (the ancestral village of 1988 presidential candidate Michael Dukakis), is the exceptionally lovely fishing port of Skala Sikaminias, The novelist Stratis Myrivilis used it as the setting for *The Mermaid Madonna.* If you've read the book, you'll recognize the tiny chapel at the base of the jetty. The author's birthplace and childhood home is in Sikaminia, a corkscrew road above.

Molyvos

★ ⑯ *61 km (38 mi) west of Mytilini, 17 km (10½ mi) southwest of Skala Sikaminias.*

Molyvos, also known as Mithimna, is a town you may dream about long after you leave. Before 1923 the Turks made up about a third of the population, living in many of the best stone houses. Today the houses are weighed down by roses and geraniums; the red-tile roofs are required by law, and the street cobbles are mandatory. Because of the town's visual charms many artists live here. Although new hotels have been banned in the old town, Molyvos swells with tour groups in summer; you may want to stay overnight in nearby Petra.

Come before high season and ascend to the **Byzantine-Genoese castle** for a hypnotic view down the tiers of red-tile roofs to the glittering sea. At dawn the sky begins to light up from behind the mountains of Asia Minor, casting silver streaks through the placid water as weary night fishermen come in. The grapevine-sheltered lane that descends from the castle passes numerous Turkish fountains, some still used. ⊠ *Above town,* ☎ *0253/71803.* 🎫 *Free.* ☉ *Tues.–Sun., dawn–sunset.*

The Arts

FESTIVAL

The best-known celebration on the islands is the **Molyvos Theater Festival,** held July through August. With the castle as backdrop, artists from all over Europe stage entertainment that ranges from a Dario Fo play to contemporary-music concerts. For tickets call ☎ 0253/71323; for information call the Molyvos tourist office (☞ Visitor Information *in* The Northern Islands A to Z, *below*).

Dining and Lodging

$$ ✗ **Gatos.** Gaze at the island and the harbor from the veranda, or sit inside and watch the cooks chop and grind in the open kitchen. Fish plates are limited; a better bet is the kokkinisto with garlic and savory onion. The beef fillet is tender, the lamb chops nicely grilled. Breakfast is also served. ⊠ *Main pedestrian st., Molyvos,* ☎ *0253/71661. No credit cards. Closed Nov.–Mar.*

$$ ✗ **Medusa.** This restaurant in a traditional stone house on the wharf
★ offers some interesting specialties, including *pita thalassinon* (seafood pie), *mydia akhnista* (steamed mussels), and *kalamarakia yemista* (squid stuffed with rice). The owners provide flawless service and quality at a low price. ⊠ *Molyvos Harbor, across from Ayios Nikolaos chapel,* ☎ *0253/72080. MC, V. Closed Nov.–Apr.*

$$ 🏨 **Aeolis.** This cluster of beach bungalows offers all the comforts of a resort complex. From the raised pool area (preferable to the mediocre beach), guests have a view of the sea as well as of Molyvos castle. Most of the bungalows have two or three beds, thick armchairs that fold out, and French doors onto a veranda. Kick back in the lounge's deep-seated sofas near the fireplace and potted plants. A hotel shuttle service runs up to town, as does the local bus. ⊠ *Outside Molyvos on rd. to Eftalou, 81108,* ☎ *0253/71772,* 🖷 *0253/71773. 28 rooms with bath. Restaurant, bar, snack bar, pool. MC, V. Closed Nov.–Mar.*

$$ 🏨 **Sea Horse.** After you've had enough of the touristy ambience uptown, descend to this modest hotel overlooking the busy harbor. Despite the traditional wood-and-stone exterior, the rooms are modern. Light sleepers should be warned of the din from nearby bars and cafés. Breakfast, served in a ground-floor breakfast room, is Continental (à la carte items are available). ⊠ *Molyvos Harbor 81108,* ☎ *0253/71320,* 🖷 *0253/71374. 13 rooms with shower or bath. Bar, cafeteria. No credit cards.*

Outdoor Activities and Sports

TENNIS

Hotels near Molyvos with courts to reserve include **Sun Rise Bungalows** (⊠ Efthalou, ☎ 0253/71713), **Alkeos** (⊠ Mithimna, ☎ 0253/71002), **Aphrodite** (⊠ Mithmna, ☎ 0253/71725), **Delfinia I Hotel and Bungalows** (⊠ Mithimna, ☎ 0253/71373), and **Olive Press** (⊠ Mithimna, ☎ 0253/71246).

Shopping

FINE ARTS

In Molyvos, the **Athens School of Fine Arts** (⊠ In Krallis Mansion near town center) occasionally holds sales of its paintings.

Petra

⑰ *55 km (34 mi) northwest of Mytilini, 5 km (3 mi) south of Molyvos.*

Petra stretches along the shore of a large sandy bay fringed by tamarisk trees. Its oldest section still retains traditional stone houses with overhanging balconies, which the government now preserves. Atop a giant monolith (Petra means "rock" in Greek) is the 18th-century church **Panayia Glikofiloussa** (Virgin of Tenderness), reached by climbing 114 steps. The less ambitious may want to stroll the **beach,** visit **Ayios Nikolaos** church (⊠ Off the sq.), with its 16th-century frescoes, or tour the intricate **Vareltzidaina mansion** (⊠ Near marketplace). ⊠ *On the rock.* ⌸ *Free.* ⊙ *Tues.–Sun. 8–3.*

Lodging

$$$ ⌸ **Clara.** A superior hotel of its class, completed in 1991, Clara has a
★ striking contemporary reception area in cool whites, pastel pinks, and gray. The bungalows all have spacious verandas with simultaneous views of Petra, Molyvos, and the sea, and with their comfortable gray beds, steel-blue covers, and pink curtains, they are a cut above the usual. Guests (mostly German package groups) can hop the shuttle bus to explore Petra, float in the large L-shape pool, or play a few sets of tennis. A buffet breakfast is served out on the terrace. ⊠ *Avlaki, south of Petra, 81109,* ☎ *0253/41522 through 41524,* ℻ *0253/41535. 45 rooms with bath. Restaurant, bar, pool, wading pool. AE, MC, V.*

$ ⌸ **Women's Agricultural Tourist Cooperative.** You can immerse yourself in island life by rooming with a Greek family, or by working in the fields for the cooperative. All rooms include breakfast. The cooperative also runs an excellent restaurant (lunch only) on the town square, with fish and meat dishes and *kotomakaronakia* (a local specialty of chicken and noodles baked in cream). ⊠ *Main Sq. (restaurant, office: Mon.–Sat. 9–3:30), Petra 81109,* ☎ *0253/41238. 100 rooms, most with bath. No credit cards.*

Skalohori

⑱ *58 km (36 mi) west of Mytilini, 3 km (1¾ mi) south of Petra.*

Skalohori is set beautifully in a valley, with tiered houses facing west toward the Aegean sunsets. Until recently the volcanic northwestern part of Lesbos around Skalohori and Andissa was home to wild horses, believed to be the last link with the horse-breeding culture of the Troad, mentioned by Homer.

⑲ The **monastery of Ayios Ioannis Theologos,** or Moni Ipsilou, was founded in 800 and rebuilt in the 12th century. Of special note are the small collection of 12th-century manuscripts, icons, and textiles; the tiles embedded in the facade; and the outstanding wood-lattice ceiling. ⊠ *On summit of extinct volcano.*

Sigri

⑳ *93 km (57¾ mi) west of Mytilini, 4 km (2½ mi) south of Skalohori.*

Sigri is built around a lovely cove; at water's edge is a small but impressive **Turkish castle** (⊠ Waterfront) with the sultan's monogram over the gate. Despite the claim of a **petrified forest** (⊠ Between Sigri and Eressos), or trees fossilized up to 20 million years ago by volcanic ash, it's not worth the search. The underwhelming site looks like a bunch of stumps. If you're interested, take a look at the specimens in **Sigri's Square,** or at **Ipsilou** (⊠ Below monastery).

Beaches

Some of the most spectacular sandy beaches and coves are in the southwest. Exceptional dark-sand beaches stretch from **Sigri** to **Skala Eressou.**

Skala Eressou

㉑ *89 km (55¼ mi) west of Mytilini, 15 km (9¼ mi) southeast of Sigri.*

Attractions in this charming village of two-story, 19th-century stone and shingle houses include **castle ruins** and the 5th-century church, **Ayios Andreas.** The church has a mosaic floor (currently covered) and a tiny adjacent **museum** housing local finds from tombs in the ancient cemetery. ⊠ *Harbor,* ☎ *0253/53332.* ⊡ *Free.* ☉ *Tues.–Sun. 8:30–3.*

The poet Sappho was born in the 7th century BC supposedly in ancient **Eressos** (⊠ 1 km/⅔ mi north of Skala Eressou). Dubbed the Tenth Muse by Plato because of her sensual lyric poetry and new poetic meter, she ran a school for young women. Though she was married and had a daughter, she is reputed to have been homosexual because her surviving poetry is dedicated to her students.

Sappho's works were burned, and only fragments of her books survive. Despite its erotic reputation, Sapphic meter was in great favor in the medieval ages and used in hymns, especially by Gregory the Great. Today, besides European and Greek tourists, many lesbians come here to visit her birthplace. (The word "lesbian" derives from Lesbos.)

Beaches

Some of the island's best beaches are in the vicinity of Skala Eressou. Especially popular is the **town's beach** because it is wide and sandy, with a small island within swimming distance.

Dining

$$ ✗ **Bennetts'.** Max and Jackie Bennett's place has seating on elevated wooden platforms, near the illuminated resort. This British-run establishment offers an unusually full menu of Greek and Western meat and vegetarian specialties. When listless from Greek food, you'll appreciate such novelties as lasagna, mushrooms in garlic sauce, and apple crumble smothered in cream. ⊠ *Skala Eressou, at east end of beach,* ☎ *0253/53624. No credit cards. Closed Nov.–Apr.*

Kalloni

40 km (24¼ mi) west of Mytilini, 4 km (2½ mi) northeast of Skala Eressou.

㉒ This agricultural market town is rather quiet, but 5 km (3 mi) northwest of Kalloni is the sprawling 16th-century **Limonos monastery,** patrolled by peacocks and the tenants of the sanitarium here. Three stories of cells ring the courtyard. A bishop has collected a jumble of plates and doodads in a sort of **folk-art museum upstairs,** but more interesting is the ground-floor treasury of Byzantine manuscripts. Women are not allowed in the main church. ⊠ *On northern outskirts of village.* ⊡ *100 dr.* ☉ *Daily 9–1 and 5–7:30.*

Agiassos

★ **㉓** *28 km (17½ mi) southwest of Mytilini, 10 km (6¼ mi) northeast of Kalloni.*

Agiassos village, the prettiest hill town on Lesbos, sits in an isolated, wooded valley near the middle of the island at the foot of Mt. Olympus, the highest peak. (There are 19 mountains in the Mediterranean named Olympus, almost all of them peaks sacred to the local sky god, who eventually became associated with Zeus.) Despite its recent discovery by tourists, Agiassos remains a special settlement with gray stone houses, cobblestone lanes, a medieval castle, and shops selling local handicrafts, particularly wood crafts. The church of **Panayia Vrefokratousa** was founded in the 12th century to house an icon believed to be the work of St. Luke.

NEED A BREAK? | Stop at one of several cafés in the winding streets of the old bazaar area past the church of Panayia Vrefokratousa. On weekend afternoons sip an ouzo and listen to a santoúri band, featuring hammered dulcimer, accompanied by clarinet, drum, and violin. As locals dance rather haphazardly on the cobblestones, you might be tempted to join in the merriment.

Dining

$ ✕ **Dagieles.** If nothing else, you must stop here for a coffee made by
★ owner Stavritsa. And you should try the *kolokitholouloudo* (stuffed squash blossoms) and the dishes that entice the local police here throughout the winter: *kritharaki* (barley-shape pasta), kokkinisto, and *varkoules* ("little boats" of eggplant slices with minced meat). For a few short weeks in spring the air is laden with the scent of overhanging wisteria. ⌂ *Agiassos near bus stop,* ☎ *0252/22241. No credit cards.*

Plomari

② 42 km (26 mi) southwest of Mytilini, 20 km (12½ mi) south of Agiassos.

Plomari, the second-largest town on Lesbos, is set in a cliff face. This cheerful mix of package resort and quiet fishing village is known for its potent ouzo and its happy Scandinavian crowd. Not unexpectedly, there's a lively night scene on the harbor, where tourists gather after a long day at the beach.

Vatera

② 53 km (33 mi) east of Mytilini, 6 km (3¾ mi) west of Plomari.

The village of Vatera is said to have one of Lesbos's most beautiful beaches, a 9 km-long sandy strip of sparkling water, lined with tamarisk trees, and framed with green hills. Local families favor the relaxed atmosphere of the area. You can sit and enjoy the view of the cape of Ayios Fokas, with its newly excavated temple of Dionysus.

Beaches

The **town beach** is idyllic. In the southeast, there is a good sand/pebble beach at **Ayios Isidoros** (⌂ Near Plomari). A sandy beach southeast in **Gera Bay** (⌂ Just south of Skala Polihnitos) is another good choice.

Lodging

$$ ▦ **Vatera Beach.** This low-key but well-designed hotel has all the makings of a higher-category lodging. Rooms in the four white-and-blue buildings have their own entrances, balconies, and a sea view. Small groups can visit in winter, when a fireplace and central heating make it a treat. Most of the food for the hotel's restaurant is raised or grown organically: fruits, vegetables, rabbits, and even pigs. ⌂ *Vatera beach 81300,* ☎ *0252/61212,* 𝖥𝖠𝖷 *0252/61164. 25 rooms with shower or bath. Restaurant. No credit cards. Closed Nov.–Apr.*

$ ⌂ **Dionyssos.** On the sloping southern shores near Vatera Beach, replete with fig, poplar, willow, and walnut trees, this is one of the island's best campgrounds. ⊠ *Vatera Beach,* ☎ *0253/61340. 105 RV sites and 10 tent sites. Bathrooms, hot showers, pool, windsurfing, disco, gas station. Closed Oct.–Apr.*

CHIOS

Homer called this island, which almost touches Turkey's coast, "Craggy Hios." It may not seem to offer much charm when you first see its modernized capital, and consider the results of its many misfortunes: the Turkish massacre of 1822; major earthquakes, including one in 1881 that killed almost 6,000 Chiotes; severe fires, which in the 1980s burned two-thirds of its pine trees; and through the ages, the steady stripping of forests to ax-wielding boat builders. But look a bit deeper. Chios will surprise you.

Allied to Athens during the Persian Wars, Chios later became independent. Emperor Constantine scooped up spoils when Rome invaded, and after the fall of Byzantium other pillagers included pirates, Venetians, Catalans, and Turks. The Genoese ruled during the 14th century, but Chios became part of the Ottoman Empire in 1566.

The name Chios comes from the Phoenician word for mastic, the resin of the *Pistacia lentisca,* evergreen shrubs that with few exceptions thrive only here, in the south part of the island. Every August incisions are made in the bark of the shrubs; the sap leaks out, permeating the air with a sweet fragrance, and in September it is harvested. This aromatic resin, which brought huge revenues until the introduction of petroleum products, was used in varnishes, waxes, cosmetics, and in the chewing gum used by odalisques in the Ottoman harems.

Until charter tourism began in the late 1980s, Chios prospered mainly from its export of mastic. It is also home to the elite families that control Greece's private shipping empires: Livanos, Karas, Chandris; even Onassis came here from Smyrna. The island did not seem to need tourists, nor to draw them.

Yet Chios intrigues, with its deep valleys, uncrowded black pebble beaches, intact *mastikhohoria* (villages where mastic is produced and processed) (☞ Pirghi and Mesta, *below*), Byzantine monasteries, and haunted, deserted villages—remnants of its poignant history. It remains unique even among these special islands, and as travelers are finding, it is well worth a visit.

Chios Town

❷❻ *24 km (15 mi) northeast of Pirgi.*

The main port and capital, Chios town, or Chora (which means "town"), is a busy commercial settlement on the east coast, across from Turkey. Aside from some fishermen's boats with their nets spread out before them, the modern waterfront is crowded with private yachts. But in the evening, the cafés overflow with ouzo and good cheer, and locals proudly promenade along the bay side.

The capital is noisy, crowded with half the island's population, but its fascinating heart is the **bazaar district** (⊠ Sprawling south and east of Platia Vounakiou, main sq.). Merchants hawk everything from local gum and fresh dark bread to screeching monkeys.

The **old quarter** (⊠ On northern highlands) is found inside the *kastro* (fort), built in the 9th century by the Byzantines. Note the old wood-and-plaster houses on the backstreets, typically decorated with latticework and balconies. This was the old Muslim and Jewish neighborhood, and decaying monuments, fountains, and mosques remain. Under Turkish rule, the Greeks lived outside the wall; the gate was closed daily at sundown.

The **Byzantine Museum,** inside the 15th-century Giustiani mansion, has airy rooms hung with frescoes from Nea Moni and Panayia Krina church (☞ *below*). ⊠ *Just inside old quarter in Giustiani mansion,* ☎ *0271/ 22819.* ⌣ *Free.* ☉ *Tues.–Sun. 9–3.*

In **Platia Frouriou** (⊠ In the fort's small sq.), look for the **Turkish cemetery** and the large **marble tomb** (with the fringed hat) of Kara Ali, chief of the Turkish flagship in 1822. Along the **main street** are elegant **Ayios Georgios** church (closed most of the time), which has icons from Asia Minor; houses from the Genoese period; and the **remains of Turkish baths** (⊠ North corner of fort).

NEED A BREAK?	Try a Chiote snack of sheep's milk yogurt and thick honey or rice pudding. The food is fresh and authentic at the unnamed **little dairy shop** (⊠ Corner of Roihou and Veneizelou, behind Appolonio lodgings).

In 1822, in the tiny **prison** (⊠ Just inside main gate) 75 leading Chiotes were jailed as hostages before they were hanged by the Turks, part of the worst massacre committed during the War of Independence. The Turks, who drove out the Genoese in 1566, had been fond of the island for its mastic, which they chewed in the company of their harems to sweeten their breath.

But Chios, spurred by Samians who had fled to the island, joined the rest of Greece in rebellion. The revolt failed, and the Sultan retaliated: The Turks killed 30,000 Chiotes and enslaved 45,000, an event depicted by Delacroix in The Massacres of Chios. The painting shocked Western Europe and led indirectly to support for Greek independence.

Copies of the Delacroix hang in many places here, including the dusty **post-Byzantine museum** housed in a mosque. On the mosque, note the *tugra* (the swirling monogram of the sultan that shows royal possession). Although the tugra is common in Istanbul, it is rarely seen elsewhere, and its presence indicated the favor Chios enjoyed under the sultan. ⊠ *Platia Vounakiou,* ☎ *0271/26866.* ⌣ *Free.* ☉ *Tues.–Sun. 10–1.*

The **archaeological museum** has been shut since an earthquake damaged it in late 1992; it is due to reopen in 1997. The collection ranges from proto-Helladic pottery dug up in Emborio to a letter from Alexander the Great addressed to the Chiotes and dated 332 BC. ⊠ *Michalon 10,* ☎ *0271/26664.*

The **Philip Argenti Museum** is the most interesting collection in town, housed on the top floor of the **Korais Library,** one of Greece's largest. It holds self-serving portraits of the family that endowed it, and more copies of the Delacroix painting, but also some fascinating costumes, embroideries, implements, and engravings evocative of earlier times. ⊠ *Koraii 2, near cathedral,* ☎ *0271/23462.* ⌣ *Free.* ☉ *Weekdays 8– 2, Fri. 5–7:30, Sat. 8–12:30.*

The Arts
Chios usually is host to a summer conference at the **International Society of Homeric Studies** (⊠ 5 Heroon Polytechneiou St., ☎ 0271/44391).

Beaches
Karfas beach (⊠ 8 km/5 mi south of Chios town) fronts a shallow sandy bay.

Dining and Lodging

$$ ✕ **Bel Air.** With its black-lacquer chairs, rows of potted plants, piano, and wall of mirrors, the decor is a step up from most tavernas. It's open 24 hours a day. The menu changes often: Look for *soupies me sevgola* (cuttlefish stuffed with mountain greens) and *soupa petropsaris* (rockfish soup). The schnitzel is stuffed with Edam and topped with onion-mushroom sauce. ⊠ *Aegeou 118 near Chandris Hotel, Chios town,* ☎ *0271/29947. MC, V.*

$$ ✕ **O Hotzas.** This spacious taverna, reputed to be the capital's best, ★ has a medieval interior with a beamed ceiling, brass implements, and family portraits. Most dishes are deep-fried, but you may also nosh on succulent lamb with lemon sauce, and many vegetable dishes. The squid is always reliable, and it's delicious with the homemade retsina or ouzo. For dessert, order yogurt with homemade cherry or quince preserves. ⊠ *Yioryiou Kondili 3, Chios,* ☎ *0271/23117. No credit cards. Closed Sun. No lunch.*

$$$ 🏨 **Chios Chandris.** On the water, this big, bustling, and boxy member of the Greek hotel and ship chain is considered the capital's best. The pool and stone terrace by the sea, lunch buffets, disco, and friendly social staff make for the most resortlike atmosphere on the island. Rooms are comfortable in shades of Aegean blue, but best are the balconies, with views of the mountains or of the caïques and fishing boats plying the harbor. ⊠ *Prokymea, between port and beach, 82100,* ☎ *0271/25761 and 25765,* 🗏 *0271/25768. 156 rooms with bath. Restaurant, 2 bars, pool, meeting rooms. AE, MC, V.*

$$$ 🏨 **Erytha.** Perched on a rock above a quiet bay like a minivillage, this new hotel on Karfas beach is sleek and high tech, designed with primary colors and tile floors. Mosaic walkways lead to gardens, terraces, and the beach below. No-nonsense rooms provide built-in furniture, TVs, and balconies. Weekly social activities and programs can augment your vacation. It is about 6 km (3¾ mi) from Chios town, and 3 km (2 mi) from the airport. ⊠ *Karfas 82100,* ☎ *0271/32311/16,* 🗏 *0271/32182. 81 rooms with bath. 2 restaurants, bar, air-conditioning, minibars, indoor pool, fitness center, meeting room. AE, MC, V. Closed Nov.–Apr.*

$$$ 🏨 **Golden Sand.** Three boxy white buildings contain simple rooms with carved-wood furniture and almost always a sea view. The hotel has some extras such as a game room, a playground, and a huge buffet breakfast. On "Greek night" in summer, tour groups arrive for Greek music and dancing. It is conveniently at mid-beach near Chios town, 4 km (2½ mi) from the airport. ⊠ *Beach Rd., Karfas, 82100,* ☎ *0271/ 32080, 0271/32081, or 0271/31010;* 🗏 *0271/31700. 108 rooms with bath or shower. Restaurant, air-conditioning, bar, piano bar, pool, beauty salon, playground. AE, MC, V.*

$$–$$$ 🏨 **Fedra.** From the moment you enter this neoclassical former mansion, painted ocher and planted with jubilant flowers, you feel at home. A pension run by a playwright, it is an appealing, inexpensive choice. All the rooms have baths and air-conditioning and heating. The summer outdoor bar generates some noise, so ask for a back room. Off-season, a piano bar warms up the place. ⊠ *M. Livanou 13, Chios 82100,* ☎ *0271/41129 or 0271/41130. 10 rooms with bath. Café. MC.*

$$–$$$ 🏨 **Kyma.** Begun in 1917, this neoclassical villa was completed in 1922, when it served as General Plastiras's headquarters after the Greek defeat in Asia Minor. From here he ordered the deposition of the king and the court-martial of six cabinet ministers. A modern cement addition only slightly mars the stone facade and grillwork. Some rooms have whirlpool baths. The only problem is noise from the street below. With the great breakfast, parting with bed won't be so bad if you are fond of fresh Chios tangerine juice. ⊠ *Chandris 1, Chios 82100,* ☎ *0271/44500,* FAX *0271/44600. 59 rooms with bath. Air-conditioning. No credit cards.*

$ ⚠ **Chios at Ayios Isidoros.** This is one of the better official campgrounds. Found here are all of the amenities and a beach site that looks across to Asia Minor. ⊠ *Ayios Isidoros, Chios,* ☎ *0271/74111 through 74113. 100 RV sites and 8 tent sites. Bathrooms, hot showers, tennis court, disco, playground. Closed Oct.–May.*

Outdoor Activities and Sports

SAILING

In Chios you can moor in Kardamila, Limnia, and Chios town. In Chios town call (☎ 0271/27286) for fuel; call (☎ 0271/27377) for water; repairs are available in the harbor. A new yacht marina is near completion at Vrondados.

Shopping

LOCAL CRAFTS

It's no surprise that gum is a best buy here; the brand is Elma. It makes a fun stocking stuffer and conversation piece. You can also find an unusual mastic liquor called *mastíha,* and gliko koutaliou, the sugary goo served on a spoon in water—a favorite with children.

In Chios town, the **women's cooperative** (⊠ Chios town, ☎ 0271/ 32000) sells traditional woven fabrics and rugs made from multicolor rags; it's open weekdays 9 to 9. In the village of Kallimasia is a popular **art cooperative** (⊠ 4 km/2½ mi south of Chios town, ☎ 0271/51– 180), which sells cloth dolls in Chian costumes; it's open Monday through Saturday 9:30 to 12:30 and 3:30 to 6:30.

Vrontados

4 km (2½ mi) north of Chios town.

㉗ **Daskalopetra** (Teacher's Rock), where Homer is said to have taught his pupils, is just above the port of Vrontados. Archaeologists believe this lectern is actually part of an ancient altar, but today you can sit on it and muse about the *Iliad* and *Odyssey.*

North of Teacher's Rock are several sites of historic interest. The 19th-
㉘ century monastery of **Panayia Myrtidiotissa** (Our Lady of the Myrtle) (⊠ On shoreline) overlooks the Aegean past the villages of Pandoukios. **Langada** (⊠ At nearby Delphinion) is where a 5th-century BC Athenian naval base was unearthed. **Kardamila** (⊠ 28 km/17½ mi north of Chios town), a former ship-owner enclave, actually has two villages,
㉙ upper and lower. **Nagos** harbor, a swampy area, is the site where a ruined temple of Poseidon was found early this century.

Beaches

In these parts try **Yiosonas** and wooded **Nagos** beaches. Many of the northern beaches are windy and deserted.

Volissos

㉚ *42 km (26 mi) northwest of Chios town, 4 km (2½ mi) west of Vrontados.*

Homer's birthplace is thought to be at Volissos, though Smyrna, Colophon, Salamis, Rhodes, Argos, and Athens also claim this honor. This pretty, narrow-laned northern village is today half-empty, with only a few hundred inhabitants. Solid stone houses march up the

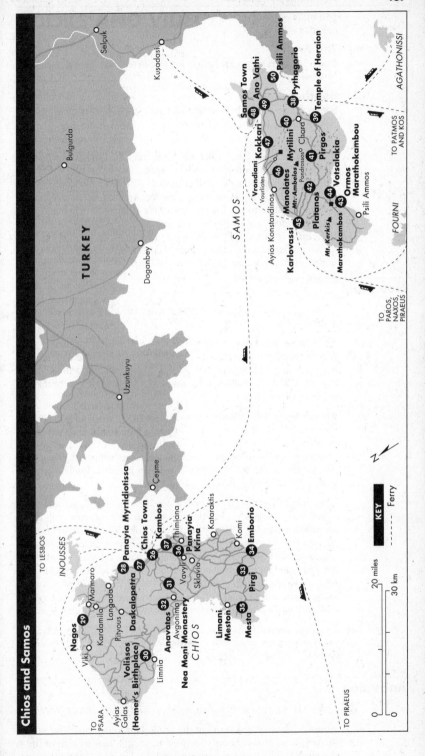

Chios and Samos

TURKEY

Selçuk

Kuşadası

Bulgurda

Doganbey

Uzunkuyu

Çeşme

SAMOS

Samos Town
Ano Vathi
Psili Ammos
Pythagorio
Temple of Heraion

50
49
48
38
39

Vrondiani Kokkari
Mytilini
Chora
Pirgos
Marathokambou
Ormos

47
40
41
42
43
44
45
46

Manolates
Mt. Ambelos
Platanos
Votsalakia

Pondrosso
Vourliotes
Ayios Konstandinos
Mt. Kerkis
Marathokambos
Psili Ammos

TO PATMOS AND KOS

FOURNI

AGATHONISSI

TO PAROS, NAXOS, PIRAEUS

INOUSSES

TO LESBOS

Panayia Myrtidiotissa
Chios Town
Kambos
Thimiana
Panayia Krina

28
27
26
37
36

Vavyli
Sklavia
Kataraktis
Komi

Marmaro
Langada
Nagos
Kardamila
Pityous

29

Volissos
(Homer's Birthplace)
Daskalopetra
Anavatos
Nea Moni Monastery

30
31
32

Viki
Ayias
Galas

TO PSARA

Avgonima
Limnia

CHIOS

Limani
Meston
Mesta
Pirgi
Emborio

35
33
34

TO PIRAEUS

KEY

Ferry

20 miles

30 km

N

mountainside to the Genoese fort, where Byzantine nobles were once exiled.

The Arts

In summer, arts events are held in historic Vrontados, during the annual **"Homeria."**

Beaches

Some of the best beaches on the island are in the vicinity, including **Limia** (⊠ 2 km/1¼ mi south of Volissos).

Lodging

$$ 🏠 **Village Houses.** Since 1987, energetic Stella Tsakiri has overseen the meticulous restoration of 11 medium-size houses, preserving where possible such vernacular touches as unworked tree trunks supporting a sleeping loft. Yet all modern conveniences are present, and each unit, designed for two to five people, has a fully equipped kitchen and a terrace with sweeping views—you're just under the half-ruined Byzantine castle. It's ideal for families on a get-away-from-it-all holiday. ⊠ *Volissos village, Chios 82100,* ☎ *0274/21421,* 𝔽𝔸𝕏 *0274/21521. 11 units with bath. Air-conditioning.* No *credit cards.*

Nea Moni

17 km (10½ mi) west of Chios town, 59 km (36½ mi) southeast of Volissos.

★ ㉛ The island's most important monument, and one of the finest examples of mosaic art anywhere, is the 11th-century **Nea Moni monastery** (⊠ High in mountains of Nea Moni). Emperor Constantine Monomachos VIII built it where three monks had found an icon of the Virgin in a myrtle bush.

The octagonal *katholikon* (medieval church) created by architects and painters from Constantinople exemplifies the artistic ideas prevailing during the 11th century in that city. Its distinctive three-part vaulted sanctuary has two narthexes, with no buttresses supporting the dome. This design, a single square space covered by a dome, closely connected with Constantinople, is rarely seen in Greece.

The church's interior gleams with colored marble slabs and mosaics of Christ's life, austere yet sumptuous, with azure blue, ruby red, velvet green colors, and skillful applications of gold. The saints' expressiveness comes from their vigorous poses and severe gazes, with heavy shadows under the eyes. On the iconostasis hangs the icon—a small Virgin and Child facing left. Also inside the grounds are an **ancient refectory, a vaulted cistern, a chapel filled with bones of Turkish massacre victims,** and a large **clock** still keeping Byzantine time, with the sunrise reckoned as 12 o'clock. ⊠ *In mountains.* ☉ *Daily 8–1 and 4–8.*

En Route   Heading toward Anavatos via the Nea Moni side-road junction, the main road turns southwest to **Avgonima,** from which there is an expansive view of the west coast.

Anavatos

㉜   *16 km (10 mi) west of Chios town, 5 km (3 mi) northwest of Nea Moni.*

About 50 houses still stand in the semi-abandoned, medieval village of Anavatos. In this heavily fortified town, the biggest sign of life is the farmers who come to gather pistachios. In 1822, during the revolution, 400 women and children threw themselves over the cliff here rather than surrender to the Turks.

Pirgi

33 *24 km (15 mi) south of Chios town, 22 km (13½ mi) southeast of Anavatos.*

At one time Chios's half-dozen or so mastic villages prospered on the sales of mastic gum and were spared by the Turks because of it. Today they depend on tangerines, apricots, olives—and tourists. Pirgi is the largest of the mastic villages.

Filled with more than 50 churches, Pirgi could be a graphic designer's model. Many of the houses along Pirgi's tiny arched streets are adorned with *xysta* (like Italian sgraffito). Especially lavish are the designs on houses near the main square, including the **Kimisis tis Theotokou** church (Dormition of the Virgin) (⊠ Near main sq.), built in 1694.

The fresco-embellished 12th-century church **Ayii Apostoli** is a very small replica of the earlier Nea Moni katholikon. The 17th-century frescoes that completely mask the interior, the work of a Cretan artist, have a distinct folk-art leaning. To get in, ask at the main square to find the current doorkeeper. ⊠ *In town, northwest of sq.* ☉ *Tues.–Thurs. and Sat. 10–1.*

About 50 people named Kolomvos live in Pirgi, claiming kinship with Christopher Columbus, known to have been from Genoa, the power that built the mastikhohoria (some renegade historians claim Columbus was really born on Chios).

Beaches

From Pirgi it's 8 km (5 mi) southeast to the glittering **black volcanic** **34** **beach** near **Emborio.** Known by locals as Mavra Volia ("black pebbles"), the cove is backed by jutting volcanic cliffs; the calm water's dark-blue color created by the smooth pebbles.

Shopping

CERAMICS
In the small mastic village of **Armolia,** 20 km (12½ mi) south of Chios town, pottery is a specialty.

Mesta

★ **35** *28 km (17½ mi) southwest of Chios town, 11 km (7 mi) west of Pirgi.*

Mesta is the island's best-preserved medieval mastic village, a labyrinth of twisting vaulted streets linking two-story, stone-and-mortar houses, which are supported by buttresses against earthquakes. The striking, somber village sits inside a system of 3-foot-thick walls, and the outer row of houses also doubles as protection. This fine example of 14th-century defense architecture was useful against the many pirates and marauders who plagued Chios through the centuries. Most of the narrow streets lead to blind alleys; the rest lead to the six gates; the one in the northeast still has an iron grate.

One of the largest and wealthiest churches in Greece, the 18th-century **Megas Taxiarchis** commands the main square, its vernacular baroque and rococo features combined in the late folk-art style of Chios.

Beaches

Escape to the string of **secluded coves** (⊠ Between Elatas and Trahiliou bays) with good swimming; a **nudist beach** (⊠ About 2 km/1¼ mi north of Lithi) with fine white pebbles is among them.

Dining and Lodging

$$ ✕ **O Moreas sta Mesta.** The proprietor spends winter and spring gathering herbs and greens from nearby hills and seashores. Typical are *kri-*

tama, to give salads a tang, and *horta* (greens like swiss chard and dandelion sautéed with lemon and oil) for his excellent *hortopita* (a pie made with horta). Unusual for a taverna, there's excellent brown bread, and a potent, semisweet red wine made from raisins. The goat fricassee must be ordered in advance, and *ksifias* souvlaki (swordfish chunks on a spit), *domotokeftedes* (fried tomato patties), and *hirino krasato* (pork simmered in wine) are usually available. ⊠ *Mesta Sq., Mesta, Chios,* ☎ *0271/76400. No credit cards.*

$ ✕ **Limani Meston.** This taverna has something for every budget: mostly magirefta in summer, with a few inexpensive fish. Meats include homemade sausage, whole roasted piglets (order ahead), and lamb or beef on the spit. You can sit outside among the ivy and blossoms, where Mesta's working harbor unfolds before you; or on colder days, enjoy the fireplace with the locals. ⊠ *Mesta Harbor, 3 km (2 mi) from Mesta village,* ☎ *0271/76367 or 0271/76265. No credit cards.*

$$ 🏠 **Traditional Settlements.** These medieval fortified houses, built into
★ the maze of Mesta village, give a feel for life in a mastikhohoria. There are four two-story houses with rooms: The Argyroudi house has two rooms and a kitchenette under a vaulted baby-blue ceiling, decorated with vase-adorned alcoves and village furniture. The houses were built with small exterior doors and windows, but they face inward to a courtyard. Mr. Pipidis makes all the arrangements; call him in advance. ⊠ *Built into maze, Mesta 82100,* ☎ *0271/76319. 8 rooms, most with bath or shower. No credit cards.*

Nightlife
BAR
Karnayio (⊠ Leoforos Stenoseos, outside town on rd. to airport) is a popular spot for dancing.

En Route   On the way to Chios town, near Vavili, is the 12th-century **Panayia**
36   **Krina** (Our Lady of the Source) (⊠ On rd. to left marked TO SKLAVIA), where three layers of frescoes spanning six periods were discovered. The very earliest period is represented by portraits of the saints facing the entrance; most of the restored frescoes hang in the Giustiani mansion in Chios town (☞ *above*). The church is rarely open, but the finely worked exterior makes the trip worthwhile.

Kambos

37   *4 km (2½ mi) south of Chios town, about 29 km (18 mi) northeast of Mesta.*

Mastodon bones were found here in the Kambos region, a fertile plain of citrus groves, which is perfect for cycling through. Since medieval times, wealthy Genoese and Greek merchants built ornate, earth-color, three-story mansions. Behind a forbidding wall adorned with a coat of arms, each is a world of its own, with details such as pebble-mosaic courtyards and **manganos** (waterwheels). Some houses are crumbled, and some still stand, reminders of the wealth, power, and downfall of an earlier time.

Lodging
$$$$ 🏠 **Villa Argentiko.** The ancestral estate of the Italo-Greek counts Ar-
★ genti de Scio has become one of Greece's classiest inns. Luxury cottages scattered about the manicured grounds accommodate a maximum of 16, with balconies, Victorian furniture, and marble-clad bathrooms. At breakfast, you can sip fresh-squeezed tangerine or orange juice, while planning a leisurely stroll or painting excursion through the groves, where a manganos fills a square pool stocked with water lilies and carp.

Dinner can be ordered à la carte. A swimming pool and two more suites are planned for the future. ✉ *Kambos district 82100,* ☎ *0271/31599,* FAX *0271/31465. 1 room with bath, 5 cottage suites. Outdoor café. No credit cards. Closed Nov.–Apr. except by arrangement.*

SAMOS

Samos is the most southern of this group of four north-Aegean islands, and of all the Greek islands, it's the closest to Turkey, separated by only 3 km. It was, in fact, a part of Asia Minor until it split off during the Ice Age. The felicitous landscape has lacy coasts, and mountain villages perched on ravines carpeted in pink oleander, red poppy, and purple sage. Samos's mountains, geologically part of the great spur that runs across western Turkey, make for surprising twists in the landscape.

Ancient names attest to the sweet virtues of Samos, known as the Island of the Blessed: Homer called it Hydrele, or the watery place, for its many clear springs; it has also been coined Anthemis, or "blooming flowers," and Kyparissia, "full of pine trees."

Although in the last decade Samos has become packed with charter tourists in July and August, it is large enough to let you escape the crowds easily. For those who approach from the west, Mt. Kerkis seems to spin out of the sea, while in the distance Mt. Ambelos guards the terraced vineyards that produce the famous Samian wine.

Plutarch writes that Anthony and Cleopatra came to Samos "giving themselves over to the feasting," that artists came from throughout the ancient world to entertain them, and kings vied to send the grandest gifts. During its heyday in the 6th century BC, the island contributed greatly to the ancient world. It was home to fabled Aesop and to Aristarchos (the first in history to place the sun at the center of our universe), to the philosopher Epicurus, and to the mathematician Pythagoras, for whom the ancient capital (formerly Tigani, or "frying pan") was renamed.

Pythagorio

38 *14 km (8¼ mi) southwest of Samos town.*

Samos had been a democratic state, but in 535 BC the town now called Pythagorio fell to the tyrant Polycrates (540 BC–522 BC), who used his fleet of 100 ships to make profitable raids around the Aegean, until he was caught by the Persians and crucified in 522 BC.

His rule produced what Herodotus described as "three of the greatest building and engineering feats in the Greek world." One is the Heraion (☞ *below*), west of Pythagorio, the largest temple ever built in Greece and one of the Seven Wonders of the Ancient World. Another is the ancient mole protecting the harbor on the southeast coast, on which the present 450-meter jetty rests. The third is the Efpalinio tunnel.

An underground aqueduct, the **Efpalinio tunnel** was finished in 524 BC with primitive tools and without measuring instruments. Efpalinos of Megara, a hydraulics engineer, set two teams of slaves digging, one on each side of Mt. Kastri. Fifteen years later, they met in the middle with just a small difference in the elevation between the two halves. The tunnel was used during the middle ages as a hideout from pirate raids, but today it is electrically lit, and though some spaces are tight and slippery, you can walk the first 304 meters (1,000 feet). ✉ *Just north of town.* 🎫 *500 dr.* ☉ *Tues.–Sun. 9–2 PM.*

Among acres of excavations, little else remains from the **ancient city** (⊠ Bordering small harbor and hill) except a few pieces of the **Policrates wall** and the **ancient theater** a few hundred yards above the tunnel. Its quiet, cobblestone streets are lined with mansions and filled with fragrant orange blossoms.

At one corner sits a crumbling **fortress** (⊠ East corner), probably on top of the ruins of the acropolis. Revolutionary hero Lycourgos Logothetis built this 19th-century edifice, and his statue is in the **church courtyard** next door. He held back the Turks on Transfiguration Day, and a sign on the church announces in Greek: CHRIST SAVED SAMOS 6 AUGUST, 1824. At night the villagers light votive candles in the church cemetery, a moving sight with the ghostly silhouette of the fortress and the moonlit sea in the background.

The small **Pythagorio Museum** contains local finds, including headless statues, grave markers with epigrams to the dead, and portraits of Roman emperors. ⊠ *Platia Pythagora, in municipal building,* ☎ *0273/61400.* 🎫 *500 dr.* ☉ *Apr.–Oct., Tues.–Sun. approximately 9–2.*

Dining and Lodging

$$ ✕ **Lito.** One of the only true restaurants lining Pythagorio's esplanade, Lito has such interesting dishes as the addictive *kolokithakia* yemista (zucchini stuffed with feta and bacon). Besides the usual grilled meats, you may savor a mixed grill with beef patties, souvlaki, liver, Mexican chicken, and fillet in Madeira sauce. Late risers can have breakfast all day. Look for the mustard-color awning and gray-and-blue chairs. ⊠ *Pythagorio Harbor,* ☎ *0273/61101. No credit cards. Closed Nov.–Mar.*

$ ✕ **Maritsa.** This simple fish tavern, on a quiet, tree-lined side street, opened in 1992 and quickly established a regular Pythagorio clientele. In the garden courtyard, you can try grilled flying fish (!), red mullet, octopus, and squid garnished with garlicky *skordalia* (a thick lemony sauce with pureed potatoes, vinegar, and parsley). The usual appetizers include a sharp *tzatziki* (tangy lemon-yogurt dip) and a large horiatiki salad, piled high with tomatoes, olives, and feta cheese. ⊠ *Last st. on right off Lykourgou Logotheti as you descend to harbor,* ☎ *0273/ 61957. No credit cards.*

$$$$ 🏨 **Doryssa Bay Hotel and Village.** If you require every comfort imag-
★ inable, this is the place for you. This pseudo-village has pastel houses (containing housekeeping apartments) with a small church, a square, *kafenion* (traditional Greek coffeehouse), and shops. Half board is mandatory, but the food at the hotel's Taverna Asterias is unusually good—sample it at Tuesday's pricey Greek night, which entails lavish spreads and traditional dancers. ⊠ *Outside Pythagorio on main rd. to Chora, 83103,* ☎ *0273/61360,* 𝖥𝖠𝖷 *Athens: 01/692–8244. 300 rooms with bath. 3 restaurants, 2 bars, air-conditioning, pool, tennis court, beach, water sports. AE, DC, MC, V. Closed Nov.–Mar.*

$$–$$$ 🏨 **Fito Bungalows Hotel.** This place exudes peace and quiet: the rooms are in a cluster of low-slung white buildings connected by tree-shaded, rose-lined walkways and are tucked between the sea and Glyfada Lake. Plain pine furniture, white walls, and verandas in the rooms add to the simplicity. A buffet breakfast is included. The water sports instructor from Doryssa Bay gives lessons on the beach. ⊠ *Pythagorio, near Potokaki turnoff, 83103,* ☎ *0273/61314,* 𝖥𝖠𝖷 *0273/61582. 86 rooms with bath. Restaurant, bar, air-conditioning, pool, beach, water sports. MC, V. Closed Nov.–Apr.*

$$ 🏨 **Galini.** You won't pay dearly for comfort at this hotel. Reached only by steps and with no cars passing in front, Galini (meaning tranquil-

ity) is aptly quiet. The large marble-adorned rooms face the town, and a few face the sea. Each floor has a refrigerator. The friendly Kanatas family serves breakfast in the garden or the dining room. ⊠ *Aesopos, off Platia Irinis, Pythagorio 83103,* ☎ *0273/61167. 16 rooms with bath. Dining room, lounge, in-room safes. No credit cards. Closed Nov.–late Mar.*

Outdoor Activities and Sports

SAILING

On Samos, **Pythagorio, Karlovassi, Ormos Marathokambou,** and **Samos town** have fuel, water, and repair services.

Sun Yachting (⊠ 9 Dosmani St., Athens, ☎ 01/983–7312) in Athens specializes in charter rentals to Samos; you can pick up the boat in Piraeus or Pythagorio for one- and two-week rentals.

TENNIS

Near Pythagorio the **Doryssa Bay** (⊠ Outside Pythagorio on main rd. to Chora, ☎ 0273/61360), **Apollon** (⊠ Outside Pythagorio on main rd. to Chora, ☎ 0273/61683), and **Princessa** hotels (⊠ Outdise Pythagorio on main rd. to Chora, ☎ 0273/61698) have courts to rent.

WATER SPORTS

On Samos many beaches have windsurfing rentals, including **Heraion, Karlovassi, Mykali, Potokaki, Tsamadou,** and **Votsalakia.**

Heraion

8 km (5 mi) southwest of Samos town, 6½ km (4 mi) southwest of Pythagorio.

★ ❸❾ The early Samians worshipped Hera, believing she was born here near the stream Imbrassos and that there she also lay with Zeus. Several temples were built on the site, the last by Polycrates, who rebuilt the **Temple of Heraion,** enlarging it and lining it with two rows of columns, 133 in all. Today, at these ruins on Samos only one column remains standing.

At the semiannual celebrations to honor Hera, the faithful approached from the sea on the **Sacred Way,** which is still visible at the site's northeast corner. Nearby are replicas of a 6th-century BC sculpture depicting an aristocratic family, whose chiseled signature reads "Genelaos made me." The originals and the world's largest kouros, also found here, are in the Samos archaeological museum (☞ *below*). The huge temple, four times larger than the Parthenon, was damaged by fire in 525 BC and never completed, owing to Polycrates' untimely death. Today, we can only imagine its massive glory. ⊠ *Near Imvisos River,* ☎ *0273/ 95277.* 🎫 *800 dr.* ☉ *Tues.–Sun. 8:30–3.*

Mytilini

❹❶ *12 km (7½ mi) west of Samos town, 9 km (5½ mi) north of Heraion.*

Mytilini, an inland village with a pretty market square, has a **paleontological museum** exhibiting local animal fossils dating back 15 million years. The prize exhibit, among the bones of ancient hippos, rhinos, and evolving three-toed horses, is a 13-million-year-old fossilized horse brain. ⊠ *City Hall,* ☎ *0273/52055.* 🎫 *500 dr.* ☉ *Apr.–Oct., weekdays 9–3.*

Dining

$ ✕ **Dionyssos (No sign).** When you tire of eating on Pythagorio's waterfront, where food is often overpriced and monotonous, take a taxi to Mytilini for inexpensive well-cooked chops, *kotopoulo* krasato (chicken in wine), lemon chicken, and the seldom-seen chicken breast on a spit. The good appetizers go well with the chilled barrel retsina, which may prepare you for the random Gypsy vendor who parks his van next to your table and pulls out stereo speakers to foist upon you. ✉ *Mytilini Sq. (Platia Kalymniou)*, ☎ *0273/51820. No credit cards.*

Pirgos

🟤 *30 km (18½ mi) west of Samos town, 14 km (8¾ mi) west of Mytilini.*

The landscape here still shows the charred signs of a 1990 fire that destroyed acres of pine forest. Hilltop **Timiou Stavrou monastery,** 14 km (8½ mi) northeast of Pirgos, is considered Samos's most important, and is worth a stop to enjoy the icons, the carved wooden iconostasis, and the bishops' throne.

Shopping

CERAMICS

Aesthetic ceramics are a specialty in the villages of **Koumaradei** and **Mauratzei.** The most popular item is the "Pythagoras" cup, which leaks when it's more than half full. It was invented by Pythagoras to ensure his students didn't imbibe during lessons.

En Route The traditional village of Pirgos and its neighbor Pandrossos, on the side of Mt. Ambelos, offer a glimpse of island life. And if you continue past Pandrossos, up over the mountain, within minutes you'll be in deep pine forest, where it is often misty even when the sun shines below. The network of dirt roads emerges on the other side of Mt. Ambelos, descending past Vrondiani monastery (1566) and the northern vineyards.

NEED A   Stop in the huge shaded courtyard of the taverna at Koutsi, 5 km (3 mi)
BREAK?   after Pirgos, for the traditional snack of yogurt and fragrant Samian honey. Clear, bubbling springs help keep this area especially green.

Platanos

🟤 *27 (16¼ mi) west of Samos town, 11 km (7 mi) northwest of Pirgos.*

Mt. Kerkis hangs in the distance and the island's undeveloped west coast plummets below as you curve around the western side of the island. Platanos is a typical hillside village, where, except for "Greek nights" staged by travel agencies in summer, not much changes from year to year.

Marathokambos

40 km (25 mi) west of Samos town, 8 km (5 mi) west of Platanos.

The village of Marathokambos stretches like an amphitheater across the lower flanks of Mt. Kerkis. In the afternoons when the haze clears, the view down to the Bay of Marathokambos is dazzling, with the island of Patmos looming on the horizon.

Ormos Marathokambou

🟤 *40 km (25 mi) west of Samos town, 5 km (3 mi) south of Marathokambos.*

Ormos Marathokambou, on the bay, still has a small caïque-building industry, and these boats make daily trips to Founi and the islet of Samiopoula. There are a few tavernas serving Samian wine, and strollers enjoy the quay, which is closed to traffic. But the port's unique attraction is at its western end: the only traffic light on Samos.

Beaches

44 Samos's longest beach, **Votsalakia** (⊠ 2 km/1¼ mi west of Ormos Marathkambos), is a pine-shaded strip of sand backed by a growing, low-rise family resort. Several tavernas serve up informal food and drink. Mt. Kerkis looms dramatically above it all. Scant crowds and lots of rays reign at **Psili Ammos** beach, 15 km (9¼ mi) southwest of Votsalakia.

Outdoor Activities and Sports

HIKING

From Votsalakia beach (☞ *above*) you can climb **Mt. Kerkis** on a path that runs past a convent, and, once above the tree line, embrace some grand views. The round-trip, including rest stops, will take most of the day.

Karlovassi

45 *33 km (20½ mi) northwest of Samos Town, 16 km (10 mi) north of Ormos Marathokambou.*

Karlovassi, Samos's second-largest harbor, is a good base for exploring the western beaches. It seems grim until you take a closer look at its neighborhoods. The area, called Paleo, spreads across a ravine above the harbor area of Limani; it is surprisingly pretty. Below the main square, richly decorated churches and elaborate neoclassical mansions, padlocked and slightly dilapidated, hint of when Karlovassi was a center of leather production. Note the empty tanneries as you drive through the coastal suburbs toward the ferry port and Potami.

OFF THE BEATEN PATH

MIKRO SEITANI AND MEGALO SEITANI – Beach lovers can easily get from Karlovassi, first by bus and then on foot, to two delightfully **secluded coves**: Mikro Seitani (pebble) and Megalo Seitani (sand). There are no stands there, and often no people, so bring your own picnic. From the port, walk or take the bus west to Potami beach (☞ *below*), where the asphalt ends. After about 10 minutes you'll come to a dirt path that veers right. Ignore it. Two minutes later, turn off at the second path going right, marked by a stone pile. The trail is steep, and it's marked with blue and white paint dots all the way to the cove. After a small farm, it winds through olive trees, giving eyefuls of the turquoise sea below. After another 15 minutes, another path bears left, but continue straight, and some 40 minutes out of Potami you'll come upon the limpid cove of Mikro Seitani. If you can manage to tear yourself away, continue to Megalo Seitani, along a path that has good views of Mt. Kerkis and in spring winds through masses of wildflowers. After about 30 minutes you'll see a path going up to the left; continue straight and you will reach Megalo Seitani in another 15 minutes.

Beaches

Along the north coast near Karlovassi are some of the island's best beaches. Two km west of Karlovassi is **Potami**, a wide pebble-and-sand beach (⊠ About 45 min by foot on the coast road from Limani, or an hour's drive on the scenic road from Paleo). It has shady bushes under which people camp, pine trees overhead, and interesting rock formations. Hidden in a reedy area halfway along the beach is a small white house where a local family serves lunch amid greenery, and under the scrutiny of the family donkey.

Dining and Lodging

$$ ✕ **Steve's.** This restaurant has quickly earned a deserved reputation for some of the best food on the island. Generous portions of standard Greek fare such as *fasolakia freska* (snap peas or green beans) and pastitsio are executed impeccably. The splendid homemade cheesecake will make you click your heels. ⊠ *Karlovassi Harbor quay, easternmost establishment on harbor,* ☎ *0273/33434. MC. Closed Dec.–Mar.*

$ ✕ Psarades. It's worth a detour to find this family-run tavern, where kittens may nip at your heels, but good, inexpensive fish is served on a terrace overlooking the waves. In spring or autumn there are trays of fresh saddled bream and grouper, and you can also order *fassolada* (bean stew), *yiouvarlakia* (rice-and-meat balls in white sauce), and pungent tzatziki and skordalia dips. ⊠ *About 100 yards east of Ayios Dimitrios you'll come to a sign for the taverna; turn left down paved driveway and continue to end, Ayios Nikolaos, 5 km (3 mi) outside Karlovassi,* ☎ *0273/32489. No credit cards.*

$$$ 🏨 Samina Bay. Without a doubt the best hotel in Karlovassi, the Samina Bay is convenient to the ferry. The hotel is spacious, with framed embroideries adding a homey touch in the reception and bar area; guest rooms have white lacquer furniture, the suites, bamboo. The polite young staff is fluent in several languages. A breakfast buffet is served on the veranda, and you can usually arrange for other meals, too. Potami beach is a 15-minute walk away. ⊠ *Main Rd., near harbor, Karlovassi 83200,* ☎ *0273/34004,* 𝖥𝖠𝖷 *0273/34009. 75 rooms with bath. Restaurant, bar, air-conditioning, pool, sauna, playground. MC, V. Closed Nov.–Apr.*

$$ 🏨 Merope. Not much to look at, this four-story '70s hotel strives for high standards at reasonable rates. Each floor has a lounge; the simple rooms have the usual pine furniture and balconies, with fantastic views above the second floor. A local bus runs to Potami beach; otherwise lounge by the pool or stroll down the street to see some of Karlovassi's fine old tobacco warehouses, some of them deserted. If you get hungry, the kitchen always has some well-prepared magirefta on hand. ⊠ *Main Rd. in Pefkakia area, by the post office, Karlovassi 83200,* ☎ *0273/32650 or 0273/32651,* 𝖥𝖠𝖷 *0273/32652. 80 rooms with shower. Bar, pool. No credit cards. Closed Dec.–Mar.*

Ayios Konstandinos

10 km (6¼ mi) northwest of Samos town, 13 km (8 mi) northeast of Karlovassi.

Shortly after Ayios Konstandinos, a peaceful, flower-crammed seaside village, begins a gorgeous piece of road with constantly changing coastal views and lush foliage—from banana plants to oak trees. You'll cross through Platanakia, flanked by two large plane-tree shaded tavernas. Walk up the road a few hundred yards to Aidonia (Nightingale), where the birdsong is heard at sunrise and sunset.

Manolates

46 *15 km (9⅓ mi) northwest of Samos town, 5 km (3 mi) east of Ayios Konstandinos through steep vineyards up Mt. Ambelos.*

The delightful village of Manolates is surrounded by forest. Squares are lined with balconied stone houses, and cats prowl the narrow streets, blanketed with whitewashed floral designs. Most hikers set out from here to gawk at coastal panoramas or to watch for birds. Steep vineyards on these lower slopes of Mt. Ambelos offer wide-ranging views and produce wines in white and rosé too. But it is the dark sweet moskhato wine about which Lord Byron wrote, "Dash down yon cup of Samian wine."

Kokkari

47 *27 km (16¾ mi) southeast of Karlovassi, 9 km (5½ mi) northeast of Manolates.*

Beyond the popular beaches of Tsabou, Tsamadou, and Lemonakia, the spectacular stretch of coast road with olive groves and vineyards ends suitably in the fishing village of Kokkari, one of the most appealing spots on the island. Until 1980, there was not much here except for a few dozen houses between two headlands, and tracts of onion fields, which give the town its name. Though now there are a score of hotels, and many German tourists, you can still traipse along the rocky, windswept beach, and spy fishermen mending nets on the quay. Cross the spit to the eastern side of the headland and watch the moon rise over the lights of Vathi in the next bay.

Beaches

Acclaimed **coves of the north coast** are the partly nudist **Tsamadou**, **Lemonakia**, and **Tsabou**; all are just a few minutes from one another, and they're to be avoided when the *meltemi* (northern winds) blow.

Dining and Lodging

$$ ✕ **Avgo tou Kokkora.** The name comes from the Greek tale of a woman who invited her son-in-law to dinner, promising such variety that there'd even be an *avgo tou kokkora* (rooster's egg). That is still the key here: Besides fresh fish and the usuals, the seaside restaurant offers *kokkoras* (rooster), *flambé bastounia tou sef* (a fried ham-and-cheese appetizer), and *glosses tis petheras* ("mother-in-law's tongue" made from beef tongue). It stays open until 3 AM. If this won't do, head for the adjacent Porto Picolo for Italian fare or Barino for a nightcap (same management). ✉ *Kokkari promenade,* ☎ *0273/92113. DC, MC, V. Closed Nov.–Apr.*

$$ ✕ **Kariatida.** Here you teeter on the water's edge, and the waiters can always squeeze in another table. The fresh-fish menu features sea bream and various incarnations of shrimp and swordfish. House specialties also include rabbit stew and *pikilia* (a medley of mixed starters). The wine list is long and well chosen. ✉ *Kokkari promenade,* ☎ *0273/92103. MC, V. Closed Nov.–Apr.*

$$ 🏨 **Olympia Beach/Olympic Village.** At this bright-white hotel you can stroll into Kokkari for a movie, yet avoid the bustle. The immaculate rooms are spare, but all look out to sea and are decorated with flowery Samian ceramics. The same owners run the nearby Olympia Village, whose apartments with a bedroom, living room, two baths, and a kitchen are ideal for families. You can walk to Tsamadou cove, favored for its shallow water, pine trees, and secluded setting. ✉ *Northwest Beach Rd., near Kokkari, 83100,* ☎ *0273/92353,* ℻ *0273/92457. 12 rooms with bath. Restaurant, bar. No credit cards. Closed Nov.–Apr.*

$$ 🏨 **Venus (Afroditi).** Your first impression is of potted plants, red marble, and wood trim—a modern interior in an unremarkable building about 100 yards from the beach. The reasonably priced rooms have wood ceilings and balconies that survey the vineyards. Breakfast is Continental or "American," which means yogurt, eggs, juice, cereal, and coffee. ✉ *In-town Rd., Kokkari 83100,* ☎ *0273/92230,* ℻ *0273/92260. 38 rooms with shower. Pool, sauna, beauty salon. AE, DC, MC, V. Closed Nov.–Apr.*

En Route   After Kokkari you pass through Malagari, the winery where farmers hawk their harvested grapes every September, hoping for a knockout vintage.

Samos Town

❹❽ *33 km (20½ mi) southeast of Karlovassi, 6 km (3¾ mi) southeast of Kokkari.*

At the head of the Vathi Bay, on the northeast coast is Samos town, the capital, also known as Vathi. In the morning at the harbor fishermen are still seen grappling with their nets to dry them in the sun, and in the early afternoon everything shuts down. Tourism does not alter this centuries-old schedule.

The stepped streets ascend from the **shopping thoroughfare,** which meanders from the port to the city park next to the **archaeological museum,** the town's most important sight. The museum's older wing has a collection of cast bronze griffin heads (the symbol of Samos), pottery, and gifts from ancient cities paying tribute. The newest wing holds the impressive **kouros from Heraion,** a votive offering to the goddess. It stands alone in the room, massive, with an inscrutable smile, the enigma of ancient Samos. It's so large (5 meters/16½ feet tall) that the wing had to be rebuilt specifically to house it. ⊠ *Platia Dimarhiou,* ☎ *0273/27469.* ◪ *800 dr.* ☺ *Tues.–Sun. 8:30–3.*

49 In the quaint older village of **Ano Vathi** (⊠ Beyond museum, to the right), 19th-century wood-and-plaster houses with red-tile roofs are jammed together, their balconies protruding into streets so narrow the water channel takes up most of the space. From here you have a view of the narrow gulf.

Beaches

50 One of the island's best beaches is sandy **Psili Ammos** (⊠ Southeast of Samos Town near Mesokambos). Closer to Samos town is **Mykali beach** (⊠ On coast east of Samos town), with a stunning view of Turkey and Mykali peak. From here you might fantasize about swimming the straits to Turkey, approximately less than 2 km (1¼ mi) across the sea.

Dining and Lodging

$$ ✕ **Apanemia.** The name of this ouzeri on the shore of Vathy bay means "the lee spot," and it's rather ambitious on choppy days, though the garden seating is pleasant. The Athenian proprietor-chef brings years of experience to the panoply of dishes—familiar Western favorites like stroganoff, cannelloni, and Greek specialties. Among the latter choose *kopanisti* (spicy cheese purée), *pastourmas* (pastrami), and mussels saganaki or ahnista (steamed in wine). ⊠ *Themistokleous Sofouli 26, Vathy,* ☎ *0273/28147. No credit cards. Closed Nov.–Apr. No lunch.*

$$ ✕ **La Calma.** Everybody always seems to be having a good time here. Maybe it's the setting, on a waterfront terrace, or maybe it's the large selection, from grilled fresh fish to traditional meat dishes. For dessert, go for the caramel custard or a glass of sweet Samian moskhato. ⊠ *Kefalopoulou 5, Vathi,* ☎ *0273/22654. No credit cards. Closed Nov.–Apr.*

$$ ✕ **The Steps.** Climb the steps and enter a courtyard draped with ivy and flowers, with candlelight, crisp-white linen, and soft music. One of the chef's specialties is the mixed plate, which gives you a chance to try the souvlaki, lamb, village sausage, and a meatball. Lamb is roasted on a spit, sliced, and served with gravy. The Krissakis family also serve exohiko, swordfish grilled with lemon-oil sauce, and sole breaded like schnitzel. To reach The Steps, turn left off the Samos waterfront and turn left between Dionyssos and Souda restaurants. ⊠ *Near Samos Harbor,* ☎ *0273/28649. No credit cards. Closed Nov.–Apr. No lunch.*

$$ ▥ **Galaxy.** Off the harbor in a very quiet neighborhood, this greenery-fringed hotel is a cheerful respite from the waterfront. Once in the courtyard, you see the pool shimmering and hear laughing from around the bar. The simply furnished rooms all have balconies overlooking the pool, the baby-palm-sprouted lawn, or the adjacent grove. ⊠ *Angeou 1, behind the Fourth Primary School, Samos 83100,* ☎ *0273/22265,* ☎ *0273/27679. 45 rooms with bath. Bar, pool. V. Closed Nov.–Mar.*

$$ 🏨 **Paradise.** Simple but elegant, this hotel is a cut above the rest, with nice details: marble, dark wood, and bird-of-paradise flower arrangements. Avoid the six front rooms; others overlook the garden and the orchards of Perivoli district, so you're treated to evening birdsong. This hotel is convenient to the bus station and within walking distance of the harbor. ✉ *Kanari 21, Samos 83100,* ☎ *0271/23911 through 0271/23913,* ℻ *0271/28754. 49 rooms with bath. Snack bar, pool. MC, V. Closed Nov.–Mar.*

$ 🏨 **Avli.** For an inexpensive alternative, take a peek at this convent school-turned-pension. Your first impression will be of space and light as you walk into the large shaded courtyard, where guests spend evenings chatting over a drink, before they retire to the former students' cells. Rooms are basic; most have their own numbered toilet cubicle close by. For private baths en suite, you must book through a tour agency. ✉ *Areos 2, 2 blocks from harbor, Samos 83100,* ☎ *0273/22939. 20 rooms, some with bath. No credit cards. Closed Nov.–May.*

THE NORTHERN ISLANDS A TO Z

Arriving and Departing

By Plane

Even if they have the time, most people avoid the 10- to 12-hour ferry ride from Athens and start their island-hopping trip by air. Most flights are one hour or less. **Olympic Airways** (☎ 01/926–9111) has at least a dozen flights a week from Athens to each of the islands in summer. Watch out for overbooking problems; if you have a reservation, you should be entitled to a free flight if you get bumped.

LIMNOS

Call the **Olympic Airways** office in Myrina (✉ Garofalidi 6, ☎ 0254/22214 or 0254/22078) or at the airport (☎ 0254/31204). The airport (☎ 0254/31294 or 0254/31202) is near Moudros Bay, 22 km (14 mi) from Myrina.

LESBOS

Olympic Airways offices are in Mytilini (✉ 44 Kavetsou, ☎ 0251/28660) and at the airport (☎ 0251/61490). The airport (☎ 0251/61212) is 7 km (4¼ mi) from Mytilini.

CHIOS

Olympic Airways has offices in the port town of Chios (✉ Prokymeia midport, ☎ 0271/20359) and at the airport (☎ 0271/23998). The airport is 4½ km (3 mi) from town. For airport information call 0271/24546.

SAMOS

Olympic Airways offices are in Vathi (✉ Kanari 5, ☎ 0273/27237), in Pythagorio (✉ Logothetou 90, ☎ 0273/61300), and at the airport (☎ 0273/61219). The busiest airport (flight information ☎ 0273/61219) is here, 17 km (10½ mi) from Vathi. More than 40 international charters arrive every week in midsummer.

By Boat

If you can't get on a flight, there's always the extensive **ferry network**, offering the consolation that you'll travel for a third of the airfare. The Greek National Tourist Organization (GNTO or EOT) office in Athens distributes weekly ferry schedules. For last-minute departure times, call the Athens port authority (☎ 01/451–1311).

CHIOS

Boats arrive daily from Piraeus. The **Chios port authority** (☎ 0271/44433) can be of assistance.

LESBOS

There are at least four boats per week from Piraeus and three per week from Thessaloniki. The **port authority** (☎ 0251/28888) is in Mytilini.

LIMNOS

Arrivals port daily in summer from Piraeus, Rafina, or Kavala. On Limnos, call **the port authority** (☎ 0254/22225) for information.

SAMOS

Ferries arrive four to nine times per week from Athens, stopping at Paros and Naxos; and most of the year two or three ferries weekly serve Pythagorio from Kos and Patmos. Ferries and hydrofoils to Kusdasi on the Turkish coast leave from Vathi. Samos has **port authority offices** in Vathi (☎ 0273/27318), Karlovassi (☎ 0273/32343), and Pythagorio (☎ 0273/61225).

Getting Around

By Boat and Hydrofoil

Hydrofoil service via Flying Dolphin is available for travel among the local islands only; it is also more expensive than ferry travel, but it's quicker. Even in low season there are several connections weekly among Samos, Chios, and Lesbos. From Limnos a boat goes two to four times a week to Lesbos and back. In summer, scheduling can be more frequent. Check ahead.

By Bus

LIMNOS

On Limnos the few buses from Myrina (✉ Platia Venizelou, ☎ 0254/22464) depart early and occasionally don't return the same day. You can, however, go from Myrina to Moudros and all points in between quite easily.

LESBOS

Lesbos's KTEL bus system (✉ Platia Konstantinopoleos, ☎ 0251/28873) is relatively expensive and infrequent, though there are several buses a day from Mytilini to Molyvos via Kalloni, and you can also get to Mandamados, Agiassos Plomari, Eressos, and Sigri.

CHIOS

Buses leave the town of Chios several times per day for Mesta and Pirgi, and three leave daily for Volissos. For information call the KTEL station (✉ Vlatarias 13, ☎ 0271/27507).

SAMOS

Samos has excellent KTEL bus service (✉ Ioannou Lekati and Kanari, near Olympic Airways office, ☎ 0273/27262), with frequent trips between Pythagorio, Samos town, Kokkari, and Karlovassi. Buses also travel at least twice daily to Ireon, Pirgos, Marathokambos, and Votsalakia beach.

By Car and Moped

A car is handiest on Lesbos and Chios, the bigger islands, but costs about $75 a day. Mopeds (about $20 a day) are the ideal way to see Samos or Limnos. You won't have any trouble finding rentals.

By Plane

Other than daily summer flights between Limnos and Lesbos, and two weekly between Lesbos and Chios, there are no direct flights between these northern islands; it's best to count on going by ferry or hydrofoil.

Guided Tours

LIMNOS

El Travel (⊠ Xristodoulidou 10, Myrina, ☎ 0254/24988, FAX 0254/22697) gives English tours to the archaeological museum and to various villages and interesting sites such as the islet of Aï Stratis.

LESBOS

Aeolic Cruises, with branches in Mytilini (⊠ Prokimea, ☎ 0251/23960 or 0251/23266, FAX 0251/43694) and Plomari (⊠ Ayios Isidoros, ☎ 0251/32009), offers a variety of island tours. In Molyvos, **Panatella Tours** (⊠ Possidonion at town entrance, ☎ 0253/71520, 0253/71643, or 0253/71644, FAX 0253/71680) has two tours that take in villages, monasteries, and other sights.

CHIOS

Ionia Touristiki (⊠ Rodokanaki 17, ☎ 0271/41047 or 0271/22034, FAX 0271/41122) organizes excursions to the mastikhohoria and other sights (one is a four-wheel-drive tour).

SAMOS

Most of the branches of **Samina** (⊠ Main office: Th. Sofouli 67, Vathi, ☎ 0273/28841; to find closest branch ☎ 0273/28842) run an island tour, a one-day trip to Patmos, and a picnic cruise.

Contacts and Resources

Emergencies

Police (☎ 100). **Ambulance** (☎ 166). **Fire** ☎ 199.

Visitor Information

LIMNOS

Tourist police, 66 Garrufalidi, ☎ 0254/22200. **Myrina tourist office** (⊠ Near port, in municipal building, ☎ 0254/24110).

LESBOS

Information offices are in Eressos (⊠ Main Sq., ☎ 0253/53214), Molyvos (⊠ Possidonios near bus stop, ☎ 0253/71347), Mytilini (⊠ Harbor, ☎ 0251/28199; ⊠ Airport, ☎ 0251/61279), and Plomari (⊠ Harbor, ☎ 0252/32535). **Tourist police** (⊠ Harbor, Mytilini, ☎ 0251/22776). **The Women's Agricultural Tourist Collective** (⊠ Petra, ☎ 0253/41238) finds rooms with farming families.

CHIOS

Greek National Tourist Organization (EOT; ⊠ 18 Kanari, Chios, ☎ 0271/44389 or 0271/20324). **Tourist police** (⊠ 37 Neoriou, Chios, ☎ 0271/44344 or 0271/44428). **The Women's Agricultural Tourist Collective** (⊠ Main Sq., Pirgi, ☎ 0271/72496) finds rooms with local families, as will **Mesta's tourist information office** (⊠ Main Sq., ☎ 0271/76319).

SAMOS

EOT: Vathi (⊠ Ikostipemptis Martiou 4, ☎ 0273/28–582), Pythagorio (⊠ Logothetou, 1 block up waterfront, ☎ 0273/61100), Kokkari (⊠ Across from OTE, ☎ 0273/92333), **Tourist police** (⊠ Vathi harbor, ☎ 0273/27980).

14 Portraits of Greece

Greece at a Glance: A Chronology

A Word about Greek Architecture

A Short Glossary of Technical Terms

Greek Mythology

Books and Videos

GREECE AT A GLANCE: A CHRONOLOGY

ca. 6000 BC Beginning of Neolithic period in Greece with introduction of domesticated plants and animals from Anatolia.

ca. 3000 BC Development of early Bronze Age cultures: on Crete called "Minoan" after the legendary monarch, Minos, and on the mainland known as "Helladic"

ca. 1900 BC Rise of important settlement at Mycenae

1900 BC–1400 BC Height of Minoan culture. On Crete the Palace of Minos at Knossos is built, which includes indoor plumbing. Its mazelike complexity gives rise to the legend of the labyrinth

1400 BC–1200 BC Height of Mycenaean power: Crete is taken, and the city of Troy in Asia Minor is sacked. At Mycenae and Pylos impressive tombs mark this warrior culture

1200 BC–1100 BC Mycenaean civilization falls, as Bronze Age civilizations of the Eastern Mediterranean collapse

1100 BC–750 BC The "dark ages": writing disappears. The legendary poet Homer narrates a history of the Trojan War and describes an aristocratic society; this oral tradition is later written down as the *Iliad* and the *Odyssey*

ca. 750 BC Establishment of the *polis,* or city-state, as the characteristic form of political and civic organization in Greece

ca. 725 BC The poet Hesiod describes rural life in *Works and Days* and establishes the pantheon of Greek gods in *Theogony*. The Olympic Games are established as a Panhellenic event, during which peace prevailed

700 BC–500 BC Colonization builds Greek city-states throughout the Mediterranean. Meanwhile, social pressures at home lead to the rule of tyrants

621 BC Dracon publishes a notoriously severe legal code in Athens

ca. 600 BC The legendary ruler Lykourgos establishes the Spartan system of a highly controlled, militaristic society. Thales of Miletus, the first Greek philosopher, starts wondering about the world

594 BC Solon is given extraordinary powers to reform the Athenian government and constitution

ca. 550 BC Establishment of the Peloponnesian League, a military alliance of city-states dominated by Sparta. The philosopher Pythagoras propounds a famous theorem and sets up a monastic colony in southern Italy; the poet Sappho of Lesbos describes a particular kind of love

508 BC–501 BC Clisthenes establishes Athenian democracy

The Classical Era

499 BC–479 BC Persian wars: Athens leads Greek states against Kings Darius and Xerxes. 490 BC: Battle of Marathon is a critical victory for Athens. 480 BC: Xerxes invades Greece; the Greek League, which includes Athens and Sparta, defeats him in a series of battles at Thermopylae, Salamis, and Plataea

478 BC–477 BC Founding of Delian League of city-states under Athenian hegemony; it will evolve into an empire

ca. 475 BC–400 BC Golden Age of classical Greek culture, centered at Athens. Aeschylus (525 BC–456 BC), Sophocles (ca. 496 BC–406 BC), and Euripides (ca.

485 BC–402 BC) form the great triumvirate of classical drama; the comedies of Aristophanes (ca. 450 BC–385 BC) satirize contemporary mores. Socrates (469 BC–399 BC) and his disciple Plato (ca. 429 BC–347 BC) debate the fundamental questions of knowledge and meaning. Herodotus (ca. 484 BC–420 BC) and Thucydides (471 BC–402 BC) invent historical writing. The Acropolis epitomizes the harmony and precision of Classical architecture and sculpture

462 BC Pericles (ca. 495 BC–429 BC) rises to the leadership of Athens and leads the city to its cultural height

460 BC–
445 BC First Peloponnesian War between Athens and Sparta ends with the "Thirty Years' Peace" and recognition of the Athenian Empire. At the height of his power, Pericles rebuilds Athens

432 BC The Second, or Great, Peloponnesian War begins when Sparta declares war on Athens

429 BC A disastrous plague kills more than one-third of the Athenian population, including Pericles

421 BC Fighting ceases with the Peace of Nicias (which proves to be temporary)

415 BC–413 BC Athens's disastrous invasion of Sicily reopens the war and sets the stage for its downfall

404 BC Athens falls to Sparta and its walls are dismantled, ending an era

398 BC–360 BC Rule of Agesilaus at Sparta, whose aggressive policies lead to its ruin

394 BC Spartan fleet destroyed by Persians

386 BC Plato founds the Academy in Athens, a school of philosophy that trains statesmen

384 BC Birth of Aristotle, the greatest ancient philosopher and scientist (died 322 BC)

378 BC Second Athenian Confederation marks the resurgence of Athens

371 BC Spartan hegemony ends with a defeat at Leuctra by the Theban army under Epaminondas

362 BC Death of Epaminondas at the battle of Mantinea ends Theban dominance, documented by Xenophon (ca. 434 BC–355 BC)

355 BC Second Athenian Confederation collapses, leaving Greece in chaos

The Hellenistic Era

351 BC Demosthenes (384 BC–332 BC) delivers the First Philippic, warning Athens of the dangers of Macedonian power

342 BC Aristotle becomes tutor to a young Macedonian prince named Alexander (356 BC–323 BC)

338 BC Alexander's father, Philip of Macedon (382 BC–336 BC) defeats the Greek forces at Chaeronea and establishes Macedonian hegemony

336 BC Philip is assassinated, leaving his empire to his son Alexander, soon to be known as "the Great." Aristotle founds his school, the Lyceum, at Athens

323 BC Having conquered the known world and opened it to Greek culture, Alexander dies of a fever in Babylon

ca. 330 BC–
200 BC Hellenistic culture blends Greek and other influences in a cosmopolitan style. Epicureanism, Stoicism, and Cynicism enter philoso-

phy; Hellenistic sculpture blends emotion and realism. At the new city of Alexandria in Egypt, Greek science and mathematics flourish with Euclid (300 BC) and Archimedes (ca. 287 BC–212 BC); Aristarchus (ca. 310 BC–230 BC) asserts that the earth revolves around the sun

The Roman Era

215 BC The outbreak of the First Macedonian War signals Rome's rise in the Mediterranean

146 BC Rome annexes Greece and Macedonia as provinces. Roman culture becomes increasingly Hellenized

49 BC–31 BC Greece is a battleground for control of Rome's empire: 48 BC: Julius Caesar defeats Pompey at Pharsalus; 42 BC: Caesar's heir Octavian defeats Brutus at Philippi; 31 BC: Octavian defeats Mark Antony at Actium and becomes, as Augustus, the first Roman Emperor

AD 125 The guidebook of Pausanias makes Greece a favored tourist stop; the Emperor Hadrian undertakes the renovation of ancient monuments

394 The Emperor Theodosius declares Christianity the official religion of the Roman Empire and bans pagan cults, suppressing the Olympic Games and closing the oracle at Delphi

The Medieval Era

476 The fall of Rome leaves Greece open to waves of invaders, though it remains nominally under the hegemony of the Byzantine emperors at Constantinople

529 The Byzantine Emperor Justinian closes Plato's Academy in Athens

1054 The Great Schism divides the Christian church into Greek and Roman orthodoxies

1204–61 Greece briefly reenters the sphere of western influence with the Latin capture of Constantinople in the Fourth Crusade

1453 The fall of Constantinople to the Ottoman Turks leads to nearly four centuries of Turkish rule

The Modern Era

1770 The Russian prince Orloff attempts but fails to establish a Greek principality

1814 The *Philike Hetairia*, a "friendly society" established by Greek merchants at Odessa (Russia), is instrumental in the growth of Greek nationalism

1821–29 The Greek War of Independence. 1821: The Greek Patriarch, Archbishop Germanos, declares Greek independence, and war with the Turks breaks out. Among those aiding Greece in her struggle is the English poet Lord Byron. 1826: A Greek defeat at Missolonghi stirs European sympathy. 1827: The Triple Alliance of Great Britain, France, and Russia intervene against the Turks and their Egyptian allies. 1829: The Turks are defeated and Greece is declared an independent state, guaranteed by the Triple Alliance

1832 Prince Otho of Bavaria is offered the Greek throne by the Triple Alliance

1834 King Otho chooses Athens as his capital

1844	Greece adopts a constitution that establishes a constitutional monarchy
1863	As a result of Otho's pro-Russian policies during the Crimean war, he is forced to abdicate and is replaced on the throne by Prince George of Denmark
1909–10	The Military League, a group of young army officers, leads a peaceful revolt and installs as prime minister Eleutherios Venizelos, who enacts a series of reforms
1912–13	Greece gains Macedonia, Epirus, and Crete as a result of the Balkan Wars
1917–18	Greece fights on the Allied side in World War I
1924	Greece is declared a republic
1935	Monarchy is restored; in the next year, King George II allows General Joannes Metaxas to establish a military dictatorship
1940	Italy invades Greece, leading to four years of Axis occupation
1946	Greece becomes a charter member of the United Nations
1946–49	Communist rebellion is defeated with U.S. help
1952	Women are given the right to vote
1963	George Seferis wins the Nobel Prize for Literature
1967	A military coup ousts King Constantine II
1974	In the wake of the Cyprus crisis, the military government collapses and the first elections in 10 years are held. Constantine Karamanlis is named prime minister. The republic is confirmed by popular vote
1980	Odysseus Elytis becomes the second Greek to win the Nobel Prize for Literature
1981	Greece joins the European Economic Community
1993	Andreas Papandreou returns to power
1994	Minister of Culture Melina Mercouri dies
1996	Former Prime Minister Andreas Papandreou dies; Costas Simitis becomes leader and wins a vote of confidence shortly after Papandreou's death, when he was elected to the position of PASOK party president, a position that Papandreou never relinquished

A WORD ABOUT GREEK ARCHITECTURE

ALTHOUGH TODAY we are able to study the remains of a great variety of ancient Greek buildings, the mental picture formed at the sound of the words "Greek architecture" is likely to be that of a temple, and a Doric one at that.

Though no city in Classical times (500 BC–355 BC) was deemed complete without its agora (or city-center), its defensible acropolis (acro = high; polis = city), its theater, gymnasium, and stadium, it was the temple of the city's patron god or goddess that was commonly given the dominant position and the greatest honor. The chief temple often stood at the highest point of the acropolis, the nucleus around which the city grew in safety, itself enclosed by fortification.

In Mycenaean Greece, 1,000 years before the Classical period, the chief building of a citadel was the king's palace, as seen at Mycenae, Tiryns, and Pylos. In these palace complexes the central feature is the *megaron*—a large rectangular room with the long walls extended to form the sides of an open porch, the roof of which was supported by columns. A single large doorway gives access to the megaron. In the center is a large hearth, the focus of the room: Around it, in a square plan, are four columns supporting the roof; in the right a raised platform for the royal throne. There are forecourts to these megara, and pillared gateways—copied from the Minoan palaces of Crete and replicated throughout Greek history. The Propylaea of the Acropolis at Athens (and of 20 other sites) derives from the Minoan gateway.

Clustered around the megaron and its forecourt are archive rooms, offices, oil-press rooms, workshops, potteries, shrines, corridors, armories, and storerooms for wine and oil and wheat—the whole forming an irregular complex of buildings quite unlike the precise, clear-cut arrangement that is later the hallmark of building in the Classical period. This irregularity, characteristic of the Minoan palaces at Knossos, Mallia, and Phaistos on Crete, was one of the influences of that earlier and foreign culture on the Mycenaeans of the mainland.

But the megaron is Greek. The king's megaron, indeed a "great room," was essentially only the ordinary man's house built large; in some ordinary houses, as at Priene, the same megaron is found. And when the shrine ceased to be a mere house-chapel in a corner of the palace complex, as at Knossos, and the god was given a house of his own, his temple had the ground plan of that porched megaron. In its full development there is a porch, or maybe a room, also at the rear, and around it all runs a peristyle of columns. Thus the Greek temple is literally the god's house, intended not for the assembly of worshipers, but as a great room to contain the statue of the god (*see* Figures A, B, and C).

The early temple builders found that sun-baked brick strengthened by horizontal and vertical timbers, if set on a stone footing, was a suitable material even for large buildings. This construction is seen at Knossos (circa 1900 BC) and at the Temple of Hera at Olympia 1,000 years later. The columns of the early temples were made of wood, and, later, when marble began to be used, constructional features appropriate to the use of timber were copied as decoration in the new material. It seems likely that the triglyph, the three-part stone slab set above the column and also above the space between columns in the Doric order, originates from a decorative wood slab that protected the beam ends of the ceiling from rain and rot—particularly when one looks at the six stone *guttae* always fixed below it, which seem to represent the six wood tre-nails, or pegs, that kept the slab in position. And the fluting of the Doric column is reminiscent of the grooves that the long strokes of the adze would make as the woodworker cut away the bark of a tree trunk before erecting it as the column.

If the origins of the Doric order are a matter of guesswork, this much is clear: that the Greeks used an elementary formula of vertical and horizontal lines of stone, so refined with skill and taste, with strict

Greek Architecture

The Megaron
Showing the development from the "House of the People" to the "House of the God"

A. TROY II

B. TIRYNS

C. OLYMPIA —
Temple of Zeus

A

Hearth

Porch

B

Columns

Hearth

Double
Porch

C

House
of the
God

The Orders of Greek Architecture

Doric

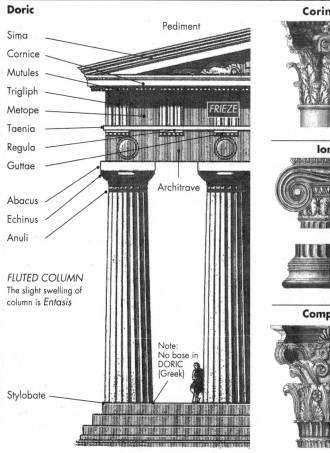

Sima
Cornice
Mutules
Trigliph
Metope
Taenia
Regula
Guttae

Abacus
Echinus
Anuli

Pediment

FRIEZE

Architrave

FLUTED COLUMN
The slight swelling of column is *Entasis*

Note:
No base in
DORIC
(Greek)

Stylobate

Corinthian

Ionic

Composite

rules of proportion, that the total effect is one of balance, symmetry, and power. At the highest development, they added a series of optical corrections to ensure that the human eye, easily misled by the effect of light and shade in alternation, saw the whole as an apparent pattern of truly horizontal and vertical lines. In fact, with the application of these optical corrections, the entire building is made up of subtly curving or inclined surfaces. These refinements called for mathematical ability of a high order in the design and for extreme skill on the part of the masons.

In the Parthenon (5th century BC), the slight swell (*entasis*) and inward slant of the columns makes them seem straight-sided and vertical (which they are not); actual straightness would cause the eye to see them as waisted, and if vertical they would seem to be inclining outward. Also, without its slight upward curve, the steps of the platform (*stylobate*) would seem to sag under the line of standing columns. In short, the Greek mind took the simple idea of the upright and the crossbar, the child's building-block technique and, in developing it to its zenith in the Parthenon, produced a masterpiece that still informs us about those ingredients in a building that make for serenity combined with power, repose with majesty.

Marble was the perfect material for buildings in which sharp edges, clear-cut outline, precision, and the beauty of uncluttered wall surfaces were desired, so that each part, functional and decorative (the sculptured metopes and pediment), might do its work, and the horizontal members could lie without stress or mortar upon the supporting verticals.

The Doric order continued in use in Hellenistic (350 BC–215 BC) and Roman times, but it is easy to distinguish Greek from Roman Dorica. The later architects dared a wider space, enough for three triglyphs, between columns; they used a base for their columns, whereas a Greek Doric column rests directly on the stylobate; they economized often by omitting the fluting in the lower part of a column (where damage most often occurred); and they reduced the size of the capital most meanly. All these Hellenistic and Roman "improvements" are seen in Delos.

The Ionic order came to mainland Greece almost certainly from Asia Minor and the islands, when the Doric order was well established both there and in the colonies of Magna Graecia (southern Italy). Ionic columns have bases; the flutes have no sharp edges to them but are separated by a substantial fillet; the columns are more tall and slender; the capitals with their beautiful spiral volutes decorative; the architrave has lost its alternating triglyphs and metopes and, in Greece proper, has a frieze of plain or sculptured stone, in Asia Minor a string of dentils to suggest the beam ends of the ceiling. If the feeling of the heavier, more austere Doric order can be described as masculine, then the Ionic is certainly feminine (and very lovely), especially suitable for such smaller buildings as the Erectheum and the Temple of Nike on the Acropolis of Athens.

The Corinthian order came later. Its first appearances were in the temple at Bassae (circa 430 BC) and in the circular building (*tholos*) at Epidauros (360 BC), where one of the perfectly preserved capitals can be seen in the museum. It is decorative and graceful, and one may contrast the simplicity of its sculptured acanthus leaves and their slender tendrils with the complications bestowed on the Corinthian capital by later Hellenistic and Roman architects, in their constant striving for magnificence.

The Classical Greeks rarely departed from the straight line and the rectangular plan; only a few circular buildings have survived; for instance, the Tholos at Delphi, the "folly" of the family of Philip of Macedon at Olympia, a temple at Samothrace built by Queen Arsinoe, and in the Agora at Athens, the building where the executive of the day lived.

Entirely aside from earthquakes, two factors have worked against the survival of the best Greek buildings. The name Marmaria ("marble quarry") for part of the ruins of Delphi reveals one reason for their destruction. There for the taking was a source of cheap marble already cut and squared. Where the ancient stones were not too big and heavy to be easily moved, a vast quantity was reused in later centuries. As recently as the 17th century the stones of the Temple of Zeus at Agrigento (Sicily) were used for the city's harbor wall.

The second factor was the need for lime and the comparative ease with which marble—statues, carved cornices, capitals and drums of columns, anything—could be burnt in a kiln and turned into cash. At one period there was a lime kiln on most of the now-famous classical sites, a kiln that devoured the greater part and left posterity the odds and ends. Perhaps because the stones of theaters are inclined to be large and of a shape useless in ordinary building, many theaters—for example, the one at Epidauros—have survived in a tolerable condition.

— Guy Pentreath

A SHORT GLOSSARY OF TECHNICAL TERMS

Acropolis: the hilltop, fortified with walls and giving protection to the temple of the patron deity and, in early times, to the king's palace, which was the nucleus of an early community living normally outside the walls.

Agora: the "marketplace" or "city-center"; here were sited the shopping and commercial facilities and the main public buildings; the accepted open space where the citizens would gather.

Ambo: the raised pulpit in a Byzantine or Orthodox Christian Church.

Apse: the semicircular recess usually in the short end wall of the long basilica or Roman law-court in which was the dais for the tribunal. When early Christians built churches on the basilica plan, the seats of the Elders were ranged around the apse to the east of the altar, as in the early church at Delos.

Archaic Period: from 700 BC to the end of the Persian Wars in the early 5th century BC.

Archon: strictly, "one who rules"; one of the chief magistrates of Athens, and in certain other city-states.

Arris: the sharp edge formed, for instance, at the meeting point of two flutes in the Doric column, a vulnerable feature of the order, rectified in the Ionic by the substitution of a flat narrow fillet between the flutes.

Ashlar: applied to masonry, of squared hewn stone.

Atrium: literally, the "place made black by the smoke" in a Roman house: a small court open to the sky, colonnaded, four or more columns supporting the roof, and rooms opening on to the colonnade. There are many fine atria or courts in the houses of Pompeii with mosaic designs on the tank tops (*impluvia*) onto which fell rain through the openings above (*compluvia*).

Bas-relief: sculpture on the surface of a slab in low relief, e.g., the Parthenon frieze.

Bema: the rostrum of a public speaker, e.g., in the agora at Corinth.

Bouleuterion: a council chamber.

Boustrophedon: an archaic method of writing, found on some inscriptions, for instance in Gortyna in Crete, where the code of laws is written not in lines from left to right, but as an ox turns with the plough at the end of the furrow and having gone from left to right, returns from right to left.

Caïque: the small trading vessel, wooden, brightly painted and rigged for sail but usually today propelled by an engine; it adds color and charm to every Greek waterfront and every passage in the Aegean Sea.

Capital: the top element of a column above the drums or monolithic shaft; the three Greek orders are the Doric, Ionic, and Corinthian.

Caryatid: the sculptured figure of a woman acting in place of a column and supporting an architrave, e.g., in the porch of the Siphnian Treasury at Delphi, or the Erectheum above at Athens.

Cathedra: the throne of a bishop in the early Church in the apse behind the high altar, e.g., at Paros.

Cavea: the auditorium of a theater usually, in Greek practice, in the hollow of a hillside. The Romans, aided by their wealth and their development of the arch and vault, usually built up theaters on arches and vaults precisely where they wanted them.

Cella: the great hall of a temple in which stood the generally colossal cult-statue of the deity.

Chimaera: a fire-breathing monster with a lion's head and dragon's after-quarters with the midship section of a goat; allegedly once a visitant to Lycia in Asia Minor; often used as a decorative design on vases of Rhodes and of Corinth whose trading connections with the East gave them familiarity with Oriental decorative motifs.

Chryselephantine: of a statue built up on a wooden core and covered with plates of gold for the clothing, and of ivory for the uncovered parts of the body, e.g., the Zeus at Olympia, and the cult-statue of Athena in the Parthenon.

Classical Period: from the Persian Wars to the unification of Greece under Philip II and the world empire of Alexander the Great, i.e., the 5th and 4th centuries BC.

Coffer: the marble ceilings of important Greek and Roman buildings were patterned and lightened by rows of sunk panels in their surface, e.g., the coffered ceilings of the Propylaea on the Acropolis at Athens.

Composite Order: of architecture, a combination of the Corinthian capital's rows of acanthus leaves with the volutes, slightly reduced in size, of the Ionic order; a late development, seen at Pergamum and Ephesus.

Corinthian Order: of architecture, differing from the Ionic only in the capital, elaborately decorated with two or three tiers of carved acanthus leaves below small volutes. The considerable advantage over the Ionic lies in the four concave sides of the abacus, which give it, in plan, a cushion shape. Supported at the pointed four corners by pairs of small volutes, this abacus solves the problem involved in the form of the Ionic capital, where the front and side views are different. The new capital was first found in the excavation of the temple at Bassae (5th century BC) and was used at Epidauros in the tholos (4th century BC).

Cult statue: the statue of a god or goddess, to house which in great dignity was the purpose of a temple. Often it was more than life-size, i.e., "heroic," or "colossal."

Cyclopean: applied to a wall constructed, not of ashlar masonry however big the blocks, but of large boulders of a size which called for giants to handle them, and with interstices filled up with small stones. Early Mycenaean walls, at Mycenae, Tiryns, and also in places on the Acropolis at Athens, were Cyclopean.

Dentils: the line of teethlike blocks of stone, suggesting the rafter ends of a flat roof, under the cornice of a building of Ionic or Corinthian Order.

Diolchos: literally, the "drag(way) across," i.e., for the portage of ships across the Isthmus of Corinth; invented by Periander in the 7th century BC. Ships were hauled on a carriage running in grooves cut on a stone track across the Isthmus,

thus avoiding the danger of the long haul around the southern promontories of the Peloponnese.

Dromos: the long horizontal passage, bordered by stone walls, cut into a small hill and giving access to a tholos, or beehive tomb, in Mycenaean Greece.

Ecclesia: the assembly of the whole male citizen body, which gave its decisive vote on policies put before it by the Boule or Council at Athens and elsewhere; later, the Christian Church.

Engaged column: a half-column (divided longitudinally), standing out on the surface of a wall.

Entablature: a term to cover all the horizontal stonework resting on a row of columns including the architrave (the lowest member), the frieze, and the cornice at the top.

Exedra: the curved marble wall, often used as a base for one or more statues, and provided with a marble bench that offered dignified and sheltered casual seating in public places.

Fillet: a flat and narrow molding on the surface of a wall, or between the flutes of an Ionic or Corinthian column.

Flutes: the vertical hollows cut into the sides of a column, which emphasized its rotundity—a device necessary in the brilliant sunlight falling on white marble—and which took off glare from the marble by the easy graduations of light.

Frieze: a band of alternating triglyphs and metopes, the central element of a Doric entablature; also a continuous band of bas-relief sculpture on an Ionic entablature, e.g., the temple of Nike on the Acropolis at Athens. (Part of the Ionic frieze, incorporated in the Doric Parthenon, is still visible inside the colonnade on the west end.)

Geometric Period: of the post-Mycenaean period when, with the Dorian invasions, the Iron Age was fully established throughout Greece and the country had settled again after a grim period of turmoil and population movement. A sub-Mycenaean, followed by a proto-Geometric period, is transitional to the Geometric period proper, which in Athens runs from about 900 BC to 700 BC. The period is characterized by its well-shaped pottery, decorated with horizontal bands of geometric patterns, later incorporating animal and human figures.

Gymnasium: physical education loomed large in the Greek curriculum, and the gymnasia were provided with spacious courts for exercise and games and with good washing rooms; there were stone benches for the sedentary school periods, e.g., at Delos and Priene.

Helladic Period: applied to the Bronze Age civilization of the Greek mainland, as Cycladic refers to that of the islands, Melos and others in the Cyclades. The period corresponds roughly with that of the Minoan civilization in Crete and, like it, is subdivided into Early, Middle, and Late periods. It was during the Late Helladic period that the Mycenaean civilization developed, first at Mycenae, then at other centers in Greece and spreading throughout the Aegean.

Hellenistic Period: conventionally, from Alexander the Great to the time of Augustus and the Roman Empire: 300 BC to 30 BC.

Herm: a square-section pillar, tapering out from ground level, about 1½ or 2 meters (5 or 6 feet) high and surmounted by the sculptured head of Hermes, bearded in the 5th century BC. They were set up in cities in large numbers as boundary marks, and also outside houses and temples, and were treated as sacred, e.g., in Delos, at the entrance to the Sanctuary of Apollo.

Hippodrome: the course for horse and chariot racing, which had to be much larger than the stadium for athletics; at Delphi, in the Pythian Games, the chariot race was held on the plain below the sanctuary.

Iconostasis: the tall continuous screen in an Orthodox church that cuts off the sanctuary with the altar from the nave and usually, from the sight of the people until the central door is opened at the crisis of the Eucharist. Icons of Our Lord, the Holy Mother, the patron saint of the church and of others are set up on the iconostasis, as its name states, for use as an avenue of worship.

Impluvium: the tank to receive the rain that fell through the open center of a Roman house-roof (the compluvium).

Ionic Order: of architecture: a development, perhaps originating in Aeolia in northwest Asia Minor; an Order more decorative and elaborate than the austere and earlier Dorica. Its columns have bases, ornamented with a variety of moldings, and are more slender, with deeper flutes and no sharp and vulnerable edges as in the Doric Order. The capital has a pair of spiral volutes extending out on either side, front and back, over a ring of egg-and-tongue molding round the top of the column; there are no triglyphs.

Kore, Korai, Kouros, Kouroi: conventionally applied to the clothed female and the nude male sculptured figures of the Archaic, pre–Persian War period: they stand erect with the weight distributed between the feet, of which the left is slightly forward, but no motion is suggested; on their faces often the "archaic smile." The best of these beautiful korai, or maidens, are in the Acropolis Museum at Athens, and of the male figures in the National Museum, where the steady progress of the sculptor's art from the purely static figure to the dynamic is readily seen and enjoyed.

Labrys: a double-axe, i.e., with two blades facing right and left; a religious symbol in the Minoan period, carved on pillars and found in great numbers in miniature as votives in sanctuaries, and in more than life-size form as religious furniture.

Labyrinth: double-axes (☞ Labrys, *above*) were numerous as religious symbols at Knossos in the Minoan palace. The palace was a most elaborate complex of rooms, passages, and staircases; hence the "place of the double-axes" gained its second and more common meaning.

Megaron: the central feature of a Mycenaean house or palace; the great room containing a large central hearth.

Metope (méh-to-pi): the plain panel, alternating with the decorated cover-plate for the roof beam-ends (the triglyphs) in the Doric frieze. In Classical times a sculptured relief decorated the plain space, the series of metopes round the temple illustrating a single theme, e.g., Greeks versus Amazons, Lapiths versus Centaurs, or the Labors of Herakles (in the Olympia Museum).

Minoan: referring to the Bronze Age civilization of Crete. Sir Arthur Evans adapted the name of the legendary King Minos of Crete to this civilization when he discovered and excavated the king's palace at Knossos.

Mycenaean: from Mycenae, the principal center of the earliest Greek-speaking people in the late Bronze Age. This civilization, at first limited to mainland sites, spread throughout Greece and across the Aegean after the fall of the Minoan empire. It collapsed only after the capture of Troy by the Mycenaeans; their return to Greece was soon followed by the destruction of their fortress centers at the hands of the Dorians, another Greek-speaking people who entered through Northern Greece, armed with iron weapons and tools.

Nike: goddess of victory, portrayed in Greek art as a winged figure descending to award victory. The earliest Nike statue was found in Delos. The most famous are the winged *Victory of Paeonius* (Olympia Museum) dated 425 BC, and the *Victory of Samothrace* (Louvre; about 320 BC).

(Early) Neolithic Period: Professor John Evans, by his excavation to the rock 7 meters (23 feet) below the Minoan levels of the Palace of Minos at Knossos, has put back the date of the earliest known human settlement in Greece to about 6100 BC, a date derived from the radiocarbon-14 test on burnt grain found on a primitive campsite.

(Middle) Neolithic Period: At the top of 4½ meters (15 feet) of accumulated soil deposit, Professor Evans found another Cretan settlement belonging to a period 1,000 years later, whose people could spin and weave. A charcoal sample submitted to the same test gave a central date of 5050 BC.

(Late) Neolithic Period: Three other groups of Neolithic settlers have left traces of their homes, habits, and craft in many parts of Greece and the Aegean: (1) The seafarers, probably from the coasts of Asia Minor, who settled in Cyprus, in Crete, and in the Cyclades about 3000 BC. The Minoans who arrived in Crete about 500 years later were probably akin to the earlier settlers; (2) a group who preferred cooler climates and settled in the plains of Thessaly and Boeotia; and (3) a group from the forest-covered North who were hunters.

Odeum: a small building in form and plan like a theater with semicircular seating. Some were roofed. Chiefly used for musical contests and concerts and other meetings. Pericles built an odeum at Athens, the roof of which was carried on many pillars, as Plutarch says. Herodes Atticus presented a large odeum to Athens that is used, with new seating, for Greek Drama festivals today.

Orchestra: the large circular space for the dancing of the chorus in a Greek theater, with an altar of Dionysus in the center. It is similar to the circular threshing-floor still seen commonly in rural Greece; for the threshing-floor, when the harvest was in and the grain stored, was the scene of the country dances and thanksgiving, the seed of Greek drama.

Ostracism: from "ostrakon"—a potsherd used as a voting paper in democratic ancient Athens. The institution of ostracism is said to have been introduced by Cleisthenes as a device to eliminate a likely-looking tyrant before he gained excessive power: first used in 487 BC. Voting was secret: each citizen scratched on a sherd the name of a citizen he wished to see banished (without loss of property and for 10 years). Hundreds of ostraka were found in the Agora excavations. In fact, none of the leading citizens who suffered ostracism look to the historian to have been embryo tyrants. Ostracism was one of the least noble or ennobling of Greek institutions.

Palaestra: a building smaller than a gymnasium, often built as a colonnade around a central court, for the training of boxers, wrestlers, and pancratiasts.

Pancration: an "all-out" contest in the athletic games in which no holds were barred: boxing and wrestling combined, whose only rule forbade biting or the gouging out of eyes.

Pantocrator: literally, "the Almighty," nearly always the subject of a mosaic or fresco dominating from its central position at the height of the dome (inside) every eye that looked upward—as is inevitable on entering a domed building where most of the light comes from the windows of the dome; e.g., the famous Pantocrator of Daphni.

Parian Marble: the marble quarries of the island of Paros produced a white, close-grained marble peculiarly suitable for sculpture; it was widely used by the leading sculptors.

Pediment: in the Greek temple, the triangular space at the vertical ends of the ridge roof, and formed by the horizontal cornice and the raking cornices of the roof; pedimental sculpture in the round was often fixed in this space.

Pendentive: the curving and overhanging triangles of stone or brickwork that transmit, to four piers below, that part of the weight of a dome that is not carried by the four arches springing from those piers; in other words, the method of carrying a circular dome on four piers, square-in-plan.

Pentelic Marble: named from its source on the mountain bordering the Attic plain on the northeast; eminently suitable for fine building both in ancient and modern times. All the finer Athenian buildings of Pericles are made of Pentelic marble; the particles of iron in it give it the famous golden tinge of color.

Peribolos: the wall of a sanctuary or *temenos*.

Peristyle: the row, or rows, of columns around a temple.

Pinakotheke: picture gallery, e.g., the north room of the Propylaea on the Acropolis at Athens.

Pithos: a large earthenware vessel, from 1¼ to 2½ meters (4 to 8 feet) high, especially used in Minoan Crete to contain oil, grain, etc.

Podium: the masonry platform on which a building (e.g., a Roman temple) might be laid.

Polygonal: of a wall made of stones with many angles, each stone being shaped and laid to fit tightly with the corresponding angles of its neighbors; an expensive but effective device to reduce the effect of earthquake.

Prophylactic: literally, "intended to guard against [evil]"; used, for example, of the eyes painted on either side of the handles of a wine cup.

Propylon, Propylaea: the dignified entrance between columns to a sanctuary or an agora or major building within an enclosure; an idea from Minoan architecture adapted by the Mycenaeans and retained in the Classical period.

Proskenion: the front of the low building that supported the stage in a developed Greek theater.

Sibyl: perhaps originally a single prophetess who wandered from center to center; but later we hear of a Sibyl at Delphi, Claros, Dodona, Cumae, etc. That an early Sibyl was important at Delphi is proved by the preservation of an outcrop of rock, left unworked in its natural state, in the midst of an area of fine building and statues, just because in early times the Sibyl had given her utterances from that improvised platform.

Stadium: a Greek running track, providing for spectators by raised earth banks. The stadium was shaped like a hairpin, one end curved and the other—the starting point—either open as at Athens and Delphi or squared as at Olympia, where a tunnel entrance was added. In the Roman period, stone seating was normal. Occasionally, as at Nicopolis, a Roman stadium was rounded at both ends. The standard length was 183 meters (600 feet), which gave a straight course for the sprint race of about 200 yards. In the 400-yard race, the runners had to round a post at the far end of the course. The two-grooved starting line is seen at Corinth (in the Agora), Delphi, and Olympia; post-holes indicate a separation of the runners at the start. It appears to have been a standing-start, at the drop of a horizontal signal arm at the top of the post.

Steatite: a stone with a soapy feel and look about it, from the Greek word for tallow; sometimes used in Minoan art for ornamental vases, and covered with gold foil.

Stele: a stone slab set up in a public place, with an inscription recording a victory, treaty, or a decree; also a gravestone. Many beautiful funeral stelai, sculptured in relief, are to be seen in the National Museum, Athens, and in the Kerameikos.

Talent: In Pericles' time at Athens, we know that the talent was equivalent in value to 6,000 drachmae, and that a normal wage for a week's work was 3½ drachmae.

Temenos: the enclosed area in which stood a temple.

Templum-in-Antis: the simplest form of temple in which "the house of the god" is the same in plan as the ordinary house; a rectangular room, with the long side walls extended to form the walls of a porch, and with two columns between the antae (or wall endings) to support the porch roof and make a fine entry to the temple, e.g., the so-called Treasury of the Athenians at Delphi.

Theater: an essential building in every city, to the Greek mind.

Thermae: the Spartans are believed to have invented the heated sweat room as a method of removing dirt from the skin, a strigil being used to scrape away the sweat, which carried the dust with it out of the pores of the skin. This process was followed by a cold plunge. Cicero refers to this kind of bath as "Laconicum." But the Greeks did not go so far as to provide great public buildings for this purpose, merely attaching limited bathing facilities to their gymnasia. The Thermae are a development of the Imperial Roman period, and very large, beautiful, and elaborate public bathing centers were built in Rome and in all the major cities of the Empire, and small ones even in some villages.

Tholos: a circular building, such as that at Epidauros, where the circular mazelike foundations can be seen, or at Delphi, where a Doric tholos has had several fallen columns re-erected; also of the numerous underground beehive tombs of the Mycenaean period, of which the so-called "Treasury of Atreus" at Mycenae is the best preserved and finest.

Treasury: the word used for the well-built, often marble, small buildings, put up by leading city-states at such pan-Hellenic centers as Delphi or Olympia; an Athenian citizen, going to Delphi, for instance, would find an Athenian official on duty in his Treasury to advise him. Doubtless festival robes and sacred vessels, etc., for use by representatives would be stored there.

Trilogy: when Greeks went to the theater to see a tragedy played, they were prepared to sit all day, for the great themes were divided into three plays that were put on in succession—e.g., the drama of Orestes in the plays *Agamemnon, Choephoroi,* and *Eumenides*—and the trilogy was concluded, for the relief of tension, with a satiric play.

Tripod: Homer writes of bronze tripods—large, three-footed vessels like cauldrons—as prizes; Linear B tablets from Knossos show a careful count of these valued objects. In Classical times we hear of their use, beautifully decorated, sometimes even made of gold, as gifts devoted to a god. On the plaster or beaten earth floor of a Mycenaean room, a three-legged vessel (or stand for a large amphora) would readily find stability. But granted this advantage to a tripod, and the possible explanation of its use as a means of storing wealth in bronze or other metals in negotiable form, the attraction of it to the Greek mind remains a mystery.

Trireme: the standard warship of the 5th and 4th centuries BC that displaced the old penteconter with 25 oarsmen a side. The trireme was about 36½ meters (120 feet) long overall, with a beam of perhaps 6 meters (20 feet) and a shallow draught. It was of light construction, liable to hog or sag at the extremities and so likely to leak in a seaway that permanent undergirding cables were fitted (if one can judge from the carved relief of the stern quarters of a trireme on the rock face at Lindos in Rhodes).

Volute: the spiral element in the capital of columns of the Ionic, Corinthian, and Composite orders; derived from the voluted ram's horns, or of Geometrical origin, or perhaps suggested by the perfect natural spiral of the seed box of one of the commonest Greek clovers.

Votive: the offering to a deity of a terracotta model, often of an animal, seems to have been a device in Mycenaean times to make the donor's prayer more likely to be remembered by the deity. Little plaques of silver embossed with a leg, eye, ear, heart, arm, etc., are today often attached to an icon on the iconostasis of a church, and are either thanksgivings or petitions for the recovery of the limb or organ so devoted.

Xoanon: a primitive wooden image, so unlike marble sculpture that it was supposed to have fallen from heaven and was accordingly deeply revered. Such an image (of Athena) was housed in the Erectheion and dressed in a new robe (*peplos*) at her great Panathenaic festival every fourth year.

— Guy Pentreath

GREEK MYTHOLOGY

MYTHOLOGY IN ITS widest sense includes legend, parable, allegory, and fable, and all fictional figures, situations, and scenes—in fact the whole non-factual, non-scientific, non-mathematical, gravity-free, miscegenetic world of the imagination and of dreams. As such it pervades almost all creative Greek art and literature. Whether we are looking at pedimental sculptures in Olympia or vase-paintings in Athens, whether we are reading the epics of Homer or the tragedies of Euripides, we are in the presence of the Greek mythopoeic mind. Even the philosophers and scientists used myths. When Plato wanted to describe the deepest truths of earth and heaven, he embodied them in myths. When the Greek astronomers charted the stars, they grouped them in mythological figures—Orion, Perseus, Andromeda, and the rest. In our own time psychologists like Freud and Jung have found names and symbols to express their discoveries in the unconscious mind with Greek mythology.

To describe this infinitely varied and variable world (for a Greek myth changed every time it was sympathetically retold), peopled with emblems of hope, fear, yearning, dim memories, patched-up misunderstandings, personifications of melting beauty or of petrifying ugliness, would be impossible here. Only a few types can be briefly mentioned.

Some myths try to answer questions about nature. How did the world and mankind first come into being? Hesiod in his magnificent *Theogony* answers with stories about Chaos and the marriage of Earth with her son Heaven, and the subsequent generations of gods and giants and men. Why do plants wither? Because Pluto takes Persephone down to Hades (and hence the wonderful myth and ritual of Eleusis). How does the sun cross the sky? In his golden chariot. What causes earthquakes? Poseidon with his trident. Who invented fire? Prometheus brought it down from Olympos. Others explore problems of human destiny. How did pain and sickness come into the world? Through the curiosity of Pandora (that other Eve). What is the nature of love? Read the myths in Plato's *Symposium*. What happens to us after death? Homer described the geography of Hades in the *Odyssey,* and dozens of other poets followed him in that macabre exploration; and the mysteries of Demeter, Orpheus, and Dionysos offered guidance across those awesome rivers and through those forlorn shades.

Quite different are the myths based on historical events supplemented, adapted, and enriched by free imagination and wishful thinking. How much is factual, how much fictional, in the legends of Troy, in the stories of the *Odyssey*, in the saga of the Golden Fleece, in the exploits of Hercules and Theseus? No one can say for certain, except when firm historical evidence gives independent proof. Archaeology has an authoritative voice in this. But the evidence of the Greek historians must be scrutinized with care: they were sometimes mythologists, too—even Thucydides.

Then there were ethical, or even frankly moralistic, myths. Is gold the best thing of all? Consider Midas. Freedom from death, then? Think on Tithonos, or the Sibyl at Cumae (shrunk with age to the size of a pea, kept in a bottle for fear of being lost, and always squeaking with her pinpoint voice "I want to die. I want to die."). Would it be a good thing for men to be able to fly? Icarus and Bellerophon did not find it so. Would you like to be married to Helen of Troy, or to Jason, the winner of the Golden Fleece? Consult Menelaos and Medea. How wonderful to be the supremely powerful and supremely popular ruler of a fabulously great city! Not for Oedipus. Well, is all human life doomed to disaster and woe? No, there are two large jars in the hall where Zeus makes his decisions, one of good fortune and one (but some think two) of ill fortune; and to most people he distributes portions fairly equally. The wisest and safest thing—and the hardest thing for Greeks—is to avoid all excess, and pride, greed, envy, and small-mindedness. But the Greek myths rarely preach directly: they prefer just to tell the story, with compassion and understanding and without useless grief.

When a genius—a Sophocles or a Pheidias or a Polygnotos—adopted these myths, they became new works of art. In less-talented hands they remained smaller and simpler, but no less memorable. Aesop's fables about Greek-speaking and Greek-thinking animals are now read mostly by children. But judgments and phrases from them—like "sour grapes," "King Stork"—remain part of our adult vocabulary and ethics. Proverbs are often shrunken myths.

To the ancient Greeks mythology was much more than a matter of literature, art, philosophy, and ethics. The whole countryside teemed with spirits and powers, to us mythical (in the sense of imaginary; but a lecturer on a Swan Hellenic Cruise has stated in print that he saw a satyr and perhaps also Pan), to them mythic (in the sense of belonging to traditional belief). Besides the loftier Olympian gods there were spirits of mountain, sea, tree, and stream—oreads, nereids, dryads, and naiads—sometimes benign, sometimes malevolent. (The Greek countryman still dreads the capricious nereids.) Pan (who gave the Christians a shape for the Devil) and the satyrs were there; and in the sea old Triton still blew his wreathed horn. In the darkness of the night or of the mind lurked figures of terror, the hideous turn-you-to-stone Gorgons, the ferocious Furies, and snatching demons, and shrivelling ghosts (one of them would take out her eye and wave it at you). Did they believe, actually and acutely, in minotaurs and chimaeras and sphinxes and centaurs and winged horses, those strange surrealistic figments embodying ancestral fears, perverse desires, dreams, visions?

Some myths are too profoundly moving and poetical to fit into any classification—Orpheus and Eurydice, Cupid and Psyche.

Divine IDs

The 12 chief gods formed the elite of Olympos. Each represented one of the forces of nature and also a human characteristic, interpreted by sculptors in their statues of the gods. They also had attributes, by which they can often be identified. The Romans, influenced by the arts and letters of Greece, largely identified their own gods with those of Greece, with the result that Greek gods had Latin names as well, by which they are known today.

— W. B. Stanford

Greek Name	Latin Name	Attributes and Associations	Symbols
Aphrodite	Venus	love, beauty	dove
Apollo	Phoebus	sun, music, and poetry	bow, lyre
Ares	Mars	tumult, war	spear, helmet
Artemis	Diana	moon, chastity	stag
Athena	Minerva	wisdom	owl, olive
Demeter	Ceres	earth, fecundity	sheaf, sickle
Hephaestos	Vulcan	fire, industry	hammer, anvil
Hera	Juno	sky, queen, marriage	peacock
Hermes	Mercury	trade, eloquence	caduceus, wings
Hestia	Vesta	hearth, domestic virtues	eternal fire
Poseidon	Neptune	sea, earthquake	trident
Zeus	Jupiter	sky, supreme god	scepter, thunder

BOOKS AND VIDEOS

Books

A. R. Burn's *The Pelican History of Greece* takes the reader from the neolithic pioneers to the splendors of Athens to the last dark days when the philosophic schools were closed, capturing the culture of an amazing people. Extremely fluid, it is written for those who are not experts in classical literature. Just as erudite and enthusiastic is the *Oxford History of Greece and the Hellenistic World*, edited by John Boardman, Jasper Griffin, and Oswyn Murray, a comprehensive but never boring view of the ancient Greek world and its achievements. A late convert to classic Greece, Peter France will engage even the laziest reader in his *Greek as a Treat* (Penguin Books); theme by theme, with a sharp wit, he introduces readers to the greats—Homer, Pythagoras, Aeschylus, Socrates, and Plato—demonstrating how they still can enrich our 20th-century lives. C.M. Woodhouse's *Modern Greece: A Short History* (Faber and Faber) succinctly covers the ensuing development of Greece, from the fall of the Byzantine Empire, to the War of Independence and the monarchy, to the ongoing struggle between the socialist PASOK party and the conservative New Democracy party. *The Greeks: The Land and People Since the War* (Penguin) by James Pettifer takes readers behind the postcard imagery of lazy beaches and sun-kissed villages to modern Greece's contradictions, as he examines the far-reaching effects of the country's recent troubled past, including civil war and dictatorship.

John Julius Norwich's three-volume account (available through Penguin) of Byzantium is a good introduction to the medieval Byzantine empire. Timothy Ware's *The Orthodox Church* introduces the Westerner to the religion of the Greek people, while Paul Hetherington's *Byzantine and Medieval Greece, Churches, Castles, and Art* provides a useful introduction to Byzantine and Frankish mainland Greece.

Unearthing Atlantis, by Charles Pellegrino, is a fascinating book about Santorini. The idyllic youth of naturalist Gerald Durrell on the island of Corfu is recalled in many of his books, such as *My Family and Other Animals,* which are written with an unpretentious, precise style in a slightly humorous vein, and are underrated as works of literature. Henry Miller's *The Colossus of Maroussi,* an enjoyable seize-the-day-as-the-Greeks-do paean that veers from the profound to the superficial—sometimes verging on hysteria—is the product of a trip Miller took to Greece, during which he experienced an epiphany.

Greece's premier writer Nikos Kazantzakis captures the strengths and weaknesses and the color of traditional Greek culture in his wonderful *Zorba the Greek;* he also wrote the classics *Christ Recrucified* and *The Odyssey.* Other modern Greek fiction will immerse readers in the joys and woes of Greece today: Kedros Books has an excellent series, *Modern Greek Writers* (✉ Gennadiou 3, 10678 Athens, ☎ 01/360−9712; distributed in the United Kingdom by Forest Books), which includes *Farewell Anatolia,* by Dido Sotiriou, chronicling the traumatic end of Greek life in Asia Minor, and *Fool's Gold* by Maro Douka, about an aristocratic young woman who becomes enamored of and then disillusioned with the resistance movement to the junta. Noted for his translations of Kazantzakis, the late Kimon Friar demonstrated exquisite taste in his superb translations of modern Greek verse, including works by C. P. Cavafy, and the Nobel Laureates George Seferis and Odysseus Elytis. Friar's *Modern Greek Poetry* is published by the Efstathiadis Group in Athens. Overseas readers may have less difficulty finding Edmund Keeley and Philip Sherrard's *Voices of Modern Greek Poetry* (Princeton University Press).

Some people like to go back to the classics while in Greece. Try either Robert Fitzgerald's or Richmond Lattimore's translations of the *Iliad* and *Odyssey* of Homer, done in verse, unlike the clumsy prose translations you probably read in school. Take the *Iliad* as a pacifist work exposing the uselessness of warfare; read the *Odyssey* keeping in mind the relationships between men and women as illustrated by Odysseus and Penelope, Circe, and Calypso. Lattimore also translated Greece's early lyric poets, Sappho and her lesser-known contemporaries, in a collection titled *Greek Lyric Poetry*. Aristophanes' play *The Wasps* is one of the funniest pieces of literature ever written. Although it isn't light reading, Thucydides' *Peloponnesian War* details the long struggle of Athens and Sparta, fought openly and through third parties, for and against democracy and autocracy. The events of the past 50 years and those of 2,500 years ago aren't so different.

Videos

A determination to live for the moment coupled with lingering fatalism still pervades Greek society. No film better captures this than Michael Cacoyannis' *Zorba the Greek* (1964; in English), starring the inimitable Anthony Quinn, Alan Bates, and Irene Pappas. Graced with the music of Mikis Theodorakis (the score won an Oscar even though Theodorakis' music was banned at the time in Greece), the film juxtaposes this zest for life with the harsh realities of traditional village society.

In perhaps the second best known film about Greece, Hellenic joie de vivre meets American pragmatism in *Never On Sunday* (1960; in English), directed by Jules Dassin. The late Melina Mercouri, a national icon, plays a Greek hooker, who in her simple but wise ways takes on the American who has come to reform her and teaches him that life isn't always about getting ahead.

The epic musical drama, *Rembetiko* (1983; English subtitles), directed by Costas Ferris and awarded the Silver Bear in 1984, follows 40 years in the life of a rembetiko (Greek blues) singer, played by smoldering, throaty-voiced Sotiria Leonardou. The film, notable for its authenticity and the music's raw energy, spans the turbulent political history of Greece and the development of *rembetika* blues, which flourished from the 1920s until the '40s as 1.5 million Greeks were displaced from Asia Minor. They brought with them their haunting minor key laments, as well as the Anatolian custom of smoking hashish; today rembetika is enjoying a resurgence with young Greeks.

Mediterraneo (1991; English subtitles) is a nostalgic, humorous depiction of life on a tiny, distant Greek island, occupied by Italian solders during World War II. The soldiers become inextricably involved with the island's vivid personalities—to the point that some refuse to leave when finally informed that the war has long been over. The movie, which won an Oscar for Best Foreign Film, features Vanna Barba, a popular Greek actress whose lusty, yet stern gaze captivates the lead role.

One of Greece's leading directors, Theodoros Angelopoulos, has made several internationally acclaimed films, including *Journey to Kythera* (1984; English subtitles) which won for Best Screenplay in the 1984 Cannes festival. Considerably shorter than most of his films, it blends the mythical with the contemporary, detailing the life of a Greek civil war fighter who returns from the Soviet Union to reunite with his son in an adventure that leaves him and his wife on a raft bound for Kythera island. Manos Katrakis, considered one of Greece's finest stage actors, performs superbly (he died soon after), and the music and striking cinematography evoke Cavafy's famous poem, "Journey to Ithaki," familiar to all Greeks: "But do not hurry the voyage at all. It is better to let it last for long years; and even to anchor at the isle when you are old, rich with all that you have gained on the way."

A recent film that portrays life in Greece since tourism hit in the late '60s is *Shirley Valentine* (1989; in English). Set amid marvelous island scenes, the story is a cautionary tale about a bored British housewife who leaves her stultifying life to vacation in Greece. Here, she regains her identity through a liberating romance with the local flirt (Tom Conti speaking abominable Greek). In England, apparently, an unusually high number of women signed up for Greek language lessons after viewing the film. Although a bit dated, since the "kamaki" (men who prey on foreign women) is no longer in full force given the increased independence of Greek women, the movie is full of humor, sharp dialogue, and dazzling shots of the Aegean.

GREEK PLACE-NAMES

Abram	Αμπράμι
Achaea	Αχαία
Acronauplia	Ακροναυπλία
Aegina, Aigina, Egina	Αίγινα
Aigaleo	Αιγάλεω
Aigion	Αίγιο
Akrotiri	Ακρωτήρι
Amfissa	Άμφισσα
Amphiareion	Αμφιαρείον
Anavatos	Ανάβατος
Andritsena, Andritsaina	Ανδρίτσαινα
Andros Town (Chora)	Άνδρος (Χώρα)
Anilio	Ανήλιο
Ano Mera	Άνω Μερά
Anoyia	Ανώγεια
Anthochori	Ανθοχώρι
Antissa	Άντισσα
Apeiranthos, Apiranthos	Απείραθος
Apollonas	Απόλλωνας
Argolic Gulf, Argolikos Kolpos	Αργολικός Κόλπος
Argolid	Αργολίδα
Argos	Άργος
Arkadi Monastery	Μοναστίρι Αρκαδίου
Armolia	Αρμόλια
Arvanitis	Αρβανίτης
Askyphou plain	Οροπέδιο Ασκύφου
Aspropyrgos	Ασπρόπυργος
Avgonima, Avgonyma	Αυγώνυμα
Avlakia	Αυλάκια
Ayassos	Αγιάσος
Ayia Marina	Αγία Μαρίνα
Ayia Paraskevi	Αγία Παρασκευή
Ayia Roumeli	Αγία Ρούμελη
Ayia Sofia	Αγιά Σοφία
Ayia Triada	Αγία Τριάδα
Ayia Varvara	Αγία Βαρβάρα
Ayii Deka	Άγιοι Δέκα
Ayii Theodori	Άγιοι Θεοδώροι
Ayioi Anargyroi	Άγιοι Ανάργυροι
Ayioi Pantes.	Άγιοι Πάντες
Ayios Ioannis	Άγιος Ιωάννης
Ayios Nikolaos	Άγιος Νικόλαος
Ayios Nikolaos Anapafsas	Άγιος Νικόλαος Αναπαυσάς
Ayios Stephanos	Άγιος Στέφανος
Ayios Titos	Άγιος Τίτος
Ayos Ermogenis	Άγιος Ερμογένης
Ayos Isidoros	Άγιος Ισίδωρος
Ayos Konstantinos	Άγιος Κωνσταντίνος
Ayos Pavlos	Άγιος Παύλος
Bassae	Βασσές
Batsi	Μπατσί
Bay of Korthion	Όρμος Κορθίου
Brauron	Βραυρώνα

Cabirion	*Καβείριο*
Cave of Psychro, Psikro	*Ψυχρό*
Chalki, Chalkio	*Χαλκί, Χαλκείο*
Cheimaros tower, Chimarou	*Πύργος Χειμάρρου*
Chios, Hios	*Χίος*
Chlemoutsi Castle, Hlemoutsi	*Κάστρο Χλεμούτσι*
Chora, Hora	*Χώρα*
Chrisovitsa	*Χρυσοβίτσα*
Christos Elkomenos	*Ελκόμενου Χριστού*
Corfu	*Κέρκυρα*
Corinth, Korinthos	*Κόρινθος*
Cyclades	*Κυκλάδες*
Daskalopetra	*Δασκαλοπέτρα*
Dervenakia	*Δερβενάκια*
Diakofto	*Διακοφτό*
Didima	*Δίδυμα*
Dodecanese	*Δωδεκάνησα*
Dodona, Dodoni	*Δωδώνα, Δωδώνη*
Drepano	*Δρέπανο*
Egina, Aegina, Aigina	*Αίγινα*
Ekali	*Εκάλη*
Elafonisi	*Ελαφονήσι*
Elefsina	*Ελευσίνα*
Eleusis	*Ελεύσις*
Elis	*Ηλεία*
Elounda	*Ελούντα*
Emborio	*Εμπόρειο*
Engares	*Εγγαρές*
Epidauros, Epidavros	*Επίδαυρος*
Epiros, Epirus	*Ήπειρος*
Eressos	*Ερεσός*
Ermioni	*Ερμιόνη*
Evia, Euboia, Euboea	*Εύβοια*
Falasarna	*Φαλάσαρνα*
Filoti	*Φιλότι*
Flerio	*Φλέριο*
Fodhele, Fodele	*Φόδελε*
Fourni	*Φούρνοι*
Frangokastello	*Φραγκοκάστελλο*
Gaidouronisi	*Γαϊδουρόνησι*
Galanado	*Γαλανάδο*
Galatas	*Γαλατάς*
Gavrion	*Γαύριο*
Gefira, New Monemvassia	*Γέφυρα, Νέα Μονεμβασιά*
Georgioupolis, Yioryioupoli	*Γεωργιούπολη*
Geropotamos river	*Γέρω Ποταμός*
Glifa	*Γλύφα*
Glyfada	*Γλυφάδα*
Gortyna, Gortys	*Γόρτηνα, Γόρτυς*
Gournes	*Γούρνες*
Gournia	*Γουρνιά*
Grotta	*Γρόττα, Γκρότα*
Gulf of Yera	*Κόλπος Γεράς*
Hania, Chania	*Χανιά*

Hephaistia	Ηφαιστεία
Heraion, Ireon	Ηραίο
Heraklion, Iraklio	Ηράκλειο
Hora Sfakia	Χώρα Σφακίων
Hydra	Ύδρα
Hymettos	Υμηττός
Idean Cave, Ideo Andro	Ιδαίον Άντρον
Ierapetra	Ιεράπετρα
Ikaria	Ικαρία
Ioannina	Ιωάννινα
Iria	Ίρια
Isthmia	Ισθμία
Kaisariani	Καισαριανή
Kalamata	Καλαμάτα
Kalambaka	Καλαμπάκα
Kalathas	Καλαθάς
Kalavrita	Καλάβρυτα
Kalloni	Καλλονή
Kaloritisa	Καλορίτισσα
Kamares Cave	Σπήλαιο Καμαρών
Kambia	Καμπιά
Kambos, Kampos	Κάμπος
Kaminia	Καμίνια
Kandia, Kantia	Κάντια
Kardamila, Kardamyla	Καρδάμυλα
Karlovassi	Καρλόβασι
Kastelli	Καστέλλι
Kastelli Kissamou	Καστέλλι Κισσάμου
Kastraki	Καστράκι
Katara	Κατάρα
Kato Zakro	Κάτω Ζάκρος
Kavala	Καβάλα
Kavasilas	Καβάσιλας
Keratea	Κερατέα
Kiato	Κιάτο
Kithairon, Kitheron	Κιθαιρών
Knossos	Κνωσός
Kokkari	Κοκκάρι
Kommos	Κομμός
Komotini	Κομοτηνή
Korfes	Κορφές
Koronos	Κώρονας
Koropi	Κοροπί
Kosta	Κόστα
Koutsi	Κούτσι
Kranidi	Κρανίδι
Kritsa	Κριτσά
Kyllini, Kilini, Killene	Κυλλήνη
Labou Mili, Lampou Myli	Λάμπου Μύλοι
Laconia	Λακωνία
Lake Voulismeni	Λίμνι Βουλισμένη
Langada	Λαγκάδα
Larissa	Λάρισα
Lasithi, Lasithio	Λασίθι

Lato	Λάτω
Lechaion	Λεχαίον
Legrena	Λεγρενά
Lesbos	Λέσβος
Libyan Sea	Λιβυκόν Πελαγός
Ligourio	Λυγουριό
Limin Hersonissos, Chersonissos	Λίμην Χερσονήσου
Limnopoula	Λιμνοπούλα
Limnos, Lemnos	Λήμνος
Limonas monastery	Μονή Λιμώνας
Lissos	Λισσός
Livadi Valley	Λιβαδιά
Loutra Killinis	Λουτρά Κυλλήνης
Loutro	Λουτρό
Makriyialos, Makrigialos	Μακρύγιαλος
Makronissos	Μακρόνησος
Malagari	Μαλαγκάρι
Mallia, Malia	Μάλια
Mandamados, Mantamados	Μανταμάδος
Manolates	Μανολάτες
Marathokambos	Μαραθόκαμπος
Marathon	Μαραθώνας
Marina Village	Αγία Μαρίνα
Markopoulos	Μαρκόπουλο
Maroussi, Amaroussion	Μαρούσι, Αμαρούσιον
Matala	Μάταλα
Megali Vrissi	Μεγάλη Βρύση
Megalo Meteoro, Metamorphosis	Το Μεγάλο Μετέωρο/ Μεταμόρφωση
Megara	Μέγαρα
Menites	Μένητες
Mesara	Μεσαρά
Mesogeion	Μεσογείων
Mesta	Μεστά
Meteora	Τα Μετέωρα
Metsovo	Μέτσοβο
Methana	Μέθανα
Mikri Vigla	Μικρή Βίγλα
Milia	Μηλιά
Miloi	Μυλοι
Mirabello Gulf, Kolpos Mirambellou	Κόλπος Μράμπελο
Mires	Μοίρες
Mochlos, Mohlos	Μοχλός
Molyvos, Mithimna, Methimna	Μόλυβος, Μήθυμνα
Monemvassia, Monemvasia	Μονεμβασιά
Moni	Μονη
Moria	Μόρια
Moudras	Μούδρας
Mt. Helmos	Χελμός Όρος
Mt. Kynthos	Όρος Κύνθος
Mt. Lykaeon	Όρος Λύκαιον
Mt. Minthis	Όρος Μίνθη

Mt. Mitsikelis	Μιτσικέλι
Mt. Ornon	Όρος Ορνόν
Mt. Panahaiko, Panakhaikon	Όρος Παναχαϊκόν
Mt. Parnis, Parnitha	Ορος Πάρνης, Πάρνηθα
Mt. Profitis Ilias	Όρος Προφήτης Ιλίας
Mt. Taygettus, Taygettos	Όρος Ταύγετος
Mt. Tomaros	Τομάρος
Mt. Zas	Όρος Ζάς, Ζεύς
Mt. Ziria, Z'npia, Mt. Killini	Ζηρια, Όρος Κυλλήνης
Mycenae, Mikine, Mikines	Μυκήνες
Myrina, Mirina, Kastro	Μύρινα, Κάστρο
Mystras	Μυστράς
Mytilinii	Μυτιλήνη
Nagos	Ναγός
Nauplion, Nafplio	Ναύπλιο
Naxos	Νάξος
Nea Epidauros	Νέα Επίδαυρος
Nea Makri	Νέα Μάκρη
Nea Moni	Νέα Μονή
Nemea	Νεμέα
Nida Plateau	Κάμπος Νίδας
Nimbros Gorge, Imbros Gorge	Φαράγγι Νίμπρου, Φαράγγι Ίμπρου
Olous	Ολούς
Olympia	Ολυμπία
Omalos Plain	Οροπέδιο Ομαλός
Ormos Marathokambos	Όρμος Μαραθόκαμπου
Paiania	Παιανία
Palaia Epidauros, Palea Epidaupus	Παλαιά Επίδαυρος
Palatia	Παλάτια
Paleochora; Paleohora	Παλαιοχώρα
Paleokastro, Palekastro, Palaikastro	Παλαικάστρο
Paleopolis	Παλαιόπολη
Pallini	Παλλήνη
Pamfila	Πάμφιλα
Panagitsa	Παναγίτσα
Panagia Hrisafitissa	Παναγία Χρυσαφίτισσα
Pandrossos, Pandroson	Πάνδροσο
Pantanassa monastery	Μονή Παντάνασσας
Pantoukios	Παντουκιός
Paros	Πάρος
Pastra	Πάστρα
Pateras	Πατέρας
Patmos	Πάτμος
Patras, Patra	Πάτρα
Patroklou	Πάτροκλου
Paximadia	Παξιμάδια
Peloponnesos	Πελοπόννησος
Pendeli	Πεντέλη
Penius River	Πήνειος
Perama, Perama Cave	Πέραμα, Το Σπηλαίο τον Περάματος
Perivleptos monastery	Μονή Περιβλέπτου

Perivoli	Μονή Περιβόλη
Petra	Πέτρα
Phaistos, Festos, Phaestos	Φαίστος
Phyle	Φύλη
Pikermi	Πικέρμι
Pindos	Πίνδος
Piraeus	Πειραιάς
Pirgos, Pyrgos	Πύργος
Pirgi Thermis	Πύργοι Θερμής
Pitsidia	Πιτσίδια
Plaka	Πλάκα
Platanos	Πλάτανος
Plataia	Πλαταίες
Platanakia	Πλατανάκια
Plati	Πλατύ
Plomari	Πλωμάρι
Polichnitos	Πολιχνίτος
Poliochni	Πολιόχνη
Poros	Πόρος
Portes	Πόρτες
Porto Heli, Porto Cheli, Portoheli	Πόρτο Χέλι
Potamia	Ποταμιά
Potamies, Potamos	Ποταμιές, Ποταμός
Pournias Bay	Κόλπος Πουρνιάς
Profitis Ilias	Προφήτης Ηλίας
Pseira	Ψείρα
Psili Ammos	Ψιλή Άμμος
Psiloritis, Ida, Idhi	Ψηλορείτης, Ίδη
Pyrgi	Πυργί
Pyrgos, Pirgos	Πύργος
Pythagorio	Πυθαγόρειο
Rafina	Ραφήνα
Repanidi	Ρεπανίδι
Rethymnon, Rethimno	Ρέθυμνό
Rhamnous	Ραμνούς
Rhodes	Ρόδος
Roussanou, Ayia Barbara	Μονή Ρουσάνου, Μονή Άγιας Βαρβαράς
Sacred Lake	Ιερή Λίμνη
Salamis, Salamina	Σαλαμίς, Σαλαμίνα
Salamis, straits of	Στενόν Σαλαμών
Samaria Gorge	Φαράγγι Σαμαριάς
Samos	Σάμος
Sangri	Σαγκρί
Sarakiniki Sarakina	Σαρακήνα
Saronic Gulf, Saronikos Kolpos	Σαρωνικός Κόλπος
Septsae, Spetses	Σπέτσες
Sigri	Σίγρι
Siteia, Sitia	Σητεία
Skala Eressou	Σκάλα Ερεσού
Sklavia	Σκλαβιά
Sklavokampos	Σκλαβοκάμπος
Souda Bay, O. Soudas	Ορμός Σούδας
Sougia, Souyia	Σουγιά

Sounion	Σούνιο
Sparta	Σπάρτη
Spetses	Σπέτσες
Sphaka	Σφάκα
Spinalonga	Σπιναλόγκα
Stavros	Σταυρός
t'Apilarou castle	Κάστρο Απαλυρού
Tatoi	Τατόι
Thanos	Θάνος
Thessaloniki	Θεσσαλονίκη
Thessaly	Θεσσαλία
Thimiana, Thymiana	Θυμιανά
Thorikos	Θορικό
Thripti	Θρυπτή
Timios Stavrou, Timiou Stavrou	Τίμιου Σταυρού
Tiryns, Tirinthos	Τίρυνς, Τίρυνθος
Tolo	Τολό
To Nissaki	Το Νησάκι
Toplou monastery	Μονή Τοπλού
Tragaia Valley	Τραγαία
Trahia	Τραχειά
Trikala	Τρίκαλα
Tripolis, Tripoli	Τρίπολη
Troezen	Τροιζήν
Tsabou	Τσαμπού
Tsamadou	Τσαμαδού
Tylissos	Τύλισος
Tzermiado	Τζερμιάδο
Vai	Βάι
Varia	Βαρειά
Varkiza	Βάρκιζα
Varlaam	Μονή Βαρλαάμ
Varybobi	Βαρυμπόμπη
Vatera	Βατερά
Vathi	Βαθυ
Vavili	Βαβίλοι
Virgin Odegetria Church	Παναγία Οδηγήτρια
Volissos	Βολισσός
Voni	Βόνη
Votsalakia	Βοτσαλάκια
Voula	Βούλα
Vouliagmeni	Βουλιαγμένη
Vouraikos Gorge	Φαράγγι Βουραίκος
Vranas	Βρανάς
Vrisses	Βρύσες
Vrondiani monastery, Moni Yronda	Βρονδιανή, Μονή Βροντά
Vrontados	Βροντάδος
Xylokastro	Ξυλόκαστρο
Za Cave	Σπήλαιο Ζά, Ζεύς
Zagora	Ζαγορά
Zakhlorou	Ζαχλωρού
Zakro, Zakros	Ζάκρος
Zoumberi	Ζούμπερι

GREEK VOCABULARY

The phonetic spelling used in English differs somewhat from the internationalized form of Greek place names. There are no long and short vowels in Greek; the pronunciation never changes. Note, also, that the accent is a stress mark, showing where the stress is placed in pronunciation.

Basics

Do you speak English?	Miláte angliká?
Yes, no	Málista *or* Né, óchi
Impossible	Adínato
Good morning, Good day	Kaliméra
Good evening, Good night	Kalispéra, Kaliníchta
Goodbye	Yá sas
Mister, Madam, Miss	Kírie, kiría, despiní
Please	Parakaló
Excuse me	Me sinchórite *or* signómi
How are you?	Ti kánete *or* pós íste
How do you do (Pleased to meet you)	Chéro polí
I don't understand.	Dén katalavéno.
To your health!	Giá sas!
Thank you	Efcharistó

Numbers

one	éna
two	dío
three	tría
four	téssera
five	pénde
six	éxi
seven	eptá
eight	októ
nine	enéa
ten	déka
twenty	íkossi
thirty	triánda
forty	saránda
fifty	penínda
sixty	exínda
seventy	evdomínda
eighty	ogdónda
ninety	enenínda
one hundred	ekató
two hundred	diakóssia
three hundred	triakóssia
one thousand	hília
two thousand	dío hiliádes
three thousand	trís hiliádes

Days of the Week

Monday	Deftéra
Tuesday	Tríti
Wednesday	Tetárti
Thursday	Pémpti
Friday	Paraskeví
Saturday	Sávato
Sunday	Kyriakí

Months

January	Ianouários
February	Fevrouários
March	Mártios
April	Aprílios
May	Maíos
June	Ióunios
July	Ióulios
August	Ávgoustos
September	Septémvrios
October	Októvrios
November	Noémvrios
December	Dekémvrios

Traveling

I am traveling by car . . . train . . . plane . . . boat.	Taxidévo mé aftokínito . . . me tréno . . . me aeropláno . . . me vapóri.
Taxi, to the station . . . harbor . . . airport	Taxí, stó stathmó . . . limáni . . . aerodrómio
Porter, take the luggage.	Akthofóre, pare aftá tá prámata.
Where is the filling station?	Pou íne tó vensinádiko?
When does the train leave for . . . ?	Tí óra thá fíyi to tréno ya . . . ?
Which is the train for . . . ?	Pío íne to tréno gía . . . ?
Which is the road to . . . ?	Piós íne o drómos giá . . . ?
A first-class ticket	Éna isitírio prótis táxis
Smoking is forbidden.	Apagorévete to kápnisma.
Where is the toilet?	Póu íne í toaléta?
Ladies, men	Ginekón, andrón
Where? When?	Póu? Póte?
Sleeping car, dining car	Wagonlí, wagonrestorán
Compartment	Vagóni
Entrance, exit	Íssodos, éxodos
Nothing to declare	Den écho típota na dilósso
I am coming for my vacation.	Érchome giá tis diakopés mou.
Nothing	Típota
Personal use	Prossopikí chríssi
How much?	Pósso?

I want to eat, to drink, to sleep.	Thélo na fáo, na pió, na kimithó.
Sunrise, sunset	Anatolí, díssi
Sun, moon	Ílios, fengári
Day, night	Méra, níchta
Morning, afternoon	Proí, mesiméri, *or* apóyevma
The weather is good, bad.	Ó kerós íne kalós, kakós.

On the Road

Straight ahead	Kat efthían
To the right, to the left	Dexiá, aristerá
Show me the way to . . . please.	Díxte mou to drómo . . . parakaló.
Where is . . . ?	Pou íne . . . ?
Crossroad	Diastávrosi
Danger	Kíndinos
Drive slowly!	Sigá!
Look out for the train (railroad crossing).	Prosséxte to tréno.

In Town

Will you lead me? take me?	Thélete na me odigíste? Me pérnete mazí sas?
Street, square	Drómos, platía
Where is the bank?	Pou íne i trápeza?
Far	Makriá
Police station	Astinomikó tmíma
Consulate (American, British)	Proxenío (Amerikániko, Anglikó)
Theater, cinema	Théatro, cinemá
At what time does the film start?	Tí óra archízi ee tenía?
Where is the travel office?	Pou íne to touristikó grafío?
Where are the tourist police?	Pou íne i touristikí astinomía?

Shopping

I would like to buy	Tha íthela na agorásso
Show me, please.	Díxte mou, parakaló.
May I look around?	Boró na ríxo miá matyá?
How much is it?	Pósso káni? (*or* kostízi)
It is too expensive.	Íne polí akrivó.
Have you any sandals?	Échete pédila?
Have you foreign newspapers?	Échete xénes efimerídes?
Show me that blouse, please.	Díxte mou aftí tí blouza.
Show me that suitcase.	Díxte mou aftí tí valítza.
Envelopes, writing paper	Fakélous, hartí íli
Roll of film	Film
Map of the city	Hárti tis póleos
Something handmade	Hiropíito

Wrap it up, please.	Tilixteto, parakaló.
Cigarettes, matches, please.	Tsigára, spírta, parakaló.
Ham	Zambón
Sausage, salami	Loukániko, salámi
Sugar, salt, pepper	Záchari, aláti, pipéri
Grapes, cherries	Stafília, kerássia
Apple, pear, orange	Mílo, achládi, portokáli
Bread, butter	Psomí, voútiro
Peach, figs	Rodákino, síka

At the Hotel

A good hotel	Éna kaló xenodochío
Have you a room?	Échete domátio?
Where can I find a furnished room?	Pou boró na vró epiploméno domátio?
A single room, double room	Éna monóklino, éna díklino
With bathroom	Me bánio
How much is it per day?	Pósso kostízi tin iméra?
A room overlooking the sea	Éna domátio prós ti thálassa
For one day, for two days	Giá miá méra, giá dió méres
For a week	Giá miá evdomáda
My name is. . . .	Onomázome. . . .
My passport	Tó diavatirió mou
What is the number of my room?	Piós íne o arithmós tou domatíou mou?
The key, please.	To klidí, parakaló.
Breakfast, lunch, supper	Proinó, messimergianó, vradinó
The bill, please.	To logariasmó, parakaló.
I am leaving tomorrow.	Févgo ávrio.

At the Restaurant

Waiter	Garsón
Where is the restaurant?	Pou íne to estiatório?
I would like to eat.	Tha íthela na fáo.
The menu, please.	To katálogo, parakaló.
Fixed-price menu	Menú
Soup	Soúpa
Bread	Psomí
Hors d'oeuvre	Mezédes, orektiká
Ham omelet	Omelétta zambón
Chicken	Kotópoulo
Roast pork	Psitó hirinó
Beef	Moschári
Potatoes (fried)	Patátes (tiganités)
Tomato salad	Domatosaláta

Vegetables	Lachaniká
Watermelon, melon	Karpoúzi, pepóni
Desserts, pastry	Gliká *or* pástes
Fruit, cheese, ice cream	Fróuta, tirí, pagotó
Fish, eggs	Psári, avgá
Serve me on the terrace.	Na mou servírete sti tarátza.
Where can I wash my hands?	Pou boró na plíno ta héria mou?
Red wine, white wine	Kokivó krasí, áspro krasí
Unresinated wine	Krasí aretsínato
Beer, soda water, water, milk	Bíra, sóda, neró, gála
Greek (formerly Turkish) coffee	Ellenikó kafé
Coffee with milk, without sugar, medium, sweet	Kafé gallikó me, gála skéto, métrio, glikó

At the Bank, at the Post Office

Where is the bank? . . . post office?	Pou íne i trápeza? . . . to tachidromío?
I would like to cash a check.	Thélo ná xargiróso mía epitagí.
I would like to change some money.	Théol na aláxo hrímata.
Stamps	Grammatóssima
By airmail	Aëroporikós
Postcard, letter	Kárta, grámma
Letterbox	Tachidromikó koutí
I would like to telephone.	Thélo na tilephonísso.

At the Garage

Garage, gas (petrol)	Garáz, venzíni
Oil	Ládi
Change the oil.	Aláksete to ládi.
Look at the tires.	Rixte mia matiá sta lástika.
Wash the car.	Plínete to aftokínito.
Breakdown	Vlávi
Tow the car.	Rimúlkiste tó aftokínito.
Spark plugs	Buzí
Brakes	Fréna
Gearbox	Kivótio tachitíton
Carburetor	Karbiratér
Headlight	Provoléfs
Starter	Míza
Axle	Áksonas
Shock absorber	Amortisér
Spare part	Antalaktikó

INDEX

Fodor's Travel Publications

Available at bookstores everywhere, or call 1–800–533–6478, 24 hours a day.

Gold Guides

U.S.

Alaska

Arizona

Boston

California

Cape Cod, Martha's
Vineyard, Nantucket

The Carolinas & the
Georgia Coast

Chicago

Colorado

Florida

Hawai'i

Las Vegas, Reno,
Tahoe

Los Angeles

Maine, Vermont,
New Hampshire

Maui & Lāna'i

Miami & the Keys

New England

New Orleans

New York City

Pacific North Coast

Philadelphia & the
Pennsylvania Dutch
Country

The Rockies

San Diego

San Francisco

Santa Fe, Taos,
Albuquerque

Seattle & Vancouver

The South

U.S. & British Virgin
Islands

USA

Virginia & Maryland

Washington, D.C.

Foreign

Australia

Austria

The Bahamas

Belize & Guatemala

Bermuda

Canada

Cancún, Cozumel,
Yucatán Peninsula

Caribbean

China

Costa Rica

Cuba

The Czech Republic
& Slovakia

Eastern &
Central Europe

Europe

Florence, Tuscany
& Umbria

France

Germany

Great Britain

Greece

Hong Kong

India

Ireland

Israel

Italy

Japan

London

Madrid & Barcelona

Mexico

Montréal &
Québec City

Moscow, St.
Petersburg, Kiev

The Netherlands,
Belgium &
Luxembourg

New Zealand

Norway

Nova Scotia, New
Brunswick, Prince
Edward Island

Paris

Portugal

Provence &
the Riviera

Scandinavia

Scotland

Singapore

South Africa

South America

Southeast Asia

Spain

Sweden

Switzerland

Thailand

Tokyo

Toronto

Turkey

Vienna & the Danube

Fodor's Special-Interest Guides

Alaska Ports of Call

Caribbean Ports
of Call

The Complete Guide
to America's
National Parks

Family Adventures

Fodor's Gay Guide
to the USA

Halliday's New
England Food
Explorer

Halliday's New
Orleans Food
Explorer

Healthy Escapes

Ballpark Vacations

Kodak Guide to
Shooting Great
Travel Pictures

Nights to Imagine

Rock & Roll Traveler
USA

Sunday in New York

Sunday in
San Francisco

Walt Disney World,
Universal Studios
and Orlando

Walt Disney World
for Adults

Wendy Perrin's
Secrets Every Smart
Traveler Should
Know

Where Should We
Take the Kids?
California

Where Should We
Take the Kids?
Northeast

Worldwide Cruises
and Ports of Call

WHEREVER YOU TRAVEL, *H*ELP IS NEVER FAR AWAY.

From planning your trip to providing travel assistance along the way, American Express® Travel Service Offices are always there to help.

Greece

American Express Travel Service
2 Hermou Street, Syntagma Square
Athens
1/3244976

Acteon Travel Agency (R)
Port Square
Ios
286/91343

Greek Skies Travel (R)
20A Capodistria Street
Corfu
661/33410

Delia Travel Ltd. (R)
At The Quay
Mykonos
289/22322

Adamis Tours (R)
23, 25th August Street
Heraklion
Crete
81/246202

Albatros Travel (R)
48 Othonos Amalias Street
Patras
61/220127

X-Ray Kilo (R)
Main Square
Fira-Santorini
286/23401

Rhodos Tours Ltd. (R)
23 Ammochostou Street
Rhodes
241/21010

Travel

http://www.americanexpress.com/travel

American Express Travel Service Offices are found in central locations throughout Greece.